THE UGLY LAWS

Whereas the streets and sidewalks of the City of Chicago contain numerous beggars, mendicants, organ grinders and other unsightly and unseemly objects, which are a reproach to the City, disagreeable to people upon the streets, an offense to business houses along the streets and often dangerous,
Therefore be it ordered,
That the Mayor at once take steps to remove from the streets all beggars, mendicants and all those who by making Exhibition of themselves and their infirmities seek to obtain money from people on and along the streets.

Ald Peevey
Alvin Hulbert

THE HISTORY OF DISABILITY

A series edited by Paul K. Longmore and Lauri Umansky

The New Disability History: American Perspectives
Edited by Paul K. Longmore and Lauri Umansky

Reflections: The Life and Writings of a Young Blind Woman in Post-Revolutionary France
Edited and translated by Catherine J. Kudlick and Zina Weygand

Signs of Resistance: American Deaf Cultural History, 1900 to World War II
Susan Burch

The Radical Lives of Helen Keller
Kim E. Nielsen

Mental Retardation in America: A Historical Reader
Edited by Steven Noll and James W. Trent, Jr.

Helen Keller: Selected Writings
Edited by Kim E. Nielsen

The Ugly Laws: Disability in Public
Susan M. Schweik

THE UGLY LAWS

DISABILITY IN PUBLIC

SUSAN M. SCHWEIK

NEW YORK UNIVERSITY PRESS NEW YORK & LONDON

NEW YORK UNIVERSITY PRESS
New York and London
www.nyupress.org

HALF TITLE ILLUSTRATION: Aldermen propose Chicago's first ugly law, May 1881. From the Proceedings Files of the Chicago City Council. Rpt. in Robert E. Bailey and Elaine Shemoney Evans, *From the Ashes, 1872–1900: A Selection of Documents from the Proceedings Files of the Chicago City Council* (Springfield: Illinois State Archives, 1990).

LIBRARY OF CONGRESS CATALOGING-IN-PUBLICATION DATA
Schweik, Susan M. (Susan Marie), 1956–
The ugly laws : disability in public / Susan M. Schweik.
p. cm.—(The history of disability)
Includes bibliographical references and index.
ISBN-13: 978-0-8147-4057-6 (cl : alk. paper)
ISBN-10: 0-8147-4057-X (cl : alk. paper)
1. People with disabilities—Legal status, laws, etc.—United States—History. 2. Beggars—Legal status, laws, etc.—United States—History. 3. Discrimination against people with disabilities—Law and legislation—United States—History. 4. People with disabilities—United States—History. 5. Beggars—United States—History. I. Title.
KF480.S39 2009 346.7301'3—DC22 2008048094

New York University Press books are printed on acid-free paper, and their binding materials are chosen for strength and durability. We strive to use environmentally responsible suppliers and materials to the greatest extent possible in publishing our books.

Designed and typeset by Charles B. Hames

Manufactured in the United States of America

10 9 8 7 6 5 4 3 2 1

CONTENTS

Preface vii
Acknowledgments ix

Introduction 1

I THE EMERGENCE OF THE UGLY LAWS

1 Producing the Unsightly 23
2 Getting Ugly 40
3 The Law in Context 63
4 The Law in Language 89
5 Dissimulations 108

II AT THE UNSIGHTLY INTERSECTION

6 Gender, Sexuality, and the Ugly Law 141
7 Immigration, Ethnicity, and the Ugly Law 165
8 Race, Segregation, and the Ugly Law 184

III THE END OF THE UGLY LAWS

9 The Right to the City 207
10 Rehabilitating the Unsightly 230
11 All about Ugly Laws (for Ten Cents) 255
Conclusion 279

Appendix: The Ugly Laws 291
Notes 297
Bibliography 351
Index 405
About the Author 431

PREFACE

This book had its start during a talk at UC Berkeley by Tobin Siebers, the well-known scholar in (among other things) literary disability studies. I work as an English professor at Berkeley, where I have been one of a group of scholars actively involved in developing an interdisciplinary disability studies program. We had invited Tobin to speak, and during the course of his lecture he briefly quoted the wording of the American ordinance (already very familiar to me) that is now my subject here. I felt the usual outrage, and allowed myself the usual shock, produced by invocations of the ugly words of "ugly law," which, as I understood it, had prohibited "diseased, maimed, and deformed persons" from appearing in public. Then my disability studies colleague Fred Collignon, a professor of city and regional planning with a long history not only of academic work on disability policy but of experience in city government, leaned over and whispered to me, "Do you know, was that law ever actively enforced?" I didn't know; it suddenly struck me as a problem that I didn't. So I went to find out. This project emerged from the moment of that whispered question—an exchange between a city planner and a literary critic that in itself exemplifies some of the interdisciplinary range of disability studies.

The ugly laws are also known, somewhat more accurately, as "unsightly beggar ordinances." *The Ugly Laws* tells the story of the figure of the "unsightly beggar" as he (and she) emerged across multiple forms of discourse and knowledge, particularly in the 1880s and 1890s. Like the so-called tramp, the subject of a similar and interconnected cultural panic during the same period, unsightly beggars were "made up," as Tim Cresswell puts it in his study of vagrants. Following Ian Hacking, Cresswell argues that tramps were more like gloves than horses, made up, that is, "like manufactured objects. . . . [T]he category 'glove' and the thing 'glove' emerged more or less simultaneously" (13). In part, this study concerns the making up of the unsightly beggar, who was produced from the same raw social material (the same political economy and material infrastructure) that generated the tramp.

I have also sought to examine this "glove" from another angle. In a 2004 speech, Jürgen Habermas, tracing some of the autobiographical roots of his intellectual work, described his early childhood experiences of being born with a cleft palate, undergoing surgery in infancy, and dealing with social exclusion by his fellow schoolchildren because of his resultant speech impairment. These experiences, he argued, played a critical role in forming his thinking on the importance of public space and the political public sphere, subjects of crucial importance to an analysis of the ugly law. Meditating on "the deep-rooted reciprocal dependence of one person on the other" and the "intersubjective structure of the human mind," Habermas, too, uses the image of a glove: "What I am getting at here is an image of subjectivity which you may imagine as a glove turned inside out to discern the structure of its fabric, a glove woven from the strands of intersubjectivity" (3). If the "unsightly beggar" of *The Ugly Laws* is like a glove, I have tried to make it like a glove turned inside out, scrutinized under the lenses offered by the disability movement, examined—to take up the enduring image offered by the title of one movement journal—at its ragged edge.

The strands I examine here are textual. In the course of research for this book, I have at times visited actual places—the house in Berkeley where mendicant writer Arthur Franklin Fuller published his autobiography of ugly law, certain still extant street corners in Chicago and Los Angeles marked as the turf for particular disabled beggars in 1894 or 1913. And I have interviewed real people—a judge in Omaha who encountered the last known "unsightly beggar" to be arrested (in 1974), disability activists today. But my general aim has been to interview a discourse; my subject is the *discursive* unsightly beggar.

"It's hard to get real excited about winning the right to beg," a New York City lawyer commented after winning a 1990 case, later overturned, that affirmed the right of panhandlers to beg in subways (Mitchell, 210). What follows is not a celebration of begging in any form. It is, however, an attempt to elucidate as fully as possible the mechanisms that create "unsightly beggars" and "unsightly persons," in the hope that in the long run all vestiges of the culture of the American ugly laws will disappear.

When I ran an early version of this project by my friend Mark Limont, he told me about his experience as a kid "who walked funny and was stared at." He described a childhood memory of seeing an obviously disabled man on the street and feeling fury and humiliation, wishing the man would go home and not embarrass him. "We all write our own ugly laws," he said. "And then we have to write through them."

What follows is my effort to write through ugly law.

ACKNOWLEDGMENTS

My first thanks go to Carolyn Dinshaw and Janet Adelman, both of whom gave me encouragement at the earliest stages of this book. Lennard Davis and Simi Linton introduced me to disability studies when I came upon the bibliography they compiled for *Radical Teacher* in 1995, and they have been teaching me ever since. I owe Rosemarie Garland Thomson and Paul Longmore my deepest debt and gratitude, not only for their own invaluable work and for their critical help with mine but also for the models of intellectual integrity and generosity that they have provided. I am also indebted to every one of my fellow participants in the NEH-funded institute on disability studies in the humanities that Rosemarie and Paul organized.

This book was written in dialogue with three scholars and dear friends who read drafts of chapters, gave crucial suggestions, and offered critical advice: Deborah Clarke, Anne Finger, and Mark Sherry. I am immensely grateful for the extraordinarily generous guidance of readers of the entire manuscript: Douglas Baynton, G. Thomas Couser, Petra Kuppers, Barrett Watten, and the anonymous reviewers. Cathy Kudlick was my ideal reader; her unerring criticism made this book far better, even if it couldn't turn me into a historian.

Many people at U.C. Berkeley have helped with this project. I am grateful to the faculty in the Berkeley English Department, particularly Ian Duncan, Mitch Breitweiser, Elizabeth Abel, Lyn Hejinian, and Stephen Goldsmith. Other colleagues at Berkeley who provided help at key moments include Janet Broughton, Daniel Boyarin, Dan Perlstein, Tim Clark, Marianne Constable, and all of the participants in the 2002 Townsend Center Initiative Grant Seminar. I would also like to acknowledge the steady assistance of the administrative staff members of the English Department, the Institute for Regional Development, and Undergraduate Interdisciplinary Studies.

I have been fortunate to collaborate with a group of faculty at Berkeley who by helping make disability studies happen created a vital intellectual context for my work here. Thanks to all of the members of Berkeley's disability studies advisory board, and in particular to Lawrence Cohen, Catherine Cole, Linda Krieger, Celeste Langan, Ray Lifchez, Jennifer Miller, Paul Rabinow, Steve Rosenbaum, and Nancy Scheper-Hughes. I have benefited greatly from work with many people alert to disability issues on the Berkeley campus; special thanks to the librarians and oral historians at the Bancroft Library's Disability Rights and Independent Living Movement project.

I would like to thank all of the scholars who participated in the Ed Roberts Postdoctoral Fellowship Program at U.C. Berkeley, especially the ones who commented in detail on parts of this book. I am also grateful to all of the participants in the Greater Bay Area Disability Studies Consortium, including Julia Epstein, Ruth Frankenberg and Mary Felstiner. My students in the disability studies courses I've taught over the years have helped enormously with the shaping and refining of this book. To the colleagues in disability studies whom I met first as my graduate students I am especially grateful. Special thanks to Dominika Bednarska, Gretchen Case, Rebekah Edwards, Michele Friedner, Hillary Gravendyk Burrill, Kris Loutensock, Anna Mollow, Paul Murphy, and Ariel Osterweis Scott. Ellen Samuels inspired and challenged me in many ways. I am one of the many people who owe Christine Hong a great debt for her kindness and the keen intelligence of her conversation.

Above all, I thank a group of U.C. Berkeley co-workers who created and sustained the structures within which I came to do this work. They have given me examples of engaged scholarship that have changed this book and changed my life. Fred Collignon's influence will be obvious from the first page. Fred, Katherine Sherwood, Georgina Kleege, Devva Kasnitz, and Marsha Saxton: I can't thank you enough.

Natalie Abbott, Melissa Cottrell, Juno deMelo, Rosa Martinez, and Charles Legere gave me indispensable research help. I was privileged to have Mike Ervin's assistance with research in Chicago. Thanks also to Judge Walter Cropper for taking time to talk with me about the 1974 Omaha case. Emily Teplin and Simon Stern did their best to help me understand American law and legal citation, and I am also grateful for help provided by Dean Rowan.

All of us who work in disability studies know what a vibrant intellectual community we share in. I don't have room to cite everyone who contributed to the making of this book, but here's a beginning to the list of those I thank: Emily Abel, Ron Amundson, Michael Berube, Laurie Block, Brenda Jo Brueggemann, Susan Burch, Brad Byrom, Lisa Cartwright, Eli

Clare, Michael Davidson, Jim Ferris, Lakshmi Fjord, Brigham Fordham, Carol Gill, Dan Gillette, Terry Galloway, Sander Gilman, Joseph Grigely, Kim Hall, Laura Hershey, Martha Stoddard Holmes, Alison Kafer, Steven Kurzman, Dennis Lang, Riva Lehrer, Victoria Ann Lewis, Kristin Lindgren, Lynn Manning, Leroy Moore, Neil Marcus, Paul Steven Miller, Sagit Mor, Corbett O'Toole, Katherine Ott, Robert McRuer, David Mitchell, Stuart Murray, Ruth O'Brien, Martin Pernick, Penny Richards, William Roth, Harilynn Russo, Carrie Sandahl, David Serlin, Tom Shakespeare, Alice Sheppard, Russell Shuttleworth, Tobin Siebers, Sharon Snyder, Robin Stephens, Jean Stewart, Susan Squier. Thanks also to Rachel Adams, Jack Batterson, Bonnie Berry, Perry Duis, and Claire Sears for their scholarship and help. Without the work of Robert Burgdorf Jr. this book simply couldn't exist.

These friends, among others, have supported and influenced this project, and I thank them with love and admiration: Ayse Agis, David Alpaugh, Evan Alpaugh, Lucy Blackmer, Phil Bolda, Ramsay Bell Breslin, Mary Lou Breslin, Elizabeth Flora, David Gilbert, Ray Grott, Jim Grow, Jenny Kern, Ralf Hotchkiss, Bob Holtermann, Suzanne Ingley, Denise Sherer Jacobson, Neil Jacobson, Debbie Kaplan, Scott Leubking, Mark Limont, Daphne Muse, Kalima Rose, Anthony Tusler, Dianne Walker, and my friends on McGee. I will always be grateful to Chris Taaffe, who saw this book through the good, the bad, and the ugly.

This work could not have been completed without the support provided by the University of California, U.C. Berkeley, and the Doreen B. Townsend Center for the Humanities. I am grateful to the National Institute for Disability Research and Rehabilitation for its support of Berkeley's postdoctoral program in disability studies, which greatly enriched my understanding of the issues at stake in this book. Thanks also to the librarians and archivists at the Library of Congress, the Columbia University Rare Book Library, the New York Public Library, the Municipal Archives of New York, the New-York Historical Society, the Newberry Library, the Chicago Public Library, the Chicago Historical Society, the University of Illinois Chicago Special Collections, the Municipal Archive at Chicago City Hall, the Columbus Public Library, the Columbus Historical Society, the Columbus Metropolitan Library, the Ohio Historical Center Reading Room, the State Library of Ohio, the Western Reserve Historical Society in Cleveland's Special Collections, the Denver Public Library Department of Western History/Genealogy, the Denver Historical Society, the Historic New Orleans Collection, the Louisiana Division of the New Orleans Public Library, the

New Orleans Historical Society, the Louisiana State Museum, the library at Tulane University, the Omaha Public Library, the Douglass County Historical Society, the California History Society, the San Francisco History Room at the San Francisco Public Library, the Buffalo Public Library Special Collections, the Buffalo Historical Society, the University at Buffalo Law Library, the South Carolina Historical Society, the Los Angeles City Archives, the California State Library, the Countway Library Rare Book Room at Harvard, the Motion Picture Archive at George Eastman House, and the Bancroft Library. Thanks especially to the Interlibrary Loan staff at UC Berkeley. I am grateful to NYU Press and particularly to Eric Zinner, Ciara McLaughlin, and Despina Papazoglou Gimbel.

Thanks with all my heart to my family, both Schweiks and Taaffes, for their love and support.

Some of the people to whom I owe deep thanks did not live to see this book's completion: Nick Howe, who suggested the image on the cover; Harlan Hahn, Marian Scott-Hill, Judith Greenwood; and Jessie Alpaugh, the entirely beautiful.

Finally, I thank Emma McElroy for her patience over the years this book took to write and for the crucial ways in which she helped with the research. Most of all, I am grateful for the love and joy she has brought me.

For Emma

Don't fail to note the man behind the handicap!

Photograph from the "Cleveland Cripple Survey" of man driven off the streets of Cleveland by the unsightly beggar ordinance, circa 1916. (Welfare Federation of Cleveland, *Education and Occupations of Cripples Juvenile and Adult: A Survey of All the Cripples of Cleveland, Ohio, in 1916*. New York: Red Cross Institute for Crippled and Disabled Men, 1918)

INTRODUCTION

In Cleveland, Ohio, sometime before 1916, the man whose photograph is on the facing page lost his job. He stands smiling in the photo, wearing white tie and newsboy's cap, holding a stack of papers, a young man with clubbed hands and feet and a steady, confident gaze into the camera's eye. A 1916 report by the "Committee on Cripples of the Welfare Federation of Cleveland" records the story of how this man sold newspapers until "the enforcement of a statute."[1] The statute in question was a version of the subject of this book: the ugly law. I think most readers will agree with me that this man's ugliness is not obvious. In fact, he is notably a conventionally appealing person, full of pluck and charm.

A version of the statute that changed this man's life appeared in Chicago decades earlier, in 1881. In the *Chicago Tribune* on May 19 of that year, an article announced that Alderman Peevey had prepared a new ordinance, one that he would submit to the Council that week. "Its object," wrote the *Tribune*, "is to abolish all street obstructions." Peevey was on the Council's West Side Streets and Alleys subcommittee, which dealt with matters such as sidewalk improvement and street widening, and the *Tribune*'s emphasis on "street obstruction" makes it sound at first as if the "ugliness" in question concerned inanimate objects, such as "piles of bricks." But the street obstructions turn out to be human. A woman in 1881 Chicago had lost her job in a woolen-mill after being caught in a carding machine and injured. Attempting to support herself and her two children, she stood on the street, playing a hand organ. The ordinance, wrote the anonymous *Tribune* reporter, would "stamp" Alderman Peevey as a "public benefactor": "He proposes to abolish the woman with two sick children who . . . grinds 'Mollie Darling' incessantly on a hurdy-gurdy on a street corner." Peevey's ordinance passed, and Chicago ratified the American ugly law:

> Any person who is diseased, maimed, mutilated, or in any way deformed, so as to be an unsightly or disgusting object, or an improper person to be allowed in or on the streets, highways, thoroughfares, or public places in

> this city, shall not therein or thereon expose himself to public view, under the penalty of a fine of $1 [about $20 today] for each offense. (Chicago City Code 1881)

Peevey did not invent the wording of this ordinance. As city administrators commonly do, he looked for models, and these words were already available for the taking. Fourteen years earlier, in the earliest instance I have found, they show up in the code book of the young city of San Francisco. Just two years after the end of the Civil War, in July 1867, the *San Francisco Morning Call* reported the arrest of "a poor, half demented fellow, named Martin Oates," a former Union soldier who had, "while in the field, been stricken down with paralysis, leaving him a perfect wreck." Turned out of the army, Oates had landed on the streets and was taken into custody while San Francisco awaited the completion of its new almshouse ("Sad Sight"). A few weeks earlier, in anticipation of that almshouse, the San Francisco Board of Supervisors had already passed a law that the *Call* described as an "order to prohibit street begging, and to prohibit certain persons from appearing in streets and public places" ("Board of Supervisors"). The certain persons in question were those like Martin Oates, "perfect wrecks," or, in the words of the city, "diseased, maimed, mutilated, or in any way deformed." In San Francisco, significantly, the law was folded into a longer prohibition against begging in general.

Using more or less identical language, in the years that followed cities around the country passed or attempted to pass versions of the ordinance. Many versions of these statutes made clear in their titles that city leaders aimed the laws at a very particular target, the person who "exposed" disease, maiming, deformity, or mutilation for the purpose of begging. This book is about American ways of identifying, representing, knowing, correcting, and disciplining the "unsightly beggar."[2]

My aim is threefold: first, to provide a fuller account of the story of unsightly subjects than has yet been written; second, to rethink aspects of U.S. culture through the insights of disability theory (and in turn to rethink aspects of disability studies through an encounter with the history of the American ugly); and finally, to illuminate the conditions of disability—and municipal law's constitution of those conditions—in the late nineteenth century and at the century's turn, so as to better understand law, culture, and disability in the present. "Hidden and disregarded for too long," disability theorist Simi Linton has written of disabled people, "we are demanding not only rights and equal opportunity, but we are demanding that the academy take on the nettlesome question of why we've been sequestered in the first place" (73).[3] This book's history of one dramatic legal effort to compel that sequestration takes on that question—and shows how intricately tied it is to other nettlesome American questions, local and national.

I have come to think that it was probably more the norm than the exception for this law to show up on the code books of American cities sometime in the nineteenth or very early twentieth century. As I noted, the first ugly law I have found appears surprisingly far west—San Francisco—and surprisingly early, in 1867. Portland, Oregon, passed a similar law, with different wording, a few months before Chicago's in 1881. The ordinance seems to have been welcomed particularly from the 1880s on in midwestern cities with strong, networked cultures of reform, towns bound to each other and the rest of the nation by railroad ties. In 1889, Denver and Lincoln passed ordinances more or less identical to Chicago's and San Francisco's, Omaha sometime between 1881 and 1890, Reno sometime before 1905. In the mid-1890s, at the height of the worst economic depression in U.S. history to that date, an intense second wave of ugly laws appeared. Columbus enacted one in 1894. Northern cities also adopted or considered versions of ugly law. Pennsylvania passed a state version of the law. New Yorkers, inspired by Pennsylvania, made an unsuccessful attempt to pass a city ordinance in 1895. There is evidence that the law swept along the West Coast a little later, during a Progressive-era last gasp; Los Angeles considered passing one as late as 1913. Though as far as I know most southern cities did not pass the law, New Orleans had a statute very much in the spirit of the ugly law (though with significantly different language) as early as 1879, and its police began to enforce it strictly in 1883; at that time a local paper reported on the new get-tough policy with approval, emphasizing that it was "gratifying to know that New Orleans is aligning herself in this matter with other American cities" ("End to Street Begging"). This pattern—enactment, reenactment, crackdown, malaise—vexed all cities seeking reform through the ordinance. What most aligned them, in fact, as I show, were not the law's successes but its failures, the impossibility of removing the unsightly in the form of persons.

In what follows I frequently refer to the "ugly law" in the singular. Doing so allows me to underscore a certain strong and unified project shared by and across various city cultures, involving both a judgment about bodily aesthetics and the use of law to repress the visibility of human diversity in social contexts associated with disability and poverty—what we might call the sighting/citing of the ugly. At the same time, though, the singular "ugly law" implies more coordination than occurred. The law(s) might be better thought of as a kind of civic contagion. The singular acknowledges local histories as aspects of a single outbreak; the plural reminds us of its multiple cases.

This contagion was, it has been argued, peculiarly American. So British scholar Stuart Murray suggests. "Disability disturbs," writes Murray, "and it disturbs the sense of self in U.S. contexts in special ways," since the American tendency to conform, always in sharp tension with ideologies of liberty, is threatened "by the ways in which disability offers its characteristically double movement: a seemingly anomalous and deviant version of humanity that nevertheless focuses all too uncomfortably for many on the central issues of the human condition." Murray's proof is "the so-called 'ugly laws' that prohibited people with noticeable physical disabilities from visiting public spaces."

The general impulses I describe here are in fact by no means limited to the United States (see McKinley; Kim; and Degener for recent examples in Eritrea, North Korea, and Germany); nor are they limited to the turn of the last century.[4]

In Murray's England, back in 1729, a London merchant suggested whippings, workhouses and the establishment of a national institution for "receiving and strictly confining . . . People . . . who wander about to extort Money by exposing . . . dismal sights." This included "creatures that go about the Streets to show their maim'd Limbs," as well as a wider group:

> If any person is born with any Defect or Deformity, or maimed by Fire . . . or by any inveterate Distemper which renders them miserable Objects, their Way is open to London, where they have free Liberty of shewing their nauseous sights to terrify People, and force them to give Money to get rid of them. (Ribton-Turner, 187; Compton, 39)

Surely in this language of "miserable Objects," "exposing," "dismal," and "nauseous sights," we find cultural seeds of later U.S. ugly law. C.J. Ribton-Turner's expansive 1887 survey of English and European statutes concerning begging to that date provides many other examples, summarized compactly by Compton; indeed, Ribton-Turner's "Index of the Principle Varieties of Beggars" begins, under the heading "Afflicted Classes," with references to "Blind," "Cripples," "Deaf and Dumb," and "Maimed," among others. Though no English statute provided the exact template for the ugly law, English precursors existed, in scores. Again in Murray's England, now in 2004, business owners in Plymouth were reassured by city officials in language that corresponds exactly to that of ugly laws, which were usually entitled "unsightly beggar ordinances": "Any unsightly beggars are quickly removed from the City Centre" (*Checkout*). If, as Murray asserts, "disability disturbs, and it disturbs the sense of self in U.S. contexts in special ways," those ways nonetheless have a distinct family resemblance to the behavior of English police, also in 2004, who banned a beggar who displayed a wound on his neck in Camden, issuing him an "Anti Social Behavior Order" that restrained him from reentering the town (Allen).

Murray is correct, however, in emphasizing the peculiarly American grain of this attempt to control the movement of disabled people in the U.S. city through the mechanism of this specific municipal ordinance. One of the most important foundations of the ugly law involves a specifically American socioeconomic determinant: the broad cultural emphasis on individualism, which enabled the law's supporters to position disability and begging as individual problems rather than relating them to broader social inequalities.[5] As Brad Byrom puts it, "The link between disability and dependency became a problem . . . as America became increasingly urban, increasingly industrial, and increasingly confident that the United States was unique in the nations of the world, a nation where wealth and prosperity existed for all who were willing to put forth hard work" (2004, 4). The absence of eventual development of a universal, socialized health and welfare system in the United States, the relatively high U.S. standard of living compared to poorer countries, and the specific conflation of disability, socioeconomic status, and race in the American context are other important factors in the American breeding ground and memory of ugly law.[6]

Americanness extends in this context to include the reach of U.S. imperialism. In 1902, under newly stabilized U.S. occupation, the Municipal Board of the city of Manila in the Philippines passed an unsightly beggar ordinance. "All ordinances shall be enacted in English and translated into Spanish," a preface read, specifying that "the English text shall govern," so that even in Manila we find the distinctively American ugly law in its familiar cadence, "no person who is diseased" and so on (Ordinance No. 27, 1213). This was one of the very first ordinances enacted under U.S. military rule. Warwick Anderson has shown how the "distressed and assertive colonial culture" of U.S. officials sought to remake Filipino bodies, to fashion "an improved sanitary race out of the raw material found in the Philippine *barrio*," an elaborated project of hygiene reform, medico-moral uplift, and "uneven and shallow" Americanization (6, 1). The constitution of the unsightly beggar was part of this "technical discourse on bodily practice, mundane contact, and the banalities of custom and habit" that produced racialized abilities and colonial bodies in the Philippines (W. Anderson, 2). This example of ugly encroachment confirms, not complicates, Murray's assertion of the ugly Americanness of ugly law.

"As late as the early 1970s," Murray states, "some US states still had not repealed the so-called 'ugly laws,'" and although his emphasis on states rather than cities is inaccurate, his dating is correct. As far as I know, municipal enactments of the ugly law ceased by World War I, but the last documented arrest, astonishingly, happened in Omaha, Nebraska, in 1974. An Omaha policeman wanted to arrest a homeless man but had no basis for it. He combed the city code, found the ugly law still on the books, and took the man into custody on the grounds that he had "marks and scars on his body." Unsurprisingly, the arrest met with confusion and noncooperation by Omaha city prosecutors. "What's the standard of ugliness?" inquired Judge Walter Cropper, both initiating and responding to a deep conflation of "disease, maiming and deformity" with the word "ugly." "Who is ugly and who isn't?" Cropper asked. "Does the law mean that every time my neighbor's funny-looking kids ask for something I should have them arrested?" Assistant prosecutor Richard Epstein noted that criminal prosecution would require the impossible: courtroom proof "that someone is ugly" (Fogarty).

More surprising, perhaps, to some but not all of my readers, is the response by city prosecutor Gary Bucchino, who declined to file a charge against the man with marks and scars on his body but nonetheless affirmed that "the law is still active; the man just didn't meet the qualifications in my judgment" (Fogarty). This was 1974, a year after amendments to the federal Vocational Rehabilitation Act had banned discrimination against disabled people and a mere three years before the Department of Health, Education, and Welfare issued regulations to reinforce those amendments after unprecedented, militant pressure from disabled activists.

Those activists understood, of course, all the ways in which the naming and production of standards of perfection and beauty—and conversely, imperfection and ugliness—still operate and influence everyday interactions. Combating ugly law, they claimed powerful qualifications as persons "diseased, deformed, maimed and disfigured." "Spatial dissidents," in Dorn's terms, they insisted not only on exposing themselves to public view but also on occupying and radically reconfiguring public space. Such activists, and those who have come after them, have kept a version of the memory of the ordinance alive.

Citations of the statute, which usually call it the "ugly law" and often locate it in Chicago, constitute a staple feature in a wide variety of writing by disability theorists and organizers in the past thirty years.[7] These references do not generally proceed to discuss the ordinance further, after quoting it; few take up questions about what motivated the law's enactment, how the courts responded to the prohibition, or whether in fact it was ever enforced. Unmoored from its original context, the "Chicago, 1911" ordinance circulates today as both powerful rhetorical tool and literal urban legend—a legend about disability in the modern city. (A librarian of one Chicago archive still treats these legendary, oft-cited laws as if they were conventional urban legend; when approached, he says quite confidently that the ordinance is a myth. But his archives contain the ugly law's traces, and those traces have become my texts.) This book is part of that history of activist citation of the ordinance; I speak to it and within it.

The phrase "ugly law" was coined in the single source for all citations of the ordinance: a single paragraph in a landmark work of legal scholarship, Marcia Pearce Burgdorf and Robert Burgdorf Jr.'s "A History of Unequal Treatment: The Qualifications of Handicapped Persons as a 'Suspect Class' under the Equal Protection Clause," published in 1975. The authors cited a version of the wording in the Chicago Municipal Code that they said was in force "until recently," and they offered footnotes to codes in three cities: Chicago, Columbus, and Omaha. Robert Burgdorf wrote me in 2007 about what he remembered of finding out about these ordinances: "I do not recall which of the three [cities] we heard about first. If I had to guess, I would say it was probably the arrest in Omaha and the Omaha *World Herald* article that brought these kinds of laws to our attention." Offering the examples of three cities, the Burgdorfs named them ugly laws, inspired by reports of the Omaha case (855).

This article had a great deal of influence, as did (even more so) one of its authors, Robert Burgdorf Jr. His emerging knowledge of the ugly law came directly out of his involvement in a live and humming network of disability organizing. He writes, "My colleagues and I at the National Center for Law and the Handicapped (NCLH) had ties to all three cities," Chicago, Omaha, and Columbus, which were mentioned in the article.

> We had begun to do a considerable amount of work with ENCOR, the Eastern Nebraska Community Office of Retardation (now "and Developmental Disabilities"); we eventually filed a deinstitutionalization lawsuit in Nebraska, and worked with ENCOR on demonstrating the feasibility of

> appropriate community alternatives. One of the NCLH sponsoring entities was the American Bar Association, which is headquartered in Chicago; and one member of our board of directors was from Columbus. (Email correspondence with author)

In 1987, Robert Burgdorf Jr. drafted the original version of the Americans with Disabilities Act (ADA) that emerged out of the national movement growing out of this kind of organizing (the law in its enacted form was significantly revised, but it worked from Burgdorf Jr.'s template). Burgdorf, who had once been denied a job as an electrician's assistant because of his partially paralyzed arm, became a lawyer who specialized in disability law. Today he is a professor at the University of the District of Columbia, David A. Clarke School of Law. Journalist Joseph Shapiro portrays him in a section of his history of "people with disabilities forging a new civil rights movement": "He had plotted the outline of an antidiscrimination law in his head. By the time he arrived at the National Council on the Handicapped in 1984, the bill was virtually in his back pocket" (108).[8]

The Burgdorfs' "History of Unequal Treatment" was an important part of the trail of legal argument leading to the ADA. Its history of the ordinances that the authors named "ugly laws" was also influential, if the proliferation of citations is any indication. But the Burgdorfs' brief paragraph gives few leads, and some of them unstable, to the history of those ordinances. It provides a strong basis for contemporary disability rights law but a weak foundation for scholars wishing to take past ugly ordinances as signal instances of disability history.

The history of the ordinances has been reduced, distorted, and misrecognized in citations of the laws by authors following the Burgdorfs. For one thing, the ugly law was a patchy solution to a raggedy problem; as is typical for city ordinances, it seems to have been enforced rarely and unevenly. Historian Brad Byrom argues that the law was frequently disregarded by police, and a great deal of evidence suggests that this was in fact the case.[9] The possibility that on the whole the law's everyday enforcers ignored an ordinance complicates its history in ways disregarded by citations in contemporary disability rights discourses that follow in the Burgdorfs' footsteps.[10]

One of the most productively misleading aspects of the Burgdorfs' handling of the ordinance is the adjective with which they named it. Inventing "ugly" law, the Burgdorfs performed an act of advocacy very much embedded in the midseventies context, as I show. They were almost certainly inspired by the title of the Omaha newspaper article recording the 1975 arrest that they footnoted: "Begging Law Punishes Only the Ugly." It is important to note, though, that the word "ugly" appears nowhere in the wording of the ordinances they cited. The Burgdorfs, and no one else before them in print, marked the law as one involved with something "ugly."

In general I follow the Burgdorfs' example in naming the ordinance. I do so partly because, like Robert Burgdorf Jr., "I believe that the ugly laws are quite ugly," partly for the provocation of the term, and partly to honor the tradition the Burgdorfs started (letter to the author, 2007). The widespread adoption of the phrase "ugly law" throughout the disability activist community means that even if this term is not historically accurate, it has sufficient currency to identify this particular type of law.[11]

"Unsightly beggar ordinance" is a more accurate name historically, since some of these laws, though by no means all, appear under that heading in the code books, and since anxieties about begging played a crucial role in the emergence of the statutes. But titling and indexing practices differed meaningfully from city to city where this ordinance was concerned, as my list of the laws in the appendix illustrates. Neither the "beggar" nor the crime of "unsightliness" appears in all places. Columbus, Ohio, employed an interesting heading as late as 1972, for instance, filing the law under the rubric "Exposing Self When Unsightly." Here, in this contemporary version, exposure, not begging, constituted the misdemeanor, and the "when" opened up a kind of space between self and its abjection: the targeted person is not always but sporadically in a state of unsightliness. Other headers at other moments in the law's history mystified the nature of the ordinance in ways diametrically opposed to the outrageous title "ugly law." Denver in 1886, for example, indexed the law under "Deformed persons, how cared for, Section 1009," though this was followed immediately by a more directly accusatory alternative, "Shall not expose himself to public view, Section 1009," and the title in the section of the Denver code itself read "Deformed, Diseased or Maimed Persons" in 1898 and (even more bluntly) "Deformed, Persons" in 1886.

Significant differences not only in the titles but in the wording of the various city versions of the ordinance make it clear that the Burgdorfs' generic language of ugly law flattens out important regional and historical distinctions within the story of the rise, the spread, and the gradual demise of this statute. Take, for a start, the case of the actual "Chicago, 1911" municipal code. Under the heading "Exposing Diseased or Mutilated Limbs," the law begins, "Exposure of diseased, mutilated, or deformed *portions* of the body prohibited" (Brundage, Hayes, and Dierssen, 645; italics mine).

Only then follows the language we now hear quoted: "Any person who is diseased" and so forth. The Burgdorf citation is potentially misleading in its heightened emphasis on an absolute exclusion of the whole person, in any manifestation, from the public sphere. Omitting the ordinance's headline intensifies focus on the extreme prohibition of being on the street rather than the (perhaps) more moderate prohibition of certain behavior on the street. Melissa Cole has shown through her applications of the insights of queer theory to the study of disability law that the obligation to hide the very thing that might constitute oneself as "diseased" or "maimed," and the prohibition of all conduct such as limping or crawling that might identify one as "deformed," were demands potentially no less discriminatory than laws that directly target disability as a status rather than a set of behaviors (839). Still, it is often (though not always) somewhat easier to avoid exposing one's arm, say, than to avoid exposing oneself.

This is only one example from the range of differing local practices and ongoing historical developments illuminated when we look closely at the law's textual variants. Note, for instance, the early poorhouse/poor-farm clause, present in three of the laws passed in the 1880s (Chicago's, Lincoln's, and Denver's): "On the conviction of any person for a violation of this section, if it shall seem proper and just, the fine provided for may be suspended, and such person detained at the police station, where he shall be well cared for until he can be sent to the county poor house," Chicago's version read. By the 1890s, this provision disappears. At that time, another variant emerges: Columbus's ordinance (1894) and the draft New York law (1895), like the early San Francisco 1867 version, describe the target of the law as "himself *or herself*" (italics mine), explicitly designating the possibility of a female miscreant. Lincoln and Denver also hark back to San Francisco's language by adding "improper" to the list of adjectives applied to the person constructed by the ordinance; the New York draft goes even further, aiming its sights at the "imperfect." Columbus and Omaha (1890) place new emphasis on the conditions and effects of public viewing, banning "exciting sympathy, interest, or curiosity." This phrase is particularly interesting, since it does not ban performances that incite disgust or other forms of negative social reaction but rather highlights those responses that might involve a more positive connection between the disabled performer and the audience. New York's draft version, under the influence of the Pennsylvania act, adds reference to "idiots and imbeciles," expanding the scope of the law to include cognitive disability. Pennsylvania's state law is a special case whose language differs markedly, but both its emphasis on begging and its function as a model for the New York version relate it directly to the municipal laws that constitute the rest of the list.

I will have more to say about the implications of these variations. For now, a note in general on the language I myself employ. I have found it inefficient and historically inaccurate to substitute more palatable contemporary terms for the hard language of the ugly laws and their surround. This means I often use words I would not claim as my own in other contexts, not only the ugly line-up—"diseased," "deformed," "maimed," "unsightly," and, of course, "ugly"—but other terms like "cripple" and "beggar." All these words carry implicit scare quotation marks whenever they are used here. But so should other, less historically removed and seemingly more acceptable words, like "disabled" and "nondisabled" (and like "race"); in the realm of these matters, our available language does not suffice. Among the range of inadequate terms, I have chosen to use "disabled people" rather than "people with disabilities," preferring the former both for its directness and for its relation to the politicized social model of disability from which it has in part emerged.[12] I choose "nondisabled" rather than "able-bodied," since there is no such thing as an entirely, unalterably able body and since "nondisabled," refreshingly, places the "disabled" subject at the center and relegates its others to the zone of the prefix.

The United States Supreme Court continues to debate over the question of who is, or who qualifies legally as, disabled. In this book I am generally unconcerned with engaging in such debates. I have chosen to write about the ugly laws in this way to avoid any engagement with a categorical understanding of disability. "Category," as Tobin Siebers points out, "derives from the Greek kategorema, meaning a public denunciation or accusation. Categorical thought is accusatory logic" (*Mirror,* 64). Certainly the Supreme Court's ADA decisions bear out the truth of this analysis.[13] I choose rather to embrace a model of disability, broadly construed, as a political process. Hence, I focus on a particular form of political behavior, a blatantly conventionally political moment, the passing and implementation of a law, in order to understand that political event in the context of modern disability formation.[14]

The history of ugly ordinances itself encodes its own uneasinesses about categorization, built deeply into the language of the law. One noticeable aspect of each version of the statute, in any state or city, is its startling indeterminacy. We cannot know, as the muddle in the Omaha court made clear, who exactly is its target or how "unsightly" one must be to come into its sights. Hence the law might prove very useful as a way of foregrounding the inevitable ambiguity of the category of "disability."[15] The very wording of the ordinance seems to suggest this difficulty. It cannot find one term to settle the question of its own object, so the labels multiply: "diseased," "maimed," "mutilated," and then, with sputteringly anxious generality, "or in any way deformed," revolving on a slippery "so as to be," escalating from relatively medical terms like "diseased" to the discourses of aesthetics and psychology—"unsightly" and "disgusting"—and arriving in some city codes, with perfect inconclusivity, at the entirely vague "improper." Do these terms represent different things, or are they different attempts to name the same thing? "Diseased" carries associations with the social and the moral; "maimed" seems to gesture clearly toward the environmental, "deformed" toward the congenital; "unsightly" minces in the realm of the genteel, "disgusting" gets visceral. Even given the ordinary verboseness of law, this ordinance seems somehow both unusually redundant and psychologically confused. It might well be brought forward to exemplify a startling indeterminacy of scope. This is not, however, what the law has come to stand for in contemporary disability activism; rather, it represents a limit case, a certain extremity of prohibition.

There's an invented scene in John Belluso's recent history play *The Body of Bourne* in which the historical figure Randolph Bourne, the disabled social critic and writer, runs directly afoul of the ugly law when he visits Chicago. Belluso knew that this event was fictional (though his audiences on the whole do not).[16] It may be that this fictive moment, passing as disability history, stands for something telling about the ugly law: that its work was effectively imaginary (I place equal emphasis on both those words: both imaginary and effective). But if few or none were cited under the law then, why do so many continue to cite it now? It is one of my purposes in this book to show how vital it has been for disability studies to tell about the ugly ordinance as an iconographic story.

One important arena for this development has been disability arts culture. Belluso's is not the only contemporary American play to stage the ugly ordinance. The formal theater of ugly law begins in 1980 (by this I mean begins on stage, for as I show the law always carried with it its own ragged street theaters and impromptu performances). In that year, as part of a larger revue on European tour by the U.S. feminist theater collective Lilith, an American performer named Victoria Ann Lewis delivered the following monologue:

> I got polio when I was three years old. I have two different-sized legs [raises pants leg] and a limp. I am disabled.

> Being disabled is a strike against you when you look for work. I ran into trouble when I decided to become an actress . . .
>
> Actually there's a long line of disabled performers—beggars, fools, freaks in a carnival side show—they all earned their living by performing. But the excitement of the performance was in the hump on the back, the withered arm, the scarred face.
>
> I'm not a performing cripple. I'm limited on the stage by my limp. But if I concentrate really hard I can sometimes walk without a limp. [demonstrates walking and then does a somersault]
>
> Did you notice? Did you notice my limp? [begins signing] But why should I hide it. I am disabled. . . . The cripples are coming out of hiding![17]

At the center of this groundbreaking speech—one of many key moments when a new formation of disability culture made its entrance onto the contemporary stage—came this invocation of history:

> I applied to a theater school in New York City. They refused to admit me because of my limp. They said, "You could train to be a director . . . have you ever considered costuming? . . . We need some help in the office."
>
> Actually I don't blame them. If they had allowed me to perform they might have been breaking the law. It's true—there is a law in some cities of the United States today which reads:
>
> "No person who is deformed or mutilated in such a manner so as to be a disgusting object shall be allowed to display themselves to public view."[18]

Lewis went on to become the founder and director of Other Voices at the Mark Taper Forum in Los Angeles, a major venue for the development of disability community-based theater and performance art (including *The Body of Bourne*).[19] Several of the Other Voices plays were staged explicitly as "breaking the law," performing and shattering versions of the ordinance. In *P.H.*reaks: The Hidden History of People with Disabilities* (1994), for instance, a slide suddenly projected onto the back of the stage read, "1911—City of Chicago Ordinance prohibits any person who is diseased, maimed, mutilated or deformed in any way so as to be an unsightly or disgusting object from exposing himself to public view."[20] On the stage, (un)doing the history of these laws, defiantly disabled bodies in performance in productions like these and Belluso's delightedly exposed themselves to public view.[21]

Academic scholarship in what has come to be called "disability studies" has also made powerful use of ugly law. I draw on, and am inspired by, this body of work throughout this book. The brief survey that follows is only a sample of the range of texts that refer to the American ugly laws. So frequently is the Chicago ordinance cited in scholarship identified as disability studies, from 1987 to the present, that it is not surprising that one *New York Times* essay on the "blossoming culture of disability" exemplified the entire field by gesturing toward this subject. Disability studies, wrote the *Times* reporter, "unearth[s] attitudes behind laws like nineteenth-century Chicago's 'unsightly beggar ordinances'" (P.L. Brown).

One early example of this "unearthing," perhaps the first outside the world of law journals, appeared in work by an architect, a pioneering scholar-activist focused on eradicating disabling physical barriers in urban environments. In 1987, one of the most significant and underrecognized texts in the development of disability studies, Ray Lifchez's *Rethinking Architecture: Design Students and Physically Disabled People*, drew directly from the popular memory of the disability movement to invoke the law in an academic and creative context well beyond the Burgdorfs' legal framework. Following in Lifchez's footsteps, and borrowing his unusual (and historically ungrounded) emphasis on the law's concern with possible "legal liabilities" posed by the presence of disabled people in public places, British urban and disability studies theorist Rob Imrie (1996) cited the ordinance in turn to stress the hope of social change and the astonishingly rapid transformation in American attitudes toward disabled people: "Indeed, the speed of change is evident if, for instance, one considers that in 1960 many municipalities still included in their local statutes what were termed 'ugly' laws" (61–62).[22]

Simi Linton's groundbreaking summary and manifesto for a theory and method of disability studies (1998) took a reverse tack, illustrating not the promise of change but the continuity of oppression and the ongoing importance of political action. A pair of epigraphs in Linton's *Claiming Disability* suggested the still "virulent force" of disability discrimination by juxtaposing the wording of the ugly law, cited simply as "from the Municipal Code of the City of Chicago," with a more recent example of an ugly impulse: a reader's letter to Ann Landers, advocating special sections in restaurants "for handicapped people—partially hidden by palms or other greenery so they are not seen by other guests" (34).[23] Linton's openly political call to undo ugly law took a different form in the work of theologian and legal scholar M. Cathleen Kaveny (2002), whose analysis of the normative functions of laws focused on the ordinance's moral ramifications: "Assuming the citizens of Chicago internalize the normative vision of the worth of persons with disabilities presupposed by the law, how will they act in contexts not explicitly governed by it?" (339–340). In Kaveny's work of openly Catholic scholarship, the ordinance demanded a theological response; "diametrically opposed to the vision animating the Ugly Law," Kaveny concludes, "is the vision articulated by . . . John Paul II" in a papal encyclical, "Sollicitudo Rei Socialis" (358).[24]

Other scholars—their work is of obvious importance in this book—sought to illuminate the operations of the ugly law not through extrapolations into a contemporary present within which we are all citizens of a moral or political "Chicago 1911" but by reembedding the ordinance in its own local and historical contexts. These projects included clarifying the law's relation to racial and ethnic segregation and racialized physiognomic practice (Gilman, 24); to the rise of eugenics (Gilman; Snyder and Mitchell 2002); to the development of state institutions for hiding disabled people from the public view (Snyder and Mitchell 2002); to what may be the ordinance's single most pressing frame, organized charity under industrial capitalism (Snyder and Mitchell, CLD); and to the development of "sciences of the surface," "physiognomic practices," and "systems of anticipatory classification . . . based on bodily aesthetics rather than literal abilities" (Snyder and Mitchell, CLD, 41).

Finally, for some scholars the ugly law has invited more theoretical considerations of bodily aesthetics and the formal operations of the concept of disability. Rosemarie Garland Thomson's influential *Extraordinary Bodies* (1996) used the law, for instance, to emphasize that disability may be defined as much by appearance ("form") as by any limit on function (7). In the important essay "What Can Disability Studies Learn from the Culture Wars?" (2003), Tobin Siebers took a more theoretical and psychoanalytic approach, moving away from the history of individual "unsightly" bodies to argue, provocatively, that the ugly laws demonstrate that "the compulsion to maintain instances of ideal form in public buildings and streets echoes a more primordial obsession with perfect, public bodies" (198).

Let us step back from recent invocations of the ordinance and return to the Cleveland man whose photograph graces the start of this book, the man who gives a face and a public body to the targets of the ugly law. He made the following statement in 1916 regarding Cleveland's unsightly ordinance. "Although it [the law] seemed rather hard," the "Cleveland Cripple Survey" reports, "he appreciated the meaning of it, but considered it ill-advised unless some step went with it for providing other opportunity for work for cripples." What meaning was it, exactly, that this man, in his guarded, strategic protest, is said to appreciate?

This book explores the meanings I discovered when I went to look for what lay behind, proceeded from, surrounded, and constituted the texture of this law. What the ordinance embodied was disability oppression deployed and embedded, ideologically and structurally, in classed, capitalist (and also gendered and racialized) social relations. Here "disability history" and "poor people's history" profoundly intertwine. Ugly law was begging law, although contemporary American disability activism did not know this. Unsightliness was a status offense, illegal only for people without means.[25]

Writing of the historical period in which both ugly ordinances and models of eugenics emerged, Davis (2002) states, "The problem for people with disabilities was that eugenicists tended to group together all allegedly 'undesirable' traits. So, for example, criminals, the poor, and people with disabilities might be mentioned in the same breath" (35). This was (and is) indeed a serious problem for disabled people, but so too, as Mollow has pointed out astutely and as Davis's work itself illustrates, is the reverse: a historical denial of the dynamics that have linked disability, poverty, and the systems for policing and designating criminality (284).[26] What if, instead of trying to tease these categories apart, we pursue the lumping together of crime, poverty, and disability? After all, as Garland Thomson has noted, "Perhaps the most enduring form of segregation [for disabled people] has been economic: the history of begging is virtually synonymous with the history of disability" (*EB*, 35).[27] This "same breath" is the story of the ugly laws.

Readers seeking a history of the ugly laws can find its outlines here, though much of that history, too, still remains to be written. Since the purview of the ordinance has so long been reduced, falsely, to "Chicago" and "1911," I have tried an opposite, corrective mode, one that ranges (though by no means exhaustively) across many cities and a broad time span. The book focuses primarily on two historical moments, one of about half a century (1867–1920) in which the laws were generated and the second the period from 1974 to the present in which they were remembered. The first we might call the era of the unsightly, since that was the term of choice in the ordinances themselves; the second we might call the era of the ugly, as that anachronistic term, with its aesthetic implications, was powerfully overlaid onto the terrain of the ordinances.

I focus here somewhat on the mythic city of ugly law, Chicago, though with significant detours to many other cities and a few imaginary places. On occasion I focus on 1911 for a reason: it is the date embedded in popular cultural memory of the law. It is an arbitrary date, in keeping with the imaginative and dislocated aspects of most ugly law citation. My aim is not to purge the legal history of its fictitious aspects (though I trace as precisely as I can what I think happened in Chicago and the other cities) but to explore the fictive work of ugly law citation, its powerful representation of urban exclusion reduced to its essence.

Part 1 of this book explores the emergence of the ugly laws. In these chapters I examine early examples of the ordinance (and related municipal laws) and begin to explore why the ugly law came to be. No single motive can account for the development of unsightly beggar policing in American culture. The first two chapters focus on two key factors: the rise of "scientific" Charity Organization Societies, whose leaders played major roles in promoting the ordinance as a tool for the state, and the conflicts and social unrest that clustered around disabled people who begged in a free-labor society driven by what Amy Dru Stanley calls "the obligations of contract" and more or less devoid of safety nets (1992, 1272).[28] If, in this period, as Daniel Bell put it, "conspicuous consumption was a badge of a rising middle class" and "conspicuous loafing is the hostile gesture of a tired working class," displays of disease, maiming, and deformity by street beggars also constituted a gesture, one increasingly read as hostile (15). But could a blind or crippled person conspicuously loaf? "Loafing" is a category applied only with difficulty to people constituted as "not-laborers." And yet the discourse of the unsightly beggar worked hard to attach loafing to the body of the person who was diseased, maimed, and deformed. "Conspicuous," of course, was a term easily applied to exposed disabled bodies already readily subject to the stares of others. The second chapter traces histories of urban unease and class conflict over conspicuous begging and glaring disability, unrest that both responded to and sometimes provoked the devising of ugly law.

The next chapters open up a wider range of factors that converged to form a niche for the law, including the rise of eugenics and state institutions; the development of modern urban planning and maps for the city beautiful; new cultures of injury in a modernity characterized by sweeping technological changes and growing corporate power; new pressures regarding city manners and civility or the conduct of public bodies on the streets; a growing understanding of the urban public sphere as a pedagogical space; anxieties around animality in the city; temperance and prohibition movements; rhetorics of disgust. At the end of part 1, I explore at length the figure of the faker who so preoccupied the advocates of the ugly laws. In much of the unsightly beggar discourse it is simply assumed that all disabled beggars are, without exception, "sham cripples." Such assumptions, it seemed, justified the severity of ugly law. Rather than simply discounting this obviously inaccurate claim, I take imposter beggars seriously, writing a history of their presence on the streets of major U.S. cities (particularly in New York's Bowery), tracing their specific impact on urban geography, and speculating on their relations to the "real cripples" who also performed unsightly disability as a begging ritual.

Cultural memory of the ugly laws has tended to frame the subject of the ordinances as purely and abstractly disabled: ungendered (that is, male), unraced (that is, white), without nationality (that is, American), and unsexualized (that is, heterosexual, but only in default). But within each city there were many ugly laws, not one. Definitions of and penalties for unsightliness could take different forms for women than men, Italians than African Americans, and so on. The second part of the book, "At the Unsightly Intersection," ranges broadly over and between other identity categories enmeshed with the "diseased, maimed, and deformed," showing how the ordinances emerged within and worked to reinforce unstable and evolving norms of nation, race, sex, and gender. I read the laws in their historical relation to the policing of gender and sexual transgression; to nativism, anti-Semitism, and anti-immigrant legislation; and to state-imposed racial segregation.

In part 3, "The End of the Ugly Laws," I trace resistance to the ordinances both at the moment they emerged and after, unfolding briefly the negligible, almost invisible, record of legal challenges and dwelling at more length on other cultural mechanisms for sidestepping, countering, and dismantling the work of the unsightly beggar ordinances. Focusing on a group of key texts—a 1903 memoir by a disabled performer famous in his time and now all but forgotten; the rehabilitationist "Cleveland Cripple Survey" of 1916; and, finally, life-writing by "unsightly beggars"—chapters 9, 10, and 11 examine why these laws no longer appear on the books and what stopped them. The concentration on life-writing by unsightly subjects in this section is a necessary (and historically grounded) equal and opposite reaction to the creation of unsightly objects in the laws themselves. An ongoing theoretical tension at play throughout my analysis—between disability as a form of (visual) exclusion, on the one hand, and a Foucauldian account of discursive formation on the other—resolves to some extent in the examples here, as Marshall P. Wilder's and Arthur Franklin Fuller's writings suggest new lines of inquiry about (and between) poetics and disability.[29]

"As long as there is still one beggar," wrote Walter Benjamin, "there still exists myth" (505). Buck-Morss has glossed this line, commenting on

Parisian street-dwellers in the present: "to attribute their permanence . . . to some archetypal weakness (or strength) of character would be to fail to see the permanence of the social order which needs to create a myth about them in order to conceal the reason why, in an affluent and 'free' society, such poverty exists" (114). Throughout the book, I emphasize the tight interconnection between disability and begging in the history of ugly law. This is a necessary corrective to the disappearance of the beggar in certain versions of the ordinance, driven by identity politics in contemporary disability culture. But in the conclusion, I set begging aside to engage with other ugly dynamics still very much at work today. We fall into an error of equivalent magnitude to forgetting the beggar if we ignore the history and ongoing intensity of matter-of-fact discrimination against people with appearance impairments. As long as there exists "disfigurement," there still exists myth. This final section asks why, in an affluent and "free" society, such poverty of imagination regarding disability—tied inevitably to material poverty—still exists.

In a concurring opinion for the *Tennessee v. Lane* Supreme Court case in May 2004, Justice Souter brought the ugly laws into high court record. "Evidence would show," he sharply noted, "that the judiciary itself has endorsed the basis for some of the very discrimination subject to congressional remedy" by the Americans with Disabilities Act. Souter continued, listing some examples:

> *Buck* v. *Bell* (1927) was not grudging in sustaining the constitutionality of the once-pervasive practice of involuntarily sterilizing those with mental disabilities. See *id.*, at 207 ("It is better for all the world, if instead of waiting to execute degenerate offspring for crime, or to let them starve for their imbecility, society can prevent those who are manifestly unfit from continuing their kind. . . . Three generations of imbeciles are enough"). Laws compelling sterilization were often accompanied by others indiscriminately requiring institutionalization, and prohibiting certain individuals with disabilities from marrying, from voting, from attending public schools, and even from appearing in public.

Souter's final glancing allusion to the unsightly beggar ordinances functions as illustration of extreme form—the extreme form—of American discrimination against disabled persons. Did the ugly laws ever categorically bar all disabled people from appearing in public, as the justice's admirably reflective and self-critical reference suggests? The answer, I argue, is no, not simply, but I argue too that the story of the unsightly beggar ordinances nonetheless justifies and underscores the importance of building their memory into the legal record and of acting on that memory as Justice Souter does here. "Like other invidious discrimination," Souter continued, these laws, through their "lack of regard, . . . did great harm."

This book is a history of the harm done by—let us allow the phrase some force—lack of regard. It is also a history of counterforms of self-regard. Playwright Mike Ervin opens up that history in his exuberant fantasy of undoing the ugly laws, even as he acknowledges that mass resistance to the ordinances never occurred. Imagining an alternate history in which the 1960s merge with the 1880s, Ervin envisions a scenario in which the arrest of an unsightly beggar sparks "the opposite of a mass boycott,"

> with hundreds of the diseased and deformed screwing up the system by going out to engage in commerce. Maybe similar acts of blatant defiance would have sprung up in other cities. Coming up with in-your-face tactics wouldn't have been hard. Just having gangs of the maimed and mutilated having picnics and chasing butterflies in the park would have been enough to goad the authorities. Would the authorities have dispersed these picnics with attack dogs and fire hoses? How much would it have changed the course of history if they had? One can only dream. (x)

This wry "one can only dream," written by an activist for spinal-cord-injured readers in 2006, registers a present lack: disability rights still unstable or deferred, a disability movement not sufficiently mobilized, disabled people still not fully included in work, education, and other aspects of society. But Ervin's playful, openly political rhetoric also registers a desire, both to measure his community's distance from and to reclaim what it owes to the ad hoc, daily, in-your-face tactics of the historical unsightly beggar. *The Ugly Laws* traces some routes between that past figure and our present, beginning with a man who sold newspapers in Cleveland, a "half-demented" paralyzed Union soldier, and the woman who played "Mollie Darling."

PART I

THE EMERGENCE OF THE UGLY LAWS

> The actual physical limitations resulting from the disability more often than not play little role in determining whether the physically disabled are allowed to move about and be in public places. Rather, that judgment for the most part results from a variety of considerations related to public attitudes, attitudes which not infrequently are quite erroneous and misconceived. These include public imaginings about what the inherent physical limitations must be; public solicitude about the safety to be achieved by keeping the disabled out of harm's way; public feelings of protective care and custodial security; public doubts about why the disabled should want to be abroad anyway; and public aversion to the sight of them and the conspicuous reminder of their plight. For our purposes, there is no reason to judge these attitudes as to whether they do credit or discredit to the human head and heart. Our concern is with their existence and their consequences.
>
> —JACOBUS TENBROEK,
> "The Right to Live in the World:
> The Disabled in the Law of Torts," 1966

1

PRODUCING THE UNSIGHTLY

In a recent letter to me, Robert Burgdorf Jr. looked back at the moment when he and Marcia Pearce Burgdorf defined the ugly laws in print and recalled why they chose that name for the ordinance:

> As to the phrase "ugly laws," I believe it was one of us professional staff members at NCLH [National Center for Law and the Handicapped] who first used it as a shorthand. The [Omaha] *World Herald* article has "ugly" in its headline, and the article focuses quite a bit on demonstrating that a person alleged to have violated the ordinance is "ugly." But as the article describes, the Omaha ordinance was more aptly described as an "unsightly beggar" law, as it only applied to persons who were "ugly" and were "soliciting alms or exciting sympathy, interest or curiosity." The Chicago and Columbus ordinances were not limited to beggars but applied to any "unsightly or disgusting" person who showed himself in public. Accordingly, it was appropriate to refer to the overall category of such laws as "ugly laws." This terminology was chosen in the law review article with clear awareness that it was catchy phrasing with some dramatic impact; it was also an accurate characterization. Nor was the secondary meaning—that such laws are themselves repugnant and abhorrent—unintended.

The choice of "ugly law" stemmed, that is, not only from a deliberate political, rhetorical strategy but also from an analytic principle: some versions of the law, understood as *ur* versions of the core of the law, "were not limited to beggars." "Ugly" was therefore "an accurate characterization." And yet, at the same time, for at least some of the laws like Omaha's, there was another more "apt" description. In the broader history of the law, this tension, between the aesthetic term "ugly" and the more relational "unsightly," and also between the beggar and beyond-the-beggar, is not resolved simply by distinguishing between cities. The beggar is always present at the origin of the law. But this does not mean "ugly" is an inaccurate characterization.

In this chapter, I explore what is apt and accurate for an understanding of the law by beginning at three beginnings, three moments of intent when cities first constituted their unsightly beggars and embarked on the futile and endlessly productive project of managing them. Together the three city histories illuminate the persistent nexus of disability and poverty at the heart of the ugly law, as well as illustrating the complex interweaving of economic interest, social policy, and cultural (including aesthetic) imagination at work in the production not just of the unsightly beggar but of the nineteenth-century American cityscape.

SAN FRANCISCO

San Francisco's ugly law is the earliest I have found.[1] It was passed in 1867, significantly earlier than the 1880s and 1890s, when unsightly beggar ordinances were in vogue. California, writes Kevin Starr, has functioned as "one of the prisms through which the American people, for better or worse, could glimpse the future," and it may be that the ugly law is one of those prisms, an early peek into one form of modernity that later swept the nation (xiv). San Francisco in 1867 was in urban shock. It was a city under enormous sociohistorical pressure, reeling from its Gold Rush boom and subsequent bust, a conflicted urban culture shaped by multinational migration (including, crucially, Chinese immigration) and by the ongoing reverberations of the U.S. annexation of California from Mexico twenty years earlier (see Sears). Clare Sears, in her San Francisco–centered study of cross-dressing regulation, has delineated how "an increasing governmental commitment to achieving moral order through municipal law" emerged in the city after the armed coup by the elite import/export businessmen who led the 1856 "Vigilance Committee." "Vigilantes and their allies dominated local politics for almost twenty years," Sears writes, "and ushered in a wave of laws that targeted 'offenses against good morals and decency,' including cross-dressing law" and ugly law (74).

In San Francisco, at its earliest known onset, American ugly law appears as a clear subset of begging law. The San Francisco ordinance begins with a general order to "Prohibit Street Begging"; the wording of ugly law taken up later by other city councils as a stand-alone law emerges in San Francisco's code book as an embedded "section 3" of a broader antimendicancy statute—embedded but at the same time underscored. The title of the order as a whole couples two linked but also potentially distinct transgressions: "Order No. 873. To Prohibit Street Begging, and to Restrain Certain

Persons from Appearing in Streets and Public Places." To be hailed by the law one must be either begging or a "Certain Person" or both; the law prohibits begging, but to certain persons it applies total restraints. The perpetual ambiguity of ugly law lies in this heading.

Early California historians often depict the streets of San Francisco circa 1867 as packed venues populated by certain persons, by unsightly beggars and mad vagrants. "The great number of [mental] patients . . . made a frequent subject of remark among the early writers about California," wrote Josiah Royce in 1886 (309). In *Dreadful California,* Hilton Helper quotes an 1860 *Alta California* editorial: "It is really surprising to notice the great number of insane people who have been found in this city" (18). He quotes a "correspondent" who writes, "Hundreds of mechanics and laborers in a deplorably destitute condition are sauntering about the streets with nothing to do and unable to find employment" (158). Men who had come to California to strike it rich remained, at loose ends and in dire straits: "Ill-fated men," writes Helper, "who, if they had the means, would be glad to shake the dust of California off their feet" (79).

Not only Helper—whose title, *Dreadful California,* declares his bias—but other chroniclers told the story of men whom the Gold Rush made unsightly, versions of the plot that Helper encapsulates in his account of a man driven mad after failing at mining:

> His reason lost his equilibrium, and we now find him a raving maniac. More than half naked, friendless and forlorn, he wandered about the streets . . . a poor, miserable, crazy vagabond.
>
> Why, it may be asked, was there no public provision made for the removal and security of this pitiable nuisance? Simply because it was California. Here, where nothing is as it should be, this unhappy man was allowed to run at large. No one cared for him. (124)

Craddock argues that this distinctly Californian lack of care stemmed from a Gold Rush ideology that emphasized the ability of any man, whatever his prior economic situation, to make good. Despite later economic downturns, the social discourse of self-made success persisted in San Francisco, undergirding the particularly "unsympathetic attitudes toward the impoverished" that Craddock finds in the city in the second half of the nineteenth century (15). We can spot this failure of care in both the Californian problem of the broken-down miner and the Californian solution of the ordinance of 1867;

"running at large" was countered by the peculiar kind of not/"caring for" that ugly law entailed.

"Caring for" distributes itself within the wording of the San Francisco ugly law with illuminating precision. The ordinance begins as a generalized ban: "No person shall, either directly or indirectly, whether by look, word, sign, or deed, practice begging or mendicancy . . . in any public place." The supervisors specified a heavy punishment for this offense, twenty-five dollars (the equivalent of $350 today) or twenty-five days in jail or both. To counterbalance the harshness of this prohibition, a "Section 2" follows:

> On the conviction of any person for practicing mendicancy or begging, if it shall appear that such person is without means of support, and infirm and physically unable to earn a support or livelihood, or is, for any cause, a proper person to be maintained at the Almshouse, the fine and imprisonment provided for in the preceding section may be omitted, and such person may be committed to the Almshouse.

A significant change in the city's material carceral infrastructure, its newly built almshouse not only made this infirmity exemption possible; it also legitimated and in some sense prompted the harsh rule that the infirmity clause was meant to temper. With an almshouse in place, street-cleaning could proceed, justified—when proper—as caretaking. The city could purport to demonstrate its commitment to by practicing commitment of "infirm and physically unable persons."[2] (The place where this almshouse sat later became the site of Laguna Honda, "the World's Largest Nursing Facility," a nursing home that has become a central locus of protest in recent years by local and national disability rights movements. This literal location makes clear that the unsightly beggar ordinances, the history of institutionalization and incarceration in poorhouses, and the modern independent-living movement are inextricably linked.)

With the infirm and the physically unable we might seem to have crossed into the terrain of ugly law. Not so. Infirm and physically unable persons, who live in what Livingston calls the overlap "between impairment, chronic illness and senescence" that constitutes "debility," are by the Board of Supervisors' definition not unsightly beggars (6). The infirm languish in Section 2 of the world of the San Francisco ordinance. Unsightly persons squat in the zone of Section 3, where our by now familiar language ("any person who is diseased, maimed, mutilated, or in any way deformed so as to be . . .") makes its appearance. Unlike infirm and physically unable persons, who are specified by the order only insofar as they need to be exempted from it, persons designated unsightly and disgusting constitute a criminal class subject to the full force of the law. Section 3, our first known ugly ordinance, doles out to the unsightly the same hard penalty applied to able-bodied beggars, twenty-five dollars and/or days.

To be sure, mercy seemingly counters severity in the next section of the law, which provides for alternative sentencing for unsightly beggars if it "shall seem proper and just." Under such circumstances the fine would be waived. Almshouse commitment (of indeterminate length) would be substituted for the twenty-five-day jail term. Still, for the unsightly, as opposed to the infirm, the language of crime and punishment emphatically precedes the language of charity in San Francisco's ordinance.

Even at best, the unsightly beggar, like his or her infirm counterpart, might be incarcerated in an almshouse for an indefinite period of time. That was not exactly getting off easy. With the city's provision for remanding to the almshouse, San Francisco was adopting a form of Victorian-era poor-law policy. In the English poor-law system, its ideological roots dating as far back as the Elizabethans and its more recent practices heavily influential in the United States, almshouse consignment functioned as a way of regulating dependent people thought likely to be disorderly. Traditional poor relief disguised its hostility toward those whom San Francisco named the infirm and the unsightly, under the mask of charity. But the notion of social and moral deviance and therefore of moral infraction never entirely disappeared. Noting that many scholars on poor-law history have focused on the "badge of moral depravity" that the ideological underpinnings of the laws "affixed on the able-bodied poor," Paul Longmore, drawing on the pioneering work of tenBroek and Matson, shows how in fact "poor-relief and welfare policies have always inflicted a parallel moral stigma," just as intensively although sometimes inflected differently, on disabled people. Even though public policies from 1867 San Francisco to this day ostensibly follow the poor-law model of separating the "worthy" from the "unworthy" poor, those policies, Longmore writes, "have also effectively erased that distinction by marking people in both categories as unworthy." In the end, one way or another, "All are punished" (2003, 240–242).[3] San Francisco's legal sorting-out of infirm from unsightly busied city officials with distinguishing which forms of bodily difference were and which were not moral transgressions, even as the sentence to the almshouse, indefinite and indiscriminate, lumped them back together in the same punitive place, equally hidden and discredited.

Whether one was "copper" (in the color-coding of the city's almshouse records) or "Coolie" or "Native-Born" white made a difference in the sorting, determining how someone found to be a "certain person" in San Francisco would be defined (as infirm or disgustingly diseased), construed (as pitiable or deplorable), and disposed of (in jail or in quarantine or exile or given over to the harsh charity of the almshouse) ("Almshouse," 342). I have more to say later in this volume about the key roles played by race and nationality in the dynamics of ugly law in this and other cities. For now, I simply note that the same Board of Supervisors that set this ugly law in motion simultaneously and subsequently engaged in a wide variety of racialized "public health intrusions" against the Chinese in particular (Craddock, 4). These orders, which pathologized Chinese people as inherently diseased, maimed, deformed, defective, and infective, profoundly shaped the cityspace of San Francisco. In the contexts of measures like the mass quarantines of entire (and entirely Chinese) districts of the city, ostensibly to halt epidemics of infectious disease, ugly law may be understood as an interlocked attempt to map and contain deviance.[4] The Supreme Court's much later (1900) overturning of such quarantines as unconstitutional, in *Jew Ho v. Williamson,* held that San Francisco authorities had acted with an "evil eye and an unequal hand." The eye and hand of ugly law were not unrelated.

Another critical factor was at work in San Francisco in 1867. Perhaps the single most salient feature of the city's ugly law is this: the ordinance was an immediate postwar phenomenon.[5] War—the Civil War in particular—played a crucial role in the development of the ugly laws, as the case of San Francisco shows. Near to the war in time, farther from it (in miles from battlegrounds) than many U.S. places, 1867 San Francisco was, perhaps, the perfect breeding ground for postbellum ugly law: a city deeply affected but not overwhelmed by the visible injuries that large numbers of Americans sustained in the war zones.

Begging veterans entering or reentering the peacetime city told war stories with their injured bodies. San Franciscans responded ambivalently. On the one hand, military service overlaid impairment with honor—particularly Union Army service (in the week before the San Francisco Board of Supervisors passed the ugly law, local papers covered the ban on Confederate soldiers marching in the civic parade of discharged soldiers on the Fourth of July) (*Alta California,* July 1, 1867). City discourse on veterans constructed them as needy, deserving, and betrayed. A July 3 editorial in the *Alta California* declared a crisis of employment for ex-soldiers, recounting instances of men promised they could return from war to jobs left behind, only to find those promises broken (July 3, 1867, 1). This kind of narrative could give a beggar in uniform some clout.

That same year, across the continent in New York City, one amputee veteran proclaimed, "I have that mark, and so conspicuous, that all can see it. . . . No man can say, that Allen was a coward and hid from danger" (Clarke, 379). Historians who have examined photographs of amputee Civil War veterans note that the majority of men photographed enacted Allen's principle in their poses, prominently displaying tightly pinned-up empty sleeves and pants legs (Figg and Farrell-Beck, 467–468). For them, being maimed seems to have constituted a badge of honor, not unsightliness. Though Allen explicitly distanced himself from the figure of the beggar—"There is no man who has lost an arm or a leg," he insisted, "but can earn a good support with the limb left him"—veterans on the street might still exploit the right to say "I have that mark, and so conspicuous" when they asked for, or demanded, alms (Clarke, 385).

But on the other hand, war injury could be faked, and as a result disabled beggars often met with more, not less, suspicion. The newspaper being hawked at the time by amputee veterans in New York, *The Soldier's Friend,* had warned that real vets had "liberal provision" from the government, "enough, surely, to render . . . mendicancy inexcusable" (Clarke, 386). In the same July 3 issue of the *Alta California* that published concerns about unemployed vets in San Francisco, an article entitled "A Young Rascal" reminded readers of "the one-legged boy who pretended to have lost his other leg at Fredericksburg, and raised some hundreds of dollars at the Metropolitan Theatre, but who turned out to be a swindler, who had never been in the army at all, and had his leg amputated in this city on account of a white swelling." This story contains in miniature key aspects of discourse in ugly law culture that I trace at length later: the sheer excess of impairment in the scene of swindling; the redoubling performativity of begging at (as) the theater. Both the scars and the scams of postwar culture laid the ground for ugly law.

CHICAGO

Ugly laws could germinate in cities not yet undergoing the kind of exploding overgrowth that San Francisco had experienced; in 1880, Portland, Oregon, another post–Gold Rush town about to adopt a similar ordinance, still had less than eighteen thousand people (Paul, 12). But under the stresses of urban crowding, particularly in the Midwest, the unsightly beggar ordinance proved especially attractive to city councils. Chicago provides an example.

The ugly law emerged in Chicago not in 1911—the legendary year commonly cited by disability activists—but in the city code of 1881. The timing is important. As Jean-Louis Comolli has written, "the second half of the nineteenth century lives in a sort of frenzy of the visible" (122). In late-nineteenth-century America, a particular form of visibility gained attention, associated with the politics of identifying and controlling the "ugly." This disciplinary politics reflected specific social and economic developments. In the early 1880s and the years immediately before, the nation underwent a period of prolonged economic depression; many disabled veterans of the Civil War were still alive and aging; disabled foreigners were noticeably present in the city, since immigration restrictions were not as tightly developed as they soon became. All these factors pressured the streets of Chicago.[6] In May 1881, two aldermen, Alvin Hulbert and James Peevey, submitted to the "Streets and Alleys, West Division" subcommittee of the Chicago City Council a "Resolution to Remove Beggars from the Streets."[7] The "West Division" of the Council's Chicago was, as Carolyn Eastwood puts it, "from its nineteenth century beginnings and on into the twentieth century . . . a port of entry for immigrants and migrants, including French, Irish, German, Bohemian, Jewish, Italian, Mexican, African-Americans, and Gypsies." By 1910 it constituted the most densely populated district—and one of the poorest areas—in Chicago (2002, 4). In 1889, Hull-House was sited there.

Ordinarily the Streets and Alleys subcommittees confined themselves to issues like the state of the sidewalks or the placement of streets. Other subcommittees were devoted to "Legislation," to "Police" (Alderman Hulbert was a member of that one as well), and to "Health and County Relations" (that is, relations to Cook County's poorhouse and public institutions like asylums), a subcommittee that included Alderman Peevey.[8] In this case, however, ugly law, not the improvement of infrastructure (*as* the improvement of infrastructure), was spawned out of, or into, the Council's West Side streets and alleys.

The law was one of many ordinances through which the Chicago City Council wrestled with the question framed by Perry Duis in his "Whose City? Public and Private Places in Nineteenth-Century Chicago." Duis argues that Chicagoans' increasing sense of urban crowding led to multiplying attempts to regulate personal comportment (13). Like the statute books of nineteenth-century cities across the country, Chicago's were being "stocked," as Mary Ryan puts it, "with coercive and quaint rules about behavior in the streets" (62). As Sears has shown, municipal law played a more important role at the time than federal or state law in regulating everyday life.[9] Most arrests in U.S. cities at the time were prompted, Ryan writes, "by infractions of public order—failure to conform to proper street etiquette" (62). Since most of the human beings whom one encounters in the city are strangers, city dwellers depended on abstract law to handle manners problems that small-town residents addressed through more intimate and flexible social mechanisms. Like other petty behavior laws, the ugly law emerged in response to new disciplines of the body in post–Civil War urbanization.

With the stroke of Alderman Peevey's pen, the Chicago Council attempted to codify a specific etiquette of impairment for the urban zone, a guideline for what constituted decent and indecent ways of being a "diseased" or "maimed" or "deformed" Chicagoan. Advance publicity for the new ordinance, as I noted in the introduction, greeted Peevey as a "benefactor" who would "abolish" the injured woman who played "Mollie Darling" and her two sick children from the public sphere. But the same article in the *Chicago Tribune* that heralded the statute registered significant anxiety about the proper scope and function of the law. "The Alderman wants to leave the question open," wrote the *Tribune* reporter, "so far as to allow a discretion in favor of a one-legged and a one-armed soldier, if the mayor desires to permit them to grind an organ." In this proposed exemption clause, war injury (at least in the form of single amputation) trumped industrial accidents like being drawn into wool-carding machines; begging masculinity trumped begging femininity; and the mayor's mendicant or peddler permit system—which, as we shall see, coexisted (though not peacefully) with ugly ordinances in many cities—overrode blanket prohibition. The question of fairness, of worthiness, was "left open." But not for long. No mention of this kind of exception occurred in the City Council when Peevey proposed the ordinance the day after this article was published.

The resolution that Peevey and Hulbert submitted, which passed on June 27, 1881, was worded as follows:

> Whereas the streets and sidewalks of the City of Chicago contain numerous beggars, mendicants, organ-grinders and other unsightly and unseemly objects, which are a reproach to the City, disagreeable to people upon the streets, an offense to business houses along the streets and often

> dangerous, Therefore be it ordered, That the Mayor at once take steps to remove from the streets all beggars, mendicants, and all those who by making Exhibition of themselves and their infirmities seek to obtain money from people on and along the streets.[10]

Here, "begging" and "infirmity," *making* an exhibition of oneself or simply offending by existing as an "other unsightly and unseemly object," seem to constitute at least potentially separable categories, but in the end they merge: though "infirmity" gets the last word in the "Streets and Alleys" resolution, the ordinance that issued from it was from then on referred to simply as "an order for the removal of beggars." The beggar's infirmity could be, of course, sheer poverty, nothing more, nothing less. It is always perfectly possible to attribute disfigurement to the poor as a group, and the pressing destitution in the body politic is capable of embodying the unsightly in and of itself. But here the presence of "unsightliness" and "unseemliness" when coupled with "infirmity" brings us to the birth of Chicago ugly law. The first version of Chicago's ugly ordinance issues in 1881, directly as a result of this resolution. And the words in the code, now identical to San Francisco's phrasing, our familiar "no person who is diseased, maimed, deformed," bring a specific kind of infirmity to the forefront of enforcement of the law.

NEW ORLEANS

Both San Francisco and Chicago enacted what I call ugly law proper—a specific ordinance with its peculiar wording. Sometimes different language, in somewhat different contexts, appears in city ordinances with clear connections to what I am calling ugly laws. New Orleans's version is a good example. Though undeniably intended to achieve the same effects that Alderman Peevey had in mind, it phrased itself in different terms from the ugly ordinances. Peevey's Chicago law prohibited, in theory, simple "exposure," in any form, of persons diseased, deformed, or maimed. It occupied a separate space in the Chicago code books, with its own headline, calling clear attention to the problem of unsightliness. The headline of San Francisco's law referred to begging but also, separately and explicitly, to the appearance in public places of "Certain Persons." New Orleans's law focused specifically on begging, and its interest in disabled bodies was embedded deeply, almost hidden, within a long elaboration of kinds of misbehavior.

The New Orleans ordinance, passed in 1879, sought to "create, define and punish each of the offenses of being an idle and disorderly person and of being a rogue and a vagabond: and to provide for the summary trial and punishment of offenders against the provisions of this ordinance and of officers and members of the police force for failing and neglecting the duties imposed upon them by this ordinance" (#5046). Already we can spot some of the anxious dynamics at play in ugly law—punishment simultaneously entwined with definition, police indifference—but the language of the "rogue and vagabond" works in a somewhat different register. All kinds of conduct could put someone in the class of the idle, disorderly rogue and vagabond; one of them, buried in the long list, was "wandering abroad and endeavoring by the exposure of wounds or deformities to obtain and gather alms."

This language of wounds was, as far as I know, unique to New Orleans, a "wounded" city itself, still directly grappling with the aftereffects of war. Federal troops had been removed from Louisiana only two years earlier (J. Jackson, 2). But the language of "exposure" and "deformity" has obvious connections to the vocabulary of the unsightly beggar ordinances. And the politics of fear and aversion that underpin all forms of the ugly laws again motivate a normative gaze that seeks to contain and institutionalize forms of human difference that lie at the intersection of disability and poverty. What happened in New Orleans illuminates several key aspects of the proliferation of ugly laws in Chicago and across the nation in the 1880s and 1890s.

First, New Orleans shared with Chicago and its sister cities that passed ugly laws an open culture of disgust—particularly open, in New Orleans's case. In 1883 the *New York Times* reprinted reportage from the *New Orleans Times-Democrat* hailing a step-up in enforcement of the "wounded and deformed" clause of the roguery and vagabondage statute: "Street begging is confessedly a great nuisance, but when it is joined, as it has been in New-Orleans, with the exposure of deformities, disease, and sores, it is simply unendurable. . . . The whole community is shocked, disgusted and sickened that these maimed beggars may secure a few nickels" ("End to Street Begging"). Two years later, when as always the (unen)durable emerged again, the *Times-Democrat* exhorted, "The number of beggars is increasing in our streets and has already grown to be a nuisance. One old woman with a deep seated cancer on her face is a revolting sight" ("Brevities").

Second, at the moment of emergence of the unsightly beggar ordinances, New Orleans shared with its fellow revolted cities a reforming culture of compassion. Indeed, a historically particular conjunction of compassion and disgust in equal measure *produces* ugly law. The *Times-Democrat* knew what to do about the woman with a cancer on her face: "she should be sent to the hospital." More than the hospital, though, it was the presence of an almshouse—as in San Francisco—that had prompted reinvigoration of New Orleans's "wounded and deformed" clause.[11]

In 1883, when the *New York Times* picked up the news of New Orleans's crackdown on revolting beggars, it omitted most parts of the New Orleans–based coverage that framed this police action specifically within a discussion of the opening a few weeks earlier of the city's newly renovated and reopened almshouse. "The Shakespeare Almshouse . . . is at last to be used," the New Orleans local piece began. Recounting the arrest of "the numerous vagrants and beggars that have infected this city for so many years," the report assured New Orleans readers that "some dozen of our street beggars, the blind, the lame, and the halt, were sent to the alms-house, where they will be well cared for." "Well cared for" is the exact phrase used in 1880s versions of ugly law proper, such as Chicago's, Lincoln's, and Denver's: "On the conviction of any person for a violation of this section, if it shall seem proper and just, the fine provided for may be suspended, and such person detained at the police station, where he shall be *well cared for* until he can be sent to the county poor house." The task of the unsightly beggar at the outset was simultaneously both to need to be well cared for and to produce disgust, as the report of the New Orleans round-up in another local paper, titled "Corralling the Cripples," made clear. It described how "the first batch of professional beggars were placed in a charity wagon and transferred to the Shakespeare Alms House." In the longer run, care turned out to be less necessary a component than revulsion. By ten years later "well" and "care" had fallen out of the statute's explicit formulations, but the presence of new institutions continued to be a critical part of the impetus and infrastructure of ugly law.

Pressure for construction of the new almshouse in New Orleans had come in part from old and disabled people. Shortly after new mayor Joseph Shakespeare was elected in 1880, a group of old people came to City Hall pleading to be placed in the already overcrowded Home for the Aged and Infirm (J. Jackson, 137). They were told that there was no more room. In July 1881 one blind man staged a proto-demonstration of one, sleeping in the City Hall corridor until a place was arranged for him in a Baton Rouge institution ("No Place for a Poor Blind Man"). "Almost daily," the *Daily Picayune* reported in April 1882, "the sick or the poverty stricken present their pathetic petitions [to the mayor] for aid in their dire extremity. Only yesterday the writer saw an old soldier of the Crimean War and the American

Civil War, come to ask permission to sing in the streets that he might gain a livelihood by chanting the martial airs of his youth" ("Poor-House"). The almshouse opened in mid-August 1883; under the jurisdiction of a new mayor and chief of police, who orchestrated general crackdowns on street violations from confidence games to street obstruction, what the newspaper called the "corralling of cripples" occurred less than a month later.

We know the names (at least the names they gave) of the nine people in New Orleans, September 1883, who were charged with violating Ordinance 5046—that is, with being "rogues and vagabonds" of the "wounded and deformed" variety—and who were then sent on to the new almshouse: Charles Rellin, John Cotillion, Louisa Edwards, John Campbell, Carrie Arkey, Richard Wilson, James Davey, Andrew Loudon, and Rosina Sardonet—three women, six men.[12] We do not know what happened to them or whether after their arrival in the almshouse they were, or felt they were, "well cared for." We do know that the almshouse soon lost its funding base and fell into disrepair. In a 1929 study of its then-current state and extent records, all from a later period than 1883, one scholar posited, "The inmates seem quite content. They feel that after all the almshouse is a place of refuge, where they . . . are sheltered from the pangs of poverty. . . . They are free to come and go as they choose" (Janice Brown, 10). But we know from internal records that in 1903, at least, inmates were not allowed to leave the almshouse more than once a week, and the Board of Managers' minutes from later years refer to strong charges of neglect, charges made particularly by blind people (Touro-Shakspeare Almshouse Minutes). We know that the Shakespeare almshouse population had an extremely high death rate (Janice Brown, 47).

Along with the discourses of care and disgust, New Orleans shares with the cities that engendered ugly laws in the later nineteenth century an obsession with those mobile subjects called "vagabonds" here but elsewhere more commonly designated as "tramps." A national tramp scare—and for that matter, the very tramp himself—was "made up," Tim Cresswell has argued, in the 1880s and 1890s, at the same time as the acceleration of the unsightly beggar ordinances. The two figures very much intertwine. In New Orleans, one was not arrestable simply for "endeavoring by the exposure of wounds or deformities to obtain and gather alms"; one had to "wander abroad" while doing so. How wide a range "abroad" was is unclear; for the "blind, lame and halt," it might have constituted a few square yards.

A comparison between Chicago and New Orleans helps clarify one way that New Orleans's proto–ugly law strongly illuminates its ugly counterparts. (Because San Francisco's city records were largely destroyed by the 1906 earthquake, I have no means of equivalent comparison for that city.) In 1883 New Orleans we can find the names of those arrested for being criminally wounded rogues and vagabonds. Not so in 1881 Chicago. There the potential elision of issues specific to disability when the city called its ugly law simply "an order for the removal of beggars" leads to some difficulties in tracking its enforcement. Annual reports by Chicago's General Superintendent of Police to the City Council between 1880 and 1885 chart and classify all arrests made in any given year. No definite reference to arrest or citation on the basis of the ugly ordinance can be found there. But there are plenty of arrests, in the context of the tramp scare, for vagrancy. And as Caleb Foote pointed out in his still pertinent review in 1956 of "Vagrancy-Type Law," city "clean-ups" or "mop-ups" of people defined as vagrants are often justified on the grounds that "the appearance of the victims was not attractive" (631).[13]

There were also, to be sure, a large number of arrests in Chicago listed under the unhelpful umbrella category "violations of various other ordinances." Clear arrests for "violation of begging ordinance" come in increasing numbers: one in 1882, two in 1883, and a dramatic leap to twenty-five in 1884. But one arrest for the same violation occurred in 1880, before the ugly law existed, so we cannot definitively conclude that these record enforcement of the ordinance in question. The increase is suggestive, like the sharp hike in numbers referred to the County Agent for institutionalization and sent to the "County Physician" during this same five-year period—one to the doctor in 1880, forty in 1885. It may be significant too that precisely at this moment Cook County split its accounting for the poorhouse from its accounting for its asylums, as the varieties of the "infirm" came into more specific focus and, as in the case of New Orleans, more mechanisms of institutionalization became available.[14]

The difficulty in distinguishing between who in Chicago got arrested simply for begging or vagrancy and who got arrested for begging or vagrancy while disabled is frustrating, but it is also illuminating. The complex relation between two seemingly distinctive but sometimes overlapping groups, "able-bodied" beggars or vagrants and their "maimed, diseased, and deformed" counterparts, has a great deal to do with the emergence of ugly law. Panhandling provoked crises of interpretation: how did one (should one) differentiate between sturdy beggars who created mendicant personae, on the one hand, and disabled people, who also created narratives to enhance their success at begging, on the other?

This dilemma, as I show in chapter 5, illuminates the performativity of disability as a visual practice. In Lennard Davis's words, "disability is a specular moment"—spectacularly so in the context of begging (1995, 12).[15] That moment is extremely complex. The social recognition of disability is a dynamic process, involving potential not only for objectification but also for an ethics of mutual recognition. The gaze involved in recognizing disability may be a normalizing one, it may be a stare, but it also may have elements that are interactive and deeply attentive, part of an ethos of care, reciprocity, and mutual acknowledgment.[16] This fluid, contextually dependent ambivalence around disability—somewhere between abjection and equality, between revulsion and recognition, between fascination and apathy—is a key element of the social dynamic that helped to lay the foundation for the ugly laws.

In an 1896 sketch entitled "Tribulations of a Cheerful Giver," William Dean Howells, in the terms of liberal guilt emerging at that moment, grappled with the conundrums posed by scenes of almsgiving that I outline in the next chapter. "Tribulations" describes the author coming upon a man and deciding on the spot to give him some money. "I have to give, or else go away with a bad conscience—a thing I hate," Howells writes candidly. And yet, he adds, "of course I do not give much, for I wish to be a good citizen as well as a good Christian." Howells recounts his uneasy compromise between the competing imperatives of civic duty and Christian mercy. He gives the man a mere fifteen cents and leaves the scene "feeling indescribably squalid": "I perceived now that I could have taken my stand upon the high ground of discouraging street beggary and given nothing; but having once lowered myself to the level of the early Christians, I ought to have given the half-dollar" (182).

Amy Dru Stanley, invoking this scene to introduce her discussion of late-nineteenth-century American urban mendicancy, writes that "by all accounts, the most vexing specimen" for reformers "was the sturdy beggar," the one who could but did not work. "Would alms help him or sink him deeper in pauperism?" Stanley asks rhetorically, describing Howells's project in "Tribulations" as "puzzling over this subject" (1992, 1265). But it is exactly not the subject of the sturdy beggar that Howells puzzles over. It is rather his opposite. The beggar who initiates Howells's essay is anything but sturdy as his culture defined the term:

> As I came nearer I perceived that he had no hands, but only stumps . . . that . . . he was holding out in the mute appeal which was his form of

> begging. . . . he did not speak. I thought this rather fine, in its way; except for his mutilation, which the man really could not help, there was nothing to offend the taste; and his immobile silence certainly was impressive. . . . I perceived that I had been the divinely appointed bearer of half a dollar to his mutilation and his misery, and . . . I had embezzled the greater part of the money entrusted to me for him. (182)

Two repeated terms govern this encounter: "I perceived" and "his mutilation." For city dwellers in Howells's position, the essay suggests, perceiving mutilation was as vexing as spotting a "sturdy" beggar. In the postwar years, "in northern states where industrial capitalism and wage labor held full sway—but where beggars still hovered outside the bounds of commodity exchange," writes Stanley, "criminal law delivered an unequivocal answer to the almsgiver's moral dilemma" (1268). The ugly law was one such answer. But as the peculiar elision of Howells's "unsturdy," mutilated beggar in Stanley's account suggests, the answer that ugly law provided was always, necessarily, equivocal.[17]

As city officials and urban reformers sought to parse the social grammars of vagrancy and mendicancy, to make or deny distinctions between deserving feebleness and undeserving, lazy fraud, ordinances like the ugly law were one important tool in their social arsenal. Cities deployed the ordinance for multiple purposes and to varied ends. They shared this in common: each of them, at the law's inception, sought to pocket their unsightly beggars.

That figure of the pocket—Howells, I think, would have understood it—I take from the contemporary literary theorist Jacques Derrida, in his exploration of the "determined place" that the beggar occupies "in a social, politico-economic, and symbolic typology" (134). The beggar's identity, Derrida writes, is delineated by "an indispensable internal exclusion," an "exception made" that Derrida describes metaphorically as "an interior closure or cleft"—like the pocket of a coat, at once a necessary part of the social fabric and cut out of it, hidden, away from public view. "The expulsion of the beggar keeps the outside within," Derrida writes. *Unsightly* beggar laws might be said to add an extra cleft, an even deeper out-turned interior pocket, in what Derrida calls the "social category" of the beggar "in its anthropology or history" (134–135).

But whose deep pockets, exactly, was the beggar to line, to delineate, to be placed within? In this particular anthropology or history, "charity"—questions of who should get it and whether it should be given at all—was always part of the equation. Not "charity" in general or in the abstract but in one concrete and notably conflicted form: the ideologies and practices of the Charity Organization Society (COS) in its U.S. variations. Along with the development of new institutions like New Orleans's Shakespeare almshouse, the presence in a given nineteenth-century American city of a "charity organization" movement is a robust predictor of the presence of ugly law in the municipal code books. Where Charity Organization Society went, ugly law did not necessarily follow, but from the 1880s on, where ugly law occurred, Charity Organization Society leaders inevitably had a hand in the development of the social category of the unsightly beggar. In New Orleans, charity organizing took off in the summer of 1883, when a group of prominent citizens, including author George W. Cable, met to form a "conference of charities" like those that "exist in all the principal cities of the nation" ("Conference of Charities").[18] A few months later, Charles Rellin, Rosina Sardanet, and their cohort were arrested for wandering abroad exposing wounds and deformities. These two events were interconnected. To understand how, we must turn to the COS at some length.

2

GETTING UGLY

This book attempts to weave a rough but strong cloth from these gnarled strands, to give the *feel* of the disability experience. Such a cloth would not have a neat, finished selvedge, but a ragged edge. This is a good image for the way people with disabilities live, at a rough and often raveling interface with the rest of society. . . . People are scared of living on the ragged edge. . . . Ironically, it is people with disabilities who could best make them see the value of life on the ragged edge, life with some physical limitations, even if it were saddled with external barriers and barriers of attitude.

—BARRETT SHAW, *The Ragged Edge* (1994)

We have been brought to the ragged edge of anarchy.

—ATTORNEY GENERAL RICHARD OLNEY, of the Pullman railroad strike (1894)

THE CHARITABLE UGLY LAWS

The ugly laws, as San Francisco's example shows, predated "charity organization," but Charity Organization Society activities led to a proliferation of unsightly beggar ordinances in the last two decades of the nineteenth century. To a significant extent, it is where the charity organizer meets the tramp that the seeds of the ugly law thrive. It is worth our while, therefore, to focus some attention on COS ideology and practice, before turning to examine some of the particular forms of social unrest that ugly laws both provoked and attempted to quell.

The first model for the American Charity Organization movement was established in London in 1869, though COS organizers looked also to the 1852 "German Plan" of "Herr Von der Heydt of Elberfeld" as an example.[1] Founded first within the United States in Buffalo in 1873, the American COS quickly spread.[2] Soon charity organization, as Kenneth Kusmer has shown, became a "major social movement" (1973, 658). The COS across the country was devoted to promoting "scientific," organized charity and eliminating street begging and "chaotic" handouts.

In place of indiscriminate giving, the COS offered a model comparable, as Lubove has argued, "to trustification and amalgamation in business" (6). As COS leader Josephine Shaw Lowell put it,

> In a country village, the mountain springs supply the water that is a necessity of life, and from the kind hearts of neighbors flows, also, a living stream of charity . . . but in the city, unhappily, we need reservoirs and pipes, ramifying through all the streets. . . . in like manner even our love to our neighbor must be guided through organized channels. (1884, 131)

Discriminate charity, as the COS envisioned it, would be engineered as carefully as other pipelines being developed in the urban infrastructure.

In general, the Charity Organization Society promulgated the principle that Michael Katz has described: the ideal charity "would coordinate, investigate, and counsel. It would not give material relief" (1986, 78). Short of this ideal, the COS was devoted to determining "a method by which idleness and beggary, now so encouraged, may be suppressed, and worthy, self-respecting poverty be discovered and relieved at the smallest cost to the benevolent" (Watson, 188). In practice, as Kusmer has shown, repeated economic depressions for decades forced COS branches to keep engaging in supposedly temporary emergency relief work less stringent in its guidelines than they would have preferred.[3]

Organizations grouped under the COS rubric were distinguished by several methods and emphases. They insisted on "the personal touch, the bringing of the comfortable into contact with the wretched, and of the strong with the depressed" (the "friendly visit," sometimes seen as a direct precursor of professional "social work"): "each poor family," as Stephen Humphreys Gurteen put it, "shall have a kind *friend* to whom to make known any distress that shall exist and may arise, instead of having to disclose it to an official or to a stranger" (5).[4] COS leader Charles Henderson saw the institution of friendly visiting as critical for the stability of the U.S. social order:

> Such visitors go back from their visits to become students of social science . . . to combat the stupid class prejudices of employers and the rich; to represent the real facts of the home life of working people and the difficulties which keep them down; to champion all that is reasonable and just in the demands of the intelligent leaders of wage earners; and, generally, to knit the bonds of fraternity, sympathy, and justice, without which the nation will become two nations, each arrayed in hostile camps, each threatening the other and endangering the common peace, prosperity, and happiness. (1906, 154)

COS organizers stressed the development of a "positive program" to prevent donations by friends to the befriended and to "change this unnatural and abominable relation between the beggar and his patron" (Divine, 278). They intended to "cure" pauperism. William Frederick Slocum provides an example of the kind of rhetoric of disability and cure employed by COS officials in discussions of the problem of the pauper: "Pauperism is a disease upon the community, a sore upon the body politic, and being a disease, it must be, as far as possible, removed, and the curative purpose must be behind all our thought and effort for the pauper class" (5). Compare the invocation of cure in Charles Henderson's account of the first COS in London: "Its main object—the cure, as distinguished from the mere alleviation of distress" (1906, 152). In the words of Josephine Shaw Lowell, charity organization was as radical as mastectomy: "Each case is to be radically dealt with. . . . the cause of want and suffering are to be removed even if the process be as painful as plucking out an eye or cutting off a limb" (1884, 94). Here the discourse of "cure," often the subject of disability studies critique in the arena of the "medical model," has another level of complex relation to disability history.[5] Pauperism required an especially firm and unwavering hand to cure it, for it represented the last instance of poverty in its loneliest hour. As Oscar McCulloch wrote in his famous eugenicist "Tribe of Ishmael," a COS document,

> The free-swimming legs and disused organs disappear. So we have the same in the pauper. Self-help disappears. All the organs and powers that belong to the free life disappear, and there are left only the tendency to parasitism and the debasement of the reproductive system. . . . What can we do? First, we must clear up official outdoor relief. Second, we must check private and indiscriminate benevolence. . . . Third, we must get hold of the children. (14–15)

To these ends, COS organizers advocated systematic record-keeping, surveys, and research into every "case." As semiofficial functionaries in various cities—it is common to find a yearly COS report to the council or mayor inserted into late-nineteenth-century city records—they contributed to the development during this period of new methods of surveillance, which, as Bennett puts it, "precisely through their bureaucratic reduction of individuality to a set of knowable traces . . . rendered the city legible to the gaze of power" (215).[6] These bureaucratic records might seem like individual microcosms or microaggressions, but they were of course far more than that; they connected the system of surveillance to broader mechanisms of disciplinary power and control.

The projects of COS organizers were various. They often concerned themselves with finding work for the unemployed. They established rural lodges or so-called friendly inns for tramps. They endeavored to sort mendicants into "lazy" or "worthy" categories by means of a "labor test" involving wood-chopping in what were called "provident woodyards."[7] And they aimed to unmask impostures of poverty or disability: friendly visitors, Gurteen argued in a standard handbook on their functions, form "a powerful check on imposture" (4).[8]

The last task, fraud detection, was a trademark COS enterprise in the public eye. Other charity efforts differentiated themselves from the COS partly on the basis of their relatively less anxious approach to the question of fraud; as Bogan put it in his 1917 history of Jewish philanthropy in the United States, "It is far better for any philanthropic agency to be duped repeatedly than that one deserving individual should be mistreated" (79).[9] In Ben Reitman's account of going around Chicago "in the guise of a poorly dressed tramp" to ask for work, food, and a place to sleep, it is the Catholic Church—"and I'm not a Catholic," Reitman says—that most openly offers assistance and resists the fraud-check ("Charities").[10] Early historians of the COS took pains to characterize the equation of their efforts with fraud-proofing as misconception: "exposure of imposters . . . is frequently overemphasized in describing the purposes of a Charity Organization Society" (Warner, Queen, and Harper, 211). Nevertheless, imposture occupies a significant amount of space in COS public literature.

Along with fraud, COS organizers placed similarly strong public emphasis on the importance of eradicating begging. The COS precursor Chicago Relief and Aid not only mentioned fraud for the first time in its 1881 report to the Chicago City Council, at the moment when the aldermen prepared their ugly law; it also for the first time mentioned begging in explicit terms:

"This society . . . has always discouraged begging, and has frequently cautioned the public against giving any countenance whatever to those whom they may encounter upon the street" (1882, 5). In New Orleans, George W. Cable and his fellow charity organizers defined their task as the "suppression of mendicancy" ("Suppression of Mendicancy," 2). In a typical later example, organizers in Cleveland, decrying "the difficulty of securing the enforcement of the ordinances affecting street trades and street begging," published a photograph of an obviously disabled man with the following caption: "The street beggar offers a never-ending opportunity for indiscriminate giving, so often misplaced and usually detrimental to the character of the recipient" (Associated Charities of Cleveland 1911). Attempts to bring "paupers" back from the brink of the "moral Niagara of beggary"[11] were so centrally a part of the COS agenda that in 1895 an "operatic burlesque" staged as a Buffalo, New York, COS fundraiser, written by COS leader Frederick Almy, genially lampooned the group's own position. In the play, Orpheus returns from the dead to Buffalo, and when he says "I beg your pardon," the answer is "Don't beg. The Charity Organization doesn't approve of it" (37).

Begging was foregrounded by the COS for complex reasons explained by advocate Frank Dekker Watson in 1922:

> Doubtless a big factor in the attempts of many societies to rid their respective communities of the evil of giving indiscriminately to beggars was the fact that almost every citizen had been visited by the poor that beg, and they felt that it was important to *begin* their propaganda work at this point, since few had ever visited the poor in their homes. The appreciation of this pedagogical principle of beginning with the known probably explains why the suppression of begging received in the propagandist literature of the eighties a longer proportion of space than it received in the work itself. (230)

The hints in this quotation of distinctions, however unstable, between the public rhetoric and the private business of organizing charity, suggest something of the complexity, variety, and ambiguity of COS undertakings as those engaged in them saw them. Of course, these undertakings changed over time. At any given moment they were rife with contradiction.

Within any given city, even at the same historical moment, the politics, motives, and styles of different COS organizers might vary dramatically. Denver provides a good example. Two men, both ministers, Myron W. Reed and Henry Martyn Hart, paved the way through charity organizing for Denver's ugly law. Both men moved to Denver, a city with an international reputation for its healing climate, as a result of illness. Both had previous COS experience. Reed had Chicago connections (he had studied at Chicago Theological Seminary), and prior to his move to Denver he was an active COS participant in Indianapolis, where his close friend and national COS organizer Oscar McCulloch, author of the eugenics tract "The Tribe of Ishmael," led the organized charity movement (Denton). Hart, the dean of Denver's St. John's Episcopal Cathedral, came from England, where he had organized the Blackheath Mendicity Society in order to, "by terror of the gaol, drive [mendicants] to honest work" and to persuade the public "not to give" (Rainsford, 206; Hart).

Reed saw organized charity as a form of socialism. "Why not here in Denver try socialism?" he wrote. "Boston Common suits me. I prefer it to any individual backyard on earth" (58). In the era of the crisis of the "tramp," Reed viewed the eradication of tramping as part of the challenge to capitalism: "The American tramp came in the same day that the American millionaire was born. One of them will kill the other unless an intelligent society peaceably disposes of both" (13). He argued that "people in distress should receive aid to help them through their misfortunes regardless of their morality" (Denton, 77). Hart took a much harder line, more in keeping with dominant national COS ideology, founding Denver's "Investigation Office" in 1889 for the purpose of ridding Denver entirely of tramps, begging, and handouts. By the time Reed's friend McCullough came from Indiana to Denver for the next annual Colorado COS conference in 1890, a new tone of panicked hyperbole emerged in the third COS report. Calling up for his audience a vision of an "awful army" of "20,000 men, women and children supported by state aid and county institutions" in Indiana, McCullough told them,

> You shall see . . . the blind feeling and groping their way, the deaf with that pained attempt to listen, with the mumbling and muttering of the dumb . . . the ghastly company of deranged, defective, deformed, neglected orphans, sorrowful, helpless and despairing, that follow the splendid and prosperous state of Indiana, its car of triumphant progress. These are the facts with which we have to deal. . . . They are here. . . . You do not believe it? Any one of them can infect you with small pox. (74–75, 79)

Reinforced by this kind of rhetoric, Hart's vision held sway and no doubt contributed to the development of Denver's ugly law.

This is, of course, a top-down account of the COS, one focused on its own stories about itself, not a social history from below. A history from below would look very different. Take the question of fraud, for instance. As Ellen Ross points out in her study of the strategies that poor housewives used to manage their relations with charity workers in London at the turn of the twentieth century, these women were as concerned about the hypocrisy and posturing of their COS visitors as those visitors were concerned with detecting duplicity in them.[12] I am interested here in the COS's own narratives because those accounts directly influenced the making of city policy and in particular the development of ugly law.

At the same time, it is crucial to recognize that COS positions never went unchallenged, whether by rival charitable organizations such as faith-based aid groups, by dissident political groups, by beggars themselves, by actors in the criminal and court systems, or by passersby with profoundly mixed feelings. Rosemarie Garland Thomson helps us understand this range of responses when she notes the inevitable, stubborn ambivalence surrounding the broad social category "disabled" in American policy, "a grudging admission of human vulnerability in a world . . . where self-government and individual progress purportedly prevail" (*EB*, 48). "That ambivalence expresses itself," she writes, "as social stigmatization and as rigorous, sometimes exclusionary supervision of people obliged to join the ranks of the 'disabled'" (48). People conscripted into the category "unsightly beggar" no doubt met versions of this kind of ambivalence in their extreme forms. Strikingly, though, ambivalence as Garland Thomson formulates it in this instance is extremely one-sided, perhaps less an ambivalence than a valence. Its modes are purely linear and negative: stigmatization, exclusion. The history of unsightly beggarhood is better understood as a history of the kind of ambivalence that Homi Bhabha conceptualizes in the context of postcolonial studies—a story not of unilateral domination but of uncertainty, hybridity, and ongoing conflict and negotiation.[13]

DEFORMANCES

Before turning, in the final section of this chapter, to one surprising story of exactly how and why COS leaders pressed city leaders to enact an ugly law, I want to pause and consider some of the broader implications for disabled people of this kind of charity organized on this set of terms. It will be important in what follows neither to overestimate the power of the COS movement (itself, of course, as much effect as cause of broader social changes) nor to underestimate the extent to which individual upper- and middle-class men and women involved in it in various times in various cities *meant well.* I want here to accord that phrase the gravity of the genuine, to try to clear away for a moment its usual layers of condescension toward the condescending: meant *well,* sought a solution to what they rightly identified as social ills.[14] But I also want to claim the gap that the conventional phrase "*meant* well" opens between *meaning* and *doing.* This gap between what is meant and what is done often shows up anxiously in the strains of COS literature. Disability activists have long pointed out that much harm to disabled people occurs precisely in (and through) the domain of the well-meaning, or what we might call the banality of good.[15]

At minimum, well-meaning charity exacted its price of "gratitude and deference," reinforcing the asymmetrical relation between classes and between those "normal" and "defective."[16] If COS organizers, like the Hull-House leaders whom Shannon Jackson has analyzed, performed what Jackson (2000) calls "reformance," they also engaged in what we might call "deformance": dramaturgies of impairment adjustment involving the carefully orchestrated and paternalistic public exposure of the "diseased, maimed, mutilated and in any way deformed"—that is, always about to be reformed.[17] I am echoing Jackson's discussion of "dramaturgies of immigrant adjustment" (227). My negative treatment of deformance here runs counter to the innovative spirit of Jackson's model of "reformance," which covers a far subtler and more supple range of dynamics, some successful, some failed, all complex and ambiguous, as Hull-House denizens sought to model and enact "cross-class sociability." This nuanced model holds true as well for analyzing what might be called cross-ability sociability, but what I wish to emphasize here is conveyed by the difference in the coined words "*re*formance" and "*de*formance": deformance is the gift that keeps on giving deformity, perpetuating the model of the deformed object as a permanent other, even as he or she is to be continually subject to reform.

Under the jurisdiction of deformers, a disfigured body might well in fact be out in public, even as a central object, but only as an adjunct to someone else's subject; a diseased body might be a spectacle, but only under someone else's orchestration; a maimed body might be an explicit body, but someone else had to write its meaning upon it; and, most importantly, the unsightly body in deformance would invite only certain kinds of audience response, the gestures of what Jacques Donzalet calls "mandatory tutelage" and David Wagner calls "repressive benevolence."[18] The "unsightly" could not beg for food, though they could beg for a cure. The context had to be ameliorative and charitable, the goal one of disciplinary uplift (usually understood as moral or medical—or, later, rehabilitative—and, in a carefully controlled way, individual). At every point deformance reinforced the asymmetrical social relation between displayer and displayed, usually between classes, and between the nondisabled and the disabled.[19] Deformance posed itself as the giving of a gift (the gift, say, of advances in public health or better understanding of city life), but as Stedman Jones noted in his discussion of charity—"the separation of classes had produced the deformation of the gift"—what was "deformed" was not only the subject of the show but the process of the offering (251–253; see also Katz 1990, 240).

Jackson's notion of reformance emphasizes its everyday complexity, "messy and paradoxical," interactive, contextual, unfinalized, reciprocal, and continually contested (5, 8–18). Deformance, too, was an unstable mode, subject to unsettling in the course of interactions between charity or social workers and people who kept being more than unsightly "cases." Written records of these encounters, however, have a way of stabilizing deformity. Here is a sample from a Cleveland-based Associated Charities brochure:

> Somewhat unique was the case of a colored dwarf. She voluntarily gave up a questionable life and her position as snake charmer in an animal show, and came to us for refuge and honest work. She needed suitable employment and a wise friend, both of which we were able to supply. (*Sixth Annual Report*, 15–16)

The "colored" and colorful snake-charming dwarf might present a "somewhat unique" case, but the case history encapsulating her tale takes entirely drab and predictable form. Deformance stories always conclude by focusing attention where it properly belongs in these texts: on the good social worker, the wise and superior friend, whose recognition is at stake and whose embrace supersedes all other social relations.[20]

EUGENIC CHARITY

But worse harms than these stories of deformance could conduct themselves through the conduit of the well-meant. At times in COS writing—at exactly those times when it becomes most openly rhetorical (most urgently tuned to persuade, most bent on signaling its own good intentions)—the potential for these harms, and the ambivalence of the COS venture, shows up especially clearly. Consider, for instance, two classic exemplars of COS rhetoric, Warner, Queen, and Harper's *American Charities and Social Work* (1894) and Charles Henderson's *Introduction to the Study of the Dependent, Defective and Delinquent Classes and of Their Social Treatment* (1906), both written as summaries of a movement in place for decades at the time of their composition.

Where dramaturgies of adjustment failed, fantasies of eradication proceeded. A significant portion of Warner et al.'s volume devotes itself to questions of charity's relation to what we would now call eugenics. Here we can see with clarity the contradictions of the COS project. Vigorously opposed not so much to Social Darwinism per se as to Social Darwinism in its most ruthless forms, *American Charities* argues for a kinder, more reasoned cultural response—one disciplined by theology, decency, and learning—to the problem of the decline of the race.

Thus, for instance, Warner et al. advocate a hands-off approach to "the intermarriage of deaf-mutes or other defectives" on the grounds that they "will not result in the formation of a deaf variety of the human race, but rather in the extinction of the degenerate stock" (66). A section entitled "Charity as a Factor in Human Selection" counters the claim that charity promotes the survival of the unfit with a counterclaim that the "children of misfortune can be rescued from distress, without enabling the children of degradation to 'be fruitful and multiply'" (86). Acknowledging the appeal of euthanasia for the "gasping, pain-racked" bodies of "the most misshapen physically and morally" where "cure was out of the question," Warner et al. argue finally against it on these grounds: "By assuming the burden of protection we give bonds to our final interest in prevention." "Some talk," they continue, extending the discussion from illness and disability to poverty more generally, "as though extermination would be a remedy for pauperism. Possibly, but it would be a costly remedy biologically; and if we allow our instincts to compel us to forgo the use of it, we shall eventually find something better" (86–88). Later in the volume, Isaac Kerlin is quoted: "The temptation for their extinction rises to the lips of the careless, forgetful how far such a practice would be from all moral or judicial right, how revolting to every religious sentiment, and contradictory to every logical principle" (162).[21]

The lips of the careful provide cold comfort in *American Charities*. Warner et al. worry over whether, since badly administered charity increases death rates, well-administered charity might dilute the vigor of racial stock. As New York COS founder Josephine Shaw Lowell put it after returning from a national Conference on Charities in 1871 at which Richard Dugdale delivered his influential findings on "Hereditary Pauperism as Illustrated by the Jukes Family," "Better leave people to the hard working of natural laws than to run the risk of interfering with those laws in a mischievous manner" (Waugh, 116). In the end, however, the book argues emphatically with the force of a religious injunction, "charity may not cease to shield the children of misfortune." Still: "Certain it is, that . . . [charity] must, to an ever-increasing extent, reckon with the laws of heredity, and do what it can to check the spreading curse of race degeneration" (89).

Many of Warner et al.'s points are echoed twelve years later by Charles Henderson, who was a professor of sociology at the University of Chicago and the leader of the Chicago equivalent of a COS.[22] Henderson's emphasis on disability as cause and concern for charity organization is marked in his *Introduction to the Study of the Dependent, Defective and Delinquent Classes*; an entire section of the book is devoted to chapters on "Education and Care of the Blind and of Deaf Mutes," "Education and Custody of the Feeble-Minded," "Social Treatment of the Insane," and "Further Specialization of Institutions for Defectives." On the question of charity and eugenics in this context, Henderson takes up Warner et al.'s conflicted refrain:

> It is true that in some institutions, as in crowded infant asylums, charity has found a way of effectually exterminating imperfect and illegitimate children. Hospitals founded with pious intent, but managed by the incompetent, become plague-smitten, and increase mortality. But such results are not sought, the sincere purpose of philanthropy being to prolong the individual life. These illustrations do not prove that charity is necessarily cruel, but that in effect it may be. (21–22)

Like Warner et al., but with particular vehemence, Henderson makes the case against indiscriminate charity. His figures for the harm of almsgiving multiply, often dominated by images of sightlessness. "He who gives blindly, ignorantly, and thoughtlessly is as culpable as one who fires a gun into a crowd" (139), he writes at one point, and at another, "Giving without knowledge is, in its effects, like administering powerful medicines in the dark" (89).

For Henderson, the knowledge that must inform giving included, among many other things, understanding of "The Standard of Normal Man." In a remarkable passage, he acknowledges that "our image of the normal man may not be exact" but calls on intellectuals and reformers to exert "much thought and care to make it as distinct as science will permit." If charity organization required a founding standard of the normal, that template was at once intuitively obvious—"very marked irregularities or deformities are noticed even by children"—and strenuously arcane. Only by study could one discern and uphold the normate.

Normate is Rosemarie Garland Thomson's generative term, one that has become a central concept for contemporary disability studies: "The term normate usefully designates the social figure through which people can represent themselves as definitive human beings. Normate, then, is the constructed identity of those who, by way of the bodily configurations and cultural capital they assume, can step into a position of authority and wield the power it grants them" (*EB*, 8).[23] Henderson seeks that social figure in canonical art: "In the figures of Greek sculpture and of great paintings of the best schools we may discover the forms which the culture races of Europe regard as most perfect. . . . these classic models are a fairly reliable standard of comparison." But only "fairly reliable," for even the classical normate—the normate *as* classic—slides into baroque, marred by deviance, excrescence, *deformity*: even in these ideal models "artificial deformities, for particular reasons, are only too common, owing to irrational and conventional standards of taste." The representational certainty of the normal (here equated with the ideal)—"it is certain that ideal forms may be presented in art with an approximation to truth"—can only be attained by "making all necessary allowance for these exceptional departures from type" (216). Here again, in the form of a discussion of aesthetics, we can identify the ambivalences of charity organization. "Deformities" are at once "exceptional departures from type" and "only too common"; the "normal standard" thrives as type, but "conventional standards" threaten it.

At the level of the social politic, Henderson's guarantee of the "standard of normal man" over and against the "irrational" and "common" depended on eugenics. In his final arguments, "common" shifts its meaning from "vulgar" to "public and mutual": "we must resist, by all available means, the deterioration of the common stock, the corruption of blood, the curses of heredity. It must be included in our plan that more children will be born with large brains, sound nerves, good digestive organs, and love of independent struggle. We wish the parasitic strain, the neuropathic taint, the consumptive tendency, the foul disease, to die out" (340). The biggest obstacle to this plan, in Henderson's COS terms, was "the great, awkward, sentimental, unthinking Public, which never seems to learn, bribing and hiring the youth to become a tramp by means of its unsystematic, impulsive, unreflecting doles of alms and broken victuals and old clothes at the door" (86).

It is important to pause at this last quotation and dwell on the difference between COS and other responses to begging and disability. Henderson's frustration with the "great . . . unthinking Public" demonstrates a slippage: the inability of COS reformers to control people's responses to human difference; the resilience of discourses of need and freely given charity in a context of social and economic inequality. Across the country in the 1880s and 1890s, Henderson's COS predecessors attempted to stamp out the tramp by stamping out the unreflecting dole, and repeatedly they failed to achieve their ends. Ugly law emerged at the epicenter of the storm around giving and tramping.

TRAMPS, BEGGARS, AND UGLY CROWDS

The fear of the unsightly beggar emerged simultaneously with the fear of the tramp.[24] The COS played an active part in the making and the managing of both cultural panics. The tramp problem and its various "organized" solutions were particularly high on COS agendas. "The question of how to deal with the tramp is said to be of special urgency in every locality in the United States with which I am at all acquainted," wrote Warner et al. (114). The tramp "has become an institution, and appears to think that he has an inalienable right to life, liberty, and the pursuit of vagabondage" (122). Citing an 1879 Connecticut law mandating an automatic year of prison for vagrancy, Warner et al. cautioned,

> Latterly, however, there have been no convictions under this law. . . . It gives a very good illustration of what repressive legislation can and cannot accomplish in this matter. The method, if rigidly applied, may cause tramps to disappear for a time; but there is always a doubt in the minds of the community as to whether or not many cases of honest destitution are not dealt with too harshly. Such stringent laws are apt to become dead letters. (116)

The "doubt in the minds of the community" and the question of the law as "dead letter" bring us back to the ugly laws. In at least one case, the COS's frustrated dealings with "doubts in the minds of the community" in the context of tramp fear led directly to its promotion of an unsightly beggar ordinance—one dead letter answered by another. The story of COS efforts to establish the letter of an ugly law in New York City illustrates broader, if more implicit, dynamics at play in the enactment of unsightly beggar ordinances across the country.

For several decades, despite the qualms articulated by Warner et al., COS strategists regularly encouraged municipal experiments with stringent general antivagrant and antibegging legislation. Many COS efforts concentrated on the municipal level. With the prodding of COS, several cities established special forces of plainclothes vagrancy police backed by harsh begging penalties. Boston did so in 1897, Philadelphia as early as 1855, and New York City at various intervals, including in the early 1890s, in 1901, in 1914, and in 1921.[25]

Sometimes these plainclothes operatives were designated police officers. At other moments cities experimented with specially appointing COS citizens as lay-police to go among the crowds detecting and arresting beggars.[26] Either way, the COS stayed closely involved in the effort both to eradicate mendicancy and to bring all vagrants under total scrutiny. A special order sent out by New York police chief Peter Conlin to the captains of his precincts in 1897 on the "imperative necessity of taking effective measures to suppress the professional beggars and vagrants" lays out very clearly the privileged role of COS:

> You must instruct your detectives and officers assigned to duty in citizens [*sic*] clothes to be on the look out.... In this connection you must work in co-operation with the officers of the Charity Organization Society. They have special knowledge of this class and their schemes. . . . their officers may look the prisoners over, to the end that if he [*sic*] is known to them the Judges before whom he will be taken may get his full pedigree and be in a position to deal with him as he deserves. ("Special Order #2639")[27]

In Boston, first offenders were warned once they were caught and written up by plainclothes detectives; habitual offenders were arrested, registered with the Associated Charities, referred to various social services, and finally jailed for two to six months or for up to two years in the State Farm system. Denver, where antibegging policies were said to be "severe," listed thousands of arrests in one year alone, 1902 (Marsh, 414). In New York, during the first fifteen months in which the Mendicancy Squad was in force in 1890, "all beggars caught"—18,603 people—"were sent for six months to the workhouse" (Watson). In a speech to the Chicago City Club in 1910, Charles Henderson "expressed the opinion that the New York Society had grappled with the problem of vagrancy as no other organization in the country had done" (149).

But New York City's attempt to counter the growing influx of "tramps" was not as successful as Henderson's account suggests—as the repeated, spasmodic reestablishments of New York mendicancy squads makes clear. Paul Ringenbach writes that in 1890, during the COS's attempt that year at establishing an antimendicancy police squad, "the officers stopped arresting beggars except in cases of fraud, because *ugly crowds* collected and generally supported the beggar suspect against the officer" (54; italics mine). In 1901, as two COS leaders planned a meeting with the New York chief of police on how to eradicate begging, they strategized about this problem:

> I doubt very much the expediency of making a big outcry over the operations of the blind and crippled. The unthinking public are inclined to regard that as persecution. . . . the result in times past has been to encourage the beggars and to make the police officials feel the public is not with us. (Merrill, letter to Devine)

As late as 1921, when the New York police tried yet again to enforce antibegging ordinances with plainclothes officers, a similar dynamic emerged. A *New York Times* article that year offers the perspective of the detectives in the "Mendicant Squad" about the special difficulties involved in arresting the crippled beggar: "They find that the chief impediment to a general elimination of public begging is the sympathy of the public. Frequently when the detectives attempt to make an arrest . . . a sympathetic audience soon gathers. Frequently members of the Mendicant Squad have been threatened by such crowds who invariably side with the prisoner" ("Flock of Crippled Beggars").

The problem of the ugly crowd was not confined to begging arrests. In Chicago, Thale notes, people under arrest "often had to be pushed, dragged, even carried by wheelbarrow to the station house, sometimes while their friends attempted to 'rescue' them." Even after the patrol wagon was introduced, in the same year as the first ugly law, "much violence remained" (626). (It may be, in fact, that the existence of the patrol wagon enabled the bringing into being of Chicago's ugly law; it is physically harder, as well as socially more awkward, to push and drag paralyzed or blind people to the station than to transport them in an enclosed vehicle.) A sympathetic and resistant audience might gather around the scene of any arrest, but it is clear from these accounts that both cops and crowds responded with particular unease when police arrested disabled beggars.

One might think that the ugly laws would have simply exacerbated these problems, provoking even more scenes between bystanders and police. But in fact there is evidence, paradoxically, of the exact reverse—at least in the minds of some framers of the unsightly beggar ordinances. Ugly laws developed in part, in the context of the late-nineteenth-century "tramp scare," as a peculiar attempt to *prevent* public resistance to arrests of and public alliance with all beggars. This counterintuitive situation is illustrated in the surprising history of New York City's flirtation with ugly law.

In 1895, in an attempt to get around the problem of the ugly crowd and to back up the police in New York, the COS attempted to get enacted what Ringenbach calls an "antifreak bill," modeled after a law passed by the Pennsylvania legislature (54). COS leader Edward Devine wrote to Mayor William L. Strong regarding the problem of vagrants whose "deformities are exposed to the public gaze simply to excite sympathy, and as a means of begging":

> The evil has excited so much attention in Philadelphia, and especially among the medical profession, that at the last session of the Pennsylvania legislature a law was enacted forbidding such exposures in places of public resort upon the grounds of public health and public morals. The same reasons . . . apply equally to New York.[28]

The Pennsylvania law to which Devine refers was probably not the one that had been most recently passed by the Pennsylvania legislature (Act 208, in 1895, which specifically prohibited what we would now call freak shows) but the one passed by Pennsylvania's House of Representatives in 1891 (Act 276), a copy of which rests in the COS archives where this letter to the mayor can be found. Though Act 276 collapses freak show and street begging into one forbidden category, it has all the hallmarks of ugly law:

> an act. To prohibit the exhibition of physical and mental deformities. Be it enacted that whoever shall exhibit any physical deformity to which he or she shall be subject or which is produced by artificial means for hire or for the purpose of soliciting alms shall be guilty of a misdemeanor and upon conviction thereof shall be sentenced to pay a fine not exceeding fifty dollars or suffer imprisonment not exceeding six months.

The New York COS proposed an even more extreme amendment of the Pennsylvania language in its own draft of a law designed to reduce the friction encountered by antimendicancy forces, producing the most elaborate version of an ugly ordinance I have encountered, with a proposed fine of a thousand dollars for offenders:

> Be it enacted, &c, That on and after the passage of this act it shall be unlawful for any person, whose body is deformed, mutilated, imperfect or has been reduced by amputations, or who is idiotic or imbecile, to exhibit him or herself in any public hall, museum, theatre or any public building, tent, booth or public place for a pecuniary consideration or reward, or to solicit or receive charitable relief, or to go from house to house or to stand or display themselves upon any public street or place to solicit or receive alms. ("Crude Suggested Draft by CDK")

It is perhaps not surprising that in New York City an idea of the law would stretch so far that it included as its target anyone whose body was "imperfect." Kellogg's extreme version of the ordinance was never enacted despite COS efforts.

But this fragment in New York's COS archives, titled "Crude Suggested Draft by CDK [Charles D. Kellogg]," holds a partial key to the proliferation of enacted ugly law. Forwarding the draft to the mayor, Devine emphasized that a law such as the one Kellogg proposed would *aid,* not hinder, police arrests of all beggars. It would shut up, not rile up, people on the street. Clearly, if angry crowds intervening to prevent the arrest of beggars are supposed to be contained by the enactment of an ugly ordinance, the law directs itself implicitly at all begging *through the vehicle of disabled beggars.*[29] "Nondisabled beggars could be ignored as shiftless vagrants or hurried from the street," writes Brad Byrom. "Disabled beggars could not be so easily disregarded. . . . Exempting cripples from bans on begging is a tradition that existed in the earliest civilizations" (2004, 4). It is particularly in alliance with disabled beggars that other people get *ugly.* The object of control is not only the abject body with cup in hand and deformities exposed to view; it is also the militant body of the forming crowd.

In this way we may come to see the ugly law on a continuum with other means of suppressing labor organizing and social unrest, and to see that the psychoanalytic or psychological frameworks (explicit and implicit) commonly brought to bear on the ordinance are inadequate unless we supplement them with a materialist analysis.[30] In a sense, I am arguing, as Brad

Byrom has helped me understand, that the display of a limb, or a marker of blindness, while begging was (or was sometimes or could be) not only a direct means of subsistence but also a circumspect and informal means of political struggle. When "writing of the historical experiences of disabled Americans," Byrom writes, "scholars have focused on the public invisibility of the disabled person." And yet, he points out, the very public gestures of unsightly beggars paved the way for social transformation:

> The public presence of cripples along with the graphic and brazen act of displaying disfigurement . . . encouraged change in social policy and cultural beliefs. So long as the physically disabled suffered quietly in a state of dependency their plight went relatively unnoticed. . . . after 1890, as the number of beggars reached a critical mass and begging practices became more aggressive, change began to occur. . . . the more readily apparent presence of crippled beggars . . . led reformers to create the dozens of hospitals, schools, and rehabilitation facilities . . . that comprise the most lasting monuments to the rehabilitation movement. . . . By claiming public space on the sidewalks of urban centers, destitute cripples had made an effective political statement. (2004, 5, 28–29)

Rarely, before Byrom, has the cripple's begging—or the bystander's attempt to stop the police from stopping it—been granted a politics. The small scene around the beggar as a crowd gathered to join in objecting to his or her arrest was the kind of disguised, low-profile noncompliance that James C. Scott has called an "infrapolitics": "infra" because, like infrared rays, it is "beyond the visible end of the spectrum," and "infra" as in "infrastructure," a "cultural and structural underpinning of . . . more visible political action." "Infrapolitics," writes Scott, "is always pressing, testing, probing the boundaries of the permissible. Any relaxation in surveillance and punishment, and footdragging—or, we might say, insistence on begging or street trading—"threatens to become a declared strike" (1990, 201).[31] Hence the surveillance and punishment of ugly law.

The infrapolitics of disability are everywhere in history, once you begin looking for them.[32] But they are rarely noticed; when disabled people "footdrag," it is often supposed to be a natural fact, not a dilatory tactic. A full account of them would take volumes. What I wish to emphasize here is their connection in this case to other infrapolitics (as well as other more visible and organized political actions), the infrapolitics of poverty and homelessness, for instance. Byrom's point is that beggars acted in some sense as political agents, paving the way for the development of rehabilitation programs. I would add that gestures on the part of momentary allies, of those who gathered to object to the arrest of a given disabled beggar, also functioned as (relatively) silent partners of the louder forms or broader gesticulations apparent in the strike or mass march—in a sense, that we can spot here a brewing infrapolitics of pity.

I am aware of the dangers of valuing a politics of pity; after all, "no pity" has been the crucial rallying cry of the disability rights movement, and a disability studies not committed to repudiating "pity" risks replicating the sentimental oppressiveness of the slogan of the Charity Organization Societies, "not alms but a friend." Moreover, it is important to note that any infrapolitics of pity that clustered around the arrests of disabled people for begging may have resulted in the terrible backlash that *was* ugly law. It is also the case that we cannot ascribe pity as the sole motivation for these moments. Perhaps these spontaneous waves of unrest stemmed from something more like "solidarity," or from any number of other possible responses. Often the show of support would have been for someone who belonged in the neighborhood, a familiar member of the community, known to other beggars, peddlers, paper boys, shoe shiners, rag pickers, stand operators, and everyday passersby who might come to aid. We have little historical evidence on which to base any claim about motives—or for that matter any assessment of who (nondisabled or disabled, middle class or poor, male or female) was in these "ugly crowds."

In addition, in a key way, these struggles were staged by the beggar. They could not occur, to begin with, without the prior action of the disabled person who begged. Thinking of the beggar, not the intervening sympathizer, as the primary agent on the ugly law's street corner changes how we interpret the reactions of the crowd: pity becomes something that can be strategically manipulated, produced by the disabled person for his or her material ends. This is, of course, exactly what antibegging ordinances sought to stop. Note the emphasis in the account by New York's 1921 police Mendicant Squad on this aspect of the stage management of the scene of the protected beggar: "frequently when the detectives attempt to make an arrest, the panhandler, exaggerating his affliction, if he has one, or faking one if he has not, will berate the officer in the presence of impressionable spectators, . . . crowds who invariably side with the prisoner." It is the panhandler, both as performer and as director, who orchestrates the drama on the curb.[33]

These scenes when "ugly crowds" attempted to prevent arrest of disabled beggars became small theaters of collaborative infrapolitical struggle, exposing what Deborah Stone, in her classic work on disability policy, called the "distributive dilemma": the thorny problem of the balance between two distributive systems, one based on work and one on need, a dilemma that the welfare category of "disability" has evolved in order to resolve (15).[34] I am arguing for reading unsightly begging ordinances as attempts to cover and alleviate the economic contradictions between these two distributive systems in the United States. I am also arguing for understanding the "ugly crowds" around the arrests of crippled beggar as effects that uncovered and exposed those contradictions as surely as the exposure of any "diseased, maimed, deformed, disfigured" portion or person. I am arguing, in short, that in order to understand the ugly laws we need to think about poverty and class, labor unrest and capitalism.

After all, the injuries of ugly law—both those it recognizes and those that it inflicts—are capitalist deformities. Sometimes we can discern capitalist pressure on, in, and around the laws with a relatively immediate clarity. For instance, Alderman Peevey's original proposal to the Chicago City Council made a point of indicting "beggars . . . and other unsightly objects" as "an offense to business houses along the streets," presumably because business owners feared dips in profits (Bailey and Evans, 65). Similarly, when an editorial in a 1901 Brooklyn paper opined that "there are special reasons why deformities and monstrosities should be kept out of shopping districts," the reasons had to do with sales ("Undesirable Immigrants").

Other connections to the broader economic context of American capitalism are also apparent. Manufacturers marketed prosthetics to amputees, as Edward Slavishak has shown, precisely by pitching artificial limbs as tools for concealing the "unsightly and improper" injured body targeted by the ordinances. An 1881 *New York Times* article describes freak-show performers subject to an informal ugly law that keeps them off the streets for fear of eating into their theatrical profits by becoming "too familiar to the people" ("All Protests against Beggars"; Slavishak; "Dwarfs and Giants"). In a sense, ugly law forbids a form of commodity fetishism practiced by disabled people who lost or never had access to the means of production and could only commodify what they had—a withered hand, a sore, a missing limb.[35]

But the connections between ugly laws and capitalism are deeper than these and also more structural. What put unsightly beggars on the streets in numbers to begin with? Though begging, work-related injury, and stark disability oppression predate the advent of capitalist economies, certainly industrial capitalism inflicted impairments on workers at a fiercely escalated pace. The market society meant, Marta Russell writes, "that disabled people who were perceived to be of no use to the competitive profit cycle would be excluded from work" (59).[36] At the same time, the category "sturdy," with its connotations of stoop work and of thing-ness (sturdy back, sturdy table), placed the "sightly" subject in direct relation to potential exploitation of labor. In "ugly crowd" encounters, people on U.S. city streets responded to these pressures on the spot.

The contradictions in these scenes sometimes seem practically intolerable. It is one of the ironies of the history of the ugly that the very city council that had crafted Chicago's ugly ordinance, five years later, at the height of Chicago's increasingly violent "class war" and in the immediate wake of the Haymarket Riot on May 4, 1886, issued another resolution on behalf of the very police who had been supposed to enforce that ordinance, as follows:

> RESOLUTION TO PROVIDE FOR DISABLED POLICEMEN
> Whereas in the defense of peace and good order. Several members of the Police force have met with Death and a large number have received grevious [*sic*] wounds. Which may render them incapable of supporting themselves and their families, and
>
> Whereas it is one of the highest duties of Nations and Municipalities to reward and take care of those who so suffer in the support of the public welfare, and Whereas the Charter of our City does not permit of making appropriations either for rewards or for giving pensions.
>
> Therefore, Resolved that the City Council of the City of Chicago hereby requests the Mayor and advise all future mayors to employ all officers of the Police Department. Who were on the 4th day of May 1886 so maimed, as to render them incapable of performing police duty. In such positions. As they can fill. And that we pledge ourselves and all future councils as far as we can. to appropriate for the pay of those so employed a sufficient sum to make the annual pay equal to that of able bodied Policemen. (Bailey and Evans, 79)

It might therefore have been theoretically possible for a maimed (but in the terms of his day reasonably accommodated) policeman, a veteran of the Haymarket Riot, to process the arrest of a diseased, mutilated, or deformed citizen for begging while maimed in public.[37] We can begin to see, in the pressures of this document, the social vectors that moved by the close of World War I toward more organized safety-net systems of compensation and rehabilitation. But the forces at work in this resolution are part of the same struggle reenacted at five-year intervals by the city council, a struggle to patrol and discipline the streets and suppress spontaneous unrest.

The point here is not to allow "labor" or "poverty" or "economic justice" issues to overtake or obscure "disability" issues. The point is to recognize that it is precisely at this arresting intersection that the subject of the ugly law stands. Perhaps even a better metaphor than the familiar "intersection," however neatly appropriate to the city street, is Diana Courvant's figure of confluence, as in the confluence of two rivers: different currents but not entirely different matter or substance.[38]

My point is this: some COS reformers insisted that without ugly law in place, the so-called undeserving poor might mobilize more easily around and with the so-called deserving poor. As I have already noted, that insistence does not make much sense; ugly law might just as well produce ugly crowds as prevent them. But to Charles Kellogg and his fellow New York City charity organizers as they promoted his "crude suggested draft" of an unsightly beggar ordinance, the crisis was real and the plan logical. All spontaneous outcries on behalf of the "crippled beggar" had to be stopped. "Indiscriminate giving" might lead not just to chronic pauperhood but to dissent by "sturdy" and "unsturdy" beggars alike, escalating demand and unrest, direct action, political mobilization. Against this possibility, ugly law had to crack down. The cultural response to tramps and paupers, writes Michael Katz, "reflected a collective hysteria, a fear that swept through the respectable classes" beginning in the 1870s.

> The source was the spectacle of working class organizing, gathering itself for massive protest and what many feared would be a massive assault upon American social institutions. Antitramp legislation, the abolition of outdoor relief and related policies . . . all were attempts to weaken collective action, to reassert class control. (1983, 179–181)

Ugly law was one of those "related policies."[39]

The category of unsightly beggar was designed to trouble the boundaries between the deserving and the undeserving in ways aimed at shoring up the dominant social, not simply the public, order. Unsightly beggars were, in a sense, legally "not/sturdy," occupying both the position of the *un*sturdy (rickety, flimsy, frangible) and the *bad* sturdy (false, lazy, purposefully shoddy). But the transgressive instability of the "not/sturdy" social grouping was not easily quelled. Not/sturdiness continually unsettled models of social welfare and city beautification. The ugly crowds that clustered around unsightly beggars were also small challenging knots and hubs of not/sturdiness.

Ian Hacking argues, in his model of the "ecological niche" for transient illness, that a niche requires a vector of "cultural polarity: the illness should be situated between two elements of contemporary culture, one romantic and virtuous, the other vicious and tending to crime" (2). If the ugly law, as a kind of transient symptom, has a niche in Hacking's terms, then what cultural polarity allows it to flourish? On the side of virtue: the romance of safe, planned public space, with all its bodies—the genteel pedestrian free of disgust, the sequestered cripple—properly organized.[40] On the side of vice and crime: rabble rousing. The law discountenanced not only publicly being ugly but the public getting ugly.

3

THE LAW IN CONTEXT

Most if not all of the problems that civic leaders associated with unsightly persons—begging, vagrancy, contagion, sidewalk obstruction, and so on—were already forbidden by other laws in these cities (laws often used, even after the advent of the ugly laws, to arrest disabled people on the street). Supplementing those existing ordinances, the crackdown on unsightly beggars seems a peculiar kind of overkill. The story of the ugly crowd is, I believe, a necessary one for understanding this law. Without it we cannot grasp the origins and functions of the unsightly beggar ordinances at the intersection of disability history and labor history. But in itself that story is not entirely sufficient. In many ways the ugly law remains a deep enigma.

After all, city councils, COS leaders, and other counterparts who wished to bolster police authority and better rid the streets of tramps and mendicants had other mechanisms than ugly law at their disposal. They might, for instance, have created ordinances penalizing passersby for intervening when an officer arrested any beggar. They might even, theoretically—however improbably—have criminalized the act of almsgiving rather than alms-seeking. Tiedeman's 1886 legal treatise on the limitations of police power in the United States raised the possibility of this kind of legislation, if only to reject it: "It would be unwise for state regulation to prohibit obedience to this natural instinct to proffer assistance to suffering humanity. Indeed, it would seem to be an absolute right of the possessor of property to bestow it as alms upon others" (47–48). The possession of property—in the form of money, of course, but also of that less tangible cultural capital we might call "being in a position to pity"—protected bestowers. And so, instead, city lawmakers targeted the bestowed-upon, stripping them of absolute rights. They targeted disabled people.

It is not my purpose to uncover the efficient cause (in Aristotelian terms) of this strange phenomenon. I mean rather to explore the law's emergence and continuation within a thick network of overdeterminations. In this chapter I explore three of the other factors that helped bring the "unsightly beggar" into being as a criminal in need of punishment and legal intervention.

BIOPOWER AND INSTITUTIONALIZATION

At the moment of the unsightly beggar ordinance's emergence, we can see the logic of biopower that Foucault argues underlies the modern order. For Foucault, biopower assesses and ranks rather than showing itself in spectacular punishments; it "effects distributions around the norm." As a result, legal institutions are "increasingly incorporated into a continuum of apparatuses (medical, administrative, and so on) whose functions are for the most part regulatory" (1978, 143–145).[1] A continuum of apparatuses of this sort is worked in explicitly to the earliest version of ugly law that I have found, San Francisco's 1867 law, which is indexed under (among other things) "Almshouse." The 1880s versions of the ugly ordinances in Chicago, Lincoln, and Denver follow suit. Each ends with a proviso not included in the Bergdorf version that has become the standard source text for disability activists today: "Upon conviction of any person for violation of this section, if it shall seem proper and just, the fine provided for may be suspended, and such person detained at the police station where he shall be well cared for until he can be sent to the county poor farm." (Here the poor farm replaces the almshouse of 1867 San Francisco. In 1867, if it seemed proper and just, "such persons" were simply "committed"; now they are "detained," "well cared for," and finally "sent," a word without the criminal or medical connotations of commitment discourse.)

In the 1880s, then, ugly ordinances speak the language of regulatory care. Indeed, in Denver, strikingly, the law gets indexed in the code books as "Deformed persons—how cared for, section 1009," followed immediately by "shall not expose himself to public view, section 1009." Ugly law, it seems, is just what the doctor orders for the one who needs to be "well cared for." The law, of course, reserves the right to punish as well as discipline, "if it shall seem proper and just." But its dominant thrust seems to be to "effect distributions around the norm" by diverting some people into institutions. In the early years of ugly law the institution is almshouse or poor farm; only later did most states formally and clinically differentiate their "poor" from their "crippled" or "feebleminded."[2] Here is a classic instance of biopower in its modern disciplinary form.

As sociologist Edward Alsworth Ross put it in his summary of this phenomenon in 1920,

> With the vanishing of personal encounter, the passing of judicial torture, branding, stocks, pillory, whipping post and cart's tail, . . . the vanishing of public executions, the abandonment of cock-fighting and bear-baiting . . . the substitution of electricity for the horse, *the removal of the diseased, maimed and misshapen from the streets to public institutions,* the feelings are no longer calloused as of yore, and human good will is able to assert itself with its original native force. (462; italics mine)

The ugly law of biopower identifies an abnormal group in order to "care for" them.

It produces another effect as well, one in line with the later stage of this phenomenon described by Hardt and Negri, in their gloss on Foucault, as the "society of [biopolitical] control" that has developed "at the far edge of modernity" and that "opens toward the postmodern," in which the "behaviors of social integration and exclusion proper to rule are . . . increasingly interiorized within the subjects themselves" in "flexible and fluctuating networks" (23). Negri and Hardt are identifying a postmodern situation, but a related process occurs at the modern moment of ugly law. Ugly ordinances command the self-policing of a populace, checking always to ensure that it is not "unsightly" or "disgusting." To the question of the Omaha judge in 1974—"Does the law mean that every time my neighbor's funny looking kids ask for something I should have them arrested?"—postmodern biopower has an unspoken answer. What one does about the neighbor's funny-looking kids is what one does about oneself: shop at the local drugstore with its aisles of health and beauty products, contemplate the question of cosmetic surgery, respond to the pharmaceutical ads on television. What the neighbor's funny-looking kids ask for is what we all ask of ourselves, making sure, daily, that we are "well cared for"—and not careless of our appearance.[3] As Julia Kingrey puts it in her "Should Discrimination Laws Cover Ugly People," "Whatever your opinion, I hope you're not entitled to protection,"—or, in the words of *Playboy* magazine's piece on the "ugliness ordinance," "Better check the mirror before going out in Chicago" (C. Adams). It did not take an ugly law, in Pennsylvania in 2000, to ban a Labor Day parade float proposed by the Pennsylvania Federation of Injured Workers to raise awareness of the organization's concerns; in a room full of disabled union members, no one volunteered. Self-policing did the trick (Cullen).

The mechanisms of biopower are so much with us now that they are hard to see. Quick citations of the ugly law today may not help in this regard. Harking back to exercises of police repression that strike us as already archaic even at the moment of their inception, ugly laws draw their shock value precisely by appearing as strange vestiges of a long-past, crueler, cruder, far more obvious juridical model. It is, perhaps, easier—too easy?—to attend to them than to attend to the diffuse and pervasive forms of bio(medical) power in the realm of disability in the emerging new global order today.

Foucault's *Discipline and Punish* (1975) does not take up the concept of biopower; the idea emerges in his next book a year later, *History of Sexuality, Volume I* (1976). But the following passage from *Discipline and Punish* bears directly on our subject. Here is the famous distinction between the urban order that meets the leper, which works by "rituals of exclusion" and "exile-enclosure," and the urban order that meets the plague, which works by disciplinary surveillance and "correct training." At this moment Foucault meets ugly law head on:

> They [control of the leper and of the plague] are different projects, then, but not incompatible ones. We see them slowly coming together, and it is the peculiarity of the nineteenth century that it applied to the space of exclusion of which the leper was the symbolic inhabitant (beggars, vagabonds, madmen and the disorderly formed the real population) the technique of power proper to disciplinary partitioning. Treat "lepers" as "plague victims," project the subtle segmentations of discipline onto the confused space of internment, combine it with the methods of analyzing distribution proper to power, individualize the excluded, but use procedures of individuation to mark exclusion. . . . generally speaking, all the authorities exercising individual control function according to a double mode; that of binary division and branding (mad/sane; dangerous/harmless; normal/abnormal); and that of coercive assignment, of differential distribution (who he is; where he must be; how he is to be characterized; how he is to be recognized; how a constant surveillance is to be exercised over him in an individual way, etc.). On the one hand, the lepers are treated as plague victims; the tactic of individualizing disciplines are imposed on the excluded; and, on the other hand, the universality of disciplinary controls makes it possible to brand the "leper" and to bring into play against him the dualistic mechanisms of exclusion. . . . All the mechanisms of power which, even today, are disposed around the abnormal individual, to brand him and to alter him, are composed of those two forms from which they distantly derive. (198–199)

In the context of this analysis, the disappearance of the poor-farm clause in ugly ordinances—both in the city lawbooks, by the early twentieth century, and in the cultural memory—begins to seem an important symptom. City by city, municipal code by municipal code, the striking of the poor-farm provision in part reflects structural changes (the increasing separation of workhouse from almshouse and then, in turn, the proliferation of clinical medical institutions; the controversies around and investigations into abuse and mismanagement in these institutions; increasing urbanization; and so on). City by city and also in the broader, longer cultural memory, the vanishing of the poor-farm shuttle also reflects an ideological change: paradoxically, as the mechanisms for "altering" the "diseased, maimed, and deformed" multiply and disperse across a society fully invested in the seemingly kindler and gentler medical disciplining of disability, the punitive "branding" of the ugly "leper" is left to stand alone, without mitigation, in the police codes. Sometimes ugly laws get quoted today as if they made people lepers alone, in Foucault's sense; the mutual imbrication of exclusion and disciplinary control so powerfully illuminated in the passage quoted above falls out of view.

In the contemporaneous development of state institutions for the "crippled," "feeble-minded," "insane," and later the "epileptic," those spaces of exclusion, American society was inventing other available mechanisms—both subtler and stronger than municipal unsightly beggar ordinances—for segregating disability.[4] The institution called the almshouse lasted well into the twentieth century, and it could be used to cordon off disabled people with or without the mechanism of ugly law in place.[5] As late as 1902, a city like Baltimore sent every "aged, crippled or infirm" beggar arrested to the city almshouse, much as New Orleans did in the late 1870s (Marsh, 414). The census survey titled *Paupers in Almshouses* that came out in 1923 stated that "63.7% of the inmates in the almshouses of the United States in 1910 . . . had some physical or mental defect" (43).

Over time, most cities abandoned explicit almshouses clauses in the ordinance and, later, abandoned the practice of almshouse-packing, shunting "defectives" to narrower, medicalized "hospitals" and "homes."[6] By 1926, Harry Laughlin, a leading American proponent of "the eugenical sterilization of the feeble-minded," argued that state institutions accomplished what almshouses (with their revolving doors) had not: "Modern state institutions provide for the permanent segregation [*sic*], and thus do not act anti-eugenically as some almshouses have done" (227). That is, almshouses, like ugly laws, were leaky structures, ones that left too many dangerously defective people on the street too much of the time, able to freely breed their degenerate children; institutionalization solved this problem entirely (indeed, Laughlin saw no need to sterilize the institutionalized, since for him institutional segregation was total and final).[7] The ugly laws both reinforced and were impelled by a eugenic logic of segregation.[8]

Ugly law and eugenic justifications have much in common. The language of the ordinance, its framing of a person who is self-evidently, before the law, "diseased, maimed, deformed," and so on, may have bolstered (and certainly did nothing to hinder) later legal justifications for eugenic sterilization. Laughlin would defend the legality of forced sterilization by appealing to a "natural class" to which it (should be) applied:

> Anglo-Saxon law demands that the same law apply with equal force to all members of the same natural class . . . [not to] limit a class with boundaries artificial and unnatural. No more natural classes of the population than the feeble-minded, the criminalistic, and the insane can be found. Therefore the law in providing for the sexual sterilization of definite kinds of social inadequates, can easily locate a natural class fully within the demands of our constitutional prohibition against class legislation. (230)

The ugly ordinances constructed a somewhat different "natural class" than Laughlin's—more outwardly marked than inwardly warped, though twentieth-century eugenicists often enough found "stigmata of degeneration" in the institution wards—but both Laughlin and the framers of the ugly laws operated through a similar circuit of reasoning: just laws allow the targeting of "social inadequates" because *nature* knows who they are, and who they are is those who must be gotten off the street, those who are beyond the pale.[9]

Note that *this* discursive "natural class" is classless or cross-social class, in stark contrast to the on-the-street contradictions of poverty and power that I have explored in the previous chapter. Indeed, part of the force and appeal of institutional "care" (as opposed to and also of course as intertwined with ugly law), its particularly compelling solution to the problem of segregating the unsightly, must have been precisely that it seemed more wholly removed than begging ordinances from class struggles. As a solution, it seems more fully driven by disinterested (and medicalized) beneficence (though of course no history of any institution, or of modern state institutionalization in general, stands removed from the actual intensities of social class division).[10] With a mechanism like "the institution" available, unsightly beggar ordinances—however well they shored up disability segregation—seemed somewhat less necessary (and indeed, many cities and most states saw fit to do without them).

MAPPING THE CITY BEAUTIFUL

And yet ugly laws proliferated. To understand why, let us turn to another factor: growing concerns with planning and management of city spaces. And let us focus for a while on the mythic locus of the unsightly beggar ordinances, Chicago 1911. That "1911" and "Chicago" came to stand for the site of ugly law may not be accidental. The year 1911 lies squarely in the Progressive era, and a Progressive focus underscores the aesthetic aspects of the regulation of street conduct. When "deformed" people, like other "indigents" and "unfortunates," came under a reformist Progressive scrutiny intended to better their conditions "both aesthetic and hygienic," they came to light, Melissa Cottrell writes, "as *problems.* They were made to embody what was wrong with the city, all that stood in the way of its greatness, its efficiency, its health or its visual appeal."[11] They would have to be managed as much as architecture, street layout, or drainage if Progressive Chicago were to avoid what a disparaging description of the city in a St. Louis paper had called "the beaten paths of ugliness."[12]

Chicago functions as a nexus of labor unrest in the American historical imagination. But that is only one of its cultural significations. Site of the most broadly attended and influential world's fair in the United States in the nineteenth century (in 1893), Chicago became the model for the modern city plan and the discipline of city planning. The "white," "alabaster," "gleaming" model of the reconfigured urban offered by the world's fair's Chicago dream launched the national city-planning movement, a major new period of urban architectural design and construction of public monuments, and the "City Beautiful" phase of urban development that lasted through the first decade of the twentieth century.

When John Coleman Adams wrote, in his "What a Great City Might Be—A Lesson from the White City" (1896), that "in the midst of a very real and earthy city, full of the faults which Chicago so preeminently displays, we saw a great many features of what an ideal city might be," he was giving voice to a common reformist theme of the period. Adams praised the White City as a model of free uncorrupted metropolitan access:

> There was not another place in America where the American citizen could feel so much of the pride of popular sovereignty as he could after he had

> paid his half dollar and become a naturalized resident of this municipality. Once within those grounds he was monarch of all he surveyed. He could go anywhere. He could see everything. He was welcome to all that he found within those gates. He could feel for once in his life that he was not liable to be snubbed by the police. . . . It revealed to him what a mock-freedom is really his. . . . Let this "popular sovereign" try to walk the streets of his own city . . . and see how mortifying a lot is his. If he meets a policeman he cannot help feeling afraid under some very innocent circumstances, that he may be arrested merely for being out of doors. . . . The sidewalks are not his. (395)

The City Beautiful movement sparked by the White City sought to reconstitute this ideal in "very real and earthy cities," but not, of course, for unsightly beggars; the sidewalks and popular sovereignty were still not theirs. The imagined great city that might be was one without disabled beggars on the street, though histories of urban development and of Chicago's influence on normative models of good city life have not addressed the ugly law's relation to American city planning.[13]

The conjunction of health and aesthetic concerns in efforts to plan the city beautiful is well illustrated in the proceedings of the first International Municipal Congress and Exposition, a gathering of political and philanthropic members of the local body politic held in Chicago in September 1911. As Cottrell describes, the most fervent social reformers who spoke at the Municipal Congress were also the most normative in their attempt to strip the public sphere of the abject and the grotesque and to reserve it for the sanitized and regulated social body.[14] In the discourse of the first International Municipal Congress, as Cottrell puts it, "civic pride, the pressing need to plan city development, and hygiene-panic all combined to motivate the policing of city space as a way of guarding both moral and physical health."[15]

They combined as well, Cottrell notes, with aesthetic zeal. A speech at the congress called "Public Lighting" by E.L. Elliott captures the spirit of these local legislators as it extended even into the realm of the inanimate object. In a section called "The Early Arc-Lamp as Art Offender," Elliott implicitly associates deformity with both bad taste and criminality: the arc-lamp, now removed from the streets, had been "hopelessly ugly; yet thousands of these atrocities disfigured the streets by day which they villainously lighted by night." In this context, the odd phrase "ugly law," which might be said to trivialize the force and nature of the prohibition in question, comes to seem more telling than misleading. It captures some of what

Siebers has called a "political imaginary" that "enforces a mutual identification between forms of appearance, whether organic, aesthetic, or architectural, and ideal images of the body politic" (2003, 186).

The campaign to eradicate the "disfigured" arc lamp and the efforts of the planners at the First Municipal Congress participated in a mutual project designed to make the city legible, beautiful, and orderly. At every level, in every corner, Chicago would, they hoped, conform to what James Scott has called "the logic of the grid." That logic was a hallmark of what Scott defines as the "muscle-bound" ideology of high-modernist city planning: "a particularly sweeping vision of how the benefits of technical and scientific progress might be applied—usually through the state—in every field of human activity" to create a more disciplined and regular modern urban order (Scott 1998, 89; D. Harvey).[16]

There were, of course, other kinds of mappings. Consider the work of anarchist doctor Ben Reitman, who worked in Chicago not only as a founder of a "hobo college" and leader of a 1908 March of the Unemployed but as an advocate for and ally with people (particularly women) with venereal diseases (Poirier). Indeed, Reitman has given us a kind of alternative "plan," an imaginary material map of ugly law, in the form of a graphic illustration of a talk he gave entitled "Reitman's Social Geography" at a 1910 "Outcast Night" he organized. In this diagram drawn on what appears to be a bedsheet, preserved in Reitman's archives at the University of Illinois–Chicago, "Vagrant Isle," with its cities "Hoboville" and "Bumtown," floats in the same "Sea of Isolation," separated off from the land of "Respect/Ability," as "Race Prejudice Isle," "Prostitute Isle," "Criminal Island," and a cluster of "Poverty Islands" with "Disable Isle" at its center.[17] "Radical Island," with its towns "Freethinkville," "Freeloveville," "Crankly," and "Tolstoy," floats nearby between the land of Freedom and the Gulf of Doubt, with "Port Direct Action" as its nearest route to land.

The city on Radical Island most interesting for my purposes is "Crankly." *Crank* (which shows up originally in American usage in our marked year 1881), in its sense of "odd or eccentric person" who obsesses about fads, is certainly a word that could be marshaled against anarchists, freethinkers, and proponents of free love. Reitman claims it, in a dynamic we might find similar to the current embracing of the words "queer" or "crip" by their respective politicized constituencies. But there is something else going on here too: *crank*'s original meaning (from the sixteenth century on) was "a beggar feigning sickness or illness; also, the falling sickness" (the word is derived from the German *krank*, ill). Hence the related terms *counterfeit*

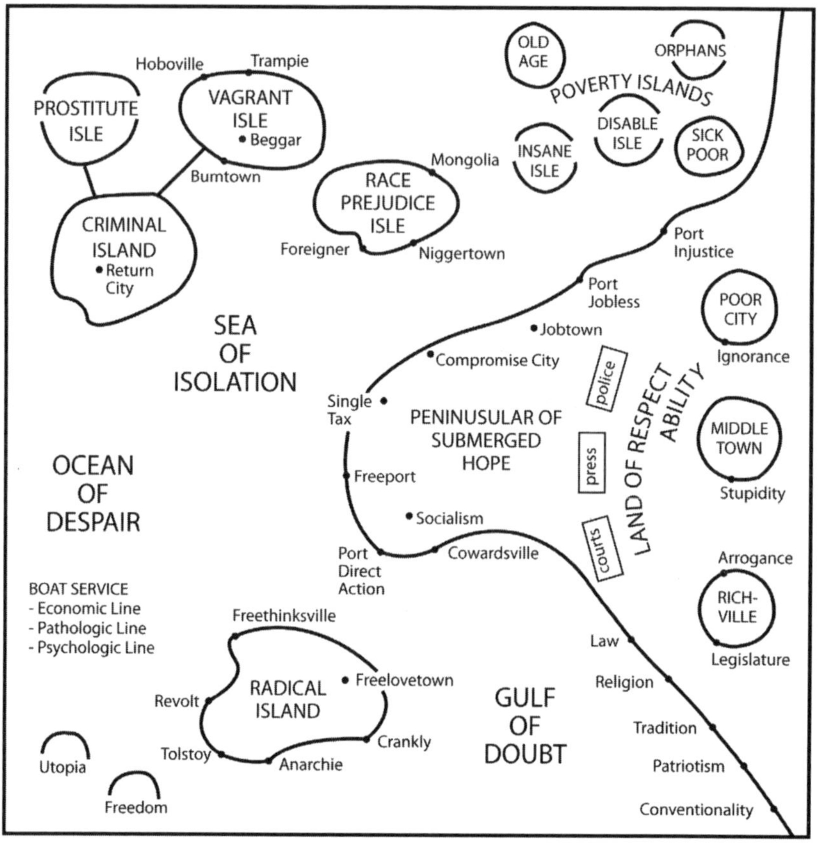

"Reitman's Social Geography," 1910. (Version by Charles Legere from author's sketch of Reitman's map on a bedsheet, drawn at a 1910 "Outcast Night," in the Reitman Papers, University of Illinois at Chicago Special Collections)

crank, described in Partridge's slang dictionary as a "sham-sick man," and *crank-cuffin* (a vagrant feigning illness; *cuffin* is from *cuff,* "a foolish old man."). In 1908, Arthur McDonald, the proponent of a national psychopathic lab, spelled out the perils of the crank in no uncertain terms:

> As in machinery we must first repair the little wheels out of gear, so in society we must first study the criminal, crank, insane, inebriate or pauper who can seriously injure both individual and community. Thus a worthless crank . . . can paralyze a whole community. (1)

Claiming the crank (the ill, the feigning ill, the one who begs, the collapse of distinction between the three where outcasts are concerned, the port of galvanizing rather than paralyzing "direct action" available to them all), Reitman blurred the borders between the politics of poverty, of sexuality, and of disability.[18] This kind of "social geography" helps us map the emergence of ugly laws as phenomena partially but powerfully impelled by response to struggles against class privilege and for economic (and on Reitman's map other, including sexual) rights.

Compare Reitman's map with another that epitomizes the opposite approach, a classic in the field of city design by an exemplar for, and collaborator with, the Progressive-era City Beautiful movement of which Burnham's famous Chicago Plan was a part. Ebenezer Howard's drawing of his "Slumless, Smokeless Garden City" in his *To-Morrow: A Peaceful Path to Real Reform* (1898) lays out Howard's influential vision of small, appealing new towns planned radially, surrounded by architectural land belts.

In this vision of the ideal city, as Imrie has noted, the diseased, maimed, deformed, and otherwise unsightly are perfectly segregated outside the urban garden: asylums for the blind and deaf, a farm for epileptics, and isolated convalescent homes all offer extra fresh air to their inmates and the promise of disability-free boulevards to everyone else (121–123). In contrast, Reitman's "social geography," neither entirely dystopian nor utopian, maps energies rather than entities, starting points rather than final destinations; his decentered map, in which the Crystal Palace of Howard's purified city becomes only a displaced "Middle Town" off to one side, takes no position as normative. Every space on this map, including "Disable Isle" and "Crankly," is politically organized and an electric venue for political organizing toward the dissolution of out-casting; and Reitman's call for grassroots, multiple "city plannings" by and for "outcasts" implicitly depends on the alliance of, and the recognition of possible links between, various abjected groups, disabled people among them, despite their isolation.

Reitman made these links as well in the group of unpublished poems he called his "Outcast Narratives," a planned sequence of one hundred flat, prosy poems each depicting a single person, many of whom (Emma Goldman and Sadakichi Hartmann among them) were his friends. Suzanne Poirier has suggested that Edgar Lee Master's *Spoon River Anthology* was Reitman's model for this anarchist lyric sequence. Perhaps, but a more direct influence is the set of "types from city streets" delineated by Reitman's fellow "Biographer of the Outcasts" Hutchins Hapgood, who helped organize the "Outcast Night" at which Reitman presented his "social geography" and

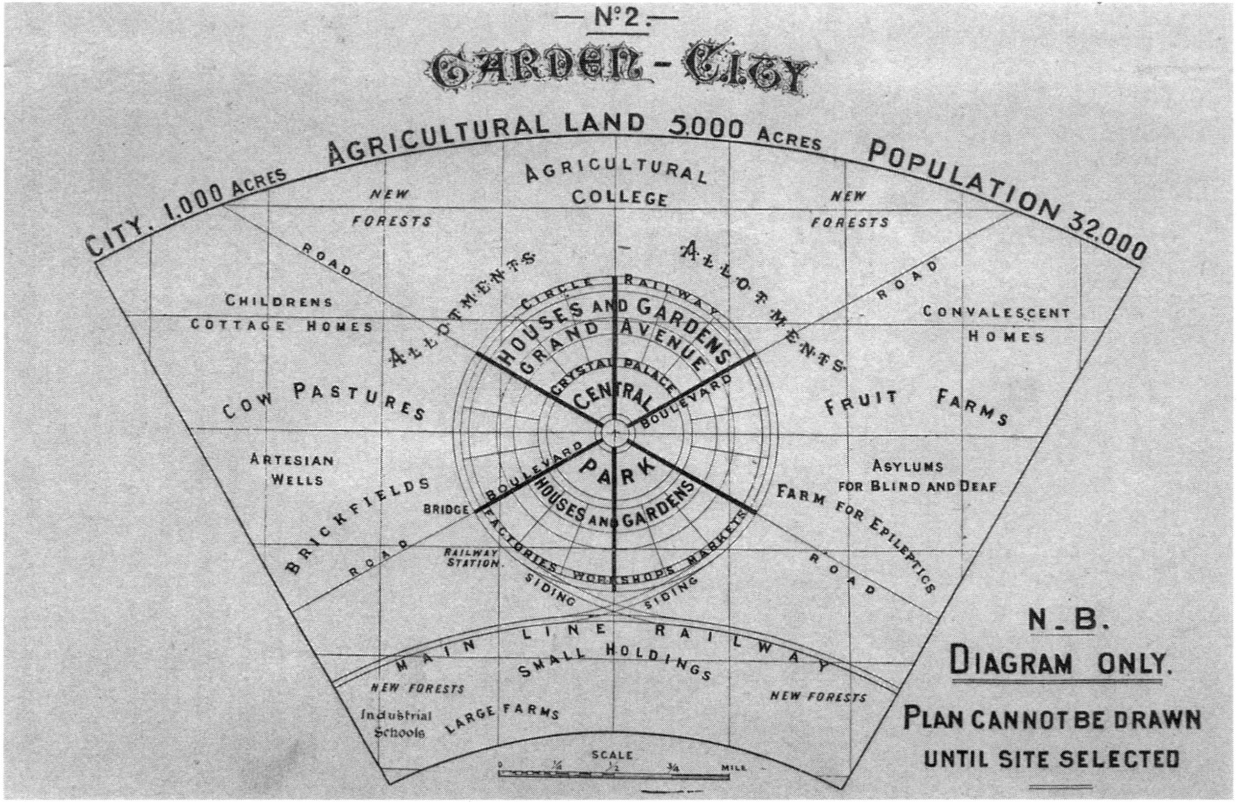

Ebenezer Howard's map for a "Slumless, Smokeless Garden City" (1898). (Ebenezer Howard, *Garden Cities of To-Morrow: A Peaceful Path to Real Reform,* 1898; rpt., London: Swan Sonnenschein, 1902)

who appears in one of Reitman's "Outcast Narratives" himself.[19] Like Hapgood, Reitman develops a series of radical sketches of various characters, "express[ing] Outcasts as he saw them": "I tried to rid the world of poverty and crime. / And I believe when you know of these things. / You too will try to rid the world of these things." His outcasts include prostitutes, street speakers and agitators, tramps, prisoners, homosexual men, and a woman teacher who refuses to sign a loyalty oath and is fired, among others. He includes an account from "Disable Isle" of a Jewish peddler, "Ike," who, after he "became a cripple, / Had to peddle shoe-strings on the street. / Then he was sent to the poor house." The sequence structure links Ike to the others. This kind of mapping, this kind of conceptual linkage, as I showed in the preceding chapter, was both a goad to and a reaction to the ugly laws.

City cultures under the grip of unsightly beggar panic, utterly fallen out of the Garden, clamped down with a different kind of map. A 1915 chart exemplifying "A Graphic Method of Illustrating Situations in Penal Institutions," included as an appendix to that year's proceedings of the American Prison Association, illustrates both the production and the dysfunction of spaces meant to contain abnormality and transgression. The map, we are told, "represents a . . . woman"—a feebleminded woman from a good family who did not have permanent custodial care in a suitable institution early in life" (Hodder and Spaulding, v).

As a "feebleminded" person, she bears an uneven relation to the direct jurisdiction of the ugly laws, but the mapping of her nonetheless tells us something about the narrative geography of the (feminine) unsightly beggar.

If this map is, is meant to be, that woman, it nonetheless does not aim to make visible some version of her interiority, some allegorical mapping of her private development or pilgrim's progress, with modern equivalents of safe cities beautiful, "feebleminded" sloughs of despond, and so forth. It is organized sequentially, moving in a kind of unhinged clockwise ring from her birth in 1871 to her lodging in a "reformatory for women" in 1914. Like Reitman's social geography of the outcast—where "Criminal Island" (with its capital "Return City") connects by bridges to "Prostitute Isle" and "Vagrant Isle" and where lines of boat service cart people from one zone to another—this map charts dynamic trajectories of movement, its back-and-forth arrows spoking to and from a central zone. But this is the map of the inmate, not the outcast. Every space is an enclosure, from the central circle of "Community," with the paternal umbrella, "Father's Home," at the hub, to the proliferating web of structures that take her in: "Private Sanitorium,"

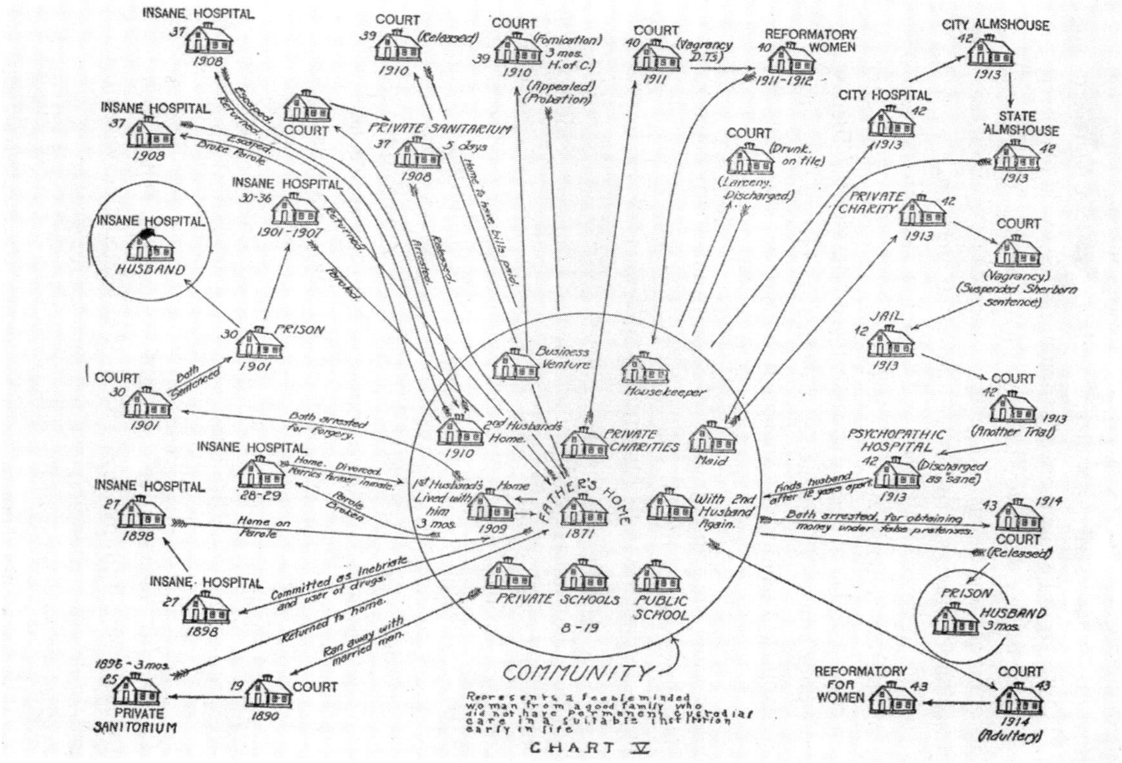

"A Graphic Method of Illustrating Situations in Penal Institutions" for the American Prison Association, 1915. (Jessie D. Hodder and Edith R. Spaulding, M.D., "Appendix. Containing Charts on 'A Graphic Method of Illustrating Situations in Penal Institutions,'" *Proceedings of the Annual Congress of the American Prison Association*. Indianapolis: Wm. B. Burford, 1915)

"Insane Hospital," "Prison," "City Almshouse," "State Almshouse," "Private Charity," "Jail," "Psychopathic Hospital," and, repeatedly, "Court." The arrows, whether they represent paths of transgressive sexuality (fornication, adultery), drunkenness, criminality, insanity, vagrancy, or poverty, all are straight roads to incarceration. As the encircling rings given over to father and even to deviant husbands suggest, patriarchy and paternalism control the siting of the woman.[20] Meant as a graphic illustration of a system in crisis—the problem here is that early intervention in a "suitable institution" did not occur, that no place can quite contain her—the infrastructure of this map nonetheless allows this woman no public space, only the fast-tracked line from one form of house arrest to another.

Public movement controlled properly; garbage disposed of properly; lamps and streets proportioned properly; disabled people ringed and sequestered and trained properly—all of this increasingly scrutinized as well as more and more vigorously managed: under such an aesthetics, actual disability as one of many forms of city irregularity seemed destined (or designed) to disappear. When it did appear, it would be tightly mapped and managed.[21] The ugly law was one of many mechanisms in the planning and policing of space in the city.

INJURY AND COMPENSATION

Another structural condition, an additional kind of legal space, played a role in making beggars unsightly and begging seemingly unnecessary and containable. When legal theorist and founder of the National Federation of the Blind Jacobus tenBroek attacked the confinement of disabled people "to their houses, asylums, and institutions" in his 1966 treatise on "the right to live in the world," he quoted what sounds like *the* legal case undoing ugly law: "Public thoroughfares are for the beggar on his crutches as well as the millionaire in his limousine" (*Weinstein v. Wheeler*, 1928; quoted in "Right to Live," 863). But *Weinstein*'s ringing declaration of principle—"Neither is it the policy of the law to discriminate against those who suffer physical infirmity"—occurs in a very specific and limited context, one reflected in the subtitle of tenBroek's essay: "The Disabled in the Law of Torts." "The blind and the halt may use the streets," the court ruled in *Weinstein*, "without being guilty of negligence if, in so doing, they exercise that degree of care which an ordinarily prudent person similarly afflicted would exercise under the same circumstances." Tort law did not undo ugly law. In fact, developments in tort law and the ideology that surrounded it may have encouraged both the acceleration of begging by disabled people in greater numbers and its equal and opposite reaction, the enactment of unsightly beggar ordinances.

U.S. culture at the moment of the emergence of the ugly laws was developing multiple new regulatory systems for managing forms of "disease, maiming, and deformity" under the category of injury. By the 1880s, Barbara Welke shows, the always-delicate balance between "the ideal of America as a nation of free men" and the reality of contingency, injury, and accident "had been irreversibly tipped" (3). Large-scale industrial technology under corporate control, modern modes of systematic record-keeping to tally "casualties," and the massive increase in rate and scope of injuries led to new understandings of the likelihood and meaning of accident. "Safety," Welke writes, could no longer "be left to individual choice.... The era of steadfast commitment to American ingenuity and independence was replaced by the era of ordered liberty, liberty assured by restraint" (3–4). The ugly laws, themselves an ordering of liberty, emerged at this juncture.

As Garland Thomson has noted, these industrial transformations, as "stable communities and older forms of production began to dissolve," and the concomitant changes in the U.S. legal system, led to a sharp increase in alms-seeking on the streets. Writing of an important 1842 court decision that defined negligence in ways that favored employers, Garland Thomson argues that injured workers "had little recourse but charity or poor relief. As long as economic resources from the public sphere were not equitably available... they not only lost their jobs but also dropped out of sight" (*EB*, 48). And/or they dropped into the glaring state of hypervisibility known as unsightliness.

If tort law under the ideology of what Garland Thomson calls "contractarian economic individualism" led to even more unsightly beggars, it also provided a new set of justifications for stopping almsgiving, and it generated new anxieties that centered, like the ugly laws, on the problem of "public view." Increasingly, Americans responded to changed economic conditions and the injuries caused by modern technologies and industry by filing lawsuits against corporations. In courts as on the street corner, struggles erupted over whether the signs of accident, injured bodies, could or should be exposed to public observation.

In *Union Pacific Railway v. Botsford*, for instance, in 1890, Supreme Court justices argued over whether the "inviolability of the person" was invaded by compulsory "exposure" if plaintiffs were forced to "lay bare the body."

Clara Botsford sued for injuries suffered when a Pullman berth fell on her. At stake in this case was her refusal to consent to a physical examination by doctors representing Union Pacific (it mattered very much, of course, that the body at risk of being indelicately laid bare here was a proper woman's). Her resistance seems the opposite of the unsightly beggar's refusal to hide signs of hurt. But other legal cases revolved around whether plaintiffs too disposed to brandish their injuries in the courtroom unfairly played on juror sympathies.[22] In both arenas, the lawsuit and the ordinance, similar cultural anxieties about how to view and how to show injury in modernity came into play.

Like the growing system of state institutions, the elaborated system of tort law offered one more reason why unsightly begging could now become obsolete. In many ways, this turn to law was the reverse of street begging; formalized, under the auspices of professionals, as scientific as organized charity, it required representation in ways that vernacular begging practices did not. The lawsuit, not the tin cup, became the sanctioned means for seeking redress, for garnering economic support, and for articulating complaint in American culture. The kinds of false claims and true rights that modernity produced, systematic and bureaucratized, promised to overtake archaic modes like begging; just compensation for injury promised to replace merciful charity.[23]

Throughout the 1880s, increasing public attention focused on another bureaucratic form of disability compensation, the Civil War pension system (first established for disabled veterans, their widows, and their minor children in 1861). As veterans aged and filed claims for pensions in larger numbers, a national political debate ignited. Should pensions continue to be granted only to men directly injured in and by the war itself? Or should they be extended to all ill and disabled veterans, solely on the basis of their honorable military service? Democrats objected to "service-based" pensions; Republicans supported the new plan. Republican Benjamin Harrison won the presidency in 1888 after a campaign intensely focused on this question.[24] In 1890, the Disability Pension Act opened the door to benefits claims by any veteran disabled in any way (as long as he could prove that "vicious habits or gross carelessness" were not the cause of impairment [Blanck, 125]). At this key moment, "Disability" decisively entered the official federal legal lexicon; as the modern association of disability with right to welfare benefits consolidated, almsgiving to beggars began to seem more and more unnecessary, and scenes of proving worthiness for aid promised to shift from the street to the offices of certifying doctors. With new systems in place to reward and care for the deserving, crackdowns on beggars could be more easily justified.

But although the courtroom, insurance office, and pension bureau became, increasingly, the sanctioned places where questions about injured bodies—and where, in a sense, the previously restless bodies themselves—were *settled,* the beggar and the tin cup still lurked there too. One 1904 handbook for doctors and trial lawyers defined itself as a tool to help them ferret out not only bold-faced fraud by plaintiffs but also the "hysterical and unconsciously exaggerated cases where . . . neurotic predisposition exists" (Hamilton, iii). A set of instructions aided readers in interpreting the "facies of the neurasthenic" (28). "There is a habitual drooping and flaccidity of most of the lower facial muscles," the author explains.

> the brow is corrugated, sometimes unilaterally—as depicted by Kirchof in his plates of insanity—or traversed by numerous wrinkles. . . . [The expression suggests] the existence of an ever-present mental image of pain rather than suffering which actually exists. This expression is more often seen in litigants whose cases are in process of arbitration or suit, and is as a rule an unconscious exhibition and therefore not to be controlled; it does not by any means imply, however, that there is a corresponding amount of suffering. (28)

In case the book's professional audience had difficulty picturing the face in question, the text provided a portrait and a helpful hint: "it can be compared to the expression of the mendicant one sees so much of in Latin countries." Under the picture of the female neurasthenic with knitted brow, the caption reads, "Facies *Mendicans*" (italics mine).

Neurasthenia, that refined form of status nervousness much in vogue, turns out to be high-class mendicancy.[25] The rise in injury lawsuits, it seems, only exacerbated the problem of the unsightly beggar, providing her upper-class counterpart with a new and even more profitable venue. I write "her" deliberately. The first two illustrations in this "book for court use" are of women. Hysterics, like neurasthenics, beg in the courts, not in the streets, like the woman written up by Raymond and Janet, whose "contraction of trunk, the result of a fixed idea" resembles "the distortion . . . that follows advanced poliomyelitis" but derives from another source:

> The patient between the ages of seven and nine sustained an injury of the left foot, which consisted of a sprained ankle due to a fall from a swing;

"Facies mendicans." (Allan McLane Hamilton, *Railway and Other Accidents, with Relation to Injury and Disease of the Nervous System: A Book for Court Use.* New York: William Wood, 1904)

and bandaging and retention for some time in an iron instrument were sufficient to develop a spasm and condition of varus. This disappeared, but reappeared with hysterical hemiplegia *after a number of years.* (Hamilton, 54; italics in original)

After viewing this picture—the naked woman blindfolded, leaning with a kind of grotesque classicism against a pedestal—it is not hard to figure out why Clara Botsford fought all the way to the Supreme Court to keep court doctors from laying her body bare. The two women in this textbook are displayed to public view to establish the terms for detecting high-strung "mendicancy." Freud had detected it in Dora:

And so it happens that anyone who tries to make [the hysterical patient] well is to his astonishment brought up against a powerful resistance. . . . Let us imagine a workman, a bricklayer, let us say, who has fallen off a

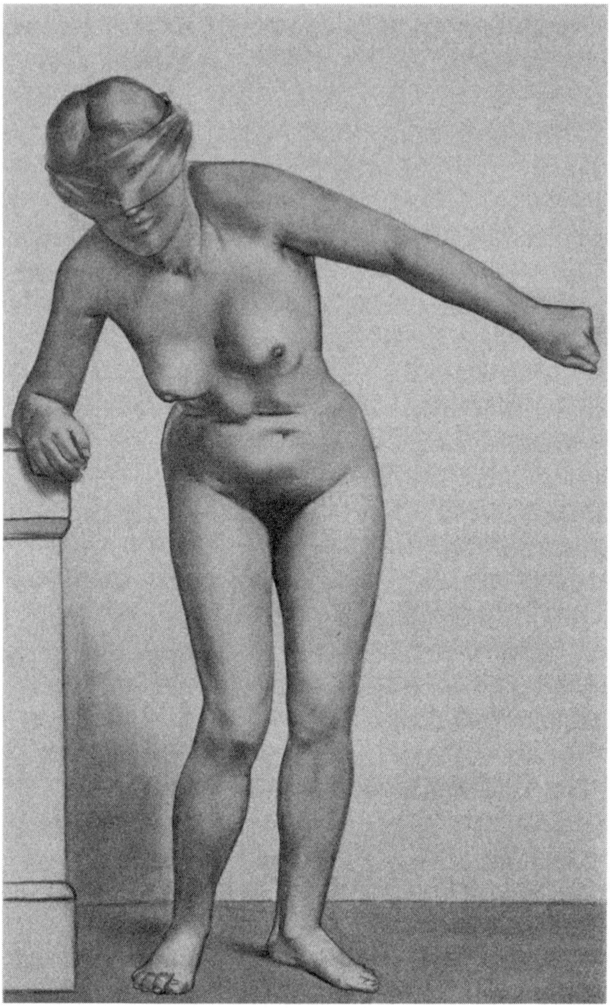

Woman "deformed by a fixed idea." (Allan McLane Hamilton, *Railway and Other Accidents, with Relation to Injury and Disease of the Nervous System: A Book for Court Use.* New York: William Wood, 1904)

> house and been crippled, and now earns his livelihood by begging at the street-corner. Let us then suppose that a miracle-worker comes along and promises to make his crooked leg straight and capable of walking. It would be unwise, I think, to look forward to seeing an expression of peculiar bliss upon the man's features. . . . he lives by his disablement. If that is taken from him he may become totally helpless. (60)

Men like Freud's workman show up too in the injury lawsuit textbooks, sometimes as neurasthenic malingerers but also as outright liars, as in this case of misread deformity in which false claiming combines with draft-dodging:

> Within a year or two in Brooklyn, a case was tried in which a carefully prepared diagnosis of amyotrophic lateral sclerosis was made by a neurologist of experience. . . . Before the end of the trial, however, it was shown that [the plaintiff] had in Russia, before his emigration to this country, inflicted bilateral wounds upon himself with a shoemaker's knife to escape military service, and the resulting deformity . . . had preceded the accident for many years. (Hamilton, 292–293)

Anxieties about such false and undeserving complaints on the part of male subjects also plagued the administration of the veterans' Disability Pension Act and its predecessor Civil War pension systems. In 1881, a general warned that soldiers who had been "rollicking with health [and] full of lusty life" at the end of the war would now be induced to discover convenient diseases "latent in their blood" if "pensions for all" were put into effect.[26] By 1894, as the pension system expanded, the *New York Times* answered a pressing question—"What Are Disabilities?"—simply with a vision of widespread fraud: "There are very few men who could not have gotten a certificate of disability. . . . The administration of the Pension Bureau made the disability pension virtually a service pension for all who were willing to reveal their ailments and swear to them," just as unsightly beggars did.

By the end of the first decade of the twentieth century, railway agents had developed national files of mugshots of personal-injury grifters like "banana peel specialists" or, more threatening yet, what Ken Dornstein calls "nature fakers, . . . freaks who tried to cash in on their genetic defects, bizarre medical conditions, unique physical capacities, or . . . preexisting injuries" in fraudulent personal-injury claims (73).[27] The figure of the unsightly beggar shares a clear connection with this kind of nature/faker, simultaneously both freak and fraud, someone who uses his or her abnormal body abnormally, exaggerating or aggravating features of that body for personal gain. Ugly law polices a subject not unlike the "Mr. Traumatic Claimant of Fakeville," formerly of "Malingerers Town and Buncoes Crossing," who was the target of the Railway Index Bureau (Dornstein, 75).

Along similar lines, the final section of the textbook for injury trial lawyers that I quoted earlier devotes itself to teaching doctors stern scientific methods for detecting simulation of a range of conditions. These might include paralysis, seizures, blindness, deafness, and the strange feigned affliction that ends the textbook, the fake dyslexia of Mrs. H.C.D. after a fall on her buttocks and the disarrangement of her hat (Hamilton, 321).[28] In this regard particularly, the ugly laws, injury lawsuits, and pension systems share a common denominator. As I show in chapter 5, just as the faking plaintiff/beneficiary increasingly preoccupied the discourse of the lawsuit and the pension, so the imposter dominated cultural constructions of the unsightly beggar.

Each of the factors I have examined in this chapter—the rise of new systems of injury compensation and imposter claimant screening, the growth of medicalized and segregatory institutions, the development of professional urban planning and reform—emerged in the material context of accelerating urbanization and industrialization, in a late-nineteenth-century nation with an unstable economy. But there were other threads as well in the social fabric that made up the ugly law. A closer look at the language of the law reveals them.

4

THE LAW IN LANGUAGE

"Any person who is diseased, maimed, mutilated, or in any way deformed, so as to be an unsightly or disgusting object, or an improper person": this person is made out of words. To start with, this person is made out of the word "person" (with the "any" signaling the broad and arbitrary reach of the law in question): a legal word, rich in discursive import. Not "any one" or "any body," but—as the *Oxford English Dictionary* puts it—"a being having legal rights, a juridical person."

If there is some comfort in remembering that this is a legal and therefore entirely "insubstantial" person, perhaps a person with rights, there is discomfort in noticing how quickly *this* person is bound back into a body and an identity: not a person *with*, for instance (as in "person with a disability") but "any person *who is*" (diseased, maimed, or what have you). This "who is" suggests that descriptors like *deformed* or *mutilated* are determined by the "natural kinds fallacy" that Silvers and Stein identify, the mistaken belief "that what *is* the case must, in fact, *be* the case": the person who is unsightly, disgusting, and improper must be unsightly, disgusting, and improper. That which is contingent is attributed to nature (226).[1] The person here is in fact precisely not the "'person' at the center of the traditional liberal theory" as Breckenridge and Vogler define him: "he is an able-bodied locus of subjectivity, . . . one who can imagine himself self-sufficient because almost everything conspires to help him take his enabling body for granted (even when he is scrambling for the means of subsistence)" (350). Unsightly = scrambling + able to take nothing for granted.

In this chapter, I explore further some meanings that cluster in this discursive and putatively natural person, in order to extend our understanding of the work done by the unsightly beggar ordinances. I focus on some words that stand out starkly in the language of the law itself—"unsightly," "improper," and "disgusting"—as well as some telling others frequently encountered in the chatter that surrounded the unsightly beggar ordinances at the time of their enactment. In each case, I range well beyond the dictionary to consider some broad dynamics in the culture of ugly law.

UNSIGHTLY, UNSEEMLY, IMPROPER

The law's emphasis not only on un*sight*liness but also on *exposure* and public *view* suggests that it represents a kind of high-water mark of problems of seeing under the new conditions of visibility in modern urbanity. In a particularly illuminating analysis of the ordinances, Rosemarie Garland Thomson focuses on their relation to visualizing as modern problem. She writes that the ugly laws constituted a

> refusal to see the disabled, a kind of bowdlerizing of the body that enacted widespread consequences for people with disabilities. Among them were the slow and conflicted demise of publicly displaying disabled people as freaks, as well as institutionalizing, segregating, and medicalizing people with disabilities. . . . even though disabled people have always been a large and significant segment of any social order, those among us whose impairments could be enlisted to symbolize disability were often hidden from public view. . . . modernity deemed disability an improper object to be looked at. (2001, 338)

Modernity, we might say, *was* controlled appearance. As Garland Thomson makes clear, ugly ordinances epitomized how modern bodies were and must be seen as they engaged with city spaces.[2]

The ordinances were obviously related to other laws in the same period that prohibited a broader range of insults to the senses, such as laws that barred people whose smell disgusted others from being in public places and the ordinances I discuss in chapter 7 that regulated noise on the street. From the "foul wound" of Sophocles's Philoctetes onward, the social exclusion and isolation of ill, wounded, and disabled people has been associated textually and culturally as much with assaults to the ears (think of Philoctetes's howling fits) or to the nose (think of his wound's stench) as with offense to the eyes. But the prohibition of appearance alone is what the ugly ordinance, at least in theory, decrees.[3] At the law's onset in 1867 San Francisco, the ordinance's headline spelled this out, defining the order as one "to Restrain Certain Persons from Appearing in Streets and Public Places."

In the later-nineteenth-century United States, combining pressures of individualism and consumerism created what Philip Ferguson calls a "broad cultural aesthetic" obsessed with problems of "appearing" and appearance. "[U]gliness became as important a judgment as beauty," writes Ferguson. "Applied to people with physical and mental disabilities, heightened attention to appearance made words such as 'repulsive,' 'grotesque,' 'dirty' and 'slovenly' into accusations of moral and mental failure as well as the more obvious aesthetic transgressions." Incurable and incorrigible ugliness entered the dangerous realm that Ferguson calls "chronicity," and the only solution was to hide it: "The proper outcome of aesthetic failure," he writes, "was permanent invisibility" (5–6).

The ugly laws thus focused on disabled people as common or uncommon *sights* on the city streets. "I say 'sight,' rather than simply 'inhabitant,'" writes Gleeson in his description of dominant conceptions in the Victorian period, "because disabled people were distinguished from the masses of pedestrians: first by the social inscriptions of difference arising from their apparent displacement, and second, by the nature of their presence in the streets" (110). These are partly mythic people, and not the whole story; in actuality the scene might be significantly complex, including, perhaps, a disabled man wearing a well-kept officer's uniform, a fashionably dressed, wealthy blind woman, and so on. It is always important not to lump all disabled people together. But Gleeson correctly identifies a pattern in the cultural imagination of poor disabled people. Neither "strolling consumers" nor "people in circulation," disabled people in poverty as Gleeson understands them experienced the street as "a place of subsistence" and as "a stage that constantly retold the story of their social difference and exclusion" (110). This is the story that the ugly law tells.

It tells, too, a story about those not subject to it: the public constructed as viewer, not viewed, as sightly and as sighting, not unsightly and disgusting. Consider, for instance, the ordinance's relation to what Kasson calls "the dialectics of social classification," the emerging standards of rudeness and refinement, acceptable and unacceptable appearance and behavior in the late-nineteenth-century United States (4). Kasson shows how, within the "proximate spaces of the new American metropolises," evolving codes of civility "helped to implant a new, more problematic sense of identity—externally cool and controlled, internally anxious and conflicted—and of social relationships. In the anonymous metropolis and within a market economy, individuals grew accustomed to offering themselves for public appraisal. At the same time they scrutinized others to guard against social counterfeits" (7).

In the cities, Kasson argues, "venturing forth" entailed increased concern about "bodily management in public. . . . Embarrassment became a normal, even an essential, part of American urban life," "a subtle and routine form of discipline" (112, 114). Etiquette books counseled would-be ladies and gentlemen on how to achieve "impeccable inexpressivity" (121). Amid this growing anxiety about either engaging in or inviting any exercise of visual intrusion, "the urban bourgeoisie was taught to overlook as much as to look," and "municipal police and detectives properly assumed" the business of surveillance (127).[4] It is easy to see how the notion of policing the unsightly emerges out of this scene—but also how ugly law, in interesting ways, overdoes this project. The idea of unsightliness, vague and other-directed, depends on an assumed axis of appropriateness and inappropriateness and on the internal vigilance of each member of the populace, a continual checking and adjusting of one's body. Ugly law *legislated* what was otherwise supposed to be (for the middle and upper classes, at least) self-regulated. Jailing and fining unsightly beggars occurred at the point where etiquette failed or could not reach; the subjects of the ugly law were understood as beyond embarrassment.

But who exactly was being managed by ugly law? The sightly (and sighted) passerby as much as the unsightly beggar. At the ordinance's onset in Chicago we can read this dynamic clearly in the push-pull work of language for labeling the problem at hand, words that emerge only to fall away. Alderman Peevey's initial resolution before the Chicago city council worried over the presence of "numerous beggars, mendicants, organ-grinders or other unsightly and *unseemly* objects, which are a reproach to the City" and "*disagreeable* to people upon the streets" (Bailey and Evans; italics mine). By the end of the council's deliberations with the mayor, the law that this resolution spawned had altered its wording in two key respects. The language of etiquette ("unseemly," "disagreeable") gives way, first of all, to more raw terms of disgust. "Unseemly," presumably, was too nice a word to be applied to the scum that played "Mollie Darling." But the well-mannered discourse of this early draft, and even more so the word "improper" in the final version, nevertheless show that politeness was at stake in Chicago's construction of its civic culture in 1881. Enforcing seemliness and sociable agreeability, it seems, was part of the council's early resolve. Note too, however, that the explicit, narrow target of Peevey's resolution ("beggars, mendicants") disappears entirely in Chicago's first published version of the ordinance, which makes no mention of beggars, diffusing its prohibition so that it applies to "any person." In the streets and public places of ugly law, all were disciplined.

Implicitly, the ugly ordinances constituted the bodies of an "everyone else" as tasteful bodies, bodies of distinction in Bourdieu's terms, whose health and attractiveness comprised a form of cultural capital.[5] The ordinances functioned as a kind of negative definition of the limits of modernist "health." Ugly laws targeted what Simon Williams, adapting Leder, calls the "dys-appearing body"—that which appears vulgar, dysfunctional, too loud in its patterns—in order to make other bodies *dis*appear, pass by on the street in silence (2003, 96).[6] At the same time, the public was also more directly disciplined, constituted as *that* which at all costs must not view *this*. Consider this account, written by Charles Henderson in 1906, of what happens if a member of the public sees an epileptic seizure:

> In sociable intercourse the epileptic is an object of dread, and no one who has witnessed the person in a convulsion can quite escape from the haunting memory of the spectacle and entirely free his mind from terror or disgust. Hence there cannot be that free, unconstrained, and natural converse which gives pleasure to society. (172)

"Hence there cannot be": this prohibition seems to function both as fiat and as natural fact, suggesting that the epileptic's seizure prevents natural sociability not only for him or her at that moment but, inexorably, for any witness, for all time; epilepsy stops the city's business forever, or at any rate constitutes it as perpetual horror.

This kind of thinking, to which the ugly laws have obvious links, often goes along with a certain kind of understanding of the public sphere. Public space, in this model, is pedagogic space; what you allow in public is what children learn is allowed in public. If you allow unsightliness a foothold, the next generation will be even uglier.[7] To display something publicly is to spread it. This was an old notion. Deaf leader Laurent Clerc had had to crusade against it when he addressed legislators in 1818: "The sight of a beautiful person does not make another so likewise. . . . Why then should a deaf person make others so also?" (17). (The idea is related to but not identical with the notions of maternal influence, which focus specifically on effects on growing fetuses, which I discuss in chapter 4.)

New versions of this theory were still developing in the late nineteenth and early twentieth centuries. A number of emerging belief systems, as Pernick has shown, held that the sight of disabled people could literally make healthy people sick. Some reviews of the Chicago-based eugenics film *The Black Stork* (1916), Pernick writes, insisted that this kind of film display of real deformity "threatened the health of all viewers" on the grounds that "powerful emotions influenced bodily health in adults" (1996, 123). *Life* magazine cartoonist and well-known Christian Scientist Ellison Hoover promoted the idea that disease was mistaken thinking encouraged by health educators who produced people's illness by displaying illness to them. In one of his cartoons, a doctor terrifies a young pupil by dangling a skull at her, gesturing toward a blackboard on which is written, "Name the Ten Most Frightful Diseases and Describe Them. Explain Why the Very Air You Breathe is Full of Deadly Germs." The caption is "The Daily Lesson" (rpt. in Ehrenreich and English, 65). Hoover's targets were Progressive-era health reformers, but the residual implications went further: better to see health everywhere; better not to be faced with sickening reminders of disease, maiming, and deformity.

At the same time, as my analysis of COS "deformances" has suggested, the era of ugly law coincides with a different notion of pedago-public space, one in which the educators whom Hoover decried held increasing sway. Here, as often, many conflicting cultural forces roiled around the ugly laws. Certain kinds of exhibition of disease and deformity were welcomed, even required by city leaders, as admonitory demonstrations for the purpose of increasing public health awareness. Take, for instance, the bulletin published by the Chicago School of Civics and Philanthropy (a Hull-House affiliate) in October 1911 as a teaching aid for those interested in promoting city welfare: a catalogue of "exhibits, lectures, motion films, slides" and so forth. Screens in which the city literally (and figuratively) projected its image of its disabilities included ones labeled "Deaf," "Blind," "Cripples," "Defectives," and a "Eugenics" series that included "Drunken Mothers," "Early Marriage," "Feeble-Mindedness," "Epileptics," and "Crippled Children." One screen produced in Chicago read, "Dental Cripples. Two defective teeth will retard a child for six months, over one-half a school year." The accompanying images display gaping children's mouths stretched open by adult hands for the public view (*City Welfare*, 30–32).

A common form of display took place in medical arenas. The political geography of Chicago charted in *Hull-House Maps and Papers* (Addams et al.) includes the story of Jaroslav Huptuk, a sixteen-year-old "feeble-minded dwarf . . . so deformed as to be a monstrosity." Huptuk had been employed, like many Chicago children, in a cutlery works, and like many Chicago children he had contracted tuberculosis in the process. Hull-House's protective campaign against child labor—"the human product of our industry is an army of toiling children, undersized, rachitic, deformed, predisposed to consumption"—brought him forward in public as an example. So did his doctors: "Dr. Holmes, having examined this boy, pronounced him unfit for work of any kind. His mother appealed from this to a medical college, where, however, the examining physician not only refused the lad a medical certificate of physical fitness for work, but exhibited him to the students as a monstrosity worthy of careful observation" (61–62). Huptuk was thus subjected to that still familiar form of deformance that contemporary disability activists name as "public stripping."[8]

Viewing in this context could be civically instructive, but displays by health reformers threatened at any minute to devolve into prurient, not pedagogical, occasions. Consider the case of the "devil baby," an incident in 1912 recounted later by Jane Addams with dismayed amusement.[9] Rumors that the women of Hull-House had in their possession a "Devil Baby," born with "cloven hoofs, pointed ears and diminutive tail" resulted in a rush of sightseers from across Chicago who "poured in all day long and so far into the night that the regular activities of the settlement were almost swamped" (67). Hull-House was hard-pressed to dispel its reputation as a kind of freak-show site. "For six months," Addams writes, "as I went about the house I would hear a voice at the telephone repeating for the hundredth time that day, 'No, there is no such baby'" and "'We can't give reduced rates, because we are not exhibiting anything'" (68). To Addams's "query as to whether they supposed we would, for money, exhibit a poor little deformed baby," a group of factory workers being turned away at the Hull-House door replied, "Sure, why not?" and "it teaches a good lesson, too" (74). Perhaps they had previously viewed a dental cripple.[10]

City leaders in the era of the ordinances struggled to encourage proper and discourage unseemly sightings of diseases, maiming, and deformity. Ugly laws faced this problem head on, as the 1890 Columbus and Omaha versions reveal explicitly, with their added proviso that the unsightly subject may not expose himself or herself to public view either for "the purpose of soliciting alms" or for the purpose of "exciting sympathy, interest or curiosity." These ordinances situate themselves as antibegging laws at first but then exceed those grounds. Even without solicitation, the sheer excitement of response of any sort (or any sort short of repulsion) must be suppressed. Surely the law cannot be separated from, must crucially be part of, a genealogy of aversion, as in the panic about epilepsy in the passage I quoted earlier. But what is at stake in Omaha and Columbus seems to be the opposite of a problem with aversion.

What kinds of excitement on the part of the public were ugly ordinances meant to preclude? In order to clarify this question, let us consider first the large range of exceptions to the prohibition—say, in Chicago 1911. Many sorts of matter-of-fact (or even heated) viewing and response seem to have been perfectly acceptable, particularly during the Progressive era, as civic boosterism promoted cities' modern novelty and do-good innovation. A certain kind of disabled body was entirely safe to display, the kind that, Herndl argues, capitalism requires: one that is productive, one shaped *through* products and paid services, and therefore the opposite of the unruly and uncanny "diseased, maimed, deformed" body of the unsightly beggar. So, for instance, the masseurs' bodies, disciplined for work, in Peter Peel's early-twentieth-century blind massage class could advertise the cutting edge of Chicago modern commerce (Viskochil).

Sports-team public relations worked similarly. In 1915 no one blinked an eye when the *Chicago Daily News* published a photo of baseball pitcher Mordecai ("Three Finger") Brown's "deformed hand." The Chicago Cubs player had been injured as a child, and the resultant configuration of his hand allowed him to throw a famously tricky curveball. Brown attributed much of his success to his "old paw," and he fascinated the public with accounts of its special efficacy. Cubs publicity never shied away from exposing the fingers of "Three Finger." His 1913 book for boys, *How to Pitch Curves,* concluded with a Whitmanesque gesture of frank and winning textual display: "Mordecai Brown's hand is reaching out to you in the distance and he is wishing you—good luck." No gothic horror lurks in this hand extending itself from the page, just a howdy and a handshake—and a good-natured, in-your-face refusal to hide from public view.

A similar dynamic occurred in the case of William Ellsworth ("Dummy") Hoy, the deaf ball player who played for the Chicago White Sox in 1901. He is credited by many people with inventing the hand signals used in baseball today by adapting American Sign Language to use with his teammates, though this may be an apocryphal story.[11] "When Outfielder Hoy made a brilliant catch," wrote Henry Furness in an 1892 *Sporting Life* piece, "the crowds rose 'en masse' and wildly waved hats and hands. It was the only way in which they could testify their appreciation to the deaf-mute athlete." Under the auspices of sport, promoters pitched the combination of prowess and impairment as a marvel, a phenomenon, a novelty, and audiences responded enthusiastically.

In another form of mass display, the Christian revival circuit, disease and disability were brought forward to the public eye as reminders that sooner or later the Savior would heal all wounds. Billy Sunday, the famous "baseball evangelist" whose career began in Chicago, sometimes mockingly imitated "King Richard III limping" in his sermons, and he frequently preached about the banishment of all impairment from heaven. But under his revival tents, openly ill and disabled people were welcome and visible. In Elijah Brown's 1914 account of a typical meeting conducted by Sunday, the event begins when a "grizzled veteran who has but one arm" bears a flag down the aisle to be personally greeted by Sunday. When later Sunday calls all those "who will accept Jesus Christ as personal savior" to come forward, the same veteran answers the call (141). Brown may have been recording the proceedings of a specific meeting, but his insistence on its typicality suggests that the deserving "grizzled veteran" plays a stock role in the revival scene, in which all people who are "diseased, maimed, or deformed" are exhorted to place themselves within the public view of Christ. As types of affliction for Sunday and other evangelists, disabled people were called on to represent in starkly dramatic form the ills of all sinners in the sight of the Lord. As Sunday put it in one reassuring invitation to backsliders, "Better to limp all the way to heaven than not get there at all"; in the public space of the revival meeting, unsightliness was a universal human condition (E. Brown, 165).

More contested, less clearly permissible displays of impairment, pleasures that teetered on the verge of the forbidden, occurred in the arena of the medicine show. Brooks McNamara describes a stock "deafness demonstration" on the medicine-show circuit in which "the ears of a deaf volunteer were briskly rubbed with Wizard Oil and then 'popped' by the medicine man" (67). In the 1880s, show doctors were instructed on techniques for healing the lame on stage by the distributors of a liniment called Modern Miracles: "Send one of your Company about town during the day looking for cripples for you to cure at night." One hapless medicine man, after one such spectacular cure in Illinois, "neglected to leave town quickly enough, and was earnestly sought after by an uncured and humiliated cripple with a gun" (McNamara, 144). During the era of ugly law, states and cities increasingly enacted legislation to ban the "quackery" of the medicine show and the disability displays that secured its ungoverned claims of healing (McNamara).

Ugly laws sought to control what Michael Sappol calls "anatomy's crowd," a public rabble that came to something called a show, no matter what its ostensible purpose, "merely to gawk at or wallow in the body's otherness." The excitement of this crowd was construed as arousal catered to by panderers, "debased sensations" (2004, 280, 299).[12] Unsightly bodies on the streets, never safely enough cordoned off in the realm of disgust, may be seen as a potential part of the delightful swirl of city mass culture for workers and immigrants, one more example of urban "visual playground," as Serlin and Lerner put it, "in which physicality became itself a tangible object to be displayed, bartered, and possessed" (106).

DISGUSTING

And yet there is that word "disgusting," indelibly part of the fabric of the law, suggesting that aversion is as much at stake as attraction. The abusive word startles, seems in a different register from the fastidious "improper" that precedes it or the relatively clinical discourse of disease and maiming. With "disgusting," ugly law takes on a feeling.

Why is the word *disgusting* in the ordinance? What ideological work did it do? Recent academic studies in the growing body of work following in the wake of William Ian Miller's *Anatomy of Disgust* (1997) provide a number of insights into the word's powerful and sometimes conflicting functions. First of all, *disgusting* suggests that the law emerges reflexively, from a deeply primal, psycho-visceral (and therefore an apparently universal) point of origin.[13] It suggests that the law knows only what Winfried Menninghaus calls a "vomitive judgment: *away* with it, from the belly" (92). "Disgust implies not just an ability to say no," Menninghaus argues, "but even more a compulsion to say no, an inability not to say no" (2). The law seems to have its own kind of raw shuddering body: law as gag reflex, a law with guts. *Disgusting* adds biological force to the ordinance, framing it as the legal concomitant of nausea.

The word's signal—good riddance—links the unsightly beggar implicitly to other core triggers of disgust: excrement, corpses, incontinence, everything that evokes organic matter falling (in Robert Rawdon Wilson's terms) "sludgewards" (xxiv) and "slimewards" (64). *Disgusting* suggests an aversion as lawful as eating—or not eating; Darwin, and many thinkers after him since 1872, located the origins of disgust in rejection of bad food.[14] So disgust is natural; it is also proto-medical, a proper health precaution in a world of permeable bodies, of possible infection and contagion. The cesspools and dumps of nuisance law are disgusting.[15] *Disgusting* mobilizes the structure that Martha Nussbaum encapsulates: "This act (or, more often and usually inseparably, this person) is a contaminant; it (or he or she) pollutes our community. We would be better off if this contamination were kept far away from us" (123). The word reinforces the impression that the law is hygiene law, impelled by what Pinker has called "intuitive microbiology."[16] Interestingly, one example used by disgust researchers Rozin, Haidt, and McCauley to illustrate the principle of contagion involves a kind of tramp scare: "although we normally handle money without thinking of who touched it before us, this strategy might not protect us in the unusual case of a dollar handed over by a vagrant" (641).

As the vagrant example suggests, disgust-thinking, which exceeds rational fear of physical contagion, is also magical thinking. With *disgusting* we enter into the realm of unreason.[17] In its disgust, its sheer "come not near," ugly law reveals itself as an apotropaic rite, a kind of spell or charm.[18] (Even the contemporary political memory of ugly law in academic and activist disability historiography has apotropaic elements: in its elimination of the history of begging from the scene of unsightliness, it too has said "come not near" to the unsightly beggar.)

Finally, as William Miller has shown, disgust is normative, "a moral response to experience, a psycho-intellectual affect," and as such it "involves distance and superiority" (294). As Miller puts it, "the avowal of disgust expects concurrence" (194). In this way, as Robert Rawdon Wilson has argued, Miller's work on disgust reveals it to be a proto-legal condition (52). Disgust's presence "lets us know we are truly in the grip of the norm whose violation we are witnessing or imagining" (W. Miller, 194). Whether that "grip of the norm" comes from within (like a stomach cramp) or without (like a parent's hand or a policeman's), and whether it is to be endorsed or bemoaned, is a matter of some study and debate in work that follows Miller's. Some recent academic work in the field roughly divides itself into camps that can be described awkwardly and inadequately as anti-disgust (such as Martha Nussbaum's argument for the elimination of disgust-principles in the operation of American law) and pro-disgust (in work such as Dan Kahan's or Sianne Ngai's, more dubious about the value or the possibility of sloughing off disgust). But no one has challenged Miller's analysis of the regulative function of naming the disgusting.

With legalized disgust, then, comes a heavy norm, as in Lord Devlin's famous idea, in 1965, that the social disgust of the ordinary "man on the Clapham omnibus" should be sufficient basis in and of itself for banning homosexual acts. We can see this norming clearly at work in the American legal record for cases at the state and federal level in the general era of ugly law (between 1880 and 1918). Judges and the laws that guide them apply *disgusting* to a number of objects (sodomy, frequently; obscenity, just as often, and also—in New Jersey—indecent letters to women; offenses of cruelty, particularly wife and child abuse and rape; alcoholism and opium addiction; sewage and other sanitary nuisances), and by far the most frequent use of the word is in the context of phrases like "I will spare you" or "we shall not recite" the "disgusting details." As the bearer (or the very embodiment) of disgusting detail, the unsightly beggar was made literally as well as figuratively unspeakable. As a Pennsylvania court put it in 1884, addressing the "loathsome habits" that made it "particularly burdensome and disgusting to take care of" a "lunatic": "A description of them could serve no useful purpose, but it is difficult to imagine a service more revolting and abhorrent" (*Appeal of Court*). In the discourse of "disgusting details," of evidence simultaneously withheld and displayed, disgust is that which *goes without saying* and cannot therefore be contradicted.[19]

Disgust is often treated as if it were a transhistorical phenomenon. But the seemingly natural state of the sensation has a history and a specific cultural location. Disgust, David Barnes notes, is both "experienced as automatic, deeply physical, and unmediated by conscious thought" and "shows distinct variation historically, cross-culturally, and even within an individual's lifetime" (112). Recent disgust theorists have acknowledged the difficulties of tracing disgust's histories. "The ambition to write a history of 'actual' disgust . . . meets with almost insurmountable difficulties," writes Menninghaus (3). Wilson makes a similar point: "the history of disgust (if it were even possible to write) would reveal an overlapping, if not wholly coterminous, history of consciousness" (xiv). Other, narrower and more mediated approaches are required: discourses of disgust can be studied. "It is only through the medium of . . . theories of disgust that some fragments of the largely mute history of this strong sensation become accessible," writes Menninghaus (3). Ugly law had no theory; but it too is a fragment in the history of disgust.

Disgust had free rein in the making of law and policy in the era of the unsightly begging ordinances. In the 1893 case *Watson v. City of Cambridge*, the exclusion of a "weak-minded" boy from school was justified not only on grounds of his disruptiveness but also by the finding that he was "unable to take ordinary, decent physical care of himself"—in short, that he disgusted his teachers and other children. At the tail end of the period of our focus (1919), thirteen-year-old Merritt Beattie, "a crippled and defective child since his birth," was also denied access to common schooling on the basis of disgust. "He is slow and hesitating in speech," reads the majority opinion in the court judgment banning Beattie from the public schools,

> and has a peculiarly high, rasping, and disturbing tone of voice, accompanied with uncontrollable facial contortions, making it difficult for him to make himself understood. He also has an uncontrollable flow of saliva,

> which drools from his mouth onto his clothing and books, causing him to present an unclean appearance. He has a nervous and excitable nature. It is claimed, on the part of the school board, that his physical condition and ailment produces a depressing and nauseating effect upon the teachers and school children. (*State Ex Rel. Beattie*)

Here the court chose to pile up evidently disgusting detail, perhaps in part to assuage the qualms involved in denying a bright child access to education with his peers. As Merritt Beattie and Thomas Watson's son could testify, and as ugly law set down in legal code, the histories of American disability and of American disgust are intimately conjoined. One of the major ways in which the disability rights movement stood ugly law on its head was by countering the discourse of disgust directed at disabled people.[20]

ANIMAL

Other terms besides the ones explicitly included in the law's language helped frame the unsightly beggar. One is strongly linked to disgust. A line of thinking in the analysis of human emotion by some of its major theorists concludes that people use disgust to ward off problems of (or with) animality. In this thesis, disgust originates, Martha Nussbaum writes, in "the belief that if we take in the animalness of animal secretions we will ourselves be reduced to the status of animals" and particularly that "if we absorb and are mingled with the decaying, we will ourselves be mortal and decaying" (89).[21] As William Miller puts it, "ultimately the basis for all disgust is us" (xiv). Inevitably, because the unsightly beggar carries animality, for "us" and toward "us," exposing it to us and us to it, the ugly law speaks the language of disgust ("no person who is . . . disgusting") right out loud.

In the late-nineteenth-century United States what the theorist calls "animality" was trouble for the alderman. After reading through the city council records for many cities in the 1880s and 1890s, I can say with some assurance that probably the single most common item on their agendas was the management of dogs. Newspapers that ignored the passage of ugly laws in their reports of council meetings paid lavish attention to measures passed at the same meetings concerning dog licensing, dog leashing, dog impounding, rabies, and so forth. There is some evidence to suggest that in cities fearful of going to the dogs, the threat of unsightly beggars who might spread disease or bite the hand that fed them got phrased at times as a problem of animal control.[22]

Certainly in the related realm of freak shows, as Rosemarie Garland Thomson has pointed out, the line between human and animal was both drawn and threatened. Cheap freak shows were as likely to display "the human-faced donkey, the three-legged rooster, and the deformed hen" as "the leopard girl" and the "poodle man," often staging the hen and the girl side by side, in open demonstration that the fascinations of anomaly crossed species lines (see "No Violation"). Garland Thomson writes in her analysis of the enfreakment of Julia Pastrana that "the visual rhetorics that governed the display of Pastrana's body questioned the traditional ontological border that divided the human and the animal into opposing and exclusive categories," citing as three key examples of these rhetorics "the emerging scientific discourse of evolution," sensationalized fantasies of bestiality, and political debates over "who was human enough to be granted . . . rights promised by democracy" (2003, 132–134).[23] "Missing Link" freaks openly provoked the question of "human and/or animal" in their audiences from the sideshow stage; unsightly beggars, probably usually less deliberately, raised (and could sometimes play on) alarm at the sight of "people living like animals" on the street.

Let us take "living like animals" as a neutral or positive term for a moment. We might say that what unsightly beggars exposed to public view was *animality*, in the sense that Ruth O'Brien summarizes:

> the able-bodied workforce must recognize its own mental and physical vulnerability. A more universal notion of the organic mind and body or "animality" should be substituted for the concept of disability in the ADA. . . . Animality underscores that homo sapiens—the human being—is made up of flesh and blood and that needs can be derived from this. . . . animality . . . associates needs not with imperfection, but with the human condition. (2005, 5–6)[24]

Or, as Martha Nussbaum puts it in her account of social scapegoating, "We have chosen these people as surrogate animals" (123). Displaying human animality, "diseased, maimed, deformed" people made that condition clear. Confronting them, others read the "human condition" as the unsightly beggar's *one* condition, as a limiting bottom line.[25]

We must be cautious, though, as O'Brien herself would recognize, about the political reverberations of the concept of *animality* if it is read, mistakenly, as a substitute term for *impairment* or *disability* instead of for *humanity.* The archives of the ugly laws reveal the price paid when already marginalized disabled people are publicly animalized.[26] In Los Angeles, for instance, a 1907 newspaper story on the growing influx of hobos quoted reports by desert brakemen "that the cripples . . . sneak into the box cars and snarl and snap like ugly dogs" ("Rags and Tags"). This kind of language helped ensure harsh welcome for disabled beggars in western cities. In a newspaper article on begging in New York City published in 1881, the abusive association of animals with human panhandlers reached what may be its shrillest pitch; the essay, titled "Canine Mendicancy," developed an elaborate satire in which stray dogs were represented as if they were unsightly people, or perhaps it is that human beggars were portrayed as feral animals.

Labels like this branded individuals as much as nameless "packs." The most striking example I have encountered comes from Atlanta, whose city council passed a one-of-a-kind ugly law sometime in the 1880s. I mean literally one-of-a-kind: the law was personalized, directed at a single man. His name was William Jasper Franklin. Paralyzed on his left side and unable to walk, he sat or lay in a wagon drawn by a goat. A reporter for the *Atlanta Constitution* described William Franklin this way in 1886: "age 36; is one of Atlanta's quaint characters. . . . his familiar petition is, 'Mister, I can't walk—give me a nickel.' . . . Sometimes he sells peanuts and matches and takes in about $1.50 a week. He claims to support his mother and father, the latter being blind." The feature in the *Constitution* recounts the emergence of Atlanta's individualized unsightly beggar ordinance as well as the typical ensuing pattern of nonenforcement: "He was such a prominent figure that city council passed an ordinance to regulate him. Some people thought his goat and himself were nuisances and they petitioned council to debar the pair from coming to the heart of the city. The ordinance was enforced for awhile, but was gradually forgotten, and the pair now wander at will."[27]

Franklin's goat played the role of what we now call a "service animal," like a guide dog. (The goat, of course, was not "trained" by "professionals" to assist Franklin; that phenomenon occurred much later, in the twentieth century, primarily in the United States and other relatively wealthy nations. Animals had not yet become service animals.)[28] The fact that the goat was barred as a nuisance serves to remind us that laws regulating whether, when, and how animals may appear in public have often—probably far more frequently than ugly law—resulted in exclusion and isolation of disabled people.[29]

William Franklin in 1886 Atlanta was not only a person with an animal or, if we risk an ahistorical lens, "a person with a service animal."[30] Franklin was also seen as an animal himself. His goat was named ("Peter"), but he himself was known in Atlanta not as "William" but as "The Goat Man." One assumes it was a practical identifier—"Oh, yeah, the guy with the goat"—but that does not entirely explain the collapse of goat into man that occurs in the name, with its hint of horns and hooves. It is easier, perhaps, to enact an ordinance barring a Goat Man from appearing in public than to enact one barring Bill Franklin. Though the "quaint . . . pair" (as if lined up two-by-two for Noah's Ark) ended up "wander[ing] at will" with the indulgence of the police, William Franklin had still been consigned to animality by a humiliating ordinance in an extreme case of ugly law.[31]

The costs of being animalized by those in power are made starkly clear in African American history. William Franklin's race goes unmentioned in Atlanta's archives, and that probably means he was seen as white, though it is possible that paralysis and "goatness" overrode racial subordination as factors worth remarking in his case. It is not surprising that the most famous goat man in American culture is both disabled and black. Many readers will be familiar with the goat-cart arrangement through the Gershwins' *Porgy and Bess.* George Gershwin based his unsightly beggar's opera on the novel *Porgy* by his collaborator, elite white (and disabled) Charleston writer Dubose Heyward, who in turn drew his inspiration for the title character from Charleston's real-life turn-of-the-century version of a goat man, the black beggar Samuel Smalls or "Goat-Cart Sam."

Punished for animality and punished by relegation to animality, made into "less of man" (or a woman), disabled beggars sometimes took on with a vengeance the categories given to them to occupy. One famous beggar, Frank Hammel, also known as "The Human Dog," was such an outlaw "Dog" that COS monitor James Forbes sent out letters across the nation warning cities about him. Issuing an alert to be on the watch for a man who "crawls along curb on all fours, with a few pencils in his hand, saying his back is broken," Forbes cautioned, "To arouse sympathy he makes false statements concerning the origin of his deformity and injury." Hammel, who was born with "muscular rheumatism," was also in fact a double amputee, but nonetheless a very undeserving beggar in Forbes's book. "Get after him," Forbes concluded his letter to other COS officials.[32] Here again we return to the inescapable suspicion of "false statements" that attends the unsightly. But Forbes's revulsion at the "Human Dog" is more than a moral disdain toward a liar. Something in these performances, conscious or not, seems almost to enact premodern rites, as if the beggar's show, The Goat and the Dog, cued into a strata of disturbingly archaic images.[33] But what seems to bother Forbes the most is the scandal of Hammel's self-display—which brings me to an additional important vector in the niche of ugly law.

FREAK

The ugly laws cry out to be placed in relation to another realm of law in which the cultural antithesis between display and concealment during this period played out: ordinances designed to control or abolish arenas of cheap entertainment where human oddities or infirmities were exhibited, such as freak shows and popular anatomical museums.[34] As Rosemarie Garland Thomson has noted, the rise of ugly law coincides with the beginning of the slow decline and the uneven suppression of the freak show. State and city laws banned "display of deformed persons for profit" or "exhibition for pay or compensation for any crippled or physically distorted, malformed or disfigured person"; new laws such as Michigan's Act 103 (1903) made it unlawful both to "expose or keep on exhibition any deformed human being or human monstrosity, except as used for scientific purposes before members of the medical profession," and to "exhibit in museums or elsewhere diseased or deformed human bodies, or parts thereof, or representations thereof, which would be indecent in the case of a living person."[35] An 1887 editorial decrying the "unsightly exhibition" of the skeleton of McKinley's assassin Goiteau had no doubt about what needed to be done: it "should be prohibited by the law at least, if not the sense of decency. . . . This nation is not a dime museum" ("Unsightly Exhibition"). Like freak-show and dime-museum suppression, ugly law was part of what Loo and Strange call "the revenge of the rubes" (649).

In the texts of some ugly or uglylike laws, the languages of freak and beggar, street and stage, overtly intertwine. We might read the trace of sideshow banner and ballyhoo, for instance, in the possibly overdetermined capital "E" that stands out in the handwritten record of Alderman Peevey's resolution to the mayor of Chicago in 1881: "at once take steps to remove from the streets . . . all those who by making Exhibition of themselves and their infirmities seek to obtain money from people."[36] (See frontispiece.) Here only the zone of operation, "on and along the streets," distinguishes begging Exhibitors from their circus counterparts. Popular columnist and answer man Cecil Adams was technically mistaken when he answered a reader's inquiry about the Chicago ugly law ("Is this for real, and what's it all about?") by treating the ordinance *perfectly clearly* as anti-freak-show legislation:

> The alleged purpose of the statute was not, as you might think, to rid the public ways of unsavory characters, but to protect the pitiful creatures from being exploited for profit—in other words, not to punish the deformed

> but to protect them. Perfectly clear? An earlier ordinance had given the City Council the power to "regulate, license, suppress, and prohibit . . . exhibitions of natural or artificial curiosities," but apparently that legislation was too much to the point to be useful.

But Adams's answer had truth to it as well. The ugly law sprang in part from protective impulses on the part of offended legislators that also spurred laws against freak "Exhibition." Though lawmakers in general made distinctions between the self-display of beggars and the exploitation of freaks by side-show owners, between "exposed" and "exhibited" persons, these lines were not always easily drawn. (Nor, as I have shown, was the line easily drawn between Adams's two terms, the "unsavory character" and the "pitiful creature.") Byrom suggests that the cross-class popularity of the freak-show form may have inspired and motivated some disabled beggars who fully understood "the public fascination with viewing impairments" (although it should be noted that beggars long before freak shows came up with the idea of exhibiting their body parts). "While the revelation of a disfigured limb may have offended the sensibilities of some," he writes, "it no doubt offered voyeuristic pleasure to others. Perhaps, then, it is most accurate to interpret the unveiling of a disfigured limb by the street-corner mendicant as part of the professional beggar's obligation to those offering alms" (2004, 16–17).

Pennsylvania's 1895 version of ugly law, Act 208, collapsed the beggar and the freak into one sentence: "Be it enacted that whoever shall exhibit any physical deformity to which he or she shall be subject . . . for hire or for the purpose of soliciting alms . . ."[37] In New York, COS leader Charles Kellogg, following suit, drafted a law prohibiting similar exhibitions "in any public hall, museum, theatre or any public building, tent, booth or public space for a pecuniary consideration or reward" or "upon any public street or place to solicit or receive alms" ("Crude Suggested Draft by CDK"). (Fines harshened when distinctions between freaks and beggars disappeared. Pennsylvania's law levied a fine "not exceeding fifty dollars" on offenders, at a time when the typical ugly-law fine was a dollar; Kellogg, under no official civic constraints, imagined a fine "not exceeding one thousand dollars," the equivalent of almost twenty-five thousand dollars today, for the law he hoped to get enacted in New York City.) When New York City police official Addison Jerome wrote to the organizing secretary of the New York Charity Organization Society in October 1895 recommending that New York follow Pennsylvania's lead and reinforce police power to shut down begging by shutting in deformity, he referred to his antibegging proposal as an "anti-freak law" (Ringenbach, 99). It is hard to say who might have been hurt more by the conflation at work here of the beggar and the freak, the beggar whose requests for help were converted into carnival spiel or the freak-show performer whose stage work was translated into whines for alms. Both were reduced to examples of disgusting bodily display.[38] Of course, helping, not hurting, was the stated aim; but poor people have often been crushed in the name of reform.

The freak and the unsightly beggar are by no means identical, despite legislative efforts like these that attempted to render them equivalent. Unsightly beggars were less disciplined than freak performers, and arguably more abject. Beggars played on pity for their plights, but "'pity' as a mode of presentation was absent" in the freak show, argues Bogdan: "Pity did not fit in with the world of amusement" (277). Beggars were usually closer to being their own bosses in the petty street economy, but they were also closer to bare life (one can die of exposure but not of exhibition). The borders between the two were indeed sometimes porous. Nickell describes sighting a subject of his research on sideshows, "El Hoppo the Living Frog Boy," in his wheelchair selling newspapers on the street, and being told by a "showman" that El Hoppo was "just some poor unfortunate . . . picked off the street and created on the spot" for a one-time exhibition (147). But the unsightly beggar plays a very different social and cultural role than that of the freak.

Freaks might in rare cases achieve star status. At the same time, the freak was governed by placement in/as spectacle. The conventions of the freak show, however tiny and seedy a show, dictate, as Susan Stewart notes, that spatially "the viewer of the spectacle is absolutely aware of the distance between self" and viewed and that "the spectacle exists in silence. . . . there is no dialogue—only the frame of the pitchman or the barker" (108–109). Freaks act as "effigies," in Roach's terms: "performed effigies—those fabricated from human bodies and the associations they evoke—provide communities with a method of perpetuating themselves through specially nominated mediums or surrogates: among them, actors, dancers, priests, street maskers, statesmen, celebrities, freaks" (1996, 36). Surrogates for no one, beggars could not be effigies. By no stretch of the imagination did they function as specially nominated mediums for the broader community. If they performed (and the next chapter will show how thoroughly the unsightly beggar was made up out of, made up by, performance), they nonetheless did not perform visibly, formally, theatrically, enough.[39] They were not contained by what Bill Brown terms "the amusement/knowledge system that translates a phenomenon into a freak" (244).

In the case of both antifreak law and ugly law, cities solidified their legal municipal cultures, what we might call their cultures of civicness, by regulating and suppressing displays of anomalous bodies too far outside civil norms and forms. As the references to indecency in the act that I quoted earlier suggest, proponents justified these efforts as guarantees of an appropriate urban culture. Suppression of unsightly beggars was one way to secure the decency of the modern urban polis.

DISSIPATIONS

In 1919, one disabled vagrant, a man who had traveled the country over many years and had a firsthand sense of exactly where and when city leaders cracked down on unsightly begging, made this observation: "During the past 17 years I have noticed that where there was booze, a red light district, gambling—a 'wide-open' town, usually the cripples and blind were not interfered with, but helped. When we get a spell of reform, we get a hard sanctimoniousness" (Fuller 1919, 62). As is often the case, Arthur Franklin Fuller (whose writing I discuss in chapter 11) turns out to be a reliable witness. The history of the unsightly beggar ordinances is indeed closely connected to the history of municipal regulation and prohibition of alcohol, not just because both emerge when "spells of reform" reflect civic willingness to police a broadening range of behavior but because a great deal of the time "so as to be an unsightly or disgusting object" turns out to mean "so as to be (or seem) inebriated."[40] A reporter on the city court beat in Louisville put it succinctly in 1884: "Such a helpless cripple would have been pitiful if he had not been so drunk" ("Victim of Drink").

"Unsightly," then, often is something like disabled plus disorderly or disabled under the influence, and "disgust" is shaped at times by the ideals of the Temperance and Prohibition movements.[41] Arthur Fuller records a debate in the Texas State legislature around 1915. "There was recently a bill up," Fuller writes, "to compel cripples and blind, etc. to keep out of the state. It was claimed they are a lot of boozefighters, gamblers, and impudent toughs; that the women are harlots and the men bawd-masters" (*Fifty Thousand Miles*, 193–194). No record exists of a Texas bill specifically addressing the problem of blind and crippled interlopers. Most likely, as the references to harlots and bawd-masters suggest, the bill in question was an act "to regulate intrastate commerce by prohibiting the transportation of women and girls for immoral and other purposes in the state of Texas, and declaring an emergency" (1915 HB 52).[42] If I am correct, "other purposes" may have referred to organized begging by disabled women. The links here between trafficking in beggars and trafficking in harlots are fascinating, and I will have more to say about these complex imbrications of unsightliness and indecency in chapter 6. Worth noting now is Fuller's emphasis on specifically masculine forms of bad behavior: gamblers, bawd-masters, impudent toughs. Imperiled women slip away, and in their place "boozefighters" step out. These rowdy cripples and blind men are drunk and disorderly, or as W.E.B. Du Bois put it in his study of Negro paupers in Philadelphia, "fast, tough, criminal and besotted" (280).

In "The Right to Live in the World" (1966), tenBroek categorically denies the possibility that a boozefighter and a disabled person could be one and the same. Commenting on an Arizona law excluding persons "of lewd or immoral character, guilty of boisterous conduct or physical violence," or "under the influence of alcohol or narcotics," tenBroek concludes decisively, "And not a blind man or a cripple is among them" (850). But in Fuller's account of the debate in Texas, "cripples and blind, etc." is the master category under which all these disreputable types are subsumed, and interestingly, Fuller endorses this claim: "The accusations," he writes, "are too generally true." Like many other disabled people attempting to make a living on the street at this time, Fuller did his best to dissociate himself from lumpen sorts as a better class of beggar or peddler. Certifying one's sobriety increased the likelihood of alms or sales of pencils. But Fuller often defended other beggars from charges that he thought were unjust, whereas here he concedes the point—despite the implausibility of this wild vision of noncompliant hordes of bawdy disabled women and pimp crips infiltrating the embattled state of Texas.

Evidence from the present day suggests that disabled people are at disproportionately high risk for substance abuse, for a variety of reasons: poverty, isolation, pain management, lack of access to treatment.[43] Evidence from the past suggests something of the kind of substance we are talking about in the context of the unsightly beggar. In the bars catering to disabled beggars that I discuss in the next chapter, the menu consisted of drinks described with typical verve in Asbury's *Gangs of New York*: "for those whose jaded palates failed to respond to the raw liquor there was a villainous mixture of water and liquid camphor. . . . There was also a hot punch compounded of whiskey, hot rum, camphor, benzine, and cocaine sweepings, which generally sold for six cents and was guaranteed to contain a case of delerium tremens in every drop" (298–299).[44] I am not arguing that all disabled people who begged were addicted to punch laced with cocaine sweepings, but I *am* noting that a history of disability on the street that ignores the traces of substance abuse is an impoverished one and, more importantly, that in American discourses of the beggar unsightly often goes out on a binge.[45] As one New York City COS worker put it in a 1902 file on one "beggar-cripple," "liquor undoubtedly furnishes in this and most similar cases the energy to cross the bridge between subjective and objective law breaking" ("James Grady, Jr., Mendicancy #1295," 2–3). For this writer, liquor created the unsightly beggar: "There are thousands of beggar-cripples in our land to-day who have become such and remain what they are by just such processes."

Policing "beggar-cripples," street cleanup and barroom shutdown campaigns often patrolled side by side. Accounts of disability discrimination in American history almost always cite the ugly ordinances, but histories of what the Burgdorfs called "unequal treatment" rarely, if ever, include liquor control laws. In the extensive compendium of "state-sponsored discrimination against persons with disabilities," including statutes from some municipal codes, that was prepared by scholars as an amicus brief for the Supreme Court's *Garrett* case, no mention is made of laws prohibiting the sale of alcoholic beverages to disabled people. Los Angeles enacted one in the Progressive era. A 1916 *Los Angeles Times* antimendicancy feature piece with special emphasis on the "sad, maimed and misshapen" represents one man's response:

> A familiar figure at Eighth and Spring streets is an old blind man who sits on a camp stool with a huge Bible written in raised script for the sightless, and from this he reads passages in a loud voice, tracing the letters with his fingers, then, after a scriptural suggestion, he shakes a tin can suggestively. . . .
>
> He is an ardent "dry," but was converted in a way which will never be placed in the annals of the Anti-Saloon League. He was accustomed to a daily care-chaser in one of the bars across the street from his stand, but one day a cripple killed one of his bartenders in the saloon, and a regulation was immediately made to serve no liquor to cripples or blind men.
>
> So he decided: "I'm going to vote dry; I'll put all the booze joints out of commission if I can't get a drink!" ("Genius of Mendicants")

It is as if, after a red-haired man killed someone in a bar brawl, a city council had banned the sale of liquor to red-haired people. The ugly laws made the disability history books, but this kind of law, with its potent brew of fear, hostility, and protectionism guaranteed to contain a case of discrimination in every drop, has never (probably simply out of ignorance) been an iconic story for the public disability rights movement.[46] Boozefighters still embarrass.

The history of these ordinances is intertwined with ugly law. Judges gave harsher sentences to beggars who were drunk and disorderly as well as unsightly. An article in the *Los Angeles Times* in July 1913 on doings in San Pedro, California, reported that "the police round-up last night was a literal compliance of the injunction of Luke xiv:21 to 'Bring hither the poor and maimed and the halt and the blind,'" recounting how "Ed Wagner, blind and deaf; Jack Logan, with one leg, and Frank Yanders, with one arm, all pleaded guilty to being drunk. All gave their occupation as lead-pencil peddlers." The subtitle to the piece was "Halt and Blind," the broader title "Police Judge Sentences without Compunction Drunken Beggars Even Though They Are Halt and Blind." A curious moment, of uncertain tone, notes that "the blind man was given a straight jail sentence," rather than being offered the option of paying a fine like his friends, "on the theory of the court that the rest would do him good." Was he being "well cared for" in the old-fashioned terms of the early ugly laws, or is this meant sarcastically? Either way, the cultural meanings of drunkenness resulted in lawmaking and sentencing "without compunction" ("Police Judge Sentences").

Arrest either under ugly law or under "drunk and disorderly" statutes could lead to long-term incarceration for disabled people. In Indianapolis, around 1915, a man who had an epileptic seizure as he stepped off a streetcar was arrested by a policeman who thought he was drunk. He remained in jail for several days, until a local doctor read about him in the paper and came forward to certify his epilepsy. As a condition of the man's release, he was institutionalized for life in Indiana's Village for Epileptics (Indiana State Board of Charities).

This man's story is easy to recognize as an extreme case of disability subjection. Boozefighters are harder to claim as disability culture heroes, even of the romantic outlaw sort. But ideas of the addict and the brawler helped shape the idea of the unsightly beggar and are an important part of the history of that idea. The image of the drunk cripple justified the ugly ordinances; so did the image of the sham cripple, to which I now turn. Like "they're all spending it on liquor," "they're all faking" worked powerfully as a formulation that undergirded the hard line of ugly law.

5

DISSIMULATIONS

> The actual practice of fraud, even when you discover it, must give you interesting question, unless you are cock-sure of your sociology.
>
> —WILLIAM DEAN HOWELLS, "Tribulations of a Cheerful Giver" (1895), 185

> "Blind Since 52. Boot and Gaitermaker."
> A Blind Man's Sign.
> "Paralyzed Since the 20th of December."
> What Was On the Other Side.
>
> —THOMAS KNOX, in Helen Campbell, *Darkness and Daylight* (1897)

WHAT WAS ON THE OTHER SIDE

The above illustration by Thomas Knox from Helen Campbell's *Darkness and Daylight; Lights and Shadows of New York Life* is meant to clinch the case. Like other chroniclers of contrast, "sunlight and shadow," "daylight and gaslight" in the large American cities of the 1890s, these two muck-and-salvation-mongers paint a picture of urban space filled with deceitfully disabled beggars. Though there is a possibility that a panhandler could be both paralyzed and blind, Knox thinks otherwise. He recounts how scamming beggars' tin signs were "sometimes printed on both sides, thus giving the beggar two tales to help him along. He displays the side that he thinks will prove to be most effective in the locality he happens to be in." In Knox's plot, the carrier of this sign is neither blind nor paralyzed. He is a "sham cripple," and his presence is a staple in the narratives of reformers in the era of the ugly law.

As I suggested in my brief discussion of fraud in chapter 2, the story of the man with the fraudulent sign reflects cultural anxieties related to the unsightly beggar ordinances. Twentieth-century political memory of the ugly laws reads "disabled people" as their target. But there is plenty of evidence to suggest that the lawmakers' sights were trained at least as much on a different category (the question of how different is my subject here): "people pretending to be disabled." As the strictures on "exhibition" in the language of many unsightly ordinances suggest, the subject of the law is not only the person who *is* "diseased, maimed, or deformed" but also the person who *seems* so, the person who "gets ugly" by disguise. The target of the law may be less a person than an act. What if we entertain the possibility that what the law forbade was something in which anyone could engage: unsightly performativity? The faker raises larger questions for theorizing disability that are the subject of this chapter.

One must work at being a nonproducer. Of the notorious faker "Chi Slim," reporter Theodore Waters wrote in 1905,

> Throwing himself into the semblance of a human bow-knot, he would crawl along the street, shaking from head to foot. No man with genuine palsy could appear worse, and it used to take him three hours, with frequent stops, to make the journey. He could keep it up no longer than that because the work was too hard. (75)

Unsightly begging *was* work, and it also *did* work.[1] It sealed the pact of pity; revealed the nonexistence of viable labor options for disabled people and exposed the lack of safety nets; confirmed the social links between impairment, incompetence, and abjection; reinforced the culture's belief in sorting undeserving from deserving—a contradictory, conflicted set of tasks. Fakers undermined and muddied, but also reinforced, the job description for "diseased, maimed, and deformed" mendicancy. The presence of imposters does not thwart our understanding of the meaning of unsightly begging. Social reformers provide some illuminating hints about disabled beggars' worlds, but we learn as much about the social production and regulation of disability, about how discourse marked unsightly bodies, when reformers confront the anxiety caused by the shameless "sham cripple."

Work in disability studies touching on the begging question has tended to resolve the relation of the genuinely to the spuriously disabled by emphasizing, rightly, that to much of the general public in the late nineteenth and early twentieth centuries the distinction was of little consequence.

Martha Stoddard Holmes's nuanced analysis of the issue in the British context concludes that the message of much Victorian reformist discourse "is that there is no real difference between imposters and those entitled to beg; in general, they are part of the same immoral culture of mendacity" (130). Because Holmes's treatment of the representation of the imposter beggar focuses always on the impact of the figure on disabled people, her argument often implicitly assumes that beggars scorned as imposters are simply truly disabled. In her exploration of the stock character of the "villainous begging imposter," for instance, Holmes argues that the type evokes "the ambivalence of suspicion, or the conviction that pathos or 'emotional excess' is fakery, a coin that disabled people use to trick the nondisabled into inappropriate giving" (8). Elsewhere, Holmes writes that in "the broad strokes of Victorian texts," the "begging imposter . . . *was a disabled person* whose economic resilience was the product of corruption and whose bodily condition did not signify complete and utter incapacity" (100, italics mine). In the service of a strong critique of "imposter beggar" rhetoric, the nondisabled imposter disappears from representation.

Similarly, Martin Norden argues, in his discussion of the fad of "fake cripple" plots in silent films (stories in which a lame man in the act of begging is startled by an inept policeman and suddenly loses his limp and runs away and the like), that to some people "beggars with feigned disabilities weren't that different from those with real ones" and that fraudulent disability stories inevitably had hard effects on disabled people (14–15). In a series of 1896 *New York Times* articles that Norden cites, New Yorkers reacted with approval to the city of Boston's imposition of harsh prison sentences on "sham cripples."[2] Each of the articles begins by indicting such imposter beggars on the grounds that they harm the cause of real "hopeless cripples." Quickly, however, as Norden points out, the distinction between simulating deformity and actually embodying it disappears. The exposés in the *New York Times* and others like them move seamlessly and dizzyingly between anecdotes about bad "sham cripples" and anecdotes about bad "true cripples" who make large amounts of money by exploiting pity for their impairment, own real estate, and have fortunes hidden under their beds.[3] In a later *New York Times* article tellingly titled "Pitiful Mendicant Gives Way to the Cunning Beggar," photographs of notorious fakers are juxtaposed with ambiguous figures who may be the genuine article, captioned, "A Typical Crippled Beggar," "Pitty [*sic*] the Poor Blind Man." It is unclear, in this context, whether any pitiable mendicant has not always already given way to cunning beggardom.

Norden quotes the New York City police chief who led the 1896 crackdown. "The law is clear about such mendicants who pretend to be deaf and dumb or afflicted in any way, and there is no reason why they should not be sent to prison," Chief Conlin argued. "There are a number of beggars who are really afflicted or deformed, and who thrust their deformities forward to the public gaze. . . . They are impudent and persistent, and will be attended to also." "Simply put," Norden writes, "beggars were perceived as public nuisances or worse who deserved to be prosecuted for their actions, and it mattered little if their disabilities were real or faked" (14–17).

But saying it mattered little may settle the question too quickly. It mattered enough to generate "sham cripple" narratives in large numbers, in film, fiction, newspaper articles, and reformist exposés. And in these texts the rhetoric that indicts "really afflicted" beggars along with the fakers—"they will be attended to also"—does not prevent the emergence of another kind of rhetoric that expresses unease about the situation of the "really hopeless." The distinction between false and true mattered enough to produce a tension between languages of care and languages of criminality, and a conflict about authenticity, that played themselves out over and over in the telling of stories of the vagrant and the beggar.

Although we have few traces of what people who begged themselves thought about begging, we have no reason to conclude that the distinction between actual and feigned impairment meant nothing for them. A truly paralyzed woman begging on the street might have experienced a faker not only (and primarily) as immediately threatening competition but also as symbolically hurtful to her reputation and her social standing. A faker, in turn, might have had a stake in not being "one of them." We cannot conclude that these differences did not matter.

The differences may, in fact, have mattered very much at the moment of the origin of ugly law. Some people's displays might have been impelled by the need for people with impairments to distinguish themselves from fakers by demonstrating real "affliction" (Byrom 2004, 15–16). Under the pressure to certify helplessness, "visible disability," Holmes writes,

> might constitute a way of being seen without being regarded as "obtruding" oneself, and of communicating without offensive clamor through the silent, modest speech of an impaired body. The visibly disabled neatly corroborated the prevailing philosophy of the COS that the deserving were identifiable. (114)

But the faker forced more obtrusive, immodest, and messy forms of corroboration. A New York writer suggests as much in his description of the city's beggars:

> The most unpleasant thing connected with this class is that the cripple . . . insists upon proving to you ocularly that there is no deceit or imposition in the case. To that end, shriveled limbs, unsightly stumps, ghastly wounds, and festering sores are revealed before you can take your money from your purse or get out of sight. When you are on your way to dinner, or to visit your beloved, or have composed in your mind the last stanza of the new poem that has given you such trouble, it is not agreeable to be confronted by some loathsome vision. You would have paid liberally to have been saved such an exhibition, and do pay promptly to be favored with as little of it as possible. . . . I have more than once observed grim smiles of satisfaction on pallid and repulsive faces when such words as "Here's something; for Heaven's sake don't show it to me!" have reached their ears.[4] (Browne, 459–460)

This passage opposes desire, pleasure-seeking, and art on the one hand to stumps, wounds, and sores on the other (an opposition that the disability arts movement and AIDS activists in the late twentieth century have worked to dismantle); it represents sensibility sustaining itself against and through the threat of shock; it emphasizes a reverse striptease in the unsightly encounter, in which people pay *not to see*. Most importantly, it reveals the triangulation that occurs in the Great Metropolis. A third figure lurks beside the "cripple" and the gentleman of sensibility: the faker, whose existence forces an exhibition of "ocular proof." A rise in chicanery in the later nineteenth century may have led to more dramatic gestures of display by people with real impairments, gestures that in turn may have provoked the ugly law. In this scenario, it mattered whether disability was real or faked.

AT THE DOCTOR'S

Both the mid- to late 1890s and the Progressive era were periods of heightened anxiety around this question of authenticity (and, not incidentally, of renewed attempts to institute or revive ugly laws in several cities), but the disability inauthenticity story was in active play long before this time and also long after.[5] This chapter mostly concerns the long stretch from the Gilded Age to World War I. At every stage, the constructed relation between "fraudulent" and "actual" disability has been a complex one, with many implications—especially so whenever disability has been constructed in government policies as "deserving of state relief."[6]

Two zones of transgression preoccupy middle-class production of the unsightly faker beggar as a type, one linguistic, the other spatial. One is the imposter's dictionary; the other, the imposter's den. Lists of the faker's "slanguage," as COS imposter-tracker extraordinaire James Forbes called it, dominate these stories. Over and over we find a tramp taxonomy of names for begging specialties. "Throw-outs" simulated paralysis, sometimes so well that "although they have been taken to Bellevue Hospital and subjected to stiff electric currents to 'shake them out' have been able to lie crippled through it all"; "dummies" or "D. and D.'s" faked deafness and were also subjected to tests by police, sometimes given ether to check if they would talk while under anesthesia; those who "chucked dummy fits" performed epileptic seizures; mute beggars gave out "dockets" with pleading poems written on them; "snake dodgers" displayed dead rattlesnakes said to have caused the loss of their limbs; "crumb throwers" tossed bread into the gutter in order to fish it out in front of passersby; and on and on.[7]

These dictionaries served multiple rhetorical purposes. They established the writers as knowing insiders and their begging subjects as inveterate outsiders. They alerted readers to be vigilant against the ever-changing, dangerously generative forms of imposture, and they taught them, too, to be suspicious of every malady. Marshaling the language of the "specialty," they emphasized the cynically professional as opposed to the spontaneous and instinctual expression of need. They located criminality and deviance not only in begging practice but in begging language. The secret cant of "throw-out" and "snake-dodger" denied—and defied—the power of doctors and policymakers to set the terms (like "diseased," "maimed," and "deformed") in which unsightly begging was discussed. In place of the ostensibly plain language of medicine and law, beggars' "slanguage"—witty, at once audacious and duplicitous—suggested that the subject of the conversation was not easily pinned down. This, as much as bilking and duping, constituted the criminal nature of imposter culture.

In addition to its languages, faking also developed its own built environments, its own geographies, and this too preoccupied reformist discourse. Faking had its *space*. New York leaders were particularly conscious at this time of the problem of the sham's location, a problem that extended in the forms that I outline here well into the twentieth century. The city's Bowery was packed, in fable and in fact, with stale-beer dens and lodging houses with names like "The Cripples' Home" catering specifically to two kinds of clientele, disabled beggars and "Bowery bums" who faked disability.[8] (Some readers will recall that the den that Fagin and Sikes frequent in *Oliver Twist*'s map of Victorian London is called the "Three Cripples.") In New York in particular, the shammers' den story came to serve as an emblem for sensationalizing chroniclers of the city's "low life" and "dark side," and this resulted in a particularly rich archive.

In the early twentieth century, the story of the "Cripples' Home" menace picked up steam. A 1907 *New York Times* piece, "Pest of Beggars Loosed on the Town: Professional Mendicants, with Made-Up Disfigurements, Return to Prey on City's Charity" notes locations of their "nests": one on Hamilton Street, one on Nassau Street in Brooklyn, one on 118th Street in Harlem, and four on the Lower East Side: "the saloons kept by Thomas Lee, or 'Chicago Tom,' on Chatham Square; the place of an ex-tramp, close by, and the saloon of 'Diamond Dan' O'Rourke in Park Row." The watching writer reported seeing beggars enter lodging houses in the evening and later emerging again, "their wounds and palsy gone, their crooked limbs straight, their sightless eyes with unimpaired vision."[9]

Two writers in particular set the terms for many rehashings of this scene. In 1905, Theodore Waters went undercover in the Bowery as a temporary beggar, tricked up in a sling, simultaneously and ambiguously faking a sham and/or a deserving cripple. He offers a lengthy account of the interiors of places like the "Cripple's Home," pianos "jangling rank accompaniments" while the habitués treated one another to drinks "bought of philanthropy," including one bar "infested with sham paralytics." "The maladies or the paraphernalia used by them in their daily calling are usually cast aside when the day's work is done, and they appear in ordinary garb at their pleasure resorts" (78).

This phenomenon—a kind of green room for the violators of ugly law—became material for another reporter and then for later-nineteenth- and twentieth-century authors writing in the tradition of the guidebook that revealed "secrets of the great city" (up to the recent accounts of Bowery "cripple factories" by Luc Sante). A long piece published in the *New York World* in 1910 reporting on raids by police captain Michael Galvin began with this long dramatic set of titles: "General Crusade Probable against Dens in Lower Manhattan Which Serve as Resorts and Refuges for Panhandlers, Criminals, Drug Victims and Desparadoes [*sic*]—Have No Counterpart Even in Worst European Cities—Maintained by Beggary, Fraud and Theft, They Fill Psychopathic Wards and Potter's Field. Sights and Scenes in Haunts of the Underdogs of the Under World . . . Thronged with the Dregs of Humanity." The reporter described in some detail the den called (in a marvelous play on the medical model) The Doctor's.[10]

In the legendary *Gangs of New York* (1927), Herbert Asbury drew heavily on the *New York World* piece to write his own version of The Doctor's. Luc Sante depended on Asbury in turn for his depiction of the Bowery scene in *Low Life* (1991). Combined, the Galvin-Asbury-Sante line offers a set of vivid details about The Doctor's interior. Presided over by Burly Bohan, "the 'Doctor' himself," who wears "flashing diamonds in his shirt bosom" (Galvin), it is lit by a single electric light, decorated only by cobwebs (Galvin) or, in Asbury's account, by the engraved portraits of fourteen presidents of the United States that hang above the bar to inspire better begging; it is loud with shouts of profanity, "hideously foolish laughter," and "the wailing of songs, . . . a degenerate's chorus" (Galvin); it is furnished with two extralong tables that function as "the rooms of the hotel," for sleepers who pay a nickel (Asbury, 300) and with a locker where "mock cripples" can store their "ingenious accoutrements, . . . fake harnesses and prostheses, elaborate swaths of bandages" (Sante, 115, following Asbury). Its clientele is made up of types like "old Tom Frizzell, a noted Bowery character who succeeded to the title of the King of the Panhandlers after Jim Farrell, blinded by the fiery concoctions which he had been imbibing for many years, had been carried screaming . . . to die in the alcoholic ward of Bellevue Hospital" (Asbury, 299). In its back room and those of its equivalents—"the Hell Hole, the Harp House, the Cripples' Home on Park Row" (Sante, 115)—operate "Fagin-style begging schools called 'cripple factories' that . . . supply the equipment and teach its use, in return for a percentage of the returns" (Sante, 115). After the day of begging, in the saloon, "the 'lame' and 'halt' . . . walk normally, the 'blind' see, and the 'deaf and dumb' converse," writes Sante, "all of them spending their receipts at the company bar, safe from the eyes of their benefactors" (121, 315).

The Bowery was not the only location for this kind of scene. In California, Frank Norris's interestingly titled "The Dis-Associated Charities" (in *The Third Circle,* 1909) offers an unpleasant story of a trick played on three blind beggars; the gag may be fictional, but the three men were historical figures on the San Francisco streets, and the setting is described as the city's version of a "Court of Miracles," a "brick house over a saloon kept by a Kanaka woman and called 'The Eiffel Tower.'" Though the saloon's customers are described as "genuine unfortunates," the reference to Victor Hugo's Parisian imposter Court, the glee with which the three blind men are conned, and the dysfunction implied by the title suggest a general atmosphere of deception (57–67).[11] Chicago socialist, settlement-house worker, and reporter I.K. Friedman set his satiric fictional representation of the imposter "Beggar's Club" (1903) in Boston. Of Chicago itself, sociologist Harvey Zorbaugh, like Herbert Asbury, wrote in the 1920s, looking back on the heyday of a fin-de-siècle disability con scene that persisted all the way into the Jazz Age. He notes that on Chicago's Clark Street there were "several old hotels and rooming-houses . . . populated largely by the physically handicapped beggar—especially the blind beggar—and by those who through simulation and 'make-up' . . . are able to ply the same trade" (111). We can assume that other large cities saw similar developments.

The phenomenon I am encapsulating in The Doctor's is represented in city histories largely by hostile witnesses. Even when The Doctor's raconteurs take stances more neutral or mischievously delighted, they show little understanding of the complex politics of disability at stake in these strange places. Recall, for instance, Luc Sante's representation of the after-hours scene at the bar, where suddenly "the 'lame' and 'halt' could walk normally, the 'blind' see, and the 'deaf and dumb' converse." Sante's unconsciously ableist lens—noticeable especially in his assumption that the actual deaf do not "converse"—sets up a firm opposition here, between the lame and the "lame," the blind and the "blind," and so on; but in fact it was not quite so simple.

ETIOLATIONS

Let us return to Norden's statement on beggars that "it mattered little if their disabilities were real or faked." There is an important aspect of this question to consider, but from a different vantage point than Norden's examination of middle-class values. How might the difference between the blind and what Sante calls the "blind" matter little to people who lived in the Bowery, matter little *from below*?

Out on the street by The Doctor's, the real lame might also perform "lameness," not only in the sense that lameness is performative, "an identity tenuously constituted in time," in Butler's familiar definition, "through a stylized repetition of acts" (about which more later), but in the more specific and conventional sense of performance, in which lameness is a put-on or theatrical guise (Butler 1988, 140).[12] The textual traces of this phenomenon come filtered through the eyes of reformist beholders, who had strong interest in attributing deception wherever begging was concerned.

But the stories of impairment performance that they tell cannot entirely be explained away as their own anxious fabrications.

A character in Alvin F. Harlow's lowlife history *Old Bowery Days* (1931), Spike O'Day, "had a wooden leg, . . . pawned it nearly every morning and redeemed it at night from the proceeds of a day's begging in a sitting position on the sidewalk" (526). In the scene of Spike O'Day, disability might be performed on the street (in this case through the sloughing off and reclaiming of a prosthesis), might be overacted and hyperbolized, by both fakers and those who could claim to be the real thing.[13] "It was art, reprehensible art, of course, but art, nevertheless," Theodore Waters wrote of the practices of New York City beggars such as "one-eyed 'Blinkie' Howard, who sat with hat in one hand and glass eye in the other," or the "one-legged youth" who stuck his good leg out so passersby would trip over it (75). An 1880 newspaper report focuses on a man named Baker, who "has a badly crippled arm, his 'fake' being to swathe the injured member in numerous wraps, and work on the sympathies of the people by showing he is disabled." Baker both *has* crippling and *fakes* it through a complex dynamic of hiding and revealing, swathing and showing ("Hard Gang").

Zorbaugh's anxious taxonomies of the disability con in *The Gold Coast and the Slum* are replete with case histories of this kind. "The flopper," he writes, "is a man or woman who has lost both legs, and sits or 'flops' along the sidewalk, begging for alms." Clearly, every legless man or woman is not a "flopper"; stylized "flopping" is dramatically performed, staged as a scene. "Flopping" is engaging in what Richard Schechner calls "twice-behaved behavior," rehearsed and then presented. Zorbaugh offers another account of a twice-behaving subject, whom he names "K." The story of K.'s chicanery knows no bounds; she goes so far as to perpetrate the sick imposture that some women commit with hair curlers. Note that K. is both blind and "blind." She belongs to a familiar category that recent disability studies work (for example by Rod Michalko, Georgina Kleege, and Tanya Titchkosky) seeks to problematize: the one who is not disabled enough to be disabled and is thereby equated with the sham.[14]

> K. is a well-known Clark Street character. She is a graduate pianist from a conservatory in a Midwestern city. Her sight having been greatly impaired, she passes as blind. . . . She has taken up the violin for street use and, as occasion necessitates, plays to street and restaurant crowds. The night before she goes to "work" she puts her hair in curlers and sits propped up with pillows all night in order not to muss her hair. One day on the street she

> came upon a blind man playing a violin. She stopped and took up a collection from the passing crowds as he played. Then she calmly walked off with the proceeds. (111)

In all these cases, the distinction between the real and the fake is fuzzy. The "flopper," Baker, Spike O'Day, and the nefarious K. both are and pretend or seem to be disabled, in degree or kind. This paradox expresses itself with force in the headline of an 1898 *New York Times* article on the notorious "professional beggar" Charles Burkawitz: "Rich Beggar's Vacation."

In the reportage on Burkawitz, the lines between real and duplicitous disability are no sooner drawn than blurred. "Burkawitz was arrested," begins one article, while "busily engaged grinding out ancient melodies on that beggars' most precious friend, the bijou hand organ, while his sightless eyes turned appealingly upward with the far-away stare of the blind." The reporter goes on, with the demeaning sarcasm typical of *New York Times* coverage of begging arrests, to portray the man's background:

> Burkawitz was brought to this country from Russia about fifteen years ago by his uncle, who hoped to use him as a remunerative object of charity.... He was descended ... from a long line of famous mendicants and inherited traits of character that were bound to stand him in good stead in new fields. The only external equipment possessed by the boy was a peculiarly repulsive appearance, his hair growing far down on his forehead, as if he had been born a helpless idiot. He did not even have a withered arm or leg.

From the sound of this account, Burkawitz already came close to qualifying as a real-life unsightly beggar. But, according to this writer, the young Burkawitz soon learned to supplement his "meager natural equipment" for begging by "feigning blindness. He would roll his eyes upward so that only the whites could be seen." On the wall of his luxurious apartment, paid for through rental income from the three tenements he is said to have bought with his begging earnings, hangs a portrait of Burkawitz that the reporter describes: "a handsome man, able to see."

Then something happened to change Burkawitz's situation. In one version of the story, he falls down a flight of stairs; when he regains consciousness, he finds "that he need not roll his eyes in order to be sightless." In another version, it is the long days of "standing for hours with his eyeballs rolled up in the sun" that produce, with ironic retribution, actual blindness: "The strain proved too much for his optic nerves, and after a time he lost his sight forever." In both these versions, the tension between "feigns blindness" and "is blind" is resolved through a linear narrative in which the faker eventually gets what is coming to him. But feigning blind and being blind are not simply differentiated by the past and the present in the *Times*'s telling of Burkawitz's story. He is said to have consulted surgeons who "told him they could perform an operation whereby he could see again" but to have "promptly decided to remain blind." In this story, how can we tell fake from real blindness, manipulation from "real affliction," twice-behaved from once-behaved identity, sightedness from unsightliness?

Burkawitz was arrested with two begging collaborators, one Joseph Buckley, "the other blind man," and Fred Allen, "the cripple." What did they think of him? Together, did they constitute or participate in some kind of community? If so, what does it have to do (if anything) with present-day ideas of "disability community"? Is Burkawitz a legitimate part of "the new disability history," and if so, on what terms? Only after he goes blind for real? Does legitimacy matter?

Imagine an axis marked at each of its ends with two opposing poles: on the one end, "shame"; on the other, "disability pride." Today activists invoke and seek to create "disability culture" as a pride culture. By no stretch of the presentist imagination can The Doctor's be said to be an 1890 Bowery equivalent or precursor of this kind of disability culture. Neither, however, can we simply mark or repudiate The Doctor's as the locus of shame (sham), particularly (but not only) because historical evidence suggests that its habitués included people with impairments as well as pretenders.

Rather, The Doctor's seems to have constituted a middle zone, remaking the boundaries and traversing the frontiers between pride and shame, authentic and inauthentic, nondisabled and disabled, meek and impudent, helpless and designing. It was, in Homi Bhabha's terms, an interstitial space. In such locations, where "subjects are formed 'in-between,'" Bhabha writes, the terms of engagement between the various parties can be "antagonistic or affiliative," but the "borderline engagements of cultural difference may as often be consensual as conflictual; they may confound our definitions of tradition and modernity; realign the customary boundaries between the private and the public, high and low; and challenge normative expectations of development and progress" (2).[15] Bhabha invokes the stairwell as a figure for this kind of "interstitial passage between fixed identifications" that "opens up the possibility of a cultural hybridity that entertains difference without an assumed or imposed hierarchy" (4). Down the stairwell into the dive of The Doctor's (or was it a street-level den arranged for better access than the average flophouse?), did such passages into cultural hybridity occur as beggars put on, sloughed off, and/or reconceived the trappings of disability, as they moved outside or between the hierarchy that placed the helpless cripple below the able body?[16] The meeting points between disability and performance in the contemporary phenomenon that gets called "disability performance," writes Petra Kuppers, "create unexpected encounters, fleeting moments, puzzles and unanswerable questions—above all . . . a flow of energy, and a way of being alive, that negates fixity" (2003, 1). Can we locate such a flow of energy on or about The Doctor's door?

These unanswerable questions should be approached with caution. For one thing, I want to be careful not to be glib about a tough and dangerous situation. If the flow of energy in sham cripple performance was a way of being (and staying) alive, it also flowed in the reverse direction. Burly Bohan, proprietor of The Doctor's, had a former life as policeman; he moved into the saloon business after being fired from the police force on charges of brutality ("Galvin's Bowery Raids"). One news article described the practices of the boss of a ring of imposters in terms that invoked both Taylorist and abolitionist discourse:

> The owner of male chattels had been quite frank. His 25 per cent of the takings of his beggars netted him about $10 a day. In return he painted fake wounds on their arms . . . and swathed them in deceiving bandages. . . . If they try to run away he puts real bruises on their brows. . . . [He] sends them out begging on the bad days when they would prefer to stay in the warm shelter of the Bowery "flop." He's an efficiency expert with a twist. ("Efficiency Engineer")

The rough culture of these dives was hard on all concerned—perhaps especially on the women, though male privilege, which did not necessarily extend to disabled men, did not protect the men from one another.[17] Costs of disabled identity were high: eugenics, sterilization, institutionalization, euthanasia, poverty and social impoverishment, exclusion, prejudice, subjection, violence, and abuse. This point needs underscoring here.

But all these costs were also borne at times by poor and marginalized people we would identify as nondisabled. That there are similarities and overlaps between the forms of subjection experienced by disabled and by nondisabled people suggests potentials for cross-identification, a coalitional possibility. The beggars and disabled people on the Bowery were so marginalized, so down and out, that the cramped Doctor's was as far as that collectivity could go or went. Still, could that little place The Doctor's have sometimes provided a safe space for unwinding that was potentially counterhegemonic for its mixed community?

One starting point for approaching this question of faking culture is the model of E. Patrick Johnson's work on "the elusive signifier called 'blackness.'" Johnson suggests that "the very thing that constitutes 'black' culture" is the "mutual constructing/deconstructing, avowing/disavowing, and expanding/delimiting dynamic that occurs in the production of blackness" (2). At times of social, cultural, and political crisis, he argues, older forms of authenticity get called into question, setting the stage for "'acting out' identity politics." "Blackness," he writes, "does not belong to any one individual or group. Rather, individuals or groups appropriate this complex and nuanced racial signifier in order to circumscribe its boundaries or to exclude other individuals or groups. . . . What happens," he asks, "when blackness takes on corporeality? Or, alternatively, how are the stakes changed when a 'white' body performs blackness?" (2). This is a productive set of questions, and I take permission from Johnson's own analysis to "appropriate" them for disability studies: How did "crippling" take on corporeality in the Bowery? How did the various individuals at The Doctor's variously appropriate the elusive signifiers of what we now call disability? (How) did "sham cripple" begging "act out" (as) a kind of quasi identity politics in the time of social and cultural crisis that produced the ugly laws? (How) were the stakes of unsightly beggar ordinances changed when an "able" body performed disability?

Say the stakes changed for the worse. Say, perhaps, that the acting-out of the fakers brought on, or at any rate helped bring on, the crackdown of ugly law. In this reading, imposters' unsightly performatives, in J.L. Austin's terms, were (to put it mildly) particularly "infelicitous." Their sham begging scenes made a mockery not only of their fooled donors but of poor people with impairments who had few or no other options besides panhandling and whose situation they played a significant role in worsening. As Austin would put it, they were doing things with the words on their signs or on their lips ("Blind Since '52," words that say without saying "I beg" and result sometimes in donation) that were "abuses, acts professed but hollow" (and in this case, rather more than others, Austin's caution not to stress "the normal connotations" of "abuse" does not apply).

Readers trained to read Austin after Derrida, Butler, and others will, of course, understand *all* performatives as "acts professed but hollow." Even, that is, when a man who has been blind since '52 holds a sign that says

"Blind Since '52," or even, for that matter, when he goes to the doctor's (not The Doctor's) and says, "I have been blind since '52," he is speaking a kind of script; he is constituting, implementing, professing a blind identity repeatedly over time, through complicated citational processes. He is in some sense *enacting* "blind" or referencing "blindness." His everyday utterances cannot be purged of every trace of the artifice that characterizes the plea "Blind Since '52" when it is performed by someone with 20/20 vision.[18] As Andrew Parker and Eve Sedgwick put it in their summary of Derrida's reading of Austin: "Where Austin, then, seemed intent on separating the actor's citational practices from ordinary speech-act performances, Derrida regarded both as structured by a generalized iterability, a pervasive theatricality common to stage and world alike" (6). Once theatricality pervades every iteration of doing "Blind Since '52," then the distinction between "hollow" blindness and "solid" blindness, as well as that between staged begging and the rest of ordinary life, become increasingly unstable.

It could be argued that the "iterability" of begging disability was exactly what provoked the ugly laws and what they banned. One of the very earliest uses of the word *iterable* in English (in 1590) employs it specifically in the legal context of licensing exceptions to law and subsequent abuse: "When license is granted to any to doe an iterable acte, otherwise against lawe, it ought to be restrained to the first acte only" (*Oxford English Dictionary*). *Disability* itself evolved as a category in policy that specified license granted to do iterable acts otherwise forbidden: to receive goods and services without working, to beg freely, to peddle without sanction. Even before the disability category emerged per se, laws and customs sometimes gave specific groups of people with impairments exceptions to rules—but often ambivalently. Begging once on the grounds of neediness may be tolerated.[19] Begging as an iterable act, though, often constitutes a problem. Remember that the *Chicago Tribune*, announcing Alderman Peevey's unsightly beggar ordinance, emphasized the "incessant" nature of the organ-grinding of the woman who played "Mollie Darling."

Proliferating fakers illustrated and exacerbated the general crisis of iterable unsightliness: too many "diseased, maimed, deformed" repeat offenders whose offense *was* ritual and repetition. The designation "professional beggar," so often applied to denigrate the group as a whole, attacks, precisely, skilled iterability. In a classic rendition of the scene I have been tracing in this chapter, the downtrodden protagonist of Upton Sinclair's Chicago exposé *The Jungle* (1906) is driven out of desperation to beg for one time, the only time, but is defeated by the professionalized skills of repeater beggars who range from (and waver between) terrifying for-reals and sinister fakers: "He was just out of the hospital—but the story was worn threadbare, and how could he prove it? He had his arm in a sling—and it was a device a regular beggar's little boy would have scorned. He was pale and shivering—but they were made up with cosmetics, and had studied the art of chattering their teeth." "Poor Jurgis might have been expected to make a successful beggar. He was . . . desperately sick-looking." But he cannot compete with the fakers or with the truly unsightly and disgusting, the "wretches" who at the end of the episode are dragged by police net into the "miniature inferno" of a detention hospital, herded together "with hideous, beastly faces, bloated and leprous with disease, laughing, shouting, screaming in all stages of drunkenness, barking like dogs, gibbering like apes, raving and tearing themselves in delirium" (275).

This passage might be said to enact a kind of encapsulated dynamic of the deep psychology of ugly law. Jurgis simultaneously qualifies as one who would fall under and as one who would fall outside the jurisdiction of the ordinance; he is both *really* ill and hurt and *merely* ill and hurt, a tolerable, pitiable, humanized form of that which escalates into "disease" or "mutilation" and "deformity." The beggars careening through this scene alternate between signs of outrageous duplicity and signs of hideous fact, between willed degeneration and inescapable contingency. What they share in common, and retain at every point, is a recidivism coded in the word "professional."[20] Here, as so often in unsightly begging discourse, "scientific professionalism" rapidly merges into the sheer misery signified by the gaping wound. The "professional" beggar and his or her frequent discursive companion the "common" beggar are one and the same; professionalism is no mark of distinction.[21] Nonetheless, the discourse of professionalism predominates in the beggar's *Jungle*; too abject misfortune is subsumed under the category of the too slick counterfeit.

Professionalism was also associated with the artifice of the prosthesis. Note that imposters could proceed not only by faking carnality (rolling up the eyes, say, to seem blind, or binding back an arm to look like an amputee) but also by manipulating technology (for example, using a white cane or publicly putting on or taking off a wooden leg). At The Doctor's, beggars relied heavily on prosthetics. Take Spike O'Day, the man who pawned his wooden leg each day to beg from a more abject and presumably more profitable position. Stephen Kurzman has described how amputees with artificial limbs pass as able-bodied and/or disclose as disabled in a process over which they exert control: "Prostheses do become visible, but often under amputees' terms of pass and trespass" (379). Spike O'Day specialized in trespass. Nondisabled fakers who rented crutches or wheelchairs out of The Doctor's cupboards trespassed if anything even more flagrantly on (and in) "amputees' terms." A strong cultural anxiety about undisciplined, irregular prosthesis drove crackdowns on "sham cripples."

In Thomas Alva Edison's 1908 film *The Thieving Hand*, an honest armless beggar, given a prosthetic arm that formerly belonged to a thief, cannot stop himself from stealing, since the hand has a will and memory of its own. The film has been interpreted primarily as a parable of modern technoanimism, in which prosthetic technology uncannily assumes the agency formerly exerted by human beings (Landsberg, 25; Sobchack, 23). This interpretation makes sense, but it ignores the particular subject positioning of the main character. Edison's plot works both by distinguishing the helpless beggar from the scheming robber and by playing on the strong association between the two. Like charity, in this formulation, prosthesis unscientifically applied is a problem, not a solution. And deregulated prosthesis—handed to just anyone, not by doctor's orders—threatens to run amok.

The fear of the professional, formalized repetition of begging, or of begging *as* formalized repetition, whether helped along with prosthetic aids or not, shows up especially clearly in U.S. newspaper reports of a supposed "Mendicants' Journal" in Paris (often, for Americans, the marked site of corrupt and stylized unsightliness). Allegedly, the journal was filled with want ads like the following: "Wanted at once, for seaside resort, a pair of helpless cripples. Good business. References given and required, also a moderate premium" ("Journal for Beggars"). This ad offends its detractors by brazenly displaying what otherwise would take place behind the closed doors of the "cripple factories," by shamelessly reduplicating the respectable discourse of employers, and by openly marking the interchangeability of "helpless cripple" role players, but also simply by putting it all in print. The impersonality of reading and the anonymity of writing intensified the scandal of begging's iterability.

This impersonality is one reason why a special intensity of anger and anxiety directs itself against beggars' written placards (such as the two-sided "Blind Since '52") and their "dockets," the messages written on cards handed out silently to passersby.[22] The docket came in for particular scrutiny. There is some evidence that down-and-out "scribes" made their living scribbling docket verse for fellow panhandlers. Asbury, for instance, describes a frequent patron of The Doctor's, called "The Scholar," who earned money for drinks by writing poems to be used by beggars passing themselves off as blind (299; see also Friedman). Pausing to reproduce the beggar's docket is a stock move in many versions of The Doctor's—partly to make fun of bad writing but more so to warn readers about writing's duplicity. I do not have space to reproduce this doggerel here, but I recommend reading it; the poems have the charm of outsider folk art (*New York Times,* Apr. 24, 1893; "Ancient Profession"; "Pitiful Mendicant Gives Way").

Unlike direct verbal pleas, beggar's dockets participated in the "promiscuous circulation, . . . anonymous negotiation and spectatorial detachment" that David Henkin argues constitutes urban modernity (ix). They could be passed on from one beggar to another; they hid behind and traded on the instability and ambiguity of print. "The bigger and blacker the headlines," bemoaned an *Los Angeles Times* piece on beggars who pretended they were the victims of accidents described in press clippings that they wore around their necks, "the more productive . . . in the silver returns," even though no one, the reporter maintained, ever read the accident reports ("This Beggar a Press Agent"). The specter of the workaday want ad in the "Mendicant's Journal" or the beggar press agent laid bare city readers' fear, as Henkin puts it, of their "increasing dependence . . . on written words, on utterances that in some sense eluded the control and exceeded the accountability of their authors" (15). This fear held true whether the "helpless cripple" at the seaside turned out to be fake or not, whether or not the beggar on the train really was a crippled orphan girl, or whether or not the bearer of the "blind" sign could read it in a shop window.

I have been suggesting that ugly law punished iterability in general. And yet I think many of us might nonetheless still want to make some kind of distinction between the iterations of—shall I say—genuinely fake unsightly beggars, on the one hand, and those of the people whom they mimicked, on the other (let us call these opposites of fakers the "for-reals," since they stood starkly for the real as they begged on street corners). Parker and Sedgwick paradoxically offer a way in here, perhaps, when they note that for Austin, as he puts it, "infelicity," hollowness, is an "ill to which *all . . . conventional* acts" are "heir." As they put it, "a performative utterance is one, as it were, that may always get sick." Continuing with the illness metaphor, Parker and Sedgwick describe Austin as imposing "a kind of quarantine" that cannot finally be maintained, when he excludes from his discussion any explicitly theatrical language such as an actor's soliloquy. Begging is borderline, neither an "ordinary" utterance like someone saying "I'm blind" to a new acquaintance nor a clearly "extraordinary" one like a speech by an actor playing Oedipus; it is in a middle ground, the staged but quotidian street. Still, even if anybody's speech act "Blind Since '52" is subject to "illness," when some (sighted) bodies wear that sign, the performance may seem especially *sick*. Ironically, "sickness" in this sense depends on normative conventions of "health" and "wellness" in other senses. (Language is not allowed the "sick role.") In this scene, the sturdiest beggar, least heir to this "ill," is the for-real, the one who is actually ill or paralyzed or deaf.

In Parker and Sedgwick's spectacular gloss on Austin, they explore his characterization of the language that he excludes from consideration. This kind of language—for instance, that spoken on the theatrical stage—is, Austin argues, "used not seriously, but in ways *parasitic* upon its normal use—ways which fall under the doctrines of the *etiolations* of language." "After all these years," Parker and Sedgwick write, "we finally looked up 'etiolation' and its cognates in our handy Merriam-Webster, and were surprised to discover the following range of definitions." What their brilliant excursion through *Merriam-Webster's* reveals is the queerness of etiolation, which involves "the act, process or result of growing a plant in darkness" but also an "effete" "overrefinement of thought or emotional sensibilities: decadence." The etiolated fleurs du mal or sickly pansies that Parker and Sedgwick pluck from their dictionary speak a certain kind of language of flowers: "We seem," they write, "to be transported not just to the horticultural laboratory, but back to a very different scene: the Gay 1890s of Oscar Wilde. Striking that, even for the dandyish Austin, theatricality would be inseparable from a normatively homophobic thematics of the 'peculiar.'"[23] Striking, too, is what Parker and Sedgwick note but underemphasize: etiolation's association with illness and disability.[24]

If we look up *etiolation* and its cognates in the *Oxford English Dictionary,* we find a somewhat different emphasis. The primary set of connotations (certainly also present in Parker and Sedgwick's *Merriam-Webster's* but less emphatically) centers around blanching and pallor; to *etiolate* is to "give a pale and sickly hue to (a human being or his skin)." Etiolation involves dissipation, but also invalidism, and although neither of these can be removed from "normatively homophobic thematics," neither can they be removed from normatively ableist thematics—or for that matter, normatively racial thematics, because, as Samuels has pointed out, pallid "invalidism" is raced as white, and so "blanching" constitutes a sickly form of white identity ("Complication").[25] (Indeed, *etiolated* surfaces as a synonym for *white* in most thesauruses.) Disability and illness, sexual artifice and perversion, and race dovetail in etiolation. We seem to be transported not just to the Gay 1890s of Oscar Wilde but also to the 1890s of The Doctor's. And here again, ironically, the less etiolated the beggar's body, the more etiolated his or her language; sturdy fakers make the most parasitical parasites on (body) language in begging performances.

Not only the thematics of race, disability, and sexuality intersect at the "etiolated"; class thematics work here as well. Reformers and muckrakers writing of the "sunlight" and "shadow," "darkness" and "daylight" of New York represented those who lived in tenements and dark alleys as quite literally etiolated, as failing to thrive because they were deprived of actual sunlight. (One reporter wrote of the stale-beer dives, "Sometimes the police will drag out the wretched inmates, who actually are blinded by the daylight" ["Phase of City Life"].) Parker and Sedgwick make etiolation queer by presenting its scientific meaning as a kind of willed hothouse process, "the result of growing a plant in darkness," but just as commonly plant etiolation implies simply an involuntary, wild form of growth when plants receive insufficient light under any adverse circumstance. (Etiolated plants are, we might say, disabled plants.) My point is not to standardize a normative version of *etiolation* or to suggest that Parker and Sedgwick distort or mislead in their account of the word but to emphasize that, like *unsightly* and *crank, etiolation* carries converging meanings and that both the question of disability and the question of choice are key parts of this key word.[26] In the worldview of "sunlight and shadow" reformism, human etiolation could be pitied as long as it was involuntary. Imposter beggars seemed to court the etiolations of the alley; their crime was to choose to fail to thrive.

TOWARD A SOCIAL MODEL OF IMPOSTURE?

In part, what I learn from thinking about imposters is what I cannot learn from imposters. For instance, while disabled people historically have had an ambivalent and complex relation to medicine and to medical symbols, disability chicanery fundamentally, often literally, depends on the simplest meanings of exactly these trappings.[27] For fakers, the crutches stored in The Doctor's cupboards signify one thing only: being part of the "deserving poor." These accoutrements—the crutch, the sling, the blind man's sign—speak to the discourse of distributive justice that Deborah Stone has outlined; they certainly speak to the performativity of disability. What they do not speak to—or of or for—is the felt world of impairment, the phenomenological parameters of impairment experience, the proprioception and carnal style of someone whose leg was amputated or whose broken arm was never set or whose eyesight was lost in a fever.[28] No doubt, a one-legged woman on her way home with her crutch to The Doctor's *was her body* differently from the way in which a woman with one leg tied up behind her, headed to the same location, *was hers* (Hughes and Patterson, 335). And certainly the symbolic medical apparatus for rent to beggars in the "cripple factories" has a cultural valence that is independent of embodied experience.

But can we be sure of this independence? Is a faker's experience entirely independent of the impaired body as "lived body" and as a social body (for, as Hughes and Patterson have eloquently argued in their critique of binary social model theory, "disability is embodied and impairment is social" [335])? From the strictest social model perspective, someone who is perceived as impaired and is stigmatized as a result is "disabled"; that is what disability means. "In our view," begins the famous British Union of the Physically Impaired Against Segregation (UPIAS) definition, "it is society which disables" (Oliver 1996, 33). The sentence goes on: "it is society which disables *physically impaired people* . . . by the way we are unnecessarily isolated and excluded from full participation" (italics mine), but nonetheless, in the purest social model, disability (as opposed to impairment) is social, plain and simple. As Tremain puts it in her strong critique of this line of thought, "Proponents of the social model explicitly argue first, that disablement is not a necessary consequence of impairment, and second, that impairment is not a sufficient condition for disability." She goes on to point out an unstated premise of the social model: that "impairment is a necessary condition for disability," as in the UPIAS quotation; "only people who *have*," she notes, "or are *presumed to have*, an impairment are counted as disabled" (2002, 41–42).

Here is a paradox: in the bluntest versions of this model, disability fakers were not exempt from social disabling. Far from it. They were not, after all, wielding their rented crutches and bandages to get access to good jobs or fuller inclusion into the social mainstream. Faking meant enacting marginalization and claiming abasement. Fakers were *presumed to have*—or in the parlance of the Americans with Disabilities Act, regarded as having—impairments and were treated accordingly. In this sense, in this model, disability imposters were disabled.

There is something unsettling about concluding that the faker is disabled by society, not least because he or she is precisely taking advantage of that society—a situation that suggests that the vectors of oppression and enablement, power and counterpower, exclusion and inclusion, are more complex than the most schematic social model can admit. In addition, fakers themselves inflicted harm by reinforcing negative images of disabled people. Susan Burch records a clear acknowledgment of this harm when she recounts how Deaf leaders mobilized against the "imposter menace" as early as 1858 and with intensity starting in 1911, advocating for state laws that penalized fakery in order to attack the public image of Deaf people as "dependent and handicapped—in short, inferior" (149).[29] The National Organization of the Deaf printed stickers contrasting mendicant charlatans with for-real Deaf people defined as their opposites: "the Deaf do not beg" (Burch, 151). This was propaganda, of course—some D/deaf people were regular habitués of The Doctor's and its kind—but for organized Deaf culture imposture constituted a grave danger precisely because the type of the downtrodden dumb beggar threatened to override every other more positive and complex view of Deaf people in American public spaces.

On the one hand, the conclusion that "disability imposters were disabled" points to the inadequacies of the social model in disability theory. It suggests the necessity for a sociology of impairment and the analysis of what Carol Thomas calls "impairment effects" within disability studies.[30] And it reinforces the need for inclusion within disability theory of issues of phenomenology and embodiment.[31]

On the other hand, the sharp heuristic tools of the strict social model allow us to take note of an interesting possibility, one acknowledged glancingly in an aside in Susan Burch's analysis: "Imposters received acrimonious condemnation from Deaf people in part because they represented a (seemingly, if not real) direct attack on the Deaf by hearing persons" (149). Could "seeming" disabled constitute only a "seeming" attack? Perhaps some fakers at The Doctor's got some sense of disability: of the hostile stare, the patronizing pity, the inaccessible stairway, and so on. Need we cast these people solely as amoral opponents of something called "disabled people"? If they garnered some experience of disability discrimination, is there any possibility that they—or we—could imagine creative uses of that knowledge, even if they were not intentionally setting out to acquire it? Is there a possibly productive hybrid experience that lies between, in our terms, "disabled" and "nondisabled"?

This kind of in-betweenness differs from the kinds of fluidity and hybridity most commonly invoked, for good reasons, in disability studies. It is not the phenomenon that Price and Shildrick describe: "The disintegrity and permeability of bodies, the fluctuations and reversibility of touch, the inconsistency of spatial and morphological awareness, the uncertainty of the future, are all features that may be experienced with particular force in the disabled body, but they are by no means unique to it" (2002, 74). It is not the instability of the category of disability explored at length by Lennard Davis (2002). It is not the point made when disability awareness workshops teach the concept of the TAB or "temporarily able-bodied," the idea that "sooner or later we will all be disabled." I will be returning to that idea, but for the moment let us notice the ways in which it does not apply here. The fakers at The Doctor's were not (or were not only) TABs (temporarily able-bodied); they were TNABs—temporarily not able-bodied. Were there understandings to be derived from this behavior? Is there any destabilizing power in the experience of being "inauthentically disabled"? In appropriating disability? Was there a productive, a positive, potential in disability chicanery?

Especially considering the overlapping experiences of subjection that I have been exploring in the last two chapters, it seems likely to me that at The Doctor's, "inauthentically disabled" people might sometimes have played the role of allies (emotional, economic, and social) to their disabled counterparts, and vice versa. Everyone at The Doctor's was marginalized, doing their best to survive in the face of social exclusion. The *New York World* reporter who investigated The Doctor's and the Cripple's Home described two groups inside, men at the bar with money for drinks and "men absolutely penniless, who beg . . . from those at the bar. . . . beggars begging from beggars—panhandlers panhandling panhandlers" ("Galvin's Bowery Raids"). Certainly such arrangements dispelled any notion of a clear boundary between the haves and have-nots, an unsettling that I am arguing may also have occurred across the binary cripple/normal divide. Of course, manipulation, bad faith, laziness, and corruption were present in The Doctor's begging scenes (as they are present elsewhere). Though I tend to be suspicious of the "millionaire beggar" stories, I have no way to prove, no way to conclude about, the authenticity of need or the possibility of cross-ability community among the various customers at The Doctor's.

My questions here are purely speculative. I remain in the dark; my arguments are necessarily, and deliberately, *etiolated.* I prefer to raise these questions rather than to abjure all speculation or to decide in advance, in a contemporary replication of the COS's sorting of "deserving" from "undeserving," that all relations between disabled people who begged and begging imposters should be understood as adversarial—or, for that matter, to decide that these two categories, "disabled people" and "imposters," were clear-cut; after all, many 1890s imposters might qualify today for ADA protection under the umbrellas of "psychiatric disability" or medical problems related to alcoholism or drug addiction or illnesses, even though these were not the signs of neediness they mocked up on the street in their enactments of the signs of supplication.

Let us risk an ahistorical parallel. In a cautious defense of the recent, much used, and very much debated practice of disability simulation—in which, say, nurses in training are put through an exercise that sounds vaguely like the doings at The Doctor's, tricking up in slings and wheelchairs and dark glasses as if participating in an eerie echo of a "cripple factory," where the aim is garnering not small change but something called "awareness"—Gary Kiger has argued that this kind of experience may result, at best, with proper ethical precaution, in "dissonance and introspection" (73).[32] Introspection on the part of 1890s faker beggars who simulated impairment may be too much to hope for in the hardscrabble world of The Doctor's, but to deny it as a possibility is to accept a model in which only acting-out, not taking-in, occurred there. Dissonance seems likely enough. Surely the fakers' daily experiences yielded some sort of inchoate or organized information. Of what sort? How to get the most money? Which city streets are worst to navigate one-legged (or, more precisely, feigning "one-legged")? How people act when they give alms to "helpless cripples"? Was every day one long "disability awareness day" for the imposters?

Fakers' uses of disability technology may sometimes have transformed their own felt worlds in ways we cannot really begin to imagine. Merleau-Ponty, focusing on the "blind man's stick," writes that to "get used to a hat, a car or a stick is to be transplanted into them, or conversely, to incorporate them into the bulk of our own body"; habit, he argues, "expresses our power of dilating our being-in-the-world, or changing our existence by appropriating fresh instruments" (143). Petra Kuppers, writing on disability, new media, and cyberspace, underscores these last two words: "It is this sense of 'fresh instruments,' acting as addenda to our body, that I want to bring" to the issues at hand (2003, 106). In the view of imposters' detractors, they indeed wielded "fresh instruments"—fresh in the sense of impudent, cheeky. But perhaps also, occasionally, if a faker settled in for the long haul with, say, a white cane, his or her body concept altered sometimes in ways not at all identical to the experiences of Merleau-Ponty's "blind man" but nonetheless palpable, experiential. The reason we cannot quite begin to imagine these possibilities is that ableism obliterates their traces; even if a tradition of faker autobiography on fakers' own terms (what might they be?) existed, the governing distinction between the blind and the "blind" makes it extremely unlikely that a bodily and kinesthetic experience of the sort generated by the fresh instruments of The Doctor's would be registered in writing, or even in consciousness.[33]

The experiences of some fakers in this regard may have been no less misleading than those of today's nursing students, about which Philip Scullion comments dryly, "if the aim is to perpetuate the tragedy view of disability then simulation may be the method for you" (558). There are some crucial differences, however, between participation in disability simulation training today and the chicanery of the "sham cripples." Unlike student nurses and the other sincere simulators on "awareness days," imposter beggars (not unlike their "for-real" counterparts) cynically and hyperbolically enacted, rather than "innocently" encountering, the "tragedy model of disability," opening up a potential space behind or outside the semiotics of the tragic, revealing tragedy as model or as script. And unlike today's student nurses and other workshop participants, imposter beggars simulated without sanction, without certification, without officially approved forms of "ethical precaution." Their simulation without discipline was precisely what made them so alarming.[34]

It is intriguing to speculate about the disabled habitués of The Doctor's who hung out with the fakers; were they employed as canny trainers and technical advisers, valued as bearers of useful practical knowledge? If so, their position could hardly have presented entirely as tragic, and the tips they imparted may have been quite informative. As often as not, they may well have been in charge, and they often worked collectively in ways that may have provided some community.

In Boston in 1895, William Jewett Tucker bemoaned the presence of an "army of cripples of every sort . . . stationed at the corners of the streets," organized by "shrewd knaves" who were probably, but not necessarily, nondisabled (179). But the most storied army or "syndicate" of cripples was defiantly cripple-owned and cripple-run: the "beggar's trust," an object of some fascination in the New York papers, that was organized in the city in the very early 1900s by a one-legged, Robin Hood–like young man by the name of Kempton, along with his "comely" companion Mary Largo ("Arrest of Beggar Band"; Spacks; Waters; "Mary Largo"). According to Theodore Waters (who may or may not be a trustworthy narrator), Kempton's exploits would be recounted by habitués in places like The Doctor's as a form of professional development training for new begging incomers. Usurping the power to regulate unsightly begging, Kempton and his crew licensed *themselves*.[35] A kind of anti-league of the Physically Handicapped, the beggar's trust is a tale for a rogue disability history.[36] Whatever else we find in the Kempton/Largo archive—and much of it is grim—we find also some brief traces of agency, creativity, and collectivity. Very brief, for after a few years the players, packed away to prison and reformatory, disappear.

At the end of the day, we know little about what happened at The Doctor's and other places like it. The stories that come down to us about these unsightly spaces usually close off the range of possibilities that I have imagined in this chapter. Most narratives of the "cripple factories" conclude with the same clinch. Daylight turns to darkness, sunlight to gaslight, and the denizens of The Doctor's return from their stint of begging to carouse. Alvin Harlow's *Old Bowery Days* (1931) wraps up its account of The Doctor's like this: "What jovial evenings the panhandlers had in their 'clubs' when the strain of the day's work was over! With the paraphernalia laid aside and the distorted faces and limbs relaxed, they joked and cursed merrily and sang rollicking, bawdy songs" (500). Filmic versions of the scene inevitably foreground this moment of *undisability*, an acting tour de force in which the transformation from object of pity to normate is disclosed and underscored. These scenes depict liminal ceremonies, in Victor Turner's sense. If, momentarily, they seem to enact a kind of underground *communitas* of "threshold people" that embraces all participants, both fakers and for-reals, in the end they conduct a ritual of transition that sorts the two groups apart and restores each of them to its familiar social place. The punch line of the fakers' party reestablishes and secures the imposter's able-bodied status (and, therefore, utter guilt). It is as if, within this plot, performing crippling as misery must be followed by performing able-bodiedness as revelry.

If, to transfer Carole-Ann Tyler's terms from the analysis of gender to the analysis of disability, impersonation is "disability with attitude"—and disability with attitude was what ugly law despised—then it is important to note that this transgressive attitude did not limit itself to fakers. Remember police chief Conlin's assailing of for-reals in his announcement of a crackdown on the sham: "There are a number of beggars who are really afflicted or deformed, and who thrust their deformities forward to the public gaze. . . . They are impudent and persistent, and will be attended to also." Both fake and for-real unsightly beggars impersonated and caricatured impairment on the streets. Unsightly begging requires a kind of "disability-face" in which participants, whether they were imposters or not, marked their bodies in stark, ritual opposition to normality, ability, and employability. At the same time, structures of fetishism drove the ugly-law culture of nondisabled COS reformers with a vengeance: "I know this man fakes, but even so his affliction offends me"; "I know this woman asking me for money is really afflicted, but all the same she is a fraud."

I write "nondisabled reformers" advisedly, with tongue in cheek, since the imposters of The Doctor's have a way of revealing that the real/fake blur does not only occur for beggars. We might say that the feigners, with their smooth, alarming passages between the able body and its other, acted to "crip" bourgeois able-bodiedness, exposed its instability and its own performativity, tripped it up, showed it up as a phantasmatic identification, in Judith Butler's terms. Able-bodiedness has always been a loaded, shifting, conflicted category, perhaps never more so than in the period of the ugly laws.

And I write "imposters . . . have a way of revealing" advisedly, mindful of Michael Rogin's proviso for the study of performance and performativity: "But reveals to whom, one wants to know, for the contemporary critic may decipher a relationship between imitation and imitated at odds with those intended by performers or received by historical audiences" (33). Imposters have a way of revealing the instability of classed able-bodiedness to whom? To us—but perhaps also, at moments, to some audiences in the era of unsightly begging law.

After all, many of the accounts from which I have gleaned the hints and traces of the subculture of The Doctor's (and of unsightly begging more generally) were garnered via a different kind of highly self-conscious shamming, the mode in which a middle-class investigator went undercover to discern and to report on the nether world of the poor. Pinkerton detectives disguised themselves to pursue lowlife suspects (Kasson, 110–111). Police donned "plainclothes" to catch beggars. Those like Theodore Waters who put on the even plainer clothes of beggars in order to capture mendicant life for privileged readers—Mark Pittenger calls these writers "down-and-outers" (27)—often began their narratives with a scene of costuming not unlike the makeup artistry of cripple factories.

Pittenger writes that "down-and-outers tried to divest themselves of the stigmata of respectability. . . . practicing 'a hang-dog position of the head,' developing 'a sort of swinging drawl of a gait'" (41). The interest in gait as well as garment suggests that these Progressive-era writers and reformers carried off their undercover missions by engaging not only in cross-class but in cross-ability transvestism (Schocket). If these practices on the one hand confirmed for down-and-outers the essential difference between the bearing of the poor (ragged and impaired) and the manners of the confidently able and respectable, they also threatened to undermine the clarity of that distinction.

Theodore Waters simulates poverty and disability. (Photograph by H. McMichael, illustration for Theodore Waters, "Six Weeks in Beggardom," *Everybody's Magazine* 12 [Jan. 1905])

Many down-and-outers, writes Pittenger, "clearly worried that this project might result in going native. . . . Middle-class 'character,' poorly adapted to dressing up in alternate personality traits to suit the moment's needs, might not bend—it might simply break" (29). Often "going vagrant" meant, in addition to class-crossing, confronting another aspect of that nether region: the "able" shading into disease, maiming, and deformity. Here, writers and readers might confront with special intensity the breakability and the bendability of bodies.

When COS chief mendicancy officer James Forbes displayed a photograph of imposter John Roche, "The Cleveland Kid," to a reporter in 1904, he commented on the inadequacy of the record: "The Cleveland Kid" is shown in the illustration posing for the society in his particular 'throw-out.' He is in the clothes of private citizen, which he wears when off duty, and the 'throwout' has not the effect which it gives with rags" ("Ancient Profession"). The "Kid" reverses the cross-class transvestism of earnest Progressive-era reformers, for no approved end. What he throws out here is category stability. The "private citizen" is supposed to have nothing to do with begging or impersonation or even, I would argue, disability; for Forbes, to be a private citizen is to be, by definition, able and financially secure, not poor and "helpless," and both privacy and citizenship are apparently denied to unsightly beggars. Why did John Roche pose for the Charity Organization Society in smart "off-duty" clothes (presumably what he was wearing when picked up) and yet in full throw-out mode? After all, COS authorities maintained that for faker beggars greater "even than the threat of a term in jail is the fear of the photographer and the newspaper artist" (Spacks, 33). Roche could have stood still, making it more difficult to identify him in action in the future; instead, he actively performed his disability sham for the camera, as if posing for a casting call rather than a mug shot. Perhaps an actor's pride motivated him (his photograph bears strong resemblance to Lon Chaney's publicity poses), and almost certainly confident defiance did, but I like to think that maybe he enjoyed "throwing-out" the "private citizen," mixing the two to remind that impairment and rags do not speak for themselves and do not necessarily coincide.

Today in the United States we do not on the whole view people in public with obvious signs of rickets, people covered with psoriasis, people whose broken arms were not set, but in the 1880s and 1890s and even further into the twentieth century these conditions were common, unremarkable. It is worth remembering that sulfa drugs and many other medical technologies on which we rely had not yet been invented in the era of the unsightly beggar laws. The amount of visual variation in gait, in bodily style, was large; there was an acceptance of tremendous risk that in the United States we can hardly fathom. In the city council boardrooms where ugly laws were framed, in the COS offices where pauperism policies were designed and implemented, in the courts where judges passed sentence, there were eyes that blurred, bodies that limped, hurt, weakened, felt their limits, and showed their scars. The architects of ugly law othered the unsightly, but they had, no doubt, their share of impairment—as well as their share of bravado, shame, and fakery. "Privilege," Shannon Jackson writes, "is a performance whose efficacy relies on the feeling that nothing dramatic is happening" (8). Policing street theaters of disability, law enforcers defined normal bodies, acceptable bodies, their own bodies, as the sites of "nothing dramatic." But dramas of disability—of revelation, concealment, exaggeration, downplaying—nevertheless took place behind the court bench as well as before it. In the end, there was no "other side" to the sign that Thomas Knox decried and that I described at the beginning of this chapter. The distinction between the "sham able" and the "diseased, maimed, deformed" may have been the biggest scam of all.

PART II

AT THE UNSIGHTLY INTERSECTION

Are persons after all not to be persons if they are physically disabled? Are members of the community to be robbed of their rights to live in the community, their certificates cancelled upon development or discovery of disability? These rhetorical questions, the hallmarks of crusade and reform throughout American history, have in our generation become the plea of the disabled as well. As with the black man, so with the blind. As with the Puerto Rican, so with the post-polio. As with the Indian, so with the indigent disabled.

—JACOBUS TENBROEK,
"The Right to Live in the World," 1966

6

GENDER, SEXUALITY, AND THE UGLY LAW

The figure that was policed by the ugly law begged at many intersections.[1] In the story of the unsightly beggar ordinances the relation between something we now call "disability" and something we call "class" was not additive but deeply connective; identities and experiences of unsightly beggars took shape within a complex web of mutually reinforcing discourses.[2] Here and in the next two chapters, I follow the by now familiar "critique of 'single-axis' frameworks" and principle of "intersectionality" developed by Kimberlé Crenshaw and others, exploring how, as Valerie Smith puts it, the apparent dominance of one term in this field of interpretation—*disability*—"masks both the operation of . . . others and the interconnections among them," even as disabled people so often disappear in critical discussions alert to other interconnections.[3] *Disability* is commonly represented as a homogeneous and monolithic category in discourses that oppress disabled people. But gender, race, sexuality, religion, and national identity are inexorably intertwined with disability and class in the culture(s) of ugly law, producing a variety of ugly identities, both at each specific moment of ordinance enforcement—each encounter between a policeman, judge, friendly visitor, or sympathetic rabble-rouser and a particular person being found unsightly—and in the broader social order that framed, ignored, fought over, and accepted the state and city codes.[4] As Nayan Shah has pointed out, studies of law and society in the late-nineteenth- and early-twentieth-century United States tend to isolate various forms of accusation, regulation, and prosecution from one another: vagrancy is understood as a separate problem from sodomy, say, or prostitution, and the designation of the unsightly beggar never even enters into the lists. Yet the history of the unsightly as what Shah calls a "distinctive social body" is tangled with other histories (2005, 705).[5]

The other histories I discuss in the next three chapters are only some of the factors at work in this intersection. The groups on which I focus here—racial others, foreign others, Jewish others, sexual others, and of course "diseased, maimed, deformed" others—all share an American genealogy.

All were marked as inferior bodies to be concealed and to be controlled. All were scrutinized with special intensity during the "tidal wave" of laws regarding "local purity" of which unsightly beggar ordinances were a part (Eskridge, 27). All were constituted through the negative discourses of racist, homophobic, and ableist eugenics, in gender-specific ways, in the tightest of interrelations, in the era of the ugly laws.[6]

These histories are often treated not intersectionally but analogically, in the manner of the epigraph from tenBroek that begins this part: "As with the black man, so with the blind. As with the Puerto Rican, so with the post-polio. As with the Indian, so with the indigent disabled." Implicit in this kind of pioneering "as with" principle, articulated here in 1966, was a developing minority model of disability, exemplified later in works such as Gliedman and Roth's *The Unexpected Minority* (1980), in which a civil rights analysis of disability oppression was heavily undergirded by explanatory analogies with race discrimination.[7] The heuristic power of these analogies for readers unaccustomed to thinking of disability in political terms was obvious at the time. Analogized to the "race question," disability could *become* a "question," in a logic of equivalence that not only compared but connected the two struggles for equality.[8] As Jakobsen has pointed out, analogy is often used to establish precedents in legal reasoning on discrimination.

When Marcia Pearce and Robert Burgdorf named the ugly law as such, that name, I believe, was doing specifically analogical work. One of the obvious rhetorical effects of the Burgdorfs' coined, ahistorical phrase *ugly law*—a set of words that never appears in any actual municipal code index—is its placement of the ordinance squarely in relation to a social model of, to a *politics* of, ugliness: ugliness understood as a political situation or process, not a personal misfortune or objective aesthetic evaluation. In the mid-1970s, when the Burgdorfs published their analysis, this politics had been gendered, to a significant extent, by second-wave feminists whose consciousness-raising turned its gaze on feminine beauty norms.[9] Just as important, the phrase recalled black activist reworkings of the power politics of ugliness. In the historical context of the 1970s, the Burgdorfs' "ugly" echoed the kind of anatomy of black ugliness and pride conducted by Chicago poet Gwendolyn Brooks in her poem "The Life of Lincoln West" or by Toni Morrison in work like *The Bluest Eye,* in which ugliness-beauty is the deep site where race/gender circuits collide. Both racial oppression and antiracist activism could mobilize specifically through a politics of ugliness, as the creators of "black is beautiful" slogans precisely understood. The Burgdorfs' name *ugly law* built on this understanding, extending the morphological emphasis of feminist and black social movements in the 1970s and expanding their critiques of idealized morphologies and restrictive norms.

The dangers of such analogy-making have been sharply summarized in recent work by Jakobsen (on the queer/Jewish analogy) and Grillo and Wildman (on race/gender analogizing). These dangers include the denial of historical and experiential specificity and complexity, colonization of one difference by another, a deceptive "affect of connection" produced by the analogy (Jakobsen), an undercutting of rather than the shoring up of alliances between social movements, overemphasis on likeness rather than difference as the basis for social change, and, perhaps most important, elision of the intersection between the two categories analogized (so that the specific situation of, say, black deaf vagrant John Doe No. 24, arrested for masturbating publicly, disappears from a minority model that can only liken disability to race or deafness to disability or sexual deviance to race and so on [Bakke]). In addition, the "disabled people are like blacks" or "ableism is like racism" analogy or its other variants reduce the relations between different kinds of subjection to mere similarity.[10] Against this principle of analogy, the idea of intersectionality poses a different model of "as with": As with the blind black man, so with—well, the blind black man. As with the indigent disabled Indian, so with the indigent disabled Indian. And is that Indian a man or a woman? And so on.

In my discussion of disability and poverty in chapter 2, I proposed replacing the now well-worn term *intersection* with Courvant's substitute, *confluence,* a more fluid term that also suggests that apparently different matters might be made of similar substances. In this section of the book, I have nonetheless retained the figure of the intersection. The street-corner metaphor, particularly apt for the situation of the unsightly beggar, sharply underscores the harm that can happen there. "[O]ne of the dangers of standing at an intersection," writes duCille, "is the likelihood of being run over" (593). It is important to note, however, that everyone at this corner is subject to the principle of intersectional identity, whether run over by it or in the driver's seat.

Let us start our exploration of these complexities and connections with one literal frame around the ugly ordinance, its textual surround. The ugly laws never stand alone in the police manuals. They always come packaged with others. Where they fall in the law books, under what general heading, preceded by which ordinance and followed by what section, tells us a great deal about how city cultures understood the meaning of making the unsightly beggar.

Columbus, Ohio, provides an illuminating example. In January, 1894, the Columbus City Council approved "An Ordinance—No. 1891," which established a large cluster of new misdemeanor offenses (*Annual Report of the City Clerk*). In the Columbus order of things, the "Unsightly Beggars" law (with a fine of up to twenty dollars and/or ten days in jail) is section 15 out of dozens of new sections enacted en masse on January 22. The sections that immediately precede it prohibit the commission of "lewd or lascivious behavior" or "indecent, immodest or filthy" acts on the public streets; "improper dress," including public nudity and wearing "a dress not belonging to his or her sex . . . in such a situation that persons passing might ordinarily see the same"; and "prostitution," including "any . . . lewd woman who . . . shall make any bold or meretricious display of herself." Then comes the ugly ordinance. The sections that immediately follow it prohibit "lewd books, picture[s] and other things" and "indecently exhibiting animals" mating.

This is not a random collection. Cities across the country, like Columbus, embedded the ugly law specifically within a matrix of codes concerning local purity: decency and exhibition, gender and sexuality.[11] The ordinances immediately prior to the ugly law in the *Chicago Code of 1911*, for instance, outlaw first the distribution of pamphlets "giving the nature and remedies of diseases peculiar to females, uterine diseases, . . . or means of prohibiting conception" and second "indecent exposure," including "wearing clothing of opposite sex." In Omaha, similarly, the law is preceded by an "indecent conduct" ordinance barring cross-dressing and prostitution and then followed by a ban on distributing lewd books. New Orleans's definition of a "rogue and vagabond" embedded its prohibition of "exposure of wounds or deformities" between strictures against exposing obscene prints to view and (by 1887) against lewd women.[12] These patterns of codification make clear that the ugly law was intrinsically tied to laws of sex and gender.

Disability-focused cultural memory of the law has tended to invoke a neutral, ungendered (or by default masculine) subject as the ordinance's target. The versions of the law that say "shall not . . . expose *himself* to public view" are cited, rather than the ones that spell out "himself or herself." The "tramp," whose ghost lurks behind ugly law, was almost exclusively discursively constructed as a male figure.[13] But the ordinance's force was inflicted on women as well as men, and its meaning was subject to gender-specific interpretation.

Unsightly defined itself differently for a woman than a man.[14] Cresswell has pointed out, for instance, that Reitman's writing on female as opposed to male tramps placed particularly strong emphasis not only on what Reitman called the women's "deformities, handicaps and injuries" but also on their "consciousness of lack of attraction and beauty," "extremes of leanness and stoutness, shortness and tallness," "extreme awkwardness—'Miss Gawky,'" "cross-eyes and eye-lesions," "excessive" or "slight growth of hair," "tiny and massive breast," and "natural appearance of being unkempt, tough and unpleasant." As Cresswell notes, Reitman made no equivalent aesthetic judgment of tramping men.[15]

Since proper femininity was understood as inherently averse to public display, a woman's disease or deformity exposed to public view was particularly transgressive (S. Ryan, 52). "A crippled woman is in a worse condition than a crippled man," ruled one judge in 1910. Not only did she lose "in the matter of physical attractiveness in respect of her chances of marriage"; her infirmity threatened her ability to support herself, because "the effect on her spirits and courage is more depressing, she feels the loss more than a man, and shrinks from the exhibition of her infirmity that is necessary to overcome its hindrances" (*Korzib v. Netherlands,* 175 F. 998 at 7). Here, the willingness of crippled men to brave being seen in public figured, interestingly, as a kind of manly hardiness, but the crippled woman who did not shrink from exhibiting herself could hardly be recognized as a woman.

Feminist disability studies has explored how gendered norms of appearance and attractiveness interconnect with health norms for similar regulatory ends. Rosemarie Garland Thomson's analysis of how body braces for scoliosis "discipline the body to conform to the dictates of both the gender and ability systems by enforcing standardized female form" is an outstanding example ("Integrating Disability," 81).[16] But these discussions do not cite the ugly law. Their focus lies primarily on women's private self-regulation of appearance through consumer practices, not on the more overtly punitive and public mechanisms like the unsightly beggar ordinances, which directed themselves with force against women whose impairments impeded or deflected the standards of the beauty system. And yet ugly law undoubtedly was one way of punishing women whose appearance violated aesthetic norms of femininity.

Not only beauty systems but pity systems were gendered. Although both begging and poverty were feminized, women and men performed mendicancy differently. Crippled mothers called up different associations and deployed different begging strategies than crippled soldiers did.[17] One genre of antimendicancy text devoted itself to defining the difference in begging tactics. For one writer in 1898, women "form an important feature of the begging fraternity" but, unlike the men, are "seldom picturesque"; women favor backdoor begging targeted at getting kitchen food from servants; the woman beggar does not fake disability because "[p]erhaps she does not need to. The general regard paid to her sex may bring her in a sufficient income without a waste of brain power"; and so on ("New York City Beggars").

Another writer in 1904, celebrating the COS-sponsored Mendicancy Bureau's expertise in "the tramp and beggar vocabulary," runs through a hierarchy of vagrants, with "Yegg *men*" (italics mine) at the top and women mentioned only at the very bottom:

> Lowest are the door-to-door beggars, "drifters" or "floaters," with the "blackhoods," the women who beg on the side streets and in front of the churches and are hard to dispose of.
>
> "Blackhood" is a name given the women beggars because they usually wear a black bonnet or hood. Everyone knows them, for they are to be found everywhere. . . .
>
> The women are most of them past middle age, wear shawls in addition to the black bonnet, and are comparatively respectable in appearance. Few people like to refuse them help because they are women and old.
>
> "But there is not one deserving among 'em," says Mr. Forbes. . . . "They . . . are hardest to handle, for they have nothing to lose." ("Ancient Profession")

It is difficult to tell, from this account, whether it was possible to be an unsightly blackhood. On the one hand, feminine blackhooding depended on "respectable appearance," an outward form obviously antithetical, in theory at least, to that of the disgusting and improper subject of ugly law. On the other hand, blackhooding depended on old age, on performing infirmity, a category that borders uneasily on the terrain of the "diseased" and the "disfigured" and the "deformed," perhaps particularly where women are concerned. In and of itself, femaleness, like age, could be deployed as a claim for alms: "few people like to refuse them because they are women and old." In the logic of ugly law, these claims made them doubly suspect. A name is needed—"blackhood"—when grandma is the wolf in sheep's clothing.

In a very different mode, one kind of disability con with its own evocative name seems to have been reserved for women (who are once again animalized, rendered as cows):

> The girl, or "cow," was playing the "high heel game" with a show of lameness. One of her shoes was built up, inside and out, like those used by sufferers from hip disease. This threw the girl's hip out of place. Her bent knee was hidden by her skirts. Struggling down a crowded street with this pitiful deformity (?) and with the aid of a crutch the money of the charitable came to her in a steady stream. . . . If the "cow" has an emaciated face and pathetic eyes she plays at being a young widow, penniless and tearful, or a nun, with all the robes and trimmings. . . . The "widow" and "nun" are not so profitable, however, as the "high-heel" game. ("Pest of Beggars"; the question mark is in the original text)

The "high-heel game" apparently required the wearing of a skirt, and hence it became a specifically feminine sham. The inside joke that the name conveys depends on its contrast to the conventional association of "high heel" with sex appeal and femme glamour. The assumption is that lame women may well be down-in-the-heels but that they cannot by any means be high-heeled—unless, that is, the shoes in question are orthopedic aids, not fashion accessories. Imposters like the notorious "Jenny Highheel" played complex games with these binary strictures; as pity sluts, they faked deformity until nightfall, when they kicked off (and up) their heels.[18]

If notions of female depravity exacerbated the disgustingness of the unsightly begging woman, notions of feminine impressionability could also mitigate her offense. A 1911 article in the *Los Angeles Times* devotes itself to the gothic tale encapsulated in its title: "Hypnotized into Madhouse: Beautiful Girl Converted into Cripple; Young Man Who Placed Her under a Lingering Spell Is Alleged to Have Employed Her as a Blind Beggar to Solicit Alms That He Took from Her." In this account, Edith Summers, "attractive" and "intellectual," a "society girl and daughter of one of Bellingham's best known families," ran away and married the wrong man, a hypnotist who mesmerized her into performing "the acts of a blind person" and later those of a "cripple" to collect alms from passersby: "she gained considerable amounts." Discovered by an Idaho physician, she came home but remained "under the hypnotic spell." Summers was brought before an examining board. "Edith told the physicians and the court the most pitiful tale ever heard in Washington's judicial circles," reported the newspaper. The court remanded her temporarily to an insane asylum, "but all the doctors agree that with care and treatment the once beautiful girl will recover." It was apparently inconceivable that a girl of such beauty and high social standing could be either a genuine unsightly beggar or a rank faker.[19]

A female unsightly beggar might also escape that category by becoming properly dependent, married to a good male guardian. A 1917 *Los Angeles Times* article featured the love story of a "chewing-gum man and paper lady." The "little crippled lady, . . . Mother Hastings," who sold newspapers, described to the reporter how Portland, Oregon, authorities had "said I was too terrible a sight for the children to see—they meant my crippled hands I guess—and said I would either have to get off the streets or go to the county farm. They gave me money to get out of town." After moving to Los Angeles, she met her future husband, who sold gum across the street from the corner where she sold magazines, when she "was left in the lurch by the man engaged to wheel her to and from her stand" and he "came to her rescue." Now, firmly inserted into a sentimental domestic narrative, her unsightliness disappears, replaced by a gaze of her own: "'Yes, I am married,' she said with a fond look at her husband. 'He takes such good care of me, too'" ("Love Blooms").[20]

Disabled men at the unsightly intersection faced a different but related set of problems, because they were presumed to need care, not to provide it in the manner of the proper breadwinner. The ugly law, which explicitly stripped its targets of humanity, turning them into "unsightly or disgusting objects," was justified nonetheless in COS rhetoric as a guarantee not only of subjectivity but specifically of masculinity. By 1902 in Columbus, as often happened in various cities, the ordinance was not being enforced. The Columbus COS mounted a campaign to revive it, pressuring the mayor to put teeth into "the law to rid the streets of beggars" in the following terms:

> Many of our citizens have for a long time been interested in the suppression of street begging, especially where crippled, maimed and blind parade their deformities in public to give emphasis to their appeal. To allow such people to be cared for *in a manner that impairs their manhood* is not in accord with the civilization of the period in which we are living. (*Associated Charities of Columbus*, 7; italics mine)

In the new period envisioned here, modernity equals unimpaired (and uncared-for) masculinity. Deformity is a parade, understood as the beggar's rhetorical device. Simultaneously cringing and flaunting, these beggars undermine manhood itself. The disabled male beggar's "to-be-looked-at-ness" apparently too closely resembled the condition of modern femininity: asking rather than taking; imploring people to feel for, with, about him, placing himself to be gazed at and in that sense possessed.[21] This appeal to save manhood from impairment must have been hard to resist. The Columbus mayor, Robert Jeffrey, readily agreed to the proposal.[22]

Disabled men on the street did their best to combat this formulation, as did Arthur Franklin Fuller, run out of Brooklyn by the ugly law, who defended himself as "'in condition, hard, strong—not effeminate or 'sloppy'" (1919, 39). Fuller sold poems on the street claiming his authority to teach manliness: "There are too many lazy-bones, / Leisure-loving, tired drones; / They oft plead sick, this shiftless clan— / Reject the call to be a man!" (1913)—unlike, presumably, the author. But strong assertions of maleness also placed the transient subjects of ugly law under suspicion. No matter how much he might "be a man," Fuller's was an interloper masculinity in Shah's terms, though Shah did not take disability into account in his own formulation; Shah describes how nineteenth-century liberal governance in the form of legal statutes tried to contain "normative American masculinity from the threats of other interloper masculinities, cast as foreign and degenerate" (2005, 704).

Unsightly begging and American manhood was almost a contradiction in terms, with one significant exception: in the figure of the war veteran, manhood and impairment coexisted in uneasy conjunction. The peak era of the ugly laws falls between two major wars (the Civil War and World War I). In the related matter of ordinances regarding the licensing of street musicians and peddlers (about which I have more to say later), a trail of case law records the ongoing controversy over the constitutionality of giving honorably discharged veterans—understood to be simultaneously both manly and disabled *as a class*—exemptions from peddling fees or from strictures against street selling. Many cities did make exceptions for male war veterans, not only of the Civil War but of a variety of conflicts. Northern states exempted Union vets; Southern states, Confederacy vets. Later, Berkeley, California, with one version of its trademark liberality, waived peddling fees for "any honorably discharged soldier, sailor or marine of the United States or Confederate States who has served in the Civil War, any Indian war, the Spanish-American war, the Philippine insurrection, the Chinese Relief Expedition or the World War who is physically unable to obtain a livelihood by manual labor" (Rhyne, Burton, and Murphy, 148).[23] Remember Alderman Peevey's qualm, at the moment of origin of Chicago's ugly law, about whether to "leave the question open so far as to allow a discretion in favor of a one-legged and a one-armed soldier, if the mayor desires to permit them to grind an organ."

Military service proved masculine citizenship, making it harder to justify and enforce ugly law proscriptions.[24] In the year of San Francisco's unsightly beggar ordinance, 1867, when almost four hundred "maimed" Union veterans submitted entries in left-handed penmanship competitions designed to prove that they were still fit "for lucrative and honorable positions," their work was displayed to the public under banners proclaiming, "We lost Our Right Hand for Our Rights, And 'tis the Left Hand now that Writes" and "Our Disabled Soldiers Have Kept the Union from Being Disabled." One entrant insisted in his essay that amputation had been "necessary, to constitute *me* a perfect man"; another defined his "veteran scars" as "richer ornaments than the purest gold." Not all the entries were this optimistic; one man wrote, "To be compelled . . . to consent to be a permanent cripple for life . . . is a matter of no small moment. We lose in a great measure our place in society" (Clarke, 389, 380, 386). But war injury offered at least a small measure of "place." It provided what Howard R. Heydon, in 1918, called "the glamour of narrative" to the disabled veteran, unless and until public war memory wore off (52).

As a result, a hierarchy of disabled street masculinity developed. Proven veterans, maimed soldiers and sailors, got the frayed red carpet in the form of free license to eke out subsistence in the street culture. Men whose impairments prevented or did not result from military service got treated like dirt.[25] At the same time, since the veteran's imprimatur could be faked, and since disease, maiming, and deformity were the tools of military malingerers as well as the badges of war heroes, men staging themselves as former soldiers on the street did not necessarily escape falling into the range of the disgusting and improper and being punished accordingly.[26]

As the treatment of the "veteran" illustrates, the consequences of the law for actual people on the streets could and did differ by gender. Arrest, or even simply the threat of the law, might lead, for example, to incarceration in a gender-segregated institution. In general, according to a government census study based on 1902 statistics, more poor men than poor women were sent to almshouses upon arrest for misdemeanors, *unless* the women "had some physical or mental defect." Women as a group could sometimes avoid the poorhouse, but disabled women were more likely than their male counterparts to end up there (Janice Brown, 38). Statistics on the Touro-Shakespeare almshouse in New Orleans show that women tended to remain there significantly longer than men (Janice Brown, 44). Women and men were often treated very differently at arrest; women arrested under the law, like all female "delinquents," were liable to strip searches and vaginal examinations (Rafter and Gibson). Laws against exposing deformity prohibited an available protective tool for homeless women, who might sometimes use deliberate eccentricity, anomaly, or unsightliness to ward off sexual harassment and assault (Merves).

What I mean, however, when I write that the ugly law was intrinsically connected to laws of gender is something broader still than these dynamics. Ugly law was part of an available arsenal of tools in the codes for controlling and punishing challenges to domestic ideology, to dominant and conventional gender roles, and to heteronormativity. It enforced and was reinforced by norms of gender and sexuality.

In ugly law, gender mattered—not just for those who broke it but for those who ordered and sustained it. Traditional structures of American gender were built into the deep surround of the unsightly begging ordinances. Take, for instance, the law's restriction of exposure to *public* view, with its implicit suggestion of some realm of *privacy* to which the diseased, maimed, deformed, and so forth are consigned.[27] Unsightly beggars occupied what Christine Stansell calls "a particular geography of sociability—the engagement of the poor in street life rather than the home," in itself taken to be evidence of "a pervasive urban pathology" (211).[28] Although some early ugly laws like Denver's openly reassigned their human targets to institutions such as the poorhouse, the primary zone of privacy and care in U.S. culture was indeed the home of the nuclear family, supported (at least in theory) by the work of an able male breadwinner and an able female caregiver. Without traditionally gendered marriage, maternity, and sisterly responsibility, the later ugly laws would have required far more explicit stipulations regarding what Denver indexed as "deformed persons, care of."[29] In the remarkable critique of ugly law written by a male unsightly beggar, Arthur Fuller, which I discuss at length in chapter 11, this dependence on traditional gender roles is made quite explicit and melodramatic: "The good woman . . . does what she can in order to be near her afflicted loved one." But "this heroic, loyal soul—this would-be rescuer" often dies young, Fuller writes, of overwork and "heavy lifting." At her funeral, her loyalty and heroism will be praised by "some of the members of the Charities":

> And the bigger the salary, the smoother the speech. In my humble opinion, it would have been better had the Charities done something to help the first party [that is, the disabled man], or helped him to help himself—or at least not "had the law on him" by refusing to allow him to sell on city streets. . . . When rich relations take a permanent drag on their hands to

prevent newspaper publicity, it would not make it very pleasant for the afflicted one. I have no rich relations. (*Fifty Thousand Miles,* 184–185)

Though many unsightly beggars were, in Martha Fineman's terms, "derivatively dependent"—that is, they begged at least in part in order to care for someone else, like the woman who played "Mollie Darling" with her two children—the law recognized them, insofar as they remained "unsightly beggars," only as inevitable dependents and as gender violators or manipulators.[30] Alongside them and apart from them, the law's "relations" or "helpers" assumed gendered positions of "care" (father-provider or angel-in-the-house).

In practice, unsightly begging ordinances gendered everyone, not only beggars but policers and passersby. Taking a hard-line stand against fraud and pauperism proved city officials' own masculinity. If they wavered, one COS leader warned, the United States would join "all nations which have prematurely passed away" because of weakness toward "parasites," "buried in graves dug by their own effeminacy" (C.R. Lowell, 138). Under ugly law there were for women two kinds of female forms, only one of which was the wretched beggar.[31] The other was the sheltered nondisabled lady viewer (or rather unviewer, the one who should not and does not desire to view). In 1896, New York City police chief Peter Conlin justified the escalation of arrest of disabled mendicants in these terms: "There are a number of beggars who really are afflicted and deformed, and who thrust their deformities forward to the public gaze, much to the disgust of ladies" (Norden, 16). For both men and women who passed by the unsightly beggar, the encounter was charged by gender and reinforced gender's terms.

The "lady viewer" and the "viewed beggar" are, of course, too neat a pair, too binary an opposition. As my polemical use of "lady" suggests, class figures in here, and most women were neither ladies nor beggars. Often there were third (or fourth or fifth) terms in the equation, as when, for instance, antibegging diatribes by the COS in New York in the late 1890s focused on the problem of women servants in the finest households indiscriminately giving out back-door alms to women beggars even as their employers ran antimendicancy campaigns out of the parlors ("New York City Beggars," 12). (Or when, in the arena of masculinity, similar texts point out that the printed cards used by beggars had union labels on them, "likely to appeal to the working man.")[32] A 1905 article on the begging habits of devious "throw-outs" with "wonderful skill in simulating deformities" focused on their harassment of women "in sweatshops . . . and at the gates of factories on paydays. . . . Their easiest prey was the working girl," not the "lady" ("No Sinecure"). That working girl occupies neither side of the lady/wretch divide. But the lady/wretch binary may help us focus, for a moment, on the position of the "diseased, maimed, deformed" woman and also of the viewer she was thought most to imperil under the regime of the ugly laws.

Mary Ryan records an earlier version of the lady/wretch encounter in her discussion of "the cartography of gender":

> Although both men and women were alerted to the dangers of the city streets, they were warned of different species of threats. By most accounts, women were exposed less to bodily harm and more to a violation of their delicate sensitivities. Perhaps the most extreme expression of this sensitivity was recorded in San Francisco in 1855 when an organ grinder was arrested and fined the hefty sum of $50 "for affrighting the women and children of Henry Street into 'conniption fits' by exhibiting a monster in the shape of a deformed Indian. The sight was truly disgusting." The regulation of begging on the street was also construed as a mode of protecting sensitive females. When a beggar displayed a decrepit arm, by way of demonstrating to passers-by that he was incapable of manual labor, the *Alta California* commented that "it may be imagined how shocked ladies have been encountering these wretches in their promenades for healthy exercise." (69)[33]

Note how firmly these "shocked ladies" are placed on an ability/disability axis; it is their striving for fitness, their mobile promenade, that is most threatened by "encountering these wretches." (So much so that an encounter with "decrepitude" impairs them, producing seizures, hysteria, "conniption.") All concerned were policed by such arrests, which reinforced the model of an infantilized feminine delicacy that made all women's access to the streets contingent and provisional.[34]

Mothers, in particular, were protected and policed by the unsightly begging laws. One proponent of the ordinance argued that for "women in a delicate condition" to pass by crippled beggars "must be offensive and in some cases harmful" (Ringenbach, 54).[35] Here we can glimpse ugly law as a kind of superstitious "evil eye event" in Siebers's terms, a dynamic in which "accusation exaggerates" physical and mental differences "until they take on a supernatural dimension"; frequently evil eye fears clustered around pregnant women (*Mirror*, 27). The belief in "maternal impression" or mother's marks, the idea that what pregnant women saw would stamp and shape their children, inhered despite scientific evidence to the contrary throughout the nineteenth century in American culture.[36] According to Bondeson, more than 170 articles on maternal impression appeared in U.S. scientific journals between 1839 and 1920 (158).

Consider, for instance, the texts produced on this subject by a particularly impressionable Chicago doctor, Frank A. Stahl. In 1890, Stahl testified in *Cosmos* about a baby born without a skull as the result of her mother's witnessing a Chicago streetcar accident in which a child's head was crushed. Six years later, he elaborated on the story in the *American Journal of Obstetrics and Diseases of Women and Children*. Disability is everywhere in Stahl's treatise, not just in its explicitly imagined city streets, where the sight of injured people injures the child of the susceptible mother, but deeply woven into its rhetorical fabric. Stahl's proof of the ordinary mother's normal(ized) impressionability depends rhetorically on comparison with two "insensible" pregnant women: a "blind and deaf" mother and an "idiot" mother:

> Let us suppose a case, one that occurs very often. A woman, pregnant, narrowly escapes a runaway; she is seized by fear, trembling, a faintness. When the doctor arrives he announces an abortion. . . . Let us again suppose that our woman was blind and deaf. What must be the conclusion?—namely, that she would have remained in total ignorance of the runaway and that she would not have had an abortion. This—and it is not presuming too much—favorable condition was maintained then. Why? Because . . . no rays of intelligence, no impressions were transmitted to her sensibilities, piercing the darkness of her intellect, consequently there was no emotion, no activity, nothing but passiveness and uninterrupted gestation. ("Maternal Impressions," 512)

Some possible policy implications of this statement (encouraging more pregnancies by deaf and blind women? blindfolding and earplugging pregnant women?) are not of course pursued by Stahl, who values "passiveness and uninterrupted gestation" without the coincidence of impairment, whether fetal or maternal.[37] The hypothetical blind and deaf mother flickers briefly in the text as a surprising kind of public health model, then disappears, reabsorbed into the generalized mass of city sights potentially disturbing to (all too) sighted and hearing mothers.[38] In her place, the hypothetical "idiot mother" comes forth to clinch the case for feminine impressionability. Stahl cites Sequin's "Idiocy and Its Treatment" (1886) to make the case that "while the mother is in a mental state of idiocy,

'Impressions will sometimes reach the fetus in its recess, cut off its arms and legs, or inflict large flesh wounds before birth—from which we surmise that idiocy holds unknown though certain relations to maternal impressions'" ("Maternal Impressions," 514). Here the implication seems to be not only that "idiot" mothers are mysteriously (especially?) impressionable but that *all* pregnant mothers bear the idiot's risk, vulnerable to influences beyond conscious control. In "The Maternal Impression in Twin Pregnancy," Stahl went on to "prove" this theory by way of an explanation of Harry Stillwell Edwards's strange novel *Sons and Fathers.*

Despite attempts to debunk Stahl's arguments by scientists like Dr. Marcus P. Hatfield in the *Transactions of the Illinois Medical Society* (1894), both folk and professional belief in the susceptibility of pregnant women to sights of deformity continued unabated throughout the period of ugly law enactment.[39] Even an article attempting to put the notion to rest like J.M. Fort's piece in the Chicago edition of the *Journal of the American Medical Association* in 1889 reinforced the knotted web of femininity, impressionability, and deformity where the pregnant woman was concerned:

> I admit that in a large majority of instances of pregnancy, especially in women of nervous temperament, the mental faculties act in an exaggerated sphere. . . . The brain does not always give forth a white light, but by perversion the thoughts are made prismatic. They indulge in, or give way to morbid sentiments, and irritable moods, which seem to transform or revolutionize their entire character. . . . Not infrequently the mind is distorted or, as it were, deformed by morbid apprehensions. . . . This abnormal mental condition . . . often gives rise to functional disorders of the senses. . . . Now, engraft upon such a mental condition, if you will, the belief or opinion that deformity or abnormality to her offspring may result from impressions. . . . it behooves us as medical men, it behooves husbands, fathers and brothers, it behooves mothers, sisters and friends of the pregnant woman to caution, admonish and to guard her faithfully against every contingency which would even in the remotest degree be calculated to bring about or result in such a calamity. (542)

For Fort, the pregnant woman, already deformed by her morbid apprehensions, might be doubly deformed (and dangerously "revolutionized"?) by seeing the unsightly. The popular notion of maternal impression was called on, even by its detractors, to justify the segregation and control of both poor disabled women "wretches" and their opposites, "ladies" understood as vulnerable and enfeebled by pregnancy and femininity, (potentially) expectant mothers, deserving shelter, who might otherwise dangerously, inadvertently glimpse deformity.

The doctrine of maternal impression both supported and was undergirded by an intensively medicalized model of pregnancy and more generally of female trouble. In 1902, when a group of New York doctors from the Academy of Medicine organized to call for ugly law, the person they rallied to defend from pestering beggars "who insist . . . on exposing to her gaze a horribly distorted limb" or other "distressing sight" was not just a "nervous and delicate woman." She was someone already under a doctor's care by definition: "the feeling aroused in *the patient* is one of fear and disgust rather than of pity. The result . . . is mental shock and often an ineffaceable impression that does incalculable mischief" (Spacks, 33; italics mine). The presence of unsightly beggars turned all women into doctors' patients.

It is important, however, not to overestimate the persuasive force of doctrines of maternal influence in the niche of ugly law. Ideologies and practices that relegated women to the shelter of the private sphere were not uniformly promulgated or generally enforced. American Victorian separate-sphere ideology, "the rough scaffolding that shaped gender ideals," as Catherine Kudlick puts it, was by no means identical to the messy practice of fin-de-siècle gendered life (2001, 191). In the 1890s, when the majority of U.S. ugly ordinances were passed, white American women entered universities and white-collar jobs in record numbers, sparking and taking part in debates about their health and comfort as they moved more freely in the public arena. In 1895, an article entitled "What Would Happen If Paris Was Under a Government Founded on Love of Beauty" imagined a utopian city in which a government "inimical to ugliness" bans "criminally hideous things" and failures to sufficiently conceal "deformity"; the "execrable assault . . . against aesthetics" under attack here consisted not of unsightly begging but of women bicycling.

During the broad period of ugly law spanning from the late 1860s (but particularly from the 1880s on) through the Progressive era, the notion of maternal impression was hotly debated by U.S. doctors, and the eventual inclusion of female researchers such as Belle Gurney and Jennie Gray in these very discussions (both published on the topic in medical journals, in 1907 and 1911, respectively) itself proves that fears of impressed mothers' birthing monster babies hardly kept women out of the public sphere. Women themselves invoked the doctrine of maternal impression for their own ends; Dr. Belle Gurney's contribution to the medical debates, for instance, culminated in the argument that the sexual repression of women led to an "abnormal sexual appetite in the unborn" and that pregnant women should be permitted a free range of sexual activity: "Have we not always heard of the unsatisfied infant due to some ungratified desire of the mother? If these laws could be understood and practiced, many diseases could be eradicated."[40]

In practice, in fact, the ugly laws of the late nineteenth and early twentieth centuries opened the public sphere to privileged women as much as they cordoned it off. Although no woman I know of played a major role in brokering the passage of ugly ordinances in the various cities, women involved with COS and other volunteer activities—working to eradicate begging, carrying out friendly visits, advocating for municipal housekeeping, proselytizing in the evangelist missions, and so on—took to the streets and public places of the city as their causeways just as they took them up as their causes.[41] As Parsons, Elizabeth Wilson, and Heron have argued, during this period newly roving and visible women, bicyclists and shoppers and office workers, appeared on the urban scene, and something like the possibility of a *flâneuse*, the feminine equivalent of Baudelaire's strolling urban observer, may have emerged for the white female figure.[42] COS women reframed their own urban motility, proceeding through the city as purposive investigators, participants, reformers. By 1915, a disgruntled male observer defined charity organization as "an army of busy bodies, mostly women," who were "becoming more and more involved in a mess of inspection, supervision, chaperonage, espionage and surveillance" at the expense of the children they neglected at home—if they had children (Armstrong).

Ugly crowds who got in the way of police arrests also seem to have been composed of a high percentage of women, or so male-authored defenses of antimendicancy campaigns imply. A 1902 account of beggars who deployed "hideous deformities" in the streets of New York concluded, "If sympathetic women will refrain from rushing to the police station to raise complaint against an officer every time a beggar is arrested" and "if the same class of people will refrain from paying the fines and appealing to the magistrates, . . . the evil can be entirely suppressed" (Spacks, 33). At moments like this, the menace policed by ugly law seems to be as much unbridled female sympathy and women's meddling as the sight of the street cripple.[43]

Let us turn now from the law's relation to gender norms and focus on its relation to sex and gender violations. The shadow double of the mobile female reformer (whether she promoted or protested the arrest of beggars) is the streetwalker, who loiters near the province of the ugly law in the city codes of Columbus and other cities, her "bold and meretricious display of herself" reconfigured in the ugly ordinance's prohibition against "expos[ing] him or herself to public view." Streetwalkers raised "the possibility that poor women might use their bodies unconventionally," writes Nicole Hahn Rafter, and they thereby "threatened the biological understanding of gender as fixed and immutable" (248); as much as unsightly beggars, they were an intensive focus of increasingly eugenics-centered COS campaigns.[44]

This argument is suggestive in regard to the ugly ordinances; it may provide one key to why these laws are indexed in the zone of gender and sexual transgression. Unsightly begging, like prostitution, involved poor people "using the body unconventionally," not only displaying what was properly hidden but commodifying it, getting paid. "[L]ike sex," writes Petra Kuppers, "disabled bodies are disavowed, shut away from the mainstream, locked into bedrooms"—and her footnote goes directly to the mythic terrain of our ordinance: "Often literally: up until the 1970s, the 'ugly laws' were in force in certain parts of the US, decreeing that people with 'unsightly' difference were banned from public places" (2003, 44, 145). Quite literally locked into bedrooms, that is, but also in another sense: disability *is* the realm of the forbidden "quite literal," as "sex" is. Nothing necessarily marked this form of transgression by gender, but it may be that cities came down particularly hard on women "exhibiting deformity" (as Lincoln, Nebraska, titled the offense it banned with ugly law), just as "dangerous" women bore the brunt of bans on streetwalking and later the brunt of forced sterilization.

As Amy Dru Stanley has argued, the prostitute "stood as the beggar's legal counterpart, outside the world of legitimate contracts."

> There were the same images of clamoring poverty, over clever streetfolk and gullible victims. There was the same vocabulary objecting to "tramps on the sidewalk, who annoy the passersby." There was the same anxiety about mistaken identity. . . . There was the same mistrust of bodily appearances, the sense that prostitutes hid their physical deformities while beggars falsely advertised theirs.

Stanley goes on to make a distinction between the two: "Coupling beggars and nightwalkers as the most debased members of the underworld, the street scenes depicted both as carriers of disease. Yet they represented the beggar's contagion as purely moral, the streetwalker's as both physical and moral, emanating from a body corrupted by degenerate sexuality" (1998, xiii). In the municipal codebooks of this period, ordinances against begging as such did not usually lie right next to ordinances against streetwalking, but ordinances against *unsightly* begging invariably did; the close consort of the unsightly beggar and the night walker suggests that, like the prostitute's, the "diseased, maimed, and deformed" beggar's imagined contagion combined moral and physical threat.

Prostitution and promiscuity come directly under ugly jurisdiction when the law's first term—"no person who is *diseased*"— is understood as common code for people (women, poor women, women of color, lesbians, and also male "sex perverts" and newsboys and tramps generally) infected with gonorrhea and syphilis.[45] Official city rhetoric often made direct linkages between sexual transgression, ill health, and appearance that disgusted: health campaigns located the origin of the "diseased" and the deformed in the bodies of tainted women, in the practice of masturbation, and in homosexuality. "Diseased" and sexual deviance went hand in hand.

The coincidence of unsightly begging and sexual deviance occurs not only in city codebooks but also in COS records; see, for instance, the strange archives of New York's COS "special agent" James Forbes, who pursued mendicancy, disability, and lesbian sexuality in equal and obsessive measure, as Rebekah Edwards's work on the matter vividly details. In tourist "slumming" guidebooks and reformist tracts, too, the tracks of disability and queerness are often inseparable.[46] Sociologist I.L. Nascher's 1909 *Wretches of Povertyville*, for instance, ends its catalogue of degradation with the following remarks: "There is still one class of wretches, male and female," writes Nascher—his "still" suggesting that what follows will be his final example—"we hardly dare mention lest we tread upon forbidden ground."

> This class is composed of those whose propensities, viler than animal since they have no counterparts in the animal kingdom, place them outside of any human category. They call themselves "faeries." Such a wretch, born of human parents, in the semblance of man gives himself a female appellative, imitates woman's voice and ways, and as far as he dares wears woman's attire. . . . This effeminate creature is in love with an equally despicable wretch of his own sex.
>
> There are women of the same class, masculine women who imitate the opposite sex as much as possible. . . . They assume a gruff voice, and in

> time lose their natural tone of voice, associate with the "faeries" and in their social intercourse with the latter take the part of a man in his relations to a woman.
>
> They patronize resorts like the Palm . . . and there give exhibitions of their bestial practices. (109–110)

Then, with no transition whatsoever, *Wretches* segues into a discussion of "professional begging," with emphasis on the "crippled beggar," real and fake, leaving it ambiguous whether he or she also belongs to the class one hardly dares to mention. Apparently the mapper of Povertyville felt no need to differentiate clearly between faerie exhibitors of bestial practice and unsightly exhibitors of disease, maiming, and deformity.

Being arrested under ugly law for exposing oneself to public view (by the 1950s, the heading of the Columbus ordinance became "Exposing self when unsightly, etc.") recalls, in part, the association of nakedness with need, with being at the mercy of the elements, as in "She died of exposure."[47] It also recalls, of course, another mode of deviance—the kind that is commonly meant in the line "He was arrested for exposing himself." Behind the exposed disabled beggar stand hints of other exposers, "savages" (as in the history of clothing laws enforcing the cover-up of "half-naked" Indians or insufficiently clothed slaves) and "perverts": the male masturbator (with his strong links to that disability category the "feebleminded" menace), the female stripper, the exhibitionist.[48] This last category in particular was commonly associated with impairment in the late nineteenth and early twentieth centuries. In French doctor Thoinot's treatise on *Medicolegal Aspects of Moral Offenses*, translated for an American audience by American M.D. Arthur Weysse in 1913, the chapter on "this morbid type" broke it down into subcategories. "Exhibitionists are met with," Thoinot reported, among "idiots and imbeciles" and also in that odd grouping then called the "general paralytic" and among "cases of senile dementia," "alcoholics," "degenerates," and "epileptics." Indeed, Thoinot maintained, the sole symptom of a certain form of epilepsy was a tendency toward acts of "immodest exhibition" (351–352, 357).

The unsightly beggars and indecent exposers identified by law shared a modus operandi: uncovering the body and displaying its forbidden part(s) for antisocial ends. It makes a kind of sense, then, to follow the one law with the other. City ordinances prohibiting "indecent exposure of the person" are interestingly vague about what this "person" is, this one or thing that should not have been shown. "Person" often seems to mean the entire offender, the self who acts indecently, but it has also been narrowly construed as a euphemism for penis and, somewhat more broadly, as "the exhibition of those parts of the body which instinctive modesty, human decency, or natural self-respect require to be kept covered in the presence of others" (Yaworsky). These parts in any city's cultural repertoire could theoretically have included an amputee's stump or a sick person's sores, the parts covered (literally as well as figuratively) by ugly law, but in practice they were not parts of the "person" indecently exposed. Indecency glanced at pleasure; unsightliness, at pain. Indecency carried a hint of power; unsightliness was powerlessness. Conversely, even if someone harassed on the street by a man exposing his "person" might have considered him diseased, deformed, and disgusting, in the law's eye the penis could be indecent but never unsightly. Penises did not come under ugly law's jurisdiction. The two laws neared each other but did not merge.

The same was true with breasts, though at moments they seem to come closer to direct inclusion in the unsightly target range. In a 1886 news feature for Boston readers on the "peculiar methods" of "The Beggars of New York," right next to "harmonium player of Fourteenth Street" with his sign "I am Blind, Palsied and Cannot Move My Legs," appears the woman who "displays her breast on the most frequented streets up town," practicing a "system of wayside nursing . . . so that the child may imbibe the nutriment while the parent grows fat upon compassion" (6). Writer Mike Ervin's historical instincts were exactly right when he titled his recent political satire on the ugly laws after the *Guinness Book of World Records*: "Our Top Story: 3700 Women Breastfeed at Once." Commenting on this new form of twenty-first-century street theater, Ervin writes,

> Women who have participated in these events most often say they're drawing attention to the health benefits of breastfeeding. But it's also been done as a political protest against those who are freaked about public breastfeeding. . . . Sometimes societies get so uptight about ideas of unsightliness that it's damn near impossible for certain of their members not to be subversive. Even a mother feeding a baby is somehow perceived as a threat to the foundations of civility. This all reminds me of the latter part of the 19th Century when city governments passed laws trying to keep us unsightly disabled folk off the streets.

The point is that disabled bodies on the street are simply behaving naturally, that they have an organic right to be there, and to be.

But the woman begging by exposing her breast also bears a strong resemblance to the more deliberately subversive and artificial "lewd woman who . . . shall make any bold or meretricious display of herself" prohibited from appearing in public in the Columbus city code book immediately before the ugly law (and followed, in turn, by the next subject of prohibition, "lewd books"). That is, when exposed breasts are lumped together with exposed blindness, palsy, and paralysis, the unsightly beggar ordinances may be understood as prohibitions on the sort of displays of (un)natural bodily functions commonly called "porn"—on a kind of pornography of disability. In this sense, views of the breast, the paralyzed arm, the amputated leg, and so on are all contested commodities, in Margaret Jane Radin's well-known sense of that term, glimpses of body parts uneasily commodified on the underground market instead of being held inviolate and private. This possibility, this scandal of commodification, begged for the regulation of the ugly law, despite attempts by parties on both sides of the exchange to configure the scene as entirely outside the market—kind donors meeting grateful pleaders, not buyers and sellers.

The curious fact that in the city codes ugly law usually goes hand in hand with strictures not only against indecent exposure and lewd books but also against cross-dressing reinforces the association between divulged deformity and sexual or gender transgression.[49] As Clare Sears has demonstrated, cross-dressing law resembled ugly law (as well as racial segregation laws, which I address later) in one key way: it was fundamentally "a technique of spatial regulation" (1) focused on defining a site, a public sphere, where the cross-dresser, like the unsightly beggar, could not appear. Such laws "produced a public/private divide" (x), Sears argues, through which "practices" like cross-dressing or displaying disease would be managed.

"[C]ross-dressing law marked the launch of a new municipal regulatory trend," Sears writes, focused "on the public visibility of problem bodies" (112). Ugly law followed suit; in San Francisco it emerged two years after the city's first anti-cross-dressing ordinance. Sears's work on city law and the cross-dresser shows how the ugly laws are part of a "dense legal matrix that dictated the kinds of bodies that could move freely through city space—and the types of bodies that could not" (135). All the strategies that Sears says cities used to contend with what she calls "problem bodies"—removal, exclusion, confinement, concealment, distribution, modification, and transparency—were applied to disabled bodies, but the rule of "transparency" may be particularly pertinent as we think about the tight links between cross-dressing and unsightly begging. As I discussed in the preceding chapter, unsightly beggars were presumed fakers. People thought to assume wounds or scars or crutches just as a man, say, might assume a woman's guise violated the principle that bodies should be guileless, self-representative, readily legible.

When Lawrence Jackson, in the Chicago summer of the ugly law in 1881, was fined one hundred dollars and sent to jail for cross-dressing in a "black alpaca dress which . . . fitted him nicely," he was described in one newspaper as "the negro who was caught promenading on Clark street in female attire" (*Chicago Inter-Ocean,* July 18, 1881). Another local daily put it more dramatically: "Lawrence Jackson, the brazen-faced darky" (*Chicago Daily News,* July 16, 1881). Neither of these papers, both of which covered the city council meetings in some detail, mentions the passing of our ordinance; neither records an instance of arrest under the ugly ordinance in their regular selective coverage of "Chicago criminalities" in the months immediately following the law's enactment. For whatever reason—opposition to the rival *Tribune,* which had trumpeted Alderman Peevey's law, or class interest—unsightly beggars, unlike fascinating cross-dressers, were under the radar for the *Inter-Ocean* and the *Daily News.* But all the papers dwelt in detail on Jackson.

Lawrence Jackson had nothing to do with ugly law. He has more in common with his later 1930s black Chicago drag-queen counterparts than with the woman who played "Mollie Darling."[50] (In Jackson's case, racism multiplied the pleasures of disgust for the newspaper's intended readers; Jackson's was specifically the brazen-face of a "darky." In chapter 8, I return to the blackening of brazenness when black unsightly beggars encountered white policing.) But Jackson and that woman have some things in common. Both were expelled from the Chicago public sphere. Like Jackson, the subject of ugly law was also constructed as "brazen-faced," not only exposed to public view but purposively, transgressively, exposing.

Indeed, the ugly law's emphasis on exposure (don't show, don't peep) can be understood, borrowing from the register of gay discourse, as a ban on *flaming* disability. The ordinance places disease and deformity in the region of those *fl* words laden with queer and more generally sexual associations: *flouting, flaunting, flagrant.* Setting it in this context helps us understand something critical about the unsightly beggar. The crime here was, in Kenji Yoshino's influential terminology, a failure to *cover.* Maybe persons diseased, maimed, and deformed could not pass (like "passersby"), but at the very least they were obliged to avoid obtrusiveness, just as gays and lesbians today are urged not to "flaunt." In the matrix of ugly law, a woman with an amputated leg would be allowed on the public street—if the stump, ideally, was hidden or at any rate if she minimized any problems associated with it.[51] Unsightly beggars broke that rule; deliberately making impairment and poverty loom large, they *un*covered.

The city regulation books where ugly laws are codified hint at forces of attraction to, not just repulsion at, uncovered unsightliness. The ugly law's specific emphasis on the public threat, the immodesty, of the disabled body exposed to strangers places it squarely in the category of the American laws suppressing bodily display that Alan Hyde has analyzed, such as bans on exposure of women's breasts, nude sunbathing, the striptease, and so on. If this grouping seems counterintuitive, it is perhaps because we have been so well trained to think of "deformity" in contradistinction to "desire" (131–150). Unconsciously, it seems, Columbus and other cities that placed ugly laws next to laws concerning gender and sexual transgression knew differently. "Differentiation . . . is dependent upon disgust. . . . But disgust always bears the imprint of desire," as Peter Stallybrass and Allon White put it. The faint imprint in the law books is in where the ordinance is placed.

7

IMMIGRATION, ETHNICITY, AND THE UGLY LAW

Manifest deformity posed a supposed threat not only to notions of gender and conventional sexuality but also to notions of American national integrity. Massive immigration in the late nineteenth and early twentieth centuries meant an upsurge in the ranks of people who, as Welke puts it, "had nowhere to turn when they found themselves disabled" (74).[1] A tensely conjoined mixture of ableism, biologized racism, and nativism emerged in American culture, an equation of the unsightly with the alien and the alien with the beggar. New systems of screening for the diseased, maimed, deformed, and mendicant developed at U.S. borders. In 1881, for instance, New York State passed a law requiring "a vigilant inspection" of steamships arriving from abroad "to prevent the landing of mendicants, cripples, criminals, idiots, &c" ("Tax on Immigration," 4). Although ugly laws tend to be remembered as local (as, say, a Chicago problem) or universal (as an example of centuries of disability oppression), their operations were neither that small nor that large. They took place within a broad but historically specific national crisis concerning the effects of immigration and the need for exclusive "anticipatory classification" of undesirables (Snyder and Mitchell, CLD, 41).

The record of twentieth-century appeals to the U.S. Supreme Court contains multiple cases in which key language like the chain of adjectives in ugly law appears. *Zartarian v. Billings* (1907) rules on "persons afflicted with a loathsome or a dangerous contagious disease" (5). A 1924 case affirms a 1917 legal definition of excluded classes that sounds like a lineup in the unsightly beggars' docket: "idiots, imbeciles, feeble-minded persons, paupers, professional beggars, diseased persons, criminals, polygamists, anarchists, prostitutes" (*Commissioner of Immigration,* 265 U.S. at 528). Both cases, unsurprisingly, concern immigration into the United States. The panic over immigration provided an easy—a too-easy—explanation for the existence of the unsightly beggar. Beggars were "visible signs," writes Kenneth Kusmer, "of the breakdown of local control that accompanied the rise of urban industrial society in the nineteenth century. Those who responded most antagonistically . . . sought scapegoats, the most convenient of whom were the waves of immigrants pouring into this country" (2002, 8).

Rhetorics of the domestic and its opposite often linked encountering the ugly with encountering the alien. When Frank Stahl, the "maternal impression" theorist, described the incident in which a mother's witness of a streetcar accident purportedly affected her unborn child, it is not coincidental that he employed the discourse of the foreign: "at the time of experiencing the shock two things were especially uppermost in the woman's mind: 1. The crushed head of the foreign child. 2. Her own developing child" ("Maternal Impressions," 509). Perhaps the child killed by Stahl's legendary streetcar is an immigrant child. Perhaps he is simply "foreign" because he is not the mother's own. Either way, his status as a stranger is underscored. In a similar vein, Stephen Crane's fictional account in 1899 of a rural infant, born with no arms, who becomes fodder for sensationalist journalism imagines the baby's "semi-human" mother as speaking "in a foreigner's dialect" (*Active Service*, 123).

So, too, when members of the Academy of Medicine organized in 1902 to push for enactment of an ugly law in New York City, invoking the example of "a nervous and delicate woman" pestered by a beggar exposing the "ineffable impression" of a "horribly distorted limb," their plea on her behalf was not directed at just any old unsightly beggar. For these doctors, unsightliness was a foreigner's dialect, an Old World disorder. "Until 1901 the beggars of Greater New York seemed to be content with ordinary methods," wrote Clifton Spacks, a reporter covering the physicians' campaign. But "since the news of the richness of the field spread to foreign shores," new methods of begging were showing up in town:

> Twisted and misshapen limbs, hands and features are made the most of from a spectacular point, just as has been done for ages in Italy and Spain and parts of France. The man with the wooden leg, or with no arms, is now superceded by hideous creatures who are apparently bereft of nearly every particle of likeness to humanity. (33)

This "business of exciting pity by prominently displaying," Spacks claimed, was a "fashion" abroad. No matter that for decades chroniclers of New York's gaslight and shadows had been recording the sensational unsightlinesses of the city's homegrown beggars. The doctors prescribed ugly law for an un-American ill, a newly imported kind of begging, the "carefully managed display of hideous deformities or loathsome sores" that Spacks defined as "the European 'exposure' method."

Spacks's audience of New Yorkers at the turn of the century, whipped up by the speeches of Assistant Commissioner of Immigration Edward F. Feeney, had been recently scandalized by rumors of Ellis Island bribes paid to secure the admission of European "cripples and people with disgusting faces and diseases" who planned to "trade on the sympathies of women" in Manhattan shopping districts ("Undesirable Immigrants"). But the problem of hideous, inhuman creatures pouring through the gates of Ellis Island was not simply a concern for shopkeepers worried about the appearance of Park Avenue. It was a national problem; it bore on the basic composition of the nation.

The first epithet in every known version of the unsightly begging ordinance except for Denver's, "diseased," suggests an immediate link between the work of the ugly laws and an operation of federal immigration law emerging at the same time, mass exclusion in the name of the health of the public body.[2] (Denver's case is of interest; a famed site of rest cure for people with tuberculosis, many of whom comprised the town's elite, the city shied away from sick-baiting.) "The usual script for plague," Sontag has famously written in the context of thinking about AIDS, is that "the disease invariably comes from somewhere else" (135).[3] Immigration screeners tried to spot prospective unsightly beggars, among others, in order to protect the body politic, "the 'general public' so familiar to us from contemporary discussions of AIDS," as Alan Hyde puts it, which "purifies itself by identifying, specularizing, and abjecting the foreign, polluting Other" (250).

The peak years of the unsightly begging ordinance occurred at the same time as intensifying measures for exclusion of undesirable immigrants. In the western states, the rise of ugly laws coincided with anti-Chinese agitation. In 1872, five years after San Francisco passed its ugly law, California legislators passed a law placing restrictions on the entrance of any immigrant "lunatic, idiot, deaf, blind, cripple or infirm person" who was not a member of an already resident family; the law was targeted against disabled Chinese people.[4] In 1882, only a few months after Chicago passed its unsightly beggar ordinance, the U.S. Congress acted in quick succession first to ban Chinese immigration and then to ban the entrance of "paupers" and "the insane" into the country. By 1891, federal immigration law required medical officers to certify (and generally to exclude) all immigrants who had a "*loathsome* or dangerous contagious disease" (italics mine), and in the realm of the loathsome (defined, in circular fashion, as "a disease which excites abhorrence in others") immigration law meets the unsightly ordinances' "disgusting object" (Fairchild, 14, 24).[5] At Angel or Ellis Island, any immigrant body might be understood as inevitably diseased, infectious, and loathsome, a danger to the entire nation. Visibly disabled immigrants, if they made it past the borders at all, posed a particular threat. Douglas Baynton's important work on the systematic exclusion of disabled people at the point of entrance to the United States demonstrates that American immigration law *was*—in policy and practice—ugly law writ large.[6]

At the same time, other laws including ugly ordinances functioned in part as federal immigration policy writ small. Just as, in Baynton's words, the idea of disability was "instrumental in crafting the image of the undesirable immigrant," so, too, the idea of uncontrolled immigration was instrumental in crafting the image of the unsightly beggar ("Defectives," 45). When national border policing failed, officials called for backup local measures. States set up roadblocks and checkpoints to enact their own versions of medicalized nativism.[7] In 1907, Alabama, for instance, passed laws prohibiting entrance into the state "of persons of an anarchistic tendency, of paupers, of persons suffering from contagious or communicative diseases, of cripples without means and unable to perform mental or physical service, of idiots, lunatics, persons of bad character, or of any persons who are likely to become a charge upon the charity of the State, and all such as will not make good and law-abiding citizens."[8] But a great deal of the policing of persons originally from abroad who were "likely to become a charge upon charity" took place at the municipal level, through the ugly law and by other means.

Prosecutors and judges in local courts attempted to do their best to stifle not just begging by individual unsightly immigrants but also, more broadly, unsightly immigration. In 1879, for example, a judge in New York sentenced Francesco Nuzzo to six months in jail as part of the city's crackdown on the *padrone* system, in which children were taken from Italy as indentured servants to assist Italian street musicians. (This kind of trafficking persists into the present, as in the case in New York City in 1998 in which dozens of Deaf Mexicans were virtually enslaved as part of a begging ring.)[9] Nuzzo had brought over thirteen-year-old Saverio Felliti to beg for him. Saverio had "a badly deformed foot and walked with the aid of a crutch," according to records kept by New York's Society for the Prevention of Cruelty to Children; he was, therefore, the Society argued, "a good card among imported monstrosities, . . . a perfect bonanza in the begging trade." The judge who sentenced Nuzzo framed his offenses not so much in the rhetoric of child-saving or antitrafficking as in a discourse that combined ableism, nativism, and classism: "it is an object of interest to the community, that the importation of human monstrosities from Italy to this country, for the purpose of mendicancy, should be promptly suppressed" (Zucchi, 129).

Saverio Felliti, thirteen-years-old, was an object for this judge, an imported item subject to trade embargo like rancid olive oil. He was also a monster, but not the kind of monster that Foucault has argued "calls law into question and disables it" (as opposed to the category of the "disabled person," for whom, Foucault argues, "the law in some way provides" and who poses no challenge to the law's foundations).[10] Is Felliti a "disabled person" in Foucault's terms? Yes and no. He has a place in U.S. immigration law: no place; he is provided for—with no provisions. His story reminds us that disability's place in civil law is always, shall we say, provisional at best, unstable if not unsettling, and never more so, of course, than when the civil law rules on those who are not citizens.

Unsightly begging ordinances offered more systematic programs for suppressing monstrous imported mendicancy at the local level than individual court rulings did. The first American ugly law that I know of was in San Francisco, 1867; the last attempt to pass one that I have found was in Los Angeles, 1913; and although there may well have been others earlier and later, this California frame calls attention to the ways in which external as well as internal nomadic subjects—immigrants and cross-border migrants as well as vagrants—not only rub shoulders but are created hand in hand with unsightly beggars. Both cities turned to ugly law at times when, as far as city leaders were concerned, too many unemployed foreigners packed the streets.

Cosmopolitan San Francisco faced (and was formed by) its immigration crises early and intensively, in the Gold Rush and its bust and aftermaths. In 1913 Los Angeles, the newly formed municipal commission charged with eradicating begging and overseeing charity singled out two groups for special attention, disabled beggars and the "aliens, chiefly Mexicans, many of whom, brought by the railroads were discharged when no longer needed and did not return home," Mexicans, that is, suddenly rendered unfit when employers no longer welcomed their low-wage labor.[11] In short, the commission seems to have been designed to target beggars who were exactly the kind of boundary-crossers eloquently linked by Anzaldúa in her borderlands theory: "the squint-eyed, the perverse, the queer, the troublesome, the mongrel, the mulatto, the half breed, the half dead, in short, those who cross over, pass over, or go through the confines of the 'normal'" (3).[12]

As the dual charge of the commission in Los Angeles suggests, ugly laws not only worked in tandem with but were directly related to other spatial solutions for managing the foreign. Borders and border checks policed those who crossed over, passed over, and went through; when "those who" was seen also as "that which," *disease* crossing, passing and going through the confines of the normal, another spatial fix came to the fore, the quarantine zone. Because the unsightly begging ordinances explicitly mapped and managed place, showing who (the unsightly person) could not be where (in public), they may be linked to other attempts to remake urban space as nondiseased and nondisabled space: to histories of the ghetto and anti-Semitic associations of Jewish bodies with impurity and contagion; to the "mapping of deviance" in Chinatowns, where "Chinese" unsightly diseases—smallpox, leprosy—were supposed to be contained, hidden, inspected (Craddock, 10).[13] Reports of concentrations of disease in the "Lower East Side" or the "Mexican quarter" or the "Chinatown" or the "Little Italy" of various cities reassured readers not only that disease came from somewhere else but also that it could be segregated (Molina, *Fit to Be Citizens*, 87). Public space—white space, citizens' space—could be cordoned off from the danger of contagion and the sound, smell, and sight of disease, all of which were carried flagrantly by the intruding, uncontained, unsightly foreign beggar.

At times, that threatening beggar was simply a generalized foreigner, someone who came from *everyplace* else. Foreign groups, east and west, north and south, often blended indeterminately into one another in middle-class nativist accounts of mendicant outsiders. "The beggar in ninety-nine cases out of a hundred is an importation," wrote G. W. Whippert in 1891, following the assertion with a list of just some of the places where mendicants, including "cripples made to order," came from: "Mafia-ridden Sicily," "squalid . . . Warsaw," "the gutters of Jolly Vienna," "struggling Ireland" (3). I.K. Friedman's fictional *Autobiography of a Beggar* (1903) derived its coarse humor exactly from the clustering and interactions of various criminal and degraded classes at the scene of begging, with a particularly strong emphasis on confused comedies of disability and immigration. Friedman's beggar narrator, Mollbuzzer, writes his memoir for an "anterpologist" who offers him twenty-five dollars for his story. As Mollbuzzer's slapstick picaresque unfolds, his putative ethnography trains its sights on a variety of fellow travelers. Foremost among them are the subjects of ugly law:

> The trade of a beggar is beset with more difficulties than any on earth. . . . The absence of one leg, even of two, is a decided aid to his calling; if he be blind, his chances for good pay are still better; if he be deaf, dumb, and blind, crippled and maimed, his chances are of the best. The more crippled he is, the higher will he be paid. To be a successful beggar, then, one must be hungry, be ill-clad to the point of rags; one must have a starving wife and children; one must be ever willing to work, yet never able to find work, and one must be a cripple. There is no royal road to beggary. (4)

Mollbuzzer's dealings with crippled beggars overlap and coincide with a crudely racist set of other encounters: a Duke-and-King-like adventure into "joining de circus," in which a black tramp is coaxed "inter playin' de Honoluler King" in a sideshow; "A Tale Ef A Pigtail" set, like many begging narratives at the turn of the century, in a Chinatown; and a dizzying, culminating plot involving "De Chinee Kid An' De Hand-Organ," in which a "man ef bizness" who supplies beggars with "hand-organs, . . . beggar signs, crutches, locations, . . . pencils, . . . shoe-strings," and other accessories trades a Chinese boy for an Italian organ-grinder's monkey. Though this final story's humor depends on a series of cultural suspicions and misunderstandings, its structure emphasizes the interchangeability of "Chinese" and "Italian"; both boy and monkey are literally packed and shipped in the same crate.

Like general anti-immigration discourse, antipathy toward specific immigrant groups mobilized easily around the figure of the unsightly beggar. Ugly law offered a compact package of medicalized and moralized language ("diseased," "disgusting," sometimes "improper") with which, at any given moment and location, to define a particular ethnic and racialized difference, to saturate that difference with significance, and to convert social inequity into seemingly natural occurrence.[14] Many marked ethnic groups were associated at one time or another with a tendency to produce unsightly beggars. When New York City police assigned two plainclothes detectives to "ferret out begging tricks" at dives like The Doctor's, they chose two detectives whose ethnicity was repeatedly specified in the ensuing press coverage—"Howry, a Greek, and Sasillio, a Russian"—presumably to reassure readers that by virtue of their national backgrounds they looked the part (see for instance "Detectives Ferret Out"). Immigrant groups linked to the cluster of defects that ugly law intended to correct—poverty, degeneracy, begging, vagrancy, and disability—varied from city to city, decade to decade. In Buffalo, home of the first American COS, organizers focused initially on Polish immigrants, who came there to beg, as one COS leader put it, "in a state of debasement difficult to understand" ("Proceedings at the Second Annual Meeting of the COS of the City of Buffalo"). Other groups—Slavs, Irish, Greeks, Syrians, Gypsies, Cyprians, Bohemians, and so on—in turn might be the focus of any given city's official formulations of pauperism.

Begging was often Orientalized in antimendicancy discourse, as was vagrancy. Even the simple presence of the "Oriental" on the street, not in any way begging but behaving as a consumer, could be cause for concern, as in an 1893 report from Theodore Dreiser about young lady tourists scandalized by the "manner in which the inhabitants of the Orient and Eastern Europe" left the confines of Chicago's Columbian Exposition to "travel about the streets of the city, stroll through its parks and enter its stores . . . almost anywhere . . . where one may go of an evening": "These Turks, Arabs, Hindoos, Japs, Egyptians and others, . . . as ugly as many of them are, . . . will smirk and grin upon observing the slightest glance in their direction" (136).[15]

Begging made the scene more ominous. In Los Angeles in 1913, at the moment when the city was contemplating passing an ugly law and lumping its unsightly beggars with unemployed Mexican laborers, news on begging alternated between accounts of the threat of "blind, epileptic and malformed" panhandlers, stories of shiftless Mexicans, and reports about a new problem: "Persian Mendicants Invade Southern California." Readers were warned that after the completion of the Panama Canal beggars from Persia would "come in droves . . . unless they get the cold shoulder, the icy hand and the grand bounce." These "shrewdest of all beggars" ("Spot Them," one headline proclaimed) are said to have practiced a particularly Oriental ruse, a kind of reverse unsightliness. The story went that Persian imposters, limping on crutches and seemingly "suffering from some terrible injury," were smuggling large quantities of gold by hiding it under filthy rags wrapped around their ostensibly swollen legs ("Shrewdest of All Beggars"). Fortunes of gold, filthy rags, veiled dissembling—a range of Orientalist effects came into play here.

In an 1892 report by officials in U.S. embassies around the world on how other countries controlled and regulated paupers, one counsel wrote from Jerusalem, "An Oriental country without beggars is inconceivable," and another wrote that in the Philippines, by definition, "the uncultivated native is a vagrant" (*Special Consular Report*, 547). One disapproving cultural commentator writing in 1894 assured his readers that "Orientalism will have nothing to do with chartered charity boards, and thinks that a gift slipped into the hand of poverty has the highest redeeming power"; in this case "Orientalism" was synonymous with Judaism ("New Publications").

But two years later, Jewish writer Israel Abrahams distinguished Jewish culture from the "Oriental" precisely on the basis of its rendering the unsightly beggar unnecessary:

> Deep-rooted in the Jewish heart lay the sentiment that poverty had rights as well as disabilities, and the first of those rights demanded that the poor need not appeal for sympathy by exhibiting their sorrows. In this characteristic the Jew was never Oriental, but struck out an original line of his own. Like Coriolanus, he might have exclaimed, against an alleviative or fraternal service bought by exposure and publicity:—"I cannot/Put on the gown, stand naked, and entreat them,/For my wounds' sake, to give their suffrage." (307)

Despite their differences, both quotations share two repudiations: of ugly begging and of the Oriental, understood as one and the same.

As Abrahams's assertion illustrates, leaders from targeted immigrant ethnic groups rejected association with the taint of the unsightly beggar. Much like the advocates in the deaf and blind schools who worked hard to dissociate impairment from begging, immigrant associations strategically and prudently repudiated every trace of the tramp. As modal subjects, if not yet necessarily modal citizens, they refused to be reduced collectively to "sorrows," to "wounds," and to the exhibition of suffering as the price of suffrage.[16] Often they claimed a superior ethic of care. Sometimes others claimed it for them, too, paradoxically reinscribing racial difference and obscuring urgent dynamics of poverty by denying the very possibility of unsightly begging within a given subcultural group. Both "Jews" and "the Chinese" got caught within this bind.

An early version of model-minority discourse stressed the nonexistence of beggars in the population of Chinese laborers.[17] "I never saw a Chinese beggar. I never saw a lazy Chinaman," wrote Joaquin Miller. The economy demanded—with severity—severely able-bodied Chinese workers. Already generally subject to what Craddock calls the "sanitary assault" of public health incursions, Chinese people who were ill and disabled had good reason to avoid exposure to general public view. "Chinatown became," in Craddock's words, "a reactive space, a space to hide from white hostility, escape police surveillance, defend against the intrusion of public health officials, and reappropriate social practices inscribed as pathological" (247).

In San Francisco at the outset of its ugly law, unsightly beggars were therefore precisely not Chinese. But their unsightliness is nonetheless connected to the dynamics of Chineseness in the American city. Later, in cities like New York, the "cripple factories" and beggars' dives of sunlight-and-shadow narratives were often located in or near Chinatown's mythic packed and dark, morally threatening, spaces.[18] Oto Mundo's 1898 adventure tale *The Recovered Continent: A Tale of the Chinese Invasion* (inevitably tagged as "bizarre" by the critics who remember it, in part because its hordes-invading plot involves a conqueror who is not Chinese at all but rather an American "idiot" changed by mad science into an evil genius) seems not quite so bizarre in the context of the culture's insistent alignment of the idiot, the unsightly, the contagious, and the Chinese alien.[19] In William Norr's 1892 *Stories of Chinatown,* set around the Bowery, we find another version of a den called The Doctor's, this one run by an "ugly, pock-marked Chinaman" who serves up opium, white-slaved girls and Chinese medicines in equal measure (73).

In order to locate the unsightly beggar in a Chinatown "chop-suey joint," poet Harry Kemp surmised in 1923, all you had to do was close your eyes (or as he put it, "fold your sight," epicanthicly): "If you but fold your sight you are away / In some quaint yellow corner of Cathay / . . . where there plies / His trade the beggar with self-blinded eyes." The streets of U.S. Chinatown in Kemp's formulation consisted of a mendicant's lice infestation or fever dream: "The streets with chattering hordes are oversped / Like swarming vermin in a beggar's head" (Greever and Bachelor, 225–226).[20]

Similar complexities attend the conjunction of "beggar" and "Jew." Like "Chinaman" and "beggar," "Jewish" and "beggar" were not words likely to be combined in the dominant cultural grammar. Mark Twain went so far as to argue in 1899 that "Jewish beggar" was practically a contradiction in terms:

> A Jewish beggar is not impossible perhaps; such a thing may exist, but there are few men that can say they have seen that spectacle. . . . Whenever a Jew has real need to beg his people save him from the necessity of doing it. The charitable organizations of the Jews are supported by Jewish money and amply. The Jews make no noise about it; it is done quietly; they do not nag and pester and harass us for contributions; they give us peace, and set us an example—an example which we have not found ourselves able to follow.

This idea that "the Jews have no beggars" has a long history; Lancelot Addison had attempted to debunk it in 1685, attributing the misconception to the "regular and commendable" practices of poor relief through which the Jews "much concealed their poverty" (Abrahams, 307). The idea is not unconnected to the corollary myth that all Jews are rich, and it is thereby intertangled with American anti-Semitisms. At the same time, Twain's praise of exemplary Jewish charity functioned as a deliberate counter to anti-Semitism, much like Henry Ward Beecher's 1887 praise of Jewish social virtue: "Are they in our poorhouses? In which? Are they in our jails? Where?" and so on (203).[21]

Twain wrote, from a position of ignorance, in the most general of terms; his remarks applied to "The Jew," anywhere and for all time: "The Jew is not a disturber of the peace of any country." "Men" in Twain's "few men" apparently applies only to gentiles. But though "few men" like Twain saw the spectacle of Jewish begging, within modern Jewish cultures, as Israel Abrahams described in his account of Jewish history in 1899, house-to-house begging was common. In modernity, "irrepressible crowds of pushing beggars," he wrote, could be found in many cities waiting outside synagogue doors. Although he insisted that imposter cripples had vanished from Jewish culture by the Middle Ages and that "the number of Jewish cripples and confirmed invalids" in Jewish history was tiny, Abrahams had no doubt that Jewish beggars disturbed Jewish peace: "To-day the Jewish beggar . . . is a persistent and troublesome figure in modern Jewish society," he concluded (310–311).

In non-Jewish urban culture, according to Twain, this persistent figure was invisible. Even in the realm of representation, he claimed, no Jewish beggars exposed themselves to public view: "The Jew has been staged in many uncomplimentary forms, but, so far as I know, no dramatist has done him the injustice to stage him as a beggar." But just a few years later, British Jewish writer Israel Zangwill's popular farcical novella *The King of Schnorrers* paraded the figure with a dramatic flourish for American readers. *Schnorrer,* related to a German word for joke or story, is a Jewish German term for a particularly presumptuous Jewish beggar "having some pretensions to respectability"; schnorrers give "the impression, with an assumption of condescension, that they [are] doing a favor in rendering an opportunity to their rich neighbors to perform a worthy deed by making a contribution" (Jacobs and Eisenstein). Zangwill presented his larger-than-life schnorrer as central to his culture, a dominant figure, the very opposite of an invisible man.

Zangwill's insolent protagonist, a master at his art, stands out as an extraordinary beggar; he has pedigree, is erudite, and is a sort of elevated con man.[22] But Zangwill's 1893 portrayal of eighteenth-century London ghetto life comments on the contemporary cultural situation of the plain beggar, as in the following passage, which turns the Charity Organization Society rhetoric of "friendly visiting" on its head: "I always hold strongly that the rich should be visited in their own homes," the King of Schnorrers insists.

> I grieve to see this personal touch, this contact with the very people to whom you give the good deeds, being replaced by lifeless circulars. One owes it to one's position in life to afford the wealthy classes the opportunity of charity warm from the heart; they should not be neglected and driven in their turn to write checques in cold blood, losing all that human sympathy which comes from personal intercourse—as it is written, 'Charity delivers from death.' But do you think charity that is given publicly through a secretary and advertised in annual reports has so great a redeeming power as that slipped privately into the hands of the poor man, who makes a point of keeping secret from every donor what he has received from the others? (72)

Zangwill's acerbic portrait of the Schnorrer King places strong emphasis on intra-Jewish conflict, something Twain's discourse of "The Jew" cannot admit. In one aspect, though, he seems to agree with Twain. The novella suggests that in modern urban Jewish history there can be no unsightly schnorrer. One passage describes the group of schnorrers waiting at the end of services outside a London synagogue:

> Their woebegone air was achieved almost entirely by not washing—it owed little to nature, to adventitious aids in the shape of deformities. The merest sprinkling boasted of physical afflictions, and none exposed sores like the lazars of Italy or contortions like the cripples of Constantinople. Such crude methods are eschewed in the fine art of *schnorring*. A green shade might denote weakness of sight, but the stone-blind man bore no braggart placard—his infirmity was an old established concern well known to the public and conferring upon the proprietor a definite status in the community. He was no anonymous atom, such as drifts blindly through Christendom, vagrant and apologetic. (2)

Both Zangwill and Israel Abrahams had good reason to make "unsightly" or "crippled" and "Jewish" the meaningful contradiction in terms. American anti-Semitism marked all Jews, not just sick or hurt beggars, as unsightly, applying idioms of disgust across the board, as in Hawthorne's account of his dinner with the first Jewish lord mayor of London: "I never beheld something so ugly and disagreeable, and preposterous, and laughable, as the outline of his profile; it was so hideous and Jewish"; as in Hay's description of Jews in the Vienna ghetto: "This coquetry of hideousness is most nauseous"; as in Twain's conclusion to his "defense" of "the Jew" in *Harper's*: "By his make and his ways [the Jew] is substantially a foreigner wherever he may be, and even the angels dislike a foreigner" (quoted in Michael, 110, 116, 114). When the words *Jewish* and *cripple* combine in American popular culture, they tend to produce effects like those in populist leader Donnelly's 1890 novel *Caesar's Column,* with its sinister mastermind character:

> He was old and withered. One hand seemed to be shrunken, and his head was permanently crooked to one side. The face was mean and sinister; two fangs alone remained in his mouth; his nose was hooked; the eyes were small, sharp, penetrating and restless; but the expanse of brow above them was grand and noble. It was one of those heads that look as if they had been packed full, and not an inch of space wasted. His person was unclean, however, and the hands and the long finger-nails were black with dirt. I should have picked him out anywhere as a very able and a very dangerous man. He was evidently the vice-president of whom the spy had spoken—the nameless Russian Jew who was accounted "the brains of the Brotherhood." (116)

In defense against this kind of formulation, Zangwill put forward the uncrippled schnorrer and his generous Jewish culture, with its contrast to the "anonymous atoms" of "Christendom."

In the large U.S. cities of strangers in the era of ugly law, the problem was not solved so simply, and nervousness about the anonymous atom did not confine itself to the realm of Christian problems. An 1896 article in the *American Hebrew,* reprinted in the *New York Times,* promised its readers that Jewish charity organization had only just then "sounded the death knell of the beggar" (*New York Times,* Dec. 12, 1896, 6). Through the efforts of United Hebrew Charities, the essay announced, the Jewish beggar was finally "an unknown character upon our streets." As usual, the death knell rang too soon. Nine years later, a COS officer reported that "in Greater New York now, there are at large . . . 100 Jewish 'shnorrers'" ("No Sinecure"). At the same time, New York anti-mendicancy officers pursued a "high-class artist" of a beggar, "really a Polish Jew," who "lived in comparative respectability" and whose assumed name, Count Marion Francois Leon d'Este, was as impudently aristocratic as that of Zangwill's Sephardic schnorrer king, Manasseh Bueno Barzillai Azevedo da Costa.

Many urban anxieties about immigrant beggars, including intragroup tensions like those in the Jewish communities of New York, played out in contestation over immigrant peddlers. The line between peddling and begging, as I discuss further in later chapters, was perpetually thin and wavering, particularly where disabled people were concerned. A blind pencil seller or newspaper vendor could always be charged with trading on pity. But peddling came under fire on its own, not just as a cover for alms-seeking. In Chicago in the ugly year of 1881, the longer-established German Jewish community reacted with alarm to the influx of newer Russian and Eastern European Jewish immigrants who made up the majority of Chicago's Jewish peddlers.[23] An editorial in the Jewish Chicago paper *The Occident* in 1881 proposed strong measures to quash this surge of peddling:

> Over thirty of the Russian refugees that have come to Chicago have already applied to the mayor of the city for licenses to peddle. If at the rate these men come here they are thus encouraged by a few of their countrymen, . . . all our Chicago thoroughfares will be lined with Russo-Polish hucksters and peddlers.
>
> We suggest to the Russian Refugee committee to make it the imperative rule not to give a meal or lodging to those having purchased a license. . . . the refugees should not be allowed to cast odium upon Judaism in Chicago by this early beginning and overrun our cities with a peddlers horde; it would simply be a disgrace to us. To show how persistently these small rapacious traders urge their countrymen into the paths of low barter, nearly all in making application for license have signed their name in Hebrew. (Quoted in Eastwood 1991, 27–28)[24]

Here, by definition, peddlers are not only embarrassing but immoral subjects, crooked and loose, "simply . . . a disgrace." Since peddling was the only form of marginally sanctioned economic participation available to many disabled people, under such sanctions a disabled Russian refugee would have been vulnerable indeed.

The same year, Chicago's city council grappled with suppressing the unsightly beggar and the immigrant peddler side by side. Hailing the advent of Alderman Peevey's ugly ordinance in 1881, the *Chicago Tribune* welcomed the law as a way to rid the city of "the fellows who yell ba-na-naas, and all other nuisances of like character." These fellows were Italian immigrants; many men newly arrived from Italy went into the street fruit-peddling business. Joseph Kirkland's 1892 "Among the Poor of Chicago" described them this way: "dark-skinned pedlers [*sic*] as they troll forth, in the sonorous Italian tones, "Banano-o! Fi, Ri, Banano-o-o-o" (200).

Italians on Chicago's streets clearly posed a problem for the city council; the same week that Peevey introduced the ugly ordinance, Italian fruit-stand vendors were petitioning the mayor to rescind another recently passed order "for removal of the fruit stands from the curb stones" (*Chicago Inter Ocean,* May 18, 1881). "The Italian won't go," reported the *Chicago Times* on May 18, 1881, describing Mayor Harrison's failed attempt, "at the solicitation of a number of business firms," to prohibit the vendors from blocking sidewalks. The *Tribune*'s collapse of the ugly law into the antivending law suggests that at least some Chicagoans perceived both ordinances as directly related to each other, mutual attempts at street control bound up with issues of citizenship, national identity, and ethnicity.

Cultural memory of ugly law, focused on the static words in the municipal codes (and on seeing disability), has obscured the politics of immigration at the dynamic moment of the ordinance's inception. Intent on the "diseased and maimed," we do not see "the Italian"—or rather, perhaps, we do not *hear* that grinding organ that accompanies the prospect of displayed deformity.[25] But the Italian will not go. The few Chicago papers that report on Alderman Peevey's ugly proposal to the city council inevitably link begging and Italian-style busking, as in this mention in the *Times*: "Alderman Peevey offered an order directing the mayor to remove mendicants and organ-grinders from the streets" (May 18, 1881).

The presence of these organ-grinders in this report of Peevey's order suggests that the ugly ordinances, always closely tied to peddling laws, played a part in regulating not only what could be seen but what could be heard in Chicago and other cities. In "Peddling Noise: Contesting the Civic Soundscape of Chicago," Derek Vaillant traces the late-nineteenth- and early-twentieth-century "coalition of anti-noise activists determined to wipe out street cries" (257). These efforts bear a close resemblance to those of the coalition of ugly-lawmakers determined to wipe out the unsightly and control the city sightscape; both campaigns, as Vaillant puts it, sought to "transform the city as a sensory as well as an economic realm," to use sensory reforms as "subterfuge for interfering with alternative modes of urban economic life" (257, 267). Vaillant shows how sonic policing in

Chicago targeted peddlers' sound as *foreign* sound, cries made by "populations newly deemed to be unacceptably loud or 'noisy' in public" (259). In 1889, the Chicago city council went so far as to consider a proposal that all peddlers had to be American citizens (266).[26] Antinoise reformers subscribed, Vaillant argues, "to a civic discourse that subtly but unmistakably attempted to naturalize a regimen of sounding 'American.' . . . aural profiling demarcated an important regulatory arena in which marginalized publics, including, but not limited to, immigrants, non-native speakers and street workers, were shunted to the far side of the fault line of civic inclusion and exclusion" (275). Along that fault line, too, ran the tremors of the ugly laws; looking American, like sounding American, required "certain behaviors and not others, and by extension, certain persons and not others," not noisy ones, not unsightly ones (275).

When we forget about the noise made by, the songs and cries and verbal appeals of, unsightly beggars or the peddlers with whom they were often associated, several problematic consequences ensue. For one, by overemphasizing the appearance of "diseased, maimed" people we underestimate or ignore their voices, replicating the very reduction to unsightly objectification that we cite the ugly law in order to decry. In addition, as I detail in chapter 9, raised voices are more likely than displayed bodies to be legally construed as "expression" and thus potentially subject to constitutional protection. Furthermore, a disability studies perspective reminds us that "sounding American" has been a barrier and burden not only for immigrants and nonnative speakers but for the "marginalized public" with speech and communication differences and impairments—deaf people, people who stutter, people whose cerebral palsy or dystonia affects their ability to be readily understood, and so on—whose specific experiences of aural profiling and voice policing go unrecognized within the common vision-centered version of the story of the ugly laws.

Finally—most important for my purpose here—a soundless scene of ugly law makes it easy to forget the "foreigners" whose presence in the cities played a crucial role in galvanizing new ordinances regulating how bodies arranged and performed themselves in the streets. Vaillant shows how the sounds of peddling and organ-grinding signified a "powerfully shared," specifically immigrant experience. Turn-of-the-century peddlers and their customers were, he points out, "disproportionately poor immigrants and Eastern European Jews who had fled . . . Russia in the 1880s," the group targeted in the German Jewish *Occident* editorial I have already described.

> Others had escaped joblessness and poverty in Greece or southern Italy. The cries and shouts of peddlers testified to group survival and resilience in the face of challenge. . . . Peddlers fought against the sanitized reform soundscape as a double threat to their livelihood as well as their claims to cultural self-determination. (Vaillant, 258–259)

Eastwood's study of Chicago's Jewish street peddlers makes clear that although peddling was a new form of work for some recent immigrants (who were drawn to it by the small amount of capital required, the minimum need for English, and the economic independence it allowed), many others had already engaged in exactly this form of petty trading prior to coming to the United States (1991, 11). The sounds of both peddling and begging resonated of Old World street economies that had no place in civic plans for the modernized American city.

Like the German Jewish writers of *The Occident,* Italian American leaders in Chicago sought to authorize themselves as assimilable, upwardly mobile, unexceptional U.S. citizens by actively supporting bans on any work for Italians that smacked of (or sounded like) Old World begging. One of their targets was organ-grinders, whose playing of music for no fixed price, as Zucchi has pointed out, threatened the binary distinction between work and mendicancy (7). In 1887, the Chicago-based paper *L'Italia* announced the formation of "an Italian association for the suppression of rag pickers and organ grinders," successfully pushing the city council to prohibit organ-grinding in September 1888. When, unsurprisingly, the police failed yet again to enforce this law, writers in *L'Italia* denounced the "secret orders" of ward politicians whom they held responsible (Nelli, 143–144).

Unsightly begging ordinances were especially closely tied to laws designed to curb organ-grinders and other street musicians, many of whom were marked doubly, as foreign and as disabled (particularly blind). In New York City history we can trace this link to street music with particular clarity. In 1895, New York businessmen organized to challenge Mayor Strong's decision to issue permits authorizing the playing of hand organs by "crippled applicants." They wrote to Strong requesting "that you will give instructions to your proper officers to have licenses refused . . . to all deformed and mutilated persons to peddle articles, or to play upon hand organs, or otherwise to display their deformities upon the public streets of the city" (Executive Committee, letter to Strong). In a private memorandum, antiorgan activists spelled out their concerns about the annoyance of players of musical instruments on the street:

> They are as a rule either blind or crippled. . . . Some of the most persistent have been arrested . . . but discharged by the Police Justices, they claiming that they being cripples were entitled to a stretch of the imagination, and call an accordion or a wheezy orgumentto [*sic*] a hand organ. In the consequence of that ruling some of the Avenues and principle streets are becoming infected with the blind and maimed. ("Illustrative Cases")

In anti-immigration discourse, America was to worker as foreign was to unsightly beggar, as host to infecting parasite, a nation on the verge of transmogrifying into an unscientifically disorganized United States of Charity, its resistance ground down by a perpetual whining organ. "There has been—and continues to be—a steady influx of professional beggars . . . lured to these shores by the tales they have heard of money to be made from 'those stupid Americans,'" a Brooklyn paper reported in 1902. "The tales told to them . . . have been to the effect that any lame, halt, or blind person—or anyone who could simulate affliction—could make more money in Greater New York in a week than could be made in Europe in a year. And these tales are absolutely true" (Spacks, 29).

Not that the distinction between insider and foreigner mattered much anymore in the case of unsightly begging. "The regular native beggars," New York city police complained in the same report, "used to content themselves with looking miserable and asking for alms" (Spacks, 29). Now, under the contagious influence of the "European 'exposure' method," secretly keeping warm in cold weather with "Chinese pocket-stoves" inside their coats, even the regular native beggars behaved like (always had been?) irregular aliens, displaying and feigning afflictions and grinding away at organs. Note that the ethnically unmarked woman slated for "abolition" by ordinance in the *Tribune* announcement of Chicago's ugly law, the one who played the popular American song "Mollie Darling" incessantly, did so on a "hurdy-gurdy," a barrel organ, an instrument strongly associated with immigrant Italian buskers.[27]

Americans during the long era of the unsightly beggar ordinances faced complex changes well outlined by Longmore and Miller: "the rapid shift to an industrial economy and urban society; the new imperialism abroad and new immigration at home; the rise of national corporations, labor unions, and other large-scale institutions; the corresponding shrinking importance of local face-to-face communities; the diminishing capacities of individuals to shape their lives within the emerging, mass modern order" (61). Add to these changes the ideological force of biological racialism and eugenics.

Under these pressures, the unsightly beggar and the menacing immigrant inevitably met and merged. No wonder the figure of the unsightly immigrant developed. After all, begging was an extreme form of what the Immigration and Naturalization Service was meant to prevent, being "a public charge." It was being a charge with no one in charge of you; it was being a public charge *in* public. Progressive-era sociologists might attempt to rewrite this script, arguing from their research that practically all tramps and beggars were native sons, but the repetition of the argument suggests the stubbornness of the assumption: unsightly begging, like plague, came from somewhere else.

8

RACE, SEGREGATION, AND THE UGLY LAW

Three strands of legal discourse defining forms of what Anthony Paul Farley has called "nobodyness" intertwine with the ragged edges of ugly law. The first concerns prohibition of prostitution and indecency. The second involves control of immigration. The third we traditionally associate with race. The ugly laws are part of the story of segregation and of profiling in the United States, part of the body of laws that specified who could be where, who would be isolated and excluded, who had to be watched, whose comfort mattered. Thinking about these ordinances in the terms of segregation reveals the crucial importance of space and placing in the constitution of American disability.[1] At the same time, thinking about the ordinances in relation to race shows how ugly law, like other public health and public welfare measures, provided one more tool for debasing and delimiting subordinated racial groups. What Farley terms "the poetics of colorlined space" meets its supplement in the poetics of the American ugly line, and each illuminates and helps to maintain the other.

To prove the general point that every available space could be colorlined, Farley points to the racial segregation of schools for the blind: "even blindness could be made to see color through the peculiar miracle of segregation" (113). This marvelously acerbic passage is inadequate. "Color" (that is, race), of course, as Farley would be first to acknowledge, is not only seen but sensed—heard, felt; as I show in this chapter, blind people learn and perform race as do their sighted counterparts. More problematic still, only one "peculiar miracle" gets debunked in Farley's account. Even racially integrated schools for the blind are segregated schools. Blind schools of any sort are also constituted by a peculiar miracle of segregation. Arguments for and against separate schooling for people with particular impairments have been long and complex; I cannot rehearse them here but must acknowledge them, since my point is not to decry categorically all "blind schools." What I wish to emphasize is this: by a peculiar miracle, American culture in general barely recognized these arrangements of categories of bodies in space as potentially problematic, as open to question. The ordinance was a strong expression of territoriality (Delaney, 6–7). Ugly law segregated, as did the developing state institutions that drove it and followed it.

Disability rights activists in the 1970s understood this dynamic vividly, viscerally, when their push for enforcement of regulations banning disability discrimination was met with reassurances that "special education" was "separate but equal." *Brown v. Board of Education* became a tool for disability activists as well as for opponents of race-based segregation.[2] In the long summary produced by scholars as an amicus brief in the Supreme Court's 2001 *Garrett* case, detailing the history of "intentional and irrational" state-sponsored disability discrimination in the United States, the ugly laws are placed in the section on segregation and directly compared with race-based restrictive zoning.[3]

Ugly laws in practice functioned to sort people on the streets and into institutions by race as well as disability; the two kinds of segregation were not so much comparable as inseparable. The race-making work of ugly law took many forms. As the discussions of Chinese American, Mexican American, and Jewish American histories in the preceding chapter begin to suggest, unsightly beggars were variously and intricately raced. In this chapter, I focus on the classic version of American race segregation, the black/white binary, for the evidence I have been able to uncover lies largely there.

In part, unsightly beggar ordinances denigrated and defined a certain kind of whiteness. The tramp whose presence lurks behind the ugly laws was strongly racialized in the cultural imaginary as native-born white and male. In the late nineteenth century, as the racial arrest statistics kept in cities like Chicago show, both tramp and unsightly beggar functioned primarily as forms of what Frankenberg has termed the "white Other," as spoiled whites, impoverished and inferior (192).[4] Indeed, ugly law may be interpreted specifically as a means of white trashing, in which poor whiteness or bad whiteness (filthy, debilitated, dangerous, debris) sets off the nice body of good whiteness.[5] The "person who is diseased, maimed, deformed, disfigured in any way so as to be an unsightly object" thus functions as a subsidiary "allegory of identity" within the more general category that Newitz and Wray describe: "We contend that white trash is an allegory of identity which is deployed to describe the existence of class antagonisms in the U.S." (170).

If white-trashed unsightly beggars posed the threat of and therefore bore the brunt of class hostilities too flagrantly displayed to public view, their black-trashed counterparts were likely to fare even worse. After all, in the white-dominated racial order of the late nineteenth century, any black person might be assigned unsightliness. When a white Union veteran who lost an arm in the Civil War sought to express in verse the extremity of his abjection, he knew exactly what word rhymed with lack: "I might as well be black" (Clarke, 387). In this cultural context, a poor, vagrant, unhinged, begging black man or woman seemingly banking on disgust in the open street, asking for change, was also asking for it—and "it" could mean the violent backlash of race and class antagonism as much as it meant redoubled condescension.[6]

In the name of Jim Crow, after all, strains of disability and blackness inextricably mix; the term *Jim Crow* was popularized on the minstrel show circuit by Thomas "Daddy" Rice, a white man who performed in blackface and beggar's rags, basing his "Jump Jim Crow" number on a routine performed "in 1828 by an elderly and crippled Louisville stableman belonging to a Mr. Crow" (Litwack, xiv; Hutton, 115–117; Connor). "Daddy" Rice's "I" who "weel[s] about and turn[s] about / and do[es] jis so" does so in the manner of a begging man enslaved and disabled in Jim Crow space. White audiences loved "Daddy's" profitable display of a diseased, maimed, deformed person (albeit ersatz) for public view, and the later "jis so" stories of segregation law sought to enforce and reinforce the compulsory crippling and enfeeblement of entire "colored" populations.

What Bryan Wagner calls the "ritual deformations of the black body" in southern Reconstruction-period newspaper court reports on vagrancy were deformities compounded when the black vagrant was identified as a crippled beggar too (63). Black bodies deformed by paralysis or palsy were no less, and often more, ritually deformed by the rhetoric of the court report, not only in Atlanta or Charleston but in Chicago and Denver. Saidiya Hartman's incisive summary of the culture of racial segregation makes the stakes clear:

> If the fundamental task conducted under the cover of the state's police power was the protection of the health of the populace, then, as this duty took shape in the emergent era of Jim Crow, ensuring the public health required the state to *attend to bodily matters*, particularly the policing of blackness and the tracking down of all its ascertainable traces. . . . the effect of *Plessy* [was] to preclude encounters between scandalously proximate bodies. . . . Clearly the integrity of bodily boundaries and racial self-certainty was at the heart of this anxiety, and the curative for this fear and loathing was the exclusion and subordination of blacks. (206; italics mine)

Recognizing ugly law as part of this same project—this attention to bodily matters, this preclusion of "encounters between scandalously proximate bodies," this guarding of body boundaries—does not mean misrecognizing or minimizing the monumental, obsessive, and extreme policing and subordination of blacks and blackness. If ugly law provided another stab at a curative "for this fear and loathing," it did not compete with or contradict racial segregation. Wheeled about and turned about just so, the unsightly beggar did cultural labor side by side with Jim Crow.

The two kinds of discrimination shared an uneasy reliance on visual identification. Unsightliness lay in or on skin, skin "exposed," skin "disfigured," skin that disgusted. "Skin is the principal medium that has carried the past into the present," writes Joseph Roach in his analysis of slave dances in New Orleans's Congo Square,

> a continuous odyssey mapped by the sinuous track of *Plessy v. Ferguson* through the heart of America. Skin has been and continues to be not only a document but also a performance, persisting as such notwithstanding the courageous resistance of many unwilling participants in the bogus and cruel expansion of its meanings. These meanings metastasize differences that are only skin deep into what I am calling *deep skin*, a melanoma of the imagination: skin deepens into the cancer of race when supposed inner essences and stereotypical behaviors are infected by it in the collective fantasies of one people about another. The malignancy of deep skin usually begins with a blank space or a kind of erasure, which empties out the possibility of empathetic response, but this cavity quickly fills with bizarre growths. First, deep skin becomes invisible; then, after the passage of time—the twinkling of an eye is all that is required—it alone remains visible. The consequences of deep skin are easy to deplore, difficult to escape. (2001, 102)[7]

Ugly law set next to *Plessy* or any everyday municipal race-segregation ordinance reveals a broad system of appearance demarcation in which each of these rulings participates: the investment in, the disciplining of, the anxious management of skin.[8] Race is "deep skin." Disfigurement and deformity are also deep skin. They come loaded with social as well as medical significance. Even melanoma itself is in part a melanoma of the imagination. Skin deepens, through collective fantasies, into the cancer of cancer. In the city of New Orleans that Roach studies, in 1884, a newspaper article voiced openly the collective fantasies of one people about another, calling for a sweep of the streets for unsightly beggars: "an old woman with a deep seated cancer on her face is a revolting sight" ("Brevities"). Seemingly wholly natural "deep seated" cancer is also, like race, cultural—overloaded deep skin.

That old woman was white; if not, the paper would have noted it, mugging her with additional layers of metaphor (Lubiano). People identified as black *and* disfigured were double-bound by layered deep-skin codes. Consider an antebellum case recorded in the city records of Charleston, South Carolina. The city's budget books for the year 1850 contain the story of Agnes, a young slave girl badly burned in a fire whose "unsightly appearance" so disconcerted the ladies that the slaveholder arranged to pay the city a yearly fee to keep her in the poorhouse ordinarily reserved for whites only (City of Charleston, 32). The need to hide Agnes, to keep her out of public view, was urgent enough to override the usual system that gave poor relief primarily to whites and thereby tied "the interests of lower-class whites to wealthy whites rather than to the free blacks who shared their poverty," as Barbara Bellows puts it (178). Significantly, Agnes's incarceration seems to have been motivated entirely by panic and disgust, by aesthetic revulsion, rather than by economic calculation. Nothing in the record indicates that she could not work.

But if the culture of unsightliness was bound to the culture of race by codes of instantaneous, decisive disgust, both were vexed, too, by hesitation and confusion. A closer look at postbellum dynamics of spatial segregation helps clarify this point. First, a note on what kind of space we are talking about. Unsightly beggar ordinances policed nobodyness in city space, as their emergence in Chicago out of a city council "Streets and Alleys" committee illustrates. The pavement and the street corner formed their primary terrain, and they properly belong in the subset of municipal statutes that manage troubling bodies (or what Sears calls "problem bodies") on sidewalks, like San Francisco's racist 1870 "Sidewalk Ordinance" prohibiting Chinese people from using poles to carry loads of laundry (Lai, Lim, and Yung, 10; Sears, 123). Like municipal racial-segregation laws (and, as Sears has argued, like municipal cross-dressing laws), ugly laws were a geopolitical practice (Delaney, 10) that attempted to reconfigure the spaces of urban life.

But although ugly law concerned the sidewalk, it traveled by railroad.[9] It spread regionally through cities connected by railroad networks. It spread on boxcars crowded, in the public imaginary, with hobo cripples who "snarl and snap like ugly dogs," ready to sneak out at the next stop ("Rags and Tags"). It spread on trains with passenger cars divided by gender, by class, by race, by citizenship, and by contention over where to place the bodies that inevitably occupied more than one of these identity categories.[10] Like its targets, ugly law spread from city to city. COS beggar-trackers put out red alerts from one town to another, warning of imposters with monikers like "Chicago Slim" and "The Cleveland Kid," their names demonstrating the vagrant and ever mobile nature of the unsightly beggar threat ("Ancient Profession"). As rail travel came into wide usage, the train, along with the sidewalk, became a site of anxiety about displays of disability and a locus for struggles over the social control of bodies.[11]

It is not accidental that enactment of ugly laws, which peaked in the mid-1890s, emerged with intensity at the moment of statutory Jim Crow. Before the late 1880s, Leon Litwack writes,

> custom, habit and etiquette . . . defined the social relations between the races and enforced segregation in many areas of southern life. . . . But in the late 1890s whites perceived in the behavior of "uppity" (and invariably younger) blacks a growing threat or indifference to the prevailing customs, habits, and etiquette. Over the next two decades, white southerners would construct in response an imposing and extensive system of legal mechanisms designed to institutionalize the already familiar and customary subordination of black men and women. Between 1890 and 1915, state after state wrote the prevailing racial customs and habits into the statute books. (230)

In the North, too, prevailing customs, habits, and etiquette no longer sufficed to control what was seen as the insubordinate and threatening beggar.

These crises, each a failure of custom "resolved" by statute book, were not parallel but directly intersectional. Amy Dru Stanley has shown that the abolition of slavery brought into focus "fundamental problems of dependency and discipline" in what was regarded as a free-market economy, "bequeathing a distinctive ideology and set of precepts to charity reformers in the North." Many of these architects of ugly law and other beggar-punishing ordinances had been antislavery activists. "The experience of war and emancipation not only honed efficient techniques of philanthropy but also schooled Yankees in schemes for forcing beggars to work," writes Stanley. "Just as the ideal of free labor was transported south, so its coercive aspects—articulated in rules governing the freed people—were carried north." Arguing that beggars must be held "fast within the world of exchange, . . . charity reformers gave new moral legitimacy to labor compulsions that came perilously close to slavery," such as the sentences to hard labor meted out under vagrancy law to offending paupers (1992, 1283, 1288, 1293).[12] As Hartman puts it, "The contradictory aspects of liberty of contract and the reliance on coercion in stimulating free labor modeled in the aftermath of the Civil War were lessons of emancipation employed against the poor" (138). Unsightly beggars emerged within this evolving new system of labor compulsions, both as wrenches in the works (those marked confusingly and categorically as unable to labor, though labor they must) and as "wretches" to be warehoused in literal buildings "designed to institutionalize," to borrow Litwack's terms, "already familiar and customary subordination."

Unsightly beggar laws and other more informal policies regarding the public behavior of disabled people developed within the nexus of race-segregation law. No one knew this better than people who rode on the knife edge of both the colorline and the unsightly line when they traveled by railroad, like the ragtime pioneer John William Boone ("Blind Boone"). Boone's experience is illustrative of the shift from custom to statute, of the complex intersections between race and disability and between beggar-policing and race-profiling in the public spaces of the railroad cars, and of the confusions that attended all these dynamics.

In 1915, Melissa Fuell, the African American "Teacher of Wide Reputation, Lecturer, Author" who had traveled years earlier in Blind Boone's famous Concert Company, published a biography entitled *Blind Boone: His Early Life and His Achievements.* Boone was born in 1864 and grew up in Missouri. In the late 1870s, in his early teens, young, black, blind Willie Boone "made up his mind," Fuell writes,

> to steal away from home alone and try to make a mark in the world for himself. . . . He knew so many of the train crews, and he felt that he could gain their consent to play for the passengers. . . . At first all went well. The porters were kind and would help him to get transportation. Passengers gave him heavy tips and he liked his work, immensely. He liked to walk up and down the aisles of the big trains, playing his harp and singing funny songs. How he would smile when a funny passenger would drop money into his hat. (60)[13]

How he would smile! Fuell's imaginative excursion into Boone's gleeful transport speaks a language provocatively glossed by Anthony Paul Farley: "Race is a form of pleasure. . . . Absolute power produced dependency;

dependency produced sycophancy; and sycophancy produced the race-pleasure that supported the entire enterprise of the colorline" (99, 119). In Willie Boone's blackness and his blindness, he was literally and doubly minstrelized (Farley: "Law creates the black body through minstrelization and criminalization. . . . Minstrelization leads to pity and pity to charity and charity to dependence and dependence to subalternation" [120, 122]). For someone like Boone, a poor person, a blind person, a child, minstrelization had real benefits; "free transportation for unfortunates" allowed him to gain mobility through disability. Under the law of minstrelization, with the help of black porters, Blind Boone strategically occupied a zone of licensed subaltern wiggle room that we might call the space of Tiny Tim Crow.

But within this structure "[m]instrelsy, of course," writes Farley, "leads to criminality, and vice versa," and around 1880, simultaneous with the development of the ugly laws, new statutes criminalizing scenes of passenger-car charity put an abrupt end to Boone's busking. The voices clamoring for these new laws will by now sound familiar. Writes Fuell,

> alas, for poor Willie, things soon changed. The world became filled with worthless characters who watched every chance to rob the honest laborer. They came in every form and disguise, some pretending that they were crippled, others paralyzed, but the most of them pretending blindness. So numerous were these fakers that the public became threadbare with every tale of woe. Of course, the real sufferers had to be punished for these faking tramps.
>
> Railroad companies became more rigid and made laws prohibiting free transportation of unfortunates. Passengers complained of being molested, hence the privilege of any one seeking aid from them, on the train, was positively denied. (60)[14]

This shift in policy, driven by imposter panic, changed Willie Boone from tolerated minstrel to out-and-out tramp: "although he was blind," Fuell writes, "he had such a determination to succeed, that he began to bum his way" (60). By the time he was a well-known adult performer, when Boone toured across the country by railroad with his musical company, Tiny Tim Crow had given way to hard-line Jim Crow. In Fuell's discussions of Boone's troupe's travels, she is careful to note whether the cars they rode in were segregated or mixed.

In several key respects, the ugly laws and the shift in railroad policy toward "unfortunates" shared a logic given full articulation in the signal ruling on U.S. racial segregation, *Plessy v. Ferguson*. All three attempted to resolve social tensions with administrative solutions. All three proceeded on ostensible behalf of elite (white) ladies in need of protection from harassment. All three claimed to secure public comfort and freedom from annoyance. All three were provoked by crises in assignment of identity. Writing of Jim Crow law, Cell remarks, "The most impressive characteristic of segregation was a complex fabric of structural ambiguity" (3), and that ambiguity was woven into ugly law and railroad begging policy as well. On the railroad, the crisis of legibility centered specifically in the problem of the conductor's discretion: how reliable was his perception, how trustworthy his seat assignments of passengers? In city streets, the problems of reading the scene were more broadly distributed. Were crippled beggars sham or for-real? Was the blind unfortunate kid riding free in the train car actually unfortunate or faking it? Was light-skinned Homer Plessy in the right railroad car, where he belonged, or was he assuming a false identity?[15]

Confronted with the impossibility of verifying such matters, ugly law, like *Plessy*, proceeded nonetheless to demand the clearest cut of categorical arrangements. "No person who is diseased . . . shall appear in public." "No person shall be permitted to occupy seats in coaches other than the ones assigned to them, on account of the race they belong to." Neither raced bodies nor disabled bodies could be properly legible; there were false signs and hidden backgrounds; and yet they had to be read. In the world of *Plessy v. Ferguson* and the municipal beggar ordinances, you *cannot* know for sure who belongs where, and you *must* know for sure, with a vengeance.

Like *Plessy*, and like southern vagrancy law, unsightly begging ordinances dealt in broad strokes that maximized police power, particularly over nonwhite people. Writing of the category that Blind Boone occupied once he began to "bum his way" in the box cars after he could no longer busk his way in the first-class cars, Bryan Wagner provides a broader view. Black vagrancy, he writes, "was not so much a pure product of state practice as an ideological mechanism that created the appearance of identity where none existed and thereby generated resources of power that could be dispensed by state functionaries for the purpose of racial control" (12). Similarly, ugly law created the appearance of identity where there was none, cramming together, as if in one passenger car, the person with tuberculosis, the one with the scar or the tumor or the amputated arm, the one who has seizures, and putting into their hands a tin cup filled with ill-begotten gains and overflowing with meaning.[16]

At the same time, however, ugly law, like the vagrancy laws to which it is so closely related, left plenty of room for interpretation. The critical "so as to be" clause in the unsightly beggar ordinances—"no person who is diseased, maimed or deformed . . . *so as to be* an unsightly or disgusting object"—opened up a textual loophole, one written right into the law, explicitly allowing for the discretion always available to functionaries where vagrancy was concerned. Because, as I have noted, under the regime of white supremacy "unsightly and disgusting" could apply to any "colored" person, disabled or not, "so as to be" functioned in part as an available form of white privilege.[17] Like vagrancy law in the postbellum South, ugly law in the North was used as a form of labor control, and it too could be employed selectively for the purpose of racial control.

The first term in the ugly law, "diseased," once again seems especially loaded in this context, just as it did in the context of the law's application to immigrant subjects under suspicion of contagion. Race too played a significant role in the symbolic economy of "disease." As Nelson and McBride have detailed, the concept of disease has long been tied to racial hierarchization, and the barrage of statistics brought forth in the name of sociomedical racism in the late nineteenth and early twentieth centuries hammered home the point that "blacks posed a major health menace" (McBride, 10, 12; Nelson, 86). One white physician widely quoted maintained that blacks were, "like the fly, the mosquito, the rats, and mice, an arch-carrier of disease germs to white people" (quoted in Gamble, n.p.).[18] In "Chicago, 1911," the physician who had recently issued the first report of sickle cell disease in a paper on one of his black patients could have picked up the *Journal of American Medicine* and read these warning words written by a southern doctor: "If Negro health is a political menace, then the diseased one is doubly a social menace, and the invasion of the South by the North forty years ago has brought about an invasion of the North, and that by the man they freed" (quoted in Wailoo, 14). In many forms of discourse at the turn of the century, accompanied (or unaccompanied) by many different explanations, disease was—as one southern public health official put it with particular but not atypical bluntness—"today almost a synonym for the word 'Negro'" (Bardin, 77).[19]

A high percentage of the black people in the cities of ugly law (albeit still a relatively small number) would have fallen into the marked categories "diseased, maimed, deformed, and mutilated." In a contribution to the recent study *Unequal Treatment,* Byrd and Clayton describe the situation for African Americans in the decades after the Civil War:

> Black health plummeted due to the Civil War collapse of the slave health subsystem. Deleterious effects were compounded by the preexisting slave health deficit, abandonment of African Americans by the mainstream health system, and continuation of racially discriminatory health policies and treatment. In lieu of emancipation, the war and its aftermath represented a health catastrophe for African Americans as their health status fluctuated wildly until 1910. This led influential biostatisticians such as Frederick Hoffman, as well as many in the medical profession, to confidently predict black extinction by the year 2000. (471)

This top-down account of policy and of conventional white-dominated medicine ignores both the "storehouse of healing knowledge" and the "clear comprehension of the harmful potential of white medical care" that African Americans brought out of their histories of enslavement. It does not address the postemancipation politics that shaped doctors' and statisticians' assessments in both North and South and the intertwining of discourses of "racial health" with ongoing debates over and assumptions about race relations.[20] But Byrd and Clayton sum up clearly the African American health crisis in the late nineteenth century.

Throughout the twentieth century and into the new millennium, African Americans faced and still face "persistent or worsening, wide and deep, race-based health disparities compared with either the white or the general population. . . . For a plethora of reasons," Byrd and Clayton conclude, "African Americans have experienced the worst health status, suffered the worst health outcomes, and been forced to utilize the worst health services of any racial and ethnic group" (476).[21] *Unequal Treatment*'s massive gathering of evidence for disparities in healthcare provides stark evidence of racism's disabling impact in the present that hint of its impact in the past. One of the book's most shocking findings is its evidence that, in a few cases only, minorities are more likely, not less likely, than whites to receive certain surgical procedures. The procedures they are more likely to receive are the less desirable ones—such as amputation, "which African Americans undergo at rates 3.6 greater . . . than their white Medicare peers."[22] As Sherry (2007) points out, in this case racism literally, directly produces disablement, and there is no reason to believe that such dynamics would have been any less in play in the United States in the last decades of the nineteenth century.[23] The bland public health discourse in *Unequal Treatment* ("slave health deficit") does not mask the disabling situation imposed on African Americans on the streets of a city like Chicago or New York in this period.

How many disabled African Americans would have come directly under the purview of the unsightly beggar ordinances is unclear. I have already discussed how Brian Wagner has shown in his work on vagrancy ordinances in the decades after the Civil War that misdemeanor laws of this kind functioned (particularly in the South) as a highly effective method of modern racial control and subordination.[24] The relative paucity of African Americans in, say, Chicago in 1881 may be attributed in part to the powerful work of the southern vagrancy statutes, which sought to immobilize black people, keep them in their place. Kerber, for instance, has shown in her *No Constitutional Right to Be Ladies* how "the obligation not to be a vagrant . . . weighed particularly heavily on African-American women in the late nineteenth century" (51), and we can assume that the "obligation not to be an unsightly beggar" applied as well. But Kusmer argues for greater numbers of culturally acknowledged "black vagabonds" (2002, 138–140), and although black tramps were rare, according to the later social studies of the 1910s and 1920s, that does not in any way mean that misdemeanor laws outside the South that clustered around vagrancy were not used against black people.[25]

Indeed, a portrait of COS-spawned efforts to crack down on begging in New York City in 1904 begins with the chase of an African American man. "'That's Florida Shine and we want him bad,' said Chief Mendicancy Officer James Forbes one day last week to a woman who had just described a colored beggar she had just passed on one of the elevated station stairways" ("Ancient Profession"). *Shine* was a general term for African American beggars, and Theodore Waters's 1905 "Six Weeks in Beggardom" offers a roster of Bowery beggars with names like "Baltimore Shine, Washington Shine, etc." (78).

In the late nineteenth century, faker rumors centered on a scam particular to black unsightly beggars who identified themselves as former slaves.[26] White, middle-class writer Alvin Sanborn's cheerfully patronizing undercover account of living among beggars in a Boston lodging house in 1893 includes among the lodgers "a one-legged negro" as well as the imposter "Honey, a fat and grizzled negro, born and bred in New York City," who "'makes a good thing' by claiming to have been a slave 'befo' de wah'" (72, 80). "What does the exposure of the violated body yield?" Hartman asks at the beginning of her *Scenes of Subjection: Terror, Slavery, and Self-Making in Nineteenth-Century America*. Sanborn's fat and happy Honey trivializes—is designed to trivialize—this question. But his allegedly false claim to violation suggests that the history of slavery displayed like (and often literalized as) a wound and a scar functioned as some northern beggars' currency, a sign of deservingness, exactly the kind of indisputable demand for compensation that fueled unsightly begging as a cultural system. Like war veterans, survivors of slavery could narrate as well as display their disease or maiming or deformity, inscribing meaning on their bodies to increase the likelihood of alms.

The "massive public health voluntarism" in black-run hospitals, social work associations, and charity organizations that developed in African American urban communities at the turn of the twentieth century aimed, like its white-run counterparts, to eradicate all forms of street begging (McBride). Du Bois's social survey *The Philadelphia Negro* (1889) used COS records for the section on "pauperism" and emphasized the problem of "unsystematic" almsgiving (271). Black leaders like Reverend H.H. Proctor spoke the discourse of the friendly visitor at conferences examining "Problems concerning Negro City Life": "we may cast a coin at a beggar to quiet a disturbing conscience. But to give ourselves,—that is the gift that costs. To go into the homes of the people and, as did Philip with the eunuch, to sit with them. . . . That is the only solution" (4). Such projects served dual purposes, as Nelson argues; they sought both to provide access to emerging black-controlled social work services for poor black people and to counter racial ideologies that rendered all African Americans as actual or potential unsightly beggars.[27]

But the troubling presence of black beggars exposing signs of disease, maiming, and deformity did not disappear. The stretch of ugly law—and even more so, of the type of beggar it designated—extends into the later period of the Great Migration. In 1890, only 14,000 Chicago residents were black; by 1930, nearly 240,000 black people were Chicago residents (Mumford, xviii). In 1915, the leading African American newspaper, the *Chicago Defender,* listed as evidence that "Chicago Leads the World in Race Progress" the fact that "there is not a colored beggar in Chicago"; but within a few years the *Defender* was regularly running standard features on the scandalous activities of fake cripples and beggars' syndicates ("Chicago Leads"; "Pays Crippled Men 3$ a Day"; "Luck Frowns on Beggars"). When Freund conducted his research on "Begging in Chicago" (with separate sections on "Crippled Beggars," "Blind Beggars," and "Deaf Beggars") for his M.A. in sociology at the University of Chicago in 1924, a high percentage of the sixty-one beggars he interviewed were, as he put it, "colored." By this point in Chicago history, the population of unsightly beggars was significantly, if not largely, black.

Freund's case histories offer a small archive of urban black disability history. In his narrative we find, among others, J. Bond, "colored and blind," who uses a placard reading "Blind—Homeless—Injured in Factory—Doctors trying to restore sight"; "Julia Flam (10 years old), colored," who "was seen leading her blind grandfather about on a begging tour of the West Side streets. She was comically, yet attractively, dressed in ill-fitting rags"; and "Billie Willis, a colored boy," who "was overrun by an auto on Wabash Avenue when five years of age and it was necessary to amputate his leg at the thigh. . . . He could get a dollar any time by appearing with his crutch at the entrance to the White City Amusement Park" (59, 63, 78).

Freund frequently marked the race of his white subjects as well, sometimes as a sign of relative approval ("Red Crane," who begs with his crutches laying before him, has two children, "rosy youngsters"), sometimes as a record of a finding that clearly interested him, the existence of cross-race sociability in the begging subculture (81). His narrative of Harry Dixon, a "thirty year old white man who sat in his wheelchair at the entrance to the 'L' station at Roosevelt Island," is a good example. "Although white," Freund writes, Harry Dixon "hired a colored boy of 22 to be his companion—to share his room, wheel him about and otherwise serve him. . . . He found his friends among the colored people among whom he lived" (80). Dixon's story offers a more complex view of the economics of unsightly begging than the usual stereotype of abject, homeless poverty; he uses his income resourcefully to pay for in-home personal care assistance. It also—if its account of Dixon's relation with the unnamed "colored . . . companion" who is both servant and friend can be trusted—provides a glimpse of a mixed-race space in race-segregated Chicago, a kind of "interzone," in Mumford's terms, like but not identical to the Progressive-era spaces that Mumford locates, in which black-white sexual subcultures showed "how the color line was drawn—and how it was crossed."[28] The story of how interzones of disability or cross-race impairment subcultures were shaped and used by their marginalized occupants, whether beggars or companions, is yet to be written.[29]

Of course, the story of the trusty colored companion to the ill white person does not necessarily transgress traditional social norms; after all, the "nurse's exemption" in *Plessy v. Ferguson* permitted black servants to travel with white children or invalids in whites-only cars. However low white unsightly beggars might be placed in urban hierarchies of value, those who employed black assistants could use whiteness as a conceit. Arthur Franklin Fuller, unsightly beggar extraordinaire, whose writing I have much praise for in chapter 11, practiced a crude racism of this sort that must be taken into account over and against any celebration of his disability politics, which turn out to be—of course—white disability politics.[30] One of the books he sold on the street described his assistant as a "cross-eyed old negro," proving, I suppose, that Fuller could dish out unsightliness as well as deny it; another book contains a hideous poem attacking another assistant for his laziness in openly racist terms ("Bud," *A Book of Poems*). A blind man peddling his autobiography on the streets in 1878 similarly capitalized on his whiteness:

> The reader may be curious to know whether we who are without sight can hear the difference between the qualities of a negro's voice, and the voices of the white race. Whenever I am asked this question I answer emphatically, yes. There is a thin, empty, fuzzy tone about a negro's voice, that denotes shallowness of character, feebleness of intellect, and grossness of tastes and feelings, while the voice of a white man is commonly clear, ringing, resonant, or deep, firm and commanding.... Of course there are exceptions to this general rule, and the grandest I ever knew is the cultivated voice, mind, and manners of Frederick Douglass ... yet his voice is decidedly negro.... In women the difference is still more pronounced. (L. Hall, 211)

Unsightly whites accompanied by black assistants could, if they chose, deploy antiblack racism in order to distinguish their own superior position from that of their attendants, accruing—if not the wages of whiteness—at least whiteness's alms.[31]

Dynamics of assistance were not, of course, always cross-racial. And assistance abounded. Arthur Fuller's writings, the story of white Harry Dixon and his "colored companion," and many other narratives collected by Freund in the 1920s suggest that there is no particular reason to image the subject of ugly law as an isolato surrounded by strangers. The companion who wheels Dixon about and the ten-year-old Julia who accompanies her blind grandfather are only two of the many figures who accompany Freund's beggars, as caregivers, hangers-on, friends, moochers, or conspirators, in "Begging in Chicago." Here is "Walter James, blind, and colored," who

> hit upon a rather unique method of alms collection as a means of supporting his family of four. He was seen making a terrific noise on an accordion

> as he walked slowly down the street. Four colored boys between ten and fifteen years of age, each armed with a tin cup, solicited every passerby on behalf of the blind man. . . . The boys enjoyed their work immensely, as it was a group activity and paid well. (32)

James, like many other assisted/employer beggars in Freund's thesis, brought along with him his own friendly (and potentially ugly) crowd. Unsightly begging was a collective enterprise.[32] In fact, its motivation was often to get cash to pay attendants, at a time when no other "independent living" alternatives to institutionalization existed. This phenomenon was by no means limited to Freund's African American disabled beggars, though the presence of structured, supportive kin networks in African American communities under poverty conditions may have made it especially likely that communal or accompanied begging would occur.[33]

In the American lode of songs in which unsightly begging finds significant expression from inside—that is, in the work of black blind blues musicians—panhandling is a markedly relational art. Among American arts traditions, blues is notable for claiming disability. It might even be argued that to a significant extent impairment *constituted* the blues. As Broomer puts it,

> Jazz usually cultivated grandeur in its naming—King Oliver, Duke Ellington, Count Basie, the Pres' Lester Young, and Lady Day. . . . The blues, however, had an eye for the quickly noted disability. Apart from some early singers with regal titles . . . the blues celebrated the infirm (Peg Leg Howell and Cripple Clarence Lofton). (1)

Hence the widely circulated Internet joke on "how to be a blues musician": "Make your own Blues name (starter kit): a. name of physical infirmity (Blind, Cripple, Lame, etc.)." "Blind" was the most common. If disability played a significant role in blues practice, so too, literally, did begging. Many blind blues singers (Blind Willie Johnson and Blind Willie McTell are two examples) panhandled in the streets.[34] And almost inevitably, stories of blind black blues, no matter how lonesome, include scenes of accompaniment.

Take the legends of Blind Lemon Jefferson. At the peak of his career the biggest-selling black blues singer, Jefferson was a Texas street musician (eventually transplanted to Chicago) who played with a tin cup tied to his guitar, the very epitome of the "unsightly beggar." Chicago Alderman

Peevey must have been turning in his grave. Leadbelly accompanied and performed with Jefferson on the streets of Dallas; when Blind Lemon played with Josh White on street corners, White employed a tambourine as a collection plate, calling out "Help the Blind." Accounts of Jefferson conflict, emblematically, on the question of whether he asked others for assistance, playing out cultural contradictions and anxieties over dependence and overcoming. Lightnin' Hopkins testifies that Blind Lemon "didn't allow no one to lead him. He say then you call him blind. No, don't call him blind. He never did feel like that." But a Leadbelly lyric states otherwise: "Blind Lemon was a blind man, He'd holler—'Catch me by the hand'—oh baby, 'And lead me all through the land'" (quoted in Uzzel, 24–27).

Ambiguities surround Jefferson's relation to "leading" but not to begging. His "Tin Cup Blues" claims begging as self-reflexive subject, even as his actual tin cup claimed it as performance, and the subject it portrays is not an isolated man:

> I stood on the corner and almost bust my head. (2)
> I couldn't make enough money to buy me a loaf of bread.
> My girl's a housemaid and she earns a dollar a week. (2)
> I'm so hungry on pay day, I can't hardly speak.
> Now gather round one, people, let me tell you true facts. (2)
> That tough luck has struck me and the rats is sleepin' in my hat.[35]

In Blind Lemon's hands, blues is insightful begging. If this song says, implicitly, "help the blind," from its first line it also says more directly, "This is what it's like to be in the position of the one who begs saying, 'help the blind.'" If it holds out the tin cup, it also traces that cup's interior and its surround. "Tin Cup Blues" challenges the ethos of ugly law head-on, verse by verse, representing begging as driven by poverty and need and telling the beggar's story as "true facts" rather than falsehood. In addition, it portrays this disabled beggar—with his "girl" and his call for "people" to gather round the "one"—as a relational subject, not antisocial but social.[36]

The ugly ordinances were meant to quash this kind of informal street economy and care nexus. Instead of paying or playing with their "companions," people like Blind Lemon, Harry Dixon, and Walter James would find themselves under the jurisdiction of guards. Being "blind, colored" instead of "blind, white" had consequences. Both jail and "care" (the poorhouse, the hospital, the other "institutions") distributed themselves differently for disabled white and disabled nonwhite subjects. Here we return full circle to the "peculiar miracle" of segregation; unsightly beggars were commonly partitioned along colorlines. In early-twentieth-century Cleveland, for instance, where arrested panhandlers were referred to Associated Charities and a beggar who "is a physical wreck is placed in an institution," the Holy Cross House opened its doors only to "crippled and invalid white children"; the Eliza Jennings home admitted only "Protestant incurable" women "of satisfactory character" (no unsightly beggars there); Rainbow Cottage cared for the "crippled and convalescent . . . of any nationality, color or religion," but only if they were minors.[37] We know from the later case of "John Doe No. 24," a black deaf (and eventually blind) man arrested by the police for vagrancy in 1945 and consigned for decades to the Lincoln State School and Colony for the Feebleminded in Illinois, that black inmates were forced to the bottom of Lincoln's pecking order. White guards gave black prisoners the most menial jobs and the harshest treatment, such as the "jail ward" in which inmates deemed troublemakers were made to shovel tons of coal (Bakke). One assumes conditions were no better for nonwhite inhabitants of Lincoln earlier in the century.

Under these circumstances, it is not surprising that some of the clearest traces of resistance to the policing of disabled beggars show up in the black press, though not, as far as I know, until well into the twentieth century. The headline of a 1921 *Chicago Defender* article describing one "legless" man's resistance to arrest by a "mendicant squad" makes no bones about the racial dynamics of the scene: "Bites White Man's Leg." A 1936 *Defender* piece with similar racial emphasis, "Jail 4 Whites for Defense of Beggar from Cop in Loop," memorializes the action of one seriously ugly crowd:

> Four white people were surreptitiously jailed Monday for defending a helpless one-legged Race beggar from attacks by a policeman in the Loop.
>
> Several hundred white people took part in the incident in which they attacked the policeman, Leonard Orlowski, plainclothes man . . . who said he was one of several assigned to rid the loop of mendicants. . . .
>
> According to the policeman, Lewis attempted to escape on his one foot. Orlowski said he was unable to control the crowd and arrest Lewis at the same time so he kicked the beggar's one leg from under him and then arrested the four. . . . Hundred [*sic*] of the spectators followed the police wagon to central station where they registered protests that Orlowskie could have performed his duty without being brutal.[38]

Here we have a bit of intriguing information about an ugly crowd's composition: the four objectors, three of whom were fined a dollar each for disorderly conduct, included two women, one of whom is described as "Mrs. Ruth Kuntz, 40 . . . executive of a downtown advertising agency." This incident got a fair amount of coverage and sparked protest against "inhuman treatment" in the white press as well; there, predictably, the beggar is "colored," the bystanders racially unmarked ("Arrests Beggar for 28th Time"; "Loop Beggar Arrested"; "Policeman and the Beggar"). For *Defender* readers, well used to stories of police brutality, a "Race beggar's" white allies made the scene newsworthy.

With Ruth Kuntz, Ben Lewis, and their fellow protestors we enter into the final section of this book, "The End of Ugly Law." Another story from the *Defender* serves as an even more compelling pivot, a record of how a black disabled beggar talked back to his accusers that made the paper's front page in 1924. The title was "Blind Beggar Defends Self at the Bar: Sightless, Eloquent, but Loses Case." It recounts the day in court of James Bradfield, "a tall, thin, shabby-looking individual, blind and homeless, at least that is what one gathers from reading a sign made of cardboard which hangs from around his neck as he makes his sightless way to and fro in the city of Chicago." Arrested for begging by an officer who behaved, the *Defender* notes with a straight face, "in a very gentlemanly manner, according to the ethics of Chicago policemen," Bradfield maintained that when he retrieved his confiscated possessions at the jailhouse, several hundred dollars had been stolen from him. He argued, in a line of defense about which I have more to say in the next chapter, that he never asked for money and therefore was no beggar. Bradfield chose to represent himself in court, and he is described as a witty self-advocate who at one point refused to answer a prosecutor's question "on advice of counsel."

But it was not Bradfield's jokes that made the *Defender*'s headlines. It was his insistence that the court recognize him. In his closing argument,

> He threw up his hands to the heavens and bewailed the fact that he was blind and couldn't see the dirty cowards who on account of his affliction brutally assaulted him without provocation. His voice trembled as he spoke of his longing only for liberty, the one thing that was continually threatened on account of his helplessness. His voice fairly filled the room as he boomed out how his father and his grandfather fought for liberty and of how he himself climbed San Juan hill and fought for liberty and after 60

> years in this world he was continually being denied the right to enjoy his liberty. The courtroom was absolutely still for a minute after his big voice had died down . . . and then court adjourned until 2 o'clock, when the verdict would be delivered.
>
> At 2 o'clock the courtroom was full of people who had been attracted by the sound of Mr. Bradfield's voice in argument and who were interested as to the outcome of the case. . . . the bailiff read the verdict of the jury, which was guilty. A $5 fine was imposed upon the defendant. He promptly made a motion for a new trial, which was overruled, as was his appeal for arrest of judgment; he then prayed an appeal which was allowed in 20 days. As he was under $200 cash bond he was released and slowly he was led away to the elevator—a tall, big, shabby old man—blind, but undaunted in his determination to enjoy his liberty.

This story obviously spoke to *Defender* readers. On page A1, it recorded events already of interest to the community, as the packed courtroom attests. Part of the appeal lay in the figure of the black military hero claiming his central role, along with his Civil War forbears, in the nation's guarantee of the promise of liberty. Bradfield had enacted a drama of masculinity. But as much as that, I think, what must have struck a chord here was an aspect of James Bradfield's proclamation that we might now identify as black blind disability theory—a theory, that is, of intersectionality:

> His deep rumbling voice took on more volume as he told them that he didn't expect to have more rights than other people because he was a blind man and a black man at that: that he only wanted his rights as an American citizen: to be protected by the courts the same as any other citizen.

The theory lies partly in the grammar. "Because he was a blind man *and* a black man." A "black man *at that*." Being blind and black is more than being both/and; it is being at that, living in the weightier, more complicated, heightened state of "at that." Whatever blindness brings, the phrase implies, blackness will bring it more so. We might expect "at that" to mean "even worse," but on the surface at least the entire sentence contradicts that reading. Blackness "at that" seems to invite or demand more privilege and compensation (however intermixed with pity and contempt): "he didn't expect to have more rights because . . ." Refuting notions of blackness and blindness as essentialized states of exception, Bradfield refused to base his call for justice on an identity claim, a beggar's exemption on the grounds of race and disability. Instead, he made what Yoshino calls a "liberty claim," emphasizing what he had in common with "any other citizen," the right to protection by the court (188). In doing so, this legally indicted beggar, for one moment in a courtroom in Chicago, placed African Americans (and all Americans at that) at his intersection.

PART III

THE END OF THE UGLY LAWS

Personal liberty, in this basic sense of the right not to be unjustly or causelessly confined, has been taken as a fundamental, natural, and social right in Chapter 39 of the Magna Carta and the due process clauses of federal and state constitutions. If the disabled have the right to live in the world, they must have the right to make their way into it. . . . A right on such terms to the use of the streets, walks, roads and highways is a rock-bottom minimum.

—JACOBUS TENBROEK,
"The Right to Live in the World," 1966

9

THE RIGHT TO THE CITY

> The right to the city is like a cry and a demand.
>
> —HENRI LEFEBVRE, "The Right to the City," 1999

At the dramatic climax of Belluso's biographical play *The Body of Bourne* (2003), Belluso's forebear, disabled writer Randolph Bourne, openly challenges Chicago's ugly law. From the outset of Belluso's play, Bourne has grappled with his relation to the categories policed by the unsightly beggar ordinance. The actual historical figure Bourne, as Longmore and Miller have noted, had himself, in the lightning space of two years between 1911 and 1913, revised his landmark essay "The Philosophy of Handicap" to replace every instance of the ugly law's stark word "deformity" with new terms, "handicap" or "disability" (64).[1] In Belluso's dramatic biography, the first scene begins with Bourne's narration of his own birth: "I will be called 'deformed' when I am born. 'Crippled' and 'hunchbacked.' There are other names, other names which will be given to my body. But what will I do, with these names?" (4). The play follows Bourne through the development of his career as an intellectual and social critic, repeatedly stressing Bourne's fear of appearing on stage in public. In Belluso's version of his life, Bourne is finally persuaded to deliver a public speech in Chicago opposing U.S. involvement in World War I. He brushes off police threats to arrest him for delivering the speech, saying, "I'm just a harmless cripple," and is answered "That's the point exactly." The ugly ordinance, he is told, will be used to prevent him from speaking (101). In a critical scene, Belluso's Bourne flouts the law and appears in spotlight at the Chicago City Club, comparing the war to a disease and insisting, "I will allow my body to be seen" (103).

As I noted at the outset of this book, no such moment actually happened. Devising it, Belluso commemorates and celebrates what did happen: a long history of everyday resistance to being marginalized that disabled people have practiced, individually and collectively, throughout the twentieth century, finding matter-of-fact ways of being in public, avenues for getting there, means of claiming a right to the city. (Even to have to declare or celebrate that right is an indignity. In a recent essay, Aguilera tells of the "café lady" who approached him and a wheelchair-riding co-worker to praise them for their inspirational courage merely in appearing in their local coffee house ["Café Lady"].)

It is no accident that Belluso's Bourne refutes the ugly law in spotlight, on a stage. This self-referential device recognizes the history of the unsightly beggar ordinances as a history of performance and of the prohibition of performance. Bourne's City Club platform is the opposite of a freak show. His primary aim is not to display his body but to participate in civic discourse, to help shape the body politic. He is using his body as a means for participating in political struggle—not in the objectified manner envisioned by those who might regard it as abhorrence but instead in a subjective, passionate, and articulate defense of universal human dignity. He refuses to conceal himself or to allow other people's malice, disgust, or patronization to exclude him. Belluso invents a very contemporary scene, a back-projection from the assertive street theaters of the disability rights movement onto Bourne's time, in order to stage the present; Bourne's speech is the speech of ADAPT's activism, of current war resistance by many disabled people.[2] In this moment, the theater of disability rights struggle, tied to a broader politic, emerges.

Today citing the unsightly begging ordinance facilitates cries and demands in the present. The crude elements of ugly law may be broken down roughly as follows: the call for harsh policing; antibegging; systematized suspicion set up to winnow the deserving from the undeserving; suppression of acts of solidarity by and for marginalized urban social groups; and structural and institutional repulsion of disabled people, whether by design or by default. None of these has disappeared since the demise of formally enacted unsightly beggar ordinances. At the same time, daily, since the Burgdorfs named the laws and brought their history to light in 1975 (and well before that), people have worked, individually and collectively, to put an end to the elemental legacies of ugly law.

Recent urban studies scholars who invoke the spirit of Lefebvre's slogan on "the right to the city" do not include the history of such disability struggle in their glosses on the complex meaning of that right, though Lefebvre's analysis has resonance in a disability context.[3] When Marxist Lefebvre himself analyzed segregation in his 1967 manifesto, he focused first and foremost on the working class. "Only the working class can become the agent, the social carrier and support," Lefebvre wrote, of "a transformed and renewed *right to urban life*" (158, italics in original). In Don Mitchell's ringing tribute to and application of Lefebvre, *The Right to the City* (2003), Mitchell concentrates on public demonstrators, migratory workers, and "the homeless." Jeff Ferrell examines the "extreme urban subcultures" of "graffiti artists, young people, radical environmentalists and the homeless" in his 2001 "history of resistance to urban spatial controls" (19). Disabled people belong, of course, to all these groups, but the cries and demands of the disability movement do not register in these analyses. Neil Smith's 1996 study of the contemporary "revanchist city," an urban space increasingly resegregated and without a working (as opposed to a merely simulated) public sphere, makes no mention of how disabled people have been structurally excluded from sites of meaningful urban interaction; neither does Andy Merrifield's work (2002).

Mitchell quotes Sennett's powerful critique of the growing desire for frictionless, unimpeded, unconfronted passage through urban centers: "resistance is a fundamental necessity of the human body. Through feeling resistance, the body is roused to take note of the world in which it lives. . . . The body comes to life when coping with difficulty." But the disability implications of this passage are ignored, even though Sennett himself underscored them by including a story about passersby reacting nervously to a man with a prosthetic limb who stops to light a cigarette in public (16–18). Nowhere in this particular line of radical urban studies is there a glimpse of the profound insight of the disability movement: that the body of the city comes to life when it actively and deliberately copes with the *resistance* of impairment and of disability activism.

At the same time, as the erasure of begging in the cultural memory of ugly law suggests, the largely (but by no means exclusively) white, middle-class disability rights movement has not attended to the histories of vagrancy that played so large a part in the attack on the unsightly beggar. Today's struggles to erase the vestiges of ugly law also include the many forms of organizing that combat antihomeless city ordinances, which, like ugly law before them, raise "a politics of aesthetics above the politics of survival," enacting what Don Mitchell has called the neoliberal "annihilation of space by law." "By redefining what is acceptable behavior in public space, by in effect annihilating the spaces in which homeless people *must* live, these laws seek simply to annihilate homeless people themselves," writes Mitchell (167, 189). Remember the *Chicago Tribune*, 1881: "Alderman Peevey . . . proposes to abolish the woman with two sick children who . . . grinds 'Mollie Darling' incessantly." The most powerful examples of recent resistance to the legacy of the unsightly beggar ordinances reflect profound engagement at that very meeting ground of poverty, urban marginalization, and disability where ugly law culture first began to germinate. But that is a story for another book.

This final section of this book will trace the arc of the early development of that struggle. In the conclusion, I touch briefly on the 1970s, when the Burgdorfs named ugly law and a gathering social movement made disability history. But I focus here primarily on the late 1910s and early 1920s, when unsightly beggar ordinances disappeared from city council agendas, and earlier, when cities debated enacting the ordinances. What historical equivalents of the self-conscious and defiant "I will allow my body to be seen" or of "You cannot refuse to see these bodies" or "This is not the correct way to address the problem of disabled people begging" occurred at the time? Who, if anyone, said an outright no to the ugly laws? What opposition can we find in 1881 or 1895 or 1910?

BEGGING THE QUESTION

Let us start where ugly law started, at the level of city policy. Municipal skirting or dismissal of the unsightly beggar ordinance often took the quietest form: a city simply did not have one on its books. Many American cities did not pass ugly laws. In some cases, perhaps, city councils could not be bothered, but chances are good that in other cases the idea of law was floated and quietly rejected. We know that COS officials in New York drafted a version of the ordinance, but it got nowhere. Other cities that became COS strongholds—Buffalo and Indianapolis, for instance—never passed and as far as I know never publicly debated passing the ugly law.

Even cities that attempted to suppress public exposure of disabled bodies in the act of begging on the street invariably allowed and even sanctioned exposure of those bodies in other settings. Sometimes this occurred as a matter of official regulation. Peddling permit systems put into place by aldermen and mayors in many of these cities worked in tandem, and often at odds, with unsightly begging ordinances. What ugly laws forbid, peddling laws undid: begging while deformed (or *as* deformed) was criminal, but selling pencils while deformed was licensed, and as often as not for disabled people the license costs were waived. No municipal government in any American city that had an ugly ordinance on its books single-mindedly enforced the letter of the law; as I have shown, no government *could* enforce that letter as one unified entity, since many actors (police, magistrates, social workers, each with their own agendas and reactions) had to be involved. Moreover, no city leader or group of leaders could entirely fix and determine the spirit of the law. Under the narrowest interpretation of the law's intent—as a prohibition on begging alone or on begging plus exhibition, not as a removal of or general intervention into the lives of poor disabled people—licensed peddling was less a loophole than a commonsense solution.

COS leaders and some other reformers, however, saw unsightly peddling as a ruse for begging, and they did their best to lobby mayors to abolish peddler permitting and fee waivers.[4] Mayors often did not comply. At the turn of the century, Warner, Queen, and Harper argued that the "work of freeing the streets of mendicants is very much limited by the practice in most cities of giving licenses for petty peddling on the streets, or for operating musical instruments of the hand-organ type" (211).

New York's Mayor Grant, for instance, instituted an organ-grinding license system in 1889, issuing a set number of permits, three hundred, according to the following principle of selection: "those who needed most to resort to the hand organ for their support should be the first, . . . and the able-bodied fellows will have to stand back and take their chances of getting in after the blind, the lame, the Grand Army men and the aged are supplied with licenses" ("Organ Grinders' Licenses," 8). The first six licenses granted by the new "Organ Grinders' Clerk" all went to disabled men. In 1905, the Chicago City Council authorized the mayor to grant free sixty-day, renewable peddling permits to needy persons (many of them undoubtedly disabled) who were recommended by ward aldermen. Before long, the requirement of a recommendation was discontinued, and a clerk in the mayor's office issued permits at his own discretion. The clerk regarded the free license, one critic wrote, "as a charity to poor people. His statement is that one can judge by the appearance of the people as to their deservedness" (Freund, 102). This dynamic seems almost the polar opposite of ugly law; the appearance of disease or bodily anomaly might well improve instead of hindering a person's chances of free access to the street economy.

When Freund studied people he identified as beggars in Chicago in 1924 (many of whom he described as having "physical defects"), he focused extensively on a free peddling system that had effectively quashed the functions of ugly law. In a section on "Blind Beggars," he tells the following story: "The Juvenile Protective Association first recorded the case in 1918 when Mr. Cook was discovered begging on the street with his two-year-old son. . . . A police officer was called but refused to interfere because Mr. Cook had a license to peddle" (55). Later comes the narrative of "Walter James, blind and colored," who "also held a free peddler's permit. The article for sale, when any was offered, was a single soiled copy of a printed poem of which he was the author. 'The Chattanooga' was an irregular bit of verse which made no sense. One copy was all he had and filled all demands" (64). By the twentieth century, many of the struggles enacted around and through unsightly beggar ordinances clustered instead around peddling regulations, and in fact the peddling permit mechanisms had in themselves become a major reason why ugly laws were not enforced.[5]

What about opposition to the ugly laws by the people whom they targeted? Certainly, again very quietly, individual people simply strategically ignored the existence of the ordinances. Perhaps they claimed beauty practices, refusing to be profiled as unsightly, like the unnamed woman, "immobile for most of her life, suffering from rickets, osteoarthritis, and cerebral palsy," who was buried, as archeologists unearthing almshouse gravesites at New York's Snake Hill recently discovered, "with an array of personal items including a jar of cold cream, a can of talcum powder, a mirror, a hairbrush and curlers, lipstick, a toothbrush, and the remains of a toiletry case" (Romey, 46). Perhaps they defiantly displayed their bodies, like Harry Gravell, a legless former motorman who went about "with a trumpeter and an automobile" campaigning against the judge who had denied him a jury trial for his injury suit against Toledo Railways, proclaiming "I want to save other poor cripples from his power."[6] Perhaps, more quietly, they engaged in what we might call "disrememory," after blues musician Blind Boy Fuller—the pretense or actual practice of not remembering as a form of noncompliance. According to a welfare department report on Fuller, when he was accused of "playing for money on the streets, although he . . . had been told it was 'strictly against the rules,' he was asked if the form for [welfare] application had been read to him but he said he 'disremembered'" (Bastin, 235). The welfare examiners terminated Fuller's benefits. In such welfare regulations, vestiges of ugly law lingered long after cities ceased enacting ordinances—and so, too, surely, did practices of tactical disremembering.

Certainly, too, as I have already suggested, individual people being picked up on unsightly begging charges sometimes attempted to resist arrest, either by appealing to passersby or by taking matters into their own hands. In New York, which had no ugly law per se but where police chief Conlin nevertheless made a point of cracking down on "impudent," "really afflicted and deformed" beggars in 1896, John Bourne, who had "a palsied leg" and who had been arrested six times in the previous four years for begging, "assaulted Officer S. by striking him on the head with his crutch" during his arrest ("Illustrative Cases," 2). Here is a Bourne who historically did challenge the policing of his body and insist, at risk, that he would allow his body to be seen—a very different figure, under far more wretched circumstances, than Randolph Bourne in John Belluso's play. In John Bourne's case (and one assumes many others) such protest was ineffectual: he was sentenced to six months in prison.

Occasionally we find traces of other, more organized contestation against the rhetoric of unsightly begging by people who were made into its subjects. Sometimes this contestation took overtly criminalized forms. In 1903, the *New York Times* reported that city COS officials had received a threatening phone call after they instigated the arrest of a "band" of beggars "who . . . deliberately defied them." All the beggars were "one-legged," according to the *Times*, except Chauncy Homer, "not a cripple" but "able . . . to simulate paralysis with a skill that has often deceived physicians." Witnesses verified that the group had been "soliciting alms from the passing crowd." The COS maintained that this was a front for even more nefarious schemes: "The plan, it is said, is for the cripple to go to a promising town, beg until he learns of establishments which carry considerable cash . . . and then inform a band of burglars" ("Arrest of Beggar Band"). The positioning of disabled beggars as organized felons reinforced the idea that disabled poor people are always a social menace: not only did they represent an ideological threat to the capitalist ethos of hard work and self-reliance and sturdy bodies as instruments of production, and a eugenic threat to the genes of the nation; now they also represented a criminal threat to the social and economic life of the community.

This kind of alleged cripple espionage, this crippled intelligence agency, loomed as a danger in exact proportion to the misleading, putative helplessness of the unsightly beggar, whose access somehow to privileged economic data goes unquestioned in the story. But the *Times*'s "picturesque" one-legged beggars proved openly thuggish. James Forbes, who answered the COS phone, "received the message of defiance," which threatened that any person who interfered with the gang "would do so at his peril." "It was in a voice he recognized," he reported to the *New York Times*. Precisely: the call attempted futilely to deter not only COS interference but COS *recognition*, the society's persistent castigation of defiant beggars "of the most dangerous class" ("Arrest of Beggar Band"). When the city police discontinued the COS-sponsored mendicancy squad several years later, patrons of a Bowery saloon much like the Doctor's celebrated by burning James Forbes in effigy ("Detectives Ferret Out").

In 1911, George Gray, "the legless newsboy of Times Square," tried a more socially sanctioned form of protest against the same COS officer, James Forbes, suing for twenty-five thousand dollars in damages for libel after Forbes *recognized* Gray in print as the very type that needed COS intervention: "the runaway boy who goes on the road to see the world, lost both legs while a tramp; returned to New York and became a street beggar." Forbes's article, co-written with Silas McBee and published in an Episcopal church publication, worked clearly in the genre of deformance, holding Gray forth as a model of successful COS reform: Forbes boasted that Gray was "[i]nduced to lead an honest life under the auspices of the National Association" and now "maintained himself honorably."[7] (In a similar vein, Forbes's obituary in the *Times* described his work setting up "scores of crippled beggars . . . in self-respect as newspaper vendors" ["Late James Forbes"].)

George Gray, however, did not need to derive his self-respect from James Forbes; he had no desire to be held up as the COS's poster newsboy, and he objected to the insinuation that he had ever lacked "a reputation for honesty and integrity." He refused, in short, to be made for one moment into an unsightly beggar. His libel case against Forbes and McBee was fought through multiple appeals. In the end, for reasons I have not been able to discover, he somehow failed to satisfy one of the elements of libel, and he lost, required to pay ten dollars in costs for his trouble. Gray's difficulty contesting Forbes's interpellations was compounded by the *New York Times* coverage of the case, which erroneously reported his name not as George but as James, Forbes's own first name.[8]

THE LEGAL RECORD

In the broader legal arena, where we would find whatever formal principled defenses occurred for people like John Bourne or his less antagonistic begging counterparts, disturbingly little opposition shows up on record.[9] The archive of nuisance law yields evidence of objection to subjective assessments of unsightliness, but only in regard to property, not persons: "The law will not declare a thing a nuisance because it is unsightly and disfiguring . . . nor because it is unpleasant to the eye and in violation of the rules of propriety and good taste. . . . No fanciful notions are recognized. The law does not cater to men's tastes nor consult their convenience merely"

(*Woodstock Burying Ground Ass'n v. Hager*, 68 Vt. at 432 [1896]). "It is quite clear that the law does not recognize any legal right in any one to . . . maintain that an unsightly or ill proportioned edifice is a nuisance because it offends his eye, or his too cultivated taste" (*Stotler v. Rochelle*, 83 Kan. at 788 [1910]). Marshaled in defense of cemeteries and piggeries, "unsightly erections" and "unsightly gulches," "appearances" and "incumbrances," spite-fences and cars driven on Sunday, this principle was applied to "things" declared nuisances but not to human beings.

One gratifying 1921 case does assert disabled people's right to public space, but the judges deny the memory of the ugly laws. In *Blackman Health Resort v. City of Atlanta*, the proposed construction of a resort had been blocked by the city on the grounds that the new building would make a nearby park "an annex for crippled and deformed persons" and that "to permit the erection of the building would cause crippled, deformed, and diseased people to be near the Tenth Street public school" (151 Ga. 507). The board of education and the PTA had lobbied for denial of the building permit. The Georgia Supreme Court ruled that by refusing the permit the mayor and council had abused their discretion: "It would seem that public parks of a city were intended for the free use of sick persons, cripples, invalids, and convalescents, as well as persons enjoying perfect health, children, and their nurses" (151 Ga. 507). This reasonable ruling proceeds by insisting that limits on crippled, deformed, and diseased people's right to the city are unprecedented: "So far as we are aware, it has never been suggested that any one or more of these classes can be arbitrarily prohibited the use of a public park directly or indirectly, or that their presence is unwelcome" (151 Ga. 507).

The rights protected here were those of invalids, not beggars. Long trails of case law contesting general municipal begging, peddling, and vagrancy ordinances are there to be followed, but I have found no legal challenge specifically to an unsightly beggar ordinance. Various American courts across two centuries have mulled over the question of whether municipal bans on appeals to passersby to buy goods or give alms constitute a violation of the First Amendment, following the lead of one mid-nineteenth-century judge who associated the crying out of hawkers with political outcry, "which some lexicographers conceive that the derivation of the word would seem to indicate" (Rhyne, Burton, and Murphy, 7). This argument, frequently made about vocal soliciting and peddling, was far less frequently applied to cases involving wordless gestures of begging. It was never extended explicitly into the terrain of ugly law. The emphasis in the ordinances on appearances rather than words made appeals to overturn the law on First Amendment grounds highly unlikely. Disabled bodies "spoke" volumes, spoke if anything too loudly, on the streets of ugly law cities. But they never spoke freely, and they never were imagined to speak politically.

Occasionally we find the presence of disabled bodies in legal challenges to begging prohibitions, but these bodies inevitably function only as exceptions to, not as the grounds of, First Amendment claims. They *frame* the large questions at stake, but the questions are not theirs. They appear, but not on their own behalf. Take, for example, a case from the present, the ruling in *C.C.B. v. Florida*, a 1984 Florida Supreme Court decision holding that cities are not "entitled to absolutely prohibit a beggar's exercise of his freedom of speech" (458 So.2d at 50). The court in *C.C.B. v. Florida* bolsters its case by noting that a prior California court decision on the constitutionality of an antibegging statute cites comments of the legislative committee report that had enacted California's antibegging statute in 1961 to the effect that "the blind or crippled person who merely sits or stands by the wayside" was excepted from the ambit of the law (*Ulmer*, 55 Cal. App. 3d at 266 [1976]). Here the right of the "blind or crippled person" to beg wordlessly is defended not as speech but as the outside of speech, mute and passive, "mere." The disabled body represents a permissible form of silent begging that appears in contrast to the prohibited, actively verbal, form. No disabled party was involved in challenging the law in either the California or the Florida case, and the courts blandly assumed that no disabled person could be charged under the statute.

When disabled bodies do "speak up" in the history of American begging law, however, anything they say can be used against them. This is illustrated in a case directly preceding and very much related to the development of unsightly beggar ordinances, in which a New York appeals court ruled that disabled bodies in and of themselves could in fact constitute a form of speech—begging speech—and that the exercise of this kind of speech was punishable. (This was not a First Amendment case; here the constitutionality of begging law itself went unchallenged.) In the matter of *Haller* (1877), we find the narrative of Frank Haller,

> a boy about ten years of age, and a cripple, unable to stand, and obliged to move on his hands and legs. At the time of his arrest, he had been moving down Broadway on the sidewalk, from John Street to Wall Street . . . when he was stopped and taken into custody by the officers. As he passed along the sidewalk the officer saw him holding out his hand to several persons, and

> receiving money from them, but he did not hear him speak to any of him. It is claimed that this silent action on his part was not "begging alms" or "soliciting charity" within the meaning of the statutes. (*Haller*, 3 Abb. N. Cas. at 66)

The court rejected this claim, affirming that the antimendicancy statute in question "does not necessarily require proof of spoken words to constitute begging." In fact, the judges argued, "in many instances words are far less effective to accomplish the end than simple acts. The deaf and dumb man, real or pretended, who stands with a placard on his breast, and with extended hat or hand, is a solicitor of charity as completely as though he spoke to passers by" (*Haller*, 3 Abb. N. Cas. at 67). Gesture could constitute begging, as the theoretical deaf man (real or—note—pretended) functions to epitomize.

But the ruling went further still. At the farthest reach of the "matter of Haller," the law prohibited not only street behavior but, potentially, *being* on the street for disabled people.

> Every one whose diseased or crippled condition appeals to sympathy, and who places himself in a position to attract attention, or passes along the street calling attention by sign, act or look to his unhappy condition, and receiving from those who observe him the charity which he is obviously seeking, is a solicitor of charity within the meaning of the law. . . . Indeed, the class of silent beggars who exhibit deformities, wounds or injuries which tell plainer than words their needy and helpless condition are the most successful of solicitors for charity. (*Haller*, 3 Abb. N. Cas. at 67)

The language of exhibiting deformity brings us to the brink of ugly law, and here, as in the unsightly beggar ordinances, *acts* of appeal seem to be the problem: "placing himself in a position," attracting attention, "calling attention," "seeking obviously." (The *Haller* ruling begins, in fact, with "act" talk: "The act of a cripple . . . is 'begging for alms.'") At the same time, however, because disease or crippling might inevitably, and without any deliberate invitation, draw the stares of passersby, or because they might engender unsolicited sympathy simply by being seen as "unhappy, . . . needy and helpless condition[s]," *Haller* verges on ruling that disabled people, no matter how they behave, *embody* begging.[10] This decision paves the way for ugly law. Indeed, it suggests another factor at stake in the emergence of unsightly begging ordinances: the need to close the loophole that might allow disabled bodies to tell stories of poverty "plainer than words." Thus, the one example in the history of pertinent U.S. begging case law, *Haller*, that treats "diseased or crippled condition[s]" as acts of expression reads them as barred speech, not free speech.[11]

Only much later did the Supreme Court come to recognize that conduct or gesture might be protectable speech.[12] In the meantime, on the tough streets of ugly law, unsightly beggars were surely not the only people subject to arrest for prohibited nonverbal forms of solicitation. Many arrests for prostitution depended on essentially the same idea, that no proof of words spoken was needed. There were probably narcotics sales cases from the same era that also made the point.

Historically the First Amendment has offered even the open speech of disabled beggars no protection. Quite the opposite: Neilson has noted that the courts have tolerated restrictions on begging far more than on any other form of public speech, however hateful, because "begging, unlike sexual harassment or racist speech, is the one form of public speech that most often confronts more privileged members of society"—merchants, property owners, white straight men (3). Mayoral permit systems, as I have discussed, sometimes granted disabled people a limited "license to harass," but as often as not, coexisting municipal ordinances like the ugly laws contravened that permission, trapping unsightly subjects in perpetually uncertain states of exception that finally granted only one group of people "harassment" privilege: the police.

In addition, as Rabban has shown, during the era of ugly law "the widespread judicial hostility to Free Speech claims transcended any individual issue or litigant," making it all the more unlikely that a significant legal interpretation of unsightly begging as protected speech could have occurred (131). The legal record offers a sobering challenge to dreams of First Amendment legal remedy for what the Burgdorfs, in their first uncovering of ugly law, called "A History of Unequal Treatment." Like the white women and men and women of color whose sidewalk encounters Neilson has studied, most poor disabled people under the regime of ugly law experienced the courts "as offering no recourse or worse, as posing the added threat of legal repression" (16).

"It is obvious," an Ohio judge wrote in 1921, upholding the conviction of a blind man found guilty of begging, "that if such an ordinance included the blind only, its unconstitutionality would not be questioned" (*Lefever v. City of Columbus*, 23 Ohio N.P. [N.C.] at 372).[13] This judge would presumably have had no doubt, therefore, about the illegality of ugly law, and yet no one—not him, not anyone, not in his own town, which had enacted and enforced the ordinance, or anywhere else—no one I know of sought grounds of any kind to challenge the constitutionality of the unsightly beggar ordinances. Arguably, Pennsylvania's state version of an ugly law violated the Equal Protection Clause of the Fourteenth Amendment, but if so, no one noticed. Partly because, to a significant extent, the notion of the citizen presumed an able body, and probably primarily because the measure was generally regarded as protective and benevolent, no analytic framework placing ugly law in the light of the U.S. Constitution ever emerged.

As in the *Haller* case, disabled people did occasionally manage to take procedural objections to their arrests for begging to appeals courts. In Brooklyn in 1896, three disabled men found a lawyer to appeal for them in county court. Their case, a newspaper reported, was "in one respect . . . unique": "One of the prisoners had lost an arm, . . . another . . . had lost a leg, and James Thompson, colored, had no legs below the knees, being compelled to stump along with short crutches." What made the incident newsworthy was not its sideshow aspect or the opportunity for ridicule provided by this singsong lineup of cripples; magistrates regularly encountered disabled vagrants. The *lawyer's* disability sold the story—that and the novelty of a disabled lawyer defending disabled clients. Lawyer Finnerty, who "himself had but one arm," pleaded "that the men should go free. They had friends and homes." Finnerty's disability advocacy retains its dignity despite the dismissive filter of the *Brooklyn Daily Eagle* report: "Of course they [the three defendants] were unable to work," he argued. "But it was no crime to lose a limb, else the counselor himself might be arraigned on that plea" ("Three Memberless Vagrants"). Finnerty went on to become a judge himself in the Brooklyn courts. The men he defended, unsuccessful in their appeal, were returned to the penitentiary to serve out five-month sentences.

Let us loiter in Pennsylvania awhile, because the state's court records offer multiple interesting examples of such appeals. (Pennsylvania, for reasons unclear to me, seems to be an epicenter for shifts and tremors in the terrain of the disabled vagrant and beggar). These Pennsylvania cases clearly illuminate the contradictions embodied in the "acts of cripples" and their ilk as cities and courts construed them. One pertinent legal case found its way to a higher court level from Philadelphia in 1909. The man who appealed his sentence was arrested not for violating an ugly law but simply for vagrancy, and he did not challenge vagrancy law per se. General vagrancy and/or nuisance laws were often called on to achieve the same immediate ends as the unsightly beggar ordinances, whether or not ugly laws existed in a given jurisdiction. It may well be the case, too, that blind people like the plaintiff in the 1909 case were not perceived as persons exhibiting "deformities," the particular category demarcated by Pennsylvania's 1894 state law.

In the case in question, *Burnside v. Superintendent of House of Correction*, a blind Philadelphia man named Charles Burnside had been "arrested upon complaint of Reserve Officer Morrow, charged with begging in the street, and after a hearing on May 17, 1909, before D.S. Scott . . . was committed by the said magistrate to the house of correction for a period of three months." The next day Burnside filed a petition for a writ of habeas corpus, arguing that the committing magistrate had not stated formally that he was found guilty in the court transcript and therefore that he was improperly confined. A week later the higher court affirmed Burnside's charge that "the transcript of the record of the magistrate in this case is defective." For a moment, Burnside had won his case. Since all the original witnesses against Charles Burnside had regathered for the appeal hearing, the court immediately proceeded to hear testimony and rule itself on whether Burnside was in fact guilty as charged. A summary of the court's decision for a digest prepared by the West Publishing Company reads as follows:

> Where blind man, able to earn $6 per week in blind man's home of which he had once been inmate, received aid from charitable society and went on streets to beg by attracting public attention by playing small hand organ and exposing tin cup to hold alms, he is vagrant within meaning of Act of May 8 1876, P.L. 154, 18 P.S. 2032–2042, and liable to commitment to house of correction. (*Vale Pennsylvania Digest,* 4)

(This kind of summary, written by a publishing house's reporters, not a judge, is not a reliable source for legal purposes. But it tells us the facts, and it does so in language that speaks for the broader culture.)

Because Burnside appealed his case, we have a fuller record of what happened in court than cursory (and often no longer extant) city records yield for proceedings against unsightly beggars at the petty municipal level. Much of what happened, no doubt, was typical. The justices took pains to assure the public that they were not pitiless: "The great affliction of the relator appeals most strongly to us, as to every person, but our sympathy for this affliction may not be allowed to influence our judgment as to the quality of his act" (*Burnside v. Superintendent,* 18 Pa. D. 601 [1909])[14]

The persistent language of affliction in the Burnside ruling is supplemented by portrayal of Charles Burnside as nonproductive (and hence "vagrant"):

> It did not appear from the testimony, nor was it pretended, that the relator is a musician or has had any musical training. . . . That which he was doing can in no sense be construed as work or labor, nor can it be properly or truthfully said that the sounds produced by the instrument which he was playing, as described in the testimony, were intended either for the education or the entertainment of the public. (*Burnside,* 18 Pa. D. 601 at 5)

The presence of an institution for the blind tipped the balance against Burnside; the prosecution's final witness, George W. Hunt, a superintendent of the Pennsylvania Working Home for Blind Men, testified that Burnside had at one time been an inmate there, employed in the broommaking shop, and could be readmitted there at any time. (Burnside was not, however, remanded to the custody of Mr. Hunt but rather returned to the penal House of Corrections.)

Why did Burnside prefer life as a hand-organ player who lived at No. 3815 Pearl Street and begged on 8th Street in Philadelphia rather than as an inmate of the Working Home in the same city? If he testified on his own behalf, his words were not recorded. A brief reference by one prosecution witness to Burnside's family on Pearl Street suggests one possible reason. Choosing domestic life over segregated institutionalization, Burnside had stressed to others that he had a family to support.

Unsurprisingly, COS officials played key roles in incarcerating Burnside. Not one but three COS agents made a point of coming to Burnside's habeas corpus hearing to repeat the same story. Burnside had approached the Philadelphia COS after first being ordered off the streets by the police a month before his arrest, in early April. He had told them he "would have to have help," and the society had given him a total of $38.25 over the course of the next month and had delivered coal and groceries to the family on Pearl Street. In return, Burnside had promised "to remain off the streets," but still the COS officers had seen him "on the street, playing his mechanical instrument . . . and had seen a number of people drop money into the tin cup which he exhibited for the purpose" (*Burnside,* 18 Pa. D. 601). Paradoxically, the facts that might have supported finding Burnside a "deserving" case—his eligibility for COS assistance and qualification for placement in a home for blind men—weighed strongly against him, making him, in the court's view, someone who chose the indecency of begging over the more institutionalized and economically poorer (but more respectable) options offered to other disabled people.

The stakes in *Burnside* are obviously similar to those in ugly law; notice the emphasis in the court's summary on attracting public attention, on "exposing" the tin cup. Burnside's unsuccessful plea of habeas corpus reveals the difficulties that may have prevented others from challenging the unsightly beggar ordinances.

Habeas corpus is sometimes explained as "let us see the body." The body in question, that which has been forbidden to appear in public, now comes forward to demand the legal right to be displayed in court. When a beggar like Burnside has filed a habeas petition, he is arguing that he has been held (detained, imprisoned) wrongfully and that he should be allowed to appear in the superior court to contest his detention. His legal appearance counters the illegal appearances that ugly law imagines. He (or his lawyer) has the agency here, demanding in a sense like Belluso's Bourne, "I will allow my body to be seen." But there is another kind of agency encoded in the grammar of habeas corpus. *Habeas corpus*: Latin for "let us have the body." The "us" in question, the "us" who "has," multiplies where diseased, maimed, and deformed bodies are concerned. Not only the House of Corrections but also the COS and the Pennsylvania Working Home for Blind Men laid claim to the body of Burnside.

As contradictions between and within state and municipal laws illustrate, disabled beggars continued to present insoluble riddles for the State of Pennsylvania and the City of Philadelphia. Sometimes they functioned as exceptions to the rule; sometimes, as the rule's targets; sometimes both at once. On the one hand, the 1887 book of laws and ordinances in Philadelphia stipulated that ordinances banning vagrancy and begging "shall not apply . . . to any blind, deaf, or dumb person, nor shall it be applicable to any maimed or crippled person who is unable to perform manual labor" (*Digest of the Laws*, 461). Was this law "better" for disabled people than ugly law? Not necessarily: it consigned disabled people to the role of beggar, particularly deaf and blind people, whom it understood as categorically incapable of working. (By the way, the proviso also exempted women and minor children from arrest for criminal begging, in an effort to protect all three types of dependence.) Ableism runs as deep in permitted-begging as in antibegging currents in American culture. It can be said for Philadelphia's exception, however, that it sought to diminish rather than increase official harassment of disabled people who begged and that it did not deny them the street, that one "arena of society," as Merrifield puts it, "not occupied by institutions" (87). On the other hand, in 1894 the broader State of Pennsylvania enacted the only state ugly law I know of, prohibiting "the exhibition of physical and mental deformities . . . for the purpose of soliciting alms."

The state's legal history offers conflicting evidence about who was barred from doing what at the point where disability and begging intersected, conflicts fought out in the courts but never settled in the beggar's favor. Consider the case of Thomas M. Thompson. Thompson is described in an appeals court narrative as a blind man who "day after day placed himself upon" the streets of Philadelphia "for the purpose of begging, . . . calling the attention of the passers-by to his pitiable condition by playing on a small hand organ. . . . In this way he made his living" (*Thompson v. Superintendent,* 58 Pa. Super. at 465 [1914]). Almost certainly influenced by his predecessor Burnside (chances are high that they had encountered each other in the Pennsylvania Working Home for Blind Men), Thompson filed an appeal in 1914 attempting to overturn his conviction for vagrancy and his sentence of three months in the House of Correction. He appealed on two grounds: that the magistrate who committed him had failed to specify that his sentence included not only imprisonment but also hard labor, work he could not perform, and that as a blind man he was not legally subject to penalties for vagrancy.[15] Thompson's lawyer argued in his defense that an act passed by the Pennsylvania legislature in 1879 had specified that "[t]he blind and crippled are exempt from prosecution" for vagrancy (*Thompson,* 58 Pa. Super at 465).[16] The appeals court judges disagreed with this reading of the legislative record, ruling that the fifth section of that act "provides, it is true, that the act shall not apply to certain persons mentioned therein, including those who are blind, but it does not exempt those persons from the prohibitions contained in other statutes," in particular the earlier 1876 vagrancy statute, which contained no exemption for blind persons and under which Thompson had been charged (*Thompson,* 58 Pa. Super at 465).[17]

Pennsylvania lawmakers were clearly uncertain about what to do about unsightly beggars. Antibegging laws were designed to punish what Stanley succinctly calls "the withholding of labor from sale" (1998, 262), but because people we now call disabled were often understood categorically to be those people unable to work, they had, by definition, nothing to withhold. Their presence in the streets significantly troubled cultural adjudications of worthy or unworthy dependence. Defined simultaneously as those who could not contract for work and those who refused to do so, unsightly beggars posed a particularly knotty social problem (one resolved primarily by the mechanism of institutionalization, which both Thompson and Burnside resisted).

The blind vagrant in particular did hard representational labor in the annals of Pennsylvania law, caught in a tangle of conflicting significations:

as the one kind of needy person who cannot work and therefore cannot help but beg, a human "exemption"; as the one kind of ungrateful beggar who disgusted the most, a human eyesore. It is unsurprising, therefore, that two rigorous challenges to the core dynamics of ugly law emerged from the mass of blind beggars. Thompson's protest against the hard-labor provision of Pennsylvania tramp law struck at the heart of a major social contradiction. Stanley has shown how northern antibegging laws enacted after the abolition of slavery—often pushed by the same COS leaders who had been ardent abolitionists—imposed with no compunction "forcible labor as a punishment for dependence" (1998, xiii).[18] Thomas Thompson's challenge constituted a potential landmark case. Instead it vanished from the legal annals, and Thompson went to prison.

Even outside the plots of blindness and of begging, Pennsylvania court solutions to crises of unsightliness tended, however ambivalently, to push diseased, maimed, and deformed people out of public view. A 1905 Philadelphia dispute involved a NIMBY question: whether Margaret O'Hara's small "hospital for the open air treatment of consumptives" constituted a nuisance and posed the kind of threat to the "health and comfort" of her suburban residential neighborhood that was barred by a restriction in the deed to her property (*Gowen et al. v. O'Hara et al.,* 15 Pa. D. at 753). O'Hara's next-door neighbor feared contagion, but he placed emphasis also on the offense to the eye posed by the consumptive residents. He pled, and the court concurred, that the patients

> are frequently seen by passers-by occupying beds in the tents and in apparel not suitable for exposure to public view. . . . That she [O'Hara] is carrying on a business which is distasteful to the neighbors; that the tents upon the lawn are unsightly; that the sick people are constantly seen about the place, many of them showing all too plainly the frightful ravages of the dread disease afflicting them, is clearly established by the testimony. (*Gowen,* 15 Pa. D. at 755–756)

The judge who wrote this summary nonetheless found no proof that O'Hara was maintaining a nuisance or that the "consumptive camp" posed a health risk to the neighbors. Still, he ruled that O'Hara's business must close down, basing his decision on the hospital's "open air" treatment method, which meant that the people living on the property spent time outside. Unlike other hospitals, where the "administration of medicine, the giving of food, the removal of the faeces, would be done behind the walls," this site's arrangement, however "tidy, cleanly and orderly," meant that "those under canvas are more or less in view." On this basis, he decided that the sanatorium "injuriously affected" not the health but the *comfort* of the neighborhood and that it thereby violated the restriction in O'Hara's deed (*Gowen,* 15 Pa. D. at 764. No diseased person at this corner could expose him- or herself to public view from that point forward.[19]

MARSHALL P. WILDER AND THE RIGHT TO PHILADELPHIA

At about this time, also in Philadelphia, Gott Dewey, too, was denied the right to the city. Dewey's case involved a sequence of events that closely resembles those worst-fear scenarios of ugly law in which not begging but mere being on the street comes under prohibition. Around 1900, Dewey, a lawyer with a large practice, chairman of his church, and a leading figure in city charitable work, was arrested on a public nuisance charge. From early childhood, Dewey had a form of chorea that caused a great deal of involuntary movement and significantly impaired his coordination and speech. Although he had a successful legal career, specializing in drafting briefs that his partner presented in court, and although he had become a highly respected figure in his local network of communities, strangers in urban Philadelphia looked at him and saw monstrosity. "His appearance and manner were really terrifying to people that did not know him," one contemporary observer reported of the arrest,

> for in trying to avoid collision with passers-by his lack of control often caused him to act as if about to strike. The magistrate, before whom he was arraigned expressed extreme sympathy, but insisted that he keep out of the streets except when in a carriage or properly attended, and poor Dewey took the affair so deeply to heart, that afterward he kept himself almost secluded from the world. (Wilder, 89–90)

Dewey's story makes clear that it did not take an ugly law to render someone unsightly. This case, with its scenes of arrest and appearance in the courtroom, lies very close to the realm of ugly law. When signs of impairment triggered panicked disgust, both an unsightly beggar and a respected professional leader might, with the flash of a badge, be denied representational space and confined to repressive space.[20]

Gott Dewey apparently ceased organizing cultural events at his church or representing himself or others in the courts, refusing to submit to those conditions of deformance that the judge enforced when he insisted on curtailing Dewey's independent mobility by requiring the constant presence of attendants. But Dewey did not go entirely unrepresented. His story survives in a remarkable text that moves us away from the courtroom and stands as an example of one important potential site for opposition to the social world of ugly law: the realm of cultural production.

The author of the book in which Dewey's story appears was Marshall P. Wilder. Although he is little known today, at the peak of his early-twentieth-century career the name was practically a household word. Along with Napoleon, Helen Keller, and John Milton, he made Jane Addams's list of "great defectives": "Though a physical dwarf," she said of Wilder in 1915, shortly after his death, "he taught himself to be so entertaining that the world forgot his deformity and he died known as one of the world's greatest comedians" (quoted in "Defective Chicago Baby Dies"). Wilder was a performer first on the Sunday-school and Chautauqua circuits and later in vaudeville. In Anthony Slide's encyclopedia of vaudeville, which notes that Wilder was earning a hefty salary of six hundred dollars a week before his death ("and he was worth it," writes another vaudeville historian, "for he drew well"; D. Gilbert, 159), he is described as follows: "Marshall P. Wilder was a curious character, a hunchbacked dwarf" (555). Like Belluso's Bourne, Wilder was faced with the question, "I will be called 'deformed' when I am born. 'Crippled' and 'hunchbacked.' . . . what will I do with these names?" The answer, decidedly, was to allow his body to be seen in the public sphere. I have written elsewhere about Wilder's major (and now buried) place in American disability history. Here I focus simply on his story of Gott Dewey's banishment from the streets of Philadelphia, which constitutes a rare and important indictment of the culture of ugly law in the early twentieth century.

The indictment is artful, subtle, but nonetheless distinct. It comes in a chapter of one of Wilder's memoirs, *The Sunny Side of the Street,* entitled "A Sunny Old City"; this "sunny" is decidedly ironic. The city is Philadelphia, site of Wilder's childhood stint in the National Surgical Institute or "Cripple's Palace." Wilder describes at length a vivid boy culture and what Longmore calls "the camaraderie of children against adult power" in such institutions (2004, vii).

> Boys are as fond as Irishmen of fighting for the mere fun of it, so we got a lot of laughing out of fist fights between some of the patients. The most popular contestants were Gott Dewey from Elmira, N.Y., and a son of Sheriff Wright from Philadelphia. Both were seriously afflicted, though they

> seemed not to know it. Wright was a cross-eyed paralytic, while Dewey had St. Vitus's dance and was so badly paralyzed that he had no control over his natural means of locomotion. He could not even talk intelligibly, yet he had an intellect that impressed me deeply, even at that early day. He could cope with the hardest mathematical problem that any could offer; he read much and his taste in literature and everything else was distinct and refined. . . .
>
> Dewey . . . was quite proud and self-reliant, and insisted upon doing everything for himself. That he might serve himself at table, a little elevator was made for his convenience, and I was mischievous enough to disarrange the machinery so that food intended for his mouth should reach his ear. Yet he loved me dearly and dashed at me affectionately though erratically whenever we met. I was unable to get about without crutches, so I frequently fell; if Dewey were in sight, he would hurry to my assistance, with disastrous results for both of us; often Wright would offer assistance at the same time and the two would fall over each other and me and attempt to "fight it out," while I would become helpless with laughter and the three of us would lie in a heap, until some attendant would separate the warriors and set me on my feet and crutches. . . . After leaving the Institute I lost sight of Dewey, though I never forgot his hearty way of greeting me whenever he met me, a heartiness which caused him to tumble all over me and compel me to put out my arm to save him from falling. (84–87)

Wilder goes on to recount his eventual reunion with Dewey. In 1900, he writes, a Philadelphia church invited him—he was now a famous entertainer—to perform for the congregation.

> The committee of arrangements met me and said they wished to prepare me for the unusual appearance of their chairman. He had endowed the church, they told me, and was almost idolized by the people for his many noble qualities of head and heart, yet he was a paralytic and his visage was shocking at first sight. Suddenly the chairman himself entered the room and I saw my old friend. . . . At the same instant he recognized me; he dashed at me in the old way; my arm instinctively caught him as it had done hundreds of times before; the committee supposing I was frightened, endeavored to separate us, but we weren't so easy to handle. (88)

And then comes the story I have already quoted, about Dewey's arrest on nuisance charges and confinement to his home "not long after our unexpected meeting" (89).

Wilder tells about the arrest, Dewey's appearance in court, and his subsequent isolation matter-of-factly, with no obvious outrage. But in the narrative framing of the incident we can read anger and protest. Immediately after the end of Dewey's story ("afterward he kept himself almost secluded from the world"), with no transition, the first line of a new paragraph follows: "Mention of Philadelphia always suggests graveyards to me" (90). So much for the "sunny old city." Though the paragraph goes on to recount a "sunny" tale of Wilder's daily childhood airings in the carts of kindly livery drivers engaged for funerals, the sharp juxtaposition with Gott Dewey's story allows a coded meaning: "this city, which forced Dewey off the streets, is death to him and to me."

The chapter's final turn reinforces this implicit association of Philadelphia with danger and oppression rather than sanctuary or healing. "I have traveled much in foreign countries," writes Wilder, "but Philadelphia is the only place in which I was compelled to beg the protection of the American flag." What follows is a comic account of travel mishap, in the form of being caught with the wrong trousers on at a black-tie Philly event.

> [M]y figure was such that I could not be fitted from any clothing store in the city. For a moment my invention was at a standstill, but the people were not, and the hall was filling rapidly. I consulted the committee hastily, and though they were greatly amused by my suggestion, they acted upon it promptly: they moved a table to the centre of the platform, draped it with the stars and stripes, and all the people on the platform arranged themselves, so that I could be unseen as I passed behind them to the table, where only my coat and vest could be seen, the objectionable trousers being hidden by my country's flag.
>
> Small wonder that I have a merry remembrance of Philadelphia. (92)

Here is an amusing anecdote, calculated not to offend; indeed, its subject is "not offending." But in the context of Gott Dewey's story, remembrances of Philadelphia carry grimmer undertones. If Dewey, the local leader, could be made into an alien in his own hometown, Wilder and others like him who "could not be fitted" had better "beg the protection of the American flag," not that that protection was accorded to disabled citizens in Philadelphia or elsewhere in 1905, when Wilder published this memoir. The protest, though mild and hedged, is there to be discerned.

In celebrity caricaturist Carlos de Fornaro's Art Nouveau cartoon of Wilder, the vaudeville star is portrayed as tiny and portly. In the middle of

Carlos de Fornaro's cartoon drawing of Marshall P. Wilder. (Library of Congress Prints and Photographs Division, acd2a08745; reprinted with permission)

a city intersection, he is loomed over by a stylized, elongated policeman whom he confronts; behind them traffic stalls.

In a comic vein, as befits his famous subject, de Fornaro captures the hints of threat and ongoing negotiation in Wilder's own portrayal of his tenuous and hard-won access to the urban streets. Out of the immediate era of the unsightly beggar ordinances, here is one instance, in a performer's autobiography, of a direct precursor of John Belluso's and a contemporary of Randolph Bourne's disability writing: one actor and speaker affirming, within the terms of his own historic moment, "diseased, maimed, and deformed" people's inalienable right to the city.

10

REHABILITATING THE UNSIGHTLY

Compare de Fornaro's caricature of Wilder and the policeman with another cartoon from the same period, printed in the so-called Cleveland Cripple Survey in 1918, which also represents a disabled man encountering the spaces of modernity.

In this drawing, "designed and executed," we are told in an accompanying note, "by a professional cartoonist and advertising expert who has had no use of his right arm," disability literally meets the world. A well-dressed white man on crutches, on his way uphill to the mountains of Success, is greeted by a natty, beaming globe with a bow tie; the artist's caption, addressed to others following in his footsteps, reads, "It's a long, hard road, but the whole world stands ready to give you a helping hand—and the goal is sure" (Welfare Federation, 18). Whereas Wilder in de Fornaro's sardonic image faces down an adversary, this encouraging cartoon cripple, drawn by a disabled artist who (significantly) goes unnamed despite being certified as "original" and "professional," exists only to face up—to new heights, to emotional challenges, and to the task of rehabilitation in front of him. In his world, seemingly, exclusionary ordinances and threatening police have been abolished. This cartoon epitomizes the rehabilitation approach that presaged the end of ugly law, beginning as early as the 1890s and gathering steam as the twentieth century headed toward and went through World War I. Although, as I have shown, city leaders well into the 1920s—and far later—continued to argue over the disabled beggar, by the time the United States entered the Great War, city councils had lost interest in passing codified unsightly beggar ordinances.

"Rehabilitation approach," Byrom's phrase, well describes the style and ethos of the Cleveland Cripple Survey and its ilk (2001, 133).[1] (Cleveland was a model leader in this approach, as Groce has detailed.)[2] *Rehabilitation* implies a goal of re-placement into a habitat, a home, a habitus from which the subject has been dislodged. *Approach* captures the manner of the survey pretty much exactly: a continual greeting of the "cripple" that starts from a distance and moves guardedly toward, without finalized arrival. Surveying

This cartoon was designed and executed by a professional cartoonist and advertising expert who has had no use of the right arm, which has been entirely paralyzed from birth

Cartoon reprinted in the "Cleveland Cripple Survey." (Welfare Federation of Cleveland, *Education and Occupations of Cripples Juvenile and Adult: A Survey of All the Cripples of Cleveland, Ohio, in 1916*. New York: Red Cross Institute for Crippled and Disabled Men, 1918)

consisted of, and the Cleveland Cripple Survey structures itself as, a series of approaches. "It was not very long after we began the Survey," begins the final section of the Cleveland report,

> that we all became so interested in our quest for cripples, that we found ourselves unconsciously looking for them in our moments of leisure. So there was some excitement in our first few weeks when one of our workers who had not yet begun investigating—in fact no interviewing cripples had yet been done—came into the office and announced that while in a locksmith's

> shop for personal business, she had seen a one-armed locksmith at work there. Since this was her discovery, she was to have the first opportunity to interview him. Unfortunately, he failed to respond to any letters, and unsuccessful attempts were made to see him where he roomed. (224)

After many approaches, the questers finally made contact with their cripple, who, though he promptly told his questioners that the subjects of their study "should never be called cripples, because it made them seem different," agreed with them enough to provide them with their conclusion. After advocating for education and training for disabled people, he added, "If you have something to offer, you can usually get a job, but you must be sure that what you have to offer is of real value" (227). Like the one-armed cartoonist who illustrated the survey, this man met the rehabilitation approach with one of his own. In the Cleveland survey he is given the last word.

Like most reformers focused on disability issues in the first two decades of the twentieth century, the Cleveland surveyors were, in Byrom's terms, "social rehabilitationists" more than "medical" ones—that is, they focused more on social than on medical solutions to the problem(s) of the cripple—though as Byrom notes, the two strains in this period mostly blended in an uneasy conjunction, less two camps than differing emphases (2001, 133–135). For social rehabilitationists, unsightliness was an *attitude,* both of the viewer and of the viewed. The plotline of the story they had to tell, their progress report, involved development toward what Hinshaw called, in his 1948 history of "the emergence of a miracle," "rehabilitation: a new concept." "It might be said," Hinshaw argued, "that today we have entered the sixth stage of development." The "five stages that preceded this one" he characterized, in order, as "extermination, ridicule, asylum, physical and custodial care, and education." The sixth stage, Hinshaw wrote, entailed "planned and intensive rehabilitation of every disabled person in keeping with the facts of his total personality and his total environment" (8). If ugly law fell somewhere in the middle of Hinshaw's previous five stages—its legal enactment of ridicule designed to further physical and custodial care—then the palliative stage "we have entered today" would render it obsolete.

In this emplotment, the Great War is a benchmark episode (Zerubavel, 84–85). Certainly the war focused the nation's attention on disability, for many reasons. "Sensitive citizens" who were troubled by the growing number of "physically handicapped beggars," argued Hinshaw, "were even more troubled by the increasing numbers of men who were being disabled by war" (35). Pioneering rehabilitationist Jeremiah Milbank, for instance, is represented by Hinshaw as roused to action by the increase in the "halt, maimed, and blind he saw on the crowded sidewalks where they begged" (36); the action he took was to found the Red Cross Institute for Crippled and Disabled Men in New York City, determining that "the Institute's earliest efforts should be concentrated on helping war casualties" (38). A syndicated article published in small city newspapers across the United States in 1918 portrayed ugly law as a way of supporting the returning troops in advance:

> The public has too often confused the idea of the cripple with that of a beggar. . . . We have seen many cripples at street corners making public exhibition of their deformity. . . . The practice should have been stopped in the past; it is absolutely necessary that it be prohibited in the future. For with the expectation of our soldiers who will return disabled from the front, the public should have no excuse for associating their prospective career with that of a mendicant. ("Away with the Beggar")

As in the past, the crackdowns on unsightly beggars that were advocated in 1918 were done in the name of care; here, care meant jobs, *vocational* rehabilitation.

Even before the United States entered the war, reports from Europe had already underscored both the devastatingly disabling force of new weapons and the development of promising new advances in the medical treatment of war injury, in assistive technology, and in practices of vocational training.[3] Milbank and others planned to begin with veterans, but they were determined to harness the public concern about "soldier cripples" to serve the interests also of what Milbank's colleague Douglas McMurtrie called "congenital cases and disease cripples." The "restoration" of these civilians "is desirable in the extreme," McMurtrie argued pragmatically, "because the elimination of dependency due to physical handicap will lift a colossal burden from the agencies of philanthropic relief" (*Future Policy*, 7).

Rehabilitationists noted other reasons besides the growing presence of injured veterans for why the Great War galvanized a crisis in disability policy. "The cripple has been considered as a helpless member of society, to be pitied and maintained," wrote McMurtrie, "but to whom constructive assistance was not feasible. This attitude is in the process of change." In part, he wrote, this change was due to "the call of the able-bodied to arms." As a result, "the ensuing labor shortage necessitated the draft into industry of women and old men. . . . the rehabilitation of the disabled became a national necessity" (*Rehabilitation*, 1–2). If the war produced more disabled workers, it also, according to Hinshaw, produced more disabled beggars: "war prosperity brought them out, equipped with tin cups, in increasing numbers. Some had been shut-ins who before had not found begging profitable" (35). Either way, rehabilitationists feared that the end of the war would only increase the number of diseased, maimed, and deformed panhandlers, and they argued for immediate intervention on these grounds. "Upon the return of employment conditions to normal," warned McMurtrie, disabled workers might be "perilously near the verge of mendicancy. No pains should be spared to avert this eventuality" (*Rehabilitation*, 10).

THE CLEVELAND CRIPPLE SURVEY

"What, then, does the cripple want?" asked the authors of the Cleveland Cripple Survey, which was begun in 1915 and published after, in their words, issues faced by crippled soldiers had begun to "overshadow . . . every other thought on the subject of the handicapped at this time."[4] The survey had begun in 1913 when a group of representatives from various Cleveland charitable organizations met to discuss "conditions from the standpoint of crippled children in the city of Cleveland" (Western Reserve Child Welfare Council, minutes of meeting). The project was first assigned to the Western Reserve Child Welfare Council and later given over to a specially designated committee, at which point professional investigators were brought in (including Allen Burns, the man listed in the end as chair of the committee who went on to direct "Americanization Studies" of immigrants in Chicago, and the women who authored and oversaw the survey itself, Grace S. Harper, Amy M. Hamburger, and Lucy Wright). By this time, war-related injury had become a paramount focus for organizing and a central issue in the discourse of the Cleveland Cripple Survey. In 1918, a report on the cripple survey was titled *Social Service at Home during the War Years* and included subheadings like the following: "Association for Crippled and Disabled Faces Problem of 4,186 Industrial Cripples in Cleveland: Each Year of the War 10,000 Soldiers Were Crippled to Every Million Engaged; Great and Terrible as This Figure Seems, Disabilities Due to Routine Industrial Causes in This Country Are Even Greater" (21).

To answer the question about what the cripple wanted, these researchers turned to their human subjects, to whom they (with conditions) granted expertise:

> The Cripple Survey is . . . more than a census in purpose and in fact. It has gone to the living sources for all possible information and guidance towards a community plan for improving the condition of the crippled. Its findings represent the ready response of men and women who have had personal experience in living out a part or all of their lives under some form of physical handicap to questions of long standing in the minds of all of us. A man with double club hands and double club feet, with the added disadvantages of a meager education and no medical treatment in all his life, but who supports himself and others for nineteen years without any aid, can, if he be a thoughtful person, speak with authority of handicaps. (11)

The question "what, then does the cripple want?" posed no great riddle for those who, in the survey's terms, "speak with authority of handicaps." It was easy for all concerned to answer: cripples want employment (Welfare Federation, 135).

Compare the more complex response given sixty years later when disability movement leader Frank Bowe began his manifesto, *Handicapping America: Barriers to Disabled People,* as if answering back directly to the question:

> They want a place to live—and cannot find it. They want an education—and are turned away. They seek access to transportation on buses and subways—and cannot get on. They desire the right to vote—but cannot get in. They want entertainment—but cannot enjoy it. They seek jobs—and are rejected. They desire respect—and receive humiliation. (x–xi)

More militant and later activists reconfigured the grammar of the statement ("we want," not "they want") and added items to the list unspeakable, if not unimaginable, to the earlier answerer/questioners, like "we want recognition of our sexuality and our sexual rights."[5] If, on the one hand, the survey's formulation "cripples want employment" grappled with a central problem—"Nowhere is the disabled figure more troubling to American ideology," writes Garland Thomson, "than in relation to the concept of work" (*EB*, 46)—it also drastically delimited the range of desire for its imagined cripples.[6]

The focus on employment (and on its corollary, education for the crippled child) manifested itself at the most basic definitional level in rehabilitationist texts of the 1910s like the Cleveland survey. McMurtrie's monograph

The Meaning of the Term "Crippled" explained the choice of the term in venues such as the title of the Institute for Crippled and Disabled Men, justifying it on several grounds. From one angle, he noted, "the classification of cripple is almost coincident with the scope of orthopedic surgery"; that is, McMurtrie understood *cripple* as a concept created by, not simply responded to by, modern medicine. He rejected alternative terms for a variety of reasons. *Invalided* had "euphonic drawbacks." But the core of his argument rested on an economic analysis. Mulling over the word *disabled,* a term he said was meeting with "considerable acceptance," he rejected it because it seemed to connote "incapable of paying work." "A man is labeled by a rehabilitation school 'crippled and disabled,'" he explained, "but he should be turned out 'crippled and able.' . . . In the strict sense a writer who returns with a paralyzed left arm is crippled but he is certainly not disabled for he can return unhandicapped to the pursuit of his vocation" (3, 8–9). McMurtrie was inspired by the authors of the Cleveland Cripple Survey, who two years earlier had touted their change "in the working definition of 'cripple.'" A prior "census of cripples" in Birmingham, England, had defined the term with emphasis on restriction of "capacity for self-support." The Cleveland surveyors rejected "this double test of physical and economic handicap" in the name of emphasizing the cripple's present and future employability (Welfare Federation, 13).

For the Cleveland project, education and employment were the antidotes to unsightly beggar ordinances. They would render such measures unnecessary. Focusing on employment was a positive, radical move; as Byrom notes, "disabled beggar" was a far more familiar concept than "disabled worker." The Welfare Federation challenged tradition, Byrom writes, "by making productive workers of a social group whose dependent status dated to the earliest human civilizations and played a significant role in defining Christian charity" (2004, 2). But even as these forward-looking reformers sought to eradicate the social conditions that produced disabled beggars, their survey spoke the backward language of the ugly laws. The surveyors who went door-to-door in Cleveland were given a standardized form to fill out, checking off boxes and making brief notations as they went. (A copy of the form is included in the volume.) In the section on "Economic Condition" of the cripple in question, they were supposed to evaluate "Home Conditions" ("comfortable," "poor," "very poor") and means of support ("Earning a Living or Dependent," "Supporting Others—How Many," "Sources of Support if Dependent," "In Case of Accident, Amount of Compensation"). A final line gave them three options to check or leave blank:

"Money Obtained by Begging," "Selling Shoe-Strings or Pencils," "Exposing Deformity" (172–173). Though this last category could be employed matter-of-factly to note income derived from participation in freak shows, nothing limited it to that domain or prevented shaming check marks—rather more moralistic in implication—at both "begging" and "exposing." On the survey form, in the end, the questioning came down to the bottom line of ugly law.

Paradoxically, rehabilitationist approaches both refuted and retained impulses of the ugly laws. This contradiction shows in the treatment of the "street operator" in the Cleveland survey. The term *street operator*—not, as far as I know, widely used elsewhere in the sense that Lucy Wright and Amy Hamburger, the two named authors of the survey, used it in the survey—played a complex function. In the quantitative "Occupation Lists by Disability" section, all those surveyed are broken down first by gender, then by type of impairment ("Loss of right arm below elbow—fifteen males," "Deformity of body—forty-five females," and so on) and then by occupation. In these lists *street operating* means one thing only, as indicated by its immediate parenthetical explanation: "(begging)." But an extra section is appended to the lists, devoted solely to "stories of street operators," whose relation to the category "occupation," the crux of the problem of the "Cleveland cripple" as a generic subject, apparently demands narrative elaboration. Of the twenty-one men whose lives are described by these stories of street operation, only three, in fact, are depicted as begging.

One of them, a "Male, thirty-seven years, born in Italy," maimed and blinded in an explosion at work on the railroad, "sits on bench in Park all day, has band on his hat which reads: 'Please help the Blind.'" Another, "Male, fifty-six years, born in Poland," who "met with a train accident which resulted in amputation of both legs above knees," is described thus: "is a typical beggar and has no intention or desire to work. . . . Gives history of a wanderer; says he can speak Polish, Italian, French, and Slovenian languages, and the only job he would consider is a teacher of foreign languages." (The contradiction between dreaming of a job as a teacher and having no desire to work is not addressed within the curt bounds of this story of street operation). For the third man, "Male, twenty-nine years, born in Italy, . . . both arms are cut off below elbow," the account is briefer: "Spends most of his time begging."

The other eighteen men, with one exception ("Male, American, twenty-seven years, . . . has been exhibiting his own and his children's deformity . . . in sideshow"), were all employed in the subeconomy as street vendors, selling candy, shoestrings, pencils, newspapers, popcorn, and notions. Often when people with impairments peddled, as I have noted, this action was considered by city leaders and reformers to be synonymous with begging; the goods ostensibly on sale, such thinking went, were a mere ruse for handouts. As Bryan Wagner has argued in the context of southern policing of black vagrancy, "vagrancy laws turned actions that would be construed in other contexts as good capitalism—as signs of industry and ingenuity—into easily diagnosed symptoms of . . . pathology" (69).[7] Nonetheless the systematic evidence of concerted attempts by these disabled men to engage in labor and commerce, however small the scale, contradicts the reductive equation of "street operating" with abject mendicancy. Interestingly, the one woman in the Cleveland list who sells goods on the street is defined simply as a "peddler" and given no narrative account. Only men, apparently, could be sleazy, manipulative, mechanical "street operators."

But not all men were, not even all disabled men who peddled. *Street operator* was a porous and a slippery category. It is difficult to tell exactly what you had to do—in the parlance of ugly law—"so as to be" one (as in "any person, who is diseased, maimed, mutilated or deformed in any way, *so as to be* an unsightly or disgusting object"; italics mine). Rehabilitationists put great store in the concept of "so as to be." For them, unsightliness, like low-life "operating," was optional as well as reversible. Accordingly—but somewhat confusingly—one man portrayed within the Cleveland Cripple Survey sells newspapers on the street, just as several of the street operators do, but his story does not appear in their section. Instead, he gets an even more extended treatment in the chapter devoted to "Stories of Successful Individuals in Cleveland." His absence from the ranks of the street operators is especially surprising, since he happens to be the one man that the survey notes was targeted for arrest under Cleveland's unsightly beggar/peddler ordinance.[8] His photograph began this book, and with him we come full circle. Why was this man not construed as a "street operator"? How is it, exactly, that he functioned "so as to be" simultaneously both "successful individual" and—literally, that is, legally—an "unsightly beggar"?

A word, first, on the story of the successful individual. Great War–era rehabilitationists claimed this kind of narrative as their trademark genre. Motion study experts Frank Gilbreth and Lillian Gilbreth (both of *Cheaper by the Dozen* fame and authors of *Motion Study for the Handicapped*) called for mass production and distribution of such stories in 1917 in their "Putting the Cripple on the Payroll," characteristically measuring the social gains that would ensue in microscopic units of time:

> Those who have read the record of the marvelous work being done abroad, and of the increased number of minutes of happiness that are resulting among cripples who are enabled to become interested, productive members of the community, through this work . . . hope the wars will cease, [but] the knowledge will be useful for industrial workers forever. . . . it is hoped that some society will cause to be collected as many as possible of the histories of cases where cripples have become able to cope successfully with their handicaps. (Quoted in Welfare Federation, 84)[9]

McMurtrie put some of his formidable bibliographic skills to this task of story collection, and his Red Cross Institute sponsored regular events to which, as he described them, "cripples from all over the city . . . are invited" to watch motion pictures and magic-lantern shows "designed to arouse their ambition by showing them how other disabled men have overcome their handicap" ("Work of an American School," 18). The Cleveland survey ends with its success stories, both to body forth the project's highest aims and to supplement (or even counteract) its cold hard data with the effect of a warmer, more empowered and empowering, human face.[10]

That face takes several forms, notably in the portrait of the double amputee and municipal judge David Moylan, the only subject named within the survey. Moylan's exceptional position, well-educated and professional, is reinforced both by comments about him from other disabled men in the text and by the form his story takes, a reprint of an article from the 1909 *New York American* ("Armless Lawyer: David Moylan Overcame Heavy Odds, Educated Himself after Being Crippled on Railroad").

Granted a profile produced entirely outside the bounds of the Cleveland project, Moylan almost escapes the category of the "case" into which the other surveyed cripples are consigned. He is proudly named. They are protectively numbered (each man, for instance, in the section on street operators is referred to only by the number given to him, as in "Survey No. 2813" and so on). During Moylan's story, the voice and gaze of social work recede; the human interest feature takes over.[11]

But Moylan is not finally the "successful individual" in the text whose story—for the surveyors themselves—most spectacularly exceeds the small boxes of the Cleveland survey form. That place belongs to the newspaper seller. Even the caption under his photograph reads differently from the others. The rest of the photos of "cripples at work," including one of Moylan, have subtitles according to a strict, straightforward formula: reference

Photograph of David Moylan from the 1909 *New York American* ("Armless Lawyer: David Moylan Overcame Heavy Odds, Educated Himself after Being Crippled on Railroad"), reprinted in the "Cleveland Cripple Survey." (Welfare Federation of Cleveland, *Education and Occupations of Cripples Juvenile and Adult: A Survey of All the Cripples of Cleveland, Ohio, in 1916*. New York: Red Cross Institute for Crippled and Disabled Men, 1918)

to impairment, reference to employment. "A successful dressmaker who runs her machine with the aid of a long iron poker"; "A one-armed steeple-jack who sticks to his job"; "A judge in the municipal court who wrote his answers to the bar examination with a pencil held between his teeth." But the news seller's appealing photograph generates a different message, exclamatory, patently emotional, and directed squarely at the reader: "Don't fail to note the man behind the handicap!"

Partly this difference may be explained by the problem posed for the surveyors by this man's line of work; if paper peddling equals street operating equals begging, it is difficult to celebrate with much wholeheartedness the career of the "successful" adult newsboy. And so instead comes the appeal to the idea of "the man behind." (This is, of course, a highly problematic as well as a productive formulation; if its surface-depth model means to counter the reduction of a person to a handicap, it also locates humanity, interiority, and masculinity *outside* impairment. There can be no man within the handicap.)[12] The imagined "man behind" has a vexed relation to peddling/begging in this text. Consider the other moment when the rhetoric of "man behind" appears, in one of the survey's strongest articulations of a social theory of disability:

> [T]he cripple finds that the hardest obstacles to overcome in his whole career are often the ideas in the minds of the rest of us—our mistaken ideas about cripples. An ambitious mechanic, looking for a real job, finds himself classified with the shoestring peddler on the street, just because he has the same disability. . . . These apparently trivial things are in reality signs of a general inability to see the man behind the handicap, and are the very things that make the cripple feel he is helpless. They contribute, without doubt, towards idleness among cripples and help create the group of sensitive recluses who only wish to come out after dark and the discouraged workman who keeps his crippled hand well hidden in his pocket. (14)

This loaded passage takes several interesting turns. Note how quickly a sociological model goes psychological, shifting attention from "*our* mistaken ideas" to the cripple's (*we* are not him). A certain "damned if you do, damned if you don't" rule inheres: expose your crippled hand, and you are a street operator; hide it, and you are a sensitive recluse, a victim of an ugly law you self-inflict. Here the man behind is a mechanic; the peddler is what hides him.

And yet the slogan "Don't fail to note the man behind" gets put under the image of a peddler. Is it meant to suggest a lurking inner mechanic behind his newsboy pose? Or is news seller, in fact, a good enough occupation? Later, the surveyors try to clarify the mechanic's paradox, shifting from the language of peddling to the language of begging: "It is not a question of praise for the crippled mechanic or blame for the crippled beggar; it is a question of what he has to work with" (16). Other survey photo captions foreground physical equipment: "Successful laborer with hook appliance";

"A man who lost his right arm and foreman's position through industrial accident restored to industry by arm and hand of his own invention." But the illustrative newspaper seller stands for a different meaning of "what he has to work with." His tools are cognitive, emotional, spiritual, the materials of interiority. In the story that goes along with his photograph, the surveyors themselves also seem to find new registers of what they "have to work with." Like Moylan's, this man's narrative also disrupts the genre of the "case," but this time from within: confronting him, the survey's own voice shifts style and tone, in a dramatic and unsettling eruption of narrative subjectivity.[13]

Who narrates a survey, this survey? As I have noted, a large "Committee on Cripples" officially produced it, chaired by Allen T. Burns for the Welfare Federation of Cleveland. Grace S. Harper was the survey's first director. After "ill-health" forced her to resign, two other women, Amy M. Hamburger and Lucy Wright, coordinated the project and are listed as the authors of the report. Nine canvassers were employed, described only as "recent college graduates" and probably primarily if not exclusively female, led by five investigators, all of whom were "young women of more experience than the average canvasser" (167–168).[14] Histories of female-authored texts in the United States do not usually include the genre of the social survey, though a significant body of American women's writing has taken that form. Legible signs that women thinking about women conducted and wrote the Cleveland Cripple Survey can be found throughout (for instance, the first "Successful Individual" portrayed is a woman, a "wheel-chair dressmaker"), but it is in the story of the man-behind-the-newspaper-seller that period-specific generic conventions cry out to readers: do not fail to note the woman behind the survey. The newspaper seller's story may be read, in fact, as a version of feminine writing.

Listen, for instance, to how his section begins. It sloughs off, is no longer handicapped by, the clipped, truncated diction of the "street operator" case study, with its elided subjects ("Is dependent on wife's relatives. Home miserable, dirty and unsanitary. Question of wife being feeble-minded"). This narrative is suddenly rich in nouns and pronouns, beginning with an authorial "I":

> Quite by chance, one day, in wandering purposelessly through the square in Cleveland, I was attracted by the agility and swiftness with which one young man was securing his large bundles of newspapers from the newspaper truck. He was surrounded by a number of other newsboys who were

> all after their share. . . . Keenly interested because he seemed so business-like, I observed a little more closely, and at first was shocked to see that he had club hands and club feet. Although unable to use his hands at all, he managed to use his arms cleverly. . . . I wedged my way through the crowd, . . . through a group of boys, until I reached him. I asked if I might speak to him a few minutes. . . . He was a fine-looking young man, of rugged build and keen blue eyes, who appeared to be the personification of happiness and geniality, despite his handicap. (220–221)

Who is this "I"? Wright? Hamburger? A flâneuse, undoubtedly, one who wanders purposelessly, until a fine-looking young man catches her eye, one she cannot ignore. The survey has developed a crush, and in the process, the crippled news seller moves definitively outside the ranks of the undesirables. When I call this "feminine writing," I mean it in two different and undecidable senses: this is the stuff of conventional romance novel, and it is also wildly and unconventionally disruptive of the "masculine" linear grid of survey statistics. Surveys of this period allow a range of feelings for the "cases" they examine, from approval to disapproval, but they do not ordinarily conduct themselves through the mechanism of infatuation.

The man is boyfriend material, if strictures about cross-class dalliances (and a structure of condescension that keeps rendering a man a boy) could be set aside, and this makes it especially shocking that Cleveland's unsightly beggar ordinance was used to run him off the streets. "The only kind of work that seemed possible for this boy was selling newspapers," the survey recounts, the "I" subsiding back into committee prose, "so he secured his corner and did a most profitable business. Life seemed bright until the enforcement of the statute which prevented cripples from exposing their deformity by selling on street corners abolished this man's job" (222). On the one hand, it is no surprise that he came within the sights of ugly law; he fits the profile: poor, uneducated, the oldest of twenty-one children of illiterate Polish immigrants who spoke no English. On the other hand, his good looks and charming manner refute the basic premise of the law and reveal it as arbitrary and oppressive, within its own terms of value. Those terms say that something is seriously wrong when such a winning man is found unsightly or when a disabled man is in fact sightly.

But if the caption under this man's photograph seems to speak back to the framers of the ordinance—Do not fail to note the man behind the "beggar" whom you call deformed—the survey also speaks for them. *He* speaks for them, as well as for the survey's authors: "Although it [the statute] seemed rather hard, he appreciated the meaning of it, but considered it ill-advised unless some step went with it for providing other opportunity for work for cripples." Everyone here "appreciates the meaning"; there is no saying no to ugly law. In fact, what extricates this man from the ranks of the street operators and propels him to the head of the successful individual class seems to be, in large part, ugly law appreciation.

Not entirely. "It seemed rather hard." His voice is lost, and in his absence his narrator speaks for him. Although at times his words fall within quotation marks, this is not one of those times, and within the bounds of the survey's newfound venture into free indirect discourse ("Life seemed bright" until "it seemed rather hard"), things may not be entirely what they seem to seem. There may have been even more outrage in his speech, more vehemence, more impassioned pressure for genuine access to work and against enforced dependence, than comes through here. And it still comes through. "His family had begun to depend upon his contribution to the weekly income, and needed this money sadly. Wasn't he a full-grown man and shouldn't he contribute his share?" (223). The passage goes on to give us one of the few extant accounts I know detailing the consequences of enforcement of an unsightly beggar ordinance (the others I discuss in chapter 11). Because he had saved an impressive amount of money and built up a strong community network, this man was unusually buffered:

> With his savings of $400, he bought out a small cigar and newsstore. This proved to be a poor investment, because he was too dependent on others to help him, and the profits were not sufficient to allow him to hire help. The undertaking was consequently abandoned, and through the kindness of the druggist in front of whose store he had previously been accustomed to stand selling papers, he was given permission to use his doorway as long as he liked. This is his selling place today, and he is a man thirty-five years of age. (223)

Note that in 1916 the ordinance still had effect in Cleveland. Nevertheless, though he stood, apparently, within a doorway, this man made sure to frame his place of work as an urban public meeting space: "I am happy in my work. Think of the many types of people I meet. . . . Best of all, I am out-of-doors" (223–224).[15]

What distinguishes an unsightly beggar from a successful individual? The difference, apparently, is as shallow as a druggist's doorstep. Surgery might do the trick, and the surveyor proposes it: "I suggested to him that it might be worth while even now to consult a specialist" (223). The man rejects the idea: "my life is satisfactory to me as it is. I have a married sister with two little children to support . . . If I left home, everything would go to pieces." His refusal meets with both regret and admiration on the part of his interlocutor. For the Cleveland surveyors what made this man exemplary was character, based squarely in domestic ideology. "Perhaps his philosophy of life—thinking entirely of others and not of himself—was his unconscious reason for happiness," his fable concludes, imparting its moral lesson. Yet why similar sentiments on the part of others in the survey did not make them "successful individuals" remains unclear. "Survey No. 2970," for instance, sells pencils on the street, and his "one ambition is to earn enough money to go back to Italy, where his motherless children are living" (162). Several other men support families in "clean homes" through "street operating."

Three decades later, the rehabilitation approach had not solved Joseph Gogola's problems. Gogola, a blind man, was also a newspaper seller in Cleveland. Like the man in the Cleveland survey, he was run off the street, not by an unsightly begging ordinance but by the abolition of his job when Cleveland's newspapers abandoned the use of newsboys for sales. In 1944, he was arrested for street operation. Charged as a "common beggar," he was found guilty, and his appeal denied by the Court of Appeals:

> After this [newsboy] work was no longer available to him, he stationed himself on Euclid Avenue, . . . where, with a cigar box in hand containing a cup and some lead pencils and shoelaces, and with a sign across his chest on which was printed the word "Blind," he would attract the attention of the passers-by by making audible sounds such as "good luck" "oh, oh, oh," etc. He dressed very shabbily, carried a cane and on some occasions would use it as a means of attracting attention in addition to the sounds above indicated. Passers-by . . . would frequently drop money into the cup but seldom would take either a pencil or shoestrings. (*City of Cleveland v. Gogola,* 58 N.E. 2d at 4).

Gogola had obtained a vendor's license, purchased sales tax stamps, and reported some sales every six months to the Sales Tax Division. None of this entrepreneurial activity was regarded, in the wake of his job loss, as vocational rehabilitation. Instead, the court concluded that "defendant's activities as an itinerant vendor were being used as a cloak to cover up the beggar behind" (*City of Cleveland,* 58 N.E. 2d at 9).

The story of the Cleveland Cripple Survey newspaper seller cannot finally put to rest the contradictions of either ugly law or rehabilitation. He escaped being labeled with a survey number. But neither does he have a name in the text, as David Moylan does. In many ways, he too can only remain, perpetually, "the man behind." The rehabilitation approach exemplified by the Cleveland survey did not and could not, finally, put ugly law entirely to rest. It took the national disability rights movement that developed fifty years later to make the next key moves in that project. At the moment of the Burgdorfs' christening of "ugly law," 1970s disability activists undertook a far more systematic dismantling of the legacy of the unsightly beggar ordinances.

If that activism claimed, at times, a kind of unsightly pride, it too tended to distance itself categorically from the shameful "beggar." Halle Lewis's recent historical study of the Cleveland Cripple Survey exemplifies this ethos today—this *approach,* which is also an aversion, a backing-off. As the quotation from which Lewis draws her title suggests ("Cripples Are Not the Dependents One Is Led to Think"), her understandable emphasis on workforce access and inclusion foregrounds the ways in which "the survey committee learned—to its apparent surprise—that most disabled people had found ways to remain part of the work-based distributive system" (197). For Lewis, the survey resulted in "both gains and losses for Cleveland's disabled population": gains in access to "new forms of educational, medical and vocational assistance" for "the sizable minority who could not make their way independently," but losses for "all disabled Clevelanders," who were now hailed as the categorical "crippled," "a label they felt described them inadequately and pejoratively, depriving them of their individual identities" (200).

No doubt this was the case. But Lewis's thoroughgoing emphasis on individualism and independence so briskly sweeps away all residues of shameful begging that only a distorted history of pride remains. The success stories in the survey, Lewis argues, simply "seem more representative of disabled Clevelanders than the street operators," not just because "only 4 percent begged" (an important statistic) but also because the seven successes "built meaningful, productive lives of which their impairments were just one facet" (226–227). Who knows whether street operators ever did or could reduce themselves entirely to "just one facet"? Certainly the Polish man who dreamed of teaching four languages seems to have attempted to present himself as multitalented, beyond impairment, to his surveyors. Lewis's "seem more representative" does open ideological work. In this forming canon of

Cleveland stories, in the name of the disability rights and independent living movement, some people become ("seem") representative Americans; others are not. What histories are erased? Tellingly, Lewis's lengthy summary of the newspaper seller's tale leaves out the part about the ugly law.

THE STRANGEST UNION IN THE WORLD

Even more clearly than the Cleveland archive, records from Los Angeles help us understand the paradoxes of the rehabilitation project and the tensions surrounding the last gasps of ugly law. The story in Los Angeles begins a few years before World War I and ends at the wartime moment of the Cleveland survey. In 1913, a Los Angeles newspaper article profiled Alfred Leroy, "aged 32, minus both legs and the left hand," who sold gum on the street. Leroy was a colorful figure, the subject of periodic feature stories in the press, notably for travelling across the country by motorcycle (a souped-up vehicle designed for him by the Indian company).[16] The *Los Angeles Times* reported Leroy's response to the news "that a movement was afoot to pass an ordinance putting a stop to his business." Other beggars in Los Angeles had already gotten wind of this possibility; "I had an idea there might be some new legislation prepared about the time cripples began to come in from the East," one wrote later. "My surmise was correct, so I was pretty well prepared" (Fuller, *Fifty Thousand Miles,* 234). But Leroy is portrayed as coming out swinging. According to the *Times,* he said upon hearing the news of the coming legislation "that he had money enough to carry a legal fight to the United States Supreme Court" ("Strangest Union"). No such fight occurred; it is likely that Alfred Leroy's deep pockets existed only in COS myth.

In the title of the 1913 *Times* article that depicted Leroy, at least three threats loom. Unsightly beggars pose a problem in and of themselves; so do unsightly beggars en masse; worse yet, unsightly beggars with lawyers: "Strangest Union in the World Uncovered Here: League of Beggars, Cripples, Sightless, Epileptic and Deformed; Great Association of Mendicants, Whose Chief Is a Blind Newspaper Vendor on Broadway, Bids Virtual Defiance to Efforts to Drive Them from the Streets; Will Fight to Highest Court, They Say." Here, it seems, the dream of a serious legal challenge to the ugly law verged on reality.

"Realizing the . . . adroit manner in which" beggars "disguised their mendicancy behind licenses to sell gum, pencils or shoestrings on the street," the *Times* reported, the newly formed Municipal Charities Organization, led by Milbank Johnson, had just begun "steps to eradicate the evil and sweep from the public view of Los Angeles the crippled and sightless unfortunates." A month earlier, in a pattern by now familiar to readers, the city had put into effect a harsh general antibegging ordinance, triggered particularly by but not exclusively targeted at itinerant members of the Industrial Workers of the World (IWW) who seemed to pose a special threat, both social and political, as well as at the growing numbers of unemployed workers from Mexico.[17] Despite this crackdown, "at least fifty crippled or blind beggars" were still "working in the city streets under this disguise" as putative peddlers. A freak-tramp panic gripped the city as it prepared for the coming months: "Other cripples working their way across the continent ahead of the onrushing winter, are desirous of reaching the land of sunshine where they may continue to beg until spring, under one pretense or another." In Los Angeles, unsightly beggars were as seasonal as laborers.

The "pitiful tales" of these mendicants "reflected a delicate condition which the city finds almost impossible to cure." Los Angeles officials saw only one solution: an ugly law. "The City Attorney's office is combing the law for the basis of an ordinance," reported the *Times*. "It was . . . suggested that the health department rigidly enforce legislation that prohibits the undue exposure of physical deformities in public places." Assistant City Attorney Westover was deputized by the Municipal Charities Commission, which in Los Angeles was an official municipal entity rather than a private nonprofit organization, to gather models of such legislation from other cities.

In this late emergence of the impulse toward ugly law, it is worth noting, the ordinance was clearly understood in the Progressive-era terms of public health; the "health department," not the vice department, comprised the law's province. The twentieth-century modernity of Los Angeles's ugly moment shows itself most clearly in the phenomenon of the beggar's union. This is not—exactly—the kind of league of rogues gathered at The Doctor's, the outlaw band of ballads and beggar's operas. Those gangs of cripples, no matter how much they exemplify what is wrong with the new metropolis, always seem vaguely medieval, anachronistic, timeless. The "strangest union in the world uncovered here" in Los Angeles in 1913 is a modern committee of beggars, "organized leisure," as the *Times*'s subtitle put it, with its model (this was its scandal) organized labor and lobbying, not organized crime. Nor is this strangest union under the legitimizing auspices of rehabilitationist charity like that other British, terribly unfortunately named, Guild of the Brave Poor Things.[18] They were poor all right, and some of them were brave, but this group formed itself on the wrong side of pity's tracks.[19]

Repeatedly, the *Times's* sensationalized report describes Municipal Charities commissioners as "uncovering" this "most remarkable union," as if unsightly beggars had been insufficiently available to public view. This is a standard move: beggars always occupy a shadowy underworld, even if their wounds and sores are too much in the light. But in actuality this group had made itself known, matter-of-factly, in the manner of any above-board civic delegation representing the interests of its members.

> The union is composed of beggars—crippled, sightless, or deformed.
>
> It has at least one walking delegate, probably many, its members pay dues and it is founded on a freemasonry that solidifies it into an organization at once unique and powerful in its class. . . .
>
> The attention of the commission was called to the widespread organization when the walking delegate for the union, a blind newspaper vendor on Broadway, called to ascertain if any action was to be taken against cripples who procured city licenses to sell trivial things on the streets.
>
> "I am president of the organization," he said, "and have been retained by the members to attend to their business." . . .
>
> Dr. Milbank Johnson, head of the commission, said yesterday that the man represented himself to be the authorized spokesman for the strange craft and said that he was paid dues by the members for his "professional work."

In short, if this report can be believed, unsightly beggars had organized. Among other things, the president of the group was charged with "lobb[ying] against ruinous legislation." In chapter 3, I made a tongue-in-cheek comparison between the outlaw crippled beggar subcultures of the Bowery and the dignified political activism of the 1930s League of the Physically Handicapped, the latter a clear precursor for later disability movements. Here is another, far less ironic, predecessor for LPH action, a trace of cross-disability political organizing from the American city's raggedest edge.[20] Speaking the language of officers and of authorization, this "walking delegate" spoke not as a successful (or unsuccessful) individual but as a representative.

In response, city officials both magnified and trivialized the image of unsightly beggars collectively representing themselves. On the one hand, the Municipal Charities Commission imagined the "strange union" as a vast international conspiracy, a cabal "whose headquarters in Los Angeles reaches to all parts of the United States and is in touch by correspondence with Europe." This beggar's grapevine "works by sign and symbol," they alleged, keeping "the unfortunates apprised of conditions—where the field is open and where it is closed"; but more than that, the strange union was said to maintain a "clearinghouse" in Los Angeles for that purpose, a kind of information headquarters for the syndicate.

On the other hand, the Municipal Charities commissioners reduced the politics of the blind newspaper vendor and those he represented to two simple dynamics: pathos and pest control. By the end of the *Times* article, the sinister beggars' clearinghouse is replaced by another:

> The office of the Associated Charities, where these strange creatures come to tell their troubles, is a clearinghouse of grief. The attitude taken by the Municipal Charities Commission is that those unfortunates are a public menace; that cripples, epileptics and others who are permitted to roam the streets under city license have a deleterious effect upon humanity in general. It is believed that the streets must be ridded of these creatures, who are defiant and audacious under legal recognition.

In the semantic "clearinghouse," the word itself, conflicting meanings negotiate. The clearinghouse, a bankers' institution for the adjustment of mutual claims, takes parodic form when "cripples, epileptics and others" claim begging (as a right, a share, a stake, a demand, an interest), in ways not unrelated to Simi Linton's use of the term in *Claiming Disability*. Against the possibility of a beggar's or an other's institution deciding how claims get settled, the Charity Organization Society asserts its legitimacy. In fact, one of the illustrative sentences for the word *clearinghouse* in the Oxford English Dictionary directly invokes it: "The Charity Organization Society is a central exchange or clearing-house for all the single relief associations."[21] The COS as definitive clearinghouse adjusts the claims of various relief associations, but it also, as the immediately following definition in the OED suggests, gives or withholds clearance for poor people: "What is wanted is first a human clearing house, or, in other words, compulsory examination of all immigrants."[22] In the COS clearinghouse of grief, grief is not so much vented as tested. Unsightly beggars, "defiant and audacious under legal recognition," are either cleared or—more likely—cleared out.

In 1913, Los Angeles unfortunates were cleared either for institutionalization or, under the influence of the growing rehabilitationist approach, for employment. According to the *Times*, "as soon as the anti-begging ordinance went into effect, the walking delegate of this strange craft advised all his followers to apply for positions with the Associated Charities. Nearly fifty applications were filed. Each application stated what kind of work the applicant desired." Alfred Leroy, the motorcyclist/gum-seller, is said to have applied for a job as "bank president" ("Strangest Union"). We know very little about what the disabled people who approached the Municipal Charities Commission as an organized group made of these attempts at job placement, because the extant records, with the important exception of the autobiography by Arthur Fuller that I discuss in the next chapter, are written only by the authorities. We do not even know the name of the group's president, who seems to have made a genuine effort to facilitate job-seeking by its members; in its place we get only the name of the outrageous rebel, the flamboyant Alfred Leroy.

By COS accounts, the plan to place the "unfortunates" in "legitimate employment" failed: "few of them want it." We do not know what jobs they were offered, under what conditions. Testimony from one man placed in the position of "unsightly beggar" suggests some of the problems in this kind of exchange. Arthur Franklin Fuller was at one point approached with an offer to be "well cared for" by being set up in the newsstand business, just as the litigating "legless newsboy of Times Square" had been by James Forbes. But Fuller, a practiced salesman, represents himself as dubious and protective of his mobility—"I have since observed others who were thus cared for. They are usually given a stand on some place already overworked, or a back street where few people pass"—and the plan fizzled (*Fifty Thousand Miles,* 171). Fuller's explanation cannot simply be taken at face value, without other corroboration. But we do know, in the case of the situation in 1913 Los Angeles, that whatever civic solution disabled beggars or peddlers faced—institutionalization, employment, or ugly law—the problem had been defined by city authorities in hostile terms, put bluntly by the *Los Angeles Times*: "take the unfortunates out of sight." Under such auspices, it is no surprise that disabled beggars balked, either individually or in "strange union."

The city of Los Angeles continued to struggle with the ongoing problem of employment for disabled people. The Municipal Charity Commission's 1914 report described a brief experiment, a sheltered sewing workshop for "handicapped women." "Our experience here," the commission concluded,

> showed plainly the necessity of providing some form of labor for the handicapped men and women who, under present conditions, have no resource except public relief or begging. If Los Angeles can provide a means of self-

> support for its own handicapped who hold legal residence here, it will be quite possible to remove from the streets the many deformed and disabled who as itinerant merchants selling trifles, exhibit their miseries in order to secure the wherewithal by which to live. (*Second Annual Report,* 54)

Here is the rehabilitation approach: jobs do the work of ugly law. But the same report made clear that the provision of labor was not the business of the commission's approved employment bureau: "In rare instances employers have been prevailed upon to hire handicapped applicants. . . . These cases are merely incidental to the larger work of the bureau" (54). A year earlier, the commission's official report defended this situation: "Criticism has been made of the Bureau on the ground that it does not find employment for the crippled or sickly. It does not claim to do so. Their problem is an entirely different one and must be met in a different way and with different means." However helpful or unhelpful these different ways and means might be, they too defined their goal in terms unlikely to win over unsightly beggars. The 1914 Municipal Charities Commission report stated outright its motives for dealing with "the many deformed and disabled who . . . exhibit their miseries": to prevent "conditions which are now a source of displeasure *to all who see them*" (53, italics mine).

The commission itself, as it turns out, was short-lived. Formed in May 1913, a few months before it went after the "strange union" of disabled beggars, it came into existence simultaneously with the strict new begging law and was charged to implement that ordinance, with "specially trained officers equipped to meet the specific disability which causes dependence" by "curative care or discipline," as well as to oversee organized charity in the city (Municipal Charities Commission, *Second Annual Report,* 33). In September 1913, a scandal erupted when the commission exposed forgery and graft within Los Angeles's Associated Charities—a development closely followed by Arthur Fuller, who foregrounded it in the autobiography *Fifty Thousand Miles* that I discuss in chapter 11. By 1916, the commission's third and final report described a "serious set-back": the Supreme Court of California had ruled that some basic provisions of the penal ordinance the Municipal Charities Commission was charged to enforce were unconstitutional because they gave the commission arbitrary power, with no clear standard for deciding who could or should not solicit alms (Municipal Charities Commission, *Third Annual Report,* 54). The case, *Ex parte Dart,* involved a challenge by the Salvation Army to the city's power to regulate its charitable activities. The commission, no longer able to function, shut down soon after. But this was no victory for the opponents of ugly law. In fact, the court made clear that only givers of charity like the Salvation Army, not takers like the unsightly beggar, were protected from the exercise of arbitrary power: protected religious "charitable work is not to be confounded with beggary, which imports personal gain" (*Ex parte Dart*, 172 Cal. at 65–66).[23]

Soon a new municipal entity formed, the Social Service Commission. By 1917, under the pressures of World War I, the commission's rehabilitionist approach made clear that Los Angeles had just passed the historical moment of officially enacted unsightly beggar ordinances. Under the sponsorship of the new organization, Mertice Buck (Knox), coauthor of several books on work for disabled people, conducted a "Survey of the Handicapped in Los Angeles" very much like the Cleveland Cripple Survey. "The handicapped mendicant vendors and itinerant musicians of the streets of this city have presented a distressing problem for years," she wrote, and then went on, in a verb tense that signalled that ugly law was already a thing of the past, "It was not just to divert them from securing even a precarious livelihood without offering some substitute" (56). Some found jobs, Buck wrote, or negotiated stipends which may have allowed them to avoid institutionalization. So ugly law was dead—but long live ugly law: "Note," Buck continued: "The adult blind, deaf, and crippled beggars on the streets are being investigated one by one. A few have been sent to the County Farm as vagrants; another aged deaf man will be sent soon" (56).

Why the delay in the case of the "aged deaf man"? Perhaps because of problems of communication or moral qualms. Perhaps because of time needed for conversations with the local Deaf community; this was a period of strenuous repudiation of begging and peddling by Deaf leaders. "Those of us who are deaf and dumb never beg," said James F. Meagher two years earlier, in a speech reported in the *Los Angeles Times*. "Real deaf mutes are not idlers. They work" ("Says the Deaf Are Not Beggars").[24] "Very few deaf and dumb persons have ever had to take County Aid or apply for work," Buck reported in her survey, "for the excellent reason that most of the adult mutes coming here have had vocational training" (56). Not so the "aged deaf man," who was perhaps late-deafened. Nothing in Buck's language hints that he faked hearing loss, and yet—a confirmed beggar—he was not a "real deaf mute." The law that convicted him was not real ugly law. But in the aftermath of his encounter with police and charity, as he did real hard labor at the County Farm, it made no difference which law put him there.

As Buck's final note on the jailing of blind, deaf, and crippled vagrants and as the trace of the language of the unsightly beggar ordinances in the reformist Cleveland Cripple Survey suggest, to some extent Progressive-era remedies for the problem of disability offered ugly "new labels on old bottles," as Patterson put it in his influential *America's Struggles against Poverty in the Twentieth Century* (1981). Writing of progressive social environmentalism generally, Patterson argued that the progressives'

> philosophy of prevention . . . in some ways sustained nineteenth-century practices that distinguished, often harshly, between the deserving and the undeserving poor. The progressive glorified the work ethic, usually by making the poor as miserable as possible when they got relief. For all their environmentalism, they still tried to change the needy—to take the poverty out of people as well as to take the people out of poverty. (23)

Rehabilitationism aimed for this end too, for all its stress on environmental factors: to *change* the unsightly—not only to take people out of disabling situations but to take the disability out of people. In the medical version of this paradigm that came to predominate as the twentieth century wore on, unsightliness was surgically, not legally, removed.[25] In the social version of the early twentieth century, as in the nineteenth century, right thinking on the cripple's part was a key factor in what would solve the problem of exposed deformity, wrapping it up neatly. Either way, in the rehabilitationist program the aim is in one sense to make disability vanish. Rehabilitation, writes Stiker, "marks the appearance of a culture that attempts to complete the act of identification, of making identical. This act will cause the disabled to disappear and with them all that is lacking, in order to assimilate them, drown them, dissolve them in the greater and single social whole" (128). Just as ugly law desired.

Can a law "desire"? I do not mean that each human shaper of each city's ordinance aspired to this end; for many, as I have argued throughout this book, what had to disappear was quite simply begging, not disability. But the stark words of the law articulate a harsher desire. In the next and final chapter, I turn to writing by some people who desired differently.

11

ALL ABOUT UGLY LAWS (FOR TEN CENTS)

MENDICANT PIECES

Long before the Burgdorfs remembered the unsightly beggar ordinances for the disability rights movement in their landmark 1975 essay, unsightly beggars themselves wrote and printed their own histories of unequal treatment. You can find a cache of these forgotten texts (collected by Marc Selvaggio) at Harvard's Countway Library of Medicine, in the rare book reading room named after Oliver Wendell Holmes, whose descendent of the same name, as a Supreme Court justice, defended the First Amendment and authored, too, the infamous decision legalizing forced eugenic sterilization in 1927 ("Three generations of imbeciles are enough").[1] The justice spoke his father's irascible tongue; Holmes Senior had written in 1891, "I take from the top shelf of the hospital department of my library—the section devoted to literary cripples, imbeciles, failures, . . . the weak-minded population of that intellectual almshouse" (301). So it is ironically fitting that writing by "literary cripples" can be found in the Wendell Holmes room, though these are hardly the texts Holmes had in mind.

Under Holmes's portrait I read through this collection of what rare book dealers call "mendicant literature," which was arranged at the Countway by impairment types: "You're going through it at a fast clip," one librarian commented to me, "the lame, the halt."[2] Paul Longmore and Lauri Umansky have noted that the "historical trail" of disability is shaped by the "dispersal of the records through disability-specific channels" (21); I saw this at work at the Countway, as an originally mendicancy-specific collection was initially divided in the cataloguing into archives of blindness, deafness, and so forth.[3] "There's something for everyone here," another Harvard librarian said, apparently amused at my interest, as she brought me a catalogue organized alphabetically, "[Amputee]" followed by "[Blind]" and then "[Crippled]." Here in the Countway, presided over by dreams of free speech, by ghosts of eugenics, and by the medical catalogue of impairment, mendicant literature speaks of the ugly law.

At the Countway (and not only here, for this kind of vagrant publication distributed itself across the country) it becomes clear that the ugly law in fact generated literature directly and distinctively. With the word *literature* I am not referring to the investigative reportage written by COS authorities or police agents, though this constitutes a significant part of the textual history of the not-person who was diseased, maimed, and deformed so as to be an unsightly or disgusting object. Nor am I referring to the work of relatively privileged disabled advocates like Marshall P. Wilder. Ugly laws produced disabled mendicant texts. Mendicant disability literature emerged elsewhere, of course, not only after the existence of or at the sites of ugly laws; but the presence of ugly laws spurred its production. Where unsightly begging was legally forbidden, peddling life stories became a way for poor disabled people on the street to ward off charges of "operation" or vagrancy, to claim a visible means of support and thereby a legitimate authority, and to establish their right to the city. Mendicant literature not only provided income; it also functioned as a first line of defense against arrest.[4] This was true at any time in any city that barred participation by disabled people in the subsistence economy through the mechanism of any ordinance (vagrancy charges, bans on street obstruction, manipulation of the license system, and so forth), including ugly law.

Disabled people on the streets frequently sold formulaic texts, bits of ephemera.[5] But mendicant writers also wrote their own more complex and extensive stories, often multiple book-length volumes, that they themselves distributed. They often sought to put their own stamp on the genre. Under the right circumstances—an available amanuensis, a sympathetic printer, money for paper, enough time, permission to settle for a while, a street corner of one's own, avoidance of jail—mendicancy spurred disability life writing of surprising intricacy and detail.[6]

Like slave narratives (and perhaps, in some cases, directly influenced by slave narrative form), these life stories often begin or end with endorsements, especially by doctors, certifying their authenticity and testifying to the good character of the author.[7] Like slave narratives, they offer sensationalized accounts of suffering bodies. Most importantly, these mendicant pieces, like slave narratives, were performative utterances, in the sense Bérubé has explained in his comparison between the slave narrative and published writing by people with cognitive or developmental disabilities. Slave narrative announces "its author's very capacity for—and accomplishment of—the fact of self-authorship," Bérubé notes, "on which could be based further claims for what are now human rights. . . . the act of self-authorship establishes the life-writer as, at bare minimum, someone capable of self-reflection and self-representation" (340).[8]

The "unsightly beggar" who wrote (and self-published) the book on ugly law. (Arthur Franklin Fuller, *An Odd Soldiery: The Tale of a Sojourner; Being an Autobiography of Arthur Franklin Fuller, a Soldier of* MIS-*fortune.* Fort Worth, Tex.: Anchor, 1914, p. 208)

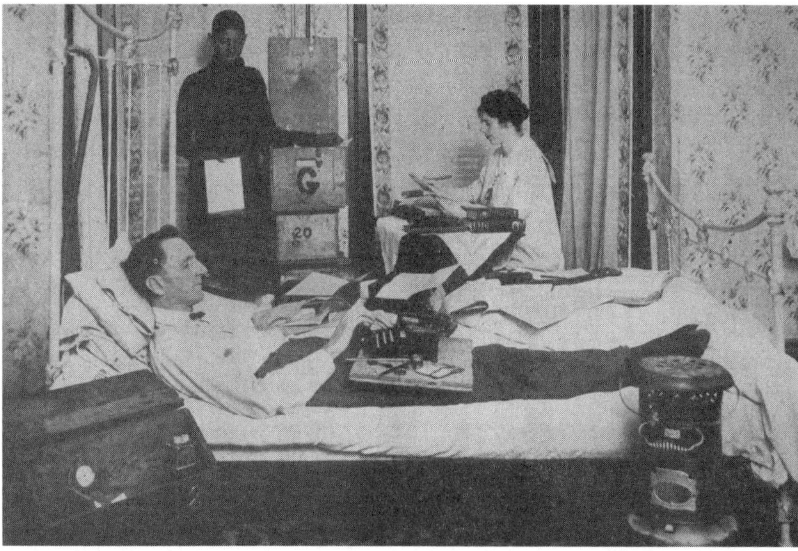

Arthur Franklin Fuller at work on one of the many books he sold on the street. (Arthur Franklin Fuller, *An Odd Soldiery: The Tale of a Sojourner; Being an Autobiography of Arthur Franklin Fuller, a Soldier of* MIS-*fortune.* Fort Worth, Tex.: Anchor, 1914, p. 93)

The writers whose work I address in this chapter were not marked as what we would now call developmentally or cognitively disabled; there is no "feeble-minded" category in the Countway catalogue of American mendicant literature. People with cognitive disabilities who begged on the streets did so in conditions so adverse to their claims that the existence of such a text seems highly unlikely. But Bérubé's point applies to mendicant writers in general and to those who were physically disabled in particular; for them, too, as Bérubé puts it, "that 'bare minimum' [of capacity for self-representation] is actually the crux of the matter, a meta-claim from which all other claims follow" (340).[9] Making this meta-claim, beggars who presented themselves as authors demonstrated their dignity as well as their need, in texts nonetheless massively constrained and mediated by the scene of panhandling and its economic and social surround.

In general in mendicant literature, and with special intensity in its disability subgenre, text and author were inseparable. What the policeman called "vagrancy" and "exposure" was reconstituted by the disabled mendicant author as a publicity tour. Lansing Hall wrote that he had been "induced . . . to offer" his books "to the public in person" (7). William Campbell explained his purpose in writing: "to put myself squarely before the public" (i). The act forbidden under ugly law, exposure to public view, reconstructs itself in mendicant disability literature as a sealing of trust. Trickster sellers might fool gullible buyers by vending texts that seemed to offer accounts of their own visible impairments but that had actually been written by others. So, for instance, Charles Cummings, who "lost his limbs while employed as brakeman," as his fine print informs us, sold a war-injury story doubly titled ALL ABOUT IT, FOR 10 CENTS and *The Great War Relic*, presumably to buyers who thought they were helping support a wounded Civil War veteran.[10] But this scam nonetheless was predicated on the implicit pact between writer/marketer and reader/buyer in the moment of mendicant bookselling: disabled self-publishers promised a direct link between the story of the text and the story of the writer's own body. Their pamphlets would, in the words of one beggar author, "embody my experience," and in turn that narrated experience was literally embodied by the texts' vendors (Newton, 1). The text came with (even as it discreetly supplemented or substituted for) bodily display. The "it" one could read all about was there, on view for all to see.

But viewers lacked the backstory, the how-come, and mendicant literature aimed to supply this demand. Writers frequently marketed their books as preemptive answers to prying onlookers.[11] Of the impudent questions of passersby, Cummings wrote, "Any refusal on my part to give them polite answers always caused the inquirers to call me the sassiest cripple they ever saw. On the account of the above actual experience, I have decided to answer all who inquire as they are answered in this little book—ALL ABOUT IT." The fact that "it," which cost ten cents, was in fact "all about" war experiences not connected to Cummings's injury may only have increased his reputation as a sassy cripple, but this does not seem to have worried Cummings in the slightest. As Cummings's openly intractable "sassiness" suggests, mendicant literature frequently and radically exceeds the simple bounds of mendicant acts.

Mendicant acts involved clear formulae, tried and true pitches that were, of course, employed by writers positioned as unsightly beggars. Narratives of misery and misfortune are common. Hence Charles Williams, offering up the exciting tale *Terrors of a Blizzard, by One Who Has Had the Experience*, subtitled his volume in order to underscore his bad luck: *Or How I Lost My Feet, Written by the Loser.* Hence Thomas Doner's 1880 *Eleven Years a Drunkard* offered its marvelous subtitle, *Having Lost Both Arms through Intemperance, He Wrote This Book with His Teeth as a Warning to Others.* But winning discourse appears equally frequently and predictably. "I class my exhibition educative to young and old," A.J. Murphy prefaces his story of quadruple amputation, "simply showing to you that though under heavy misfortune, a man can be happy and satisfied in life, if he has manly courage enough to lay his misfortune aside" (1). The author of *My Life Story: Yours Truly, Kitty Smith* plays out this dialectic in alternating chapter headings in her version of the genre: "What Perseverance and Determination Can Do" followed by "I am Armless, Helpless and Homeless."[12]

Producers of these texts situated themselves as alms-seekers by emphasizing that they had no other alternative for gainful employment (see, for instance, Hagans, Williams, Campbell, Hall, Bowen). But mendicant writers also justified their offerings as quality merchandise, worthy of sale in the everyday market of economic competition. And some of the writing in the Countway collection goes far beyond the requirements of subsistence literature. In the most striking examples of texts in this genre the "it" the text tells "all about" is not blindness, amputation, paralysis, and so forth; nor is "it" the eked-out, sharp, and basic need of the beggar reduced to begging. "It" is expansive, garrulous, social, and political. If, as Longmore and Umansky put it, the "'medical model,' powerful though it has been in shaping the life experiences of people with disabilities, has never gone uncontested" (22), neither, these texts illustrate, has the "mendicant model."

Some mendicant literature is a literature of contestation. In it, marginalized disabled historians wrote marginal disability history.

One might expect mendicant literature to narrate single tales of woe and overcoming, but as often as not community effects predominate. Texts in the Countway Library collection often come illustrated with photographs not just of the author but of his or her (usually his) disabled friends. The authors' strategies of address speak to as well as for these friends. At times, speaking in the collective first-person plural, these texts confront head-on the impossibility of writing a history of the "us"—writing unsightly history—for what mendicant writer Lansing Hall called "the world of eyes" (12). Occasionally mendicant pieces seem to turn away from these worlds of eyes entirely, staging themselves for stretches as beggar writing for beggars.

In a 1938 radio episode of Orson Welles's *The Shadow,* a society of disabled beggars, threatened by petty extortionists, join together with The Shadow's help to defend themselves. "[M]ake your signs of distress . . . using the symbols you use in communicating with one another," The Shadow instructs them; disabled beggars in Lamont Cranston's town employ some kind of special coded graffiti scrawled on alley walls as their underground communication system, a visual "beggar's grapevine," apparently undeterred by the fact that a large number of them are blind. Moments in the Countway collection of mendicant literature almost seem a version of this secret language. A number of the texts contain long lists of cities evaluated for their kindness or hostility to unsightly beggars. Though these lists function obviously as appeals to the civic pride of almsgivers, they also read like insider's tips, as if each little booklet constituted a kind of Baedeker for vagrants, with trip-adviser warnings about the worst cities and the best.[13] At such moments, these texts seem to participate in what Beverley has described as a kind of "testimonial practice in subaltern cultures, a practice which includes the arts of . . . storytelling, gossip and rumor" (81), here captured on the page perhaps for (and certainly by) disabled people on the street and on the road.

Subaltern they were, by any definition; Spivak's succinct one in her famous "Can the Subaltern Speak" will serve: "subaltern—a person without lines of social mobility" (38). Legal unsightly beggarhood might be defined as the denial of social mobility to people understood as already, by nature, immobilized. With some defiance, these writers charted lines of mobility in their books—if not upward, at least outward ("fifty thousand miles backridden," as Arthur Fuller put it).

Can the unsightly beggar speak? These ephemeral texts have largely vanished, a few handfuls preserved by dedicated collectors like Selvaggio. Even when purchased, they may have gone unread as often as not. I found *Fifty Thousand Miles Back-Ridden* in the card catalogue of the Los Angeles central public library; a librarian who went in search of it in the stacks thought at first that the copy must have burned in a long-ago fire, because no one, he told me, had ever checked it out. Moreover, since mendicant literature by its very existence distinguishes itself from and defends its seller against the charge of begging—as a commodity offered for sale, a token of economic participation, an offering rather than a taking—it cannot by definition be the "speaking" of the illegitimized "beggar," only of the legitimate not-beggar.

Nonetheless, to a startling extent mendicant pieces (particularly the ones by white men) aimed, however futilely, to speak out—to represent *for* the diseased, maimed, and deformed, to make the broad social phenomenon of unsightly begging political, explicable, and understood. Some of these texts openly protested the poorhouse or almshouse systems, challenging the claim in the 1880s ugly laws that people incarcerated there were simply "well cared for." Some writers talked back to charity organization and developed open critiques of the dynamics of deformance, seeking and affirming a warmer and more complicated mutual exchange between donor and beggar or buyer and book-peddler.[14] But some writers went further, openly challenging the edicts and representations of the law and the police. In the Countway, after four years of research on this book, I found for the first time an archive of direct textual resistance to city laws and policies regarding disabled beggars, written by the beggars themselves.

Williams's *Terrors of a Blizzard, by One Who Has Had the Experience* (circa 1907) introduces itself as an answer to an obvious question: "In 1880 I had the misfortune to lose my lower limbs from freezing, and my appearance, going, as I have been compelled to most of the time, on my knees, seems to arouse the curiosity of every person I meet" (1). But the history of the blizzard and of Williams's impairment occupies only a small portion of the pamphlet; much of it is given over instead to records of police harassment. Along with two other disabled men, Williams traveled from town to town "over the H&D of the Milwaukee railroad" selling stationery, or trying to. The story of his travels comes to a standstill in Faribault, Minnesota, where the mayor (Williams makes sure to call him out by name: "a fellow by the name of Townley") ordered that he pay a daily license fee (and past-due fine) in order to continue selling. Williams triumphantly records the gathering of an ugly crowd of respectable businessmen who went in delegation to the mayor to protest on his behalf. The mayor refused to back down, but Williams, with sly civility, gives himself the punchline: "being well advertised through the mayor's acts, I was well patronized" (10–11).[15]

Herbert Kohr's *Around the World with Uncle Sam* (1907) describes the toll taken by mayoral peddling-permit systems for disabled people and by the conflict between those systems and city ordinances (the ugly law among them) that forbade street selling and begging. Kohr testifies to the anxieties produced by the logic of exception that defined the uneasy status of licensed unsightliness. Licensing disabled beggars or peddlers made their presence provisional by definition; a permit carried with it the threat of its withdrawal at any time. Cities often had multiple, confusing, and blatantly contradictory mechanisms for the social control of disabled street operators. Kohr, an army veteran who became disabled later after a workplace explosion burned, blinded, and maimed him, sold pencils from town to town, often in the company of other blind peddlers. His account of his experience in an unnamed "eastern city" is jovial enough, but it describes with clarity how coexisting permit exceptions and outright ugly bans forced him and others like him into a constant state of good-cop/bad-cop interrogation:

> On our way home we passed through an eastern city, where we were stopped by the police and not allowed to sell. . . . I proceeded to the mayor's office, but he referred me to the chief of police. . . . He informed me that the city council had just passed a strict ordinance, prohibiting any sales in the city. But being kind hearted he at length gave me permission. We had much amusement in making sales, for after selling for an hour or more, we would be met by some guardian of the law, who would send us to the mayor's office; he would laugh and send us out again. (196)

Kohr's book ends here, after an explanation that he has taken up autobiography because "perhaps that might afford an opportunity for a little easier method of making my own way. There is always a way for those who are willing to help themselves, even though they are seriously handicapped" (197).

These texts map the terrain around the unsightly beggar ordinances but do not mention them directly. There is one text, however, that confronts the handicap of ugly law head-on: Arthur Franklin Fuller's first-person narrative, *Fifty Thousand Miles Back-Ridden*. *Fifty Thousand Miles* is a significant and entirely buried American autobiography, part of what Verter has called the literature of "subterranean lives" in "alternative America," life writing that "assert[s] the integrity of lives lived over lives imagined or, worse, denied, . . . not by conforming to conventional norms but rather by requiring a reassessment of those norms."[16] In 1915, Fuller told the story of the ugly law, demanding that reassessment. At the same time, he gave a clear account of why dissent against unsightly beggar ordinances by people marked as unsightly beggars barely exists.

THE MAN WHO WROTE THE BOOK ON UGLY LAW

Born in 1880, Fuller was the son of genteel choir directors, and as a young man he did a brief stint as an Episcopalian choir director himself. He slipped uneasily into the ranks of the subaltern after a series of injuries and illnesses and chronic pain left him in the shape described in words painted on his wooden cart: "Cannot Walk or Sit—Spinal and Heart Trouble—Down Since 1899" on the side, "Must Earn a Living/Patronize Me" on the front. "Sells Books and Music—His Own Productions," the signs continued.

Elsewhere Fuller described the sight of him in the third person: "a queer-looking little cut-wagon, in which lay at full length a man with an earnest, alert countenance. . . . Everyone spoke well of 'that crippled man, Mr. Fuller.'" I have already mentioned Fuller's racist relations to his paid assistants. Fuller's class positioning was equally elitist. He portrayed himself as a cut above "most of the traveling cripples and afflicted," whom he described as "elementals and uneducated" (*Wrestling the Wolf*, 30).

Fuller is an odd candidate to be the radical defender of unsightly beggars. "Odd" is his own word: one of his many books bears the title *An Odd Romance* (1915); another, the first volume to *Fifty Thousand Miles Back-Ridden*'s second, is titled *An Odd Soldiery* (1915). Both "odd" books use war language to figure Fuller's disability. He subtitled *An Odd Romance* with *The Story of a Brave Little Soldier* and *Odd Soldiery* with *Being the Autobiography of Arthur Franklin Fuller, a Soldier of* MIS*-fortune*. *Odd Soldiery* develops this strained martial metaphor at great length; the chapter titles describing the onset of impairment and skirmishes with doctors move from "War Declared" through "One More of the Enemy's Batteries Silenced" to "Overtures for Peace." Between odd and soldier Fuller situated himself, calling attention to his queerness even as he attempted to claim (in miniature, and in MIS-appropriation) the normative power of the heroic veteran.

Unlike most of the other authors and sellers of the mendicant literature in the Countway's collection, Fuller could not point to one medically

Arthur Fuller on the street. (Arthur Franklin Fuller, *An Odd Soldiery: The Tale of a Sojourner; Being an Autobiography of Arthur Franklin Fuller, a Soldier of* MIS*-fortune.* Fort Worth, Tex.: Anchor, 1914, p. 201)

Fuller and anonymous assistant, circa 1914. (Arthur Franklin Fuller, *An Odd Soldiery: The Tale of a Sojourner; Being an Autobiography of Arthur Franklin Fuller, a Soldier of* MIS*-fortune.* Fort Worth, Tex.: Anchor, 1914, p. 162)

conclusive trauma that disabled him. As a result, the first volume of his autobiography, *Odd Soldiery*, is dominated by struggles with the discourse of hypochondria. Querulous in tone, repetitive in structure, *Odd Soldiery* attempts to ward off charges of duplicity and delusion. "Therefore," Fuller challenges his audience at one point,

> to any doctor, healer, scientist, or fool who will undertake to prove that I am deceived about my condition—self-hypnotized—or that I am a fake and making game of the public, he can have $1000, on presentation of substantial proof of this success; provided that if he fails he will pay me the same amount and all expenses, when he has had sufficient time to see plainly who is the chump. . . . One of the several hob-goblins which this child of trouble would flee is the man who conceitedly announces, "I can cure Fuller." . . . Friend, I am not deceived about my condition—nor am I deceiving you. (91, 100)

Under the pressure of medical certification, much of *Odd Soldiery* devotes itself to charts of symptoms—pulse rates, nightmares, bladder trouble. This book of complaints seems designed primarily to attest to the author's incapacity and need:

> The purpose of this book is merely to state facts regarding my experience and physical condition. Physicians . . . have frequently been patrons, and I need to avoid making enemies. This book is written for my *defense* and if any man will do me the honor to consider its contents from cover to cover, with unbiased mind, he can hardly fail to realize that I have set forth only the facts and have presented the truth. . . . It would be impossible to tell it all—to fairly represent, just what I have to endure. And even if I could tell it, there would no doubt be still someone who was *skeptical*. (75; italics in the original)

At the same time, Fuller strove to establish his legitimacy in another way as well, certifying himself not only as disabled but also as normal. If the book aims to prove his worthiness of charity and accommodation, it also aims to prove his worthiness of conventional respect. This dynamic plays out clearly in the photos he includes, especially in the complex interplay of the one captioned "A clever picture which eliminates evidences of invalidism for those who like to think of him as musician, composer, author, poet, rather than as a cripple."

A clever picture which eliminates evidences of invalidism for those who like to think of the author as Musician, Composer, Author, Poet, rather than as a cripple.

Arthur Franklin Fuller. (Arthur Franklin Fuller, *An Odd Soldiery: The Tale of a Sojourner; Being an Autobiography of Arthur Franklin Fuller, a Soldier of* MIS*-fortune.* Fort Worth, Tex.: Anchor, 1914, p. 113)

This portrait of the artist as a not-unsightly man attempts to slough off disablement, much as the Cleveland Cripple Survey encouraged readers to find "the man behind the handicap." But because his diagnosis was unclear, Fuller's situation differed significantly from the Cleveland newspaper seller's. He needed to place himself into the realm of "handicap" even as he needed to escape it. Thus, his emphasis in the caption on cleverness of the photographic trick reassures readers that he does deserve alms, that he cannot work, that he truly is a cripple. Combined, the photograph and caption pose him as a fake well person—a far cry from the sham cripples of COS legend. In this complex scene, Fuller simultaneously differentiates himself from "cripple," demonstrates his normality (even his ideality), protests the social construction of the "cripple," and certifies his disability—an intricate dance of identification and disidentification. These dynamics constitute the very personal political task of the first volume of Fuller's autobiography.

But in the second volume, *Fifty Thousand Miles Back-Ridden,* an older Fuller comes into his own as a broader social critic. *Fifty Thousand Miles* organizes itself geographically rather than chronologically, as a vagrant travelogue, the disabled tramp tale that the title suggests. Midway through the book, Fuller describes in detail an encounter with a COS official when he arrived in Brooklyn from Jackson, Mississippi, via Chicago in 1910. The episode begins with an explanation of how the author negotiates the responsibilities of being in public:

> The first few months I spend in any city of size, I am so much of a curiosity, that with slight encouragement or excuse, the Public gather round my vehicle as though I were some newly discovered specimen of pre-historic existence and must needs be inspected with care. In order to avoid congesting traffic, obstructing the sidewalk, distracting attention of the buying public from the show windows of progressive merchants, I have the attendant wheel me a few paces, then stop a moment while I call out my challenge to the kindly disposed to "Buy something." (161)

Here already we find the effect of ugly law discourse in reverse. Fuller presents himself as a civic citizen, mindful of the needs of merchants (at least of the "progressive" variety), ally of the Streets and Alleys subcommittee of the city council. The effect increases as the narrative pays an (un)friendly visit to a charity official, describing the man with the same clinical tone and physiognomic obsession with which COS case histories record encounters with beggars:

> We were proceeding along in this fashion when a small, sharp featured man in a gray suit stepped along side of my attendant and said, "Take him around the corner—I want to talk with him." . . . I wondered what he could be and what he had to say. . . . This man wore glasses through which peered small, pale blue eyes. His chin was strong, the lips were thin, the nose aggressive. I could not guess him out, but fancied he might be a newspaper reporter who wished to do me and his paper a little mutual good. . . . The

> little man produced a tablet and pencil . . . "Are you under the care of any doctor here?" he inquired artfully. (166)

To which Fuller records his response: "I am tired of being experimented with" (166).

The "little man" is John D. (Fuller erroneously names him J.F.) Godfrey, who worked for both the Bureau of Charities and the Brooklyn police department and collaborated closely with James Forbes across the bridge. Both men's portraits are included, facing each other squarely, in a 1905 *New York Times* article on their joint efforts to eradicate "mendicant parasites" with special attention to the problem of the crippled beggar ("No Sinecure"). "During Mr. Godfrey's period of service," the *Times* reported, "he has investigated something like 2,000 cases of professional beggars whose records are now on file." Men like Godfrey, "familiar, as officers of the Mendicancy Department naturally are, with every piece of beggardom can tell almost infallibly from personal knowledge plus complete records just who is the latest panhandler gathered in the mendicancy corral, unless he happen to be a new light on the metropolitan horizon, in which case his pedigree and history are as carefully inquired into and mapped out as if he were the heir to a title or a fabulous fortune."

Whereas the *Times* article provides a totalizing celebration of Godfrey's vigilant surveillance and his "infallible" beggar radar, Arthur Fuller's version of what it means to come under Godfrey's sights proceeds quite differently. The passage takes intensely dialogic form, in almost novelistic detail, as the beggar and the policeman square off.

> [Godfrey] leaned upon the roof of my vehicle and said, "Now I want you to go home—to your room, and stay there, and not come out on the streets this way any more." . . . "And if I persist?" I questioned.
>
> "I will arrest you if I see you on the streets again," replied Godfrey, curtly.
>
> "On what charge?"
>
> "Vagrancy."
>
> It was evident the situation was serious. I hoped to see better how I stood by questioning further, so I ventured:
>
> "My understanding of the word 'vagrant' is beggar. I am not begging. Here are books and music of my own writing for sale. It is necessary for me to earn a living." . . .

> Mr. Godfrey continued obdurately: "Yes I know all you would say. But I am hired by a society of rich people for the express purpose of keeping persons like you off the streets. I have been here about two years now and flatter myself that Brooklyn is pretty clean of this sort of thing."
>
> I replied heatedly: "This is sure getting to be a great country if it is now a crime for a man to market his own productions—particularly when he is unable to do anything else, and is doing his best to make an honest and independent living."
>
> Mr. Godfrey rested his weight on one foot and gazed down the street saying: "Well I appreciate all that. . . . But we do not want it and will not tolerate it in Brooklyn. . . . It does not look well." (166–167)

Shown a permit by a local alderman licensing Fuller to sell on the streets, Godfrey dismisses it in capital letters: "'This Permit is absolutely no good. These big Politicians have an idea they can about run the Universe. . . . I know every Judge in this City and I know they back me up. . . . when I set my mind to get a man off the streets he goes,' ripped out the little man in the gray suit, bending his stony gaze upon me" (168).

Here the chapter ends, but as the encounter with Godfrey spills over into the next one ("Ch. XXIV. Mr. Godfrey Explains"), the book's loose episodic structure ceases, and confrontation with the ugly law becomes its core and spine. "It was easy to see there was nothing to be gained by antagonizing the representative of charity, law and order," Fuller begins. "So I proceeded mildly." "Mr. Godfrey's explanation," in return, is the logic of ableism reduced to its most basic opposition. Fuller argues,

> "Well all I can say is that I can prove all I claim—that I am physically unable to fill any wage-earning position. . . . It seems to me pretty hard to have such a cold-blooded proposition forced upon me, showing that the worse a man needs a little consideration or privilege, the harder it is to get."
>
> Mr. Godfrey explained: "If you were a well man there would be no objection to your selling your books and music on the streets or anywhere else if you could. But you cannot do it here in your condition." (168)

At this moment full-blown ugly law shows its face. It is Mr. Godfrey's final explanation. The ordinance's language comes mediated and distorted, as it must have actually come to Fuller on the street, but nonetheless there is no mistaking it. "I was told," Fuller says,

> that the authorities were hard on unfortunate folk in the North and East, but I could not believe but that the circumstances connected with my case would be a passport to the privilege I need. . . ."
>
> "I do not remember the exact wording," the plain clothes man explained, "but in the penal code there are clauses which provide that 'no person shall be allowed to use any affliction to foster business or obtain money, or in any way make capital of it by making any indecent exposure or displaying a sign advertising his affliction.'" (173)

And here in this autobiography, for once, an unsightly beggar answers ugly law on the record, glossing for himself the meaning of his body as a text of crippled/man/writing:[17]

> "My signs are not for the purpose of affecting the sympathies or pocketbook of the public, but that all may know that I am wheeled because I cannot walk and lie down because I cannot sit. Before they were painted I was frequently taken to be a lazy man or a new-fangled peanut and popcorn machine. The signs say 'sells' that all may know I do not beg. They refer to what I sell in order to furnish those police who are willing to interpret the law to my protection that I am selling my own productions, periodical publications, on which there is no license. I admit the signs do help my business, but not nearly enough to make up for the hindrance my afflictions impose."
>
> "Our point of view," replied Mr. Godfrey, "is, of course, exactly opposite to yours." (173)

A full-scale exposition of Fuller's point of view ensues. *Fifty Thousand Miles* moves beyond counterattack on Godfrey to a strenuous general critique of COS ideology and practice. "Why should a cripple or afflicted man be compelled to have the public begged for him—why should he not beg himself?" Fuller queries (180). In his rewriting of the language of exposure, it is the hidden unsightliness of organized charity that needs to be held up to public view:

> To some readers, the position taken by the Bureau of Charities . . . may appear fair and just. But that is the trouble and danger. It is their business to make things appear right. They work quietly, gaining the co-operation of people and police and city authorities in such a way as to avoid exposure to public sentiment. (177)

To counter the discourse of the COS, *Fifty Thousand Miles Back-Ridden* wrote unsightly history in two ways: in the assertive mode of forensic debate but also in the investigative mode of social science—a kind of cripple's survey designed to supplant and counteract the surveying of street cripples done from above. "A Charity Agent unguardedly told me that this is the plan," Fuller wrote: "—get the newspapers to publish articles which will control the surge of public sentiment and send it against the Poor" (190). Fuller himself had been represented in some of these articles, and at least once, after a Topeka, Kansas, newspaper described him as a secretly wealthy man, he "sought redress" in some fashion but, by his account, "was treated with scant courtesy—even threatened" (*Wrestling the Wolf,* 23).[18] As he traveled by freightcar in his wooden cart back and forth across the country, he kept a lookout for newspaper stories attacking unsightly beggars and made it his own "business to investigate every cripple and blind man" in cities where those attacks occurred. In Fort Worth, for instance, he countered a feature on secretly wealthy beggars by conducting his own survey, the results of which, he asserted, proved that "not one of them owned anything except one" (*Fifty Thousand Miles,* 190). Some chapters of *Fifty-Thousand Miles* consist of interviews with other disabled street people.

Fuller talked back to ugly law by debunking its underlying assumptions and potential motives, developing a radical kind of "odd" theory. In one interesting passage in *Fifty Thousand Miles,* he turned the doctrine of maternal impression on its head, not to reject it but to give it a crip spin:

> Excuses are given the Public—not reasons—why stringent measures should be passed and enforced. One I have met is that of pre-natal impressions. Probably the City Physician somewhere got it up. You know it is a pretty poor theory that cannot find somebody to support it. It is known that a pregnant woman can "mark" her child through sudden strong emotion. . . . There is of course evidence to support this contention. But mothers who are so impressionable as to be liable to bring forth deformed or diseased offspring by seeing unsightly afflicted persons on the street selling, are so impressionable as to get the same result from some other cause—a picture show, or a novel, or baneful suggestions of old women. . . .
>
> Whereas, if prospective mothers have right habits of thought and think thoughts of mercy, love, compassion, benevolence and kindness at the sight of the unfortunates on the streets, and reject evil impulse, receiving instead an impression of industriousness, patience, fortitude in the face of

> handicaps, their offspring will be most desirably "marked" and the presence of a beggar be a blessing rather than a curse. (196–197)

Elsewhere he included a photograph to demonstrate how little space his cart took up on an "ordinary city sidewalk" (200); insisted that he made sure not to attract crowds and that in any case "the stoppage is not longer than if a lady dropped her purse" (197); attacked the unsightly beggar ordinances on health grounds, arguing that they forced street sellers into the ostensibly private doorways of abandoned buildings (in his later book *Wrestling the Wolf,* 12); defended against charges of vagrancy ("This man has traveled from coast to coast . . . not because he is a tramp or rover by choice or nature, but because he has never found a community where the people could . . . be led to buy more than once or twice" [*Wrestling the Wolf,* 4]); and placed the ordinances in the context of other laws that targeted poor people (*Fifty Thousand Miles,* 198).

The final volume of Fuller's autobiography, *Wrestling the Wolf* (1919), devotes itself almost entirely to accounts of his various and unsuccessful attempts to find and sustain paid employment. Although these stories certainly are meant to function as defenses of begging and as simple sales-pitches, they offer critical, powerfully articulate reflections on the politics of work and disability. Describing his problems getting work as a musician in Los Angeles, Fuller developed an anatomy of ableism, redefining the able body as sheer "physique and gall": "The pianist could not play nearly as well as I, even in dance music. But these folks have well, normal bodies, and that makes all the difference in the world. Often physique and gall get by and go over the top rather than conscientiousness and art and real ability" (29).

In another eloquent passage on work disincentives and charity patronization, a manifesto for the principles of independent living emerges:

> I have been living in this body about 34 years and do not allow that anyone else knows better than myself, what I want or need and know that proper care and food and comfort are not furnished according to the whims of inmates of charity institutions. . . . I prefer street work to basket weaving or other jobs provided by The Charities, at $4 a week in an institution. . . . to consent to be committed to such a place would be to consent to be, as it were, buried alive—to a living death—the death of individuality, citizenship and personal independence. . . . This is my individuality. I despise charity, so-called. I only ask for justice. (25–26)

Fuller repeatedly pointed out the instability of the category "beggar"; one chapter of *Fifty Thousand Miles*, "Seeking a Definition," is devoted to interrogating the word. "Even though it be true," he wrote, "that I have accepted money for which I gave nothing but a smile and a thank-you, I maintain I am no beggar. Because I have put every particle of strength I have been able to muster, into trying to qualify for a livelihood" (177). Appealing to his readers, he emphasized the contingency of their own relation both to the opposition between beggars and givers and to the sightly/unsightly binary:

> Sometimes people are heard to say "Oh, isn't that dreadful. Such cases are so shocking and unsightly, they ought not to be permitted on the streets." Yet when there is no other way, what shall a man do? Fancy yourself in such a situation—no home, no friends able to give you a home and take care of you and utterly unable to fill any wage-earning position. . . .
>
> I am confident the American Public do not intend to permit laws to be formed which disenfranchise and afflict one of their own kind—especially if they can be brought to realize they may be so situated themselves. Surely the Public will make it their business to see that when a man gets down (as all must, prior to death, except those who pass out by accident, apoplexy, or heart failure)—when a man gets down so he cannot make a living at his former trade or profession he does not lose his Rights and be rendered an alien, an outcast, an object of suspicion and subject of persecution. . . . Now, the list is growing constantly, of cities where an unfortunate who is unable to do anything else, can not go and work on the streets, soliciting the Public. . . . what will he do when all the cities "tighten up"? It is only a question of time until that occurs. (177, 187)

Marshaling echoes of Shakespeare and the Bible, Fuller's rhetoric meets this crisis in high gear: "Friends, neighbors, brothers, fellow-human-beings! I would not do so unto you" (187).

But the texts that Fuller cites most often, as his language of "rights" suggests, are those of the Founding Fathers.[19] "When a boy at school," he writes,

> I learned the Declaration of Independence and grew up to think the U.S.A. a free country. I did not dream that any citizen or person who had ever read it could be so mean as to step to the telephone and stir up the police

> to enforce the law and get me off the streets or out of town. I did not know, and can scarcely now believe, that such a law was ever made. (175)

And then Fuller, in the service of his own declaration of independent living, quotes the first lines of the Declaration, following it with his own statement of a truth he thought self-evident: "I have long labored under the delusion that I had the right to sell on the streets. And I still believe that the public do not know that when they see a blind man, a cripple or afflicted person selling or begging, he is doing so by the toleration of the Police Department—because they are kind enough to suspend the laws" (176). Moving from the Declaration to the Constitution, *Fifty Thousand Miles* reaches toward an early version of a critical disability legal theory. "The Constitution of the United States allows," Fuller wrote, "or should allow, a man to market his own labor without license." But

> I have not the money to contest the matter in court. [A]n individual would be a poor match for a big corporation like the city of Los Angeles. The latter would stop at nothing to win. . . . because I am in such a fix as places me absolutely at the mercy of the Law-Makers and the Law-Enforcers, as well as the Public, I am not to be allowed as much chance to fight for "life, liberty and the pursuit of happiness" as those who have been spared losing the most precious thing in life—health—the ability to come and go and enjoy one's self. (192)

According to his own account, Fuller did in fact seek out a lawyer in 1918 after a run-in with a Santa Monica ordinance explained by a policeman in the following terms: "If we did not have [this law], we would be overrun with blind and cripples, every day" (*Wrestling the Wolf*, 55). The lawyer discouraged him from pursuing the issue further. In *Fifty-Thousand Miles,* Fuller wrote of his decision not to challenge the Brooklyn ugly law:

> From what I am told, it was fortunate I did not enter a law contest with Godfrey. He would have won in all the lower courts in all probability. It would take $600 or more to carry it to the higher courts. I would still be at a disadvantage. . . . they would always have the point of "menace to public safety and himself" and "obstructing the sidewalk." (223)

Instead, this man repeatedly defined as an unsightly beggar "under legal recognition" fought ugly law not in the courts but on its other turf, the street.[20] He appealed to a public sphere of two, buyer and seller, an intimate dyad below the police radar unless an ugly crowd was needed: "If a policeman is seen talking to me, unless there is a pleasant expression on his face and mine, it might mean that anyone who had the nerve to try to succor me, might do well to 'listen in' and let it be known that a few people are 'for' me. Otherwise, this is confidential—not for aimless conversation. Just between ourselves—you and me" (163). It is important that Fuller sold his autobiographies "just between you and me" in public urban spaces, in a begging or peddling posture, violating the ugly laws in the very act of distributing a political critique of their existence. He put his asking for money where his mouth was. These texts do not simply defend begging. They embody and practice begging. In a very explicit way, they have—are—mouths to feed. Fuller not only defied ugly law; he undid it, by refusing both the prohibition against begging/exposing and the opposition between the unsightly beggar and the proper person on the streets and public ways.

It is still possible today to get a public view of Arthur Franklin Fuller. Chances are not bad that your local library includes one of his many books illustrated with photographs of his life on the streets. You can see him on film as well. For a brief time, among his many efforts at finding steady employment, he sought out work in the motion picture industry and got small parts in two Cecil B. DeMille films. *We Can't Have Everything* is lost, but a copy of *Till I Come Back to You* is stored at Eastman House at Rochester, New York.

Till I Come Back To You (1918) is one of DeMille's World War I films, a propaganda piece centered on the romance triangle of a heroic Allied spy behind the lines, "Yvonne the little Belgian wife of the Prussian Officer," and Yvonne's evil husband, von Krutz. In one scene, intertitled "At the American Prison Camp," the scheming von Krutz, captured by U.S. troops, "sees in a wounded German waiting to be 'exchanged'—his opportunity to escape." Fuller, who lies on a bench throughout the scene, plays one of a group of wounded Germans. The rest stand in a line with their disability markers prominently displayed. Von Krutz, combining fake cripple and POW escape plots, changes places with an extra who wears his arm in a sling and marches off with the other exchanged prisoners, leaving Fuller behind with the actor playing the American on guard duty. The guard points at Fuller, calling for stretcher-bearers, and with this emphatic reminder of Fuller's immobility the scene ends. DeMille clearly wants to underscore Fuller's paralysis. Fuller's presence guarantees a certain wartime authenticity; here is the real thing, the genuine disabled playing the genuine wounded, certifying the film's utter opposition to everything von Krutz represents. But Fuller does not stay still for his moment of fame. Whether under DeMille's direction or of his own accord, he turns his head on screen, at the moment when the guard hails him, and stares full-face, intently, at the camera.

It is ironically fitting that this trace of Fuller's moving presence takes place in a scene of policing. His own writing suggests that he often found himself at the American prison camp.

Above a facsimile of Arthur Fuller's signature, *Fifty-Thousand Miles Back-Ridden* ends its discussion of the ugly law with a template for the future and a model of accomplishment:

> My quarrel, contention, and rebuke is for whoever it may be that causes oppressive laws to be made; those who persecute the afflicted and the stranger within the city's gate; those who represent to the public that drastic legislation is made to punish imposters, the obnoxious, malicious, vicious and unworthy, and then apply the law without discrimination. . . .
>
> My object in this book is to urge moderation in legislating—a nobler thought, a better attitude toward the infirm and aged; a spirit of co-operation and helpfulness; practice of the Brotherhood of Man. (238)

From the vantage point of the back-ridden (and the back-written), Fuller's public gets a new view of the ugly law and more. "I look back to note what the ten books I have issued have done for me," Fuller concluded. "They have put my financial and physical conditions before the public." More importantly, they have "held up a mirror," he wrote, "that each community might see itself and its neighbors" (238). Fuller's radical mendicant literature turned the public gaze back on itself. Writing about the phenomenon that has occupied this book's attention, he did not call it an "unsightly beggar" law. His name for it phrased the problem entirely differently. He called it the "Charity Ordinance."

Seventy-five years later, in 1991, the man who named the ordinance the ugly law, Robert Burgdorf, assessed the recent passage of the Americans with Disabilities Act in these terms: the legislation "reflects the civil rights view of persons with disabilities not as unfortunate, afflicted creatures needing services and help, but as equal citizens, varying across the spectrum of human abilities, whose over-riding needs are freedom from discrimination and a fair chance to participate fully in society" (426–427). Fuller back-rode the ugly laws; in his wake, disability activism in the later decades of the twentieth century overrode them. The laws played a part

Arthur Franklin Fuller plays a wounded German soldier in Cecil B. DeMille's *Till I Come Back to You* (1918). (Reprinted by permission of the Motion Picture Archive at George Eastman House, Rochester, N.Y.)

Fuller being left behind in *Till I Come Back to You.* (Reprinted by permission of the Motion Picture Archive at George Eastman House, Rochester, N.Y.)

in the ADA debate, written into the congressional record as an example of state discrimination against persons with disabilities (S. Rep. No. 101-106, at 7 [1989]). Once again, disabled people testified against the unsightly beggar ordinances, but this time, precisely not for ten cents. Burgdorf, writing of the ADA in the *Harvard Law Review*, put it this way, invoking an activist slogan: “You Gave Us Your Dimes, Now We Want Our Rights” (426).

CONCLUSION

On October 18, 1973, after nearly a century, the *Chicago Tribune* once again turned its attention to the ugly law. The article was titled in no uncertain terms: "A Law That's an Offense." "Repeal was urged yesterday," reported Edward Schreiber,

> of a provision of the city code banning from public places any person "who is diseased, maimed, mutilated, or in any way deformed so as to be an unsightly or disgusting object."
>
> The measure, enacted in 1939, was described as an "affront to everyone" as the City Council Health Committee unanimously voted to recommend repeal to the full council. . . .
>
> Ald. Paul T. Wigoda [49th], co-sponsor of the proposed repeal with Ald. Marilou Hedlund [48th], said his research has failed to discover why the measure was enacted, and that several organizations representing handicapped persons have asked for repeal of it.
>
> "It is cruel and insensitive," Wigoda said. "It is a throwback to the dark ages."
>
> Mrs. Hedlund observed, "If this were enforced, it would have banned Franklin Delano Roosevelt from visiting Chicago."
>
> Dr. Olga Brolnitsky, chief epidemiologist for the city Health Department, described the provision as barbaric. She said it hasn't been enforced and isn't needed to help prevent spread of communicable diseases.

Here are the terms in which ugly law gets repealed:

1. It must be rendered prehistoric—that is, pre-American history (it is a "barbaric" "throwback" to the "dark ages").

2. It must produce counterfactual scenarios (here, concerning FDR) that reiterate an identity-politics-based understanding of the work of the ordinance.

3. Whereas it began in the Streets and Alleys Committee, it must now be routed through epidemiology and the Health Committee. After all, issues

in the 1970s affecting disabled people, as Mary Lou Breslin puts it, were inevitably "thought to be understood by bureaucrats . . . involved in health, education and welfare, as opposed to peace, freedom and justice," and as opposed to matters commonly referred to the "streets" in 1970s protest culture (117).

4. It must speak the language of personal feeling and misconduct ("cruel," "insensitive"), not of economic, social, and structural conditions. "Everyone" feels these things. This is a common strategy. Descriptions of disability-based social prejudice and institutionalized discrimination are often understood as "insensitive." The language sidesteps the reality of social injustice, reducing it to a question of compassion and charitable feelings. Disability is—as it is so often—depoliticized.[1]

5. It must misremember its history ("the measure, enacted in 1939").

6. In short, not unlike the law it is undoing, the repeal must obliterate the traces of the unsightly *beggar.*

7. And, importantly, it happens because of pressure from disabled people organized as a cross-disability collective, a movement—from people who have had a stake in remembering or reconstructing Chicago's ugly law.

The "organizations representing handicapped persons" that reframed the law solely in terms of the history of "handicap" did so for good reason. "Perhaps the clearest example of state-sponsored disablism," writes Sherry, was the existence of "the (now defunct) 'ugly laws' in America. . . . But we should not assume that disability discrimination is a thing of the past. Disabled people continue to experience discrimination in a wide range of areas, including the built environment, the labour market, education, welfare, health and support services, literature, the media and the leisure industry" (2004, 781).[2] (Sherry's point that ugly law is the clearest example of state-sponsored disablism is debatable; compulsory institutionalization and sterilization are also good candidates.) For disability activists in Chicago, campaigns to repeal the already defunct law and others like it were a means to far larger ends in the present.

This disability-specific politics emerged at a key turning point in American history. A year before Chicago's repeal, in 1972, the first Center for Independent Living was founded in Berkeley, California.[3] In the same year as the repeal, 1973, the new version of the federal Rehabilitation Act included a surprising and little-discussed clause inserted by quietly activist congressional staffers, buried in Section 504 of its Title V, that prohibited recipients of federal aid from discriminating against any "otherwise qualified handicapped individual." Within the year, the Burgdorfs were writing their "History of Unequal Treatment." The Education for All Handicapped Children Act passed in 1975. By 1977, disability advocates nationwide had mobilized to insist that the federal government sign a forceful, meaningful version of guidelines for implementing Section 504. The networks that emerged out of this activism sustained a growing national cross-disability rights movement that led to the passage, in 1990, of the Americans with Disabilities Act.[4]

Chicago disability activists who demanded that their city council repeal the law in 1973 inadvertently sealed the public association between their particular city and an ordinance that had actually had multiple locations.[5] Another newspaper piece played a role in popularizing the notion that Chicago was the base of ugly law. Well-known columnist Mike Royko followed the *Tribune*'s coverage of the repeal with commentary of his own, in a piece of deadpan humor provocatively titled "A Law City Should Keep" and even more provocatively beginning, "The City Council intends to repeal my favorite old-time ordinance." "The aldermen say the ordinance is cruel and inhuman," Royko continued. "That may be so. But they are acting hastily." Even more outlandishly, he launched into a modest proposal affirming that if "at least part" of the ordinance were retained, "it would make this a much better place to live."

Of course, Royko made clear at the outset, the first part of the ordinance, "that which bans people who are diseased, maimed, mutilated," should be repealed. But "there has been a crying need," he went on, "to get people off the streets who are 'unsightly,' 'improper,' and 'disgusting' objects." First and foremost among these objects, he proposed, were the members of the city council themselves. He called for the arrest of all politicians who march in Chicago's Saint Patrick's Day parade:

> Anyone who has seen them come wheezing down the street, toting their bulging wallets, would agree that many of them are unsightly, some of them are disgusting, and all of them are improper every chance they get.
>
> Many's the time I've stood on the curb and heard citizens remark: "Look at that improper-looking object—What is it?" They are amazed when I tell them the object is an elected official. . . .
>
> The aldermen say they want to repeal [the ordinance] out of a sense of decency and compassion. I guess it is possible for aldermen to display those emotions. Wolves have been turned into house pets. But I suspect they are looking out for themselves. They feel threatened by the ordinance. Any time an alderman darts out of City Hall . . . he is on a public way.

> And chances are he is plotting something improper. They have to make a living.

Enforcing the ordinance, Royko maintained, would sweep the streets of many undesirables, including television weathermen, Spiro Agnew (who had recently resigned from the vice presidency), and "men who wear the new F. Scott Fitzgerald–style clothes." With tongue in cheek, Royko mourns the law's demise: "I thought it would be a fine opportunity for some young policeman to make a name for himself, herding them into a paddy wagon with an 'Up you go, you unsightly, disgusting objects.' But none did" (116–117).

Royko's humor is a delight, and I will try not to be too heavy-handed with it. I do want to suggest that his handling of the law in this column, which had a quite large readership, had some specific cultural effects. Royko spoke the broad language of Chicago populism; in the column, city history buffoons itself, with a cast of old-time crooked ward politicians and Keystone cops all mixed up with Watergate cynicism and 1970s pop mockery. Nothing in the piece positions Royko as a champion of a new disability rights campaign (or for that matter as a detractor), but there is a kind of theory implicit here—a demonstration at the very least of the social construction of unsightliness and a playful slide from minoritizing to universalizing discourses that has implications, however understated, for the understanding of disability.

Royko's complete decoupling of "unsightly" from "diseased, maimed, mutilated," like the title of the article about the then-recent Omaha arrest case "'41 Begging Law Punishes Only the Ugly," resembles the Burgdorfs' naming of the "ugly" law a year later in the *Santa Clara Law Review*. Whether the authors took a universalizing approach like Royko or a minoritizing one like the Burgdorfs, all three of these mid-1970s texts focused attention on a politics of ugliness that they pinpointed at the core of the ordinance. Clearly, that appearance-centered focus did powerful work at this moment; we can locate the official undoing of the ugly laws with some precision, beginning around 1973.

The influence of this approach still shows in formulations like the following, from a 2005 legal essay entitled "The Prevalence of 'Look'ism in Hiring Decisions: How Federal Law Should Be Amended to Prevent Appearance Discrimination in the Workplace": "Several cities once enforced 'ugly laws,' which prevented disabled, physically maimed, *or very unattractive people* from appearing in public" (Zakrewsky, 453; italics mine).[6] This is a strong reading of the ugly laws, one that emphasizes meanings signified specifically by the cultural work of *ugly,* deeply tied to questions of appearance and attractiveness (and in particular to meanings attached to the face) that are never entirely separable from but not identical to ideologies of disability. As I have tried to show throughout this book, that strong reading errs in failing to take into account the ordinances' specific links to antimendicancy policy. It obscures dynamics around class and vagrancy that historically entwined unsightliness with disability and both, inexorably, with begging. But what the reading sacrifices in historical accuracy it makes up for with forceful political advocacy, of a sort still very much needed in the present. Wendell notes that the "power of culture alone to construct a disability is revealed" particularly clearly by facial scarring and other kinds of "disfigurement," because this kind of bodily difference causes "little or no functional or physical difficulty" but nevertheless constitutes "major social disabilities," and for this reason an emphasis on the "ugly" does powerfully explanatory political work (44). Moreover, for some people with appearance impairments, there sometimes might as well be active "ugly" laws.[7] Even after the demise of the unsightly beggar ordinances, it can be—well—still ugly.

"Disfigurement" has always been a significant part of the history of the unsightly in law, policy, and culture.[8] Remember the enslaved young woman Agnes's incarceration in the segregated basement of a Charleston poorhouse in 1850 after being badly burned; remember the repulsion on record in New Orleans in 1880: "an old woman with a deep seated cancer on her face is a revolting sight." When Frank Norris wrote his sequence of "Little Dramas of the Curbstone" (1909), the horror he represented in the following mother-and-son scene lay not so much in what the son is imagined as incapable of doing or in what the mother is imagined in having to endure as in the way the boy *looks.* If the unsightly figure (or dis-figure) is "made up," in Cresswell's and Hacking's sense, like a glove—a glove, in Habermas's sense, that should be "woven from the strands of intersubjectivity"—this particular reduction to nothing but an ugly face paves the way for utter refusal of the possibility of the son's participation in intersubjectivity, and for the glove to be brutally "discarded":

> Blind and an idiot! Blind and an idiot! Will you think of that for a moment, you with your full stomachs, you with your brains, you with your two sound eyes. Do you fancy the horror of that thing? Perhaps you cannot, nor perhaps could I have conceived of what it meant to be blind and

> an idiot had I not seen that woman's son in front of the clinic, in the empty, windy street, where nothing stirred, and where there was nothing green. . . . His hands were huge and white, and lay open and palm upward at his side, the fingers inertly lax, like those of a discarded glove, and his face—
>
> When I looked at the face of him I know not what insane desire, born of an unconquerable disgust, came up in me to rush upon him and club him down to the pavement with my stick and batter in that face—that face of a blind idiot—and blot it out from the sight of the sun for good and all. (20)

These days, this desire to "blot it out" is not commonly quite so openly expressed.[9] But legalized discrimination against capable people with facial anomalies in our postugly era is still remarkably widespread.[10]

Take, for instance, Samantha Robichaud's legal fight. In 2003, the Equal Employment Opportunity Commission (EEOC) filed a lawsuit accusing RPH Management, owners of a McDonald's restaurant in Alabama, of violating the Americans with Disabilities Act by refusing to promote Robichaud to manager because of her appearance. Robichaud was born with a large birthmark covering her face; she testifies that her boss told her, "You will never be in management here because I was told you would either make the babies cry or scare the customers off" (Greenhouse; "EEOC Sues").

The outcome of this case is both mysterious and telling. It garnered a fair amount of coverage, including a piece in the *New York Times Magazine,* titled "Going to Great Lengths," expressing worry that the EEOC "is effectively trying to define ugliness as a disease" (Postrel). RPH paid Robichaud a financial settlement. A 2006 legal brief provides a summary of what transpired in court; the question at hand by that point no longer had to do with attorney's fees between the EEOC and RPH. The EEOC civil rights claims were dismissed on the grounds that the EEOC had failed to proceed properly with required mediation between Robichaud and RPH prior to filing the complaint.

Early on, RPH had offered to settle for back pay but not to offer any damages for pain and suffering, in part, their lawyer explained to the EEOC, because Robichaud had told her manager at McDonald's that she had had to deal with "negative public reactions for her entire life." This is all we are told in the legal brief, but we can try to tease out the implications of this lawyer's line of reasoning. There is more than a hint of the faker and her legal corollary the whiner here too; the suggestion is, of course, that Robichaud is taking advantage. Two other implications emerge. First, in the "negative public reactions for her entire life" model, Robichaud suffers perpetually anyway. Therefore the bad behavior of her boss does no more damage than anyone else's interaction with her; everyone—that is, no one—bears responsibility for this damage. But second, there is no damage, because in this model Robichaud copes perpetually anyway. Bearing her stigma, bearing up, she is understood to be beyond pain and suffering.

Understandably, Robichaud considered RPH's offer an insult and its explanation, in itself, an injury. The EEOC quit conciliating and went to court. In the legal finding that the EEOC stopped mediating improperly, too quickly, we encounter the inevitable third hidden implication of RPH's lawyer's statement. That is, the statement means nothing, because, as the 2006 brief sums up a lower court ruling, "every litigator" surely knows "that negotiators' first offers are rarely their last offers, and that parties tend to commence negotiations by advancing 'inflated demand[s]' and 'stingy offer[s].'" Reading this account, I think I understand why Robichaud and the EEOC did not simply take the lawyer's words as the ritual initial stingy offer. In the EEOC's "Conciliation log," Robichaud's reaction to the lawyer's statement is described: she is said to have "testified repeatedly" that hearing about it "felt like being slapped or kicked in the face" ("EEOC Sues"). In the face—where, once again, pain and suffering registers. I do not consider Robichaud's call for recognition and respect "in the face" an inflated demand.

Robichaud's suit illustrates that contemporary scapegoating of disabled people need not take blatant forms. Quieter forms of scapegoating work more efficiently, as in the subtle violence in the rhetoric of the reasonable, probing question in the commentary on Samantha Robichaud's lawsuit by an academic dean of business. Mulling over the "disquieting issues" raised by the case—"balancing an individual's right to just returns for doing a good job against an employer's responsibility to make decisions that achieve financial and organizational benefits"—Olian considers:

> Sure, the easiest solution would be to promote Robichaud to an alternative job where her performance would shine and business interests would not be jeopardized. But what if that option isn't available? . . . where's that line between fairness and openness to individuals of all shapes and kinds, and employers' legitimate rights to exercise their business needs? The case of Samantha Robichaud falls right on that line.[11]

Classic ugly law proceeded by drawing clear lines and firmly placing people outside or inside them; today's exclusions convert people into cases, ones that fall perpetually, inexorably, right on "the line," a thick gray area you cannot erase or thin. (Note, too, that the "case" is "of Samantha Robichaud," not "of" her boss.)

The case of McDonald's and RPH underscores why the Burgdorfs chose and why I have continued to use that fighting word "ugly" to name the law. But here, in this conclusion, I am ready to repeal the term. After all, the ordinances whose history I have traced ruled out in advance any number of responses to the person they declared unsightly. Among other things, they disallowed what Scarry calls "the pleasure-filled tumult of staring" (74), during which a beautiful object may be suddenly made or discovered to be present, perhaps one that formerly had been "confidently repudiated as an object of beauty" (16). Refusing the possibility that an anomalous body might be seen in public and found pleasing, the law policed the sites of beauty as much as the situation of the ugly. "At the moment one comes into the presence of something beautiful," Scarry writes, "it greets you. . . . it is as though the welcoming thing has entered into, and consented to, your being in its midst" (26). Consider these words alongside the photograph that began this book, the image of the man in Cleveland who was subjected to exclusion by an ugly law. Perhaps it is precisely his greeting, the call of beauty figured forth in this picture, that the ordinance forestalled.[12]

Or rather, his greeting raises another possibility: the undoing of "ugly/beauty" categories. In much of this book the aesthetic has presented itself as a form of social control; the ugly law creates its "ugly" through a process related to other city beautification efforts inscribed in class logics, like gentrification or broken window theory or gated communities. But the aesthetic also intersects with other city traditions, with urbanism and class politics, as in the work of Benjamin and Lefebvre. My goal in this book has been to move past the demonstration of regimes of social control and into more affirmative notions of the display of the disabled body as a site of social comprehension and of agency. A radically different vision emerges in the Cleveland news seller's offering of papers. His self-presentation or Arthur Fuller's autobiographical writing, to take just two examples, embody a politics of reclaimed urban experience, utterly refusing the ugly/beauty distinction.

What do we encounter when we look back to, when we look back at, the face of the unsightly beggar? Ending this book with this greeting, the Cleveland newsman's half-outstretched hand, I am drawing on Levinas's notion of the "face," both his account of the face's ethical demand and his insistence on its unrepresentability.[13] "The thought that is awake to the face of the other human," he writes, is not a representation of that other. It is, however, "nonindifference." It is not a thought *of* but a thought *for*, and "for" does not mean taking over thinking like the scientific charity organizer but proceeding with the understanding that the other, "as neighbor and unique," is going to remain "indiscernible to knowledge" (1996, 166–167). In this passage, Levinas writes a kind of incantation of the face:

> Face which is not dis-closure, but the pure denuding of exposure without defense. Exposure as such, extreme exposure to death, to mortality itself . . . The nudity of pure exposure, which is not simply the emphaticalness of the known, of the disclosed in truth: exposure which is expression, first language, call and assignation. . . . The face as the extreme precariousness of the other. Peace as awakeness to the precariousness of the other. (167)

Judith Butler, drawing on Levinas for a nonviolence theory, calls attention to the way these last two lines deliberately "do not quite accomplish the sentence form. . . . both statements are similes, and they both avoid the verb, especially the copula" (2004, 135). I will follow that model and avoid that too-simple "is" in my own formulation. The unsightly beggar as the face. Unsightliness as precariousness. Exposing to view as a call, even as the very beginning of language. The ordinance as form of defense against being in proximity, being made awake, to the face of the other.

For Levinas, as Butler emphasizes, the "face," exposing precariousness, at once triggers and puts a restraint on aggression. And therefore this encounter produces the struggle "at the heart of ethics" between violence and nonviolence (2004, 135). Samantha Robichaud clearly understood her case against RPH as a fight at the heart of those ethics. Remember her answer to the dismissal of her "pain and suffering" and the simultaneous reduction of her life to nothing but pain and suffering. It felt like being kicked in the face.

Reading a recent summary of Levinas's formulations and Butler's argument, I was therefore not surprised to find that although the discussion focused on current global geopolitical struggles, it suddenly swerved toward a local scene and a familiar, vaguely archaic, name. Meditating on why the calling of the "face" spurs thoughts of violence, Angela McRobbie writes,

> Crudely, one part of us (psychically) does not wish to be burdened by the responsibility, one wants to be able to shrug it off, one wants to wish away

> the presence of he or she who suffers . . . , stonily ignore the woman with tiny child asking money from passengers on the London underground, see the removal of such people from the streets and public transport, and see an end to these violent threats of otherness that disrupt our otherwise comfortable existence.

One wants, in short, McRobbie writes, "to kick the unsightly beggar" (79).

Still here, not removed, neither historically nor geographically, the persisting unsightly beggar remains an available figure and an agitating occasion. That occasion on the street (if not the page) is always more complex than the suffering and kicking dynamic at stake in McRobbie's confession, as one final turn to the past may remind us. Around the same time that COS organizer Charles D. Kellogg sat down in New York to write his "crude suggested draft" of an unsightly begging ordinance for the city, author Stephen Crane was drafting a sketch eventually published in the *New York Press* in 1894. The piece appeared in print under the headline "When Man Falls / A Crowd Gathers / A Graphic Study of New York / Heartlessness. / Gazing With Pitiless Eyes / "What's the Matter?" That Too Familiar Query."

The incident Crane describes involves neither begging nor deliberate exposure, but it does combine many of the elements I have traced in this book. An Italian immigrant, marked as such by the narrator (he is described as "mumbling the soft syllables" and "walking with the lumbering peasant's gait," those "the's" establishing him as type), strolls through the East Side with his young son, "blinking their black eyes at the passing show of the street" (107). Very quickly, this becomes a version of the scene at the core of this book, a scene not of transversal, like the flâneur's, but of obstruction. The shop windows are "a-glare," angry and illuminated, and when the man has a seizure, his own "glare" draws a fascinated crowd to take over the animated staring across the course of a single objectifying sentence:

> Through his pallid, half closed lids could be seen the steel colored gleam of his eyes that were turned toward all the bending, swaying faces and this inanimate thing upon the pavement burned threateningly, dangerously, whining with a mystic light, as a corpse might glare at those live ones who seemed about to trample it under foot. (106–108)

Like a charity organizer, the narrator claims to be repelled by the crowd of "peering ones" (110) by "the madness of their desire to see the thing" (109), though his story magnifies their stare; unlike a COS officer, he distances himself also from those others who react "with magnificent passions for abstract statistical information" (109); and when the crowd turns ugly, interfering with the unsympathetic policeman who first comes to tell the "human bit of wreckage at the bottom of the sea of men" (110) to move along and then hides him to the onlookers' dismay in an ambulance, Crane's sketch records it all with the strange combination of imperturbability and overinvolvement that Fried identifies.

Fried writes that the sketch's "*ostensible* occasion, the witnessing of a man in the throes of an epileptic seizure, would seem to fall short of justifying the intensity of feeling that, both in the action of the sketch and in the urgency of its prose, is everywhere in play" (106; italics mine). But we have seen throughout this book that this "overdraft of intensity," as Fried puts it, was not peculiar to Crane; it was broadly characteristic of American culture, provoked by exactly such real occasions on the streets of U.S. cities. Kellogg's contemporaneous "crude suggested draft" of an unsightly beggar ordinance for New York City, with its massive one-thousand-dollar fine and its stipulation that "it shall be unlawful for any person, whose body is imperfect or has been reduced . . . to exhibit him or herself," was, in this sense, a very typical overdraft.

Crane's sketch in draft was more fine-tuned. On a press clipping of the piece now housed in the Crane collection at Columbia, near the archive where Kellogg's idea for an ordinance is filed, Crane's handwriting replaces the title I quoted earlier ("When Man Falls/A Crowd Gathers" etc.) with what was presumably his own preferred title: "When Men Stumble." The difference is small but important. The elaborate title in the *New York Press* refers in telegraphic headline shorthand to the specific Italian man who had a seizure on a specific day on the East Side (not, as one might initially conclude, to a generic Miltonian humankind). But Crane's alternate title "When Men Stumble" has a broader reach. The unused title, written in the margins, refuses for a moment to distinguish between "one," one of us, and the other whom one wants to kick. Anyone can stumble; here we are all potentially unsightly, or rather we are all beyond the unsightly and its opposites.

This book has told the story of a petty ordinance, barely enforced, small-minded, and obscure. I have aimed to show how large and how ongoing the implications of that story are. The law, remembered powerfully by one social movement alone as a legend and a lesson about disability, turns out to be about much more: about class antagonism, the distribution of wealth, and the routine suppression of resistance; about authenticity and masquerade;

about how distinctions between genders and races and between Americans and others have been sorted out by Americans (and others); about bodily vulnerability and animality; about political action.

Broad principles about identity and politics and performance are illuminated by this story. I have considered how an identity understood as an exclusion or a victimage is actually profoundly connected to forms of agency; the ugly laws were motivated not simply by appearance politics but by the need to control the economics of the underclass and group behavior within it. I have explored how identity is relational and how it depends, always, on specific discursive constructions between and among identities. And I have shown how identity occurs precisely at the intersection between negativity (exclusion, prescription, regulation) and emancipation. In addition, this book explores how people deal with the emergence of new regimes such as the modern ugly law. What are regimes at the level of everyday interactions, and how do they sustain themselves? What performances generate the kind of official politics that produce, and are produced by, something like an ordinance, and how then are those performances questioned and modified everywhere?

Exploring these broader questions does not mean turning away from the disability-specific call of the Chicago activists who pushed in 1974 for repeal of the ugly law, or of the Burgdorfs and their fellow staffers at the National Center for Law and the Handicapped when they turned a word from an Omaha news story about a beggar into a watchword for a disability movement. I have tried throughout this book to show how much more we understand when we begin to face the history of disability.

APPENDIX

THE UGLY LAWS

CITY OF SAN FRANCISCO, CALIFORNIA

DATE: 1867

INDEX CATEGORY: "Begging, street, prohibited, penalty." (Also indexed under "Almshouse, maimed or deformed persons exposing themselves to be committed to and infirm persons begging to be committed to.")

TITLE: "Order No. 783. To Prohibit Street Begging, and to Restrain Certain Persons from Appearing in Streets and Public Places. Approved July 9, 1867."

TEXT: "Section 1. No person shall, either directly or indirectly, whether by look, word, sign, or deed, practice begging or mendicancy in or on any of the streets, highways or public thoroughfares of the city and county of San Francisco, nor in any public place. Any person who shall violate the provisions of this section, shall be deemed guilty of a misdemeanor, and on conviction thereof, shall be punished by a fine not exceeding twenty-five dollars, or by imprisonment in the county jail not exceeding twenty-five days, or by both such fine and imprisonment.

"Section 2. On the conviction of any person for practicing mendicancy or begging, if it shall appear that such person is without means of support, and infirm and physically unable to earn a support or livelihood, or is, for any cause, a proper person to be maintained at the Almshouse, the fine and imprisonment provided for in the preceding section may be omitted, and such person may be committed to the Almshouse.

"Section 3. Any person who is diseased, maimed, mutilated, or in any way deformed so as to be an unsightly or disgusting object, or an improper person to be allowed in or on the streets, highways, thoroughfares or public places in the City or County of San Francisco, shall not therein or thereon expose himself or herself to public view. Any person who shall violate the provisions of this section shall be deemed guilty of a misdemeanour; and on conviction thereof, shall be punished by a fine not exceeding twenty-five dollars, or by imprisonment in the county jail not exceeding twenty-five days, or by both such fine and punishment.

"Section 4. On the conviction of any person for a violation of any of the provisions of the next proceeding section (3) of this Order, if the same shall seem proper and just, the fine and imprisonment provided for may be omitted, and such person be committed to the Almshouse.

"Section 5. It is hereby made the duty of the Police Officers to arrest any person who shall violate any of the provisions of this Order."

UPDATE, 1878: The San Francisco ugly law is separately indexed as "maimed, diseased or mutilated person not to appear in public places."

CITY OF NEW ORLEANS, LOUISIANA

DATE: 1879

TEXT: New Orleans passes a law seeking to "create, define and punish each of the offenses of being an idle and disorderly person and of being a rogue and a vagabond: and to provide for the summary trial and punishment of offenders against the provisions of this ordinance and of officers and members of the police force for failing and neglecting the duties imposed upon them by this ordinance." Offenses include "wandering abroad and endeavoring by the exposure of wounds or deformities to obtain and gather alms." Immediately before this clause is a stricture defining a rogue and a vagabond as someone who exposes obscene prints to view.

UPDATE, 1887: The "exposure of wounds" crime is followed by a definition of a "lewd woman" as a rogue and vagabond. Over time "lewd women" falls off and on the list.

CITY OF PORTLAND, OREGON

DATE: circa Jan. 6, 1881

CONTEXT: "Sec. 22. [No heading.] If any person or persons shall exhibit or cause to be exhibited upon the street or in any house or public place within the city any crippled, maimed, or deformed person they shall be deemed guilty of a misdemeanor and upon conviction thereof before the Police Court shall be fined not less than twenty dollars nor more than two hundred dollars."

TEXT: "Sec. 23. [No heading.] If any crippled, maimed, or deformed person shall beg upon the streets or in any public place they shall upon conviction thereof before the police court be fined not less than twenty dollars nor more than two hundred dollars."

CITY OF CHICAGO, ILLINOIS

DATE: May 1881

CONTEXT: City Council resolution that preceded enactment of Chicago's first law: "Whereas the streets and sidewalks of the City of Chicago contain numerous beggars, mendicants, organ grinders and other unsightly and unseemly objects, which are a reproach to the City, disagreeable to people upon the streets, an offense to business houses along the streets and often dangerous, Therefore be it ordered, That the Mayor at once take steps to remove from the streets all beggars, mendicants, and all those who by making Exhibition of themselves and their infirmities seek to obtain money from people on and along the streets."

TEXT: "Any person who is diseased, maimed, mutilated, or in any way deformed, so as to be an unsightly or disgusting object, or an improper person to be allowed in or on the streets, highways, thoroughfares, or public places in this city, shall not therein or thereon expose himself to public view, under the penalty of a fine of $1 for each offense. On the conviction of any person for a violation of this section, if it shall seem proper and just, the fine provided for may be suspended, and such person detained at the police station, where he shall be well cared for, until he can be committed to the county poor house."

UPDATE, 1911: "Exposing Diseased or Mutilated Limbs. Exposure of diseased, mutilated, or deformed portions of the body prohibited. Any person who is diseased, maimed, mutilated, or in any way deformed, so as to be an unsightly or disgusting object, or an improper person to be allowed in or on the streets, highways, thoroughfares, or public places in this city, shall not therein or thereon expose himself to public view."

UPDATE, 1911 Police Manual: Law bans not only public exposure of those "whose deformity is such as to excite public curiosity" but also "pictures or any article" associated with these forbidden attractions.

CITY OF DENVER, COLORADO

DATE: 1886

INDEXED CATEGORY: "Deformed persons, how cared for, Section 1009," followed by "Shall not expose himself to public view, Section 1009"

TEXT: "Any person who is diseased, maimed, mutilated, or in any way deformed, so as to be an unsightly or disgusting object, or an improper person to be allowed in or on the streets, highways, thoroughfares, or public places in this city, shall not therein or thereon expose himself to public view, under the penalty of a fine of $1 for each offense. Upon conviction of any person for violation of this section, if it shall seem proper and just, the fine provided for may be suspended, and such person detained at the police station where he shall be well cared for until he can be sent to the county poor farm."

CITY OF LINCOLN, NEBRASKA

DATE: 1889

TEXT: "Any person who is diseased, maimed, mutilated, or in any way deformed, so as to be an unsightly or disgusting object, or an improper person to be allowed in or on the streets, highways, thoroughfares, or public places in this city, shall not therein or thereon expose himself to public view, under the penalty of a fine of $1 for each offense. Upon conviction of any person for violation of this section, if it shall seem proper and just, the fine provided for may be suspended, and such person detained at the police station where he shall be well cared for until he can be sent to the county poor farm."

STATE OF PENNSYLVANIA

DATE: 1891

TEXT: "AN ACT. To prohibit the exhibition of physical and mental deformities. Be it enacted that whoever shall exhibit any physical deformity to which he or she shall be subject or which is produced by artificial means for hire or for the purpose of soliciting alms shall be guilty of a misdemeanor and upon conviction thereof shall be sentenced to pay a fine not exceeding fifty dollars or suffer imprisonment not exceeding six months."

(Section 2 provides similar fines and jail terms for "Any person having the care or custody of an insane person or of a minor child subject to any mental or physical deformity who shall exhibit such insane person or minor for hire or for the purpose of begging.")

CITY OF COLUMBUS, OHIO

DATE: Jan. 22, 1894

TEXT: "An Ordinance—No. 8191" established a cluster of new misdemeanor offenses, including Section 15: "Unsightly beggars. Whoever being in any way diseased, maimed, mutilated or deformed, so as to be an unsightly or disgusting object, shall expose himself or herself to public view upon any street, sidewalk, or in any public place for the purpose of soliciting alms or exciting sympathy, interest or curiosity shall upon conviction thereof be fined not exceeding twenty dollars, or be imprisoned not more than ten days, or both."

UPDATE, 1952: Law still on the books: "Sec. 29.10: Beggars—Exposing self when unsightly, etc." (Then same language as above.)

CITY OF OMAHA, NEBRASKA

DATE: 1890

TEXT: Same as Columbus, Ohio, above.

CITY OF NEW YORK, NEW YORK

(drafted; never enacted or as far as I know officially proposed)

DATE: 1895

TEXT: "Be it enacted, &c, That on and after the passage of this act it shall be unlawful for any person, whose body is deformed, mutilated, imperfect or has been reduced by amputations, or who is idiotic or imbecile, to exhibit him or herself in any public hall, museum, theatre or any public building, tent, booth or public place for a pecuniary consideration or reward, or to solicit or receive charitable relief, or to go from house to house or to stand or display themselves upon any public street or place to solicit or receive alms; and whosoever shall exhibit such mental or physical deformity or mutilation . . . shall be sentenced to pay a fine not exceeding one thousand dollars, or suffer imprisonment not exceeding six months, or both, in the discretion of the court."

CITY OF MANILA, THE PHILIPPINES

DATE: Mar. 18, 1902

TITLE: "Ordinance No. 27: An Ordinance Related to Vagrants, Including Mendicants, Gamblers and Prostitutes."

TEXT: "one . . . who wanders abroad and begs or places himself in the streets or other public places to beg by look, word, or sign, or to receive alms; or who, being diseased, maimed or deformed so as to be an unsightly or disgusting object exhibits himself in a public street or place . . . shall be deemed a vagrant, and, upon conviction thereof, shall be punished by a fine not to exceed one hundred dollars ($100) or imprisonment not to exceed six months, with or without hard labor, on the streets or elsewhere, or both, for each offense."

CITY OF RENO, NEVADA

DATE: circa Aug. 20, 1905

CONTEXT: "An ordinance concerning breaches of the peace, fighting, riots, affrays, injury to property, malicious mischief, disorderly persons, lewd or lascivious cohabitation or behavior, begging, carrying deadly weapons, and resisting an officer within the City of Reno; to restrain and punish the same.

"Section 11. No person shall, either directly or indirectly, whether by look, word, sign or deed, practice begging or mendicancy, within the limits of the city of Reno."

TEXT: "Nor shall any person who is diseased, maimed, mutilated, or in any way deformed, so as to be an unsightly or disgusting object, or an improper person to be allowed in or on the streets, highways, thoroughfares, or public places in this city, shall not therein or thereon expose himself to public view. Any person violating any of the provisions of this section shall be liable to a fine of not more than fifty ($50.00) dollars or the imprisonment in the city jail not more than fifty (50) days, or to both such fine and imprisonment."

NOTES

NOTES TO THE INTRODUCTION

1. Welfare Federation of Cleveland (commonly referred to as the "Cleveland Cripple Survey"). Cleveland appears not to have had an official ugly law—that is, one on the books. And yet this man clearly came under the jurisdiction of some rule that acted like ugly law. Byrom (2004) treats the statute referred to here as "similar" to ugly law because it was aimed not just at beggars but "at cripples who made their living selling items . . . on street corners." This distinction turns out to be so nebulous that it can hardly be maintained; and by the end of the paragraph Byrom himself calls this law ugly law (15). The lack of a paper trail underscores the high likelihood that even some official (much less, of course, quasi-official or ad hoc) policing of the unsightly beggar left no record. I am much indebted to Byrom throughout this book.

2. I am indebted here to Cresswell's study of "ways of knowing" the tramp in U.S. culture during the same time period. See also Shah 2005, 713.

3. A note on what I mean by "disability" and "disabled." For a summary of the history and politics of definition of the term, see J. Epstein, 13–17. Oliver's *The Politics of Disablement* provides an important template (1–9). I follow Oliver and many others after him in my use of the phrase "disabled people" (xiii–xiv). I proceed here with the sense that—as Garland Thomson puts it in *EB*—disability "is an overarching and in some ways artificial category. . . . The physical impairments that render someone 'disabled' are almost never absolute or static." Rather, they are "dynamic, contingent conditions" (15). See also Kudlick 2003. The idea that disability is contingent and dynamic is not a new insight, though the political ends to which it is put are a recent phenomenon. In his 1880 census survey of the "defective, dependent and delinquent classes," Wines noted, "The difficulty of enumerating the defective classes with any approach to accuracy is very great. In the first place, there are no distinct boundary lines between normal and abnormal conditions. . . . similarly, it is difficult to say at what stage of impaired vision one becomes blind, or of impaired hearing deaf" (1660).

4. See Loberg on similar legislation in late-nineteenth- and earlier-twentieth-century Berlin, which established a commercial code banning peddlers who were "disfigured in a repulsive way" (13).

5. On disability and U.S. individualism, Garland Thomson 1996 is a basic source, especially 41–44 and 46–49.

6. Writing of the present, Beuf notes that "the person whose appearance is impaired, who stands out because of obvious flaws or disfigurements, is perceived as a deviant in the United States. In undeveloped or poor countries, where extreme poverty, lack of medical attention, malnutrition and neglect, and the consequences of physical trauma prevail, it is common to see the limp caused by a childhood fall, the bent limbs of malnutrition, the cheek scarred by the untreated injury of several years ago, the face misshapen by improper dental development. But in America such sights are rare. The physically-impaired or disfigured person in America is deviant in two regards: failing to live up to the cultural standard of beauty, and failing to conform to the United States standard of 'normal' or unexceptional appearance" (7).

7. In the classic collection of essays by the leading historian of disability, Paul Longmore, for instance, the law is indexed as "*Chicago* unsightly beggar ordinance" (2003, 265; italics mine). At a key moment in the recent film *The Music Within* (2007), a biography of American disability activist Richard Pimentel, Pimentel and his friend Arthur Honeyman are shown being arrested for violating the ugly law in Portland, Oregon, in the early seventies, an incident that galvanized Pimentel to political action. A summary of the episode on David W. Boles's Urban Semiotic website, "Enforcing the Ugly Laws" (May 1, 2007), records the details—a waitress in a pancake house demands that Honeyman leave because he is disturbing customers, the men refuse and are arrested—but transfers the action to its mythic site, Chicago. See http://urbansemiotic.com/2007/05/01/enforcing-the-ugly-laws.

8. On Burgdorf's role in drafting the ADA, see J. Young; Zames and Fleisher, 90; Scotch, 175.

9. Byrom suggests this in a dialogue on the ugly laws archived at the disability studies resource www.mailbase.ac.uk/lists/disability-research/1998-10/0135.html. Kusmer (2002) discusses the problem of nonenforcement; see especially 82–83. See Byrom's source, Heydon; Freund, 89; "Sham Cripples"; "To Get Rid"; and examples of ugly laws in the city codebooks that end with peculiar, anxious stipulations that police must arrest violators (San Francisco, *General Orders*, 1869; the New Orleans version in *Jewell's Digest*, 341). Of course, even unenforced laws exert effects. Working-class deaf writer Pauline Leader, writing about her childhood in the early twentieth century, conveys this chillingly when she writes of her mother's "tales of the policeman who had said that I must not be allowed out." Given a scrap of paper on which this prohibition is recorded, Leader writes, "It is impossible to merely read the words with my eyes. They enter me" (91–92). See Strange and Loo, 6–7; B. Wagner, 5; Gusfield, 8.

10. Lack of police and court enforcement did not limit itself to this law alone. See Stead, 312; Harrison, 3. Chicago itself was hardly idiosyncratic or dysfunctional in its nonenforcement; in heterogeneous cities, police forces historically have often enforced or ignored laws according to the community standards of

individual neighborhoods. Police who worked in, or who perhaps themselves came from, certain beats might well show indifference to laws enacted by middle-class legislators who themselves lived elsewhere, in wealthier and more suburban districts. Legislatures are particularly prone to pass symbolic laws in cases in which a given interest group's belief about the proper may conflict with views held by significant segments of the population, or perhaps even a majority of the people. Nonenforcement in these circumstances, as Frederick Collignon once said to me, may be "good and normal policing, and good and normal public administration." The casual and intermittent application of municipal ordinances designed to regulate many different kinds of individual behavior reminds us not to overread the implications of lax administration of ugly law. In large part, it was simply business as usual. See Loo and Strange, 640–642; and Dean, 153.

11. "Ugly" is by no means an ahistorical term, except in narrow reference to the wording of the ordinance. When social critic Randolph Bourne argued in 1911 that "the handicapped" understand "the feelings of all the horde of the unpresentable and the unemployable, the incompetent and the ugly, the queer and crotchety people who make up so large a proportion of human folk" (350), he was articulating a theory of ugliness entirely in keeping with the Burgdorfs'.

12. For critical analysis of the "social model of disability" and its opposition to a "medical model" (and the related impairment/disability distinction), see Stiker; Hughes and Paterson; Barnes, Mercer, and Shakespeare; Crow; the authors in Corker and Shakespeare; Williams 1999 (see especially 810); Tremain 2005; Titchkosky 2007; Thomas 2007, 120–129; Sherry 2005; Snyder and Mitchell, CLD, 6; and Kasnitz and Shuttleworth.

13. Analyses of the Supreme Court on the question of the definition of disability include Francis and Silvers; Krieger; and O'Brien 2004.

14. I am echoing, and drawing my inspiration from, Hogan's model of analyzing class. The link between class formation and disability formation is not accidental.

15. In 1984, the Florida Supreme Court disagreed, concluding that the words "crippled or physically distorted, malformed, or disfigured" are not ambiguous. *Gardner v. Johnson* upheld the constitutionality of a law prohibiting exhibition of animals described by these adjectives. Each of the words, the court maintained, "has a plain and ordinary meaning which can be readily understood." Johnson had presented evidence that police officers, when shown photographs, did not agree on which animals were crippled, malformed, and so on. Fordham discusses this case. On the ambiguity of the disability category, and the oddly "bipolar" nature of American disability law (in which the courts have provided "stark yes or no answers" to the question of who counts as disabled, in the very face of that ambiguity), see Colker, 165 and throughout. On the ambiguity of descriptors of physical appearance see Berry.

16. In the Mark Taper Forum's playbill for *The Body of Bourne*, Paul

Longmore, whose scholarship on Bourne forms an important background for Belluso's play, places Bourne and ugly law in proximity but makes it clear that that conjunction is speculative: "In New York, Randolph Bourne was spurned as a luncheon guest because of his 'unsightliness.' In Chicago, he might have been arrested for daring even to appear in public" (6). See the similar analysis in Longmore 2003, 36. In the same playbill for the Mark Taper production of *The Body of Bourne*, Victoria Ann Lewis is credited with bringing the play to fruition. Both Lewis and Longmore played significant roles in introducing the ugly law within contemporary American disability culture. My thanks to the dramaturg for this production, Pier Carlo Talenti, for sending me a copy of this program.

17. From *Moonlighting*, by Lilith, a Women's Theatre, 1980, partially reconstructed from memory by Lewis, personal communication to the author, Apr. 4, 2002.

18. With the phrase "made its entrance" I mean to recall the title of A. Benjamin. On disability performance arts cultures, see Lewis 2005; Sandahl and Auslander; Kuppers 2001; Kuppers 2003; Darke, 131–142.

19. Other Voices, founded by Lewis in 1981, describes itself as follows: "Other Voices is dedicated to the empowerment of the disability community in the American theatre." See Lewis 2005.

20. For the text of *P.H.*reaks*, including this scene, see Lewis 2005.

21. Lewis 2006 provides a history of organized disability political theater.

22. Lifchez's emphasis on legal liability may have been influenced by Jacobus tenBroek's approach in work like "The Right to Live in the World," backread into the operations of the ugly law.

23. After Landers told off a "Chicago Reader" who complained at the sight of a disabled woman in a restaurant, she printed a raft of hostile letters in response. "Has it occurred to you that . . . it is not their divine right to burden the general public with their problems?" wrote F.Z. from Columbus, Ohio. "Would you believe that there are many handicapped people who take great pleasure in flaunting their disability so they can make able-bodied people feel guilty? I, for one, refuse to fall into that trap," began a letter from California. "The sight of a woman in a wheelchair with food running down her chin would make me throw up. I believe my rights should be respected as much as the rights of the person in the wheelchair. . . . maybe even more so, because I am normal and she is not," D.L. weighed in from Greenville, Mississippi. Thanks to Simi Linton for passing on her copy of this column.

24. The passage quoted by Kaveny is, "Solidarity helps us to see the 'other'—whether a person, people, or nation—not just as some kind of instrument, with a work capacity and a physical strength to be exploited at low cost and then discarded when no longer useful but as our 'neighbor,' a 'helper' (cf. Gen 2:18–20) to be made a sharer, on a par with ourselves in the banquet of life to which all are equally invited by God." The capitals in Kaveny's phrase "Ugly Laws" are in her original.

25. I am drawing on Kerber's 1999 discussion of vagrancy as status offense (54) and John Sutton's discussion of the "elastic status" of madness. The case of the Cleveland newspaper seller might seem to contradict my formulation here—he did, after all, have a job and managed to save some money—but his economic situation was still precarious.

26. This denial does not apply to psychiatric disability, where the connections between discourses of mental illness, dangerousness, criminality, poverty, and social exclusion are well established, not only in Foucault's work but, in the U.S. context, in Perlin's work (2000) on "sanism."

27. Garland Thomson goes on, quoting from Compton's important unpublished paper: "Much of American disability legislation has attempted to sort out this conflation, termed by Tom Compton the 'vagrant/beggar/cripple' complex" (35).

28. See also Stanley 1998.

29. I am indebted to Barrett Watten here; thank you, Barrett.

NOTES TO CHAPTER 1

1. Compton writes, intriguingly, that the "best clues to the lives and status of cripples in post-revolution America are local and municipal rules which have come down to us as 'ugly laws.' These originated in the towns of the first 13 colonies and moved westward with the pioneers" (50). This may be the case—Compton's historical research was extensive—but the only source he cites for this particular assertion is the Burgdorfs' essay, which mentions only the late-nineteenth-century Chicago, Omaha, and Cleveland laws. I have so far been unable to find any versions of ugly law prior to San Francisco's. But the history of attempts in England to clamp down on disabled beggars, well detailed by Compton, suggests that it is possible that similar efforts occurred in the Northeast earlier in the century.

2. P. Ferguson helps contextualize this relatively late adoption of the almshouse/poor-law system in relation to the broader historical development and demise of the U.S. almshouse; see especially 21–43.

3. In their classic work on disability and the U.S. welfare system (1966), tenBroek and Matson went back to English poor law and the early years of the American almshouse to describe a then (and still) ongoing concept of "the characterological causation of poverty and dependency." In the eyes of poor law and the space of the poorhouse, they wrote, "there are not broad social problems of poverty or injustice to be solved but only individual wrongs. . . . And the proper corrective, in most cases, is some form of punishment" (833). As Ferguson puts it, the almshouse system established "formalized custodialism in its most vicious forms that tied economic failure . . . to moral categories and individual inadequacy"; the almshouse needs to be understood as a form of abandonment;

and "treatment in the almshouses can only be described as abominable" (24, 21). Longmore expands on this theme in his *Why I Burned My Book*, particularly in the important chapter of the same name, a scathing indictment and meticulously documented illustration of the "long history" of an "institutionalized system of social humiliation" from the almshouse and before to the present (240). My thanks to Paul for reminding me of the abusive function of San Francisco's almshouse clause.

4. Gostin provides crucial general context for these regulatory activities (213 and elsewhere). Craddock powerfully analyzes the history of disease control as racial control and the spatial mapping of deviance in San Francisco, and I am indebted to her.

5. The effect of the war should not, however, be overestimated. Like the emergence of the tramp, the emergence of the unsightly beggar generally coincides with the growth of industrial capitalism (and its consequent economic downturns) in an increasingly urbanized United States. "While the war produced a particularly noteworthy number of physical disabilities," writes Byrom, "the total number of persons injured in the war paled in comparison to the number of people disabled in non-military mishaps" (2004, 11) such as industrial accidents.

6. On conditions in Chicago at this time, McCarthy provides a general overview, 27–28. See also Hogan, 1–50.

7. For background on Hulbert, see the 1892 *Biographical Dictionary*; on Peevey, see C. French. Hulbert's and Peevey's committee assignments, and the record of deliberations on this resolution by the "Streets and Alleys, Western Division" subcommittee, are in the 1882 *Council Proceedings*, 52. On the demographics of the City Council, see Duis 1999, 138–139. The City Council exerted major influence at this time. Teaford writes, "As late as 1898 a student of Chicago's city government concluded that 'the municipal history of Chicago has emphasized . . . the supremacy of the common council during more than a half century of municipal activity'" (22).

8. Peevey's "Health and County Relations" subcommittee of the Chicago City Council by the next year, 1882, had its counterpart at the county level in a "City Relations" subcommittee of the Cook County Board of Supervisors, after a reorganization and subdivision of the county's Committee on Public Charities. The early to mid-1880s were a time of strenuous reorganization of those of Cook County's institutions that provided for and monitored the poor, the sick, the disabled, and other potential recipients of public assistance. James Brown describes these changes in detail. On county care of dependents, see Pierce, 23.

9. See also Friedman; and T. McDonald. My thanks to Sears for pointing me to these analyses.

10. This document is reprinted in manuscript facsimile and transcribed into print as "Document 21—Resolution to Remove Beggars from the Streets" (May

23, 1881) in Bailey and Evans, 65. Prior to this resolution, at the end of 1880, the Citizens' Association of Chicago (an alliance of prominent Chicagoans founded six years earlier, after the fire) had included for the first and only time in its annual report this section: "Unlicensed Peddlers are another of those nuisances which ought to be, and have been, to a certain extent, abated. They obstruct the sidewalk, annoy passers-by, and interfere with the trade of those who pay taxes and rent. Yet we find many of our own members who will petition the police authorities to allow them to continue their illegal traffic as a measure of charity. We cannot but think that such charity is ill-judged." *Annual Report of the Citizens' Association,* 17. Though there are no disability markers in this language, the sudden interest here in charity and the question of street obstruction and annoyance seems clearly linked to the logic of ugly law.

11. The new almshouse (officially the Touro Shakespeare Almshouse) was funded through the "Shakespeare Plan," a scheme by which large gambling houses paid donations to the city in order to be allowed to stay in business. It opened on August 13, 1883. The ingenious Shakespeare plan was soon declared illegal, however, and funding dwindled rapidly. By 1900 the home was "in desperate need of repair." See J. Jackson, 41, 137–38; and Janice Brown.

12. Records of the Second Recorder's Court, Sept. 11. 1883, in the city archives of the New Orleans Public Library; see also "Corralling the Cripples." None of these names turned up in examination of Louisiana census records of birth and death records for Louisiana Parish.

13. Foote's vividly detailed account and indictment of vagrancy procedures in the Philadelphia Court in 1951 speaks both to the past of ugly law and to our present.

14. *Report of the General Superintendent of Police . . . 1881–85,* 22–28; *Report of the General Superintendent of Police . . . 1880,* 14. On the functions of the County Agent at this time, see James Brown, and on the splitting of accounting for the poorhouse from asylum accounting, Brown also provides an account (80).

15. Davis stresses that surveying the body is a central part of "consolidating the hegemony of normalcy" (1995, 48). Visible disability, he argues, has a particular relation to citizenship: "to be visibly disabled was to lose one's full nationality, which should be an invisibility, a neutrality, a degree zero of citizenry existence" (95). Davis suggests that disability disrupts the gaze, so it must be "regulated, rationalized, contained" (129).

16. See Levin's introduction to *Modernity and the Hegemony of Vision,* 1–29, especially page 13.

17. Stanley's piece seems implicitly to acknowledge this equivocality. For all its emphasis on the case of the sturdy beggar, its first illustration is Jacob Riis's 1888 photograph "Blind Beggar," another figure with at best a highly ambiguous relation to the category of the sturdy.

18. See also Arlin Turner.

NOTES TO CHAPTER 2

1. On the British COS, see Chinn, 105; L. Rose; Bailward; Woodroofe; Humphries, 50–63 and 172–174; Ribton-Turner, 327. On the "German Plan," see Slocum, 9–10.

2. On the U.S. COS, see Watson; Katz 1990, E. Schneider, 138–143; Abramovitz, 150–171; Ginzberg, 196–202; Kusmer 2002; Margolin; Lubove; D. Wagner, 46–68.

3. Abu-Lughod; Feder; James Brown, 78–80 and 116–121.

4. Watson, 208. The argument that the "friendly visit" prefigured "social work" is a common one. But Kusmer argues that Charity Organization Societies, which had both "retrogressive" and "transitional" functions, were not direct factors in "the making of modern social welfare policy" (1973, 657).

5. On the rhetoric of cure, see Cheu. Byrom (2001) analyzes the discourse of the "work cure" in a related context.

6. Bennett is writing about detective fiction (the development of which may be linked to COS narrative).

7. On "friendly inns and provident woodyards" and debates about their pros and cons as charitable tools, see Warner, Queen, and Harper, 117, 120–122; Piven and Cloward, 25; Feder, 169–170; Kusmer 2002, 74–75; and Hoch and Slayton, 56.

8. Kusmer (2002) gives an account of the various methods of the Charity Organization Societies—and, importantly, of popular opposition to the COS by "local philanthropies" refusing to be "organized." Boyer provides a Foucauldian analysis, 20–31.

9. Bogan's chapter on "Resident-Dependents" provides some leads to specifically Jewish efforts at setting up disability rehabilitation structures in the early twentieth century (for instance, an "endeavor to publish an accurate Yiddish and Hebrew literature for the Jewish blind" [44]). See also the attack on the COS, "$230,000 for Expenses; $95,000 for Charity," published in the *Jewish Criterion* in July 1911, and Eastwood 1991, 28. Some Jewish charity rhetoric of the period more closely resembles COS style; see, for instance, the *First Annual Report of the United Hebrew Charities of Chicago for the Year 1888–89*. On opposition to the COS generally, see Humphries, 62. On Salvation Army opposition, see Spain, 103–113.

10. Catholic charities differed in their response to COS structures and philosophy. Boston Irish poet John Boyle O'Reilly summed up the Catholic critique of COS as follows: "The organized charity scrimped and iced, / In the name of a cautious, statistical Christ." This poem is quoted in Trattner (84) in the context of a general discussion of opposition to the COS. In some cities, the Society of St. Vincent de Paul refused to join organized charity, but in many cities it nonetheless maintained strong informal ties to COS groups. Eric Schneider summarizes historians' debates over the question of whether Catholic social welfare differed significantly from the COS variety (229).

11. On the "moral Niagara," see Gurteen, keynote address, 10.

12. Another excellent example of doing charity history "from below" is in the same volume as Ross's article: Katz 1990. Emily Abel has done extensive work fleshing out what this history from below might look like in a context especially pertinent here: the imbrication, in COS social work, of poverty knowledge with medicalization.

13. See Sherry's analysis (2005; 2007) of ambivalence and his critique of the notion of oppression for disability studies.

14. Susan Ryan explores related issues in an earlier period in her analysis of the "grammar of good intentions" in the "antebellum culture of benevolence."

15. The sharpest general critique of social work's well-meaning that I have found is Margolin (5–7 and throughout). Work in disability studies on the problem of charity includes Longmore 1997, 2005; Hevey; Finger; and M. Johnson. Snyder and Mitchell's analysis of the emerging sway of charity in the early nineteenth century is closely related to my subject here; see their chapter on Melville in CLD.

16. I have drawn on Katz 1990 here. The key text on charity and the deformations of gift-giving is Stedman Jones. See also Katz's discussion of COS as "a way of reuniting classes in a deferential and dependent relationship" (1983, 52).

17. On a related topic, see Moeschen's discussion of the demonstrations organized earlier in the century by administrators of asylums to display the talents of the "deaf/dumb and blind."

18. Donzalet is quoted in Polsky, 58–59; D. Wagner, 13. For an analysis of the continuation of similar dynamics through the twentieth century, see Losecke. Wagner's critique of charity has a great deal to offer disability studies, though he cites none of the obvious disability studies work related to his argument, such as Longmore's "Conspicuous Contribution" or Drake. My use of the term "explicit body" is meant to echo, with ironic anachronism, Rebecca Schneider's analysis of contemporary performance art.

19. For my analysis of this "asymmetrical" relation, I am indebted to Katz (1983).

20. Garland Thomson's analysis of the "benevolent maternalism" of earlier, mid-nineteenth-century humanitarian social reformers is pertinent here: *EB*, 81–102.

21. Kerlin was superintendent of the Pennsylvania Training School for Feeble-Minded Children and at one time chair of the National Conference of Charities and Correction's committee on idiocy. Trent discusses his career at some length.

22. For background on Henderson, see Getis, 55, 58–61; and Hogan, 16–17.

23. Davis (1995) has also played an influential role in establishing American disability studies as "normalcy studies." Kuppers analyzes the concept of the normate (2003, 7). See also Sherry's (2005) discussion of the centrality of the idea of the normal in U.S. disability studies.

24. On the tramp scare, see Cresswell; Ringenbach; Kusmer 2002; and Byrom 2004 for disability-specific analysis. According to Kusmer, "it is impossible to overstate the hostility of the educated public to the tramps in the 1870's and 80's" (2002, 43).

25. On Philadelphia's antimendicancy squad, see Kusmer 2002. A typical example of New York's repeated efforts to reestablish or reinvigorate antibegging policing is described in the *New York Morning Sun* article of May 14, 1914: "Police to Rid City of Beggars: Mendicancy Squad Revived to Aid Worthy Causes." Marsh's survey of "Methods Employed by American Cities to Eradicate Vagrancy" provides an illuminating table of municipal efforts to police vagrancy and begging, with a great deal of space devoted to categories related to disability, such as the presence and number of institutes in each city "for Crippled and Blind Adults" and "to teach Blind and Crippled Children Trades."

26. A report by the COS committee on mendicancy in 1895 maintains that COS detectives "warned, arrested and otherwise personally dealt with" over seven hundred beggars and also "to some considerable extent stimulated the police to do their duty as well." Relations between the COS and the police were complex, and discussions concerning the structure and management of plainclothes mendicancy units were often heated; see, for instance, the flurry of complaints in 1908 as accusations of police incompetence and inappropriate COS interference were traded back and forth in New York City, recorded in the Community Service Society/COS Papers (Box 108, "Committee on Mendicancy").

27. See also a similar general order two years later by Chief William S. Devery (General Order No. 32, Mar. 11, 1899) in the same archive.

28. Not all Pennsylvania doctors supported the bill. An essay by doctors in the *Medical Record* reprinted in the *New York Times*, entitled "The Freaks Find a Defender," argues, "We very much doubt the wisdom of such a bill. The desire of ordinary people to see the freaks of nature enables many unfortunate people to gain a comfortable livelihood," as well as to "experience a certain degree of pleasure in the wonder they incite. This may not be a very high type of feeling, but it is innocent and perhaps it is less harmful than that which the belle feels over her figure or the beau over the fit of his clothes or the politician over the newspaper glorifications of his statesmanship."

29. There is evidence, unsurprisingly, that people with disabilities constituted a large percentage of vagrants. The first major published study of American homelessness, Solenberger 1914, emphasized the high rate of disability in the survey group.

30. Readers will notice that throughout this book I downplay psychoanalytic approaches to the making of the unsightly beggar. Kristeva's theory of abjection, or the Lacanian/Zizekian idea of the Real, can be very productively brought to bear on this subject; but that would be a different project from the historicist and materialist one that I am engaged in here.

31. Kelley's application of the notion of infrapolitics in *Race Rebels* introduced me to Scott's work. On infrapolitics, Kelley writes, "Whether or not battles were won or lost, the mere threat of resistance elicited responses from the powerful which, in turn, shaped the nature of the struggle" (33); one such response, I am arguing, was ugly law. Wright briefly takes up Scott's notion of infrapolitics in the related context of resistance to arrests for homelessness. I am grateful to Brad Byrom for suggesting I look to the model of infrapolitics.

32. I am echoing Doug Baynton's line about disability and history (2001, 52).

33. On begging and performance, see Kusmer 2002, 83, and Gilmore's sections on begging as "one-act play," "plain pantomime," and "tableau" in his chapter "The Mendicant Art," 33–38.

34. On Stone's demonstration that "disability turns out to be a central rather then peripheral matter to the development and maintenance of modern welfare states," see Barnes and Mercer's introduction to *Exploring the Divide.*

35. The language of capital occurs with some frequency in unsightly beggar discourse. A 1920 article in the *New York Evening Sun,* for instance, addresses the problem of crippled beggars: "Clearly if they are unable to support themselves they ought to be taken care of. But the capitalization of deformity should be stopped." The same text refers later to "permit[ting] them to make capital of their deformities" ("Beggars Coming Back").

36. In Marx's words, under this system, "Time is everything; man is nothing; he is at the most, time's carcase [*sic*]" (41). Diseased, maimed, deformed people begging on the streets gave time's carcass noticeably literal form. At the same time as relentless industrial speed-ups and assembly-line production pushed disabled people further out of the work arena, the increasing medicalization of disability and the ideology of the "normal" and of "correction" helped ensure that out of the unsightly "unfit," tidy profits could still be made. Emerging charity industries, of which COS was a forerunner, and the bigger and bigger business of the new professionally staffed institutions consolidating at the peak of ugly law enactment, would prove that principle. Turn-of-the-century American industrial capitalism emerges as a central factor in the social fabric that produced the ugly laws. See Russell's synthesis of these issues in *Beyond Ramps* and Jean Stewart's work, particularly her unpublished talk "Disability, Capitalism and War," delivered at the World Social Forum in Mumbai, India, January 7, 2003. See also Russell and Stewart's joint essay and Roth 2002, 86–87. Kusmer provides a packed, informative analysis in a few paragraphs of the relation between industrial accidents, disability, and mendicancy in the United States at this time (2002, 104). On exclusion of disabled people from the capitalist labor force, Oliver's work is foundational. Oliver's work in turn builds on the foundation of work by Finkelstein. Gleeson details how "space was manipulated in ways that ensured maximum productivity from those bodies valorized by the market" (101) in a work pertinent to this whole chapter. Titchkosky, discussing the importance of

attending to "the specific background situation against which the typically different [e.g., the 'disabled'] shows up at all," points as one of several key backgrounds (others include the "heteronormative demand") the "hyper-individualism of capitalism" (2007, 128).

37. Joseph Kirkland's "Among the Poor of Chicago" (233) portrays one policeman, "one of the severely wounded" police in what Kirkland calls the "Anarchist Riot," who in 1895, "now too much shattered to do more than light tasks about the station," worked as a messenger at the West Side police headquarters.

38. Talk presented at the Queer/Disability Conference at San Francisco State. Courvant's image of confluence helps get around some of the theoretical and political problems identified by Jakobsen in her discussion of the ambivalence of the term "alliance": "Alliances assume the existence of separate, autonomous movements which might come together to form an 'alliance'; but alliances also require the subversion of the autonomy upon which they depend. As the case studies show, attempts to form alliances by first establishing autonomous movement . . . will tend to fail because the basis of alliance—the complex interrelation among issues and movements—has been undercut by the assertion of autonomy" (2003, 26).

39. For a twentieth-century Depression-era comment on the use of vagrancy law to quell working-class organizing, see Tillie Olsen (publishing under the name Tillie Lerner), "Thousand-Dollar Vagrant," an autobiographical account of being arrested on a vagrancy charge with one-thousand-dollar bail for Communist Party organizing. Thanks to Rebekah Edwards for pointing me to this little-known essay.

40. Byrom argues for the importance of the ideology of the "shut-in"—the proper sick or disabled person behind closed doors until recovery—in this period (2004, 17).

NOTES TO CHAPTER 3

1. On biopower and disability, see Tremain 2005, xvi, 4–7; Kuppers 2003, 5–6.

2. On these shifts in/to institutionalization, see Rothman; Katz 1983; and Braverman. Garland Thomson, invoking Foucault, directly relates the ugly laws to institutions for custodial segregation of disabled people, in *EB*, 35.

3. As Davis puts it, "care *of* the body is now a requirement for existence in a consumer society. We are encouraged and beseeched to engage in this care," which "involves the purchase of a vast number of products for personal care and grooming, products necessary to having a body in our society. . . . In addition, the body is increasingly becoming a module onto which various technological additions can be attached. . . . The aim and goal, above all, is to make this industrial-modeled, consumer-designed body appear 'normal'" (2002, 27). The goal may in fact be less to make the body appear "normal" than to maximize cultural capital in terms of

looks, but Davis's formulation of the Foucauldian "care of" is an important one. Compare Crawford's (2000) discussion of the imperatives for corporeal control in Williams, Gabe, and Calnon. See also Williams 2003, 33; Berry; and MacGregor's analysis in 1951: "Advertisements . . . inform, indeed threaten, us that we will never find a job, husband (wife), or friends with 'that unsightly skin'" (632).

4. Gleeson treats Foucault's concept of the "space of exclusion" (1995, 199) in a disability studies analysis, 108.

5. At the same time, as Byrom notes, the nineteenth-century institutional structures "almshouse" and "poorhouse" were on the decline after 1890 (2004, 13–14)—a factor that certainly helps explain the removal of the poorhouse clause in later versions of ugly law.

6. At first, many of these institutions were specifically for children. Byrom details the development of "hundreds of institutions . . . created with the intent of providing mobility impaired children with services ranging from medical care to moral training" (2004, 3).

7. Citing the census survey *Paupers in Almshouses,* Janice Brown wrote in 1929, "Only a comparatively few people go to the almshouse with the idea of making it their future home. Poorhouses are usually places of temporary shelter. Of the almshouse population in 1910, 30.5 per cent had been in such institutions less than a year" (46).

8. See Katz's (1983) account of eugenic discourse around the figure of the tramp, 92–93.

9. For example, on the "stigmata of degeneration—asymmetries and deformations" identified by managers of New York's Crane Colony for epileptics in 1895, see Dwyer, 266; see also A. McDonald 1908, 16–17. The classic source is Lombroso; see, for instance, Lombroso and Ferrero. On the conjunction of eugenics and aesthetics where ugly law so clearly lies, see Pernick 1997 and the extended treatment in *The Black Stork*; see also Snyder and Mitchell, CLD.

10. In the British context, where class division is more openly marked and remarked, we have the testimony of Elmslie in 1911: "the segregation of physically defective children is necessary only amongst the poorer classes, amongst those children who are educated by the public education authority, and whose parents, if the child remained at home, have neither the leisure to teach him themselves nor the means to provide a governess or master for that purpose. The same groups of children will, amongst the well-to-do, remain at home and be taught privately" (7). In the American context, see the account of the care system set up at home for the "carefully guarded son of a well-to-do merchant occupying a costly mansion not far from the southern boundary of the Central Park" in the *New York Times* (May 24, 1885, 4). The thirty-year-old man is described as "a physical monstrosity . . . not found in the museums."

11. The phrase "both aesthetic and hygienic" is Wacker's, in his "Chicago Plan," 40.

12. *St. Louis Spectator* (Sept. 30, 1882). Carl Smith (208) quotes this article in his discussion of a project related to the Chicago Plan: planning for the model Pullman community (later home of the famed Pullman strikes) on Chicago's south side.

13. I am indebted here, as elsewhere, to Fred Collignon's comments on this work in manuscript. On the Columbian Exposition in Chicago in 1893 and its influence on city planning, see Burg; J. Gilbert; Spain, 16–17, 49–54. The gleaming city model at the center of the Exposition abutted freak-show display of disabled and exoticized bodies; on this aspect of the Exposition, see Bill Brown. On the City Beautiful movement, see Boyer and the compact discussion in Serlin, "Rethinking," 145.

14. In *Geographies of Disability,* Gleeson quotes a phrase I echo here in an analysis from Dorn (on a project beginning in Europe in the seventeenth century): "a public sphere stripped of the grotesque." But as Gleeson goes on to point out, "the abject, grotesque bodies of industrialism managed to resist this sanitization of the public sphere by clinging to the interstitial public spaces such as the street and fairgrounds" (111).

15. Burnham and Bennett's famous *Plan of Chicago,* a major landmark in modern urban reform, was published just two years earlier, in 1909.

16. On disability and the modernist project, see Snyder and Mitchell, CLD, 4.

17. I first encountered Reitman's map in Cresswell, who brilliantly analyzes it, 70–80. Cresswell's visual rendition of the map is inaccurate in a few details. For instance, what appears in his version as a seamless phrase—"Land of Respectability"—is broken in Reitman's drawing, where it reads "Land of Respect," with "Ability" directly below it. Perhaps Reitman enjambed the word simply because he ran out of space in writing it, but the separation out of "ability" opens up the possibility of a political pun that calls attention to the "ability/disability" axis in the dynamics of the respectable. See the corrections in the rendition in this volume done by Charles Legere from my sketches.

18. Compare the Christian Socialist Denver COS leader Myron Reed: "I like the word crank. It is suggestive. A crank is a thing that brings hidden obscure values up and into the light" (187).

19. Poirier, 77; Hapgood. The program for the Outcast Night that Reitman organized with Hapgood is in the University of Illinois–Chicago Reitman archives, as are the "Outcast" poems.

20. On "the hegemony of paternalism," see Hahn 2003, 39–40.

21. By 1944, rehabilitationist T. Arthur Turner openly listed "the aesthetic motive" as one reason "for Tolerance of Infirmity" (the others being "Influence of Parental Love," "Co-Operation in the Struggle for Survival," "Reciprocal Protection," and "Influence of Religious Training"). "Care of the handicapped," Turner wrote in a classic articulation of deformance principle, "is not entirely unselfish

on the part of those who engage in it. In most of us there is an irresistible impulse to create, to bring order out of chaos" (9).

22. L.S. Teller provides a summary of many cases from this period, including a strangely fascinating index with entries like "Bowed leg, display of," "Foot amputated from body, display of," and "Pus, display of." Courts in general ruled that there was no error in permitting plaintiffs to expose disease, maiming, and deformity to the jury's public view.

23. This pattern is related to the phenomenon that Goodman describes: "in the late nineteenth-century the institutionalization of charity went hand in hand with the trend in legal reform that relieved the law of its jurisdiction over acts of good Samaritanism and replaced bystanders with designated rescuers—police and fire officials, and other trained emergency professionals" (110).

24. The classic history of the Civil War pension system and social debates surrounding it is Skocpol's. Blanck provides a thorough disability-focused discussion.

25. "Neurasthenia . . . [was] a mark of distinction, of class, of status, of refinement. Neurasthenia struck brain-workers but no other kind of laborer. It attacked those, such as artists and connoisseurs, with the most refined sensitivities. It affected only the more 'advanced' races, especially the Anglo-Saxon. . . . The disease became such a marker of status and social acceptability, in fact, that it could be coveted" (Lutz, 6).

26. M.M. Trumbull, "Pensions for All," *Popular Science Monthly* 39 (1881): 721, 723; cited in Blanck, 129.

27. The term "nature faker" was more commonly applied as a slur against the alleged pretensions of nature writers, famously Jack London.

28. Compare Gottlieb.

NOTES TO CHAPTER 4

1. Silvers and Stein draw here on Amsterdam and Bruner's argument in *Minding the Law*: "'cripple' becomes a less natural category to the extent that prosthetic technologies become available; it is a particularly natural category when a culture not only lacks technological resources but regards physical afflictions as punishments for one's misbehavior in a prior life."

2. The word *unsightly* has a long American history, and it well predates modernity. Sermons on Acts 3:7 often refer to Peter's healing of an "unsightly" beggar. What I am suggesting is that *unsightly* takes on additional meaning as the policing of the visual comes to the fore in this historical period.

3. Atlanta's city council in 1903, for instance, passed an ordinance barring "persons who carry odors" from traveling on streetcars. (This ordinance had a particularly obvious class valence; odors especially targeted were those "which

emanate from persons who work in factories" ["An Olfactory Crusade"].) As recently as 1972, a rule proposed by the Air Traffic conference stated, "persons with malodorous conditions, gross disfiguration or other unpleasant characteristics so unusual as to offend fellow passengers should not be transported by members." See R. Scott, 155. That contemporary disability activism has so often cited the ugly law and not the history of such cases is telling. The law's visual prohibition seems to be an especially stark and at the same time particularly richly metaphoric sanction. A disability politic centered on the "malodorous" might certainly be too narrow, or possibly too dangerously close to the abject. On the policing of odor and offensive bodies, see A. Hyde, 252–257. Weigman's critique of contemporary American culture's overemphasis on visibility and the definition of "the heterogeneity of the social as the [viewed] presence of an eccentric body" is pertinent here.

4. So, for instance, in the week after San Francisco passed its ugly law, a crime report in the city paper the *Dramatic Chronicle* (July 18, 1867, 1) objected vehemently to other press coverage of a murder scandal that had emphasized the head size of the accused murderer, "small almost to deformity"; "these statements are fanciful and untrue," the *Chronicle* insisted: "The young man is no worse-looking than the average of young men in his condition of life." "Deformity" had to be carefully quantified and was not a term to be used lightly.

5. What seems ludicrous and impossible about ugly law is, in part, its attempt to legislate the unlegislatable, what Bourdieu calls bodily hexis, the "permanent dispositions" and "durable manner[s] of standing, speaking and thereby feeling and thinking" that "are placed beyond the grasp of consciousness" (94) and hence cannot be made explicit by law. Simon Williams (2003) follows Bourdieu in an illuminating discussion of health as social capital.

6. The body that "passes us by in silence" is Sartre's from *Being and Nothingness*. Cf. Tom Shakespeare: "a situation where disabled people are defined by their physicality can only be sustained in a situation where non-disabled people have denied their own physicality" (96). See also Crawford's discussion of how the "'healthy self' is sustained in part through the creation of 'unhealthy others'" (1994, 1348).

7. My thanks to Martin Pernick for this point.

8. "By and large," writes Lisa Blumberg in her classic essay on the subject of public stripping, "disabled people . . . want to be provided with a medical service—not render one" (75), but the display by medical practitioners to medical practitioners of people with conditions such as spina bifida or dwarfism continues the tradition of rendering to this day. For examples of the transgressive reappropriation of public stripping by contemporary disability artist activists, see Courvant 1999 and the solo autobiographical performance pieces by Greg Walloch recorded by Killacky and Connolly in their film *Crip Shots* and analyzed by Sandahl. See also Kuppers 2003, 38–42.

9. Addams tells the story of the devil baby both in 1916 and in 1930. This second account is reprinted in 1960, 66–82.

10. Compare the comic justification of freak display in Alden's *Among the Freaks*, a fictional collection of stories told by the purported owner and manager of a dime museum in Chicago. On a two-headed girl viewed by "the very best classes of Boston" the narrator states, "They made out . . . that the girl had something to do with philosophy, and that her two heads proved something or other that Mr. Emerson used to teach" (56)—Emersonian individualism, perhaps?

11. On Dummy Hoy, see the two-part series in *Deaf Life* 5 and 6 (Nov. and Dec. 1992). On the hand signals, see Bjarkman; and Ritter.

12. Loo and Strange's discussion of Canadian regulation of traveling shows during this same period is useful in contextualizing this kind of bourgeois effort "to civilize plebian entertainment and rough amusements" as a broad historical mobilization in Europe and across North America "against working-class profane and disorderly conduct" (640).

13. "Psycho-visceral" is Robert Rawdon Wilson's term, vi.

14. For Darwin, disgust referred to "something revolting, primarily in relation to the sense of taste, as actually perceived or vividly imagined" (253). On this line of thought, see Rozin, Haidt, and McCauley, 637–653; W. Miller; and M. Nussbaum, 87.

15. Compare Delaney's analysis of how Supreme Court rulings on the legality and reasonability of race segregation have implicitly or explicitly depended on the idea "that black people were like slaughterhouses, brickyards, livery stables . . . in some significant respect" (133).

16. Quoted in Susan Miller, 5. Miller's psychoanalytic reading of disgust begins with a focus on the idea of the "transmittability of the fouled, disgusting state as advancing disgust's ability to protect us from physical infection" (2).

17. Rozin et al. argue that disgust fears of contamination involve "sympathetic magic." As Martha Nussbaum puts it, disgust's "thought-content is typically unreasonable, embodying magical ideas of contamination, and impossible aspirations to purity" (14).

18. "Come not near" is the wording of Shakespeare's apotropaic fairy lullaby in *A Midsummer Night's Dream*, an enjoinment to snakes and spiders. Menninghaus discusses the apotropaic in the context of disgust, 84.

19. Hence Oscar Wilde's futile reply to the theatrically disgusted Justice Wills after sentencing at the conclusion of his third trial: "And I? May I say nothing, my lord?" See H. Montgomery Hyde. The unsightly beggar and the grossly indecent sodomite have much in common as subjects of disgust, links I explore in chapter 6.

20. Take, for instance, the organizing that culminated in the successful 1977 "Section 504" sit-in by disabled protesters and allies at the HEW headquarters in San Francisco, an action that secured enforcement of federal regulations

prohibiting disability discrimination and that laid the groundwork for the national cross-disability rights movement that led (among other things) to the passage of the American with Disabilities Act. The powerful symbolic work of the 504 victory could be drawn on now to undo the symbolic work of the unsightly beggar ordinances. Whether the protestors knew the specific history of ugly law or not, they talked back to it. In the well-publicized hearing organized inside the Federal Building during the occupation, Joan Tollifson described to the audience of congressmen and HEW representatives the past that the activists countered: "I was really afraid growing up that physically I was inadequate, physically I was ugly. . . . I had totally internalized the oppression. . . . And also, I was programmed not to associate with other disabled people." Cece Weeks spoke of the present: "Now people walk by this building and actually see you here and give you the power signal, thumbs up. I am now hopeful mothers won't snatch their children away and say "Don't look.'" "Voices of 504," 9. On the 504 action, see R. Shaw; Barnartt and Scotch; and Zames and Fleischer.

21. Theorists of disgust who explore its relation to animality include Angyal and W. Miller.

22. For "bite the hand that fed them" I take inspiration from Mitchell and Snyder's meditations on disability (and disability studies) as forcibly "feral" in CLD.

23. See also Jennifer Mason's discussion of Pastrana, 61–66.

24. O'Brien's "animality" derives from philosophical precursors that include the work of Donna Haraway and of Alasdair MacIntyre in his *Dependent Rational Animals*.

25. Understanding this point links the issues at stake in this book to recent work by Carey Wolfe and others on "speciesism" and animal rights. "The discourse of speciesism," Wolfe writes, "will always be available for use by some humans against other humans as well, to countenance violence against the social other of *whatever* species—or gender, or race, or class" (117). Or bodily form or ability. Disability studies does not need to replicate this speciesism or repudiate the "animal" in order to defend the dignity and humanity of people treated like dogs.

26. So do the archives of American racism; see, for instance, Hancock's recent discussion of the use of animal imagery for welfare recipients by congressional representatives in the 1996 welfare reform debate. Like the welfare queen whose image Hancock deconstructs, the unsightly beggar was a form of public identity shaped by "the politics of disgust."

27. Article in the *Atlanta Constitution*, June 1886, quoted in Garrett, 106.

28. The development of "service animal" programs in "the wealthiest countries" is addressed in Litvak and Enders, 716.

29. Today this still holds true. Although recent research on service dogs has shown that "dog users showed improvements in self-esteem, internal locus of control, psychological well-being, increase in school and work attendance, and

a dramatic decrease in paid and unpaid personal assistance hours," the category of "service animal" remains ambiguous and contested. Even when the distinction between service animals on the one hand and pets or strays on the other is relatively straightforward, as in the case of the use of guide dogs by people with vision impairments, the regulation of animals may result in the exclusion of people. A recent example occurred in Baltimore in 2002, when a newly hired blind elementary school teacher, Janet Mushington, was denied the right to bring her guide dog into the classroom because of a "no animal" policy and consequently could not take the job. She sued the district, charging violation of the ADA. "The Americans with Disabilities act is intended to open the doors of employment opportunity for people with disabilities," commented Ralph Boyd Jr., assistant U.S. attorney for civil rights. "When an employer refuses access by a person with a service animal, it closes the door on that opportunity." See the section in tenBroek's "The Right to Live in the World" entitled "The Rights of Dogs and the Rights of Men," 852–859.

30. That phrase "with a service animal" is interesting; "with" simultaneously renders the animal as contingent to and as necessary to the person, the necessity conveyed through echo of another tag, the "person with a disability."

31. William Franklin was not by any means the only "goat man." A similar goat-cart, used by a man photographed in 1890 in Schenectady, New York, can be viewed on the Disability History Museum website. As late as 1936, officials in another Georgia city were complaining about Artemus Thomas, "a negro," that when he "has been arrested for drunkenness, his goat has had to be taken into custody for participating in the celebration." The police, a newspaper article reported, "wish Artemus wasn't a cripple" because of his goat's expensive appetite ("Imprisoned Goat").

32. James Forbes to Mrs. M.A. Rhett, Feb. 25, 1903. See also Waters's (1905) account of the "repulsive appearance" of the "Human Dog" (78).

33. Thanks to Petra Kuppers for this point.

34. On what Fretz calls "one of the paradoxes of the tension-filled nineteenth century," the simultaneous existence of sequestering institutions (and prohibition laws) and freak display, see Fretz, 102, and Sears's illuminating work on freak shows and the democratic policing of gender.

35. Information on the 1903 Michigan law may be garnered from a court case prosecuting several doctors for violating it: *People v. Kennedy et al.* (May 29, 1913). On the demise of the freak show, see Garland Thomson, EB and *Freakery*; also see Bogdan, 62–67, and Duis 1998, 207–209. On the lingering traces but also the inevitable decline of anatomical museums, see Sappol 2002 and 2004. The freak show laws that I quote here are California's Penal Code 400 (1874) and Florida's Code 867.01, pertinent because each was subject to a major contemporary legal challenge (*Galyon v. Municipal Court for the San Bernardino California Judicial District*, 1964, and *World Fair Freaks and Attractions v. Hodges*, 1972). See Fordham.

36. Reproduced in facsimile in Bailey and Evans.

37. *Laws of the General Assembly* (1895), Act 208. The voting record on the act (here referred to as House Bill No. 496)—it passed unanimously—may be found in the *Journal of the House* (1896), in the records for May 27.

38. Alden's *Among the Freaks* ventures at one point into an explanation of why "freaks" supposedly have little brains: "You see 'freaks' make their living by careful cultivation of their bodies. Naturally, their minds are no sort of use to them" (80–81). This twisted inversion of the culture of physical cultivation, in which aberrant bodily features and functions are encouraged through practice as self-improvement, was attributed to unsightly beggars as well.

39. Compare Bill Brown's comment on the moment when Stephen Crane's character Henry Johnson, rendered "the monster" (in the novella of that name) after his face is disfigured, stares at the townspeople who stare at him: "The monster's eye metaphorizes the general breakdown in visual authority provoked by a monster's existence outside the structure of the freak show" (234). Unsightly beggars similarly disrupted structures of looking safely contained by freak shows.

40. As Derrida puts it, "by reason of their very marginality, by reason of their exteriority in relation to the circulation of labor and to the productions of wealth, by reason of the disorder with which they seem to interrupt the economic circle of the same, beggars can signify the absolute demand of the other, the inextinguishable appeal, the unquenchable thirst for the gift," a thirst, he writes, suggested in "Baudelairian situations" where the beggar and addiction intermingle (137). Since unsightliness, if anything, accentuates the beggar's marginality and exteriority, it is no surprise that extreme thirst and addiction emerge in the unsightly beggar's story.

41. Later, in the mid-1930s, the newly forming Alcoholics Anonymous resolved to exclude unsightly beggars. Beggars, tramps, and asylum inmates "were definitely out," reports one early member: "Yes, sir, we'd cater *only* to pure and respectable alcoholics! Any others would surely destroy us. Besides, if we took in those odd ones, what would decent people say about us? We built a fine-mesh fence right around A.A." (Alcoholics Anonymous, 140). Soon, with profound consequences, AA undid its fine-mesh ugly law.

42. The bill was introduced on January 15, 1915, and appears in committee report (with a recommendation not to pass it) on January 25. They were not all that alarmed; the "declaring an emergency" line is standard bill language at that time.

43. See, for instance, the materials of the Substance Abuse Resources and Disability Issues center at Wright State University, Ohio.

44. See also the vivid account of substance abuse in "Galvin's Bowery Raids," Asbury's primary source.

45. Du Bois's treatment of paupers in *The Philadelphia Negro* is typical in this regard; the chapter is entitled, simply, "Pauperism and Alcoholism."

46. I have been told but have been unable as yet to verify that until 1996 there

was a provision in the Illinois State liquor code making it illegal to serve alcohol to disabled people. If this law did not actually exist, it stands as an example of legend making in the disability movement; my hunch is that it did exist, because (as in the case of ugly law) disability movement activists have made a point of remembering this kind of history.

NOTES TO CHAPTER 5

1. On being work and doing work, see Tyler. Derrida's analysis of the social category of the beggar emphasizes the work the beggar does: "he does not work. *In principle*, begging produces nothing, no wealth, no surplus-value. The beggar represents a purely receptive, expending, and consuming agency, an *apparently* useless mouth. One must indeed say, as always, *apparently*, for in fact he can play a role of symbolic mediation in a sacrificial structure and thereby assure an indispensable efficacy. . . . the fact that he does not work and does not produce does not mean he is inactive" (134).

2. "Sham Cripples"; "Prison for the Beggars."

3. See, for instance, "Rags and Tags: Hobo Influx Grows Apace," in the *Los Angeles Times* (1907). The article begins as an exposé of imposters, with subheadings like "Sores Painted On," but moves eventually into an indictment of "Cripples Cruel": "Some of the most cruel and criminal of the visitors are the actual cripples."

4. The year this passage was written, 1869, is earlier than the peak of ugly-lobbying in New York in the mid-1890s (though close in time to the enactment of San Francisco's ordinance), but the dynamic described here had certainly not abated by the time of the "sham cripple" scandals of 1896.

5. The story is active to the present day, of course, and in new forms; for an illuminating consideration of disability fakery on the Internet (in the well-known case of Sanford Lewin, who posed online as a disabled woman), see Goggin and Newell, 113–115. For analysis of the phenomenon in the period just before the ugly laws, see Ellen Samuels's discussion of the "disability con" in Melville's *Confidence Man* (1857) and its contexts ("From Melville to Eddie Murphy"). Samuels distinguishes the disability confidence man from the figure of the faker beggar; I am less sure that the two can be separated. See also Susan Ryan's thorough discussion, especially pp. 52–59. One of the most familiar examples from just before the period that I cover here is a passage from Mark Twain's *The Prince and the Pauper* (1881), set in the harsher period of the early modern English poor laws but bearing in its social commentary on Twain's American present. Twain's slumming prince wakes in a run-down barn to a find the "motliest company" of tattered no-longer-blind-and-crippled beggars casting aside their patches and crutches in a drunken orgy (109). It is, Twain writes, "a grim and unsightly picture."

6. Stone's *The Disabled State* is the text to consult on this point. On begging's

connection to deception in the public understanding and the perceived blurring of "boundaries between the real and the fake," see especially p. 33. Garland Thomson discusses the policing of faking in another foundational text in disability studies, *EB*, 48–49: "at least since the inception of the English Poor Laws in 1388, the state and other institutions concerned with the common welfare have molded the political and cultural definition of what we now know as 'physical disability,' in an effort to distinguish between genuine 'cripples' and malingers, those deemed unable to work and those deemed unwilling to work."

7. Knox, in Campbell, 598; "Pitiful Mendicant Gives Way to the Cunning Beggar"; Zorbaugh, 111; "Fit-Faint Faker"; Sante, 315; Kusmer 2002, 84.

8. On stale-beer cellars, their homeless clientele, and the sham deformed, see T. Anderson, 359–360; the *National Review*'s 1887 "Homes of the Criminal Classes"; the *New York Times*'s "Father . . . Made $100 a Day Outfitting Fake Cripples." Asbury provides a long list in *Gangs of New York*, 298.

9. Diamond Dan O'Rourke's salon was either at 180 or 158 Park Row (or at both at different times). Thomas Conley's was at 184 Park Row. Thomas D. Sullivan's occupied 7 and 8 Chatham Square.

10. "Galvin's Bowery Raids." Thanks to Emma McElroy for her help in tracking down this article.

11. The three beggar/peddlers appear in various histories of San Francisco, with enough additional information to make it clear that Norris's piece is not the single source; see, for instance, Cowan, Bancroft, and Ballou, 30.

12. Siebers analyzes this process, with a detailed taxonomy of its multiple contemporary forms, in "Disability as Masquerade." Welke's treatment of disability performativity in the context of nineteenth-century injury lawsuits explores a related phenomenon, 234–237, 246.

13. On overacting and hyperbole in the context of gender performance, see Doane; and Tyler.

14. All these works address the sight/blindness binary specifically. See also Brueggemann.

15. Sherry makes a strong case for the importance of Bhabha's work as a model for disability studies in his "(Post)colonizing Disability": "Bhabha's examination of subtle forms of resistance, such as the displacement, distortion, dislocation and ambivalence generated by the process of colonial domination is far more complex than the simple models of unilateral 'oppression' which can be found in many disability studies texts. . . . Bhabha stresses that it is important to identify those in-between moments that initiate new sites of identity, new collaborations, and new conflicts over identity. Again, this sophisticated approach to forms of domination and alterity is markedly different from the approach of disability scholars, who tend to favor simplistic models of oppression and uncritically regard minority discourse as signs of political strength and unity, rather than ambivalence" (19). As Sherry puts it in *If I Only Had a Brain*, "rather than finding

an undiluted, 'authentic' voice of opposition among marginalized groups, it is far more common to uncover both resistance and complicity. . . . disability studies could benefit from identifying a fluid continuum of subject positions with regard to impairment and disability identities" (170). In conversation with Sherry, Snyder and Mitchell also look to Bhabha's figure of the stairway (and develop a critique of the use of an emblematic image of inaccessibility, the stairs) in CLD, 205.

16. The stairway is a staple feature in representations by middle-class authors of the site of The Doctor's and places like it. Crane's depiction of Park Row and Chatham Square in "An Experiment in Misery" takes its readers "up the steep stairway" to a lodging house packed with men "who exhibited many deformities" (251, 234); Swaffield warned his audience that to "get into these pestilential human rookeries you have to . . . ascend rotten staircases which threaten to give way beneath every step"; and according to Gregory Jackson, Jacob Riis narrated his stereopticon virtual tours of the Five Points district by showing pictures of "descent down steep stairs into damp, verminous cellars" and announcing, "we've descended into the underworld."

17. I am drawing on Higbie's work on hobo rough culture; although hoboes, he argues, "enjoyed the social advantages of being men, . . . male power did not always benefit them. They were both perpetrators and victims of the physical violence that was an element of male power generally" (15). In some accounts of the rough culture of places like The Doctor's, the threat of violence is embodied particularly in the presence of seamen who frequent the bars. Though sailors, as Newman notes (111), were very often scarred or disfigured as the result of their "arduous work and difficult life" at sea, they tend to show up in imposter dive narratives as volatile outsiders unaware of the cripple scam and therefore as particularly dangerous.

18. As Tremain puts it, "The testimonials, acts and enactments of the disabled subject are performative in so far as the 'prediscursive' impairment which they are purported to disclose or manifest has no existence prior to, or apart from, those very constitutive performances" (2002, 42). See also Corker and Shakespeare, 10; and Price and Shildrick, 1996. Snyder and Mitchell historicize the performativity of disability in CLD: "Disabled people are recognized as those who must adeptly manipulate suspicious and surly social belief systems about their potential masquerades of incapacity and parasitism. Nineteenth-century capitalism thus produced disabled people as ever-visible actors on a debasing stage" (42–43).

19. Langan's analysis (46) of Jean Jacques Rousseau's problem with a crippled boy who begs too often and too insistently, transforming free compassion into debt, is apropos here, and her general analysis of Rousseau's "playing the beggar" provides a rich background for the all too thin and impoverished textual examples available in the *New York Times, Everybody's Magazine,* and New York guidebooks that this chapter takes as its field.

20. On the "professionalism" of beggars as "a perversion and a parody of

Americans' growing investment in the worth of occupational expertise," see S. Ryan, 56.

21. Official city reports in the period of ugly law sometimes tabulate the number of "common beggars" (as well as "common prostitutes") arrested; see, for instance, the *Annual Report of the Public Service Division of Charities, Correction and Cemeteries of the City of Cleveland* (1906). The adjectives seem largely redundant, but they serve to open up, implicitly, a space for uncommon beggars and prostitutes—presumably those who commit the act against their will and one time only.

22. The understanding of writing itself as potentially unsightly, in the case of the sign around the neck or the card handed out, had an effect worth mentioning here: exposing a text could be as criminal as exposing a sore, placing some deaf (or fake-deaf) beggars under the jurisdiction of ugly law when otherwise they would have fallen outside its scope.

23. "Dandyism" is a category that has been mobilized for disability studies in Kuppers's analysis of the work and persona of contemporary UK rock musician, performer, and "Thalidomide Warrior" Mat Fraser. For Kuppers, finding a way to make sense of Fraser entails being transported exactly back to the "Gay 1890s of Oscar Wilde." Fraser, Kuppers argues, "dandifies disability": "Disability, culturally linked to invisibility and the 'ugly,' needs reperforming, reclaiming, remapping if it is to appear in the registers of the beautiful. The narcissistic body, beautiful *against* 'nature,' is created" (2002, 191). Illuminating on disability images today, Kuppers's concept of dandifying does not apply to what was going on at The Doctor's. But we can see both the figure of the dandy and the figure of the unsightly beggar as two examples of appearance/behavior/identity being marked as unruly and in need of surveillance on the urban streets. For analysis of controversies about dandies' exhibiting themselves in public, see Kasson. Kuppers makes additional connections between disability and something like dandification, in her marvelous treatment of a passage in Benjamin's discussion of Baudelaire describing a flâneur who walks a turtle in the arcades. She relates this figure of the turtle walker to the disability performer: "Like the trickster, often out of place or tone, the turtle's slow pace subverts the city's rhythm by its presence. . . . In uneasy alignment, dialogues of being in space develop. Within the larger gameplan of city life, turtle walking in the city is a minor, tactical insertion into a systematic whole. . . . Performance makes a new cityscape" (2003, 2–3). The unsightly beggar, sham or for-real, is a quintessential turtle walker in Kuppers's sense, in the tradition of disabled performers who, as she puts it, "use public spaces outside the theater in order to challenge ever more effectively the concept of allocation and categorization" (2003, 1–2).

24. I am engaged here in a project shared by Diedrich in her use, for different ends, of the same passage from Parker and Sedgwick in order to "move the other way—back from 'queer' to 'ill'" (44).

25. Invalidism functions, that is, much as Carter argues neurasthenia (understood as a sickness of "well-bred white people") functioned: "weakness seems to have worked as a racial asset" (44).

26. On norming by dictionary, see Davis 2002, 102–118.

27. On the complex range of possible reactions by disabled people to assistive technologies today, see, for instance, Iwakuma; Frank; and Siebers, "Disability as Masquerade." Ott, Serlin, and Mihm explore the issue in the realm of prosthetics.

28. I take these terms from the important critique and manifesto by Hughes and Patterson.

29. In distinguishing *Deaf* (with a capital *D*) from *deaf* (lowercase *d*), I am following the convention first proposed by James Woodward in 1972. The lowercase *deaf* refers to an audiological condition; uppercase *Deaf* refers to a particular group, people who share a common culture and American Sign Language as their common language. See Padden and Humphries, 2–5, and Woodward.

30. Here again Hughes and Patterson is the starting point for thinking of what a "sociology of impairment" might entail. On "impairment effects," see Thomas 2007 and the dialogue between Thomas and Corker, 20 and 29. Corker responds by emphasizing the "ontological consequences" of impairment "that interact in complex ways" with social organization (21).

31. See, for instance, Petra Kuppers's discussions of Merleau-Ponty and phenomenology in *Disability and Contemporary Performance*.

32. On debates over the ethics and efficacy of disability simulation exercises, see Scullion; French 1992, 257; Pfeiffer; and the ongoing discussions on the international "disability research" email discussion list administered by the Center for Disability Studies at Leeds that analyze why simulation fails.

33. Readers who want clarification of the meanings of the word *ableism* might start with Levi's discussion.

34. Another set of terms in present disability discourses may have potential but undecidable relation to the past of the fakers at The Doctor's: the labels *devotees, wannabes, disability pretenders,* and most recently, *people with Body Integrity Identity Disorder* or *transabled.* In contemporary parlance, "devotees are nondisabled people who are sexually attracted to people with disabilities"; *wannabes* "actually want to become disabled, sometimes going to extraordinary lengths to have a limb amputated," a practice recently renamed "self-demand amputation" (Bruno; Lingis; N. Sullivan). The *pretender,* perhaps the most pertinent catchword here, "describes a nondisabled person who lives as if he or she has a disability, using medical equipment or paraphernalia (i.e., wheelchairs, crutches, braces, taping limbs together)" (Ham 2003; see also Sean O'Connor's discussions of "transability"). For analysis of these phenomena see Guter; Kafer; Duncan's film *My One-Legged Dream Lover*; N. Sullivan. Raymond Aguilera begins his "Disability and Delight: Staring Back at the Devotee Community" by contrasting the text of the ugly law (cited as "City of Chicago Ordinance, circa 1911") with a

March 2000 personals ad placed by a "good-looking gay white professional male" looking for a partner who was "injured, leg in a cast, bandaged, on crutches, or in neck brace." "Quite a change over the past eight decades," writes Aguilera. But there is some evidence that versions of these categories emerged as early as the first decade of the unsightly beggar ordinances. See Bruno; and "Professor William H. Pancoast," *New Orleans Times-Democrat,* Sept. 20, 1884. It may be that The Doctor's drew its share of what we would now call devotees and pretenders. It may be that a few of the genuine amputees lost limbs not quite by accident. It may even be that at some level municipal crackdowns on imposters, "cripple factories," and unsightly begging were prompted in part by a vague, dawning cultural fear that something besides begging, something volatilely transgressive, something like mayhem, might be happening at The Doctor's. On the concept of mayhem and its relation to these issues, see Harry Benjamin and the work of Nikki Sullivan.

35. See Loo and Strange on the phenomenon in which "the objects of formal regulation themselves" conduct "orderly enterprises" to monitor their own grifts, creating a "rival illegal social order" as rule bound as city officials' versions (645).

36. Longmore and Goldberger have given us the history of the depression-era disability organizing of the LPH.

NOTES TO CHAPTER 6

1. I use "figure" in the sense glossed by Garland Thomson in *EB*, 140.

2. Disability studies work on "simultaneous" and "multiple" oppression is pertinent here, though the underlying models are different from the idea of intersectionality; see, for instance, Stuart; Fawcett, 47–53.

3. The term *intersectionality* is Crenshaw's. The quotations here are from Valerie Smith's powerful application of intersectionality to interpretation, xiv, xv, xviii.

4. Cf. Shakespeare's exploration of the "variety of disability identities" (10).

5. Compare the body exhibited in nineteenth-century anatomy museums as Sappol describes it: "The disowned body . . . linked to sexually desiring (and desired) females, the working class, criminals, and non-Europeans, exemplars of the social consequences of undisciplined desire, analogous to or emblematic of deformity and disease" (2002, 308).

6. On eugenics, race, and nativism, see Blackmar, and the recent analysis by Snyder and Mitchell, "The Eugenic Atlantic," in CLD.

7. On the minority model of disability, see Stroman. Hahn's work a little later than Gliedman and Roth's, in the 1980s, was crucial in formulating this model, and it is worth noting that he returned repeatedly to questions of aesthetics and the beauty/ugly divide; see Hahn 1985 and 1988.

8. On the logic of equivalence, see Laclau and Mouffe; also Jakobsen, 66.

9. On the influence of feminist consciousness-raising on the practices of the disability rights movement, see Roth 2002, 60.

10. Grillo and Wildman. I am indebted to Jakobsen throughout this discussion of the politics of analogy. See also an essay used by Jakobsen: Crosby, "Language and Materialism."

11. Not all cities did so; some followed an alphabetical system of listing ordinances.

12. The 1887 version of the New Orleans law goes so far as to add "Lewd Women" to its general title ("Idle Persons, Vagrants, and Lewd Women," among whom wounded and deformed beggars were a subgroup). *Jewell's Digest*, 1887, 464.

13. There were female tramps, but in lesser numbers, and their presence is obscured in representations of the vagrant. See Cresswell's chapter "Gendering the Tramp"; McCook 1894; and Kusmer 2002, 106–107 and 140–141. Kerber has an excellent discussion of U.S. women's relation to vagrancy law, 47–80.

14. On women and the ugly, see for instance Iris Marion Young: "while a certain cultural space is reserved for revering feminine beauty and desirability, in part that very cameo idea renders most women drab, ugly, loathsome or fearful bodies" (123). Young's general analysis here directly pertains to the situation of the ugly laws. Tseelon has argued that women's embodiment is caught up in a "beauty paradox" among other paradoxes: women signify beauty but embody ugliness (5–6).

15. Reitman, 281–283; Cresswell, 106–107. Compare the gendered formulations of "aesthetic criminology" described in an 1893 article: "In respect of aesthetical physiognomy, criminals differ a little from ordinary persons except in the case of female criminals, who are almost always ugly, if not repulsive," and some male forgers and swindlers have "the face of an old woman" ("Criminology").

16. See also Garland Thomson's analysis of femininity and disability in *EB*, 27–29.

17. In a different context, Okeley's study of gender difference in how gypsy men and women in England deployed begging and street conduct provides a variety of examples.

18. Jennie Highheel's story appears in "Ancient Profession of Street Beggar." Compare the narrative of Virginia Wilson in "Pitiful Mendicant Gives Way." Some analysis of the fashionable form of the high heel in feminist disability studies argues that high heels disable women. Garland Thomson writes, "Feminine cultural practices such as . . . stiletto high heels . . . impair women's bodies and restrict their physical agency, imposing disability on them" ("Integrating Disability," 89). This kind of thinking reverses the opposition of the dame's high heel to the lame high heel that the "high-heeled game" mocks. Kusmer (2002) writes about the high-heel scam and other specifically feminized modes of begging fakery, 84.

19. Compare "Wiles of Beggars Pay Well, She Says," in which a woman caught

begging whose left side is paralyzed is treated relatively gently by authorities after she tells her story: "He has had me under his influence. . . . He made me beg."

20. Compare Alden's revision of Hawthorne's "The Birth-Mark" in *Among the Freaks.* Here a dime museum Bearded Lady who considers herself "a disgusting sight" quits the museum after marriage to the museum's Giant in order to keep house, "which is what every woman freak that was ever born is always longing to do," and then dies on the operating table when a doctor tries out a "new way of removing beards," to the horror of the museum's manager ("you are proposing to destroy twenty thousand dollars of paying capital") and to the mortal grief of her loving husband, who dies soon after. The story is Hawthorne revised under the pressure of freak-show capitalism and a freak ethic of mutuality, pertinent here because of the way conventional marital domesticity trumps the ugly.

21. "Femininity as to-be-looked-at-ness" is Mulvey's famous formulation. Rosemarie Garland Thomson's work continues to explore dynamics of disability and to-be-looked-at-ness.

22. Compare Helen Keller's "Pity and tears . . . do not . . . save the manhood of blind men," quoted in Kudlick, 2001. For a broader context in which to place the rhetoric of masculinity and civilization here, see Bederman.

23. Most courts found exemptions for war veterans unconstitutional, with some interesting exceptions; in *State v. Montgomery* (1899), the court found that a statute exempting Civil War vets from paying licensing fees "was both patriotic and constitutional" (Rhyne, Burton, and Murphy, 67). The leading case for the opposite position involved Chicago (*Marallis v. Chicago*), in which the court explained its objection to such exemptions: "All persons holding such discharges were declared exempt . . . without regard to the length or character of military, naval, or marine service, their sound or debilitated condition of body and their affluence or poverty" (Rhyne, Burton, and Murphy, 67). In other words, the case hinged in part on the question of whether all veterans were as a class disabled. In *Farley v. Watt,* the court had argued that they were: "Those who were classified and called away were handicapped. . . . they constituted a distinct class distinguished from the mass of society—a class created by deprivation of equal opportunity in civil pursuits at home and marked by disability incident to defense of the country abroad" (Rhyne, Burton, and Murphy, 66). Gerber (2000 and elsewhere) provides an important overview of issues concerning disabled veterans.

24. Compare Carroll Smith Rosenberg's discussion of attitudes toward begging in the early-nineteenth-century United States. She argues that Americans in the first decades of the nineteenth century "accepted, in some cases appeared to approve, street begging, that anathema of later urban philanthropists"; she cites an author praising in particular the sight of "a maimed and disabled soldier, begging through our streets, when the liberal hand of charity has been opened to assist him" (28–29).

25. Serlin writes of the cultural distinction between "the 'tragically' disabled

and the congenitally 'deformed'" in the context of veterans' history in his essay "Queerness and Disability in U.S. Military Culture": "This delineation relied in part on the difference between disability induced by modern technology or warfare and disability induced by heredity or illness. . . . The former kind of disability confirms one's service to the modern state, to industrial capitalism, to warfare: it helps the veteran's body preserve patriotic values and masculinity" (161). As an 1893 newspaper article put it, the disabled soldier by definition could not be a beggar; any money given to him was wages earned by "the arm that lies bleaching on the hillside under the southern sky; for the ear that no sound can reach," and so on ("To the Old Soldiers"). In contrast, disability from birth or acquired through illness "marks one's rejection," Serlin argues, "from competent service to society: it confirms that the disabled body is hopelessly queer and inimical to patriotic value or normative manly competence and productivity" (161). See also O'Brien 2004, 7, and Skocpol's extensive treatment of this issue.

26. On links between military malingerers and unsightly beggars, see Dornstein, 62–67.

27. This structure lingers in U.S. law today, as shown by Melissa Cole Essig's analysis of the ADA and the obligation to keep disability private, in "Gimp Theory and the ADA's 'Feedback Loop.'"

28. Stansell is addressing an earlier time period, but her analysis applies here.

29. On marriage and the "ideally independent" family as structures through which American culture attempts to manage the problem of dependency, see Fineman.

30. Sanborn provides one account of this kind of derivative dependency: "Mrs. McCloskey—familiar as a basket-beggar to many householders—is the most disgusting creature in the alley; she is blear-eyed and dripping-eyed, pimply-faced and smutty-tongued. She is very loyal to her husband, who has been in the insane asylum for the last thirteen years. . . . she will not give a thought to leaving this country till she has 'taken her husband's bones away.' She takes the best care she knows of her three motherless grandchildren" (155). On derivative and inevitable dependencies, see Fineman, 35–45. When "unsightly beggar" discourse recognizes derivative dependency at all, it is seen as manipulation, as in this account from the *New York Times* in 1898: "Women support entire families in this way. They have their regular customers to whom they go. . . . A woman frequently finds that begging is so easy that when the need is past she keeps up the practice" ("New York City Beggars"). Meanwhile, when a male tramp in this article takes "a female hobo under his wing" as his "homekeeper," the reporter goes on to doubt whether "any expression regarding masculine protection is appropriate when applied to this degraded stage of humanity."

31. With "female forms" I mean to invoke one of the most important texts in feminist disability studies and in disability studies generally, Thomas's *Female Forms*. A large body of feminist disability studies on which I am implicitly

drawing in this section includes Saxton and Howe; Wendell; Fine and Asch; Herndl; Fawcett; Carlson; O'Toole; Kudlick; Hall; and the work of Garland Thomson.

32. "It is the workingmen who give," this piece asserts, arguing that unsightly beggars "know the different pay days of the big manufacturies and follow them" ("Ancient Profession"). See also "Hard Times Too Much for the 'Begging Squad.'" Kusmer (2002) provides a fascinating account of working-class/underclass solidarity between beggars and the workers they approached, 84–85.

33. It is possible that the "monster in the shape of a deformed Indian" was a woman, perhaps even the famous Julia Pastrana, the Mexican Indian exhibited as human curiosity around the world under the labels "Female Nondescript," "The Baboon Lady," "The Marvelous Hybrid or Bear Woman," and "The Ugliest Woman in the World," beginning in the United States in the same year, 1855. (More likely, since Pastrana's serial showmen traveled as impresarios, not organ-grinders, the San Francisco man who pimped the "deformed Indian" may have been attempting to capitalize on Pastrana's fame with a local imitation.) Garland Thomson provides a complex analysis of the various meanings attached to and fought out over Pastrana in "Making Freaks," an important example of work that treats disability, gender, race, nationality, and sexuality as intricate and inseparable factors in cultural production. See also Bondeson; and Hunter, 35–36, for an account of the film about Pastrana, *La Donna Scimia,* and of the later doings of Pastrana's husband, who toured with a second woman named Marie Bartels and renamed "Zenora Pastrana."

34. Parr's analysis is pertinent here: "In recent times geographers have begun to document and theorize body (and mind) differences under the heading of disability, with emphasis on ways in which society and its spaces may be seen as 'ableist.' . . . Such critiques . . . link with work by feminist geographers concerned with the idealized 'body spaces' of women, which can also be seen as 'disabling'" (60). Scobey's "Anatomy of the Promenade" in nineteenth-century New York discusses how anxieties about bourgeois women, "like the proverbial canaries in the coal mine," stood for more general anxieties: "the bourgeois woman . . . figuratively condensed the class requirements and sexual risks of polite sociability" (205).

35. See also "Due Notice," 2.

36. On the history of ideas of maternal impression, see Connor, 101–118, and Todd, particularly 44–63. According to Bogdan, one 1889 encyclopedia of diseases of children had an entire chapter on the subject (110–111). The 1900 *Index-Catalogue of the Library of the Surgeon-General's Office* (Washington, D.C.: Government Printing Office, vol. 5) contains scattered references to mother's marks in its many entries of scientific articles on maternal impression. Groce writes that examples of maternal impression explanations for deafness "crowded the nineteenth-century scientific literature" and provides several interesting examples

(1985, 118–120). Gallaudet, for example, argued that "epidemics" of congenital deafness could be attributed to "maternal anxiety. . . . This is particularly the case in a country that is the seat of war" (quoted in Groce 1985, 120), and Groce records other examples of the more classic direct impression theory (in which the birth of one deaf child is attributed to the mother's sight of another). The notion of maternal impression continued into the twentieth century, as in this example from a 1926 eugenics manual: "During Pregnancy, What to Avoid: Pregnant mothers should avoid thinking of ugly people, or those marked by any disease: avoid injury, fright and disease of any kind. Also avoid ungraceful position and awkward attitude, but cultivate grace and beauty in herself. Avoid difficulty with neighbors or other trouble" (Jefferis and Nichols, 107). My thanks to Lennard Davis for alerting me to this passage.

37. Catherine Kudlick's analysis of blindness and gender in the turn-of-the-century United States pertains here: "For blind women . . . disability compounded the disadvantages already associated with being female—helplessness, dependence, frailty—but without a social payoff, for even in a world that celebrated female virtues, it made women too feminine" (2001, 202).

38. I am drawing here on Georgina Kleege's analysis in "Blindness and Visual Culture" of the "hypothetical blind man" in philosophical discourse.

39. Bondeson records various moments at which disability policy was governed by the vagaries of the ideology of maternal impression (149). King Frederik IV of Denmark, for example, segregated disabled people as a prenatal health precaution.

40. Compare arguments against corseting in this period, which also employed the fear of deformity to advocate for loosening constraint on women's bodies, as in B.O. Flower's argument in "Fashion's Slaves" (1891): "A possible genius deformed and dwarfed by the weight of a fashionable dress; a brain which might have been brilliant rendered idiotic by the constant pressure of a corset; . . . a child . . . condemned to drag a weakly, diseased, or deformed body through life, with mind ever chained to the flesh, through the heartless imposition which fashion imposed upon his mother!" (rpt. in Smith and Dawson, 283). More generally, feminists and suffragists linked women's emancipation to eradicating child deformity. Victoria Woodhull, for instance, argued that "marriage itself, as a structure, posed a danger to children by sexually enslaving their mothers. . . . The offspring of such an arrangement would always risk serious debility" (quoted in Richards, 74).

41. See Spain on middle-class women's creation of a "voluntary vernacular" in the built environment during this period. Spain, drawing on the work of Maureen Flanagan, argues, "Crudely stated, men emphasized economic growth and progress (the City Profitable), while women invoked religiosity and domesticity for the benefit of strangers (the City Livable). Men and women both built the industrial city" (13). Cumbler, examining the histories of two Massachusetts towns,

writes that the membership of late-nineteenth-century charity organizations "was primarily women" (98) and that over time, when women had more organizational power, they shifted policies both toward greater concern with conventional women's issues like child care and away from an emphasis on frauds and cheaters.

42. E. Wilson 1991 and 1992; Heron; Parsons. Wilson argues the possibility of the flâneuse against Wolff's claim in "The Invisible Flâneuse" that "the flâneur can only be male." On the flâneuse debate, see McDowell's very useful *Gender, Identity and Place,* 152–156. On the flâneur in U.S. culture, see Brand.

43. These gender/class dynamics may be seen as related to those charted by Rosemarie Garland Thomson in her discussion of a slightly earlier mid-nineteenth-century "compensation model," in which "disability is interpreted as a lack that must be compensated for by the 'benevolent maternalism' of the middle-class women"; see *EB,* 81–102.

44. On the "prostitute body" as the nineteenth century's "paradigmatic disorderly body," see Hooper.

45. My thanks to Lynn Sacco for pointing out the general use of the term *diseased* as a euphemism for people infected with sexually transmitted disease (personal communication). On anti-venereal-disease organizing, see Burnham. Like the man in Cleveland whose photo is reprinted in the introduction, many disabled boys and men worked selling newspapers. COS organizing to shut down the "newsboy" trade emphasized the frequency among them of "loathsome diseases . . . incurred from constant contact with . . . degraded minds." M. Adams, 8.

46. As recent a text as Carter's *The Heart of Whiteness,* admirably devoted to analyzing the intersection of sexuality and race in the construction of the "normal American," surprisingly ignores disability. In Carter's terms, normality "becomes a subject for critical analysis simultaneously along both racial and sexual axes of difference and power" (26) but not along a disability axis. This omission seems particularly problematic because Carter has clearly encountered some disability studies scholarship, or so a briskly patronizing reference suggests (30). But other recent work attends to the simultaneous interaction of queerness and disability. The special issue of GLQ, edited by Robert McRuer and Abby Wilkerson, on queer theory and disability studies explores the implications of linking the two fields, as does Robert McRuer's work generally and much of Corbett O'Toole's. Currah's short essay offers a summary and manifesto on the topic. I am indebted to Mark Sherry for discussions of his paper "Queer/Crip Theory: Transgressing the Margins" (delivered at the Center for the Study of Sexual Culture, University of California at Berkeley, Jan. 22, 2003) and his essay "Overlaps and Contradictions between Queer Theory and Disability Studies." Terry and Urla contextualize James Forbes's attempts to track (and measure) Elizabeth Duval in ways illuminating for disability and queer history: "Efforts to measure the ears of criminals, the clitorises of prostitutes, and the facial contours of 'perverts' fuelled a feverish desire to classify forms of deviance, to locate them in biology and thus

to police them in the larger social body. The somatic territorializing of deviance, since the nineteenth century, has been part of a larger effort to organize social relations according to categories denoting normality versus pathology, and national security versus social danger" (1). See also Cresswell, 107–109. Lombroso and Ferrero's *Criminal Woman, the Prostitute, and the Normal Woman* (1903) epitomizes the complex ways in which the tracking of the lesbian, the criminal, and the disabled woman occurs all at once.

47. "[W]e are not 'allowed' or encouraged in our culture, nor indeed in any other known cultures, to either exhibit ourselves or to observe the bodies of others, except in highly restrictive and codified contexts. . . . Nakedness is a lure to intimacy and proximity because it invites the other's care and solicitude. Nakedness is a state of vulnerability, not simply because one is open to the elements, at the mercy of the environment, unprotected, but also because one is prone, more prone than usual, to the affect and the impact of the other" (Grosz, 194).

48. On charitable efforts to enforce the cover-up of Indian bodies, see David Wagner's chapter "Charity, Philanthropy and the Indian." For one example of an ordinance stipulating that the bodies of enslaved people must be kept covered, see *Digest of the Ordinances of the City Council of Charleston* (1818), 191.

49. As Paul Longmore has suggested to me, if the law's nearness to cross-dressing strictures in the codes suggests links to gender transgression, it also may bring to mind a distant connection to another history of laws prohibiting deceptive attire as a way of policing class and status: medieval and early-modern sumptuary laws. Whether ordinances regarding clothing ever spelled out the proper outfit for a beggar I do not know. But it is intriguing to consider "unsightliness" as a kind of clothing.

50. See R. Ferguson, 31–43, on alternative gender and sexual relations and African American culture in the 1930s.

51. Extending Yoshino's paradigm, Melissa Cole Essig argues that disability status is protected under recent interpretations of the ADA only to the extent that conduct that is constitutive of disability identity is covered. Cole; Essig.

NOTES TO CHAPTER 7

1. Nativist suspicion of the foreign beggar began earlier. Susan Ryan discusses texts from the 1850s warning of foreigners who, as one editorial put it, "put on the dress of beggars" (59). But antimendicant nativism escalated in intensity as the century wore on.

2. Sennett, Gilman, and Shah, among others, have helped us understand attempts to find spatial solutions to the problem of "disease" that place the ugly law in context as yet another way of remaking urban American space as nondiseased and nondisabled space. As each of these scholars has shown, these spatial strategies have links to histories of anti-Semitism, particularly to the association of

Jewish bodies with impurity and contagion, as well as to anti-immigration policies. See Sennett, 215, 227, and the entire chapter on the creation of the ghetto in Venice; Gilman, 24. On strategies (both narrative and material) for containing contagion, and on the racist functions of nineteenth-century public health regulation, see Shah 2001.

3. Sontag suggests the inevitability of the diseased/alien equation: "there is a link between imagining disease and imagining foreignness. It lies perhaps in the very concept of wrong, which is archaically identical with the non-us, the alien" (136). See also Alan Hyde's chapter on "diseased bodies," 241–251.

4. Title VII, Chapter 1 of the California Political Code. See Chan, 98–99, and Byrom 2004, 6–7.

5. The definition of *loathsome* comes from the 1910 book of instructions "for the medical inspection of aliens."

6. Baynton's scholarship offers a key example of the kind of "joint conversation" that Molina calls for (as does Molina's own): "Studies of race and immigration and of disability provide a unique opportunity to understand the fallacy of the modal subject [of American identity]. . . . we need to conduct a *joint* conversation, one that deliberately reaches across the separate, isolated spaces—academic, private, and public—that are and have been the typical sites of discourse" ("Medicalizing the Mexican," 24). See also the chapter "Trying to Come Home to America: A Historical Illustration of the Classifications of Disability in U.S. Immigration Law" in Jaeger and Bowman.

7. "Medicalized nativism" is Molina's phrase, in "Medicalizing the Mexican," 7.

8. 1907 Ala. Acts 313 (app. 9). Similarly, Missouri passed a law in 1901 prohibiting bringing children with incurable diseases or "of feeble mind" into the state. 1901 Mo. Laws 132 (app. 163).

9. See Buck, 51; Bales, 163–164; Haines and Rosenblum, 348.

10. "Disability may well be something that upsets the natural order, but disability is not monstrosity because it has a place in civil or canon law. The disabled person may not conform to nature, but the law in some way provides for him. Monstrosity, however, is the kind of natural irregularity that calls law into question and disables it. Law must either question its own foundations, or its practice, or fall silent, or abdicate, or appeal to another reference system, or again invent a casuistry" (Foucault 2003, 64).

11. Municipal Charities Commission, *First Annual Report,* 67. Molina notes in her study of health and immigration politics in Los Angeles, "Medicalizing the Mexican," that "until the mid-1920s, Mexican immigrants crossed the border with relative ease (the border patrol was not created until 1924), and their health status was an issue only sporadically" (26); the economy of Southern California depended on Mexican labor, so Mexican immigrants were not on the whole represented as unfit, likely to be public charges, unsound, and so on. Hence, to some extent the problem of the unemployed Mexican begging

on the street was cordoned off from the problem of the unsightly beggar, though the two exist in close proximity here. Molina offers a complex account of these dynamics (and of configurations of race and public health clustered around Chinese and Japanese bodies in Los Angeles) in *Fit to Be Citizens.* Mexicans in Mexico have long been associated with begging in U.S. discourse; as far back as 1825, one Mr. Poinsett, reporting on his travels in Mexico, remarked that he "met more miserable squalid beings clothed in rags and exposing their deformities and diseases to excite compassion than I have elsewhere seen," and one reviewer of his travelogue concurred that this "degree of mendicity" could be ascribed to "the extreme fertility of the soil" (rev. of *Notes on Mexico,* 16).

12. See Shah's (2005) related use of Anzaldúa, 722, and McRuer's discussion of the ways in which Anzaldúa's work speaks to disability studies, 37–39.

13. See also Shah 2001.

14. See Molina, *Fit to Be Citizens,* 8.

15. Bill Brown analyzes this passage, pointing out that the enfreakment of the Exposition facilitated "recalcitrant performativity" on the part of the "peoples of the world" gathered in Chicago—a recalcitrant performativity not unrelated, I would add, to the unsightly beggar's. Brown notes, too, that this scene exposes "the fragile containment of Chicago's immigrant population" (232).

16. On the modal subject's constitution as nondisabled and challenges to that conception, see Molina, "Medicalizing the Mexican," and Breckenridge and Vogler.

17. A similar principle applied to Japanese American beggars. A California paper in 1897 found this report newsworthy: "A Jap begging for bread is rather an uncommon spectacle, but that was just what was to be seen on the streets of Woodland today" ("Jap Begging," 1). Compare the title of the 1923 article in the *Los Angeles Times,* "Chinaman Is Jailed as Beggar"; apparently the very existence of "Chinaman" and "Beggar" in the same phrase was newsworthy.

18. On Chinatown as moral threat, see Lui, 90.

19. On the "bizarre" nature of the text, see McAllister; Franklin; and Lyman. The idiot-turned-genius solves various ideological problems for Mundo; the device ensures that the Asiatic hordes (allied, too, with an Ethiopian darky who speaks fake Chinese "better than if he had pretended to be deaf and dumb" [209]), incapable of empire-building themselves, are led by a white man—but one with depths of defect.

20. Kemp's poem is one of several that people a city street with unsightly beggars in close conjunction with foreigners in a collection defined as an "urban anthology." See also Edgar Lee Masters, "The Loop," and T.A. Daly's Italian-dialect verse "Da Colda Feet," in Greever and Bachelor.

21. For other examples from the time period of this kind of rhetoric, see Michael.

22. My thanks to Edna Nahshon for her help in understanding Zangwill's schnorrer figure.

23. On the tension between German Jews in Chicago and the new Jewish immigrants, see Meites; and Cutler.

24. A similar dynamic occurred in Germany under the pressure of the entrance of Jewish beggars who arrived there from Russia and Poland after train systems had been established. An 1897 Jewish German article about "Foreign Beggars' Organizations" says of these refugees, "the more experienced they are, they add crippled and blind people to their ranks; they forge begging letters; they say they have been expelled from Russia, and this word 'expelled' works wonders and is an unending source of income" (quoted in Bornshtain). Thanks to Chava Boyarin for translation of these lines.

25. Vaillant comments on the general emphasis on sight over sound in urban studies: "Although ways of seeing . . . are well established in urban studies, the subject of sound . . . has only recently begun to come into its own" (259).

26. Other cities responded similarly. In 1894 the city council of Buffalo asked the mayor to pass a similar ordinance banning peddling permits for anyone who was not an American citizen. *Proceedings of the Council, City of Buffalo, 1894*, 11, 1365.

27. On the predominance of Italian street organists, see Zucchi; and Cohen and Greenwood.

NOTES TO CHAPTER 8

1. I am drawing here on Delaney's formulation regarding "the centrality of 'space,' 'place' or geography in the historical constitution of race" (3). Delaney shows how "spatial configurations are not incidental to power relations such as those predicated on race but are integral to them. . . . such relations are what they are because of how they are spatialized" (7). The same holds true for disability, in—for instance—the spatial configuring of special education classrooms, segregated institutions, and stairways.

2. Ferri and Connor do an excellent analysis of the intricate intersections between American racial and disability segregation in "Tools of Exclusion." Disability rights activist Judith Heumann's powerful invocation of *Brown v. Board of Education* in her testimony at the congressional hearing held during the famous Section 504 action ("Before there was a Section 504 . . . there was Brown vs. Board of Education") can be seen on film in "The Power of 504," available from the Disability Rights Education Defense Fund in Oakland.

3. Horwitz, Field, Minow, and other scholars, amicus brief in support of respondents, *University of Alabama at Birmingham Board of Trustees v. Patricia Garrett*, 531 U.S. 356 (2001). Compare Thurgood Marshall's analogy between forced disability institutionalization and racial segregation in his opinion in the Supreme

Court's *Cleburne* case: "a regime of state-mandated segregation and degradation . . . that in its virulence and bigotry rivaled, and indeed paralleled, the worst excesses of Jim Crow" (473 U.S. at 462 [1985]).

4. Rafter's discussion of "the feebleminded" as white Others in this period has influenced me here and offers another pertinent context: "The Criminalization of Mental Retardation" (250). See also Stallybrass and White's discussion of the representation of the "low other," 3, and Ching's application of the concept in the American context, 120. On white trash as a social category, see Newitz and Wray; and Wray and Newitz. The authors of the most extensive survey of conditions for disabled people done during the era of ugly law, the so-called "Cleveland Cripple Survey," wrote that "[t]he colored have a comparatively insignificant place in the problem of Cleveland cripples"; the majority of their tabulated cases of disabled "street operators" was defined as white and immigrant (Welfare Federation of Cleveland, 24). The situation was sometimes reversed in southern cities. At the turn of the twentieth century, the Charleston chief of police noted with civic pride that "as far as this city is concerned . . . begging on the streets is confined mostly to aged and crippled negroes." (W.A. Boyle, letter to Mrs. M.A. Rhett, Nov. 5, 1902). When Paul Kellogg, an editor of *Charities* magazine, wrote in 1902 to Rhett, the secretary of Charleston's Associated Charities, requesting information "as to mendicancy and its problems" in Charleston, he approached her with a clear preconception about what the answer might be: "What is the special type, or types, of beggar most promenant [*sic*] locally. . . . Any 'local color' as to methods, characteristics, places or plying of calling, etc. that you may add will be very interesting. Outside of its picturesque features, this gathering of information should be of real service." For city leaders, "aged and crippled negro" mendicants, if properly managed, constituted an unthreatening, even a winning, form of local color, like the black women who sold flowers out of baskets on the street.

5. Bouson's analysis of "white trash shame" and "white trash shamelessness" in the context of contemporary writer Dorothy Allison's work makes this link explicitly when Bouson discusses the ugly laws, 113. Unsightly mendicancy functioned in ways similar to (and intersecting with) the functions of "feeblemindedness" that Stubblefield has identified: "an umbrella concept that linked 'off-white' ethnicity" and "poverty," understood as "the signifier of tainted whiteness" (162).

6. I mean "unhinged" in its colloquial sense, but also in the metaphoric sense employed by Hale: "With freedom, African American identity became unhinged for the first time collectively from the taint of slavery, from its dialectical place as the antithesis of citizenship" (15).

7. See also Slaughter; and I. Young (1990), 123. Martin Sullivan comes at epidermal politics from another angle in his discussion of "maintaining the integrity of the skin" and the policing of "self-neglect" in the rehab ward (36).

8. On "demarcation," I am again inspired by Bryan Wagner's work,

encapsulated in the title of his dissertation: "Disturbing the Peace: Black Vagrancy and the Culture of Racial Demarcation."

9. A variety of factors deterred those identified as feeble from boarding passenger cars at all, including, of course, problems of economic means and physical access. In the years before establishment of on-board diners, "the old and infirm," according to Mencken, "were barred from eating [at meal stop concessions] at any time," presumably because of the dangers of stampeding passengers rushing to get fed in the short time allowed. A British traveler recounting his railroad journeys in the 1850s noted, "One circumstance particularly struck me during my travels in the United States and that is that I scarcely ever saw a decrepit traveler or one suffering under severe physical infirmity" (114). Although by the 1880s railroads "were able," as Richter puts it, "to position themselves as saviors rather than destroyers of individual and national health," as purveyors of vacations and restful sightseeing, many disabled people, however privileged, were still excluded from the recuperative rails, segregated de facto if not by statute (155).

10. On division of passengers by gender, see Welke; Elizabeth Abel; and Richter. Legal ambiguities surrounding the use of "ladies' cars" led black women to bring a majority of the legal challenges to racial segregation on the rails, until Jim Crow statutes excluded them from the category of the "lady" and denied them, as Abel puts it, "the benefits of gender ideology" (447). On division of cars by class and citizenship status, see Richter.

11. Condit has argued that the "train became a mobile equivalent, a special kind of microcity moving over the ground" (x). For a summary of work relating and contrasting railroads to cities, see Richter, 14.

12. In the discourse that Stanley traces, mendicants in need of punishment are always, necessarily, "able-bodied" beggars. But those beggars' counterparts, the diseased, maimed, deformed, unsightly ones, also came in for hard labor sentencing, as I show in chapter 9, even as they were constituted as persons categorically unable to labor.

13. My thanks to Jack A. Batterson for the reference in his book that led me to this text, and even more so for his generous responses to my research questions.

14. According to Arthur Franklin Fuller, who should know (he traversed the country by railroad in a cart lying on his back), this new policy was the result of the Inter-State Commerce Law: "Before the Inter-State Commerce Law was made, sometimes a railroad conductor would carry me a few miles without collecting fare. Now I not only pay for every inch I travel, but some railroads will not carry me except I have an attendant" (*Fifty Thousand Miles*, 198).

15. On the power of conductors to assign identity and the inevitability of misidentification, see Welke, 312–313.

16. I am influenced here by Bryan Wagner's comment on southern vagrancy law: "Being vulnerable to arbitrary arrests for vagrancy, then, is something like occupying a permanent seat on a segregated train car" (10).

17. On white-over-black, see Farley.

18. See also S. Epstein, 37; Washington, 133.

19. Bardin was writing specifically of tuberculosis. See also McCord.

20. These quotations are from two important studies: Fett; and Wailoo, 14.

21. See also Bryan, 139–140. Sheila Miller provides some background on specific impairments.

22. Gornick et al. (1996), cited in Smedley, Stith, and Nelson, 74. Fett gives significant historical background for this pattern of amputation in her *Working Cures*, 28–29.

23. It is not coincidental that the first person to have three limbs amputated successfully (in an operation performed by a nineteenth-century Alabama doctor, James Buckner Luckie) was a black man, very possibly an experimental subject with no prior injury; see his photograph in Worden, 47. This historical context helps explain the intense resistance to amputation taught to interns and nurses by Daniel Hale Williams in the first American black-run hospital; see Buckler's biography of Williams.

24. See also Cresswell's succinct survey of race and arrests for vagrancy in *The Tramp in America*, 39.

25. On the whiteness of the "tramp," see Cresswell, 39. Kusmer's counterargument in *Down and Out, On the Road* is on pp. 138–140; see also 106–107.

26. Susan Ryan's discussion of black "duplicitous others," "blackface begging," the "disturbing slippage between the figure of the oppressed slave and that of the conniving beggar" (64) and the "anxious and possibly foolish whiteness" of "benevolent white Americans" (76) provides important background and an exemplary analysis of the dynamics that I describe here. It is worth noting that Fitzhugh's infamous defense of slavery *Cannibals All* (1852) reprints an article from the *Edinburgh Review* of that same year describing the nefarious ways of faker beggars (here called "Lurkers"), including "The Sick Lurk" and "The Deaf and Dumb Lurk." Fitzhugh's point was that the problem of the pauper could be solved only by the beneficent controls of slavery. But from there it is a short slide to the "ex-slave lurk" and the duped abolitionist or clueless Northern almsgiver.

27. Du Bois, for instance, indicted racial discrimination within the organized charity movement: "Fifty-nine of the charities mentioned in the Civic Club Digest discriminate against colored persons." Some did so covertly, a practice that Du Bois argued was "very unjust, for it makes it seem as though the Negro had more help than he does. . . . the managers of many of these enterprises find it by far the easiest method silently to draw the color line." At the same time, Du Bois indicted Negro beggars and the charities that he saw as reinforcing their position: "Of direct almsgiving, the most questionable and least organized sort of charity, the Negroes receive probably far more than their just proportion, as a study of the work of the great distributing societies clearly shows. On the other hand, protective, rescue and reformatory work is not applied to any great extent among them" (356–357).

28. See also Roderick Ferguson's discussion of "the intersection of the black and the nonblack" neighborhoods in Chicago, 40–41. Enforced ugly law might effectively bar access by disabled people to the sex districts that Mumford describes, to the extent that those places were understood to be "public" thoroughfares.

29. Susan Nussbaum's play *No One as Nasty* explores complexities of race and class dynamics within disabled employer/personal-care-assistant relationships in the contemporary context.

30. On whiteness and disability, and the whiteness of disability studies, see C. Bell.

31. As in Roediger's famous *The Wages of Whiteness.*

32. Indeed, for Browne, writing in 1869, unsightly begging was inevitably done in the company of attendants: "The sick and crippled are attended, *of course,* by someone who does the talking and describes the woe. And this companion of misfortune is either a relative of the afflicted or an employe [*sic*] who receives a proportion of the receipts for his services" (459).

33. The presence of companions for the African American disabled people who begged reflects a continuity with the "relational vision of health" in plantation slave communities that Fett has traced. See also Stack's classic *All Our Kin.*

34. Uzzel discusses the high percentage of blindness among blues singers.

35. Quoted in Uzzel, 23. My thanks to Leroy Moore for pointing me to "Tin Cup Blues" and opening up the subject of blind black blues tradition in relation to the ugly laws.

36. Similar cultural work was performed in the tradition, frequently directly linked to blues music, of African American pegleg dancing by amputees (often hoboes), whose vestiges in the late twentieth century are well captured in Davenport's documentary film on dancer/musician Peg Leg Sam Jackson, *Born for Hard Luck.*

37. *Cleveland Directory of Charities and Social Work,* 60–61. On referral to Associated Charities, see "Hark, Hark, the Dogs Do Bark."

38. The variant spellings of the policeman's name are in the original. Three articles in the *Chicago Tribune* list his name as Leon Orlowski ("Arrests Beggar for 28th Time"; "Loop Beggar Arrested"; Lurie).

NOTES TO CHAPTER 9

1. "A Philosophy of Handicap" is the 1913 title, replacing the earlier "The Handicapped"; I have chosen to refer to it by the later title both because it reflects Bourne's final authorial intention and because it is by far the more interesting name. See Longmore and Miller for a full discussion of Bourne's revisions and their implications.

2. ADAPT is an acronym both for American Disabled for Attendant Programs

Today and Americans Disabled for Accessible Public Transit. ADAPT advocates for community-based personal assistance and accessibility on public transit and in public spaces. For ADAPT history, see Johnson and Shaw; and Caldwell and Biandi.

3. For instance, Lefebvre's contrast of the crucial "right to the city" with what he identified as a pseudo-right to nature/leisure might be placed in dialogue with his urbanist predecessor Ebenezer Howard's "Garden City," in which "asylums for the deaf and blind," "convalescent homes," and a "farm for epileptics" are placed in an agricultural zone outside the urban center, or with the plan devised by Progressive-era Cleveland city planner Cooley, who imagined a "farm colony" where "all the city's charges . . . might be cared for." "The land furnishes the largest opportunities for the aged and defective," wrote Cooley. "Upon the land the men past their prime, the crippled, the weak can always find some useful work," a task impossible, he thought, within the bounds of the industrial city. Lefebvre, 158. On Cooley's farm colony plan, see the account in the autobiography of the famous Progressive Cleveland mayor Tom L. Johnson, 175.

4. On COS attempts to block the issuing of permits, see Ringenbach and the NYCOS papers held at the Columbia University Rare Book Library.

5. Efforts to close the peddling escape valve occurred in many different quarters. Like the Italian leaders in Chicago who pressed the city to ban fruit peddling by Italians, some Deaf leaders not only publicly repudiated but called for sanctions against peddling and begging. A note bemoaning deaf vagrant peddling printed in the *American Annals of the Deaf and Dumb* in 1859 came with the following editorial preface: "We are happy to say that the educated deaf-mutes do as a body thoroughly disapprove of the vagrant course of life to which a few of their number addict themselves" (Chamberlyne, 237). See also Gannon, 255–259; *Deaf Mute's Journal,* Mar. 24 and Mar. 27, 1899; and Burch, 149–155. As national Deaf organizations developed, ostracism of deaf peddlers by deaf educators and leaders intensified. "In 1913, for example," Robert Buchanan writes, "some leaders in the NAD [National Organization of the Deaf] favored making it a crime for deaf adults to 'ask for assistance on account of deafness'" (Buck, x). Buchanan's foreword to Buck (2000) notes of contemporary U.S. culture, "Indeed, it may be as accurate to say that among many deaf adults, the term peddler is as much epithet as occupation" (Buck, xv). But peddling did not entirely cease, as Buck's account illustrates and airport travelers importuned to buy trinkets can attest. Buck's autobiography is a rich resource on the history and ethics of deaf peddling. See also the representation of the deaf peddler/beggar character and the controversies he causes among members of a "Metro Club of the Deaf" (circa 1980) in Bragg and Bergman's Deaf theater production *Tales from a Clubroom,* which includes lines like the following: "We respect him because he always fools the hearies. They always take advantage of the deaf, but that peddler, a deafie, takes advantage of them for a change" (37–38).

6. Gravell's story is contained in the records of proceedings against lawyer Charles Thatcher, who accompanied him around Lucas County in Ohio in their campaign against the judge; see 80 Ohio St. 492, 89 N.E. 39, 7 Ohio Law Rep. 116, 23.

7. The "National Association" here is Forbes's Association for the Prevention of Mendicancy and Charitable Imposture, formed after Forbes broke with the COS; for the history of his dismissal, see the as yet unpublished work of Rebekah Edwards.

8. "Legless Newsboy Sues"; *Gray v. Forbes*; Forbes and McBee.

9. I am grateful to Simon Stern for his invaluable help with this section on the pertinent legal record. All errors are, of course, my own.

10. As Longmore puts it, "whether local ordinances banned or allowed alms seeking, all regarded cripples as natural beggars" (2003, 58).

11. A recent dissent by Judge Norris in the record of *Roulette v. City of Seattle* (1996) does make a possible case for reading some kinds of impairment in a related context as street expression protected by the First Amendment. The case involved a First Amendment facial challenge (rejected by the Ninth Circuit Court of Appeals) to a Seattle ordinance prohibiting sitting or lying on the sidewalk. Norris argued for the "possibility that a beggar's message is dramatized by sitting," quoting a ruling by Judge Wilken in the case of *Berkeley Community Health Project v. City of Berkeley*: "One message which may be communicated by the act of sitting on the sidewalk is the message that the solicitor is in serious need . . . [and] too weak, ill, or defeated by circumstances to stand" (*Roulette,* 97 F. 3d at 314–315). Norris warns that under the court's ruling "an unsightly beggar symbolizing the failure of our society to achieve economic justice may not sit, even to add power and content to his message" (*Roulette,* 97 F. 3d at 316).

12. As I understand it, the term *expressive conduct* came out of *Tinker v. Des Moines School District* (1968), which recognized that high school students were entitled to wear black arm bands to protest the Vietnam War. Fordham has recently argued that freak-show or sideshow displays of disabled bodies are and should be understood as protected expressive conduct.

13. The court here applies one of the "counterfactual schemes" that Best has shown were "common to turn of the century equal protection law, . . . those interrupted itineraries (between cause and effect, past and present) that spawn scenarios characterized by alternative chronologies, historical contingency, and fictive suppositions" (218). Here, as in the cases involving racial segregation analyzed by Best, counterfactualism provided "that 'fuzzy logic' that enabled the courts to imagine a separate-but-equal (alternative and parallel) universe" (227).

14. This kind of rhetoric, in which the court demonstrably steels itself against its sentimental impulses, occurs too in a case in Columbus in which a man argued that his blindness should exempt him from begging prohibitions: "As an expression of human kindness, society may be reluctant to exclude the worthy

blind from begging when in distress or in need, but . . . [i]f it is legal for a blind person to beg, it is legal for any person to beg, and if all are permitted to beg social conditions sink to the level of the tribe, our institutions disintegrate, and the government fails in those purposes for which it is organized" (*Lefever,* 23 Ohio N.P. (N.C.) at 374.

15. On the kind of grueling work that Thompson was forced to perform, see Stanley 1992, 1278.

16. The Act of April 30, 1879 (P.L. 33), titled "To define and punish tramps," specifies clearly in the fifth section, in language echoing the Philadelphia city ordinance passed two years earlier, "This act shall not apply . . . to any blind, deaf, or dumb person, nor shall it be applicable to any maimed or crippled person who is unable to perform manual labor" (*Laws of the General Assembly,* 1879).

17. It appears that Thomson's lawyer, John N. Landberg, ran unsuccessfully as a Socialist candidate for the Pennsylvania Congress in 1914 and was barred in the late 1930s after being convicted for fraud against securities dealers. He self-published a book called *Social Dramas,* which I have not seen; there is a copy in the Library of Congress. Thanks to Simon Stern for these leads on Landberg.

18. See also Hartman, 138.

19. In the landmark Supreme Court case of *Cleburne v. Cleburne Living Center, Inc.* (1985), which involved neighborhood opposition to the licensing of a group home for cognitively disabled people, the Court rejected this kind of NIMBYism. But on the ambiguous implications for disabled people of *Cleburne,* Hahn provides an important note of caution (2003, 40–41).

20. Merrifield's analysis of the concept of representational space in Lefebvre is pertinent here.

NOTES TO CHAPTER 10

1. Works that provide both history and theory of the "rehabilitation approach" include Stiker's important discussion, 121–190; McRuer, 110–116; Snyder and Mitchell's eloquent challenge in CLD; and the critique of traditional rehabilitation by DeJong, 20–24. Byrom writes, "War, progressive 'child-saving' efforts, charity reform, workman's compensation laws, and a general concern for social justice all played a role in the development of the rehabilitation movement. As the movement gained momentum in the 1910's, orthopedic surgeons gradually came to dominate the movement. Yet, at its outset the rehabilitation movement was driven as much by medical laymen as doctors and other medical professionals—individuals inspired to action by the public presence of disabled beggars more so than any other single cause" (2001, 3–4).

2. "[A] group of internationally oriented professionals in the Cleveland area" was hard at work on disability issues by the early 1920s," Groce writes. "In 1922 in the nearby town of Elyria, Ohio, Edgar Allen had founded an organization

initially called the International Society for Crippled Children. This would eventually give rise to two organizations: the National Easter Seals society and what is today Rehabilitation International" (Groce 1996, 7). Although she was not involved in the Cripple Survey, leading rehabilitationist Bell Greve was based in Cleveland (see Groce 1996). At the same time, Cleveland was a model in the development and charity and innovative municipal organization. Both the first Community Chest and the first Community Foundation developed in Cleveland (Tuennerman-Kaplan, 5). On Cleveland disability history, see H. Lewis.

3. As the Cleveland Hospital Council put it, "The experiences and triumphs of orthopedic surgery during the war have opened the eyes of the laity and of the medical profession to the infinite possibilities for human salvage, for prevention of deformity and dependency, and for the re-establishment of function in those disabled in the spinal column or in the extremities, such possibilities having been in the past hardly conceived of outside of a few groups of leaders in the profession" (Cleveland Hospital Council, 197). The progress in the approach to disabled soldiers was, however, uneven; in World War II, burned American pilots were sometimes met with open public demands that they be "kept on their own grounds and off the streets" (Valentine).

4. The first meeting of the group took place on October 23, 1913 (Western Reserve Child Welfare Council, minutes of the meeting). They were particularly concerned about the problem(s) of what they called "double defectives"—the exclusion from the State Institute for the Feeble Minded of children who were crippled or blind (Western Reserve Child Welfare Council, "Work Done for Children in the City of Cleveland"; see also container 1, folder 1, in the same archive for other in-house documents pertaining to the survey). Accounts vary as to who instigated this meeting. By some accounts it was initiated by Mrs. E.M. Williams, who was president of the Sunbeam Circle for the Practical Education and Training of Cripples. The Sunbeam Circle (later the Sunbeam Association) ran a hospital school for crippled children as well as sheltered employment workshops primarily for girls and young disabled women. See "Crippled Girls Learn to Sew"; and "Crippled Julia Gets New Start: Alien Girl, After Operation on Foot, Studies to Become Self-Supporting." Mrs. Williams's husband, a well-known industrialist and philanthropist, eventually became chairman of the ensuing Committee on Cripples. According to historian William Ganson Rose, Alpha Robbins (Mrs. Ray S. Gehr), who went on to become the executive secretary of the Association for the Crippled and Disabled in Cleveland (an organization formed in response to the Cripple Survey), originally suggested that a survey be conducted (759). Robbins did not attend the initial meeting, however, and I have found no other corroboration of Rose's version. The Sunbeam Circle was the major funder for the survey effort. See the papers of the Western Reserve Child Welfare Council, Container 1, Folders 4 and 5. For background on survey planning, see also the Cleveland Federation for Charity and Philanthropy Papers (MSS. 3788, Container

8, Folders 190 and 193) at the Western Reserve Historical Society, Cleveland, Ohio; Cleveland Federation for Charity and Philanthropy, *The Social Year Book,* 145; Kaiser, 161–169; and "New Chance for Cripples in Study Just Begun," 1. On the broader genre of the social survey, see Bulmer, Boles, and Kish Sklar; A. O'Connor (39); and on African American surveying of "cripples in Harlem," see "Urban League Interested." Halle Lewis provides a good general background on the Cleveland survey specifically, 201–202.

5. On "we" and the "politics of pronouns," see Garland Thomson's foreword to M. Mason, x.

6. Consider how troubling the conjunction of disability and work is in the following formulation. The *New York World,* in 1916, covered the new rehabilitationism: "Work for the Infirm Proves a Great Boon." A boon, yes, but a puzzling one: "One of the strangest inducements to the infirm to learn some kind of handiwork," reported an astonished reporter, "is the money received for the result of their labor." I confess that I have also labored under this strange inducement.

7. I have omitted the word "racial" in this passage to make a more general point, but that omission obviously elides a great deal of complex differences and similarities between northern and southern vagrancy laws, antitramp discourses, constructions of the beggar, and spatial practices; Wagner's work focuses on the South, but see his discussion of differences in rhetoric and political economy between the two regions on p. 109.

8. The account in the Cleveland survey leaves no doubt that there was a version of ugly law in place there: "the enforcement of the statute which prevented cripples from exposing their deformity by selling on street corners abolished this man's job" (222). I have been unable to verify the existence of a pertinent ordinance in the extant municipal law books between 1880 and 1918, and the old city council records were unavailable during my research stint in Cleveland. Either the law was published in a volume of ordinances I have been unable to locate or the "statute" to which the survey refers was enforced through some less formal mechanism; if the latter case holds true, it raises the possibility that other cities had ugly policies that left no trace in the municipal records.

9. The famous biography of the Gilbreths by their children, *Cheaper by the Dozen,* not only does not mention Frank B. Gilbreth's disability and extended hospitalization but also actively presents him—until the final surprise twist when he dies young—as a kind of counterinvalid who will not allow himself or his children to be ill and who emphasizes his and their hearty "pioneer stock." In fact, many of Gilbreth's children had been born before he was hit hard by rheumatism at the outset of World War I, only a short time before this article was published. In a preface to the Gilbreths' *Motion Study for the Handicapped* (1920), W.O. Owen offers his account of Gilbreth's hospitalization: "One of the most interesting experiences of my life was to go to this Hospital [Walter Reed] and see this man bedridden, utterly unable to move any single joint in his entire body without

pain, scarcely able to move at all, his mind working all the time with some new problem, questioning me concerning my work, making suggestions as to better methods. . . . The last thing on his mind was his own physical condition" (vii). The Gilbreths' work on motion study for the handicapped, continued by Lillian after Frank's death, no doubt drew in part on their personal experience of this episode.

10. Titchkosky (2007) analyzes present-day versions of the successful individual narrative (which she calls "the story of the abled-disabled individual"); see especially 207 and the entire chapter "Overcoming: Abled-Disabled and Other Acts of Normative Violence," which includes a discussion of the "look beyond" rhetoric of the Cleveland survey's "man behind" formulation.

11. Moylan is listed as a judge in the Cleveland municipal court in Avery, 1:447.

12. Here again we can read Bowe's 1978 introduction of disability rights to the mainstream as a direct counter to the Cleveland survey. "Just as we cannot seem to see the man *in* the policeman," Bowe writes (italics mine), "so imposing are the uniform and the cultural expectations that go with it, so we cannot see the woman in the wheelchair" (ix). This artful and conciliatory example of 1970s rhetoric also throws a wrench of sorts in ugly law, allying rather than opposing policing and disability.

13. Halle Lewis notes that the survey was "essentially a dialogue between reformers and disabled Clevelanders" (198); I take this moment in the text as a central part of that dialogue.

14. Cleveland women were heavily involved in initiating and following up on the results of the survey, including the officers of the Sunshine Circle (especially Mary Raymond Williams), the civic leader Belle Sherwin, Clara Sherwin of Rainbow Cottage, Selma Sullivan, and later Alpha Robbins (Gehr) and Bell Greve. Although men (J.H. Garfield of the Child Welfare Council, Edward M. Williams, and Allen T. Burns) took on high-profile roles to garner approval of and publicize the survey effort, the bulk of the work most likely was done by women.

15. See Byrom 2004 for a related discussion of the narrative of the newspaper seller. The move into the doorway in order to get around ugly law was not unique to this man. Arthur Fuller, whose work I treat at length in chapter 11, describes his identical strategy in Denver, sometime between 1915 and 1919. Fuller's mood is far less cheerful: noting sardonically that the arch over the entrance to the *Denver Post* building was carved with "O Justice! When exiled from other climes, come find a welcome here," he wrote, "Could not but reflect that if a little of said justice had been accorded me, I would not have had such a struggle, dodging police, . . . would likely not have had that sick spell as I could then have chosen my place of selling and not had to go into that dirty, dark, unsunned hole I was obliged to sell from" (*Wrestling the Wolf*, 13).

16. Fellow "street operator" Arthur Franklin Fuller describes Leroy and press

coverage of Leroy in his 1919 *Wrestling the Wolf,* 81. It is an anxious and defensive depiction, driven, one senses, by nervousness about Leroy as a kind of supercrip favored by the newspapers. Fuller comments on the press's change of heart toward Leroy, who he implies truly is well off and "has pull."

17. "The establishment of a Municipal Charities Commission authorized to examine solicitors of alms, or beggars as they are sometimes called, and to issue permits only to worthy and meritorious persons may relieve housewives from the appeal of an I.W.W. who rings the front door bell" ("Permits for Beggars"). On Mexicans, see Municipal Charities Commission, *First Annual Report,* 67. On ordinances blocking Wobbly access to the streets, see Rabban.

18. On the Brave Poor Things organized by Sister Grace Kimmins, described as a "social union of the crippled, the deformed, the blind, and the partially paralyzed," see Booth, 205; Vicinus, 66; and Stoddard Holmes, 26.

19. The nod to the title of the famous black feminist manifesto is tongue-in-cheek and deliberate: *All the Women Are White, All the Men Are Black, but Some of Us Are Brave.* By this reference I do not mean to assert that black women were necessarily part of the "strangest union"; the gender of its members (aside from male) is uncertain, as is its racial composition, though almost certainly it was dominated by white men. If being "brave" is what happens at any site of marginalized and intersecting identity, then the model of politicized "bravery" may extend beyond its partially figurative substitution for the words "black women." The bravery claimed by a "some of us" always differs in meaning from the bravery imposed on the "poor thing" from outside, as in "be brave."

20. Tremain reflects a common understanding of disability history when she writes, "Beginning in the Great Depression, and over the last thirty years in particular, people classified as 'handicapped' or 'disabled' have developed sociopolitical conceptions of disability to counter medicalized approaches" (2005, 1). A case can be made that the "strangest league" offers one example (there may be others, maybe even many others) of sociopolitical organizing in a modern mode predating the 1930s. Arthur Franklin Fuller's work (see chapter 11) certainly represents such an understanding.

21. *Harper's Magazine,* Sept. 1883, 634/2, cited in the OED. The language of the clearinghouse shows up repeatedly in COS literature, as in an example from an essay on charity association as the application of business principles to charity work, in which the Associated Charities is described as "a department store," a "Dun's or Bradstreet's," "a popular militia," a "trust," and, yes, a "clearinghouse" of charity (Marquis).

22. *Daily Chronicle,* Dec. 10, 1903, 6/7, cited in the OED.

23. For background, see "Army's Forced to Surrender."

24. See also "No Cheer for Fake Mutes" and "Makes Him Talk," both in the *Los Angeles Times,* 1915.

25. Linker writes, "unlike eugenicists who wanted to sterilize the unfit and

legislate the removal of 'defectives' from city streets, orthopedists did not shun men with permanent disfigurements. . . . Indeed, their professional survival relied on a steady population of people who would either be born with physical deformities or acquire them in adulthood" (101). Two orthopedic surgeons quoted by Linker argued in a 1916 AMA journal that they could turn "boastful, consuming, idle derelicts" into "happy, productive, wage earning citizens" (103).

NOTES TO CHAPTER 11

1. Mark Willis has commented eloquently on the painful and ironic conjunction of these two aspects of Holmes's legal theory.

2. "Mendicant pieces are books and pamphlets written by handicapped or penniless persons, usually telling their life story, and peddled by them to earn a living," writes Robert G. Hayman, quoted at the beginning of the Schoyer's Books catalogue. Schoyer's books (now Marc Selvaggio Books) works out of Berkeley, California; the collection by Marc Selvaggio at Schoyer Books of American Mendicant Literature is now housed in the rare book room of the Countway. I am indebted to Selvaggio for his scholarship and dedication in amassing this remarkable collection, and also to Peter Brigham Howard for alerting me to the existence of the collection at Harvard. On mendicant literature, the usual source is Cumming. Fabian devotes a chapter to mendicant writing and self-publishing in the United States in the early nineteenth century, exploring what can be learned, in that historical context, "by exploring connections between behavior so socially marginal as begging and behavior so culturally central as writing" (12).

3. The Schoyer's Books catalogue of the collection was subdivided by impairment category. Harvard now catalogues the collection with subject headings that point to both disability and begging.

4. Selling one's own writing from the position of the "author" could function as a way of deflecting the label of "peddler" as well as that of "beggar." So, for instance, Charles Waddell, who was in no way marked as disabled, legally challenged his obligation to pay for a peddling license in order to sell his book (probably the race-purity tract *Race Problem*) on the street (and lost his case). *Conway v. Waddell* (1909).

5. The Schoyer's Books collection contains multiple examples of the "Blind Man's Appeal," deaf peddling, and "Good Luck to the Purchaser. Souvenir of the Cripple" cards.

6. Commenting on the rise in published life writing by disabled people coincident with the flowering of the disability rights movement in the late twentieth century, Couser notes that such autobiography "should be seen, then, not as spontaneous 'self-expression' but as a response—indeed a retort—to the traditional misrepresentation of disability," a retort produced by and within a very particular historical context (2006, 400). Though the traces of disability mendicant

literature are very small compared with the contemporary "disability renaissance" that Couser addresses here, they also represent a historically specific response and retort.

7. The two "sets" of writings are not parallel but intersectional. Harriet Wilson's *Our Nig*—a novel, but a text with strong connections to life writing and slave narrative—was shopped to the publisher with an appeal very much in the terms of disabled mendicancy: "Deserted by kindred, disabled by failing health, I am forced to some experiment which shall aid me in maintaining myself and child without extinguishing this feeble life" (2).

8. On obstacles to the very existence of disability autobiography, see Couser (1997), on whom Bérubé is drawing, especially p. 183.

9. "[O]ne can see why autobiography is a particularly important form of life writing about disability," writes Couser. "[W]ritten from inside the experience in question, it involves self-representation by definition. . . . With particularly severe or debilitating conditions, particularly those affecting the mind or the ability to communicate, the very existence of first-person narratives makes its own point: that people with condition 'X' are capable of self-representation" (2006, 400–401). Begging and impoverishment may be seen as particularly severe and debilitating condition X's. In his earlier *Recovering Bodies,* Couser writes, "Written self-representation may appeal especially to disabled people precisely because, by shifting the grounds of interaction, it offers an alternative to what sociologists call the 'low-power' scripts of everyday interaction" (1997, 216).

10. Cummings was a Civil War veteran but not war injured. His pamphlets were apparently popular, since many copies are extant today. Cumming suggests in his survey of mendicant literature that thirty-five thousand copies of this text sold between 1866 and 1887.

11. "[D]eviations from bodily norms often provoke a demand for explanatory narrative in everyday life. Whereas the unmarked case—the 'normal' body—can pass without narration, the marked case—the scar, the limp, the missing limb, or the obvious prosthesis—calls for a story. . . . people with anomalous bodies are often called upon to account for them sometimes quite explicitly: they may be asked, 'What happened to you?'" (Couser 2006, 400).

12. This text took the form of a begging letter; the copy at the Countway was mailed to a woman in Vermont, who was asked to return it if she did not want to pay for it. Begging letters as often as not were signed by men, but women like Smith could stamp the form in properly feminine mode, underscoring their shrinking from public display.

13. Writing in 1907, Herbert O. Kohr both certified his own temperance and warned other disabled peddlers that Philadelphia city-dwellers were not buying: "There seems to be a great deal of trouble with crippled men who sell articles in the city. Many of them drink and carouse, thus making it difficult for those who do not" (197). He also counseled against visiting Altoona and Pittsburgh. A few

years later, Arthur Franklin Fuller, who had traveled across the country selling his writing on the streets, cautioned readers with mobility impairments to avoid San Francisco—"the sidewalks are twisted and uneven from the earthquake"—but recommended a nearby city: "in Berkeley, people were so kind and good I seldom spent as much as $1 per week while there. Even boys who wheeled me quite a ways, did not charge for their help" (*Fifty Thousand Miles*, 233, 214).

14. See, for instance, Uriah Hagans's objection to being forced to make brooms in the blind home shop instead of studying music (18, 22); Harvey A. Fuller's extended critique of institutionalization; and B.B. Bowen's call for education instead of institutionalization, his reversal of the charges of fraud in accusation of fraudulent charity organization, and his strenuous critique of the dynamics of deformance.

15. "Sly civility" is Bhabha's concept.

16. Bradford Verter, prospectus for the "Subterranean Lives: Chronicles of Alternative America" book series of "first-person accounts by members of oppositional or stigmatized subcultures" at Rutgers University Press.

17. I am alluding here to Spivak's landmark essay on the subaltern, in which "speech" at its most urgent is bodily, nonverbal, the story told by a woman's menstrual period: "Bhubanesari attempted to 'speak,'" Spivak writes, "by turning her [menstruating] body into a text of woman/writing" (308). So, too, the exposed bodies of the subjects of ugly law "spoke." The tracks of sexual difference in the archive of the Countway, and the specific situation of the woman/cripple/writing, are too complex to explore in this context and must be my subject elsewhere.

18. Fuller also appears in "Genius of Mendicants," *Los Angeles Times* (1916). Fuller appends to *Odd Soldiery* testimonies to his character, some of which, he claims, were published in newspapers, such as this one by F.P. Griffith in the *Riverside Daily Press* (1914): "There are many brave souls struggling under life's heaviest handicaps to . . . maintain their individuality as citizens. And great and prosperous cities through the agency of their associated charities . . . bid them begone from the streets. . . . Is it not time that we have a different point of view? Mr. Fuller's 50,000 miles, traveled on his back, will not have been in vain if we can help his fellow countrymen to attain it" (153–154).

19. Compare the claims to national identity in the post–Revolutionary War mendicant writers Fabian discusses.

20. Fuller's decision not to challenge the law in court may be compared to a principle of the Wobblies, who were often arrested during this same period for various offenses closely tied to ugly law (such as begging, vagrancy, and sidewalk obstruction) and who were also the direct targets of Los Angeles's Municipal Charities Commission (see "Permits for Beggars"). Rabban notes that Wobblies "rarely sought appellate review of their convictions in part because they lacked

sufficient financial resources, but primarily because they preferred the pressure of direct action over recourse to a legal system they ridiculed as a tool of the employing class" (82).

NOTES TO THE CONCLUSION

1. I am indebted here to Paul Longmore, who noted to me, after reading a draft of this conclusion, that on the Supreme Court's *Tennessee v. Lane* case the *New York Times* editorialized in favor of Lane on the grounds that inaccessible courthouses were "insensitive" (not unjust).

2. *Ableism* and *disablism* are often used interchangeably in disability theory; to some extent the choice between the two is governed by national linguistic differences (*ableism* seems to me to be the term of choice in the United States). Arguably, there are ideological implications in the difference between the two words—Sherry and the late Mairian Corker have suggested that the use of *ableism* obscures the range of disabilities that are not conventionally understood as "physical" (e.g., sensory, cognitive, or psychiatric disabilities)—but I have not been persuaded by the argument.

3. The independent living movement did not originate in this center but closer to Chicago, at the University of Illinois at Urbana-Champaign. After World War II, the campus, under the leadership of Tim Nugent, developed accessible housing and transportation services for disabled veterans. But Berkeley's Center for Independent Living, and (but not only) its charismatic leader Ed Roberts, played an important role in articulating a model for the principles and practices of "independent living."

4. Scotch provides a thorough discussion of these developments, as do the oral histories in the Bancroft Library's "Disability Rights and Independent Living" series. See also Shapiro; R. Johnson; R. Shaw; Barnartt and Scotch; Zames and Fleischer. Pimentel et al. make direct links between the ADA and the ugly law in the first line of their book: "Perhaps the best way to put the ADA in perspective is to examine the following ordinance" (1).

5. According to Pimental et al., the Omaha ordinance was also repealed, in 1976, "after lobbying efforts by the Easter Seals Society and upon advice from the city prosecutor that similar ordinances had been found unconstitutional by the United States Supreme Court" (1). As Robert Burgdorf Jr. suggested to me, presumably the Supreme Court reference is to the decision in *Papachristou v. City of Jacksonville* (1972), in which Justice Douglas authored a decision striking down a vagrancy law and used strong language condemning many such laws, particularly for criminalizing activities that are "normally innocent." I have not yet been able to verify this account of an Omaha repeal campaign, with its intriguing suggestion of late-twentieth-century organized charity mobilizing to reverse the ugly

law, but Pimentel, a disability activist, would have been well-placed to know about such activity, and the response seems likely in the wake of the publicity around the Omaha arrest two years earlier. A filmic biography of Pimentel released as this book goes to press, *The Music Within,* suggests that Pimentel's disability activism began with his own arrest, with his friend Arthur Honeyman, for refusing to comply with the ugly law after being ordered to leave a restaurant in Portland, Oregon, in 1971. If the story is true, it suggests that the Omaha arrest may not have been as anomalous as first appears. As a cultural myth, the episode compactly locates the origin of 1970s disability activism in outrage at the ugly law.

6. See also "Facial Discrimination." Recent academic discussions of "lookism" outside legal journals have tended to focus on the other American law that gets called "ugly law," the 1992 Santa Cruz city ordinance prohibiting discrimination against persons on the basis of "personal appearance." Political theorist Wendy Brown (and following her, legal theorist Robert Post) influentially (and productively, for their broader intellectual purposes) misrepresented this ordinance as the "purple hair ordinance," but the ordinance is given a far more careful and accurate analysis by Krieger in "Sociolegal Backlash" in her edited volume *Backlash against the* ADA. As I complete this book in February 2008, three Mississippi state legislators have just introduced a bill whose dynamics of appearance discrimination mark it as a direct descendent of the ugly laws, House Bill No. 282: "Any food establishment to which this section applies shall not be allowed to serve food to any person who is obese, based on criteria prescribed by the State Department of Health" (Pasquale).

7. On appearance impairment, see Beuf; Dion; the work of Kmiecek, Mauser, and Banzinger; Pillavin et al.; Berry. See also the important, pioneering work of MacGregor, the first scholar to construct disfigurement as disability, particularly her 1951 essay "Some Psycho-Social Problems Associated with Facial Deformities" ("It is the aesthetic aspect alone which makes the problems of the facial cripple unique"), which concluded in an early version of proto-disability-studies scholarship, "the problems associated with facial deformities . . . are not those of the handicapped individuals alone, but are of equal importance for the nonhandicapped. . . . It is to be hoped that the time is not too distant when the public, through education, will understand more fully the plight of one who has a marred or atypical face, and will not add to his difficulties either by rejection or by unsought sympathy" (630, 638). The number of studies published on this issue in the 1970s suggests another important context for the Burgdorfs' naming of "ugly" law.

8. Putzi analyzes a variety of pertinent examples in nineteenth-century literary representation, particularly the representation of the disfigured woman.

9. As Hahn puts it in his discussion of the "aesthetic anxiety" that disability can engender: "Paternalistic sentiments, which pervade interactions between

disabled and nondisabled people, usually seem to inhibit the examination of these feelings. In general, such emotions tend to produce aversion rather than verbal or open expression of prejudice. Yet avoidance is also a form of segregation and discrimination" (1985, 307). On certain websites, though, there are few holds barred. As I write, the website www.uglypeople.com—a site whose sole purpose is to post pictures of "ugly people"—includes several photographs of people with Down Syndrome. Someone wrote in to complain; here is that letter, posted on the site, and the reply: "Hi, this is not intended to be hate mail, I just have a concern. I think your site is hilarious. I just don't like that you have a few people with Downs Syndrome on it. I used to babysit a child who had Downs Syndrome and I would really appreciate it if you took their pictures off of your site. There aren't very many of them so I don't think it would be a great loss. Otherwise keep the funny pictures coming!" The answer: "Thank you for your consideration. We are considering removing the images of children with Downs Syndrome per your request. We haven't fully decided yet. . . . I think it would help my case if you were to send us a picture of the little retard you used to babysit. While you're at it, why don't you send me your picture too. You know . . . for the full scenario."

10. Here is one example. A professional in the field of "The Child in the Health Care Setting," Betty Wilson has been director of Child Life Services in two large hospitals and has worked as a specialist in a large pediatric practice. When she decided to do some volunteer work with hospitalized kids, three hospitals turned her down on the grounds that her face would frighten the children. (Wilson underwent major facial reconstructive surgery rebuilding a jaw that had deteriorated as the result of a bone implant she had received years earlier during surgery for cancer.) A report on Wilson's "case" in a journal for mediators gives voice to Wilson's response to others' responses to her "unsightliness." In the place of the negative intersubjectivity embodied by the ugly law—the worst prejudices one inherits by interacting with others, the self-loathing that can come from thinking through the eyes of others—Wilson offers a model of working toward an open, productive subjectivity built up from communal relations: "Betty finds that children's reaction to her is not fear or avoidance. In her 30 years of experience living with this face, she finds that children tend to be openly curious and concerned that her face hurts. If they are staring, she often reassures them. . . . She then changes the subject to focus on the child and says something like: 'Are those new red shoes?'—teaching the child something that many adults don't seem to understand: that she is not thinking of her face and that she lives a normal, interesting personal and professional life" (*Dispute Resolution Magazine*). Wilson heads an activist support group called Let's Face It; the name of the group in itself stares down ugly law.

11. On the rational bias theory underlying this kind of argument, see Berry.

12. The Positive Exposure project by collaborators Rick Guidotti, a former

fashion photographer, and Diane McLean, viewable on the Web at http:///www.positiveexposure.org, effectively enacts this greeting, using photography and video interviews to "challenge the stigma associated with difference and celebrate the richness of genetic variation." See also Sutton et al. Thanks to Natalie Abbott for pointing me to this site.

13. On greeting, see Levinas 1981, 117, and Iris Marion Young's discussion of this passage in *Inclusion and Democracy*, 58–59.

BIBLIOGRAPHY

THE ORDINANCE IN CITY RECORDS

CHICAGO

The Municipal Code of Chicago: Comprising the Laws of Illinois Relating to the City of Chicago, and the Ordinances of the City Council. 1881. Law #1612, p. 377.

Brundage, Edward, Howard W. Hayes, and George E. Dierssen. *The Chicago Code of 1911.* Chicago: Callaghan and Company, 1911. 643–645.

COLUMBUS

Annual Report of the City Clerk to the City Council of the City of Columbus, Columbus, Ohio, for the Year Ending December 31, 1894. Columbus: Westbote, 1896. 8. "An Ordinance—No. 8191, Section 15." Passed Jan. 22, 1894.

Doane, John M., ed. *Ordinances of the City of Columbus, Ohio.* Columbus: Westbote, 1896. 112.

The Code of the City of Columbus, Ohio, 1952. Charlottesville, Va.: Michine City Publications, 1952. 504.

DENVER

Hersey, Henry J. *Compiled Ordinances and Charter, The City of Denver.* Denver: Smith-Brooks, 1898.

Denver Police Department. *Denver Police Handbook.* 1899.

LINCOLN

City of Lincoln. "History of the Lincoln Police Department." http://lincoln.ne.gov/city/police/about/lpdhis.htm.

MANILA

Annual Report, War Department, of the Governor General of the Philippine Islands. Washington, D.C.: Government Printing Office, 1919.

NEW ORLEANS

Ordinance #5046, Mayoralty of New Orleans, City Hall, May 7, 1879, Administrative Series. When I viewed this it was archived at the New Orleans Public Library.

Jewell, Edwin L. *Jewell's Digest of the City Ordinances . . . of the City of New Orleans.* New Orleans: Edwin L. Jewell, 1882.

Jewell, Edwin L. *Jewell's Digest (Revised Edition) of the City Ordinances.* New Orleans: Edwin L. Jewell, 1887. 464.

OMAHA

The Revised Ordinances of the City of Omaha, Nebraska. Omaha: W.J. Connell, 1890. 347.

SAN FRANCISCO

San Francisco. *The General Orders of the Board of Supervisors.* San Francisco: Cosmopolitan Printing Company, 1869. Order No. 783 (Approved July 9, 1867).

———. *The General Orders of the Board of Supervisors.* San Francisco: Spaulding and Barbe, 1875.

———. *The General Orders of the Board of Supervisors.* San Francisco: W.M. Hinton, 1878.

THE ORDINANCE IN STATE RECORDS

CALIFORNIA

California Penal Code (1872). Title VII, Ch. 1.

PENNSYLVANIA

Laws of the General Assembly of the State of Pennsylvania, Passed at the Session of 1879, in the One Hundred and Third Year of Independence. Harrisburg: Lane S. Hart, 1879. Act No. 31, "To define and punish tramps," 33–34.

Laws of the General Assembly of the Commonwealth of Pennsylvania, Passed at the Session of 1895, in the One Hundred and Nineteenth Year of Independence. Pennsylvania: Clarence M. Busch, 1895. Act 208.

Journal of the House of Representatives of the Commonwealth of Pennsylvania. Pennsylvania: Clarence M. Busch, 1896. In the records for May 27.

TEXAS

1915 HB 52. *Texas House Journal for the 34th Legislature, Regular Session.* 177.

THE ORDINANCE IN FEDERAL RECORDS

S. Rep. No. 101-106, at 7 (1989).

MANUSCRIPT ARCHIVES

BERKELEY

Breslin, Mary Lou. Oral history in the University of California's Bancroft Library "Disability Rights and Independent Living" oral history series. Regional Oral History Office.

BUFFALO

Gurteen, Stephen Humphries. Keynote address at the fourth annual meeting of the Charity Organization Society of the City of Buffalo. In Charity Organization Society, "Compilation of Papers Relating to the Incorporation of the Charity Organization Society of the City of Buffalo." Buffalo Public Library, Special Collections.

"Proceedings at the Second Annual Meeting of the Charity Organization Society of the City of Buffalo." June 9, 1881. In Charity Organization Society, "Compilation of Papers Relating to the Incorporation of the Charity Organization Society of the City of Buffalo." Buffalo Central Public Library, Special Collections.

CHARLESTON

Boyle, W.A. Letter to Mrs. M.A. Rhett, Nov. 5, 1902. Papers of the Associated Charities Society of Charleston, S.C., South Carolina Historical Society, Charleston.

Forbes, James. Letter to Mrs. M.A. Rhett, Feb. 25, 1903. Papers of the Associated Charities Society of Charleston, S.C., South Carolina Historical Society, Charleston.

Kellogg, Paul. Letter to Mrs. M.A. Rhett, 1902. Papers of the Associated Charities Society of Charleston, S.C., South Carolina Historical Society, Charleston.

CHICAGO

Reitman, Ben. "Charities." Unpublished mss. Ben Reitman Papers, University of Illinois at Chicago Special Collections, Supplement II (Brotherhood Welfare Association Reports), n.d.

Reitman, Ben. Unpublished mss. on the "Hobo Banquet." Ben Reitman Papers, University of Illinois at Chicago Special Collections, Supplement II (Brotherhood Welfare Association Reports), n.d.

"Reitman's Social Geography." Map on bedsheet drawn at a 1910 "Outcast Night." Ben Reitman Papers, University of Illinois at Chicago Special Collections.

CLEVELAND

Cleveland Federation for Charity and Philanthropy Papers. MSS 3788, Container 8, Folders 190 and 193, Western Reserve Historical Society, Cleveland, Ohio.

Western Reserve Child Welfare Council. Minutes of meeting, Oct. 23, 1913. MSS 4632, Container 1, File 5, Western Reserve Historical Society, Cleveland, Ohio.

———. Papers regarding the 1918 report *Social Service at Home during the War Years.* Container 1, Folders 4 and 5, Western Reserve Historical Society, Cleveland, Ohio.

———. "Work Done for Children in the City of Cleveland." Container 1, Folder 1, Western Reserve Historical Society, Cleveland, Ohio.

NEW ORLEANS

Records of the Second Recorder's Court, Sept. 11, 1883. I examined these records in the city archives of the New Orleans Public Library.

Touro-Shakspeare Almshouse Minutes, 1901 (Feb. 1, 1903) and 1924 (October). When I saw these minutes, they were in Special Collections, Tulane University, New Orleans. *Note: the name appears alternately as "Shakspeare" and "Shakespeare" in various sources.*

NEW YORK CITY

"Annual Report of the Committee on Mendicancy, February 12, 1895." Community Service Society/Charity Organization Society Papers (Box 144), Columbia University Rare Book Library, New York.

Community Service Society/Charity Organization Society Papers (Box 208, "Committee on Mendicancy"), Columbia University Rare Book Library, New York.

Conlin, Peter, Chief of Police, New York City. "Special Order #2639," Feb. 2, 1897. Community Service Society/Charity Organization Papers (Box 144), Columbia University Rare Book Library, New York.

"Crude Suggested Draft by CDK [Charles D. Kellogg]." Community Service Society/Charity Organization Society Papers (Box 144), Columbia University Rare Book Library, New York.

Devery, Chief William S. General Order No. 32, Mar. 11, 1899. Community Service Society/Charity Organization Papers (Box 144), Columbia University Rare Book Library, New York.

Devine, Edward. Letter to Hon. William L. Strong, Dec. 30, 1895. Community Service Society/Charity Organization Society Papers (Box 144), Columbia University Rare Book Library, New York.

Executive Committee. Letter to Hon. William L. Strong, Dec. 30, 1895. Community Service Society/Charity Organization Society Papers (Box 144), Columbia University Rare Book Library, New York.

Forbes, James. Letter to Charles F. Weller, Aug. 31, 1906. Community Service Society/Charity Organization Society Papers (Box 108), Columbia University Rare Book Library, New York.

"Illustrative Cases" (handwritten manuscript by anonymous author). Community Service Society/Charity Organization Society Papers (Box 144, "Mendicancy—1883–1920"), Columbia University Rare Book Library, New York.

"James Grady, Jr., Mendicancy #1295" (case study). Community Service Society/Charity Organization Society Papers (Box 144), Columbia University Rare Book Library, New York.

Merrill, Charles E. Letter to E.T. Devine, Apr. 25, 1901. Community Service Society/Charity Organization Society Papers (Box 108), Columbia University Rare Book Library, New York.

Weeks, Francis. Letter to David B. Hill, June 1, 1887. Community Service Society/Charity Organization Society Papers, Columbia University Rare Book Library, New York.

SAN FRANCISCO

San Francisco Police Department. "Criminal Descriptions C 1891–1902."

COURT CASES

Matter of Haller, 3 Abb. N. Cas. 65 (1877)

Appeal of Prizer, 3 Walk. 487 Pa. (1882) (on disgusting details)

Appeal of Kost, 107 Pa. 143 (1884) (on disgusting details)

Union Pacific Railway v. Botsford, 141 U.S. 250 (1891)

Watson v. Cambridge, 157 Mass. 561 (1893)

Plessy v. Ferguson, 163 U.S. 537 (1896)

Woodstock Burying Ground Ass'n v. Hager, 68 Vt. 488 (1896)

State v. Montgomery, 92 Me. 433 (1899)

Jew Ho v. Williamson, 103 F. 10 U.S. App. (1900)

Gowen et al. v. O'Hara et al., 15 Pa. D. 753 (Pa.Com.Pl.) (1905)

Zartarian v. Billings, 204 U.S. 170 (1907)

Burnside v. Superintendent of House of Correction, 18 Pa. D. 601 (1909)

Conway v. Waddell, 90 Ark. 127 (1909)

Korzib v. Netherlands-American Steam Nav. Co., 175 F. 998, D.C.N.Y. 1910, 80 Ohio St. 492

Stotler v. Rochelle, 83 Kan. 86 (1910)

People v. Kennedy et al., 176 Mich. 15 (1913)

Thomas M. Thompson v. Superintendent of House of Correction, 58 Pa. Super. 465 (1914)

Gray v. Forbes, 167 A.D. 922152 N.Y.S. (1915)

Ex parte Dart, 172 Cal. 47 (1916)

State Ex. Rel. Beattie v. Board of Education of the City of Antigo, 169 Wisc. 231 (1919)

Lefever v. City of Columbus, 23 Ohio N.P. (N.C.) 372 (1921)

Blackman Health Resort v. City of Atlanta, 151 Ga. 507 (1921)

Commissioner of Immigration of the Port of New York v. Gottlieb, 265 U.S. 310 (1924)
Weinstein v. Wheeler, 127 Ore. 406, 413 (1928)
Marallis v. Chicago, 349 Ill. 422, 182 N.E. 394 (1932)
Farley v. Watt, 165 Okla. 6 (1933)
City of Cleveland v. Gogola, 58 N.E. 2d 101 (1944)
Galyon v. Municipal Court for the San Bernardino California Judicial District, 229 Cal. App. 2d 667 (1964)
Tinker v. Des Moines School District, 393 U.S. 503 (1968)
World Fair Freaks and Attractions v. Hodges, 267 So. 2d 817 (1972)
Papachristou v. City of Jacksonville, 405 U.S. 156 (1972)
Ulmer v. The Municipal Court, 55 Cal. App. 3d 263 (1976)
C.C.B. v. Florida, 458 So. 2d 47 (1984)
Cleburne v. Cleburne Living Center, Inc., 473 U.S. 432 (1985)
Berkeley Community Health Project v. City of Berkeley, 902 F. Supp. 1084, 1092–93 (N.D. Cal. 1995)
Roulette v. City of Seattle, 97 F. 3d 300 (1996)
University of Alabama at Birmingham Board of Trustees v. Patricia Garrett, 531 U.S. 356 (2001)
Tennessee v. Lane, 541 U.S. 509 (2004)

NEWSPAPER ARTICLES

ATLANTA

"Begging Cripples Should Be Banished." *Atlanta Constitution,* July 27, 1903, 7.
"The Passing Throng." *Atlanta Constitution,* Feb. 5, 1906.

BOSTON

"The Beggars of New York: Peculiar Methods of the Professional Mendicants." *Boston Globe,* July 27, 1886, 6.

BROOKLYN

"Due Notice." *Brooklyn Daily Eagle,* Mar. 31, 1878, 2.
"Andy Cisco: Death of the Deformed Negro Dwarf." *Brooklyn Daily Eagle,* Aug. 2, 1878, 4.
"Three Memberless Vagrants." *Brooklyn Daily Eagle,* Sept. 8, 1896, 14.
"Ridding Havana of Beggars." *Brooklyn Daily Eagle,* Oct. 30, 1898, 34.
"All Protests against Beggars Are Seasonable." *Brooklyn Daily Eagle,* Feb. 4, 1900, 18.
"Undesirable Immigrants." *Brooklyn Daily Eagle,* Aug. 25, 1901, 16.
Spacks, Clifton. "Prosperous Beggars Form a Trust to Check Rush of Pauper Mendicants." *Brooklyn Daily Eagle,* Jan. 26, 1902, 29, 33.

CHICAGO

Chicago Tribune, May 10, 1881, 3 (Carter Harrison's speech on the right to the city).
Chicago Inter Ocean, May 18, 1881, 4 (on removal of fruit stands).
Chicago Times, May 18, 1881, 6 (on Italian fruit vendors).
Chicago Tribune, May 19, 1881, 8 (on the ugly law).
Chicago Daily News, July 16, 1881, 1 (on Lawrence Jackson's arrest).
Chicago InterOcean, July 18, 1881, 8 (on Lawrence Jackson's arrest).
Chicago Tribune, May 19, 1907 (on blind organ-grinder).
"Hello! Says 'Dumb Beggar'; Cop Calls Patrol Wagon." *Chicago Tribune,* Mar. 11, 1911, 1.
"Fingers Reveal Fake Cripple . . . When Hand Is Found in Supposedly Empty Sleeve." *Chicago Tribune,* Mar. 14, 1911, 3.
"$230,000 for Expenses; $95,000 for Charity." *Jewish Criterion,* July 1911.
"Chicago Leads the World in Race Progress." *Chicago Defender,* June 19, 1915, 5.
"Urban League Interested in Cripples." *Chicago Defender,* Feb. 7, 1920, 4.
"Bites White Man's Leg." *Chicago Defender,* July 2, 1921, 1.
"Pays Crippled Men $3 a Day to Beg Alms." *Chicago Defender,* June 24, 1922, 15.
"Luck Frowns on Beggars in New York." *Chicago Defender,* Dec. 23, 1922, 13.
"Blind Beggar Defends Self at the Bar: Sightless, Eloquent, but Loses Case." *Chicago Defender,* Aug. 30, 1924, A1.
"Arrests Beggar for 28th Time; Jails Objectors." *Chicago Tribune,* July 28, 1936, 4.
"Loop Beggar Arrested 28th Time Is Fined $10." *Chicago Tribune,* July 29, 1936, 11.
Lurie, Walter A. "The Policeman and the Beggar." *Chicago Tribune,* Aug. 2, 1936, 16.
"Jail 4 Whites for Defense of Beggar from Cop in Loop." *Chicago Defender,* Aug. 8, 1936, 8.
Schreiber, Edward. "'Affront to Everyone': A Law That's an Offense." *Chicago Tribune,* Oct. 18, 1973, A1.

CLEVELAND

"Hark, Hark, the Dogs Do Bark, the Beggars Are Coming to Town." *Social Bulletin,* Jan. 6, 1915, 2.

DENVER

Letter from Denver doctor. *Denver Republican,* Nov. 14, 1888, 5.
Rocky Mountain Weekly News, Feb. 27, 1889.

FITCHBURG, MASSACHUSETTS

"Imprisoned Goat Eats Police Fodder Supply." *Fitchburg Sentinel,* Apr. 9, 1936, 3.

FREDERICK, MARYLAND

"The Unsightly Exhibition . . ." *The News,* July 23, 1887, 2.

HAMMOND, INDIANA

"Away with the Beggar." *Lake County Times,* July 9, 1918, 4. (Published also in the Lima, Ohio, *Daily News,* July 1, 1918, and the Ogden, Utah, *Standard,* July 2, 1918.)

LOS ANGELES

"A Hard Gang." *Los Angeles Times,* Aug. 21, 1880, 2.

"The Cripple Fake." *Los Angeles Times,* Mar. 4, 1890, 5.

"Journal for Beggars." *Los Angeles Times,* May 4, 1899, 4.

"Drunken Beggar Fights Cop." *Los Angeles Times,* June 6, 1905, II2.

"Rags and Tags: Hobo Influx Grows Apace." *Los Angeles Times,* Sept. 15, 1907, V13.

"This Beggar a Press Agent." *Los Angeles Times,* Jan. 2, 1911, 15.

"Hypnotized into Madhouse: Beautiful Girl Converted into Cripple; Young Man Who Placed Her under a Lingering Spell Is Alleged to Have Employed Her as a Blind Beggar to Solicit Alms That He Took from Her." *Los Angeles Times,* Apr. 27, 1911, II3.

"Three-Legged Legless Beggar Says He Can't Work." *Los Angeles Times,* July 25, 1912, 17.

Marquis, Netta. "Organizing the Social Spirit." *Los Angeles Times,* Sept. 17, 1912, II7.

"Shrewdest of All Beggars." *Los Angeles Times,* Mar. 2, 1913, II1.

"Permits for Beggars." *Los Angeles Times,* Sept. 12, 1913, II4.

"Police Judge Sentences without Compunction Drunken Beggars Even Though They Are Halt and Blind." *Los Angeles Times,* July 27, 1913, 19.

"Strangest Union in the World Uncovered Here: League of Beggars, Cripples, Sightless, Epileptic and Deformed; Great Association of Mendicants, Whose Chief Is a Blind Newspaper Vendor on Broadway, Bids Virtual Defiance to Efforts to Drive Them from the Streets; Will Fight to Highest Court, They Say.." *Los Angeles Times,* Oct. 22, 1913, II1.

"An Efficiency Engineer." *Los Angeles Times,* July 6, 1914, 18.

"Army's Forced to Surrender: Charities Commission Ousts the Salvationists." *Los Angeles Times,* Sept. 9, 1914, II3.

"Makes Him Talk." *Los Angeles Times,* Jan. 23, 1915, II3.

"Says the Deaf Are Not Beggars." *Los Angeles Times,* July 23, 1915, II3.

"No Cheer for Fake Mutes." *Los Angeles Times,* Nov. 8, 1915, II5.

Armstrong, Burl. "Milk of Kindness Is Soured by Meddlers." *Los Angeles Times,* Dec. 19, 1915, II2.

"Genius of Mendicants Defeats Beggary Law: Plain Solicitation of Alms Means Jail, So the Sad, Maimed or Misshapen Company Takes Refuge behind Chewing Gum, Shoe Strings, Music and Reading of Scriptures or Verses." *Los Angeles Times,* Dec. 24, 1916, II9.

"Love Blooms on Sidewalk." *Los Angeles Times,* Jan. 14, 1917, II2.

"Chinaman Is Jailed as Beggar." *Los Angeles Times,* Mar. 8, 1923, I10.

"Rare Type." *Los Angeles Times,* July 25, 1925.

NEW ORLEANS

"No Place for a Poor Blind Man." *New Orleans Daily Picayune,* July 18, 1881, 2.

"A Poor-House: Forcible Illustration of the Need for Such a Building." *New Orleans Daily Picayune,* Apr. 12, 1882, 3.

"Suppression of Mendicancy." *New Orleans Daily Picayune,* May 3, 1883, 2.

"The Conference of Charities: Organizing for the Suppression of Mendicancy in This City." *New Orleans Daily Picayune,* May 16, 1883, 2.

"Corralling the Cripples." *New Orleans Times-Picayune,* Sept. 11, 1883, 2.

"An End to Street Begging." *New Orleans Times-Democrat,* Sept. 12, 1883, 3; rpt. in part as "Suppression of Street Begging," *New York Times,* Sept. 16, 1883, 4.

"Professor William H. Pancoast." *New Orleans Times-Democrat,* Sept. 20, 1884, 4 (on Professor Pancoast and voluntary amputation).

"Brevities." *New Orleans Times-Democrat,* Sept. 23, 1885, 3.

NEW YORK

"The Tax on Immigration." *New York Times,* June 4, 1881, 4.

Conner, Edmon S. "An Old Actor's Memories." *New York Times,* June 5, 1881, 10 (on Jim Crow).

"The Dwarfs and Giants." *New York Times,* Oct. 23, 1881, 5.

"Canine Mendicancy." *New York Times,* Oct. 26, 1881, 4.

"Homes of the Criminal Classes." *National Review.* Rpt. in *New York Times,* Aug. 19, 1883, 3.

"An Unfortunate Showman: His Indignation When Taken for a Tramp Owing to His Deformities." *New York Times,* July 20, 1884, 7.

"A Victim of Drink." *New York Times,* Oct. 4, 1884, 5.

New York Times, May 24, 1885, 4 (on the wealthy man called a "physical monstrosity").

"Organ Grinders' Licenses." *New York Times,* Dec. 11, 1889, 8.

"Phase of City Life." *New York Times,* June 29, 1890, 12.

"The Freaks Find a Defender." *New York Times,* May 4, 1891, 3.

"Akin to Highwaymen: Methods Pursued by a Number of Professional Beggars." *New York Times,* Jan. 25, 1892, 8.

New York Times, Apr. 24, 1893, 4 (on beggar's docket).

"A Gang of Brutes Arrested: Children Deformed and Made Professional Beggars." *New York Times,* Aug. 1893, 2.

"New Publications." *New York Times,* Feb. 26, 1894, 3.

"What Are Disabilities?" *New York Times,* Mar. 31, 1894, 4.

"No Violation, Said the Justice: But Schulum Was Suspicious of the Human-Faced Donkey, the Three-Legged Rooster, and the Deformed Hen." *New York Times,* Dec. 26, 1894, 5.

"To Get Rid of Tramps." *New York Times,* Jan. 30, 1895, 16.

"What Would Happen If Paris Was Under a Government Founded on Love of Beauty." *Journal des Debate.* Rpt. in *New York Times,* Aug. 25, 1895, 4.
"Prison for the Beggars: Boston's Cure for Mendicants Who Pretend to Be Deformed." *New York Times,* Feb. 21, 1896, 9.
"Sham Cripples." *New York Times,* Feb. 23, 1896, 4.
New York Times, Dec. 12, 1896, 6 (on Jewish beggars).
"Panhandlers' Den Raided." *New York Times,* July 15, 1897, 5.
Holmes, Bayard. "How to Treat the Tramp." *New York Times,* Oct. 15, 1897, 5.
"Twelve Years a Beggar: John Daebler, Seventy-Three Years Old, Spends Thanksgiving Day in the Workhouse." *New York Times,* Nov. 16, 1897, 4.
"New York City Beggars: They Live Largely by Area-Door Charity Given by Sympathetic Servants." *New York Times,* July 17, 1898, 12.
"Rich Beggar's Vacation." *New York Times,* Oct. 12, 1898, 12.
Twain, Mark. "The Jews." *New York Times,* Sept. 3, 1899, 19.
"Feigned Blindness, Is Blind." *New York Times,* May 7, 1901, 2.
"Mary Largo, Queen of the Beggar's Trust: Life Story of the Girl Sent to Bedford Reformatory; Her Father a Spanish Sailor—Her Husband Indolent—She Ruled a Gang in the Lower Bowery." *New York Times,* Apr. 13, 1902, 24.
"An Olfactory Crusade." *New York Times,* May 14, 1903, 1.
"Arrest of Beggar Band: Mendicants Arrested Despite a Threat of Violence; Charity Organization Warned Not to Molest Them—Said to Be in League with Cracksmen." *New York Times,* June 23, 1903, 14.
"The Ancient Profession of Street Beggar as Practiced in New York To-Day." *New York Times,* June 19, 1904, MS2.
"No Sinecure Has the N.Y.C.O. Mendicancy Officer." *New York Times,* May 14, 1905, SM6.
"Pest of Beggars Loosed on the Town: Professional Mendicants, with Made-Up Disfigurements, Return to Prey on City's Charity; Fagin's Nests Filled Again with 'Yeggs,' 'Crust-Throwers' and 'Floppers.'" *New York Times,* Jan. 27, 1907, 5M4.
"Beggars Taught to Beg: An Ex-Actor Runs a College in Paris and Furnishes Disguises." *New York Times,* Sept. 8, 1907, C4.
"Hard Times Too Much for the 'Begging Squad.'" *New York Times,* Sept. 27, 1908, SM6.
"Fit-Faint Faker Won't Fool More Generous Women." *New York World,* Feb. 27, 1910, 2N.
"Galvin's Bowery Raids May Sound Knell of Notorious 5-Cent Whiskey Dives." *New York World,* Mar. 6, 1910, 6N.
"Beggar 'Blind' Boy Proves to Be a Fake." *New York World,* Mar. 20, 1910, 3N.
"Pitiful Mendicant Gives Way to the Cunning Beggar." *New York Times,* Aug. 28, 1910, SM11.
"Police Squad Out for Bold Beggars." *New York Times,* Feb. 19, 1911, 1.

"Detectives Ferret Out Begging Tricks." *New York Times*, Feb. 20, 1911, 16.
"Wiles of Beggars Pay Well, She Says." *New York Times*, Sept. 28, 1911, 6.
"Legless Newsboy Sues: Wants $25,000 Damages for Article That Said He Was Once a Tramp." *New York Times*, Sept. 30, 1911, 5.
"Porto Rico's Beggars." *New York Times*, 1912, V114.
"Police to Rid City of Beggars: Mendicancy Squad Revived to Aid Worthy Causes." *New York Morning Sun*, May 14, 1914.
"Work for the Infirm Proves a Great Boon." *New York World*, Jan. 2, 1916, N4.
"The Movie Director's Mad Quest for Types." *New York Times*, Jan. 9, 1916, X5.
"Beggars Coming Back to Town." *New York Evening Sun*, 1920. In Community Service Society/Charity Organization Society Papers (Clipping File, Box 144), Columbia University Rare Book Library, New York.
"Flock of Crippled Beggars Go to Jail." *New York Times*, May 27, 1921.
"Speakeasy Equips Beggar as Cripple: 'One-Armed Soldier' Reveals Scheme When Detectives Find an Arm under Bandages; His Friends Try It, Too; One Went Out from the Bowery as a Hunchback, Culprit Tells Court—Gets Six Months." *New York Times*, June 15, 1926, 16.
"Father . . . Made $100 a Day Outfitting Fake Cripples." *New York Times*, July 2, 1929.
"The Late James Forbes: Pioneer in the Borderland between Social and Police Work." *New York Times*, Dec. 7, 1935, 16.
McKinley, J.C. "Eritrea: African Success Story Being Writte." *New York Times*, Apr. 30, 1996, A1.
Brown, Patricia Leigh. "A New Culture Moves on Campus: Viewing Ahab and Barbie through the Lens of Disability Studies." *New York Times*, Aug. 20, 2000, WK3.
Greenhouse, Steven. "Lifetime Affliction Leads to a U.S. Bias Suit." *New York Times*, Mar. 30, 2003, A8–9.

OAKLAND

"Dear Ann Landers." *Oakland Tribune*, Jan. 26, 1974, 45.

OGDEN, UTAH

"To the Old Soldiers." *The Standard*, May 28, 1893.

OMAHA

Fogarty, James. "'41 Begging Law Punishes Only the Ugly." *Sunday World Herald* (Omaha), Apr. 21, 1974, B1.

PORTLAND

"Offenses against the City." *Morning Oregonian*, Jan. 6, 1881, 4.

RENO

"City Ordinance No. 45." *Reno Evening Gazette,* Aug. 20, 1905, 6.

SALEM, OHIO

Whippert, G. W. "Begging a Fine Art." *Salem Daily News,* May 16, 1891.

SAN FRANCISCO

"Almshouse Superintendent Contest." *Alta California,* July 1, 1867, 2.

Alta California, July 1, 1867, 2 (on ban on Confederate soldiers marching in parade).

"Board of Supervisors." *Alta California,* July 2, 1867, 2.

Alta California, July 3, 1867, 1 (on need for jobs for ex-soldiers).

"Board of Supervisors." *San Francisco Morning Call,* July 3, 1867, 2.

"A Young Rascal." *Alta California,* July 3, 1867, 2.

"Board of Supervisors." *Alta California,* July 9, 1867, 2.

"Reports and Persons Under Arrest." *Dramatic Chronicle,* July 18, 1867 ("The young man is no worse looking").

"A Sad Sight." *San Francisco Morning Call,* July 18, 1867, 1.

TRENTON, NEW JERSEY

"The Beggars' Latest Scheme." *Trenton Evening Times,* Aug. 2, 1898, 10.

WASHINGTON, D.C.

"Compelled to Pose as a Beggar." *Washington Post,* June 13, 1896, 3.

"Beggar's Tour Nets $." *Washington Post,* June 2, 1913, 1.

"Defective Chicago Baby Dies." *Washington Post,* Nov. 18, 1915, 6 (quoting Jane Addams's speech on "Great Defectives").

WOODLAND, CALIFORNIA

"A Jap Begging for Bread." *Daily Democrat,* Nov. 2, 1897, 1.

ZANESVILLE, OHIO

Martz, Andrew L. "Begging—a 100,000,000 a Year American Industry." *Zanesville Signal,* Sept. 23, 1928, 33.

OTHER BOOKS AND ARTICLES

Abbot, John Willis. *Carter Henry Harrison: A Memoir.* New York: Dodd, Mead, 1895.

Abel, Elizabeth. "Bathroom Doors and Drinking Fountains: Jim Crow's Racial Symbolic." *Critical Inquiry* 25 (Spring 1999): 446–449.

Abel, Emily K. "Hospitalizing Maria Germani." *Bad Mothers: The Politics of Blame*

in Twentieth Century America. Ed. Molly Ladd-Taylor and Lauri Umansky. New York: NYU Press, 1997. 58–66.
———. "Medicine and Morality: The Health Care Program of the New York City Charity Organization Society." *Social Service Review* (Dec. 1997): 634–651.
———. "Taking the Cure to the Poor: Patients' Responses to New York City's Tuberculosis Program, 1844 to 1918." *American Journal of Public Health* 87:11 (Nov. 1997): 1808–1815.
———. "'Very Dear to My Heart': Confronting Labels of Feeblemindedness and Epilepsy." *Hearts of Wisdom: American Women Caring for Kin, 1850–1940*. Cambridge, Mass.: Harvard University Press, 2002. 201–213.
Abrahams, Israel. *Jewish Life in the Middle Ages*. Philadelphia: Jewish Publication Society of America, 1911.
Abramovitz, Mimi. *Regulating the Lives of Women: Social Welfare Policy from Colonial Times to the Present*. Boston: South End, 1996.
Abu-Lughod, Janet L. *New York, Chicago, Los Angeles: America's Global Cities*. Minneapolis: University of Minnesota Press, 1999.
Adams, Cecil. "Appearance-ism in Chicago." Nov. 2, 1973. Archived at The Straight Dope, http://www.straightdope.com/columns/read/124/appearance-ism-in-chicago-the-anti-ugliness-ordinance.
Adams, John Coleman. "What a Great City Might Be—A Lesson from the White City." *New England Magazine* 14 (Mar. 1896): 3–13. Rpt. in *The American 1890s: A Cultural Reader*. Ed. Susan Harris Smith and Melanie Dawson. Durham, N.C.: Duke University Press, 2000.
Adams, Myron. *The Buffalo Newsboy and the Street Trades Bill*. Buffalo: Charity Organization Society, 1903.
Addams, Jane. *Jane Addams: A Centennial Reader*. New York: Macmillan, 1960.
———. *The Long Road of Woman's Memory*. New York: Macmillan, 1916.
———. *The Second Twenty Years at Hull-House*. New York: Macmillan, 1930.
Addams, Jane, and the Residents of Hull-House. *Hull-House Maps and Papers*. Urbana: University of Illinois Press, 2007.
Aguilera, Raymond J. "The Café Lady." *Bent Voices* (Nov. 2000). www.bentvoices.org.
———. "Disability and Delight: Staring Back at the Devotee Community." *Sexuality and Disability* 18:4 (Dec. 2000): 255–261.
Alcoholics Anonymous. *Twelve Steps and Twelve Traditions*. New York: Hazelden, 1952.
Alden, W.L. *Among the Freaks*. New York: Longmans, Green, 1896.
Alger, Horatio. *Hugo, The Deformed*. 1857. Rpt. by Gilbert K. Westgrad II, 1978.
Allen, Jonathan. "Ban for Beggar with 'Wound.'" *Camden New Journal*, Sept. 9, 2004.
"Almshouse." *San Francisco Municipal Reports 1867–1868*. San Francisco: John H. Carmany, 1868.

Almy, Frederick. *Orpheus and Eurydice: An Operatic Burlesque.* Buffalo: Peter Paul, 1897.

Amsterdam, Anthony, and Jerome Bruner. *Minding the Law: How Courts Rely on Storytelling, and How Their Stories Change the Ways We Understand the Law and Ourselves.* Cambridge, Mass.: Harvard University Press, 2000.

Anderson, Tyler. *Five Points.* New York: Plume, 2001.

Anderson, Warwick. *Colonial Pathologies: American Tropical Medicine, Race, and Hygiene in the Philippines.* Durham, NC: Duke University Press, 2006.

Angyal, Andras. "Disgust and Related Aversions." *Journal of Abnormal and Social Psychology* 36 (1941): 393–412.

Annual Report of the Citizens' Association of Chicago, 1880. Chicago: Hamlin and Reed, 1880.

Annual Report of the Public Service Division of Charities, Correction and Cemeteries of the City of Cleveland. Cleveland: Gardner, 1906.

Anzaldúa, Gloria. *Borderlands/La Frontera: The New Mestiza.* San Francisco: Aunt Lute, 1987.

Asbury, Herbert. *The Gangs of New York: An Informal History of the Underworld.* New York: Thunder's Mouth, 1927.

Associated Charities of Cleveland. *Fifth Annual Report.* Cleveland: Forman-Bassett-Hatch, 1905.

———. *Sixth Annual Report.* Cleveland: Calvert and Hatch, 1906.

———. *Eleventh Annual Report.* Cleveland: Associated Charities, 1911.

Associated Charities of Columbus, Ohio Annual Report. Nov. 1902–Nov. 1903.

Austin, John L. "How to Do Things with Words, Lecture 11." *How to Do Things with Words.* Ed. J.O. Urmson and Marina Sbisa. Cambridge, Mass.: Harvard University Press, 1975.

Avery, Elroy McKendree. *A History of Cleveland and Its Environs.* Chicago: Lewis, 1918.

Bahler, John F. *Thrilling Incidents in the Life and Experience of John F. Bahler, Blind Man; with Poems by His Wife; Also, Fifty Hints on Health, and Forty Recipes of Great Value.* N.p.: Published for the author, 1900.

Bailey, Robert E., and Elaine Shemoney Evans. *From the Ashes, 1872–1900: A Selection of Documents from the Proceedings Files of the Chicago City Council.* Springfield: Illinois State Archives, 1990.

Bailward, W.A. "The Oxford House and the Organization of Charity." *The Universities and the Social Problem.* Ed. J.M. Knapp. London: Rivington, 1895.

Bakke, David. *God Knows His Name: The True Story of John Doe No. 24.* Carbondale: Southern Illinois University Press, 2000.

Bales, Kevin. *Understanding Global Slavery: A Reader.* Berkeley: University of California Press, 2005.

Bancroft, Hubert Howe. *History of California 7: 1860–1890.* San Francisco: History Company, 1890.

Bardin, James. "Some Public Health Aspects of Race Relationships in the South." In *Lectures and Addresses on the Negro in the South*. Charlottesville, Va.: Michie, 1915.

Barnartt, Sharon, and Richard Scotch. *Disability Protests: Contentious Politics, 1970–1999*. Washington, D.C.: Gallaudet University Press, 2001.

Barnes, Colin, and Geoff Mercer, eds. *Exploring the Divide: Illness and Disability*. Leeds, U.K.: Disability Press, 1996.

Barnes, Colin, Geoff Mercer, and Tom Shakespeare. *Exploring Disability: A Sociological Introduction*. Cambridge, U.K.: Polity, 1999.

Barnes, David. "Confronting Sensory Crisis in the Great Stinks of London and Paris." *Filth: Dirt, Disgust and Modern Life*. Ed. William Cohen and Ryan Johnson. Minneapolis: University of Minnesota Press, 2005. 103–129.

Bastin, Bruce. *Red River Blues: The Blues Tradition in the Southeast*. Chicago: University of Illinois Press, 1986.

Bauman, H. Dirksen L. "Audism: Exploring the Metaphysics of Oppression." *Journal of Deaf Studies and Deaf Education* 9:2 (2004): 239–246.

Baynton, Douglas. "Defectives in the Land: Disability and American Immigration Policy, 1882–1924." *Journal of American Ethnic History* (2005): 31–45.

———. "Disability and the Justification of Inequality in American History." *The New Disability History*. Ed. Paul K. Longmore and Lauri Umansky. New York: NYU Press, 2001. 33–57.

———. "Immigration: Law and Policy." *Encyclopedia of Disability*. Vol. 2. Ed. Gary Albrecht. Thousand Oaks, Calif.: Sage, 2005. 914–919.

Bederman, Gail. *Manliness and Civilization: A Cultural History of Gender and Race in the United States, 1880–1917*. Chicago: University of Chicago Press, 1996.

Beecher, Henry Ward. "Jew and Gentile." *Menorah* 2 (1887): 203.

Bell, Chris. "Introducing White Disability Studies: A Modest Proposal." *The Disability Studies Reader*. 2nd ed. Ed. Lennard Davis. New York: Routledge, 2006. 275–282.

Bell, Daniel. *Work and Its Discontents*. Boston: Beacon, 1956.

Bellows, Barbara. *Benevolence among Slaveholders: Assisting the Poor in Charleston, 1670–1860*. Baton Rouge: Louisiana State University Press, 1993.

Belluso, John. *The Body of Bourne*. New York: New Dramatists, 2003.

Benjamin, Adam. *Making an Entrance: Theory and Practice for Disabled and Non-Disabled Dancers*. New York: Routledge, 2002.

Benjamin, Harry. *The Transsexual Phenomenon*. New York: Julian, 1966.

Benjamin, Walter. *Passagen-Werk: Gesammelte Schriften V*. Ed. Rolf Tiedemann. Frankfort am Main: Suhrkamp Verlag, 1972.

Bennett, Tony. *Popular Fiction*. London: Routledge, 1990.

Berry, Bonnie. *Beauty Bias: Discrimination and Social Power*. Westport, Conn.: Praeger, 2007.

Bérubé, Michael. "Autobiography as Performative Utterance." *American Quarterly* 52:2 (2000): 339–343.

Best, Stephen M. *The Fugitive's Properties: Law and the Poetics of Possession.* Chicago: University of Chicago Press, 2004.

Beuf, Ann Hill. *Beauty Is the Beast: Appearance-Impaired Children in America.* Philadelphia: University of Pennsylvania Press, 1990.

Beverley, John. *Subalternity and Representation: Arguments in Cultural Theory.* Durham, N.C.: Duke University Press, 1999.

Bhabha, Homi. *The Location of Culture.* New York: Routledge, 1994.

Billings, John Shaw. "Public Health and Municipal Government." *Annals of the American Academy of Political and Social Science* (Feb. 1891): 1–23.

Biographical Dictionary and Portrait Gallery of Representative Men of Chicago and the World's Columbian Exposition. Chicago: American Biographical, 1892.

Bjarkman, Peter C. *Baseball's Great Dynasties: The Reds.* New York: Gallery Books, 1991.

Black, Edwin. *War against the Weak: Eugenics and America's Campaign to Create a Master Race.* New York: Four Walls Eight Windows, 2003.

Blackmar, F.W. "The Smoky Pilgrims." *American Journal of Sociology* (June 1897): 490–500.

Blanck, Peter. "Civil War Pensions and Disability." *Ohio State Law Journal* 62 (2001): 109.

Blumberg, Lisa. "Public Stripping." *The Ragged Edge: The Disability Experience from the Pages of the First Fifteen Years of the Disability Rag.* Ed. Barrett Shaw. Louisville, Ky.: Advocado, 1994.

Bogan, Boris. *Jewish Philanthropy.* New York: Macmillan, 1917.

Bogdan, Robert. *Freak Show.* Chicago: University of Chicago Press, 1988.

Bondeson, Jan. *A Cabinet of Medical Curiosities.* New York: Norton, 1997.

Booth, Charles. *Life and Labor of the People in London.* New York: Macmillan, 1903.

Bornshtain, Aharon. *Ha-Kabtsanim: perek be-toldot Yehude Germanyeh* [*The Beggars: A Chapter in the History of the Jews of Germany*]. Jerusalem: R. Mas, 1992.

Bosanquet, Helen. *Social Work in London, 1869–1912: A History of the Charity Organization Society.* New York: Dutton, 1914.

Bourdieu, Pierre. *Outline of a Theory of Practice.* New York: Cambridge University Press, 1977.

Bourne, Randolph. "A Philosophy of Handicap." *Youth and Life.* Boston: Houghton Mifflin, 1913. Rpt. by Burt Franklin, 1971.

Bouson, J. Brooks. "You Nothing but Trash." *Southern Literary Journal* 34:1 (2001): 101–123.

Bowe, Frank. *Handicapping America: Barriers to Disabled People.* New York: Harper and Row, 1978.

Bowen, [B]enjamin B. *A Blind Man's Offering*. New York: Published by the author, 1847.
Bowles, David W. "Enforcing the Ugly Laws." David W. Bowles' Urban Semiotic weblog, May 1, 2007, http://urbansemiotic.com/2007/05/01/enforcing-the-ugly-laws.
Boyer, M. Christine. *Dreaming the Rational City: The Myth of American City Planning*. Cambridge, Mass.: MIT Press, 1986.
Brace, Charles Loring. *The Dangerous Classes of New York and Twenty Years' Work among Them*. New York: Wynkoup and Hallenbeck, 1872.
Brand, Dana. *The Spectator and the City in Nineteenth-Century American Literature*. New York: Cambridge University Press, 1991.
Bragg, Bernard, and Eugene Bergman. *Tales from a Clubroom*. Washington, D.C.: Gallaudet University Press, 1981.
Bragg, Lois, ed. *Deaf World*. New York: NYU Press, 2001.
Braverman, Harry. *Labor and Monopoly Capital: The Degradation of Work in the Twentieth Century*. New York: Monthly Review Press, 1974.
Breckenridge, Carol A., and Candace Vogler. "The Critical Limits of Embodiment: Disability's Criticism." *Public Culture* 13:3 (2001): 349–357.
Bregstone, Philip B. *Chicago and Its Jews: A Cultural History*. Privately published, 1935. Available in the library of the Spertus Museum, Chicago.
Brooks, Gwendolyn. *Blacks*. Chicago: David Company, 1987.
Broomer, Stuart. "Licked by All: A Postage Stamp of Robert Johnson." *Coda, The Journal of Jazz and Improvised Music* (Nov./Dec. 1995): 1.
Brown, Bill. *The Material Unconscious: American Amusement, Stephen Crane, and the Economies of Play*. Cambridge, Mass.: Harvard University Press, 1996.
Brown, Elijah. *The Real Billy Sunday*. Dayton, Ohio: Otterbein, 1914.
Brown, James. *The History of Public Assistance in Chicago 1833–1893*. Chicago: University of Chicago Press, 1941.
Brown, Janice. "A Study of the Touro-Shakespeare Almshouse." 1929. New Orleans Public Library, Louisiana Reference Collection, microform.
Brown, Mordechai. *How to Pitch Curves*. Chicago: W.D. Boyce, 1913.
Browne, Junius Henri. *The Great Metropolis*. 1869. New York: Anchor, 1975.
Brueggemann, Brenda. *Lend Me Your Ear*. Washington, D.C.: Gallaudet University Press, 1999.
Bruno, Richard. "Devotees, Pretenders and Wannabes: Two Cases of Factitious Disability Disorder." *Journal of Sexuality and Disability* 15:4 (1997): 243–260.
Bryan, Willie. *Multicultural Aspects of Disabilities*. Springfield, Ill.: Charles C. Thomas, 1999.
Buck, Dennis. *Deaf Peddler: Confessions of an Inside Man*. Foreword by Robert Buchanon. Washington, D.C.: Gallaudet University Press, 2000.
Buckler, Helen. *Daniel Hale Williams: Negro Surgeon*. New York: Pitman, 1968.

Buck-Morss, Susan. "The Flaneur, the Sandwichman, and the Whore: The Politics of Writing." *New German Critique* (1986): 99–140.

Bulmer, Martin, Kevin Boles, and Kathryn Kish Sklar, eds. *The Social Survey in Historical Perspective, 1880–1940*. New York: Cambridge University Press, 1991.

Burch, Susan. *Signs of Resistance: American Deaf Cultural History, 1900 to World War* II. New York: NYU Press, 2003.

Burg, David. *Chicago's White City of 1893*. Lexington: University Press of Kentucky, 1976.

Burgdorf, Marcia Pearce, and Robert Burgdorf Jr., "A History of Unequal Treatment: The Qualifications of Handicapped Persons as a 'Suspect Class' under the Equal Protection Clause." *Santa Clara Law Review* 15:4 (1975): 855–888.

Burgdorf, Robert L., Jr. "The Americans with Disabilities Act: Analysis and Implication of a Second-Generation Civil Rights Statute." *Harvard Civil Rights–Civil Liberties Law Review* 26 (1991): 413–522.

Burnham, Daniel, and Edward Bennett. *Plan of Chicago*. 1909. New York: Da Capo, 1970.

Burnham, John C. *Paths into American Culture: Psychology, Medicine and Morals*. Philadelphia: Temple University Press, 1988.

Butler, Judith. *Gender Trouble: Feminism and the Subversion of Identity*. New York: Routledge, 1990.

———. "Performative Acts and Gender Constitution: An Essay in Phenomenology and Feminist Theory." *Theatre Journal* 40:4 (1988).

———. *Precarious Life: The Powers of Mourning and Violence*. New York: Verso, 2004.

Byington, Lewis Francis. *The History of San Francisco*. Chicago: S.J. Clarke, 1931.

Byrd, W. Michael, and Linda A. Clayton. "Racial and Ethnic Disparities in Healthcare: A Background and History." *Unequal Treatment: Confronting Racial and Ethnic Disparities in Healthcare*. Ed. Brian D. Smedley, Adrienne Y. Stith, and Alan R. Nelson. Washington, D.C.: National Academies Press, 2002.

Byrom, Bradley. "A Pupil and a Patient: Hospital-Schools in Progressive America." *The New Disability History: American Perspectives*. Ed. Paul Longmore and Lauri Umansky. New York: NYU Press, 2001. 133–156.

———. "A Vision of Self Support: Disability and the Rehabilitation Movement of Progressive America." Ph.D. dissertation, University of Iowa, 2004.

Cahill, Spencer E., and Robin Eggleston. "Reconsidering the Stigma of Physical Disability: Wheelchair Use and Public Kindness." *Sociological Quarterly* 36:4 (1995): 681–698.

Caldwell, Joe, and Larry Biandi. "ADAPT." *Encyclopedia of Disability*. Vol. 1. Ed. Gary Albrecht. Thousand Oaks, Calif.: Sage, 2005. 34–37.

Campbell, Helen. *Darkness and Daylight; Lights and Shadows of New York Life: A Pictorial Record of Personal Experiences of Day and Night in the Great Metropolis*. Hartford, Conn.: Hartford Publishing, 1897.

Campbell, William. *Reminiscences of Squandered Days*. N.p., 1927.
Carlson, Licia. "Cognitive Ableism and Disability Studies: Feminist Reflections on the History of Mental Retardation." *Hypatia* 16:4 (2001): 124–146.
Carter, Julian. *The Heart of Whiteness: Normal Sexuality and Race in America, 1880–1940*. Durham, N.C.: Duke University Press, 2007.
Cell, John. *The Highest Stage of White Supremacy: The Origins of Segregation in South Africa and the American South*. Cambridge: Cambridge University Press, 1982.
Chamberlyne, H.M. "Vagrancy among Deaf-Mutes." 1859. *Deaf World*. Ed. Lois Bragg. New York: NYU Press, 2001. 237–238.
Chambers, Robert. *Book of Days*. London: W. and R. Chambers, 1869.
Chan, Suecheng. *Entry Denied: Exclusion and the Chinese Community in America, 1882–1943*. Philadelphia: Temple University Press, 1991.
Charity Organization Society of Denver. *First Annual Report of the Charity Organization Society of Denver, Colorado*. Denver: C.J. Kelly, 1889.
———. *Third Annual Report of the Charity Organization Society of Denver, Colorado*. Denver: Rocky Mountain News Print, 1890.
Charity Organization Society of New Orleans. *First Annual Report of the Charity Organization Society of New Orleans, La*. New Orleans: Palfrey and O'Donnell, 1897.
Checkout: Keeping Plymouth's Retailers Informed (Summer 2004). Available online at http://www.plymouth.gov.uk/ccp_checkout_summer_2004.pdf.
Cheu, Johnson. "Disabling Cure in Twentieth-Century America: Disability, Identity, Literature and Culture." Ph.D. dissertation, Ohio State University, 2003.
Chicago Bureau of Associated Charities. *Third Annual Report of the Bureau of Associated Charities of the City of Chicago, Nov. 1896–Oct. 1897*. Chicago: William C. Hollister, 1897.
Chicago Citizens Association. *Addresses and Reports of the Citizen's Association of Chicago 1882*. Chicago: Hamlin and Reed, 1882.
Chicago Municipal Markets Commission. "Report to the Mayor." Dec. 28, 1914.
Chicago Relief and Aid Society. *First Special Report of the Chicago Relief and Aid Society*. Chicago: Culver, Page, Hoyne, 1871.
———. *The 23rd Annual Report of the Chicago Relief and Aid Society to the Common Council of the City of Chicago, Oct. 31 1879–Oct. 31, 1880*. Chicago: R.R. McCabe, 1880.
———. *The 25th Annual Report of the Chicago Relief and Aid Society to the Common Council of the City of Chicago*. Chicago: R.R. McCabe, 1882.
Chicago Vice Commission. *The Social Evil in Chicago*. Chicago: Gunthorp-Warren, 1911.
Ching, Barbara. "The Possum, the Hag, and the Rhinestone Cowboy: Hard Country Music and the Burlesque Abjection of the White Man." *Whiteness: A Critical Reader*. Ed. Mike Hill. New York: NYU Press, 1997.

Chinn, Carl. *Poverty amidst Prosperity: The Urban Poor in England, 1834–1914*. New York: Manchester University Press, 1995.
City of Charleston. *City of Charleston, South Carolina, Budget*. Charleston: The City, 1881.
City Welfare: Aids and Opportunities. Chicago School of Civics and Philanthropy Bulletin No. 13, Oct. 1911.
Clare, Eli. *Exile and Pride: Disability, Queerness and Liberation*. Cambridge, Mass.: South End, 1999.
Clarke, Frances. "Honorable Scars: Northern Amputees and the Meaning of Civil War Injuries." *Union Soldiers and the Northern Home Front: Wartime Experiences, Postwar Adjustments*. Ed. Paul A. Cimbala and Randall M. Miller. New York: Fordham University Press, 2002. 361–395.
Clerc, Laurent. "Address to the Connecticut Legislature." *A Mighty Change: An Anthology of Deaf American Writing 1816–1864*. Ed. Christopher Krentz. Washington, D.C.: Gallaudet University Press, 2002.
Cleveland Directory of Charities and Social Work. Cleveland: Committee on Co-operation, 1914.
Cleveland Federation for Charity and Philanthropy. *The Social Year Book*. Cleveland: Cleveland Federation, 1913.
Cleveland Hospital Council. *Cleveland Hospital and Health Survey*. Cleveland: Cleveland Hospital Council, 1920.
Cohen, David, and Ben Greenwood. *The Buskers: A History of Street Entertainment*. North Pomfret, Vt.: David and Charles, 1971.
Cole, Melissa. "In/Ensuring Disability." *Tulane Law Review* 71 (2003): 839–884.
Colker, Ruth. *Hybrid: Bisexuals, Multiracials, and Other Misfits under the Law*. New York: NYU Press, 1996.
Comolli, Jean-Louis. "Machines of the Visible." *The Cinematic Apparatus*. Ed. Teresa de Lauritis and Stephen Heath. New York: Palgrave Macmillan, 1985.
Compton, Thomas. *The Brief History of Disability, or The World Has Always Had Cripples*. Berkeley, Calif.: Privately printed, 1992.
Condit, Carl. *The Railroad and the City*. Columbus: Ohio State University Press, 1977.
Connor, Steven. *The Book of Skin*. Ithaca, N.Y.: Cornell University Press, 2004.
Corbin, Alain. *The Foul and the Fragrant: Odor and the French Social Imagination*. Trans. Miriam Kochan. Cambridge, Mass.: Harvard University Press, 1986.
Corker, Mairian, and Tom Shakespeare, eds. *Disability/Postmodernity: Embodying Disability Theory*. New York: Continuum, 2002.
Cottrell, Melissa. Unpublished, untitled ms. on urban planning in Chicago 1911, University of California at Berkeley.
Council Proceedings, City Council for the Municipal Year 1881–1883. Chicago: W.P. Dunn, 1882.

Courvant, Diana. Talk presented at the Queer/Disability Conference, San Francisco State University, June 2–3, 2002.

———. "Strip!" *This Is What Lesbian Looks Like.* Ed. Kris Kleindienst. Ithaca, N.Y.: Firebrand, 1999. 70–79.

Couser, G. Thomas. "Disability, Life Narrative, and Representation." *The Disability Studies Reader.* 2nd ed. Ed. Lennard Davis. New York: Routledge, 2006. 399–404.

———. *Recovering Bodies: Illness, Disability, and Life Writing.* Madison: University of Wisconsin Press, 1997.

Covino, Deborah. *Amending the Abject Body: Aesthetic Makeovers in Medicine and Culture.* Albany: SUNY Press, 2004.

Cowan, Robert Ernest, Anne Bancroft, and Addie L. Ballou. *The Forgotten Characters of Old San Francisco.* San Francisco: Ward Ritchie, 1964.

Craddock, Susan. *City of Plagues: Disease, Poverty, and Deviance in San Francisco.* Minneapolis: University of Minnesota Press, 2000.

Crane, Stephen. *Active Service.* 1899. *The University of Virginia Edition of the Works of Stephen Crane.* Vol. 3. Ed. Fredson Bowers. Charlottesville: University of Virginia Press, 1976.

———. "An Experiment in Misery." 1894. *Great Short Works of Stephen Crane.* New York: Perennial, 1968.

———. *Maggie, a Girl of the Street.* 1893. *Great Short Works of Stephen Crane.* Ed. James B. Colvert. New York: Perennial, 2004.

———. "When Man Falls/A Crowd Gathers." *The University of Virginia Edition of the Works of Stephen Crane.* Vol. 8. Ed. Fredson Bowers. Charlottesville: University of Virginia Press, 1973. 868–870.

Crawford, Robert. "The Boundaries of the Self and the Unhealthy Other." *Social Science and Medicine* 38 (1994): 1347–1365.

———. "The Ritual of Health Promotion." *Health, Medicine and Society: Key Theories, Future Agendas.* Ed. Simon Williams, Jonathan Gabe, and Michael Calnon. London: Routledge, 2000.

Crenshaw, Kimberlé. "Demarginalizing the Intersection of Race and Sex: A Black Feminist Critique of Antidiscrimination Doctrine, Feminist Theory and Antiracist Politics." *University of Chicago Legal Forum* (1989): 139–167.

Cresswell, Tim. *The Tramp in America.* London: Reaktion Books, 2001.

"Criminology." *Public Opinion* (Apr.–Sept. 1893): 151.

"Crippled Girls Learn to Sew." *Social Bulletin,* Nov. 1914, 2:1.

"Crippled Julia Gets a New Start: Alien Girl, after Operation on Foot, Studies to Become Self-Supporting." *Social Bulletin,* Jan. 6, 1915, 2:2.

Crosby, Christina. "Language and Materialism." *Cardozo Law Review* 15:5 (March 1994): 1657–1670.

Crow, Liz. "Including All of Our Lives: Renewing the Social Model of Disability."

Exploring the Divide: Illness and Disability. Ed. Colin Barnes and Geoff Mercer. Leeds, U.K.: Disability Press, 1996. 55–72.

Crowley, P. "Report of the Chief of Police, San Francisco Aug. 1 1868—for the year ending June 30, 1868." *San Francisco Municipal Reports 1867–1868.* San Francisco: John H. Carmany, 1868.

Cullen, Lisa. *A Job to Die For: Why So Many Americans Are Made Ill at Work and What to Do about It.* Monroe, Me.: Common Courage, 2002.

Cumbler, John. "The Politics of Charity: Gender and Class in Late 19th Century Charity Policy." *Journal of Social History* 14:1 (Fall 1980): 99–111.

Cumming, John. "Mendicant Pieces." *American Book Collector* (March 1966): 17–19.

Cummings, Charles/George L. Reed. *The Great War Relic, or* ALL ABOUT IT, FOR 10 CENTS. Harrisburg, Pa.: Kinneard and Shade, ca. 1886.

Currah, Paisley. "Disability and Queerness: Centering the Outsider." CLAGS *(Center for Lesbian and Gay Studies) News* (Graduate Center, City University of New York) 14:1 (Winter 2004): 1–2.

Cutler, Irving. *The Jews of Chicago.* Urbana: University of Illinois Press, 1996.

Darke, Paul. "Now I Know Why Disability Art Is Drowning in the River Lethe." *Disability, Culture and Identity.* Ed. Sheila Riddell and Nick Watson. New York: Prentice Hall, 2003.

Darwin, Charles. *The Expression of Emotions in Man and Animals.* 1872. Chicago: University of Chicago Press, 1965.

Davis, Lennard. *Bending Over Backwards: Disability, Dismodernism and Other Difficult Positions.* New York: NYU Press, 2002.

———, ed. *The Disability Studies Reader.* 2nd ed. New York: Routledge, 2006.

———. *Enforcing Normalcy: Disability, Deafness and the Body.* London: Verso, 1995.

Deaf Mute's Journal. Mar. 24 and Mar. 27, 1899.

Dean, Mitchell. "A Social Structure of Many Souls: Moral Regulation, Government and Self-Formation." *Canadian Journal of Sociology* 19:2 (1995): 145–168.

Degener, Theresia. "A Survey of International, Comparative and Regional Disability Law Reform." International Disability Law and Policy Symposium, Oct. 22–26, 2000, organized by the Disability Rights Education and Defense Fund (describing the German court decision *AG Flensburg* of Aug. 27, 1992—63 C 265/92). Trans. Degener.

DeJong, Gerben. "Defining and Implementing the Independent Living Concept." *Independent Living for Physically Disabled People: Developing, Implementing, and Evaluating Self-Help Rehabilitation Programs.* Ed. Nancy M. Crewe, Irving Kenneth Zola, and Associates. San Francisco: Jossey-Bass, 1983.

Delaney, David. *Race, Place, and the Law, 1836–1948.* Austin: University of Texas Press, 1998.

Denton, James A. *Rocky Mountain Radical: Myron W. Reed, Christian Socialist.* Albuquerque: University of New Mexico Press, 1997.

D'Eramo, Marco. *The Pig and the Skyscraper.* Trans. Graeme Thomson. New York: Verso, 2002.

Derrida, Jacques. *Given Time: I. Counterfeit Money.* Trans. Peggy Kamuf. Chicago: University of Chicago Press, 1992.

Devlin, Patrick. *The Enforcement of Morals.* Oxford: Oxford University Press, 1965.

Diedrich, Lisa. *Treatments: Language, Politics, and the Culture of Illness.* Minneapolis: University of Minnesota Press, 2007.

A Digest of the Laws and Ordinances of the City of Philadelphia. Philadelphia: Kay and Brother, 1887.

Digest of the Ordinances of the City Council of Charleston. Charleston, S.C.: Archibald E. Miller, 1818.

Dimock, Wai-Chee. "Class, Gender, and a History of Metonymy." *Rethinking Class: Literary Studies and Social Formations.* Ed. Wai-Chee Dimock and Michael T. Gilmore. New York: Columbia University Press, 1997. 57–104.

Dion, Karen. "What Is Beautiful Is Good." *Journal of Personality and Social Psychology* 24 (1972): 215–220.

Dispute Resolution Magazine (published by the American Bar Association Section of Dispute Resolution) 10:2 (Winter 2004): 15.

Divine, E.T. "Organization of Charity." *Proceedings of the National Conference on Charities and Correction, 26th Session.*

Doane, Mary Ann. "Film and the Masquerade—Theorizing the Female Spectator." *Screen* 23:3–4 (1982): 74–87.

Doner, Thomas. *Eleven Years a Drunkard: Having Lost Both Arms through Intemperance, He Wrote This Book with His Teeth as a Warning to Others.* Sycamore, Ill.: Arnold & Nicholls, 1880.

Donnelly, Ignatius. *Caesar's Column: A Story of the Twentieth Century.* Middleton, Conn.: Wesleyan University Press, 2003.

Doran, John. *The History of Court Fools.* London: Richard Bentley, 1858.

Dorn, Michael. "The Travel Narratives of a 'Cripple.'" *Places through the Body.* Ed. Heidi J. Nast and Steve Pile. New York: Routledge, 1998. 183–206.

Dornstein, Ken. *Accidentally, On Purpose: The Making of a Personal Injury Underworld in America.* New York: St. Martin's, 1996.

Dorsett, Lyle, and Michael McCarthy. *The Queen City: A History of Denver.* Boulder, Colo.: Pruett, 1977. Rpt. 1986.

Douglas, Mary. *Purity and Danger: An Analysis of the Concepts of Pollution and Taboo.* 1966. London: Routledge, 2002.

Drake, Robert F. "A Critique of the Roles of the Traditional Charities." *Disability, Politics and the Struggle for Change.* Ed. Len Barton. London: David Fulton, 2001. 147–166.

Dreiser, Theodore. *Theodore Dreiser: Journalism.* Ed. T.D. Nostwich. Philadelphia: University of Pennsylvania Press, 1988.

Du Bois, W.E.B. *The Philadelphia Negro.* 1899. New York: Schocken, 1967.

DuCille, Ann. "The Occult of True Womanhood: Critical Demeanor and Black Feminist Studies." *Signs* 19:3 (Spring 1994): 591–629.

Duis, Perry. *Challenging Chicago: Coping with Everyday Life, 1837–1920.* Champaign-Urbana: University of Illinois Press, 1998.

———. *The Saloon: Public Drinking in Chicago and Boston 1880–1920.* Champaign-Urbana: University of Illinois Press, 1999.

———. "Whose City? Public and Private Places in Nineteenth-Century Chicago." *Chicago History: The Magazine of the Chicago Historical Society* (Spring 1983).

Dwyer, Ellen, "Craig Colony for Epileptics." *Mental Retardation in America: A Historical Reader.* Ed. Steven Noll and James W. Trent Jr. New York: NYU Press, 2004. 258–280.

Eastwood, Carolyn. *Chicago's Jewish Street Peddlers.* Chicago: Jewish Historical Society, 1991.

———. *Near West Side Stories: Struggles for Community in Chicago's Maxwell Street Neighborhood.* Chicago: Lake Claremont Press, 2002.

Edwards, Harry Stillwell. *Sons and Fathers.* Chicago: Rand McNally, 1896.

Edwards, Rebekah. "Archives of Certainty: James Forbes' Subjects of Surveillance." Ph.D. dissertation in progress, University of California at Berkeley.

"EEOC Sues McDonald's Restaurant for Disability Bias against Employee with Facial Discrimination." EEOC press release, Mar. 7, 2003.

Ehrenreich, Barbara, and Deidre English. *Complaints and Disorders: The Sexual Politics of Sickness.* Old Westbury, N.Y.: Feminist Press, 1973.

Elliott, E.L. "Public Lighting." *Municipal Advance.* Chicago, 1911.

Elmslie, R.C. *The Care of Invalid and Crippled Children in School.* London: School Hygiene Publishing, 1911.

Emmens, Liz. Comment on panel on "Narrative and Argument" at the Disability, Narrative and the Law Conference, Moritz College of Law, The Ohio State University, Feb. 17, 2006.

Epstein, Julia. *Altered Conditions: Disease, Medicine and Storytelling.* New York: Routledge, 1994.

Epstein, Steven. *Inclusion: The Politics of Difference in Medical Research.* Chicago: University of Chicago Press, 2007.

Erkulwater, Jennifer. *Disability Rights and the American Social Safety Net.* Ithaca, N.Y.: Cornell University Press, 2006.

Ervin, Mike. "Our Top Story: 3,700 Women Breastfeed at Once." *National Spinal Cord Injury Newsletter,* Nov. 1, 2006.

Eskridge, William. *Gaylaw: Challenging the Apartheid of the Closet.* Cambridge, Mass.: Harvard University Press, 2002.

Essig, Melissa Cole. "Gimp Theory and the ADA's 'Feedback Loop.'" *St. Louis University Law Journal* 49 (2005): 1047–1075.

Fabian, Ann. *The Unvarnished Truth: Personal Narratives in Nineteenth-Century America.* Berkeley: University of California Press, 2002.

"Facial Discrimination: Extending Handicap Law to Employment Discrimination on the Basis of Physical Appearance." *Harvard Law Review* 100 (1987): 2035–2052.

Fairchild, Amy. *Science at the Borders: Immigrant Medical Inspection and the Shaping of the Modern Industrial Labor Force.* Baltimore: Johns Hopkins University Press, 2003.

Fanon, Franz. *Black Skin, White Masks.* New York: Grove, 1967.

Farley, Anthony Paul. "The Poetics of Colorlined Space." *Crossroads, Directions, and a New Critical Race Theory.* Ed. Francisco Valdes, Jerome McCristal Culp, and Angela P. Harris. Philadelphia: Temple University Press, 2002.

Fawcett, Barbara. *Feminist Perspectives on Disability.* Essex, U.K.: Pearson, 2000.

Feder, Leah. *Unemployment Relief in Periods of Depression: A Study of Measures Adopted in Certain American Cities, 1857 through 1922.* New York: Russell Sage, 1936.

Ferguson, Philip. *Abandoned to Their Fate: Social Policy and Practice toward Severely Retarded People in America, 1820–1920.* Philadelphia: Temple University Press, 1994.

Ferguson, Roderick A. *Aberrations in Black: Toward a Queer of Color Critique.* Minneapolis: University of Minnesota Press, 2004.

Ferlinghetti, Lawrence, and Nancy J. Peters. *Literary San Francisco.* San Francisco: City Lights, 1980.

Ferrell, Jeff. *Tearing Down the Streets: Adventures in Urban Anarchy.* New York: Palgrave, 2001.

Ferri, Beth, and David J. Connor. "Tools of Exclusion: Race, Disability, and (Re) segregated Education." *TCRecord* 107:3 (2005): 453–474.

Fett, Sharla. *Working Cures: Healing, Health and Power on Southern Slave Plantations.* Chapel Hill: University of North Carolina Press, 2002.

Figg, Laurann, and Jane Farrell-Beck. "Amputation in the Civil War: Physical and Social Dimensions." *Journal of the History of Medicine and Allied Sciences* 48:4 (1993): 454–475.

Fine, Michelle, and Adrienne Asch, eds. *Women with Disabilities: Essays in Psychology, Culture and Politics.* Philadelphia: Temple University Press, 1988.

Fineman, Martha Albertson. *The Autonomy Myth: A Theory of Dependency.* New York: New Press, 2004.

Finger, Anne. "And the Greatest of These Is Charity." *The Ragged Edge: The Disability Experience from the Pages of the First Fifteen Years of the Disability Rag.* Ed. Barrett Shaw. Louisville, Ky.: Advocado, 1994.

Finkelstein, Vic. *Attitudes and Disabled People.* New York: World Rehabilitation Fund, 1980.

Fitzhugh, George. *Cannibals All! Or, Slaves without Masters.* 1852. Cambridge, Mass.: Harvard University Press, 1960.

Fleisher, Doris Zames, and Frieda Zames. *The Disability Rights Movement: From Charity to Confrontation.* Philadelphia: Temple University Press, 2000.

Foote, Caleb. "Vagrancy-Type Law and Its Administration." *University of Pennsylvania Law Review* 104 (1956).

Forbes, James, and Silas McBee. *The Churchman.* Sept. 2, 1911.

Fordham, Brigham. "Dangerous Bodies: Freak Shows, Legal Discourse, and the Definition of Disability." Available online at http:/lworks.bepress.com/brigham.fordham/1.

Fort, J.M. "Do Maternal Impressions Affect the Foetus in Utero?" *Journal of the American Medical Association,* Apr. 20, 1889.

Foucault, Michel. *Abnormal: Lectures at the College de France 1974–1975.* Trans. Graham Burchell. New York: Picador, 2003.

———. *Discipline and Punish: The Birth of the Prison.* 1975. Trans. Alan Sheridan. New York: Vintage, 1995.

———. *The History of Sexuality, Volume 1: An Introduction.* 1976. Trans. Robert Hurley. New York: Pantheon, 1978.

Francis, Leslie Pickering, and Anita Silvers, eds. *Americans with Disabilities.* New York: Routledge, 2000.

Frank, Gelya. *Venus on Wheels: Two Decades of Dialogue on Disability, Biography and Being Female in America.* Berkeley: University of California Press, 2000.

Frankenberg, Ruth. *White Women, Race Matters: The Social Construction of Whiteness.* Minneapolis: University of Minnesota Press, 1993.

Franklin, H. Bruce. *War Stars: The Superweapon and the American Imagination.* New York: Oxford University Press 1990.

French, Charles, ed. *Biographical History of the American Irish in Chicago.* Chicago: American Biographical, 1897.

French, Sally. "Simulation Exercises in Disability Awareness Training: A Critique." *Disability and Society* 7:3 (1992): 257–266.

Fretz, Eric. "P.T. Barnum's Theatrical Selfhood and the Nineteenth-Century Culture of Exhibition." *Freakery: Cultural Spectacles of the Extraordinary Body.* Ed. Rosemarie Garland Thomson. New York: NYU Press, 1996.

Freud, Sigmund. "Fragment of an Analysis of a Case of Hysteria." 1905. *Dora: An Analysis of a Case of Hysteria.* New York: Collier, 1963.

Freund, Roger. "Begging in Chicago." Ph.D. dissertation, University of Chicago, 1925.

Fried, Michael. *Realism, Writing, Disfiguration.* Chicago: University of Chicago Press, 1988.

Friedman, I.K. *The Autobiography of a Beggar.* Boston: Small, Maynard, 1903.

Friedman, Lawrence. *A History of American Law.* New York: Touchstone, 2005.

Fuell, Melissa. *Blind Boone: His Early Life and His Achievements.* Kansas City: Burton, 1915.
Fuller, Arthur Franklin. *A Book of Poems.* Berkeley, Calif.: Anchor, 1913.
———. *Fifty Thousand Miles Back-Ridden.* Fort Worth, Tex.: Anchor, 1915.
———. *The Golden Chalice and Other Poems: Poems for the Warm-Hearted and Refined.* Los Angeles: A.F. Fuller, 1939.
———. *An Odd Romance: The Story of a Brave Little Soldier.* Fort Worth, Tex.: Solar Musical and Literary Bureau, 1915.
———. *An Odd Soldiery: The Tale of a Sojourner; Being an Autobiography of Arthur Franklin Fuller, a Soldier of MIS-fortune.* Fort Worth, Tex.: Solar Musical and Literary Bureau, 1915.
———. *Wrestling the Wolf.* Los Angeles: Wayside, 1919.
Fuller, Harvey A. *Trimsharp's Account of Himself: A Sketch of His Life, Together with a Brief History of the Education of the Blind, and Their Achievements, to Which Is Added a Collection of Poems Composed by Himself.* Ann Arbor, Mich.: Ann Arbor Printing and Publishing, 1873.
Furness, Henry. Untitled article in *Sporting Life* (1892).
Gamble, Vanessa, ed. *Germs Have No Color Line: Blacks and American Medicine, 1900–1940.* New York: Garland, 1989.
Gannon, Jack. *Deaf Heritage.* Silver Spring, Md.: National Association of the Deaf, 1981.
Garland Thomson, Rosemarie. *Extraordinary Bodies.* New York: Columbia University Press, 1996. Abbreviated as *EB*.
———. Foreword. *Working against Odds: Stories of Disabled Women's Work Lives.* By Mary Grimley Mason. Boston: Northeastern University Press, 2004.
———, ed. *Freakery: Cultural Spectacles of the Extraordinary Body.* New York: NYU Press, 1996.
———. "Integrating Disability, Transforming Feminist Theory." *Gendering Disability.* Ed. Bonnie K. Smith and Beth Hutchison. New Brunswick, N.J.: Rutgers University Press, 2004.
———. "Making Freaks: Visual Rhetorics and the Spectacle of Julia Pastrana." *Thinking the Limits of the Body.* Ed. Jeffrey Jerome Cohen and Gail Weiss. Albany: SUNY Press, 2003. 129–144.
———. "Seeing the Disabled: Visual Rhetorics of Disability in Popular Photography." *The New Disability History.* Ed. Paul Longmore and Lauri Umansky. New York: NYU Press, 2001. 335–374.
Garrett, Franklin M. *Atlanta and Environs,* vol. 2. Athens: University of Georgia, 1954.
Gerber, David, ed. *Disabled Veterans in History.* Ann Arbor: University of Michigan Press, 2000.
Getis, Victoria. *The Juvenile Court and the Progressives.* Urbana: University of Illinois Press, 2000.

Gilbert, Douglas. *Vaudeville: Its Life and Times.* New York: Dover, 1940.

Gilbert, James. *Perfect Cities: Chicago's Utopias of 1893.* Chicago: University of Chicago Press, 1991.

Gilbreth, Frank, and Lillian Gilbreth. *Motion Study for the Handicapped.* Preface by W.O. Owen. London: George Routledge and Sons, 1920.

Gilman, Sander. *Making the Body Beautiful: A Cultural History of Aesthetic Surgery.* Princeton, N.J.: Princeton University Press, 2000.

Gilmore, Harlan W. *The Beggar.* Chapel Hill: University of North Carolina Press, 1940.

Ginzberg, Lori D. *Women and the Work of Benevolence: Morality, Politics and Class in the Nineteenth-Century United States.* New Haven, Conn.: Yale University Press, 1990.

Gleeson, Brendan. *Geographies of Disability.* New York: Routledge, 1998.

Gliedman, John, and William Roth. *The Unexpected Minority: Handicapped Children in America.* New York: Harcourt, Brace and Jovanovich, 1980.

Goffman, Erving. *Stigma: Notes on the Management of Spoiled Identity.* Harmondsworth, U.K.: Pelican, 1963.

Goggin, Gerard, and Christopher Newell. *Digital Disability: The Social Construction of Disability in New Media.* New York: Rowman and Littlefield, 2003.

Goodman, Nan. *Shifting the Blame: Literature, Law, and the Theory of Accidents in Nineteenth-Century America.* Princeton, N.J.: Princeton University Press, 1998.

Gostin, Lawrence. *Public Health Law: Power, Duty, Restraint.* Berkeley: University of California Press, 2000.

Gottlieb, J. Adelphi. "Feigned Diseases—Their Importance, Purpose, and Recognition." *Medico-Legal Journal* 16 (1899).

Green, Paul M., and Melvin G. Holli, eds. *The Mayors: The Chicago Political Tradition.* Carbondale: Southern Illinois University Press, 1987.

Greever, Garland, and Joseph M. Bachelor, *The Soul of the City: An Urban Anthology.* Boston: Houghton Mifflin, 1923.

Grillo, Tina, and Stephanie M. Wildman. "Obscuring the Importance of Race: The Implication of Making Comparisons between Racism and Sexism (or Other Isms)." *Critical Race Feminism.* Ed. Adrien Katherine Wing. New York: NYU Press, 1997.

Groce, Nora. *Everyone Here Spoke Sign Language: Hereditary Deafness on Martha's Vineyard.* Cambridge, Mass.: Harvard University Press, 1985.

———. "Rehabilitation in an Historic Perspective: The Work of Bell Greve." *Journal of Rehabilitation* (April-June 1996): 7–11.

Grosz, Elizabeth. "Naked." *The Prosthetic Impulse: From a Posthuman Present to a Biocultural Future.* Ed. Marquard Smith and Joanna Morra. Cambridge, Mass.: MIT Press, 2006.

Gurney, Belle. "Maternal Influences." *Index Catalogue of the Surgeon General's Office*, 1907 (30508001320).

Gurteen, Stephen Humphries. *Hints and Suggestions to the Visitors of the Poor*. Buffalo, N.Y.: Courier, 1879.

Gusfield, Joseph R. *Symbolic Crusade: Status Politics and the American Temperance Movement*. Champaign-Urbana: University of Illinois Press, 1986.

Guter, Bob. "Nasty Habits." *Queer Crips: Disabled Gay Men and Their Stories*. Ed. Bob Guter and John Killacky. Binghamton, N.Y.: Haworth, 2004.

Habermas, Jürgen. "Public Space and the Political Public Sphere: The Biographical Roots of Two Motifs in My Thought." Commemorative lecture, Kyoto, November 11, 2004. Available online at http://homepage.mac.com/gedavis/JH/kyoto_lecture_Nov_2004.pdf.

Hacking, Ian. *Mad Travelers: Reflections on the Reality of Transient Mental Illnesses*. Charlottesville: University Press of Virginia, 1998.

Hagans, Uriah. *Autobiography of Uriah Hagans*. Liberty Center, Ohio: n.p., 1906.

Hahn, Harlan. "Accommodations and the ADA: Unreasonable Bias or Biased Reasoning?" *Backlash against the ADA: Reinterpreting Disability Rights*. Ed. Linda Hamilton Krieger. Ann Arbor: University of Michigan Press, 2003.

———. "Can Disability Be Beautiful?" *Social Policy* 18 (1988): 22–31.

———. "Introduction: Disability Policy and the Problem of Discrimination." *American Behavioral Scientist* 28:3 (1985): 293–318.

Haines, Blind E. *Constitution of the United States, The Declaration of Independence, with Washington's Farewell Address: Published for the Benefit of Blind E. Haines*. Zanesville, Ohio: Zanesville Courier Office, 1864.

Haines, David W., and Karen Elaine Rosenblum. *Illegal Immigration in America*. Westport, Conn.: Greenwood, 1999.

Halberstam, Judith. *Female Masculinity*. Durham, N.C.: Duke University Press, 1998.

Hale, Grace Elizabeth. *Making Whiteness: The Culture of Segregation in the South, 1890–1940*. Charlottesville: University of Virginia Press, 19998.

Hall, Kim. "Feminism, Disability and Embodiment." *NWSA Journal* 14:3 (2002): xii–xiii.

Hall, Lansing V. *The World as I Hear It*. Dansville, N.Y.: A.O. Bunnell, 1878.

Haltunnen, Karen. *Confidence Men and Painted Women: A Study of Middle-Class Culture in America, 1830–1870*. New Haven, Conn.: Yale University Press, 1983.

Ham, Francie. "A Life for a Limb: Body Integrity Identity Disorder." *Social Work Today*, Feb. 24, 2003, 16–19.

Hamilton, Allan McLane. *Railway and Other Accidents, with Relation to Injury and Disease of the Nervous System: A Book for Court Use*. New York: William Wood, 1904.

Hancock, Ange-Marie. *The Politics of Disgust: The Public Identity of the Welfare Queen*. New York: NYU Press, 2004.

[Hanes, Elias] Rev. John Cumming. *The Coming Wars, and Distress of Nations, and*

the Final Triumph of the Righteous, Published for the Benefit of Blind E. Haynes: Including a Brief Account of His Misfortune. Pittsburgh: Ferguson & Snider, 1861.
Hapgood, Hutchins. *Types from City Streets.* New York: Funk and Wagnalls, 1910.
Hardt, Michael, and Antonio Negri. *Empire.* Cambridge, Mass.: Harvard University Press, 2000.
Harlow, Alvin. *Old Bowery Days.* New York: D. Appleton, 1931.
Harrison, Mayor Carter H., Sr. "Inaugural Address." May 9, 1881. *Chicago Illinois City Council: Journal of the Proceedings* (1881).
Hart, Henry Martyn. *Recollections and Reflections.* Denver: Gibb Bros. & Moran, 1917.
Hartman, Saidiya. *Scenes of Subjection: Terror, Slavery, and Self-Making in Nineteenth-Century America.* New York: Oxford University Press, 1997.
Harvey, David. *The Condition of Post-Modernity.* Oxford, U.K.: Blackwell, 1989.
Harvey, John. "Circumcised by a Maternal Impression." *Medical Record.* New York: W. Wood, 1888. 535.
Hatfield, Marcus. "Maternal Impressions." *Transactions of the 44th Annual Meeting of the Illinois State Medical Society.* Chicago: F.F. Pettibone, 1894.
Helper, Hilton. *Dreadful California.* 1855. New York: Bobbs-Merrill, 1948.
Henderson, Charles. *Introduction to the Study of the Dependent, Defective and Delinquent Classes and of Their Social Treatment.* Boston: D.C. Heath, 1906.
———. Speech recorded in *City Club Bulletin of Chicago* (1910).
Henkin, David. *City Reading: Written Words and Public Spaces in Antebellum New York.* New York: Columbia University Press, 1998.
Herndl, Diane Price. "Hate and the Uncanny Body: The Strange Cases of Nike, Dr. Strangelove, Faulkner and the Supreme Court." Unpublished lecture at the University of California at Berkeley, Mar. 31, 2003.
———. *Invalid Women: Figuring Feminine Illness in American Fiction and Culture, 1840–1940.* Chapel Hill: University of North Carolina, 1993.
Heron, Liz. *Streets of Desire: Women's Fiction in the Twentieth Century.* London: Virago, 1983.
Hershey, Laura. "How Dare I Call Us Crip?" *Crip Commentary: Laura Hershey's Weekly Web Column.* http://www.cripcommentary.com/cc090299.html.
Hevey, David. *The Creatures Time Forgot: Photography and Disability Imagery.* New York: Routledge, 1992.
Heydon, Howard R. "The Supremacy of the Spirit." *Annals of the American Academy of Political and Social Science* 80 (Nov. 1918 issue on "Rehabilitation of the Wounded"): 52–56.
Higbie, Frank Tobias. *Indispensable Outcasts: Hobo Workers and Community in the American Midwest, 1880–1930.* Chicago: University of Illinois Press, 2003.
Hinshaw, David. *Take Up Thy Bed and Walk.* New York: G.P. Putnam's Sons, 1948.
Hoch, Charles, and Robert A. Slayton. *New Homeless and Old: Community and the Skid Row Hotel.* Philadelphia: Temple University Press, 1989.

Hodder, Jessie D., and Edith R. Spaulding, M.D., "Appendix. Containing Charts on 'A Graphic Method of Illustrating Situations in Penal Institutions.'" *Proceedings of the Annual Congress of the American Prison Association.* Indianapolis: Wm. B. Burford, 1915.

Hogan, David John. *Class and Reform: School and Society in Chicago, 1880–1930.* Philadelphia: University of Pennsylvania Press, 1985.

Holmes, Martha Stoddard. *Fictions of Affliction: Physical Disability in Victorian Culture.* Ann Arbor: University of Michigan Press, 2004.

Holmes, Oliver Wendell. *Over the Teacups.* Boston: Houghton Mifflin, 1891.

Hooper, Barbara. "The Poem of Male Desires." *Making the Invisible Visible: A Multicultural Planning History.* Ed. Leonie Sandercock. Berkeley: University of California Press, 1998. 227–254.

Howard, Ebenezer. *Garden Cities of To-Morrow: A Peaceful Path to Real Reform.* 1898. London: Swan Sonnenschein, 1902.

Howells, William Dean. "Tribulations of a Cheerful Giver." *The Century* (Jun.–Jul. 1895).

Hughes, Bill, and Kevin Patterson. "The Social Model of Disability and the Disappearing Body: Towards a Sociology of Impairment." *Disability and Society* 12:3 (June 1, 1997): 325–340.

Humphries, Robert. *Sin, Organized Charity and the Poor Laws in Victorian England.* New York: St. Martin's, 1995.

Hunter, Jack. *Inside Teradome: An Illustrated History of Freak Film.* San Francisco: Creation Books, 1995.

Hutton, Laurence. *Curiosities of the American Stage.* New York: Harper and Brothers, 1891.

Hyde, Alan. *Bodies of Law.* Princeton, N.J.: Princeton University Press, 1997.

Hyde, H. Montgomery. *The Three Trials of Oscar Wilde.* New York: University Books, 1956.

Imrie, Rob. *Disability and the City: International Perspectives.* London: Paul Chapman, 1996.

Indiana State Board of Charities. Testimony of Amos Butler in *Proceedings of the Annual Congress of the American Prison Association, 1915.* Indianapolis: Wm. B. Burford, 1915.

International Municipal Congress and Exposition. *Proceedings.* Chicago: Chicago City Council, 1911.

Iwakuma, Miho. "The Body as Embodiment." *Disability/Postmodernity: Embodying Disability Theory.* Ed. Mairian Corker and Tom Shakespeare. New York: Continuum, 2002. 78–81.

Jackson, Gregory S. "Cultivating Spiritual Sight: Jacob Riis's Virtual Tour Narrative." *Representations* 83 (Summer 2003): 126–166.

Jackson, Joy. *New Orleans in the Gilded Age: Politics and Urban Progress 1880–1896.* New Orleans: Louisiana Historical Association, 1997.

Jackson, Shannon. *Lines of Activity: Performance, Historiography, Hull-House Domesticity*. Ann Arbor: University of Michigan Press, 2000.

Jacobs, Joseph, and Judah David Eisenstein. "Schnorrer." JewishEncyclopedia.com.

Jaeger, Paul, and Cynthia Ann Bowman. *Understanding Disability: Inclusion, Access, Diversity, and Civil Rights*. Westport, Conn.: Praeger, 2005.

Jakobsen, Janet. "Queers Are Like Jews, Aren't They? Analogy and Alliance Politics." *Queer Theory and the Jewish Question*. Ed. Daniel Boyarin, Daniel Itzkovitz, and Ann Pellegrini. New York: Columbia University Press, 2003. 64–90.

———. *Working Alliances and the Politics of Difference: Diversity and Feminist Ethics*. Bloomington: Indiana University Press, 1998.

Jefferis, B.G., and J.L. Nichols. *Safe Counsel or Practical Eugenics*. Philadelphia: Domino, 1926.

Johnson, E. Patrick. *Appropriating Blackness: Performance and the Politics of Authenticity*. Durham, N.C.: Duke University Press, 2003.

Johnson, Mary. "A Test of Wills: Jerry Lewis, Jerry's Orphans and the Telethon." *The Ragged Edge: The Disability Experience from the Pages of the First Fifteen Years of the Disability Rag*. Ed. Barrett Shaw. Louisville, Ky.: Advocado, 1994.

Johnson, Mary, and Barrett Shaw. *To Ride the Public's Buses: The Fight That Built a Movement*. Louisville, Ky.: Advocado, 2001.

Johnson, Roberta Ann. "Mobilizing the Disabled." *Social Movements of the Sixties and Seventies*. Ed. Jo Freeman. New York: Longman, 1983.

Johnson, Tom L. *My Story*. Kent, Ohio: Kent State University Press, 1993.

Kafer, Alison. "Amputated Desire, Resistant Desire: Female Amputees in the Devotee Community." Paper presented at the Society for Disability Studies Conference, Chicago, June 2000.

Kahan, Dan. "The Anatomy of Disgust in Criminal Law." *Michigan Law Review* 96 (1998): 1621–1657.

Kaiser, Clara Anne. "Organized Social Work in Cleveland, Its History and Setting." Ph.D. dissertation, Ohio State University, 1936.

Kant, Immanuel. *Anthropologie in Pragmatischer Hinsicht*. Konigsburg: Universtats Buchhanblung, 1820.

———. *Anthropology from a Pragmatic Point of View*. Trans. Victor Lyle Dowdell. Ed. Hans H. Rudnick. Carbondale: Southern Illinois University Press, 1996.

Kasnitz, Devva, and Russell Shuttleworth. "A Sociocultural Model of Impairment-Disability." *Engaging Anthropology and Disability Studies in Interdisciplinary Dialogue*. Ed. Devva Kasnitz and Russell Shuttleworth. Williamsport, Conn.: Praeger, forthcoming.

Kasson, John. *Rudeness and Civility: Manners in Nineteenth-Century Urban America*. New York: Hill and Wang, 1990.

Katz, Michael. "The History of an Impudent Poor Woman in New York City from 1918 to 1923." *The Uses of Charity: The Poor on Relief in the Nineteenth-Century*

Metropolis. Ed. Peter Mandler. Philadelphia: University of Pennsylvania Press, 1990.

———. *In the Shadow of the Poorhouse: A Social History of Welfare in America.* New York: Basic Books, 1986.

———. *Poverty and Policy in American History.* New York: Academic Press, 1983.

Kaufman, A. *Historic Supplement of the Denver Police: A Review from Earliest Days to the Present Time.* Denver: Denver Police Mutual Aid Fund, 1890.

Kaveny, M. Cathleen. "Autonomy, Solidarity and Law's Pedagogy." *Levain Studies* 27:4 (2002): 339–358.

Kelley, Robin D.G. *Race Rebels: Culture, Politics, and the Black Working Class.* New York: Free Press, 1994.

Kerber, Linda. *No Constitutional Right to Be Ladies: Women and the Obligations of Citizenship.* New York: Hill and Wang, 1999.

Kiger, Gary. "Disability Simulations: Logical, Methodological and Ethical Issues." *Disability, Handicap and Society* 7:1 (1992): 71–78.

Kim, Eun Jung. "History of Disability: Korea." *Encyclopedia of Disability.* Ed. Gary Albrecht. Vol. 2. Pp. 858–864. Thousand Oaks, Calif.: Sage, 2005.

Kingrey, Julia. "Should Discrimination Laws Cover Ugly People?" www.thefence.com, posted Jan. 15, 2001, DebateID 844.

Kirkland, Joseph. "Among the Poor of Chicago." *Scribner's* 12:1 (July 1892).

Kleege, Georgina. "Blindness and Visual Culture: An Eyewitness Account." *Journal of Visual Culture* 4:2 (2005): 179–190.

———. *Sight Unseen.* New Haven, Conn.: Yale University Press, 1999.

Kleinfeld, Sonny. *The Hidden Minority: America's Handicapped.* Boston: Little, Brown, 1977.

Kmiecek, Cynthia, Paula Mauser, and George Banzinger. "Attractiveness and Interpersonal Space." *Journal of Social Psychology* 108 (Aug. 1979): 277–278.

Knox, Mertice Buck. "Survey of the Handicapped in Los Angeles." *Annual Report of the Social Service Commission, City of Los Angeles, California July 1, 1916–July 1, 1917.*

Kohr, Herbert O. *Around the World with Uncle Sam.* Akron, Ohio: Commercial, 1907.

Krausz, Sigmund. *Street Types of Chicago: Character Studies.* Chicago: Max Stern, 1892.

Krieger, Linda Hamilton, ed. *Backlash against the ADA: Reinterpreting Disability Rights.* Ann Arbor: University of Michigan Press, 2004.

Kristeva, Julia. *Powers of Horror: An Essay on Abjection.* New York: Columbia University Press, 1982.

Kudlick, Catherine J. "Disability History: Why We Need Another 'Other.'" *American Historical Review* 108:3 (June 2003): 1–28.

———. "The Outlook of *The Problem* and the Problem with the *Outlook*: Two Advocacy Journals Reinvent Blind People in Turn-of-the-Century America." *The*

New Disability History: American Perspectives. Ed. Paul Longmore and Lauri Umansky. New York: NYU Press, 2001.

Kuppers, Petra. *Disability and Contemporary Performance: Bodies on Edge.* New York: Routledge, 2003.

———, ed. *Disability and Performance.* Special issue of *Contemporary Theatre Review.* New York: Harwood Academic Press, Summer 2001.

———. "Image Politics without the Real: Simulacra, Dandyism and Disability Fashion." *Disability/Postmodernity: Embodying Disability Theory*. Ed. Mairian Corker and Tom Shakespeare. New York: Continuum, 2002.

Kurzman, Steven L. "Presence and Prosthesis: A Response to Nelson and Wright." *Cultural Anthropology* 16:3 (2001): 374–387.

Kusmer, Kenneth. *Down and Out, On the Road: The Homeless in American History.* New York: Oxford University Press, 2002.

———. "The Functions of Organized Charity in the Progressive Era: Chicago as a Case Study." *Journal of American History* (Dec. 1973): 657–678.

Laclau, Ernesto, and Chantal Mouffe. *Hegemony and Socialist Strategy: Towards a Radical Democratic Politics.* London: Verso, 1985.

Lai, Him Mark, Genny Lim, and Judy Yung. *Island: Poetry and History of Chinese Immigrants on Angel Island, 1910–1940*. Seattle: University of Washington Press, 1980.

Landsberg, Alison. *Prosthetic Memory.* New York: Columbia University Press, 2004.

Langan, Celeste. *Romantic Vagrancy: Wordsworth and the Simulation of Freedom.* New York: Cambridge University Press, 1995.

Laughlin, Harry. "The Eugenical Sterilization of the Feeble-Minded." 1926. *Mental Retardation in America: A Historical Reader.* Ed. Steven Noll and James W. Trent Jr. New York: NYU Press, 2004.

Leader, Pauline. *And No Birds Sing.* Vanguard, 1931.

Leder, Drew. *The Absent Body.* Chicago: University of Chicago Press, 1990.

Lefebvre, Henri. "The Right to the City." *Writings on Cities.* Selected and translated by Eleonore Kofman and Elizabeth Lebas. Oxford, U.K.: Blackwell, 1999.

Levi, Sandra J. "Ableism." *Encyclopedia of Disability.* Vol. 1. Ed. Gary Albrecht. Thousand Oaks, Calif.: Sage, 2005. 1–3.

Levin, David Michael, ed. *Modernity and the Hegemony of Vision.* Berkeley: University of California Press, 1993.

Levinas, Emmanuel. *Otherwise than Being, or Beyond Essence.* Trans. Alphonso Lingis. The Hague: Nijhoff, 1981.

———. "Peace and Proximity." *Basic Philosophical Writings.* Ed. Adriaan T. Peperzak, Simon Critchley, and Robert Bernasconi. Bloomington: Indiana University Press, 1996.

Lewis, Halle. "Cripples Are Not the Dependents One Is Led to Think: Work and Disability in Industrializing Cleveland, 1861–1916." Ph.D. dissertation, SUNY Binghamton, 2004.

Lewis, Victoria Ann. *Beyond Victims and Villains: Contemporary Plays by Disabled Playwrights*. Theater Communications Group, 2005.

———. "Radical Wallflowers: Disability and the People's Theater." *Radical History Review* 94 (Winter 2006): 84–110.

Lifchez, Ray. *Rethinking Architecture: Design Students and Physically Disabled People*. Berkeley: University of California Press, 1987.

Lindberg, Richard. *To Serve and Collect: Chicago Politics and Police Corruption from the Lager Beer Riot to the Summerdale Scandal: 1855–1960*. Carbondale: Southern Illinois University Press, 1998.

Lindsey, Almont. *The Pullman Strike*. Chicago: University of Chicago Press, 1967.

Lingis, Alphonso. "The Physiology of Art." *The Prosthetic Impulse: From a Posthuman Present to a Biocultural Future*. Ed. Marquand Smith and Joanne Mora. Cambridge, Mass.: MIT Press, 2006. 78–82.

Linker, Beth. "Feet for Fighting: Locating Disability and Social Medicine in First World War America." *Social History of Medicine* 20:1 (2007): 91–109.

Linton, Simi. *Claiming Disability*. New York: St. Martin's, 1998.

Linton, Simi, and Lennard Davis, eds. *Radical Teacher* 47 (Fall 1995).

Litvak, Simi, and Alexandra Enders. "Support Systems: The Interface between Individuals and Environments." *Handbook of Disability Studies*. Ed. Gary Albrecht, Katherine D. Seelman, and Michael Bury. Thousand Oaks, Calif.: Sage, 2001.

Litwack, Leon. *Trouble in Mind: Black Southerners in the Age of Jim Crow*. New York: Knopf, 1998.

Livingston, Julie. *Debility and the Moral Imagination in Botswana*. Bloomington: Indiana University Press, 2005.

Lloyd, B.E. *Lights and Shades in San Francisco*. San Francisco: A.L. Bancroft, 1876.

Loberg, Molly. "Berlin Streets: Politics, Commerce and Crowds, 1918–1938." Ph.D. dissertation, Princeton University, 2006.

Lombroso, Cesare, and Guglielmo Ferrero. *Criminal Woman, the Prostitute, and the Normal Woman*. 1903. Trans. Nicole Hahn Rafter and Mary Gibson. Durham, N.C.: Duke University Press, 2004.

Longmore, Paul. "Conspicuous Contribution and American Cultural Dilemmas: Telethon Rituals of Cleansing and Renewal." *The Body and Physical Difference: Discourses of Disability*. Ed. David T. Mitchell and Sharon Snyder. Ann Arbor: University of Michigan Press, 1997. 134–160.

———. "The Cultural Framing of Disability: Telethons as a Case Study." "Conference on Disability Studies and the University." *PMLA* 120:2 (Mar. 2005): 1–13.

———. "Disability: The Body and the World." Playbill for the Mark Taper production of John Belluso's *The Body of Bourne*, 2001. 6.

———. Foreword. *The Hospital Poems*. By Jim Ferris. Charlotte, N.C.: Main Street Rag, 2004.

———. "The Life of Randolph Bourne and the Need for a History of Disabled People." *Reviews in American History* 13 (Dec. 1985): 581–587.

———. *Why I Burned My Book and Other Essays on Disability*. Philadelphia: Temple University Press, 2003.

Longmore, Paul, and David Goldberger. "The League of the Physically Handicapped and the Great Depression: A Case Study in the New Disability History." *Journal of American History* 87:3 (2000): 888–922.

Longmore, Paul, and Paul Steven Miller. "A Philosophy of Handicap." *Radical History Review* 94 (Winter 2006): 59–83.

Longmore, Paul, and Lauri Umansky, eds. *The New Disability History*. New York: NYU Press, 2001.

Loo, Tina, and Carolyn Strange. "The Traveling Show Menace: Contested Regulation in Turn-of-the-Century Ontario." *Law and Society Review* 29:4 (1995): 639–668.

Losecke, Donileen. "The Whole Spirit of Modern Philanthropy: The Construction of the Idea of Charity 1912–1992." *Social Problems* 44:4 (Nov. 1997): 525–544.

Lowell, C.R. "How to Adapt 'Charity Organization' Methods to Small Communities." *Proceedings of the National Conference on Charities and Correction*. Boston: Geo. H. Ellis, 1887.

Lowell, Josephine Shaw. "One Means of Preventing Pauperism." *Proceedings of the Sixth Annual Conference on Charities* (June 1879): 189–200.

———. *Public Relief and Private Charity*. New York: Putnam, 1884.

Lubiano, Wahneema. "Like Being Mugged by a Metaphor." *Mapping Multiculturalism*. Ed. Avery F. Gordon. Minneapolis: University of Minnesota Press, 1996.

Lubove, Ray. *The Professional Altruist: The Emergence of Social Work as a Career, 1880–1930*. Cambridge, Mass.: Harvard University Press, 1965.

Lui, Mary Ting Yi. *The Chinatown Trunk Mystery: Murder, Miscegenation, and Other Dangerous Encounters in Turn-of-the-Century New York City*. Princeton, N.J.: Princeton University Press, 2005.

Lutz, Tom. *American Nervousness, 1903: An Anecdotal History*. Ithaca, N.Y.: Cornell University Press, 1991.

Lyman, Stanford. "The 'Yellow Peril' Mystique: Origins and Vicissitudes of a Racist Discourse." *International Journal of Politics, Culture and Society* 13:4 (2000): 683–747.

MacGregor, Frances Cooke. *Facial Deformities and Plastic Surgery*. New York: Charles Thomas, 1953.

———. "Some Psycho-Social Problems Associated with Facial Deformities." *American Sociological Review* (1951): 629–638.

———. *Transformation and Identity: The Face and Plastic Surgery*. Oak Gove, Ill.: Eterna, 1980.

MacIntyre, Alasdair. *Dependent Rational Animals: Why Human Beings Need the Virtues.* Chicago: Open Court, 1999.
Margolin, Leslie. *Under the Cover of Kindness: The Invention of Social Work.* Charlottesville: University of Virginia Press, 1997.
Marks, Deborah. *Disability: Controversial Debates and Psychosocial Perspectives.* London: Routledge, 1999.
Marsh, Benjamin C. "Methods Employed by American Cities to Eradicate Vagrancy." *National Conference of Charities and Correction Proceedings.* 1903.
Marx, Karl. *The Poverty of Philosophy.* 1847. New York: International Publishers, 1963.
Mason, Jennifer. *Civilized Creatures: Urban Animals, Sentimental Culture, and American Literature, 1850–1900.* Baltimore: Johns Hopkins University Press, 2005.
Mason, Mary Grimley. *Working against Odds: Stories of Disabled Women's Work Lives.* Boston: Northeastern University Press, 2004.
McAllister, Edwin. "Smallpox, Opium, and Invasion: Chinese Invasion, White Guilt, and Native American Displacement in Late Nineteenth- and Early Twentieth-Century American Fiction." *Complicating Constructions: Race, Ethnicity, and Hybridity in American Texts.* Ed. David S. Goldstein and Audrey B. Thacker. Seattle: University of Washington Press, 2007. 143–156.
McBride, David. *From TB to AIDS: Epidemics among Urban Blacks since 1900.* Albany: SUNY Press, 1991.
McCarthy, Kathleen. *Noblesse Oblige: Charity and Cultural Philanthropy in Chicago, 1849–1929.* Chicago: University of Chicago Press, 1982.
McCook, John J. "A Tramp Census." *Forum* 15 (Aug. 1893): 753–756.
———. "Tramps." *Public Opinion* 16:14 (Jan. 4, 1894): 316–317.
McCord, C.H. *The American Negro as a Dependent, Defective and Delinquent.* Nashville, Tenn.: Benson, 1914.
McCulloch, Oscar. "The Tribe of Ishmael: A Study in Social Degradation." Paper read at the Fifteenth National Conference of Charities and Corrections in Buffalo, July 1888. Rpt. in *Yearbook of Charities: Work of 1888–1889.* Indianapolis: Baker and Randolph, 1890.
McDonald, Arthur. *Juvenile Crime and Reformation, Including Stigmata of Degeneration.* Senate Doc. 532. Washington D.C., 1908.
———. "A Plan for the Study of Man." *American Journal of Sociology* 6:6 (May 1901): 839–846.
McDonald, Terrence. *The Parameters of Urban Fiscal Policy: Socioeconomic Change and Political Culture in San Francisco, 1860–1906.* Berkeley: University of California Press, 1987.
McDowell, Linda. *Gender, Identity and Place: Understanding Feminist Geographies.* Minneapolis: University of Minnesota Press.

McMurtrie, Douglas. *Future Policy in Dealing with Disabled Civilians: Some Conclusions from Experience.* New York: William Wood, 1918.
———. *The Meaning of the Term "Crippled."* New York: William Wood, 1918.
———. *Rehabilitation of the War Cripple.* New York: Red Cross Institute for Crippled and Disabled Men, 1918.
———. "The Work of an American School for the Rehabilitation of the Disabled." *Boston Medical and Surgical Journal* (Jan. 1919).
McNamara, Brooks. *Step Right Up.* 2nd ed. Jackson: University of Mississippi Press, 1995.
McRobbie, Angela. "Vulnerability, Violence and (Cosmopolitan) Ethics: Butler's *Precarious Life.*" *British Journal of Sociology* 57:1 (2006): 69–86.
McRuer, Robert. *Crip Theory.* New York: NYU Press, 2006.
McRuer, Robert, and Abby Wilkerson, eds. GLQ 9:1/2 (2003). Special issue entitled "Desiring Disability: Queer Theory Meets Disability Studies."
Meites, Hyman L. *History of Jews in Chicago.* 1924. Chicago: Chicago Jewish Historical Society, 1990.
Mencken, August. *The Railroad Passenger Car.* Baltimore: Johns Hopkins University Press, 2000.
Menninghaus, Winfried. *Disgust.* Trans. Howard Eiland and Joel Golb. Albany: SUNY Press, 2003.
Merington, Marguerite. "Woman and the Bicycle." *Scribner's* 17 (June 1895). Rpt. in *The American 1890s: A Cultural Reader.* Ed. Susan Harris Smith and Melanie Dawson. Durham, N.C.: Duke University Press, 2000.
Merleau-Ponty, Maurice. *Phenomenology of Perception.* Trans. Colin Smith. London: Routledge, 1962.
Merrifield, Andy. *Metromarxism: A Marxist Tale of the City.* New York: Routledge, 2002.
Merves, E.S. "Homeless Women: Beyond the Bag Lady Myth." *Homelessness: A National Perspective.* Ed. M.J. Robertson and M. Greenblatt. New York: Plenum, 1992.
Michael, Robert. *A Concise History of American Antisemitism.* New York: Rowman and Littlefield, 2005.
Michalko, Rod. *The Difference That Disability Makes.* Philadelphia: Temple University Press, 2002.
Miller, Joaquin. Untitled article in *Harper's Weekly,* Mar. 15, 1879, 216.
Miller, Sheila D. *Disability and the Black Community.* New York: Haworth, 2002.
Miller, Susan. *Disgust: The Gatekeeper Emotion.* Hillside, N.J.: Analytic Press, 2004.
Miller, William Ian. *The Anatomy of Disgust.* Cambridge, Mass.: Harvard University Press, 1997.
Mitchell, David T., and Sharon Snyder, eds. *The Body and Physical Difference: Discourses of Disability.* Ann Arbor: University of Michigan Press, 1997.

Mitchell, David T., and Sharon Snyder. See also Snyder, Sharon, and David T. Mitchell.

Mitchell, Don. *The Right to the City.* New York: Guilford, 2003.

Moeschen, Sheila. "Suffering Silences, Woeful Afflictions: Physical Disability, Melodrama, and the American Charity Movement." *Comparative Drama* 40:4 (Winter 2006–7): 433–455.

Mogk, Marja. "Narrating Vision: Disability, Aging and Autobiography." Ph.D. dissertation, University of California at Berkeley, 2004.

Molina, Natalia. *Fit to Be Citizens? Public Health and Race in Los Angeles, 1879–1939.* Berkeley: University of California Press, 2006.

———. "Medicalizing the Mexican: Immigration, Race, and Disability in the Early-Twentieth-Century United States." *Radical History Review* (Winter 2006): 22–37.

Mollow, Anna. "Identifying Disability, Disabling Identity: Disability Studies, Identity Politics, and Postmodernism." *Michigan Quarterly Review* 43:2 (2004): 269–296.

Morales, Alfonso. "Peddling Policy: Street Vending in Historical and Contemporary Context." *International Journal of Sociology and Social Policy* 21:3–4 (2000): 76–98.

Morrison, Toni. *The Bluest Eye.* 1970. New York: Plume, 2000.

Mulvey, Laura. "Visual Pleasure and Narrative Cinema." *Visual and Other Pleasures.* Bloomington: Indiana University Press, 1989.

Mumford, Kevin. *Interzones: Black/White Sex Districts in Chicago and New York in the Early Twentieth Century.* New York: Columbia University Press, 1997.

Mundo, Oto. *The Recovered Continent: A Tale of the Chinese Invasion.* Columbus, OH: Harper-Osgood, 1898.

Municipal Charities Commission. *First Annual Report of the Municipal Charities Commission, City of Los Angeles, July 1, 1913–July 1, 1914.* Los Angeles: Diamond, 1914.

———. *Second Annual Report of the Municipal Charities Commission, City of Los Angeles, California, July 1, 1914–July 1, 1915.* Los Angeles: Diamond, 1915.

———. *Third Annual Report of the Municipal Charities Commission, City of Los Angeles, California, July 1, 1915–July 1, 1916.* Los Angeles: Diamond, 1916.

Municipal League. *Proceedings of the National Conference for Good City Government Held at Philadelphia January 25 and 26, 1894.* Philadelphia: Municipal League, 1894.

Murphy, A.J. *The Life of A.J. Murphy.* Columbus, Ohio: n.p., ca. 1900.

Murray, Stuart. "Bartleby, Preference, Pleasure and Autistic Presence." Paper presented at MLA Convention, Philadelphia, 2004.

Murrell, Thomas. "Syphilis and the American Negro: A Medico-Legal Study." *Journal of the American Medical Association* 54 (Mar. 10, 1910): 846–849.

Muscatine, Doris. *Old San Francisco*. New York: G.P. Putnam's Sons, 1975.

"Mutilation as a Trade." *Public Opinion* 15:26 (Sept. 30, 1893): 600–601.

Nascher, I.L. *The Wretches of Povertyville: A Sociological Study of the Bowery*. Chicago: Jos. J. Lanzit, 1909.

National Conference of Charities and Correction Proceedings of the 30th Annual Meeting, Atlanta, Georgia, 1903.

Neilson, Laura Beth. *License to Harass: Law, Hierarchy, and Offensive Public Speech*. Princeton, N.J.: Princeton University Press, 2004.

Nelli, Humbert. *Italians in Chicago, 1880–1930: A Study in Ethnic Mobility*. New York: Oxford University Press, 1970.

Nelson, Alondra. "Black Power, Biomedicine, and the Politics of Knowledge." Ph.D. dissertation, New York University, 2003.

"New Chance for Cripples Just Begun." *Social Bulletin* 3 (Nov. 1915): 1.

Newitz, Annalee, and Matt Wray. "What Is 'White Trash'? Stereotypes and Economic Conditions of Poor Whites in the United States." *Whiteness: A Critical Reader*. Ed. Mike Hill. New York: NYU Press, 1997. 168–184.

Newman, Simon P. *Embodied History: The Lives of the Poor in Early Philadelphia*. Philadelphia: University of Pennsylvania Press, 2003.

Newton, John. *Blind John in New York in 1861*. Montpelier, Vt.: Argus and Patriot, 1891.

Ngai, Sianne. *Ugly Feelings*. Cambridge, Mass.: Harvard University Press, 2005.

Nickell, Joe. *Secrets of the Sideshows*. Lexington: University Press of Kentucky, 2005.

Norden, Martin. *The Cinema of Isolation: A History of Physical Disability in the Movies*. New Brunswick, N.J.: Rutgers University Press, 1994.

Norr, William. *Stories of Chinatown: Sketches from the Chinese Colony*. New York: William Norr, 1892.

Norris, Frank. "Little Dramas of the Curbstone." *Wave* (Jan. 26 and Dec. 10, 1897).

———. *The Third Circle, A Deal in Wheat and Other Stories of the New and Old West*. 1909. Garden City, N.Y.: Doubleday, Duran, 1928.

Rev. of *Notes on Mexico*, by Poinsett. *United States Literary Gazette* 1:8 (1825): 16.

Nussbaum, Martha. *Hiding from Humanity: Disgust, Shame, and the Law*. Princeton, N.J.: Princeton University Press, 2004.

Nussbaum, Susan. *No One as Nasty*. In *Beyond Victims and Villains: Contemporary Plays by Disabled Playwrights*. Ed. Victoria Ann Lewis. New York: Theater Communications Group, 2005.

O'Brien, Ruth. *Bodies in Revolt: Gender, Disability, and a Workplace Ethic of Care*. New York: Routledge, 2005.

———. *Crippled Justice: The History of Modern Disability Policy in the Workplace*. Chicago: University of Chicago Press, 2001.

———, ed. *Voices from the Edge: Narratives about the Americans with Disabilities Act*. New York: Oxford University Press, 2004.

O'Connor, Alice. *Poverty Knowledge: Social Science, Social Policy and the Poor in Twentieth-Century U.S. History*. Princeton, N.J.: Princeton University Press, 2001.

O'Connor, Sean. "Talking about Body Integrity Identity Disorder." http://trandisabled.org.

Okeley, Judith. "Gypsy Identity." *Gypsies and Government Policy in England*. Ed. B. Adams et al. London: Heinemann, 1975.

Olian, Judy. "On the Job: Lawsuit Contends Birthmark Kept Woman from Promotion." *Pittsburgh Post-Gazette*, Apr. 15, 2003, Business section, 1–3.

Oliver, Michael. *The Politics of Disablement: A Sociological Approach*. New York: St. Martin's, 1990.

———. *Understanding Disability: From Theory to Practice*. New York: St. Martin's, 1996.

Olsen, Tillie (publishing under the name Tillie Lerner). "Thousand-Dollar Vagrant." *New Republic*, Aug. 29, 1934, 67–69.

O'Toole, Corbett. "The Sexist Inheritance of the Disability Movement." *Gendering Disability*. Ed. Bonnie G. Smith and Beth Hutchinson. New Brunswick, N.J.: Rutgers University Press, 2004.

O'Toole, Corbett, and J.L. Bregante. "Disabled Lesbians." *Perspectives on Disability*. 2nd ed. Ed. M. Nagler. Palo Alto, Calif.: Health Markets Research.

———. "Lesbians with Disabilities." *Sexuality and Disability* 10:3 (1992): 163–172.

Ott, Katherine, David Serlin, and Stephen Mihm. *Artificial Parts, Practical Lives: Modern Histories of Prosthesis*. New York: NYU Press, 2002.

Packard, Frank. *The Miracle Man*. New York: Grosset and Dunlap, 1914.

Padden, Carol, and Tom Humphries. *Deaf in America: Voices from a Culture*. Cambridge, Mass.: Harvard University Press, 1988.

Paine, Robert Treat. *How to Repress Pauperism and Street Begging*. New York: Charity Organization Society, 1883.

———. *The Work of Volunteer Visitors of the Associated Charities among the Poor: Its Limitations, Allies, Number of Workers, Aims, and Grand Results*. Boston: Geo. E. Crosby, 1880.

Parker, Andrew, and Eve Kosofsky Sedgwick, eds. *Performativity and Performance: Essays for the English Institute*. New York: Routledge, 1995.

Parr, Hester. "Disability." *A Feminist Glossary of Human Geography*. Ed. Linda McDowell and Joanne P. Sharp. New York: Oxford University Press, 1999.

Parsons, Deborah. *Streetwalking the Metropolis: Women, the City and Modernity*. New York: Oxford University Press, 2000.

Pasquale, Frank. "The Notion That We Should All Look the Same Is Hatred." Concurring Opinions weblog, Feb. 11, 2008, http://www.concurringopinions.com/archives/2008/02/the_notion_that.html.

Patterson, James T. *America's Struggle against Poverty in the Twentieth Century*. Cambridge, Mass.: Harvard University Press, 1981. Rpt. 2001.

Paul, Rodman W. "After the Gold Rush: San Francisco and Portland." *Pacific Historical Review* 51:1 (1982): 1–21.

Paupers in Almshouses II. Washington, D.C.: Bureau of the Census, 1923.

Perlin, Michael. *The Hidden Prejudice: Mental Disability on Trial*. Washington, D.C.: American Psychological Association, 2000.

Pernick, Martin. *The Black Stork: Eugenics and the Death of "Defective" Babies in American Medicine and Motion Pictures Since 1915*. New York: Oxford University Press, 1996.

———. "Defining the Defective: Eugenics, Aesthetics, and Mass Culture in Early-Twentieth-Century America." *The Body and Physical Difference: Discourses of Disability*. Ed. David T. Mitchell and Sharon L. Snyder. Ann Arbor: University of Michigan Press, 1997. 89–110.

———. "Film: Medical Films." *Censorship: A World Encyclopedia*. Ed. Derek Jones. Chicago: Fitzroy Dearborn, 2001. 815–816.

Pfeiffer, David. "Disability Simulation Using a Wheelchair Exercise." *Journal of Postsecondary Education and Disability* 7:2 (1989): 53–60.

Pierce, Bessie Louise. *A History of Chicago, Volume 3*. Chicago: University of Chicago Press, 1976.

Pillavin, Irving M., Jane A. Pillavin, and Judith Rodin. "Costs, Diffusion, and the Stigmatized Victim." *Journal of Personality and Social Psychology* 32 (1975): 429–438.

Pimentel, Richard, Francis P. Alvarez, Michael J. Lotito, Society for Human Resources Management (U.S.), Lewis Jackson, and Milt Wright and Associates. *Americans with Disabilities Act: Making the ADA Work for You*. Granada Hills, Calif.: Milt Wright and Associates, 1992.

Pittenger, Mark. "A World of Difference: Constructing the 'Underclass' in Progressive America." *American Quarterly* 49:1 (1997): 26–65.

Piven, Frances Fox, and Richard A. Cloward. *Regulating the Poor: The Functions of Public Welfare*. New York: Pantheon, 1971.

Poirier, Suzanne. *Chicago's War on Syphilis, 1937–1940: The Times, The Trib, and the Clap Doctor*. Urbana: University of Illinois Press, 1995.

Polsky, Andrew J. *The Rise of the Therapeutic State*. Princeton, N.J.: Princeton University Press, 1991.

Pope John Paul II. "Sollicitudo Rei Socialis" no. 39.

Postrel, Virginia. "Going to Great Lengths." *New York Times Magazine*, Aug. 31, 2003, 16.

Price, Janet, and Margrit Shildrick. "Breaking the Boundaries of the Broken Body." *Body and Society* 2:4 (1996): 93–113.

———. "Bodies Together: Touch, Ethics and Disability." *Disability/Postmodernity: Embodying Disability Theory*. Ed. Mairian Corker and Tom Shakespeare. London: Continuum, 2002. 63–75.

Proceedings of the Council, City of Buffalo, 1894. Buffalo, N.Y.: James D. Warren's Sons, 1894.

Proctor, Rev. H.H. "The Need of Friendly Visitation." *Social and Physical Conditions of Negroes in Cities*. Atlanta: Atlanta University Press, 1897.

Putzi, Jennifer. *Identifying Marks: Race, Gender, and the Marked Body in Nineteenth-Century America*. Athens: University of Georgia Press, 2006.

Rabban, David. *Free Speech in Its Forgotten Years*. New York: Cambridge University Press, 1997.

Radin, Margaret Jane. *Contested Commodities*. Cambridge, Mass.: Harvard University Press, 1996.

Rafter, Nicole. "The Criminalization of Mental Retardation." *Mental Retardation in America: A Historical Reader*. Ed. Steven Noll and James W. Trent Jr. New York: NYU Press, 2004.

Rafter, Nicole, and Mary Gibson. Introduction. *Criminal Woman, the Prostitute, and the Normal Woman*. Ed. Nicole Rafter and Mary Gibson. Trans. Cesare Lombroso and Guglielmo Ferrero. Durham, N.C.: Duke University Press, 2004.

Rainsford, George N. "Dean Henry Martin [*sic*] Hart and Public Issues." *Colorado Magazine* (Summer 1971): 206.

Reed, Myron W. *Temple Talks*. New York: Bowen Merrill, 1898.

Reik, Theodore. *Jewish Wit*. New York: Gamut Press, 1962.

Reiser, Andrew. *The Chautauqua Moment: Protestants, Progressives, and the Culture of Modern Liberalism*. New York: Columbia University Press, 2003.

Reitman, Ben. *Sister of the Road: The Autobiography of Boxcar Bertha*. 1937. Oakland, Calif.: Nabat/AK Press, 2002.

Report of the General Superintendent of Police of the City of Chicago, To the City Council, 1880. Chicago: Clark and Edwards, 1881.

Report of the General Superintendent of Police of the City of Chicago, To the City Council, 1881–85. Chicago: Cameron, Amberg, 1886.

Rhyne, Charles S., Charles H. Burton, and Charlie O. Murphy. *Municipal Regulation of Peddlers, Solicitors and Itinerant Merchants: Report No. 118*. Washington, D.C.: National Institute of Municipal Law Offices, 1947.

Ribton-Turner, C.J. (Charles James). *A History of Vagrants and Vagrancy and Beggars and Begging*. London: Chapman and Hall, 1887.

Richards, Penny. "Beside Her Sat Her Idiot Child." *Mental Retardation in America: A Historical Reader*. Ed. Steven Noll and James W. Trent Jr. New York: NYU Press, 2004. 65–86.

Richter, Amy G. *Home on the Rails: Women, the Railroad, and the Rise of Public Domesticity*. Chapel Hill: University of North Carolina Press, 2005.

Riis, Jacob. *How the Other Half Lives*. 1890. New York: Dover, 1971.

Ringenbach, Paul T. *Tramps and Reformers 1873–1916: The Discovery of Unemployment in New York*. Westport, Conn.: Greenwood, 1973.

Ribton-Turner, C.J. *A History of Vagrants and Vagrancy, Beggars and Begging.* 1887. Montclair, N.J.: Patterson Smith, 1972.

Ritter, Lawrence S. *The Glory of Their Times: The Story of the Early Days of Baseball Told by the Men Who Played It.* New York: William Morrow, 1984.

Roach, Joseph. *Cities of the Dead: Circum-Atlantic Performance.* New York: Columbia University Press, 1996.

———. "Deep Skin: Reconstructing Congo Square." *African American Performance and Theater History: A Critical Reader.* Ed. Harry J. Elam and David Krasner. New York: Oxford University Press, 2001.

Roediger, David. *The Wages of Whiteness: Race and the Making of the American Working Class.* London: Verso, 1999.

Rogin, Michael. *Black Face, White Noise: Jewish Immigrants in the Hollywood Melting Pot.* Berkeley: University of California Press, 1996.

Romey, Kristin M. "The Dead of Snake Hill." *Archeology* (May/June 2005): 42–49.

Rose, Lionel. *Rogues and Vagabonds: Vagrant Underworld in Britain, 1815–1985.* New York: Routledge, 1988.

Rose, Wendy. "Julia." *The Woman That I Am: The Literature and Criticism of Contemporary Women of Color.* Ed. D. Soyini Madison. New York: St. Martin's, 1997. 127–128.

———. "Sideshow: Julia the Lion Woman, The Ugliest Woman in the World." *A Gathering of Spirit: A Collection by North American Indian Women.* Ed. Beth Brant. New York: Firebrand, 1984.

Rose, William Ganson. *Cleveland: The Making of a City.* Kent, Ohio: Kent State University Press, 1990.

Rosenberg, Carol Smith. *Religion and the Rise of the American City: The New York City Mission Movement, 1812–1870.* Ithaca, N.Y.: Cornell University Press, 1971.

Ross, Edward Alsworth. *The Principles of Sociology.* New York: Century, 1920.

Ross, Ellen. "Hungry Children: Housewives and London Charity, 1870–1918." *The Uses of Charity: The Poor on Relief in the Nineteenth-Century Metropolis.* Ed. Peter Mandler. Philadelphia: University of Pennsylvania Press, 1990.

Roth, William. *The Assault on Social Policy.* New York: Columbia University Press, 2002.

———. "Handicap as a Social Construct." *Society* (Mar./Apr. 1983): 56–61.

Rothman, David. *Conscience and Convenience: The Asylum and Its Alternatives in Progressive America.* New York: HarperCollins, 1980.

Royce, Josiah. *California.* 1886. New York: Knopf, 1948.

Royko, Mike. "A Law City Should Keep." Oct. 19, 1973. *For the Love of Mike.* By Mike Royko. Chicago: University of Chicago Press, 2002.

Rozin, Paul, Jonathan Haidt, and Clark R. McCauley. "Disgust." *Handbook of Emotions.* Ed. M. Lewis and J.M. Haviland-Jones. New York: Guilford. 637–653.

Russell, Marta. *Beyond Ramps: Disability at the End of the Social Contract.* Monroe, Me.: Common Courage, 1998.

Russell, Marta, and Jean Stewart. "Disablement, Prison, and Historical Segregation." *Monthly Review* (July 2001): 61–75.
Ryan, Miss Amelia (A Blind Lady). *Poems.* N.p.: ca. 1890.
Ryan, Mary. *Women in Public: Between Banners and Ballots 1825–1880.* Baltimore: Johns Hopkins University Press, 1992.
Ryan, Susan. *The Grammar of Good Intentions: Race and the Antebellum Culture of Benevolence.* Ithaca, N.Y.: Cornell University Press, 2003.
Samuels, Ellen. "A Complication of Complaints." *Melus* 31 (Fall 2006): 15–47.
———. "Fingerprinting the Nation." Ph.D. dissertation, University of California at Berkeley, 2006.
———. "From Melville to Eddie Murphy." *Leviathan: A Journal of Melville Studies* 8:1 (2006): 61–82.
Sanborn, Alvin. *Moody's Lodging House and Other Tenement Sketches.* Boston: Copland and Day, 1895.
Sandahl, Carrie. "Queering the Crip or Cripping the Queer? Intersections of Queer and Crip Identities in Solo Autobiographical Performance." GLQ*: A Journal of Lesbian and Gay Studies* 9 (2003): 1–2.
Sandahl, Carrie, and Philip Auslander. *Bodies in Commotion.* Ann Arbor: University of Michigan, 2005.
Sante, Luc. *Low Life.* New York: Farrar, Straus, and Giroux, 1991.
Sappol, Michael. "Morbid Curiosity: The Decline and Fall of the Popular Anatomical Museum." *Common-Place* 4:2 (Jan. 2004).
———. *As.*
Saxton, Marsha, and Florence Howe, eds. *With Wings.* New York: Feminist Press, 1987.
Scarry, Elaine. *On Beauty and Being Just.* Princeton, NJ: Princeton University Press, 1999.
Schaak, Michael. *Anarchy and Anarchists: A History of the Red Terror and the Social Revolution in America and Europe.* Chicago: F.J. Schulte, 1889.
Schechner, Richard. *Performance Studies: An Introduction.* New York: Routledge, 2002.
Schneider, Eric. *In the Web of Class: Delinquents and Reform in Boston, 1810s to 1930s.* New York: NYU Press, 1992.
Schneider, Rebecca. *The Explicit Body in Performance.* New York: Routledge, 1997.
Schocket, Eric. "Undercover Explorations of the 'Other Half,' or the Writer as Class Transvestite." *Representations* 64 (Fall 1998): 109–127.
Schultz, Rima, and Adele Hast. *Women Building Chicago, 1790–1990.* Bloomington: Indiana University Press, 2001.
Scobey, David. "Anatomy of the Promenade: The Politics of Bourgeois Sociability in Nineteenth-Century New York." *Social History* 17 (1992): 203–227.

Scotch, Richard K. *From Good Will to Civil Rights: Transforming Federal Disability Policy*. Philadelphia: Temple University Press, 2001.

Scott, James C. *Domination and the Arts of Resistance: Hidden Transcripts*. New Haven, Conn.: Yale University Press, 1990.

———. *Seeing Like a State*. New Haven, Conn.: Yale University Press, 1998.

Scott, Rumelle L. "Case Note on Ignacio v. United States Postal Service." *Howard Law Journal* 31 (1988): 159.

Scullion, Philip A. "Disability in a Nursing Curriculum." *Disability and Society* 14:4 (1999): 539–559.

Sears, Clare. "'A Dress Not Belonging to His or Her Sex': Cross-Dressing Law in San Francisco, 1860–1900." Ph.D. dissertation, University of California at Santa Cruz, 2005.

Sedgwick, Eve Kosofsky. *Epistemologies of the Closet*. Berkeley: University of California Press, 1990.

Selvaggio, Marc. *American Mendicant Literature: Books, Pamphlets, Broadsides, Handbills, Etc.* Schoyer's Books catalogue available in Harvard's Countway Library.

Sennett, Richard. *Flesh and Stone: The Body and the City in Western Civilization*. New York: Norton, 1994.

Serlin, David. "Disabling the Flaneur." *Journal of Visual Culture* 5:2 (Aug. 2006): 131–146.

———. "Queerness and Disability in U.S. Military Culture." GLQ 9:1–2 (2003), special issue entitled *Desiring Disability: Queer Theory Meets Disability Studies*. Ed. Robert McRuer and Abby Wilkerson.

———. "Rethinking the Corporate Biosphere." *Big and Green: Toward Sustainable Architecture in the 21st Century*. Ed. David Gissen. Princeton, N.J.: Princeton Architectural Press, 2003.

Serlin, David, and Jesse Lerner. "Weegee and the Jewish Question." *Wide Angle* 19:4 (Oct. 1997): 95–108.

Shah, Nayan. "Between 'Oriental Depravity' and "Natural Degenerates': Spatial Borderlands and the Making of Ordinary Americans." *American Quarterly* 57:3 (2005): 703–725.

———. *Contagious Divides: Epidemics and Race in San Francisco's Old Chinatown*. Berkeley: University of California Press, 2001.

Shakespeare, Tom. "Disability, Identity and Difference." *Exploring the Divide: Illness and Disability*. Ed. Colin Barnes and Geoff Mercer. Leeds, U.K.: Disability Press, 1996. 94–113.

Shapiro, Joseph. *No Pity: People with Disabilities Forging a New Civil Rights Movement*. New York: Random House, 1994.

Shaw, Barrett, ed. *The Ragged Edge: The Disability Experience from the Pages of the First Fifteen Years of the Disability Rag*. Louisville, Ky.: Advocado, 1994.

Shaw, Randy. *The Activist's Handbook.* Berkeley: University of California Press, 1996.

Sherry, Mark. *If I Only Had a Brain: Deconstructing Brain Injury.* New York: Routledge, 2005.

———. "Overlaps and Contradictions between Queer Theory and Disability Studies." *Disability and Society* 19:7 (Dec. 2004): 769–783.

———. "(Post)Colonizing Disability." *Wagadu* 4 (Summer 2007): 10–22.

Shuchman, John S. *Hollywood Speaks: Deafness and the Film Entertainment Industry.* Urbana: University of Illinois Press, 1999.

Shuttleworth, Russell P. "Toward a Constructionist Approach to Disability and Sexuality and the Inclusion of Disabled People in the Sexual Rights Movement." *Sexuality Inequalities: Case Studies from the Field.* Ed. Niels Teunis. New York: Routledge.

Siebers, Tobin. "Broken Beauty: Disability and Art Vandalism." *Michigan Quarterly Review* 41:2 (2002): 223–245.

———. "Disability as Masquerade." *Literature and Medicine* 23:1 (2004): 1–22.

———. "Disability in Theory: From Social Construction to the New Realism of the Body." *American Literary History* 13:4 (2001): 737–754.

———. *The Mirror of Medusa.* Christchurch, New Zealand: Cybereditions, 2002.

———. "What Can Disability Studies Learn from the Culture Wars?" *Cultural Critique* 55 (2003): 182–216.

———. "Words Stare Like a Glass Eye: From Literary to Visual to Disability Studies and Back Again." PMLA 119:5 (2004): 1315–1324.

Silvers, Anita, and Michael Ashley Stein. "From Plessy (1896) and Goesart (1948) to Celburne (1985) and Garrett (2001): A Chill Wind from the Past Blows Equal Protection Away." *Backlash against the* ADA*: Reinterpreting Disability Rights.* Ed. Linda Hamilton Krieger. Ann Arbor: University of Michigan Press, 2003.

Sinclair, Upton. *The Jungle.* New York: Penguin, 1920.

Sixteenth Annual Proceedings of the National Conference of Charities and Correction. Boston: Geo. H. Ellis, 1889.

Skocpol, Theda. *Protecting Soldiers and Mothers: The Political Origins of Social Policy in the United States.* Cambridge, Mass.: Harvard University Press, 1992.

Slaughter, Thomas. "Epidermalizing the World: A Basic Mode of Being Black." *Philosophy Born of Struggle.* Ed. Leonard Harris. Dubuque, Iowa: Hunt, 1982.

Slavishak, Edward. "Artificial Limbs and Industrial Workers' Bodies in Turn-of-the-Century Pittsburgh." *Journal of Social History* 37:2 (Winter 2003): 365–388.

Slide, Anthony. *The Encyclopedia of Vaudeville.* Westport, Conn.: Greenwood, 1994.

Slocum, William Frederick, Jr. *The Relation of Private and Public to Organized Charity.* Baltimore: Charity Organization Society, 1886.

Smedley, Brian D. Adrienne Y. Stith, and Alan R. Nelson, eds. *Unequal Treatment: Confronting Racial and Ethnic Disparities in Healthcare.* Washington, D.C.: National Academies Press, 2002.

Smith, Carl. *Urban Disorder and the Shape of Belief.* Chicago: University of Chicago Press, 1995.

Smith, Kitty. *My Life Story: Yours Truly, Kitty Smith.* South Whitley, Ind.: n.p., ca. 1905–1910.

Smith, Neil. *New Urban Frontier: The Revanchist City.* New York: Routledge, 1996.

Smith, Susan Harris, and Melanie Dawson, eds. *The American 1890s: A Cultural Reader.* Durham, N.C.: Duke University Press, 2000.

Smith, Valerie. *Not Just Race, Not Just Gender: Black Feminist Readings.* New York: Routledge, 1998.

Snow, David, Leon Anderson, and Paul Koegel. "Distorting Tendencies in Research on the Homeless." *American Behavioral Scientist* 37:4 (1994): 461–475.

Snyder, Sharon, Brenda Jo Brueggemann, and Rosemarie Garland Thomson, eds. *Disability Studies: Enabling the Humanities.* New York: Modern Language Association, 2002.

Snyder, Sharon, and David T. Mitchell. *Cultural Locations of Disability.* Chicago: University of Chicago Press, 2006. (Abbreviated as CLD)

———. "Out of the Ashes of Eugenics: Diagnostic Regimes in the United States and the Making of a Disability Minority." *Patterns of Prejudice* 36:1 (2002): 79–103.

Sobchack, Vivian. "A Leg to Stand On: Prosthetics, Metaphor, and Materiality." *The Prosthetic Impulse: From a Posthuman Present to a Biocultural Future.* Ed. Marquard Smith and Joanna Morra. Cambridge, Mass.: MIT Press, 2006.

Solenberger, Alice. *One Thousand Homeless Men.* New York: Survey Associates, 1914.

Sontag, Susan. *Illness as Metaphor and AIDS and Its Metaphors.* New York: Anchor.

Spain, Daphne. *How Women Saved the City.* Minneapolis: University of Minnesota Press, 2001.

Special Consular Report: Vagrancy and Public Charities in Foreign Countries. Washington, D.C.: Government Printing Office, 1893.

Spivak, Gayatri. "Can the Subaltern Speak?" *A Critique of Postcolonial Reason: Toward a History of the Vanishing Present.* Cambridge, Mass.: Harvard University Press, 1999.

Stack, Carol. *All Our Kin.* New York: Harper and Row, 1974.

Stahl, Frank. "The Maternal Impression in Twin Pregnancy, as Seen in the Mystery Story, 'Sons and Fathers.'" *Chicago Medical Reporter.* Chicago, 1896. 24, 25.

———. "Maternal Impressions and Their Significance." *American Journal of Obstetrics: Diseases of Women and Children.* Vol. 33. New York: William Wood, 1896.

Stallybrass, Peter, and Allon White. *The Politics and Poetics of Transgression.* Ithaca, N.Y.: Cornell University Press, 1986.

Stanley, Amy Dru. "Beggars Can't Be Choosers: Compulsion and Contract in Postbellum America." *Journal of American History* 78 (Mar. 1992): 1265–1293.

———. *From Bondage to Contract: Wage Labor, Marriage and the Market in the Age of Slave Emancipation.* New York: Cambridge University Press, 1998.

Stansell, Christine. *City of Women: Sex and Class in New York, 1789–1860.* New York: Knopf, 1986.

Starr, Kevin. *California: A History.* New York: Modern Library, 2005.

Stead, William. *If Christ Came to Chicago.* 1894. Chicago: Chicago Historical Book Works, 1990.

Stedman Jones, Gareth. *Outcast London.* Harmondsworth, U.K.: Penguin, 1976.

Stewart, Jean. "Disability, Capitalism and War." Talk delivered at the World Social Forum in Mumbai, India, Jan. 7, 2003.

Stewart, Susan. *On Longing.* Durham, N.C.: Duke University Press, 1993.

Stiker, Henri-Jacques. *A History of Disability.* Trans. William Sayers. Ann Arbor: University of Michigan Press, 2000.

Stone, Deborah A. *The Disabled State.* Philadelphia: Temple University Press, 1984.

Strange, Carolyn, and Tina Loo. *Making Good: Law and Moral Regulation in Canada, 1867–1939.* Toronto: University of Toronto Press, 1997.

Stroman, Duane F. *The Disability Rights Movement: From Deinstitutionalization to Self-Determination.* Lanham, Md.: University Press of America, 2003.

Stuart, Ossie. "Double Oppression: An Appropriate Starting Point?" *Disabling Barriers—Enabling Environments.* Ed. John Swain, Vic Finkelstein, Sally French, and Mike Oliver. London: Open University Press. 93–100.

Stubblefield, Anna. "Beyond the Pale: Tainted Whiteness, Cognitive Disability, and Eugenic Sterilization." *Hypatia* 22:2 (Spring 2007): 162–181.

Sullivan, Martin. "Subjected Bodies: Paraplegia, Rehabilitation and the Politics of Movement." *Foucault and the Government of Disability.* Ed. Shelley Tremain. Ann Arbor: University of Michigan Press, 2005.

Sullivan, Nikki. "Integrity, Mayhem, and the Question of Self-Demand Amputation." *Continuum: Journal of Media and Culture Studies* 19:3 (Sept. 2005): 325–333.

Sutton, Erica J., Lauren Rosapep, Karen Ball, et al. "Through the Viewfinder: Positive Exposure a Year Later." *American Journal of Medical Genetics,* Part C (Seminars in Medical Genetics) 142C: 260–268.

Sutton, John R. "The Political Economy of Madness: The Expansion of the Asylum in Progressive America." *American Sociological Review* 56:5 (Oct. 1991): 665–678.

Swaffield, Walter. "Round Table: 'The Tenement House Curse.'" *The Arena* 9:53 (April 1894).

Teaford, Jon. *The Unheralded Triumph: City Government in America, 1870–1900.* Baltimore: Johns Hopkins University Press, 1984.

Teller, L.S. "Propriety of Permitting Plaintiff in Personal Injury Action to Exhibit His Person to the Jury." *American Law Reports* 66, 2d series (1959): 1334.

tenBroek, Jacobus. "The Right to Live in the World: The Disabled in the Law of Torts." *California Law Review* (1966): 841–919.

tenBroek, Jacobus, and Floyd Matson. "The Disabled and the Law of Welfare." *California Law Review* (1966): 809–840.

Terry, Jennifer, and Josephine Urla. *Deviant Bodies: Critical Perspectives on Difference in Science and Popular Culture.* Bloomington: University Press of Indiana, 1995.

Thale, Christopher. "Police." *The Encyclopedia of Chicago.* Ed. James R. Grossman, Ann Durkin Keating, and Janice L. Reiff. Chicago: University of Chicago Press, 2004.

Thoinot, L. *Medicolegal Aspects of Moral Offenses.* Trans. Arthur Weysse. Philadelphia: F.A. Davis, 1913.

Thomas, Carol. *Female Forms: Experiencing and Understanding Disability.* London: Taylor and Francis, 1999.

———. *Sociologies of Disability and Illness: Contested Ideas in Disability Studies and Medical Sociology.* New York: Palgrave Macmillan, 2007.

Tiedeman, Christopher. *A Treatise on the Limitations of Police Power in the United States.* St. Louis: F.H. Thomas, 1886.

Titchkosky, Tanya. *Disability, Self and Society.* Toronto: University of Toronto Press, 2003.

———. *Reading and Writing Disability Differently: The Textured Life of Embodiment.* Toronto: University of Toronto Press, 2007.

Todd, Dennis. *Imagining Monsters: Miscreations of the Self in Eighteenth-Century England.* Chicago: University of Chicago Press, 1995.

Trachtenberg, Alan. "Experiments in Another Country." *American Realism: New Essays.* Ed. Eric Sundquist. Baltimore: Johns Hopkins University Press, 1982.

Trattner, Walter. *From Poor Law to Welfare State: A History of Social Welfare in America.* New York: Free Press, 1974.

Tremain, Shelley, ed. *Foucault and the Government of Disability.* Ann Arbor: University of Michigan Press, 2005.

———. "The Subject of Impairment." *Disability/Postmodernity: Embodying Disability Theory.* Ed. Mairian Corker and Tom Shakespeare. London: Continuum, 2002. 32–47.

Trent, James. *Inventing the Feeble Mind: A History of Mental Retardation in the United States.* Berkeley: University of California Press, 1994.

Trotter, David. "The New Historicism and the Psychopathology of Everyday Modern Life." *Filth: Dirt, Disgust and Modern Life.* Ed. William Cohen and Ryan Johnson. Minneapolis: University of Minnesota Press, 2005. 30–50.

Tseelon, Efrat. *The Masque of Femininity: The Presentation of Woman in Everyday Life.* London: Sage, 1995.
Tucker, William Jewett. "Andover House in Boston." *The Poor in Great Cities.* Ed. Robert A. Woods. New York: Scribner's Sons, 1895.
Tuennerman-Kaplan, Laura. *Helping Others: Power, Giving and Community Identity in Cleveland, Ohio, 1880–1930.* Kent, Ohio: Kent State University Press, 2001.
Turner, Arlin. "George W. Cable's Beginnings as a Reformer." *Journal of Southern History* 17 (May 1951): 150–152.
Turner, T. Arthur. *Organizing to Help the Handicapped: A Brief Guide for the Voluntary Association for the Crippled.* Elyria, Ohio: National Society for Crippled Children, 1944.
Twain, Mark (Samuel Clemens). *The Prince and the Pauper.* 1881. New York: Signet, 2002.
Tyler, Carole-Anne. *Female Impersonation.* New York: Routledge, 2003.
United Hebrew Charities of Chicago. *First Annual Report of the United Hebrew Charities of Chicago for the Year 1888–89.* Chicago: S. Ettlinger, 1889.
Upshaw, William D. *Earnest Willie, or Echoes from a Recluse, etc.* Atlanta: Franklin, 1903.
Uzzel, Robert. *Blind Lemon Jefferson: His Life, His Death, and His Legacy.* Austin, Tex.: Eakin, 2002.
Vaillant, Derek. "Peddling Noise: Contesting the Civic Soundscape of Chicago, 1890–1913." *Journal of the Illinois State Historical Society* 96:3 (Autumn 2003): 259–260.
Vale Pennsylvania Digest 40. St. Paul, Minn.: West, 1971.
Valentine, Vikki. "War Is a Helluva Teacher." Report on National Public Radio, Nov. 8, 2006. Transcript available online at http://www.npr.org.
Vernon, Ayesha. "The Dialectics of Multiple Identities and the Disabled People's Movement." *Disability and Society* 14:3 (1999): 385–398.
Vicinus, Martha. *Independent Women: Work and Community for Single Women, 1850–1920.* Chicago: University of Chicago Press, 1985.
Viskochil, Larry A., ed. *Chicago at the Turn of the Century in Photographs.* New York: Dover, 1984.
"Voices of 504." *The Independent* (Summer 1977).
von Every, Edward. *Sins of New York as "Exposed" by the Police Gazette.* 1930. New York: Benjamin Blom, 1972.
Wacker, Charles. "Chicago Plan." *Municipal Advance: Extracts from Papers on Various Municipal Services Read at the First International Municipal Congress and Exhibition.* Chicago, Sept. 18–30, 1911.
Wagner, Bryan. "Disturbing the Peace: Black Vagrancy and the Culture of Racial Demarcation." Ph.D. dissertation, University of Virginia, 2002.
Wagner, David. *What's Love Got to Do with It? A Critical Look at American Charity.* New York: New Press, 2000.

Wailoo, Keith. *Dying in the City of the Blues*. Chapel Hill: University of North Carolina Press, 2001.

Walling, George W. *Recollections of a New York Chief of Police*. 1887. Denver: Denver Police Mutual Aid Fund, 1890.

Warner, Amos Griswold, Stuart Alfred Queen, and Ernest Bouldin Harper. *American Charities and Social Work*. New York: Thomas Y. Crowell, 1894. Rpt. 1930.

Warner, Michael. *The Trouble with Normal: Sex, Politics and the Ethos of Queer Life*. Cambridge, Mass.: Harvard University Press, 2000.

Washington, Sylvia Hood. *Packing Them In: An Archeology of Environmental Racism in Chicago, 1865–1954*. New York: Lexington Books, 2005.

Waters, Theodore. "Six Weeks in Beggardom." *Everybody's Magazine* 12 (Jan. 1905): 70–71, 76–77.

Watson, Frank Dekker. *The Charity Organization Movement in the United States: A Study in American Philanthropy*. New York: Macmillan, 1922.

Waugh, Joan. *Unsentimental Reformer: The Life of Josephine Shaw Lowell*. Cambridge, Mass.: Harvard University Press, 1997.

Weigman, Robyn. *American Anatomies*. Durham, N.C.: Duke University Press, 1995.

Welfare Federation of Cleveland. *Education and Occupations of Cripples Juvenile and Adult: A Survey of All the Cripples of Cleveland, Ohio, in 1916*. Survey commonly referred to as the "Cleveland Cripple Survey." New York: Red Cross Institute for Crippled and Disabled Men, 1918.

Welke, Barbara. *Recasting American Liberty: Gender, Race, Law, and the Railroad Revolution, 1865–1920*. New York: Cambridge University Press, 2001.

Weller, Charles F. "Friendly Visiting—a Social Force." *Charities Review* 7 (Nov. 1897): 748.

Wendell, Susan. *The Rejected Body: Feminist Philosophical Reflections on Disability*. New York: Routledge, 1996.

Wilder, Marshall P. *The Sunny Side of the Street*. New York: Funk and Wagnalls, 1905.

Williams, Charles. *Terrors of a Blizzard, by One Who Has Had the Experience: The Fate of a Mail Carrier; Or How I Lost My Feet, Written by the Loser*. Oshkosh, Wis.: Castle-Pierce Press, ca. 1907.

Williams, Simon. "Is Anybody There? Critical Realism, Chronic Illness and the Disability Debate." *Sociology of Health and Illness* 21:6 (1999): 797–819.

———. *Medicine and the Body*. London: Sage, 2003.

Williams, Simon, Jonathan Gabe, and Michael Calnon, eds. *Health, Medicine and Society: Key Theories, Future Agendas*. London: Routledge, 2000.

Willis, John Abbot. *Carter Henry Harrison: A Memoir*. New York: Dodd, Mead, 1895.

Willis, Mark. "Blowback: Three Generations of Imbeciles Are Not Enough." Paper delivered at the Disability, Narrative and the Law Conference, Moritz College of Law, The Ohio State University, Feb. 17, 2006.
Wilson, Elizabeth. "The Invisible Flâneur." *New Left Review* 191 (1992): 90–110.
———. *The Sphinx in the City.* London: Virago, 1991.
Wilson, Harriet. *Our Nig.* New York: Vintage, 2002.
Wilson, Robert Rawdon. *The Hydra's Tale: Imagining Disgust.* Edmonton: University of Alberta Press, 2002.
Wines, Frederick. *Report on the Defective, Dependent, and Delinquent Classes of the Population of the United States, as Returned at the Tenth Census (June 1, 1880).* Washington, D.C.: Government Printing Office, 1888.
Wolfe, Cary. "Animal Rights, Neocolonialism, and Michael Crichton's *Congo.*" *Arizona Quarterly* 55:2 (Summer 1999): 115–153.
Wolff, Janet. "The Invisible Flâneuse: Women and the Literature of Modernity." *Theory, Culture and Society* 2 (1985): 37–46.
Woodroofe, Kathleen. *From Charity to Social Work in England and the United States.* London: Routledge, 1962.
Woodward, James. "Implications for Sociolinguistics Research among the Deaf." *Sign Language Studies* 1:1–7.
Worden, Gretchen. *Mutter Museum of the College of Physicians of Philadelphia.* New York: Blast Books, 2002.
Wray, Matt, and Annalee Newitz. *White Trash: Race and Class in America.* New York: Routledge, 1997.
Wright, Talmadge. *Out of Place: Homeless Mobilizations, Subcities, and Contested Landscapes.* Albany: SUNY Press, 1997.
Yaworsky, Michael J. "Indecent Exposure: What Is 'Person.'" *American Law Reports* 63, 4th series (1988): 1040.
Yoshino, Kenji. *Covering.* New York: Random House, 2006.
Young, Iris Marion. *Inclusion and Democracy.* New York: Oxford University Press, 2002.
———. *Justice and the Politics of Difference.* Princeton, N.J.: Princeton University Press, 1990.
Young, Jonathan M. *Equality of Opportunity: The Making of the Americans with Disabilities Act.* Washington, D.C.: National Council on Disability, 1997.
Zakrewski, Karen. "The Prevalence of 'Look'ism in Hiring Decisions: How Federal Law Should Be Amended to Prevent Appearance Discrimination in the Workplace." *University of Pennsylvania Journal of Labor and Employment Law* (Winter 2005): 431.
Zames, Frieda, and Doris Zames Fleischer. *The Disability Rights Movement: From Charity to Confrontation.* Philadelphia: Temple University Press, 2001.
Zangwill, Israel. *The King of Schnorrers.* 1893. Hamden, Conn.: Shoe String Press, 1953.

Zerubavel, Eviator. *Time Maps: Collective Memory as the Social Shape of the Past.* Chicago: University of Chicago Press, 2003.

Zorbaugh, Harvey Warren. *The Gold Coast and the Slum: A Sociological Study of Chicago's Near North Side.* Chicago: University of Chicago Press, 1929.

Zucchi, John. *The Little Slaves of the Harp.* Montreal: McGill-Queens University Press, 1992.

FILMS

Davenport, Tom. *Born for Hard Luck.* Documentary film on dancer/musician Peg Leg Sam Jackson. University of North Carolina, Chapel Hill, 1976.

DeMille, Cecil B. *We Can't Have Everything.* Artcraft Pictures Corporation, 1918.

———. *Till I Come Back to You.* 1918. Written by Jeanie Macpherson. In the Motion Picture archive at George Eastman House, Rochester, N.Y.

Duncan, Kath. *My One-Legged Dream Lover.* Australia: Dream Lover Films. 1999.

Edison, Thomas Alva. *The Thieving Hand.* Vitagraph, 1908.

Killacky, John, and Larry Connolly. *Crip Shots.* John R. Killacky, 2001.

Mitchell, David, and Sharon Snyder. *Vital Signs: Crip Culture Talks Back.* Brace Yourselves Productions. 1997.

O'Toole, Corbett Joan. *Workshop in a Box.* Video series. 2000.

Sawalich, Steve. *The Music Within.* MGM, 2007.

RADIO BROADCAST

"The Shadow: The Blind Beggar Dies." Starring Orson Welles and Margot Stevenson. Apr. 17, 1938. Reproduced in the compact disk *The Shadow: 2 Complete Classic Radio Broadcasts.* New Rochelle, N.Y.: GAA Corporation, 1996.

INDEX

Page numbers in italic indicate illustrations

Abel, Elizabeth, 334n. 10
Abel, Emily, 305n. 12
Ability: cross-ability sociability, 47, 120, 130; in liberal theory, 85; phantasmatic, 11, 134; poverty, stigma and, 27; relation of able-bodied to unsightly beggars, 36, 334n. 12; securing of able-bodied status, 133; shading into disability, 136; temporarily able-bodied (TAB), 130; temporarily not able-bodied (TNAB), 130. *See also* Normate and normality
Abjection: ambivalence and, 37; Kristeva on, 306n. 30; public sphere stripped of, 70; social link with impairment, 109; and ugly law, 56, 306n. 30
Ableism: conjoined with racism and nativism, 165; definition of, 321n. 33, 347n. 2; and eugenics, 142; logic of, 269; reading and, 131; state-sponsored, 280
Acts, prohibition on, vs. prohibition on basis of status, 10, 217. *See also* Status offenses
ADA. *See* Americans with Disabilities Act
ADAPT, 208, 336–337n. 2
Addams, Jane, 91, 226, 313n. 9; on "great defectives," 226
Addiction, 131, 316n. 40; disability and, 105–106, 316n. 43. *See also* Alcohol
Aesthetics: aesthetic failure, 87; "aesthetic motive" for care, 310n. 21; and affirmation, 286; bodily, 3, 15, 322n. 7; city planning and, 69–71, 77, 286; criminology, gender and, 323n. 15; eugenics and, 309n. 9; as form of social control, 286; politics of, 209; and urbanism, 286
African American: Agnes (burned enslaved girl in Charleston), 188, 283; begging, 195–196, 333n. 4, 335n. 27; black charity organization, 196; blind black disability theory, 203; blues, 199–200; critique of white charity organization, 335n. 27; cross-dresser, 163; cultural association with unsightliness, 186; first hospital, 335n. 23; Great Migration, 196; healing traditions, 194; health crisis, 194; identity after slavery, 333n. 6; imposters, 196; pegleg dancing, 336n. 36; press, 196, 201–204; policing of, 187; public health voluntarism, 196; repudiation of unsightly beggars, 196; social networks, 199, 336n. 33; suspicion of white medical care, 194; Tiny Tim Crow, 191; tramps, 195; understood as health menace, 193; unsightly beggars, 185, 195, 196–97; vagrancy, 192; vagrancy law and, 195; veterans, 203; women, 195, 343n. 19. *See also* Blackness; Slavery

Age: "aged deaf man," 253; blackhoods, 146; debility, 26; "old woman with deep-seated cancer," 188, 283
Aguilera, Ray 208, 321n. 34
AIDS, 112, 167
Alabama, 168
Alcohol: Alcoholics Anonymous, 316n. 41; alcoholism, 131; boozefighters, 104–107, 345n. 13; DuBois on, 316n. 45; prohibition of sales to disabled people, 106, 316n. 46; regulation, 104–107; stale-beer dens, 113, 127; unsightliness and, 105–107; temperance and prohibition, 17, 104. *See also* Addiction
Almsgiving: COS critique of, 41–42, 50; criminalization of, 63; effect on of pension system, 79; Howells on, 37–38; moral dilemma of, 37–38. *See also* Begging
Almshouse: decline of, 309n. 5; and development of ugly law, 2, 26, 34, 39, 67, 150, 301nn. 2, 3, 309n. 7; excavation of, 212; gender difference in experience of, 150; New Orleans, 34–35, 39, 303n. 11; punitive function of, 27; racial segregation in, 28; regulatory care in, 64; San Francisco, 26–28; Victorian era poor-law and, 27. *See also* Poor house
Ambivalence: about disability, 37, 46, 305n. 13; and suspicion, 110
Americans with Disabilities Act (ADA): activism leading to, 281, 313–314n. 20; Burgdorf Jr. and, 8, 278; protection by, 130–31, 329n. 51; "regarded as" clause, 128; Supreme Court decisions on, 11, 106, 185, 347n. 1; ugly law and, 19, 347n. 4; ugly law introduced into congressional debate on, 276–277; violation of, 284, 315n. 29
Amputation: African American higher rate of, 194, 335nn. 22, 23; autobiography on, 255, 258, 259, 261; veteran, 29, 149, 150, 186; pegleg dancing by amputees, 336n. 36; prosthetics and, 123; self-demand, 321–322n. 34
Analogy, politics of, 142–143, 322n. 8
Anarchism, 40, 71, 168
Animal: animality, 97–100, 290, 314n. 24; animalization of women, 146; animal rights, 314n. 25; disgust and, 97, 314n. 21; goat man, 99–100, 315n. 31; racism and, 314n. 26; service animals, 99, 314nn. 28, 29
Anti-Semitism, 18, 175, 176–177, 329n. 2
Anzaldua, Gloria, 169, 331n. 12
Appearance: in activist memory, 215–216, 282; cultural obsession with, 86; demarcation, 187; disability defined by, 15; discrimination on basis of, 19, 282–286, 348–349n. 9; discrimination, Santa Cruz ordinance prohibiting, 348n. 6; impairment, 19, 283–286, 348n. 7, 349n. 10; link between bodily and other forms of, 71; managing, 65, 86–89; politics, 290; and ugly law, relation to begging, 25; in U.S. context, 298n. 6. *See also* Visuality and visibility
Arizona, 105
Asbury, Herbert, *Gangs of New York*, 105, 115, 124, 316n. 44, 318n. 8
Asch, Adrienne, 326n. 31
Atlanta, GA, 99, 311n. 3
Auslander, Philip, 300n. 18
Austin, J.L., 121, 125, 126
Authenticity: disability and, 111, 112, 130; and inauthenticity, 119, 318–319n. 15; older forms called into question, 121; and masquerade, 289. *See also* Imposters

Autobiography: blind, 346n. 14; disability autobiography, obstacles to, 345n. 8; faker, 131; of Fuller, Arthur Franklin, 262–276; self-authorship and, 256; solo autobiographical performance, 12–13, 312n. 8; of Wilder, 226–228. *See also* Autobiography, mendicant disability
Autobiography, mendicant disability, 256–276; community effects in, 260; and embodiment, 258–259; impossibility of beggar writing, 261; intricacy of, 256; political representation in, 261–276; and slave narratives, 256, 345n. 9; beyond subsistence literature, 259; written for other beggars, 260

Bailey, Robert, and Elaine Evans, 303n. 10, 316n. 36
Baltimore, MD, 67, 315n. 29
Barnartt, Sharon, and Richard Scotch, 314n. 20, 347n. 4
Barnes, Colin, 299n. 12, 307n. 34
Baudelaire, Charles, 157, 316n. 40, 320n. 23
Baynton, Douglas, 168, 307n. 32; 330n. 6
Beauty: city beautification, 69–71, 286; finding, ugly law as prohibition on, 286; norms, failure to live up to, 298n. 6; norms, social movement critiques of, 142; policing of, 286; practices by disabled people, 212, 320n23; undoing of beauty/ugliness binary, 286. *See also* Ugliness
Begging: beggar gangs, 132–133, 213–214, 248; beggars' union, 248; begging law, ugly law as, 16, 24, 32, 283; begging law, ugly law not reducible to, 23, 283; claiming, 250; in Cleveland Cripple Survey, 237–238; common, 320n. 21; crackdowns on, 32, 34, 44, 53–54, 55–56; cripples as born beggars, 338n. 10; Derrida on, 38, 316n. 40, 317n. 1; and First Amendment, 215–218; as free speech, 215–218; instability of category, 273; Orientalism and, 172; performance and, 58, 116–119, 307n. 33; political action and, 57; professional, 113, 122–124, 160, 319n. 20; right to beg, vii, 215–216; small percentage of among disabled people, 246; sturdy beggar, 36, 37, 60, 61, 303n. 17; Taylorism and, 120; writing and, 124–125, 320n. 22, 345n. 12
Bell, Chris, 336n. 30
Belluso, John, 12; *The Body of Bourne*, 12, 13, 207–208, 213, 226, 227, 299–300n. 16
Benjamin, Adam, 300n. 18
Benjamin, Walter, 18, 286, 320n. 23
Berkeley, CA, 149, 346n. 13; Center for Independent Living, 347n. 3
Berlin, Germany, 297n. 4
Berry, Bonnie, 299n. 15, 309n. 3, 348n. 7, 349n. 11
Berube, Michael, 256, 345n. 8
Beuf, Ann, 298n. 6, 348n. 7
Bhabha, Homi, 46, 119, 318n. 15, 346n. 15
Biopower, 64–67, 308n. 1
Blackness: "black is beautiful," 142; black-trashing, 185; black/white binary, 185; and "brazen-face," 163; cultural association with lack, 186; performance of, 121; policing of, 187; and vagrancy, 192. *See also* Whiteness
Blind/vision impaired: beggars in Chicago, 211–212; black blind disability theory, 203; "Blind Beggar" (Jacob Riis), 303; Blind Boy Fuller, 212;

Blind/vision impaired, (*Continued*) Blind Lemon Jefferson, 199, 200; Blind Willie Johnson, 199; Blind Willie McTell, 199; blindness and gender, 327n. 37; blues singers, 199–200; Boone, John William (Blind Boone), 190–91, 192; Bradfield, James (blind beggar's self-defense), 202; exemptions for, 222–23; "hypothetical blind man" (Kleege), 327n. 38; massage, 92; Norris's representation of, 283; peddling, 245; Pennsylvania Working Home for Blind Men, 222; performances in institutions, 305n. 17; political autobiography, 346n. 14; racialization of b. people, 184; resistance to arrest, 220–224; schools, 173, 184. *See also* Ten Broek, Jacobus
Blues, 199–200
Blumberg, Lisa, 312n. 8
Body: bodily hexis, 312n. 5; bodily management in public, 30–31, 86–89; of distinction, 88; dys-appearing, 89; embodiment, 127–128, 129–130; explicit, 47, 305n. 18; idealized morphology, 142–143; integrity identity disorder, 321n. 34; that "passes by in silence," 89, 312n. 6
Bogdan, Robert, 315n. 35, 326n. 36
Boston, MA, 53, 110, 116, 132
Bourdieu, Pierre, 88, 312n. 5
Bourne, Randolph, 12, 207–208, 213, 229, 299–300n. 16; "Philosophy of Handicap," 207, 336n. 1
Bouson, J. Brooks, 333n. 5
Bowe, Frank, 235, 342n. 12
Bragg, Bernard, and Eugene Bergman, *Tales from a Clubroom*, 337n. 5
Breckenridge, Carol, and Candace Vogler, 85
Breslin, Mary Lou, 280
Brooklyn, NY, 59,149, 219, 267–270
Brown, Mordechai ("Three Finger"), 92
Brown, Wendy, 348n. 6
Brown v Board of Education, as tool for disability activism, 185, 332n. 2
Brueggemann, Brenda, 318n. 14
Bryan, Willie, 335n. 21
Buck, Dennis, 337n. 5
Buffalo, NY, 171, 210, 332n. 26
Burch, Susan, 129, 337n. 5
Burgdorf, Robert Jr., 7–8, 23, 276, 278, 298n. 8; and Marcia Pearce Burgdorf, 7, 8, 23, 142, 208, 218, 246, 280, 282, 286, 290, 301n. 1
Butler, Judith, 116, 121, 287
Byrd, W. Michael, and Linda A. Clayton, 193–194
Byrom, Brad, 5, 8, 57–58, 102, 111, 230, 232, 236, 297n. 1, 298n. 9, 302n. 5, 306n. 24, 307n. 31, 308n. 40, 309nn. 5, 6, 330n. 4, 339n. 1, 342n. 15

Caldwell, Joe and Larry Biandi, 336–337n. 2
California, 24, 25
Cancer, 33, 188, 283; melanoma, 187
Capitalism, 16, 38, 59–60, 92, 213, 302n. 5, 307n. 36, 319n. 18
Care: of the body, 308n. 3; and criminality, tension between, 111; gender and, 151; institutional, appeal of, 68; on the street, nexus of, 200; regulatory, provision for in early ugly laws, 34, 64–65; superior ethic of, claimed by immigrant groups, 173
Carlson, Licia, 325n. 31
Case, genre of, 48, 242, 285–286
Catholicism, 15, 43, 300n. 24, 304n. 10
Center for Independent Living, 280

Charity Organization Society: Abolition movement, and, 189; African American, 196; and African American beggars, 195; on alcohol, 106; anti-begging measures promoted by, 53, 213, 250; British, 304n. 1; in Burnside case, 221; Catholicism and, 304; challenges to, 46; contradictory ideologies of, 44; Crane, Stephen and, 288–289; discourse countered by Arthur Fuller, 271–275; Du Bois's use of records of, 196; encounters Arthur Fuller, 267–271; fetishism and,133–134; fraud identification and, 111, 136; "German Plan," 304n. 1; history of, 41–46, 250; immigrants and, 171; Jewish, 177; major role in promoting ugly law, 15, 17, 38–39, 40, 55–56, 288; medicalization and, 305n. 12; modern social welfare policy and, 304n. 4; narrative, and detective fiction, 304n. 6; opponents of, 304nn. 8, 9, 10; opposition to peddling, 211, 337n. 4; problem of ugly crowd for, 54; racism of, 335n. 27; relation to police, 306n. 26; Salvation Army and, 304n. 9; Southern modes of control and, 189, 224; tracking of lesbians, 159; women's participation in, 157; writing by agents of, 256. *See also* Friendly visiting, COS idea of

Charleston, SC, 100, 188, 333n. 4

Cheu, Johnson, 304n. 5

Chicago, IL: African Americans in, 142, 196; African American beggars in, 196, 201–203; anti-Italian legislation in, 179; approved display of disability in, 90–93; association of with ugly law, 281; *Chicago Defender*, 196, 201–204; Chicago Plan, 73, 309n. 11, 310nn. 12, 15; *Chicago Tribune*, 39, 178, 279; City Beautiful movement in, 69–71; city council members, 30, 302n. 7; city council, power of, 302n. 7; Columbian Exposition in, 172, 310n. 13; control of fruit peddling, 178–179, 303n. 10; COS in, 50; cross-dressing arrest, 163; decency laws in, 144; enactment of ugly law in 1881, *ii*, 1–2, 29–32, 59, 64; eugenics in, 89; Haymarket Riot, 60; imposters in, 116, 117–118; institutions in, 302n. 8; interzones in, 336n. 28; Jewish communities in, 30, 178, 332n. 23; newspaper coverage, 163; ugly law in, language of, 10, 293; ugly law, legend of, in "Chicago, 1911," 7, 13, 14, 16–17, 30, 65, 207, 298n. 7; ugly law, repeal of, in 1973, 279–281; World's Fair, 69

Chinatown: as moral threat, 331n. 18; as mythic locus of unsightly begging, 174; in New York, 174; *Stories of Chinatown*, 174

Chinese, 24, 28; anti-Chinese laws and agitation, 167; beggars, supposedly nonexistent, 173, 331n. 17; cultural association of unsightly beggars with, 174; quarantine of, 28,170; unsightly beggars as precisely not, 173

Citizenship: ability and, 219; citizens' space, 170; disability and, 303n. 15; modal, 173; peddlers required to be citizens, 180; street control and, 179; ugly law bound up with, 179

City: beautification, 62; Beautiful, 17, 69–71, 73, 310n. 13; gentrification, 286; logic of grid in, 71; "muscle-bound" planning, 71; planning, 69–71, 73, 77, 310n. 13, 337n. 3; revanchist, 209; right to the, 207–208; sensory policing of, 179–180; White City, 69. *See also* Urban

Civil War: effects in New Orleans, 33, 34; pension system, 79–80, 83, 311n. 24; ugly law development in aftermath of, 2, 28–29, 30, 33, 189–190; Union veteran writing, 150, 186; veterans of, exemptions for, 149, 325n. 25
Class: asymmetrical relations, 47, 305n. 16; cross-class sociability, 47; cross-class transvestism, 134–136; disability and, 141, 309n. 10; gender and, 152; middle, and able-bodiedness, 134, 136; privilege, 309n. 10; race and, 185–186; struggles, 60, 68, 289, 290; ugly law and, 16, 59, 186, 283, 286; working, 152, 209, 298n. 9, 313n. 12, 326n. 32
Clerc, Laurent, 89
Cleveland, OH: Associated Charities, 48, 201; blind peddler arrested in, 245; model leader in rehabilitation planning, 230, 339n. 2; Progressive-era city planning, 337n. 3; race in, 333n. 4; segregation in, 201; ugly law in, 1, 297n. 1, 341n. 8; women reformers in, 342n. 14. *See also* Cleveland Cripple Survey
Cleveland Cripple Survey: cartoon in, 230, *231*; history of, 230–232, 234–247, 339n. 2, 340n. 4, 342n. 14; Lewis, Halle, on, 246–247, 342n. 13; negative effects of, 246; newspaper seller in, *xii*, 1, 15, 20, 239–245, 286, 301n. 25, 328n. 45, 342n. 15; race in, 333n. 4; rehabilitationism in, 18, 230–232, 234–247, 253, 266, *240*; on ugly law, 1, 297n. 1, 341n. 8; ugly law, reduplication of terms of, 237
Cognitive disability: target of New York's draft ugly law, 10; begging by people with, 258; writing by people with, 256. *See also* Feebleminded; Idiots and Imbeciles
Cole, Melissa, 10, 325n. 27, 329n. 51
Colker, Ruth, 299n. 15
Collignon, Fred, vi, 299n. 10, 310n. 13
Columbus, OH: begging case in 1921, 218; emphasis on exposing self in ugly law, 9, 160; problems of enforcement, 148; ugly law in, 3, 10, 91, 294–295; ugly law next to lewdness law in code, 144
Compton, Tom, 301
Corker (Scott-Hill), Mairian, 299n. 12, 319n. 18, 321n. 30, 347n. 2
Cottrell, Melissa, 70
Courvant, Diana, 61, 143, 308n. 38, 312n. 8
Couser, G. Thomas, 344n. 6, 345nn. 8, 9, 11
"Covering" (Yoshino), 163–164, 329n. 51
Craddock, Susan, 25, 170, 173, 302
Crane, Stephen, 166; and Charity Organization Society, 288–289; "An Experiment in Misery," 319n. 16; "The Monster," 316n. 39; "When Man Falls," 288–289
Crenshaw, Kimberle, 141, 322n. 3
Cresswell, Tim, vi, 35, 144, 145, 283, 297n. 1, 306n. 24, 310n. 17, 323nn. 13, 15, 329n. 46, 335nn. 24, 25
Cripple: critique of label, 246, 311n. 1; dental, 90; "factories," 114, 128, 131, 133, 134; rehabilitationist definitions of, 236. *See also* Cleveland Cripple Survey
Cross-dressing: regulation of, 24; relation to ugly law, 144, 159, 162–163; transvestism, cross-class and cross-ability, 134
Crow, Liz, 299n. 12

Cure, 42, 47, 49,93; Fuller, Arthur, on, 265; rhetoric of, 304

Darke, Paul, 300n. 18, 305n. 18
Darwin, Charles, 94, 313n. 14
Davis, Lennard, 16, 37, 130, 303n. 15, 305n. 23, 308n. 3, 321n. 26, 327n. 36
Deaf/deaf: "aged deaf man" arrested in L.A., 253; condemnation of imposture, 129; "cures" of, in medicine shows, 93; beggars, and writing, 320n. 22; Deaf/deaf distinction, 321n. 29; equated with begging, 217; eugenics movement against, 49; Hoy, William Ellsworth ("Dummy"), 92, 313n. 11; Leader, Pauline, writer, 298n. 9; maternal impression and, 89, 326n. 36; National Organization of the, 337n. 5; performances in institutions, 305n. 17; repudiation of begging, 173, 253, 337n. 5; theater, 337n. 5; trafficking of, for begging, 168
Decency and indecency, 31, 101, 104, 144, 160–161, 184
Deformance, 46–48, 90, 91, 226, 310n. 21. *See also* Display of disability; Reform
Deformity, 9, 12, 207, 312n. 4; feminist and suffragist analysis of, 327n. 40
De Fornaro, Carlos, cartoon of Marshall P. Wilder, 228–230, 229
DeMille, Cecil B., 275–276
Denver, CO: anti-begging policies in, 53; COS in, 44–45; as rest cure site, 167; ugly law in, 3, 10, 64, 151, 167, 293–294, 342n. 15
Dependence: characterological causation of, 301n. 3; derivative, 152, 325n. 30; exemptions for dependents, 222; family as means to manage, 325n. 29; female, 148; reciprocal, vii; repudiation of, 246. *See also* Independence, American ideology of
Derrida, Jacques, 38, 121, 122, 316n. 40, 317n. 1
Deserving and undeserving, 61, 109, 111, 113, 127, 130, 221, 254
Desire, 254; and disabled people, 235; and disgust, 164
"Devil baby," 91, 313n. 9
Dewey, Gott, 225–228
Dime museums, 101, 315n. 35, 322n. 5
Dion, Karen, 348n. 7
Disability: ambiguity of, 11, 299n. 15; appearance and, 15; as barred speech, 218; as begging embodied, 217; as begging speech, 216; categorization of, 11; compensation, 79–80; consignment to begging, 222; contingency of, 297n. 3; community, 119; culture, 12–13,112, 119, 312n. 8; dandyism and, 320n. 23; definition of, 11, 15, 79, 83, 122, 128–129, 297n. 3; depoliticization of, 280; disability-face, 133; distinction from impairment, 128; exemptions for, 222; flaming, 163; Foucault on, 169; history, 119; infirmity and, 32, 146; McMurtrie's definition of, 236; medical model of, 49, 299n. 12; mendicant model of, 259; minority model of, 142, 143, 322n. 7; and modern welfare system, central to, 307n. 34; nondisabled, 11, 133–134; opposed to monstrosity, 330n. 10; oppression, 16, 305, 318n. 15; Pension Act of 1890, 79, 83; place in civil law, 169; pornography of, 162; simulation, 131, 132, 321n. 32; as site of social comprehension, 286; social model of, 11, 14, 127–129, 299n. 12;

Disability, (*Continued*)
tragedy model of, 132; undisability, 133; with attitude, 133. *See also* Cognitive disability; Impairment; Psychiatric disability
Disability History Museum, 315n. 31
Disability movement: cross-disability, 280, 281; demands of, 235; disability in the city, understanding of, 209; opposition o segregation, 185; precursors for, 249; repudiation of vagrancy and begging, 209, 246, 247; Section 504 sit-in, 313–314n. 20; ugly law, undoing of, 208, 246, 276, 280, 290; ugly law, memory of, in, 7, 8–10, 12–13, 16–17, 18, 20, 144, 207–208, 279–281, 282, 290, 298n. 7. *See also* ADAPT; Burgdorf, Robert, Jr.; Center for Independent Living; Disability Rights Education Defense Fund; Eastern Nebraska Community Office of Retardation; National Center for Law and the Handicapped; Union of the Physically Impaired Against Segregation
Disability Rights Education Defense Fund, 332n. 2
Disability studies: analysis of ugly law epitomizing, 14; center for, at Leeds, 321n. 32; on charity, 305n. 15; feminist, 325n. 31; immigration studies and, 330n. 6; interdisciplinarity of, vi; on intersectionality, 322n. 2; on unsightly beggar ordinances, vi, 13–15; postcolonial studies and, 46; proto-disability studies, 348n. 7; queer theory and, 328n. 46; urban studies and, 209; white, 336n. 30
Disabled people, vs. people with disabilities, 11, 297n. 3
Disciplines of the body, 31, 64, 65, 66–67, 87–88, 308n. 3; and femininity, 145
Disease: border crossing of, 170; contagion and, 63, 94, 158, 167, 224; the foreign and, 170, 330n. 3; loathsome, 167, 328n. 45; racial control and, 28, 193, 302n. 4; sexual transgression and, 159; unsightly beggar reduced to, 170; venereal, 71, 159, 328n. 45; word omitted from Denver's ugly law, 167. *See also* Quarantine
Disfigurement, 19, 283–284; dis-figure, the, 283
Disgust, 14, 23, 33, 88, 94–97, 168, 225, 284, 313nn. 13–19; anti-Semitic, 177; and desire, 164; disgusting details, 95–96; history of, 96; and slavery, 188
"Disrememory," 212
Display of disability, sanctioned: 91–93; in civic advertisement, 92; in medicine shows, 93; opposed to "bold and meretricious," 162; public stripping, 91, 312n. 8; in sports, 92; on revival circuit, 92–93. *See also* Deformance
Doctor's, The, 115, 116, 117, 119, 120, 123, 124, 126, 127, 130, 131, 132, 133, 134, 171, 214, 248; in Chinatown, 174; sailors in, 319n. 17
Doctors and ugly law: in opposition to, 306n. 28; in support of, 55, 156, 166, 306n. 28
Dogs: city regulation of, 97; unsightly beggars compared to, 99,100
Domestic ideology, 148, 151, 245, 324n. 20, 325n. 29
Donnelly, Ignatius, *Caesar's Column*, 177
Dorn, Mike, 6, 310n. 14

Dreiser, Theodore, 172
Du Bois, W.E.B., 196, 335n. 27
Duis, Perry 30, 302n. 7, 315n. 35
Duncan, Kath 321n. 34

Eastern Nebraska Community Office of Retardation (ENCOR), 7–8
Eastwood, Carolyn, 30, 178, 181
Education, 235, 236; Education for All Handicapped Children Act (1975), 281; special, and segregation, 185
Edwards, Rebekah, 159, 308n. 39, 338n. 7
England: Charity Organization Society in, 41, 304n. 1; Guild of the Brave Poor Things in, 248, 343n. 18; poor law in, 4–5, 27
Epilepsy, 67, 89, 107; and "immodest exhibition," 160
Epstein, Julia, 297
Equal Employment Opportunity Commission (EEOC), 284
Ervin, Mike, 20, 161
Eskridge, William, 142
Essig, Melissa. *See* Cole, Melissa
Etiolation, 126–127
Eugenics: and aesthetics, 309n. 9; *The Black Stork*, 89; *Buck v. Bell*, 19, 255; campaigns focused on unsightly beggars, 158, 213; charity organization and, 48–51; Holmes, Oliver Wendell and, 255; institutions and, 67; Jukes family, 50; lumping together of undesirables, 16; nativism and, 182, 322n. 6; prostitution and, 158; racism and homophobia linked with, 142; Supreme Court upholding of, 19, 255; tramp and, 51, 309n. 8; Tribe of Ishmael, 42; and ugly law, logic of, 67. *See also* Sterilization
Euthanasia, 50, 120
Exhibition, 32, 101, 103, 109, 144; exhibitionism, 160
Exposure, 9, 12, 13, 32, 33, 86, 102, 160, 222; as beginning of language, 287; of breasts, 161; in Cleveland Cripple Survey, 237; in court cases, 78–79, 311n. 22; and epilepsy, 160; "European exposure method," 167, 182; flaunting, 148, 163; indecent, 160–162, 163; nakedness and, 329n. 47; of portions rather than persons, 9; reconstituted as publicity, 258; of violated body (Hartman), 195; of wounds, 33
Expression: freak-show performance as, 338n. 12; legal freedom of, 180, 338n. 12. *See also* First Amendment; Speech

Face: facial anomalies, discrimination on basis of, 284–285; facial scarring, 283; "Facies mendicans," 80–81, *81*; and ideology of disability, 283; Levinas on, 286–287; of the unsightly beggar, 286
Fakers. *See* Imposters
Farley, Anthony Paul, 184, 190, 335n. 17
Fawcett, Barbara, 322n. 2, 326n. 31
Feeble-minded: boy, exhibition of, 90; clinical category, development of, 64; eugenics and, 90; exclusion of, 330n. 8; Lincoln State School and Colony for, 201; menace of, 160; race and institutionalization of, 201; segregation of, 67; self-representation and, 258; white Others and, 333nn. 4, 5; woman, containment of, 75–77
Feminine: depravity of, 147; impressionability of, 147; unsightly beggar, 75;

Feminine, (*Continued*)
writing, 242. *See also* Femininity; Women
Femininity, 145, 148, 153; and begging, 345n. 12; and disability, 323nn. 16, 18. *See also* Masculinity
Feminism, 142, 143
Ferguson, Philip, 86–87, 301n. 2
Ferguson, Roderick, 329n. 50, 336n. 28
Ferri, Beth, and David Connor, 332n. 2
Fett, Sharla, 335n. 20, 336n. 33
Film: *The Black Stork*, 89; The Doctor's, filmic representations of, 133; *The Music Within*, 298n. 7; *The Thieving Hand*, 124; *Till I Come Back to You*, 275–76, 277; World War I in, 275–276. *See also* DeMille, Cecil B.
Fine, Michelle, 326n. 31
Fineman, Martha, 152
Finger, Anne, 305n. 15
Finkelstein, Vic, 307n. 36
First Amendment: disabled beggars given no protection by, 218; disabled bodies in claims, 216; Holmes's defense of, 255; judicial hostility to claims, 218; protection of begging and, 215–218. *See also* Expression; Speech
Forbes, James, 100, 113, 136, 146, 159, 195, 213, 214, 268, 315n. 32, 338n. 7
Fordham, Brigham, 299n. 15, 315n. 35, 338n. 12
Foucault, Michel, 18, 64–67, 169, 301n. 26, 308n. 2, 309nn. 3, 4, 330n. 10
Francis, Leslie Pickering, 299n. 13
Frank, Gelya, 321n. 27
Frankenberg, Ruth, 185
Fraser, Mat, 320n. 23
Fraud. *See* Imposters
Freaks: Alden, W.L., *Among the Freaks*, 313n. 10, 316n. 38, 324n. 20; as effigies, 103; "find a defender," 306n. 28; relation to unsightly beggars, 102. *See also* Freak-shows
Freak-shows: capitalism and, 59; Cleveland Cripple Survey on, 237; at Columbia Exposition, 310n. 13; demise of, 86, 101, 315n. 35; gender and, 324n. 20; human/animal blurring in, 98; institutionalization and, 315n. 34; laws pertaining to, 315n. 35; opposite of, 208; Pennsylvania "anti-freak" bill, 55; suppression of, related to ugly laws, 55, 86, 101–104. *See also* Freaks
French, Sally, 321n. 32
Fretz, Eric, 315n. 34
Freud, Sigmund, on Dora and mendicancy, 81, 83
Freund, Roger, 196–197, 198, 199, 211, 298n. 9
Fried, Michael, 289
Friedman, I.K., *Autobiography of a Beggar*, 116, 125, 170
Friendly visiting, COS idea of, 41–42; called into question, 46; concept reversed, 176; as prefiguration of social work, 304n. 4
Fuller, Arthur Franklin: autobiography of, 263–276; and category "cripple," 266–267; charge of hypochondria and, 263, 265; citing Constitution, 274; citing Declaration of Independence, 274; classism of, 263; cripples survey by, 271; critical disability legal theory of, 274; critique of COS, 270–272; defense against charge of begging, 270; defense against charge of fraud, 265; defense of masculinity by, 149; in DeMille films, 275–276; on disabled boozefighters, 104, 105; *Fifty Thousand Miles Back-Ridden*, 260, 261,

262–263, 267–272; on gender, disability, and poverty, 151–52; on independent living, 272; on L.A.'s consideration of ugly law, 247, 252; maternal impression and, 271; modernity of, 343n. 20; newspaper coverage of, 346n. 18; "odd" and, 263, 271–272; *Odd Soldiery*, 263, 265; opposition to ugly law, 267–275, 342n. 15; racism of, 197–198; on railroad travel, 334n. 14; reclaimed urban experience and, 286; subalternity and, 260; on vocational rehabilitation, 251; *Wrestling the Wolf*, 272, 274; 257, 264, 266, 277; writing for disabled audience, 346n. 13

Gannon, Jack, 337n. 5
Garland Thomson, Rosemarie, 15, 51, 78, 86, 98, 101, 145, 235, 297n. 3, 301, 305n. 20, 308n. 2, 315n. 35, 318n. 6, 322n. 1, 323nn. 16, 18, 324n. 21, 326nn. 31, 33, 328n. 43, 341n. 5
Gender, 31, 144–157, 290; himself or herself clause in ugly law, 10, 144. *See also* Feminine; Femininity; Masculinity; Men; Women
Gerber, David, 324n. 23
Germany, 297n. 4, 304n. 1, 332n. 24
Gilbreth, Frank, and Lillian Gilbreth, 238–239, 341n. 9
Gilman, Sander, 15, 329n. 2
Gleeson, Brendan, 87, 307n. 36, 309n. 4, 310n. 14
Gliedman, John, and William Roth, *The Unexpected Minority*, 142, 322n. 7
Goggin, Gerard, and Christopher Newell, 317n. 5
Groce, Nora, 230, 326n. 36, 339n. 2
Guter, Bob, 321n. 34

Habermas, Jurgen, vi, 283
Hacking, Ian, vi, 62, 79–80, 283
Hahn, Harlan, 310n. 20, 322n. 7, 339n. 19, 348n. 9
Hall, Kim, 326n. 31
Hard labor sentences, 339n. 15; and disability, 334n. 12; legal objection to, 223; and slavery, 190
Hartman, Saidiya, 186, 190, 195, 339n. 18
Hawthorne, Nathaniel, 177; "The Birth-mark," 324n. 20
Haymarket Riot, policemen disabled in, 60, 308n. 37
Health, 70, 89; modernist, 89; racial disparities in, 194; as social capital, 312n. 5
Henderson, Charles, "The Standard of Normal Man," 41, 49, 50–52, 305n. 22
Herndl, Diane Price, 92, 326n. 31
Heteronormativity, 151, 308
Heumann, Judith, 332n. 2
Hevey, David, 305n. 15
Hogan, David, 299n. 14, 302n. 6, 305n. 22
Holmes, Martha Stoddard, 110, 111, 343n. 18
Holmes, Oliver Wendell, 255
Homelessness, 209, 306n. 29, 307n. 31; anti-homeless ordinances, 209
Homosexuality, 75, 95, 159–160
Honeyman, Arthur, account of arrest for violating ugly law, 298n. 7
Howard, Ebenezer, 73–74, 74, 337n. 3
Howells, William Dean, "Tribulations of a Cheerful Giver," 37–38, 108
Hughes, Bill, and Kevin Patterson, 128, 299n. 12, 321n. 30
Hugo, Victor, *Hunchback of Notre Dame*, 115
Hull House, 30, 90, 91
Hybridity, 46, 119, 129–30

Hyde, Alan, 164, 167, 312n. 3, 330n. 3
Hysteria, 80, *82*

Identity: categories, ambiguity of, 188, 191–193; politics, 121, 203–204, 290, 318n. 15
Idiots and imbeciles: eugenics and, 19; idiot leader of Chinese hordes in *Recovered Continent,* 174; idiot mother, 154; Norris's representation of idiot, 283, Sequin on, 154–155; specified in ugly law, 10. *See also* Cognitive disability; Eugenics, *Buck v. Bell*; Feeble-minded
Immigration, 24, 30, 165–183, 184; in Cleveland Cripple Survey, 243; federal exclusion of disabled immigrants, 168; immigrants as inevitably disabled, 168; increase in late nineteenth century, 165; law, as ugly law, 168; lumping together of immigrants, 170; migratory workers, 209; municipal involvement in policing, 168; nomadic subjects, 169; padrone system, 168; policing, related to policing of unsightly, 178; represented by Crane, 166, 288; screening, 165; state exclusion, 168; studies, and disability studies, 330n. 6. *See also* Chinese; Mexicans; Nativism
Impairment, 29, 127, 137, 209; archives arranged according to, 255; effects, 129, 321n. 30; and masculinity, 241; relation to disability, 128; sociology of, 129, 321n. 30
Imperfect: children, effectual extermination of, 50–51; in draft of New York City ugly law, 10, 56
Imposters, 17–18, 108–137; African American, 195, 335n. 26; in autobiography, 258; COS policing of, 43, 58; COS seen as, 46; cranks, 71; cross-dressing and, 162; in court cases, 80–83; Deaf condemnation of, 129; escaping military service, 83; fake well person, 266; female, 146–147,158; Fuller on, 276; imposter's dictionary, 113; medical detection of, 84; "Mr. Traumatic Claimant of Fakeville," 84; nature fakers, 83, 311n. 27; on the Internet, 317n. 5; Persian, 172; on railroads, 191; "sham cripples," 108, 109, 110, 111, 115, 121, 124; veteran, 29, 150; vs. for-reals,125, 133. *See also* Authenticity
Imrie, Rob, 14
Independence, American ideology of, 78, 246, 247, 325n. 29
Independent living: first Center for Independent Living, 280; history of, 347n. 3; movement, link to ugly law, 26; unsightly begging as means for, 199
Indiana, 45, 107; Indianapolis, 45, 210
Individualism: ability/disability and, 342n. 10; American, 46, 78, 86, 297 n. 5; capitalism, and, 308n. 36; freak shows and, 313 n. 10; Fuller's claim of, 272; overemphasis on, 246; successful individual, concept of, 238–247, 342n. 10
Industrialization, 165, 302n. 5, 307n. 36; industrial accidents, 59–60, 302n. 5
Industrial Workers of the World (IWW), 248, 343n. 17, 346n. 20
Infrapolitics, 57–58, 307n. 31; of pity, 58
Injury, 77–78; personal injury fraud, 83–84
Institutionalization: eugenics and, 67–68; of feeble-minded woman, 75–77; forced, 221–222, 250; freak display and, 315n. 34; history of, linked to ugly law, 26, 36, 68–69, 86, 190;

laws compelling, 19; performance and, 305n. 17; regulatory function of, 64–65; 66–68, 308n. 2; segregation and, 185; solution to contradictions around work in U.S. culture, 223; state-sponsored ableism and, 280
Intersectionality, 61, 141, 143, 185, 189, 203–204, 322nn. 2, 3; *But Some of Us Are Brave*, 343n. 19; and confluence, 61, 308n. 38
Intersubjectivity, vii, 283
Invalid, 236; Fuller's staging of self as, 265; ideology of the shut-in, 308n. 40; legal protection of, 215; raced as white, 126, 321n. 25.
Italian: anti-Italian legislation, 179; fruit-stand vendors, 179; immigrant represented by Crane, 288; immigrants in Chicago, 179; *L'Italia*, newspaper, 181; street musicians and busking, 179, 182, 332n. 27; suppression of organ grinders, organizing for, 181
Iwakuma, Miho, 321n. 27

Jackson, Shannon, 47, 48, 137
Jaeger, Paul and Cynthia Ann Bowman, 330n. 6
Jakobsen, Janet, 142, 308n. 38, 322n. 8, 323n. 10
Japanese Americans, 330–331n. 11, 331n. 17
Jewish: beggars, supposedly nonexistent, 173, 174–175; begging, 175–178; blind, 304n. 9; charity organization, 177; community in Chicago, 178; "cripples," 177; cultural association with contagion, 170; cultural distinction from the Oriental, 173; cultural equation with the Oriental, 172; German, relation to other Jewish immigrants, 178, 332nn. 23, 24; ghetto, 170, 176; intra-Jewish conflict, 176; Others, 141; peddler, Reitman's representation of, 75; peddlers, noise policing of, 180; philanthropy, 304n. 9; repudiation of begging, 173; Russian Jewish refugees, 178; Schnorrer, 175–177; theater, 175; United Hebrew Charities, 177; unsightly beggar, impossibility of, 176; Zangwill, Israel, 175–177. *See also* Anti-Semitism
Jim Crow: and disability, 186, 333n. 3; original figure of, 186, 187; popularized by Daddy Rice, 186; statutory, 186, 187, 189, 191, 192, 333n. 3, 334n. 10. *See also* Segregation; Tiny Tim Crow
Johnson, E. Patrick, 121
Johnson, Mary, 305n. 15; and Barrett Shaw, 337n. 2
Johnson, Roberta, 347n. 4

Kafer, Alison, 321n. 34
Kasnitz, Devva, 299
Kasson, John, 87, 320n. 23
Katz, Michael, 41, 61, 304n. 2, 305nn. 12, 16, 19, 308n. 2, 309n. 8
Kaveny, M. Cathleen, 14, 300n. 24
Kelley, Robin, 307n. 31
Kellogg, Charles D., "Crude Suggested Draft" of New York City ugly law, 56, 61, 102, 288, 289
Kerber, Linda, 195, 301n. 25, 323n. 13
Kerlin, Isaac, 49, 305n. 21
Kiger, Gary, 131
Killacky, John, and Larry Connolly, 312n. 8
Kingrey, Julia, 65
Kleege, Georgina, 117, 327n. 38
Knox, Mertice Buck, 253
Krieger, Linda, 299n. 13, 348n. 6

Kudlick, Catherine, 156, 297, 324n. 22, 326n. 31, 327n. 37
Kuppers, Petra, 120, 131, 158, 300n. 18, 305n. 23, 308n. 1, 312n. 8, 315n. 33, 320n. 23, 321n. 31
Kurzman, Stephen, 123
Kusmer, Kenneth, 41, 165, 195, 298n. 9, 304nn. 2, 4, 7, 8, 306nn. 24, 25, 307n. 33, 318n. 7, 323nn. 13, 18, 326n. 32, 335n. 25

Labor: control, ugly law as selective form of, 193; history and disability history, ugly law at intersection of, 17, 63; organizing and unrest, 17, 56, 59, 61; unions, as model for organized begging, 247–249
Landers, Ann, 14, 300n. 23
Langan, Celeste, 319n. 19
Law: annihilation of space by (Mitchell), 209; begging, 215–219, 222, 223; habeas corpus, 222; lawsuits, injury and compensation, 78–84; liberty claim in, 203–204, 205; natural class theory in, 68; nuisance, 214–215; modern disability formation and, 11; person, definition of, in, 85; state legislation (*see* Alabama; Missouri; Pennsylvania; Texas); statute, shift from custom to, 189–190; sumptuary, and ugly law, 329n. 49; tort, 77–79; unofficial, 297n. 1, 298n. 9; vagrancy, 192, 219–22, 223–224. *See also* Americans with Disabilities Act; *Brown v. Board of Education*; Legal cases; Municipal law; Poor law; Supreme Court, U.S.; Ugly law
League of the Physically Handicapped, 132, 249, 322n. 36
Lefebvre, Henri, 207, 208–209, 286, 337n. 3, 339n. 20
Legal cases: *Berkeley Community Health Project v. City of Berkeley*, 338n. 11; *Blackman Health Resort v. City of Atlanta*, 215; *Buck v. Bell*, 19, 255; *Burnside v. Superintendent of House of Correction*, 220–222; *C.C.B v. Florida*, 216; *Cleburne v. Cleburne Living Center*, 332n. 3, 339n. 19; *Ex parte Dart*, 252–253; *Farley v. Watt*, 324n. 23; *Gardner v. Johnson*, 299n. 15; *Gogola v. City of Cleveland*, 245; Gott Dewey's, 225–226; *Gowen et al v. O'Hara*, 224; *Gray v. Forbes*, 214; *Haller*, 216–218; *Jew Ho v. Williamson*, 28; *Korzib v. Netherlands*, 145; *Lefever v. City of Columbus*, 218, 338n. 14; *Marallis v. Chicago*, 324n. 23; *Papachristou v. City of Jacksonville*, 347n. 5; *Roulette v. City of Seattle*, 338n. 11; *Stotler v. Rochelle*, 215; *Tennessee v. Lane*, 19, 347n. 1; *Thomas M. Thompson v Superintendent*, 223–224; *Union Pacific Railway v. Botsford*, 78–79; *University of Alabama v. Garrett*, 106, 185, 332n. 3; *Weinstein v. Wheeler*, 77; *Woodstock Burying Ground Ass'n v. Hager*, 215; *Watson v. City of Cambridge*, 96; *Zartarian v. Billings*, 165. See also *Brown v. Board of Education*
Lesbians, 159–160, 329n. 46
Levi, Sandra, 321n. 33
Levinas, Emmanuel, 286–287, 350n. 13
Lewis, Halle, 246–247, 340n. 2, 341n. 4, 342n. 13
Lewis, Victoria Ann, 12–13, 300n. 17–21
Lifchez, Ray, 14, 300n. 22
Limont, Mark, vii
Lincoln, NE, 3, 10, 64, 158, 294
Linker, Beth, 343n. 25
Linton, Simi, 2–3, 14–15, 250, 300n. 23
Little people, 48, 90, 226–229

Litvak, Simi, and Alexandra Enders, 314n. 28
Litwack, Leon, 186, 189, 190
Livingston, Julie, 26
Loberg, Molly, 297n. 4
Lombroso, Cesare, 309n. 9, 329n. 46
Longmore, Paul, 27, 226, 299–300n. 16, 329n. 49, 338n. 10, 347n. 1; on charity, 305n. 15; and Goldberger, David, 322n. 36; and Miller, Paul Steven, 182, 207, 336n. 1; and Umansky, Lauri, 255, 259; *Why I Burned My Book*, 302n. 3
Loo, Tina, and Carolyn Strange, 101, 298, 313n. 12, 322n. 35
Los Angeles: attempt to pass ugly law, in 1913, 3, 169, 247–253; Fuller in, 252, 272; Municipal Charities Commission, 169, 247–253, 330n. 11; newspaper coverage of disabled beggars, 107,148; Persian mendicants in, 172; policing of Mexicans, 169, 330n. 11; prohibition of sale of liquor to disabled people in, 106; response to hoboes in, 99–100; "Strangest Union in the World" in, 247–253
Lowell, Josephine Shaw, 41, 42, 49
Lubove, Ray, 41, 304n. 2

MacGregor, Frances Cooke, 309n. 3, 348n. 7
Manila, Philippines, 5–6, 295–296
Maps: "A Graphic Method of Illustrating Situations in Penal Institutions," 75–77, *76*; Howard's "Slumless, Smokeless Garden City," 73, *74*; mapping of deviance, 302n. 4; "Reitman's Social Geography," 71–73, *72*, 310n. 17. *See also* City
Margolin, Leslie, 304n. 2, 305n. 15
Marshall, Thurgood, 332n. 3
Marx, Karl, 307n. 36
Masculinity: and begging as contradiction in terms, 149; default, 144; disabled men on, 149, 150, 203; interloper (Shah), 149; "man behind," 240–241, 266, 342nn. 10, 12; in rough culture, 319n. 17; ugly law justified as defense of, 148–149, 152, 324n. 22; veterans and, 149–150, 325n. 25
Mason, Mary Grimley, 341n. 5
Maternal impression: deafness and, 89, 326n. 36; history of idea of, 326n. 36; nativism and, 166; governmental policy based upon, 327n. 39; ugly law and,153–157; women doctors on, 156–157
Matson, Floyd, 27, 301
Mayhem, 322n. 34
McCulloch, Oscar, 42, 45
McElroy, Emma, 318n. 10
McMurtrie, Douglas, 233–234, 239
McRobbie, Angela, 287–288
McRuer, Robert, 328n. 46, 331n. 12, 339n. 1; and Abby Wilkerson, 328n. 46
Medicalization: as solution to unsightliness, 244–245, 254; deformance and, 48; orthopedic surgeons and, 339n. 1, 340n. 3; poverty knowledge and, 305n. 12; profit and, 307n. 36; relation of disabled people to, 127. *See also* Disability, medical model of; Public Health, Rehabilitationism
Men: disabled, 145; in Gold Rush, as ill-fated, 25; male chattels, 120; male guardians, 148; male unsightly beggars, 148–150; malingering, 83–84; neurasthenia and, 83; tramping, 145; Yegg men, 146. *See also* Masculinity; Veterans
Mendicancy squads, 53–54, 58

Mendicant literature, 255–261, 344n. 2; as defense against arrest, 256; formula in, 259
Menninghaus, Winfried, 94, 96, 313n. 18
Mercer, Geoff, 299n. 12, 307n. 34
Merleau-Ponty, Maurice, 131, 321n. 31
Merrifield, Andy, 209, 222, 339n. 20
Mexicans: unsightly begging in U.S., 169, 172, 248, 330n. 11; workers, crackdown on unemployed, 248
Michalko, Rod, 117
Michigan, Act 103, 101
Milbank, Jeremiah, 232–234
Miller, Paul Steven, 182, 207, 336n. 1
Miller, Sheila, 335n. 21
Miller, William Ian, 94, 95, 97, 313nn. 14, 16, 314n. 21
Missouri, 330n. 8
Mitchell, David, and Sharon Snyder. *See* Snyder, Sharon, and David Mitchell
Mitchell, Don, 209
Modernity, 24, 86, 125, 148, 181, 182, 248
Moeschen, Sheila, 305n. 17
Molina, Natalia, 170, 330nn. 6, 7, 11, 331nn. 14, 16
"Mollie Darling," woman who played, 1, 31, 122, 152, 163, 182, 210
Mollow, Anna, 16
Monstrosity: boy exhibited as, 90–91; vs. disability, 330n. 10; human, laws against display of, 101; "imported," 169; "monster in the shape of a deformed Indian," 153; projection of, 225; outside the freak show, 316n. 39
Moore, Leroy, 336n. 35
Mothers, 145; benevolent maternalism, 328n. 43; breastfeeding, 161; protection of, as justification for ugly law, 153–157. *See also* Maternal influence
Mumford, Keith, 197, 336n. 28
Mundo, Otto, *The Recovered Continent*, 174, 331n. 19
Municipal law: establishing morality through, 24, 142; important role of, 31; as means of regulating comportment, 30–31; new trends of in 19th century, 162
Murray, Stuart, 4–5
Music Within, The, 298n. 7, 348n. 5

National Center for Law and the Handicapped (NCLH), 7, 23, 290
Native Americans, 142; "deformed Indian" exhibited in San Francisco, 153; and history of clothing law, 160, 329n. 48
Nativism, 165, 322n. 6, 329n. 1; medicalized, 330n. 7. *See also* Immigration
Neilson, Laura, 218
Nelson, Alondra, 193, 196
Neurasthenic, 80, 311n. 25, 321n. 25; female, 80, *81*
New Orleans, LA: almshouse in, 34–35, 67, 150; Congo Square, 187; "corralling of cripples," 35, 303n. 12; COS in, 39; law in, similar to ugly law, 3, 32–36, 292, 298n. 9; old woman with cancer in, 187; ugly law and "lewd women" in, 323n. 12
New York City, NY: anti-mendicancy in, 53–56, 306nn. 25, 26; Bowery, 18, 113–115, 117, 119, 130, 133, 174, 195, 214, 249; Chinatown, 174; Crane, on, 288–289; criminal organization of begging in, 132–133, 213–214; Haller, Frank, begging in, 216–218; hand-organ permits, 181, 211; rehabilitation efforts in, 233; sham cripples in, 108, 110–111, 113–115, 118–119; subway panhandling case in, vii; unsightly begging in, 112, 152; version of ugly law, 3, 10, 56, 102–103, 106, 295; ugly

law not enacted, 210. *See also* Brooklyn, NY; Crane, Stephen; Forbes, James
Newsboys, 159, 245, 251, 328n. 45. *See also* Cleveland Cripple Survey, newspaper seller in
Noise: legal regulation of, 86, 179; and "aural profiling" (Vaillant), 180; and sensory reform, 179
Norden, Martin, 110, 111, 152
Normate and normality, 51, 133, 170, 297n. 3, 305n. 23, 307n. 36, 308n. 3, 328n. 46; abnormal individual, 66
Norris, Frank, 115; "The Dis-Associated Charities," 115, 318n. 11; "Little Dramas of the Curbstone," 283–284
Nussbaum, Martha, 94, 95, 97, 98, 313nn. 14, 17
Nussbaum, Susan, 336n. 29

O'Brien, Ruth, 98, 299n. 13, 325n. 25
Oliver, Michael, 128, 297n. 3, 307
Omaha, NE: emphasis on ugliness in coverage of law, 6–7, 65, 282; influence of Omaha case on Burgdorfs, 7, 8–9, 290; ugly law enacted in, 3, 295; ugly law, language of excitement of, 10, 91; ugly law, last known arrest under, 6; ugly law, repeal of, 347n. 5;
Organ-grinders, 31, 179, 181, 332n. 27; licensing of, 211
Other Voices (Mark Taper Forum), 13
O'Toole, Corbett, 326n. 31, 328n. 46
Ott, Katherine, 321n. 27

Padden, Carol, and Tom Humphries, 321n. 29
Paris, France, 124, 156
Parker, Andrew, and Eve Kosofsky Sedgwick, 122, 125, 126, 127, 320n. 24
Parr, Hester, 326n. 34
Passing: and covering, 163–164; and trespass, 123–124
Pastrana, Julia, 98, 314n. 23, 326n. 33
Patrol wagon, introduction of, and ugly law, 54
Pauperism: COS plans for cure of, 42; Du Bois on African American, 196, 316n. 45; extermination and, 49; hereditary, 50; and immigration restriction, 167
Peddling: and begging, 178, 245; in Berlin, 297n. 4; in Cleveland Cripple Survey, 237–238, 241; deaf, 337n. 5; Jewish, 75, 178,180; sanctions against, 178, 303n. 10, 337nn. 4, 5; sound of, as foreign, 180. *See also* Peddling permits
Peddling permits, 31, 181, 210–212, 303n. 10, 337n. 4; contradicting ugly law, 210–212; discussed in autobiography, 262; invalidated, 269; for veterans, 149
Peevey, James, 1–2, 30, 59, 88, 122, 149, 178, 210
Pennsylvania: Act 208 (freak law, 1895), 55, 102; Act 276 (ugly law, 1891), 3, 10–11, 55–56, 102, 294, and Fourteenth Amendment, 219; contradictions in legal treatment of disabled beggars, 222; doctors' relation to ugly law in, 306n. 28; idiots and imbeciles specified in ugly law in, 10; as key site for conflicts concerning disability and begging, 219; legal exemptions for disabled people in, 222, 339n. 16
Performance: of begging, 307n. 33; dandyism and, 320n. 23; in film enactments of imposter beggers,133; history of ugly law as history of, 290; of infirmity, 146; privilege and, 137; skin as, 187; solo autobiographical,

Performance, (*Continued*) 312n. 8; theatrical, 12–13, 207, 336n. 29; "twice-behaved behavior" (Schechner), 117; vaudeville, 226, 228; of ugly law in disability culture, 12–13; of unsightly begging, 29, 36, 58, 116–120, 133; of war injury, 29
Performative utterances, 121, 125, 256
Performativity: and begging, 29, 36; definition of, 116; of disability, 37, 127, 319n. 18; recalcitrant (B. Brown), 331n. 15; unsightly, 109, 121–122
Pernick, Martin, 89, 309n. 9, 312n. 7
Person: as euphemism for penis, 161; disability and the, 139; indecent exposure of, 160; legal concept of, 85; in liberal theory, 85; "with a disability," 315n. 30
Personal care assistance: begging as source of income for, 197; to subjects of ugly law, 198–200, 336n. 32
Pfieffer, David, 321n. 32
Phenomenology, 127, 129, 131
Philadelphia: anti-mendicancy policing in, 53, 306n. 25; arrests of blind beggars in, 220–224; consumptive hospital in, 224; doctors advocating ugly law in, 55; Dewey, Gott, arrest in, 225–228; exemptions for disabled people, 339n. 16; unfriendly to disabled peddlers, 345n. 13; vagrancy court in, 303n. 13; Wilder, outrage of, 228
Philippines, 172. *See also* Manila
Ph*reaks, 13, 300
Pimentel, Richard: account of arrest for violating ugly law, 298n. 7, 348n. 5; on ugly law and ADA, 347n. 4
Pittenger, Mark, 134, 136
Pity: beggar's manipulation of, 58; beggars vs. freaks and, 103; gender and, 145, 147, 324n. 22; infrapolitics of, 58; minstrelization and, 191; "No Pity," 58; pact of, 109; "pitiful creatures," 102; "Pitiful Mendicant Gives Way to Crippled Beggar," 110; pity sluts, 147; trading on, 178; transformation from object of to normate, 133; vs. solidarity, 58
Plague: Foucault on, 66; Sontag on, 167; and unsightly begging, 183
Playboy, on ugliness ordinance, 65
Plessy v. Ferguson, 186, 187, 192; nurse's exemption in, 197
Poirier, Suzanne, 71, 73, 310n. 19
Police: arrests by, 53, 54; 212–213; disabled, 60–61; NYC Chief Conlin, 111, 152; NYC Captain Galvin, 114–115, 120; nonenforcement of law by, 8, 33, 181, 211–212, 274, 298–299nn. 9, 10; plainclothes, 53, 134, 171; resistance to arrest by, 54–55, 56, 57, 58, 201–202, 213–214; in silent film, 110
Poor house: burned enslaved girl consigned to, 188; history linked to ugly law, 26, 36; poor farm, 64; poor house clause in ugly law, 10, 27, 67; race and, 200–201; regulatory care in, 64. *See also* Almshouse
Poor law, English, 27, 301nn. 2, 3, 318n. 6
Porgy and Bess, 100
Portland, OR, 3, 29, 148, 292
Positive Exposure Project, 349n. 12
Post, Robert, 348n. 6
Poverty: in affluent society, 19; COS response to, 41–43, 305n. 12; and disability, nexus of, 16, 19, 120, 210; disfigurement as characteristic of poor people, 32; infrapolitics of, 57; poor relief, 27; and psychiatric disability, 301n. 26; Reitman on, 72, 73,75; and ugly law, 59, 61, 68

Pregnancy, 153–156; medicalized, 156
Pretenders, disability, 321n. 34
Price, Janet, and Margit Shildrick, 129–130, 319n. 18
Progressive Era, 69, 90, 106, 112, 136, 183, 197, 248, 254
Prosthetics, 117, 123–124, 209, 321n. 27
Prostitute: bodily measurement of, 328n. 46; as paradigmatic disorderly body (Hooper), 328n. 44; prostitution law and ugly law, 158–159; Reitman and, 72, 75; ugly law indexed near laws concerning, 144
Psychiatric disability: ADA and, 131; gender and, 147; in Gold Rush California, 25; "Hypnotized into Madhouse," 147; hysteria, 80–83; insane, institutions for, 67, 76, 77; madness, elasticity of concept, 301n. 25; poverty and criminality and, 301n. 26; pregnancy and, 155, 156
Psychoanalytic: frameworks brought to bear on ugly law, 15, 56, 306n. 30; reading of disgust, 313
Public health: display of disability, 90; hygiene panic, 70; incursions into Chinatowns, 28, 173; as means of subordination, 184, 186, 329–330n. 2; race and, 184, 186; transgressive sexuality targeted by campaigns, 159; as venue of ugly law, 248, 279–280
Public sphere: disability and, Habermas on, vii; as pedagogic space, 89; private sphere and, 151, 162; spatial regulation in, 162, 209, 310n. 14; white, 170
Public view, 86, 151. *See also* Public sphere; Visuality and visibility

Quarantine, 28, 170. *See also* Disease
Queer: boundary-crossers, 169, 331n. 12; crank and, 71; in military culture, 325n. 25; queerness and disability, 328n. 46; theory in understanding of ugly law, 163–164; *See also* Eugenics, homophobia linked with; Homosexuality; Lesbians

Race: anti-racism, 142; cross-race sociability, 197; culture of unsightliness and, 188; degeneration, 50; disgust and, 188; eugenics and, 141–142, 322n. 6; as form of pleasure (Farley), 190; mixed-race space, 197; race-based health disparities, 194; race-making work of ugly law, 185; racism, 141–142, 165, 182, 186; producing disablement, 194; racial control, ugly law as form of, 18, 193; ugly law and, 5, 184–204; vagrancy and, 195, 335nn. 24, 25; of white unsightly beggars, 198. *See also* Blackness; Whiteness
Radin, Margaret Jane, 162
Rafter, Nicole, 158, 333n. 4; and Gibson, Mary, 151
Railroad: free transportation on, 191; inaccessibility of, 334n. 9; injured workers suing, 212; as microcity, 334n. 11; passenger injury on, 78–79; policing of fraud on, 83–84; porters, 191; segregation on, 334n. 10; ugly law traveled by, 188–189
Red Cross Institute for Crippled and Disabled Men, 233, 236, 239
Reform: begging and, 37; on disabled beggars, 109, 116, 127; fetishism and, 133; reformance (Jackson), 47; reformist discourse, 110, rehabilitation and, 230–254; spells of, 104; surveillance and, 43. *See also* Charity Organization Society; Deformance
Rehabilitationism, 230–254; aesthetic motive in, 310n. 21; analysis of, 339n. 1;

Rehabilitationism, (*Continued*) approach, 230, 252; and charity, 248; concept of unsightliness in, 238; and deformance, 48; development of, 60; making disability vanish, 254; social vs. medical, 232, 254; vocational, 233; Vocational Rehabilitation Act of 1973, 6, 280
Reitman, Ben, 71–75, 144, 310nn. 17, 19, 323n. 15; "Outcast Narratives," 73; "Reitman's Social Geography," 71–73, 72
Reno, NV, 3, 296
Resistance: to arrest, 212–213; in autobiography, 261–262; of Burnside, Charles, 220–222; in cultural production, 226–229; of Dewey, 225–226; difficulty of, 263; by disabled people, 207–208, 209, 210, 212–214; of Fuller, 262–276; of Gray, George, 214; of Leroy, Alfred, 247, 251; organized criminal, 213–214; procedural objections in appeals court, 219–224; to spatial control, 209; suit for libel, 214; suppression of, 289, 307n. 31; of Thompson, Thomas, 223–224; to ugly law, in autobiography, 262–276; of Wilder, 226–229
Riis, Jacob, 303n. 17, 319n. 16
Ringenbach, Paul, 54, 55, 103, 153, 306n. 24, 337n. 4
Roach, Joseph, 103
Roberts, Ed, 347n. 3
Robichaud, Samantha, 284–286, 287
Roediger, David, 336n. 31
Rogin, Michael, 134
Roth, William, 142, 307n. 36; 322n. 7, 323n. 9
Royko, Mike, "A Law City Should Keep," 281–282
Russell, Marta, 60, 307n. 36
Ryan, Susan, 145, 305n. 14, 317n. 5, 320n. 20, 329n. 1

Salvation Army, 252–253
Samuels, Ellen, 317n. 5
Sandahl, Carrie, 300n. 18, 312n. 8
San Francisco, CA, 24–29; anti-Chinese measures, 28, 167, 170, 173, 188; Gold Rush, 24, 25; immigration crises, 169; imposters in, 29, 115–116; news articles in, 28–29, 312n. 4; Norris story set in, 115–116, 318n. 11; ordinances on "problem bodies" (Sears), 162; sidewalk ordinance, 188; ugly law in, first known, 2, 24–25, 64, 291–292, 298n. 9; ugly law, language of, 10
Santa Cruz, CA, the other "ugly law" in, 348n. 6
Sante, Luc, 114, 115, 116, 318n. 7
Sappol, Michael, 93, 315n. 35, 322n. 5
Sartre, John Paul, 312n. 6
Saxton, Marsha, and Florence Howe, 326n. 31
Scarry, Elaine, 286
Schechner, Richard, 117
Schoyer Books, 344nn. 2, 3, 5
Scotch, Richard, 347n. 4
Scott, James C., 57, 71, 307n. 31
Scullion, Philip, 132
Sears, Claire, 24, 31,188, 302n. 9, 315n. 34
Section 504 of Rehabilitation Act of 1973, 280, 281, 313–314n. 20, 332n. 2
Segregation: and appearance demarcation, 187; centrality of to power relations, 332n. 1; by class, 188, 209, 334n. 10; conceptual difficulty of, 189, 334n. 10; economic, 16; of disabled people, 86, 327n. 39, 332n. 3; disability segregation, lack of un-

derstanding of, 184; by gender, 150, 155, 188, 334n. 10; institutionalization and, 67–68; in institutions, 200–201; intersections between racial and disability, 332n. 2; racial, 162, 188–189, 313n. 15, 334n. 10; railroad, 188, 191, 334n. 10; segregation law, ugly law indexed as, 185; separate but equal, 185; ugly law and, 18, 184–185; of unsightly beggars by race, 185. See also *Brown v. Board of Education*; Jim Crow; *Plessy v. Ferguson*

Selvaggio, Marc, 255, 261, 344n. 2

Sennett, Richard, 209, 329n. 2

Serlin, David, 310n. 13, 324–325n. 25; and Jesse Lerner, 106; on prosthetics, 321n. 27

Sexuality: lewd, 144, 162, 323n. 12; masturbation, 159, 160; perverts, 159, 160; sexual rights for disabled people, 235; sodomy, 313n. 19; ugly law enforced by norms of, 151; unsightly begging, coincidence with sexual transgression, 159–164; women's, containment of, 77, 156–157. *See also* Homosexuality

Shah, Nayan, 141, 297n. 2, 329n. 2, 331nn. 12, 13

Shakespeare, Tom, 299n. 12, 312n. 6, 319n. 18, 322n. 4

Shapiro, Joseph, 8, 347n. 4

Shaw, Barrett, 40

Shaw, Randy, 314n. 20, 347n. 4

Sherry, Mark, 194, 299n. 12, 305n. 13, 318n. 15, 328n. 46, 347n. 2

Shuttleworth, Russell, 299n. 12

Sidewalks: obstruction, 63; policing of, 188; sidewalk ordinance, 188

Siebers, Tobin, vi, 15, 70–71, 153, 318n. 12, 321n. 27

Silvers, Anita, and Michael Ashley Stein, 85, 299n. 13, 311n. 1

Sinclair, Upton, *The Jungle*, 122–123

Skin, 187; deep skin (Roach), 187; epidermal politics, 333n. 7

Skocpol, Theda, 311n. 24, 325n. 25

Slavery: and covering, 329n. 48; history of, displayed as scar, 195; imposter survivors, 195–196; as purported solution to pauperism, 335n. 26; slave narratives, relation to mendicant disability autobiography, 345n. 7; and unsightliness, 188

Smell, legal regulation of, 86, 311n. 3

Smith, Valerie, 141, 322n. 3

Snyder, Sharon, and David Mitchell, 15, 165, 299n. 12, 305n. 15, 309n. 9, 310n. 16, 314n. 22, 319nn. 15, 18, 322n. 6, 339n. 1

Sobchack, Vivan, 124

Sontag, Susan, 167, 330n. 3

Souter, Justice David, on ugly law, 19

Space: and constitution of disability, 184; and constitution of race, 332n. 1; interstitial, 119, 310n. 14; mixed-race, 197; "poetics of colorlined" (Farley), 184; spatial dissidents (Dorn), 6; territoriality and disability, 185. *See also* City; Maps; Quarantine; Segregation; Street

Speech: barred, disability as, 218; begging, disability as, 217; bodily, 346n. 17; and communication impairment, 180; freedom of, 180, 215–218; racist, 218. *See also* Expression; First Amendment

Spivak, Gayatri Chakravorty, 260, 346n. 17

Stanley, Amy Dru, 17, 37, 158, 189, 224, 301n. 28, 303n. 17, 334n. 12, 339n. 15

Status offenses, 10, 16. *See also* Acts, prohibition on
Stedman Jones, Gareth, 48, 305n. 16
Sterilization, 67–68, 120; Supreme Court upholding of compulsory, 255, 280. *See also* Eugenics, *Buck v. Bell*
Stern, Simon, 338n. 9, 339n. 17
Stewart, Jean, 307n. 36
Stigma, 27, 285; stigmata of degeneration, 309n. 9
Stiker, Henri-Jacques, 254, 299, 339n. 1
Stone, Deborah, 59, 127, 307n. 34, 317n. 6
"Strangest Union in the World," 247–250
Street: culture, 310n. 14; disabled people in, 87, 151; economy, 179, 181, 200; extreme subcultures in, 209; operator, 237–238, 245, 333n. 4; streetwalker, 158
Stroman, Duane, 322n. 7
Stuart, Ossie, 322n. 2
Sullivan, Nikki, 321–322n. 34
Supreme Court, U.S.: ADA cases, 11, 106, 185, 332n. 3, 347n. 1; beggar's resolution to fight ugly law up to, 247; debate over definition of disability, 11; on free speech, 218, 255; immigration cases, 165; overturning anti-Chinese measures, 28; on segregation, 185, 313n. 15, 332n. 3, 339n. 19; on ugly law, 19; on vagrancy, 347n. 5
Survey: from below, 271; Cleveland, 230–232, 234–247; as form of American women's writing, 242; genre of, 242, 341n. 4; Los Angeles, 253; narrative voice of, 242

Ten Broek, Jacobus: and Matson, Floyd, 27, 301n. 3; on poor law, 301n. 3; "The Right to Live in the World," 21, 77, 105, 139, 205, 300n. 22, 315n. 29
Texas, legislation to regulate intrastate commerce, 104
Thomas, Carol, 129, 299n. 12, 321n. 30, 325n. 31
Tiedeman, Christopher, 63
Tiny Tim Crow, 191
Titchkosky, Tanya, 117, 299n. 12, 307n. 36, 342n. 10
Tollifson, Joan, 314n. 20
Trafficking, 104–105, 120,168
Tramps: eugenics and, 52, 309n. 8; female, 323n. 13; male, 144, 319n. 17; "made up" (Cresswell), vi; from minstrel to, 191; racialization of, 185; Reed's socialist analysis of, 45; Reitman on, 72, 75; tramp scare context of ugly law, vi, 35, 52, 55, 306n. 24; venereal disease, association with, 159. *See also* Vagrancy
Tremain, Shelley, 128, 299n. 12, 308n. 1, 319n. 18, 343n. 20
Trent, James 305n. 21
Twain, Mark (Samuel Clemens), 174, 177, 317n. 5
Tyler, Carole-Ann, 133, 317n. 1, 318n. 13

Ugliness: gender and, 144–145, 323n. 15; growing emphasis on in later nineteenth century, 86; in Omaha case, 6, 8–9, 23; politics of, 142, 282, 283; postmodern, 65; Randolph Bourne on, 299n. 11; sighting/citing of, 3; of ugly law, 9, 23; undoing of ugly/beauty binary, 286; urban, 69; "what's the standard of," 6; women and, 323n. 14. *See also* Beauty
Ugly crowds, 54–56, 58, 60, 61,199, 275, 289; as targets of ugly law, 54–59,61–62; white defense of black beggar

in, 201; women's participation in, 157, 202
Ugly law: ambiguity of, 25; Americanness of, 4, 5–6; and anti-freakshow legislation, 101; as apotropaic rite, 95, 313n. 18; basic elements of, 208; as "Charity Ordinance," 276; cities that did not enact, 210; coined as term, 9, 23, 142, 348n. 7; consequences of enforcement, 244; constitutionality of, 347n. 5; contemporary citation of, 8–9, 12–13,179; disability studies on, 14–16; discourse in reverse, 267–268; emphasis on the visual, 312n. 3; era of, 16; era of the postugly, 284; fines for, 102; first known enactment of, 2, 24–29, 64, 291–292, 298n. 9; Fuller's critique of, 267–276; generation of literature in response to, 256; historical summary of, 3; indexing of, 9; introduced in Congressional ADA debate, 278; language of, 9–12, 91; last known arrest for, 6; as legend about disability, 7,13, 14, 16–17, 30, 65, 207, 298n. 7; minimal history of legal opposition to, 214–219, 346n. 20; noise policing in relation to, 180; nonenforcement of, 8, 33, 211; overdetermination of, 63; poor house clause in, 10, 27, 67; possible earlier existence of, 301n. 1; psychology of, 123; repeal of, in Chicago, 279–280; repeal of, in Omaha, 347n. 5; smell policing in relation to, 86; "so as to be" clause, 193, 238; spread of, 3–4; Supreme Court on, 19; text of, 291–296; as transient symptom, 62; ugly law culture, 210; ugly law proper, 32; variants in language, 9–10
Undercover investigation, 114, 134–136
Union of the Physically Impaired Against Segregation (UPIAS), 128
Unsightliness: all of us as potentially unsightly, 289; applied to beggar, vi, 2, 3, 23; as attitude, 232; as clothing, 329n. 49; era of, 16; history of the term, 311n. 2; vs. indecency, 161; in nuisance law, 214–215; as precariousness, 287; in the present, 288; in Progressive era, 254; skin and, 187; unseemliness and, 31–32, 88; writing as unsightly, 320n. 22
Unsightly beggar: "one wants to kick the," 288; ordinance, 2, 9; organization of, 249; putative isolation of, 198. *See also* Ugly law
Urban: planning, 69–71; urbanization, 30–31,165, 302n. 5. *See also* City
Urban studies, 208–210, 286; neglect of disability studies analysis in, 209

Vagrancy, vi, 36, 54, 95, 253, 283, 306n. 25; and disability, 306n. 29. *See also* Tramps; Vagrancy law
Vagrancy law, 141, 193, 303n. 13; bookselling used as defense against, 256; as racial control, 195; Southern, 192; ugly law, for purposes of, 219; used to quell working class organizing, 308n. 39. *See also* Law
Vaillant, Derek, 179–180, 332n. 25
Verter, Bradford, 262–263, 346n. 16
Veterans: African American, 203; autobiography, 258, 262; begging, 28–29, 34–35; disabled, 30, 145, 150, 196, 324n. 25; fraudulent, 29; legal exemptions for, 31, 149, 324nn. 23, 24; ostracism of disabled, 340n. 3; pensions for, 79; racialization of injury of, 186; rehabilitation of, 232–234; rhetoric, Fuller's use of, 263; self-defenses for begging by, 202;

Veterans, (*Continued*)
Union veteran writing, 150, 186; World War II, burned pilots ostracized, 340n. 3. *See also* Rehabilitationism; War
Visuality and visibility: citizenship and, Davis on, 303n. 15; frenzy of the visible (Comolli), 30; gaze, 37, 43; in city sightscape, 179; overemphasis on in disability studies, 180; policing of, 311n. 2; race and, 187; staring, Scarry on, 286; Thomson, Garland, on, 86, 324n. 21; "to-be-looked-at-ness," 148; ugly law emphasis on, 86–87; visual identification, 187; visual playground, city as, 93. *See also* Appearance

Wagner, Bryan, 186, 192, 195, 298n. 9, 333n. 8, 334n. 16, 341n. 7
Wagner, David, 47, 304n. 2, 305n. 18
Wailoo, Keith, 193, 335n. 20
Walloch, Greg, 312n. 8
War: heroism claimed in court, 202–203; overestimation of effects of, 302n. 5; resistance to by disabled people, 208; ugly law era between wars, 149. *See also* Civil War; World War I; Veterans
Waters, Theodore, 109, 114, 117, 132, 134, 195, 315n. 32, *135*
Watten, Barrett, 301n. 29
Weeks, Cece, 314n. 20
Welfare system, U.S., 79, 113, 301n. 3; COS prefiguration of, 304n. 4; disability as central to, 307n. 34; racism and, 314n. 26; and vestiges of ugly law, 212
Welke, Barbara, 78, 318n. 12, 334nn. 10, 15
Wendell, Susan, 283, 326n. 31
Whiteness: alms of, 198; delimited by unsightly beggar ordinances, 185; deployed by white unsightly beggars, 197–198; disability studies and, 336n. 30; poor relief for, 188; white disability politics, 198; "White Other" (Frankenberg), 185; white privilege, 188, 193, 197; white supremacy, 193; white trash as social category, 333nn. 4, 5; white trashing, 185. *See also* Blackness
Wilde, Oscar, 126, 313n. 19, 320n. 23
Wilder, Marshall P., 18, 225–229, 256, *229*
Williams, Simon, 89, 299n. 12, 309n. 3, 312n. 5
Willis, Mark, 344n. 1
Wilson, Harriet, *Our Nig*, 345n. 7
Wobblies. *See* Industrial Workers of the World
Women: autobiography of woman beggar, 259; bicycling, 156; blackhoods, 146; breastfeeding, 161; of color, 159; containment of feebleminded, 76–77; crippled, condition worse than for crippled man, 145; disease and, 159; disfigurement and, 348n. 8; doctors, 156; exemption from arrest for begging, 222; experience of arrest, 150; female forms, 152, 325n. 31; flaneuse, 157, 243; high-heel game, 147, 323n. 18; homeless, 151; hysteria and, 80–81; ladies, 152, 153, 155; lewd, 144, 162, 323n12; old, 146, 188; in public sphere, 156–157, 327n. 41; reformers, 157; servants, 152; sexuality of, 157; sheltered workshops for handicapped, 251; Smith, Kitty, 259; supposed delicacy of, 153; and ugliness, 144–145, 323n. 14; white, protection of, 192; woman/cripple/writing, 346n. 17;

wretches, 153, 155. *See also* Lesbians; Maternal impression; Mothers; Prostitute
Work: contradictions in American ideology regarding, 235; "cripples at," 239; disability defined as inability to, 223; disabled worker as radical concept, 236, 341n. 6; disabled workers, 246; discrimination against, 315n. 29; rehabilitationist prioritizing of, 235, 250; unsightly begging as, 109; wartime work by disabled people, 233–234
World War I: Bourne's opposition to, 207; in film, 275–276; rehabilitation in aftermath, 60, 232–234, 247, 340n. 3

Yoshino, Kenji, 163–164, 204, 329n. 51
Young, Iris Marion, 323n. 14, 333n. 7, 350n. 13
Young, Jonathan, 298n. 8

Zakrewsky, Karen, 282
Zames, Frieda, and Doris Zames Fleischer, 298n. 8, 314n. 20, 347n. 4

ABOUT THE AUTHOR

Susan M. Schweik is Professor of English and co-director of the Disability Studies Program at the University of California, Berkeley. She is the author of *A Gulf So Deeply Cut: American Women Poets and the Second World War* (1991).